arihant
SUCCESS AND NOTHING LESS

Be a TOP SCORER
in ISC Exams 2025

i Succeed

15 Sample Question Papers

with Quick Study Notes

Mathematics 12th

AUTHORS
Prem Maharishi
Sunil Rathore

Arihant Prakashan
(School Division Series)

Administrative & Production Offices

Regd. Office
'Ramchhaya' 4577/15, Agarwal Road, Darya Ganj, New Delhi -110002
Tele: 011- 47630600, 43518550

Head Office
Kalindi, TP Nagar, Meerut (UP) - 250002
Tel: 0121-7156203, 7156204

Sales & Support Offices
Agra, Ahmedabad, Bengaluru, Bareilly, Chennai, Delhi, Guwahati, Hyderabad, Jaipur, Jhansi, Kolkata, Lucknow, Nagpur & Pune.

PRICE

PO No : TXT-XX-XXXXXXX-X-XX

Published by Arihant Publications (India) Ltd.

For further information about the books published by Arihant, log on to www.arihantbooks.com or e-mail at info@arihantbooks.com

Follow us on

i Succeed

SAMPLE QUESTION PAPERS

THE **BEST CHOICE** OF TEACHERS & STUDENTS, Why?

01 Exact Exam Pattern

All Sample Papers have been designed on the actual exam format of ISC

02 Complete Syllabus

Complete coverage of syllabus through different types of questions across all the sample papers

03 Latest Specimen & Examination Question Paper

Latest Specimen & ISC examination Question Paper with detailed solutions.

04 Detailed Answers

Step-by-step answers to help you understand concepts and improve problem-solving skills.

05 All Type of Questions

Coverage of all type of exam pattern questions, analysis, understanding, application & evaluation.

Free Doubt Solving APP

To help you sort out your doubts at any time any place.

i Succeed

Mathematics 12

Course Structure
2024-25

There will be one paper of Three hours duration of 80 marks and project work carrying 20 marks.

Paper I : Theory **80 Marks**

The syllabus is divided into three sections A, B and C.

Section A is compulsory for all candidates. Candidates will have a choice of attempting questions from **EITHER** Section B **OR** Section C.

DISTRIBUTION OF MARKS FOR THE THEORY PAPER.

S.No.	Unit Name	Total Weightage
	Section A : 65 Marks	
1.	Relations and Functions	10 Marks
2.	Algebra	10 Marks
3.	Calculus	32 Marks
4.	Probability	13 Marks
	Section B : 15 Marks	
5.	Vectors	5 Marks
6.	Three-Dimensional Geometry	6 Marks
7.	Applications of Integrals	4 Marks
	OR Section C : 15 Marks	
8.	Applications of Calculus	5 Marks
9.	Linear Regression	6 Marks
10.	Linear Programming	4 Marks
	Total	**80 Marks**

SECTION A

1. Relations and Functions

(i) Types of relations: reflexive, symmetric, transitive and equivalence relations. One to one and onto functions, inverse of a function.

- **Relations as**
  - Relation on a set A
  - Identity relation, empty relation, universal relation.
  - Types of Relations: reflexive, symmetric, transitive and equivalence relation.
- **Functions**
  - As special relations, concept of writing "y is a function of x" as $y = f(x)$.
  - Types: one to one, many to one, into, onto.
  - Real Valued function.
  - Domain and range of a function.
  - Conditions of invertibility.
  - Invertible functions (algebraic functions only).

(ii) Inverse Trigonometric Functions

Definition, domain, range, principal value branch. Elementary properties of inverse trigonometric functions.

- Principal values.
- $\sin^{-1} x, \cos^{-1} x, \tan^{-1} x$, etc.
- $\sin^{-1} x = \cos^{-1} \sqrt{1-x^2} = \tan^{-1} \dfrac{x}{\sqrt{1-x^2}}$
- $\sin^{-1} x = \text{cosec}^{-1} \dfrac{1}{x}$; $\sin^{-1} x + \cos^{-1} x = \dfrac{\pi}{2}$ and similar relations for $\cot^{-1} x, \tan^{-1} x$, etc.

$$\sin^{-1} x \pm \sin^{-1} y = \sin^{-1} (x\sqrt{1-y^2} \pm y\sqrt{1-x^2})$$

$$\cos^{-1} x \pm \cos^{-1} y = \cos^{-1} (xy \mp \sqrt{1-y^2}\sqrt{1-x^2})$$

Similarly,

$$\tan^{-1} x + \tan^{-1} y = \tan^{-1} \frac{x+y}{1-xy}, xy < 1,$$

$$\tan^{-1} x - \tan^{-1} y = \tan^{-1} \frac{x-y}{1+xy}, xy > -1$$

Formulae for $2\sin^{-1}x$, $2\cos^{-1}x$, $2\tan^{-1}x$, $3\tan^{-1}x$ etc. and application of these formulae.

2. Algebra

Matrices and Determinants

(i) Matrices

Concept, notation, order, equality, types of matrices, zero and identity matrix, transpose of a matrix, symmetric and skew-symmetric matrices. Operation on matrices: Addition and multiplication and multiplication with a scalar. Simple properties of addition, multiplication and scalar multiplication. Non-commutativity of multiplication of matrices and existence of non-zero matrices whose product is the zero matrix (restrict to square matrices of order upto 3). Invertible matrices and proof of the uniqueness of inverse, if it exists (here all matrices will have real entries).

(ii) Determinants

Determinant of a square matrix (up to 3 x 3 matrices), properties of determinants, minors, co-factors and applications of determinants in finding the area of a triangle. Adjoint and inverse of a square matrix. Consistency, inconsistency and number of solutions of system of linear equation by examples. Solving system of linear equations in two or three variables (having unique solution) using inverse of a matrix.

- Types of matrices ($m \times n$; $m, n \leq 3$), order; Identity matrix, Diagonal matrix.
- Symmetric, Skew-symmetric.
- Operation – addition, subtraction, multiplication of a matrix with scalar, multiplication of two matrices (the compatibility).

e.g. $\begin{bmatrix} 1 & 1 \\ 0 & 2 \\ 1 & 1 \end{bmatrix}\begin{bmatrix} 1 & 2 \\ 2 & 2 \end{bmatrix} = AB$ (say) but BA is not possible.

- Singular and non-singular matrices.
- Existence of two non-zero matrices whose product is a zero matrix.

Inverse (2×2, 3×3) $A^{-1} = \dfrac{\text{adj } A}{|A|}$

- *Martin's Rule (i.e. using matrices)*

  $a_1x + b_1y + c_1z = d_1$
  $a_2x + b_2y + c_2z = d_2$
  $a_3x + b_3y + c_3z = d_3$

$$A = \begin{bmatrix} a_1 & b_1 & c_1 \\ a_2 & b_2 & c_2 \\ a_3 & b_3 & c_3 \end{bmatrix}, B = \begin{bmatrix} d_1 \\ d_2 \\ d_3 \end{bmatrix}, X = \begin{bmatrix} x \\ y \\ z \end{bmatrix}$$

$$AX = B \Rightarrow X = A^{-1}B$$

Problems based on above.

Note : *The conditions for consistency of equations in two and three variables using matrices are to be covered.*

- *Determinants*
  - *Order.*
  - *Minors.*
  - *Cofactors.*
  - *Expansion.*
  - *Application of determinants is finding the area or triangle and collinearity.*
  - *Properties of determinants. Problems based on properties of determinants.*

3. Calculus

(viii) Continuity, Differentiability and Differentiation. Continuity and differentiability, derivative of composite functions, chain rule, derivatives of inverse trigonometric functions, derivative of implicit functions. Concept of exponential and logarithmic functions.

Derivatives of logarithmic and exponential functions. Logarithmic differentiation, derivative of functions expressed in parametric forms. Second order derivatives.

- *Continuity*
  - *Continuity of a function at a point $x = a$.*
  - *Continuity of a function in an interval.*
  - *Algebra of continuous function.*
  - *Removable discontinuity.*
- *Differentiation*
  - *Concept of continuity and differentiability of $|x|$, $[x]$, etc.*
  - *Derivatives of trigonometric functions.*
  - *Derivatives of exponential functions.*
  - *Derivatives of logarithmic functions.*
  - *Derivatives of inverse trigonometric functions - differentiation by means of substitution.*
  - *Derivatives of implicit functions and chain rule.*
  - *Derivatives of Parametric functions.*
  - *Differentiation of a function with respect to another function e.g. differentiation of $\sin x^3$ with respect to x^3.*
  - *Logarithmic Differentiation - Finding dy/dx when $y = x^{x^x}$*
  - *Successive differentiation upto 2nd order.*

Note : *Derivatives of composite functions using chain rule.*

(ii) Applications of Derivatives

Applications of derivatives: rate of change of bodies, increasing/decreasing functions, tangents and normals, maxima and minima (first derivative test motivated geometrically and second derivative test given as a provable tool). Simple problems (that illustrate basic principles and understanding of the subject as well as real-life situations).

- *Equation of Tangent and Normal.*
- *Rate measure.*
- *Increasing and decreasing functions.*
- *Maxima and minima*
  - *Stationary/turning points.*
  - *Absolute maxima/minima.*
  - *Local maxima/minima.*
  - *First derivatives test and second derivatives test.*
  - *Application problems based on maxima and minima.*

(iii) Integrals

Integration as inverse process of differentiation. Integration of a variety of functions by substitution, by partial fractions and by parts, Evaluation of simple integrals of the following types and problems based on them.

Fundamental Theorem of Calculus (without proof). Basic properties of definite integrals and evaluation of definite integrals.

- *Indefinite integral*
  - *Integration as the inverse of differentiation.*
  - *Anti-derivatives of polynomials and functions $(ax+b)^n$, $\sin x$, $\cos x$, $\sec^2 x$, $\text{cosec}^2 x$ etc.*
  - *Integrals of the type $\sin^2 x$, $\sin^3 x$, $\sin^4 x$, $\cos^2 x$, $\cos^3 x$, $\cos^4 x$.*
  - *Integration of $1/x$, e^x.*
  - *Integration by substitution.*

– *Integrals of the type* $f'(x)\,[f(x)]^n$, $\frac{f'(x)}{f(x)}$
– *Integration of* tan *x*, cot *x*, sec *x*, cosec *x*.
– *Integration by parts.*
– *Integration using partial fractions.*

Expressions of the form $\frac{f(x)}{g(x)}$, when, degree of $f(x)$ < degree of $g(x)$.

e.g. $\frac{x+2}{(x-3)(x+1)} = \frac{A}{x-3} + \frac{B}{x+1}$,

$$\frac{x+2}{(x-2)(x-1)^2} = \frac{A}{x-1} + \frac{B}{(x-1)^2} + \frac{C}{x-2}$$

$$\frac{x+1}{(x^2+3)(x-1)} = \frac{Ax+B}{x^2+3} + \frac{C}{x-1}$$

When degree of $f(x) \geq$ degree of $g(x)$,

e.g. $\frac{x^2+1}{x^2+3x+2} = 1 - \left(\frac{3x+1}{x^2+3x+2}\right)$

Integrals of the type :

$$\int \frac{dx}{x^2 \pm a^2}, \int \frac{dx}{\sqrt{x^2 \pm a^2}}, \int \frac{px+q}{ax^2+bx+c}\,dx,$$

$$\int \frac{px+q}{\sqrt{ax^2+bx+c}}\,dx \text{ and } \int \sqrt{a^2 \pm x^2}\,dx, \int \sqrt{x^2 - a^2}\,dx,$$

$$\int (px+q)\sqrt{ax^2+bx+c}\,dx \quad \int \sqrt{ax^2+bx+c}\,dx,$$

integrations reducible to the above forms.

$$\int \frac{dx}{a\cos x + b\sin x}, \int \frac{dx}{a + b\cos x}, \int \frac{dx}{a + b\sin x},$$

$$\int \frac{dx}{a\cos x + b\sin x + c}, \int \frac{(a\cos x + b\sin x)}{c\cos x + d\sin x}\,dx,$$

$$\int \frac{dx}{a\cos^2 x + b\sin^2 x + c}, \int \frac{1 \pm x^2}{1+x^4}\,dx, \int \frac{dx}{1+x^4},$$

$$\int \sqrt{\tan x}\,dx, \int \sqrt{\cot x}\,dx \text{ etc.}$$

- Definite integral
  – Fundamental theorem of calculus (without proof).
  – Properties of definite integrals.

Problems based on the following properties of definite integrals are to be covered.

$$\int_a^b f(x)\,dx = \int_a^b f(t)\,dt$$

$$\int_a^b f(x)\,dx = -\int_b^a f(x)\,dx$$

$$\int_a^b f(x)\,dx = \int_a^c f(x)\,dx + \int_c^b f(x)\,dx, \text{ where } a < c < b$$

$$\int_a^b f(x)\,dx = \int_a^b f(a+b-x)\,dx$$

$$\int_0^a f(x)\,dx = \int_0^a f(a-x)\,dx$$

$$\int_0^{2a} f(x)\,dx = \begin{cases} 2\int_0^a f(x)\,dx, & \text{if } f(2a-x) = f(x) \\ 0, & \text{if } f(2a-x) = -f(x) \end{cases}$$

$$\int_{-a}^a f(x)\,dx = \begin{cases} 2\int_0^a f(x)\,dx, & \text{if } f \text{ is an even function} \\ 0, & \text{if } f \text{ is an odd function} \end{cases}$$

(iv) Differential Equations

Definition, order and degree, general and particular solutions of a differential equation. Solution of differential equations by method of separation of variables solutions of homogeneous differential equations of first order and first degree.

Solutions of linear differential equation of the type: $\frac{dy}{dx} + py = q$, where p and q are functions of x or constants. $\frac{dx}{dy} + px = q$, where p and q are functions of y or constants.

– Differential equations, order and degree.
– Formation of differential equation by eleminating arbitrary constant (s).
– Solution of differential equations.
– Variable separable.
– Homogeneous equations.
– Linear form $\frac{dy}{dx} + Py = Q$, where P and Q are functions of x only.

Similarly for *dx/dy*.

Note 1 : Equations reducible to variable separable type are included.

Note 2 : The second order differential equations are excluded.

4. Probability

Conditional probability, multiplication theorem on probability, independent events, total probability, Bayes' theorem, Random variable and its probability distribution, mean of random variable.

– Independent and dependent events, conditional events.
– Laws of probability, addition theorem, multiplication theorem, conditional probability.
– Theorem of Total Probability.
– Baye's theorem.
– Theoretical probability distribution, probability distribution function; mean of random variable.

SECTION B

5. Vectors

Vectors and scalars, magnitude and direction of a vector. Direction cosines and direction ratios of a vector. Types of vectors (equal, unit, zero, parallel and collinear vectors), position vector of a point, negative of a vector, components of a vector, addition of vectors, multiplication of a vector by a scalar, position vector of a point dividing a line segment in a given ratio. Definition, Geometrical Interpretation, properties and application of scalar (dot) product of vectors, vector (cross) product of vectors.

– *As directed line segments.*
– *Magnitude and direction of a vector.*
– *Types: equal vectors, unit vectors, zero vector.*
– *Position vector.*

- *Components of a vector.*
- *Vectors in two and three dimensions.*
- *i, j, k as unit vectors along the X, Y and Z-axes; expressing a vector in terms of the unit vectors.*
- *Operations: Sum and Difference of vectors; scalar multiplication of a vector.*
- *Section formulae.*
- *Scalar (dot) product of vectors and its geometrical significance.*
- *Cross product - its properties - area of a triangle, area of parallelogram, collinear vectors.*

Note *Proofs of geometrical theorems by using Vector algebra are excluded.*

6. Three Dimensional Geometry

Direction cosines and direction ratios of a line joining two points. Cartesian equation and vector equation of a line, coplanar and skew lines, shortest distance between two lines. Cartesian and vector equation of a plane. Angle between (i) two lines, (ii) two planes, (iii) a line and a plane. Distance of a point from a plane.

- *Equation of X-axis, Y-axis, Z-axis and lines parallel to them.*
- *Equation of XY-plane, YZ-plane, ZX-plane.*
- *Direction cosines, direction ratios.*
- *Angle between two lines in terms of direction cosines /direction ratios.*
- *Condition for lines to be perpendicular/ parallel.*

- ***Lines***
  - *Cartesian and vector equations of a line through one and two points.*
  - *Coplanar and skew lines.*
  - *Conditions for intersection of two lines.*
  - *Distance of a point from a line.*
  - *Shortest distance between two lines.*
- ***Planes***
  - *Cartesian and vector equation of a plane.*
  - *Direction ratios of the normal to the plane.*
  - *One point form.*
  - *Normal form.*
  - *Intercept form.*
  - *Distance of a point from a plane.*
  - *Intersection of the line and plane.*
  - *Angle between two planes, a line and a plane.*

7. Application of Integrals

Application in finding the area bounded by simple curves and coordinate axes. Area enclosed between two curves.

- *Application of definite integrals - area bounded by curves, lines and coordinate axes is required to be covered.*
- *Simple curves: lines, circles/ parabolas/ ellipses, polynomial functions, modulus function.*

SECTION C

8. Application of Calculus

Application of Calculus in Commerce and Economics in the following:

- *Cost function,*
- *average cost,*
- *marginal cost and its interpretation*
- *demand function,*
- *revenue function,*
- *marginal revenue function and its interpretation,*
- *Profit function and breakeven point.*
- *Rough sketching of the following curves: AR, MR, R, C, AC, MC and their mathematical interpretation using the concept of maxima & minima and increasing- decreasing functions.*
- *Self-explanatory*

Note : *Application involving differentiation, increasing and decreasing function and maxima and minima to be covered.*

9. Linear Regression

- *Lines of regression of x on y and y on x.*
- *Scatter diagrams*
- *The method of least squares.*
- *Lines of best fit.*
- *Regression coefficient of x on y and y on x.*
- $b_{xy} \times b_{yx} = r^2,\ 0 \le b_{xy} \times b_{yx} \le 1$
- *Identification of regression equations*
- *Properties of regression lines.*
- *Estimation of the value of one variable using the value of other variable from appropriate line of regression.*
- *Self-explanatory*

10. Linear Programming

Introduction, related terminology such as constraints, objective function, optimization, different types of Linear Programming (LP) problems, mathematical formulation of LP problems, graphical method of solution for problems in two variables, feasible and infeasible regions (bounded and unbounded), feasible and infeasible solutions, optimal feasible solutions (up to three non-trivial constraints).

Introduction, definition of related terminology such as constraints, objective function, optimization, advantages of linear programming; limitations of linear programming; application areas of linear programming; different types of Linear Programming (LP) problems, mathematical formulation of LP problems, graphical method of solution for problems in two variables, feasible and infeasible regions, feasible and infeasible solutions, optimum feasible solution.

Preparation Assessment Zone

Welcome to the Preparation Assessment Zone !

In this section, you'll find **ISC Specimen Paper** and **Board Examination Paper 2024** to help you assess your readiness. Attempt these papers to familiarise yourself with the exam format and identify areas that need improvement.

Progress Tracker **Tick the papers as you complete them.**

- ☐ ISC Specimen Paper
- ☐ Board Examination Paper 2024

ISC Specimen Paper

Session 2024-25

Mathematics (Code 860)

Class 12

General Instructions

1. This Question Paper consists of three sections A, B and C.
2. Candidates are required to attempt all questions from Section A and all questions either from Section B Or Section C.
3. **Section A** Internal choice has been provided in two questions of 2 marks each, two questions of 4 marks each and two questions of 6 marks each.
4. **Section B** Internal choice has been provided in one question of 2 marks and one question of 4 marks.
5. **Section C** Internal choice has been provided in one question of 2 marks and one question of 4 marks.
6. All working, including rough work, should be done on the same sheet as and adjacent to the rest of the answer.
7. The intended marks for questions or parts of questions are given in brackets [].
8. Mathematical tables and graph papers are provided.

Time : 3 Hrs.

Max. Marks : 80

Section A (65 Marks)

1. In subparts (i) to (xi) choose the correct options and in subparts (xii) to (xv), answer the questions as instructed.

(i) A matrix which is both symmetric and skew-symmetric matrix is a/ an • *Understanding*

(a) triangular matrix (b) identity matrix
(c) diagonal matrix (d) null matrix

(ii) The value of $\int a^x \cdot e^x dx$ equals • *Recall* [1]

(a) $(a^z \cdot \log_e a)e^x + c$ (b) $\dfrac{a^x \cdot e^x}{\log_e(ae)} + c$

(c) $\dfrac{a^x \cdot e^x}{\log_{ae} e} + c$ (d) $\log_e(ae)(ae)^x + c$

(iii) The trigonometric equation $\tan^{-1} x = 3\tan^{-1} a$ has solution for • *Application* [1]

(a) $|a| \leq \dfrac{1}{\sqrt{3}}$ (b) $|a| > \dfrac{1}{\sqrt{3}}$

(c) $|a| < \dfrac{1}{\sqrt{3}}$ (d) all real value of a.

(iv) **Assertion** Degree of the differential equation $a\left(\dfrac{dy}{dx}\right)^2 + b\dfrac{dx}{dy} = c$, is 3.

Reason If each term involving derivatives of a differential equation is a polynomial (or can be expressed as polynomial), then highest exponent of the highest order derivative is called the degree of the differential equation. • *Analysis* [1]

Which of the following is correct?

(a) Both Assertion and Reason are true and Reason is the correct explanation for Assertion.
(b) Both Assertion and Reason are true but Reason is not the correct explanation for Assertion.
(c) Assertion is true and Reason is false.
(d Assertion is false and Reason is true.

(v) Five numbers x_1, x_2, x_3, x_4 and x_5 are randomly selected from the numbers 1, 2, 3, ..., 18 and are arranged in the increasing order such that $x_1 < x_2 < x_3 < x_4 < x_5$. What is the probability that $x_2 = 7$ and $x_4 = 11$?
• *Application* [1]

(a) $\frac{26}{51}$ (b) $\frac{3}{104}$
(c) $\frac{1}{68}$ (d) $\frac{1}{34}$

(vi) If $\begin{vmatrix} a & b & c \\ m & n & p \\ x & y & z \end{vmatrix} = k$, then what is the value of $\begin{vmatrix} 6a & 2b & 2c \\ 3m & n & p \\ 3x & y & z \end{vmatrix}$?
• *Understanding* [1]

(a) $\frac{k}{6}$ (b) $2k$ (c) $3k$ (d) $6k$

(vii) Consider the graph $y = x^{\frac{1}{3}}$

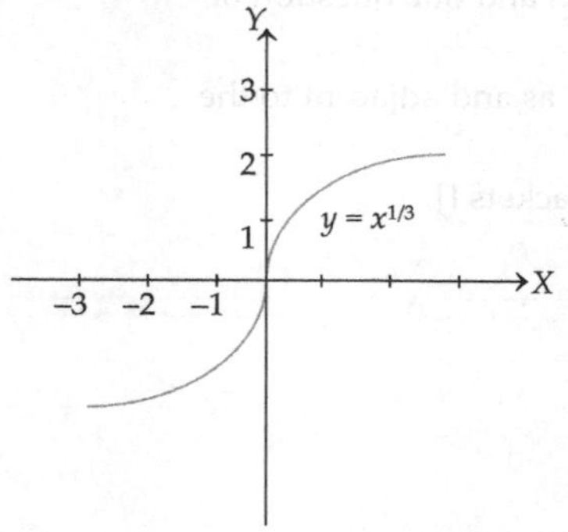

Statement I The above graph is continuous at $x = 0$.
Statement II The above graph is differentiable at $x = 0$ • *Application* [1]
Which of the following is correct?
(a) Statement I is true and Statement II is false.
(b) Statement II is true and Statement I is false.
(c) Both the statements are true.
(d) Both the statements are false.

(viii) The value of $\frac{dy}{dx}$, if $y = |x-1| + |x-4|$ at $x = 3$ is
(a) -2 (b) 0 (c) 2 (d) 4

(ix) **Statement I** The intersection of two equivalence relations is always an equivalence relation.
Statement II The Union of two equivalence relations is always an equivalence relation.
• *Understanding* [1]
Which one of the following is correct?
(a) Statement I implies Statement II.
(b) Statement II implies Statement I.
(c) Statement I is true only if Statement II is true.
(d) Statement I and II are independent of each other.

(x) In a third order matrix a_{ij} denotes the element of the ith row and the jth column.

$$A = a_{ij} = \begin{cases} 0, & \text{for } i = j \\ 1, & \text{for } i > j \\ -1, & \text{for } i < j \end{cases}$$

Assertion Matrix A is not invertible.
Reason Determinant of $A = 0$
Which of the following is correct?
• *Application* [1]
(a) Both Assertion and Reason are true and Reason is the correct explanation for Assertion.
(b) Both Assertion and Reason are true but Reason is not the correct explanation for Assertion.
(c) Assertion is true and Reason is false.
(d) Assertion is false and Reason is true.

(xi) Given two events A and B such that $P\left(\frac{A}{B}\right) = 0.25$ and $P(A \cap B) = 0.12$. The value of $P(A \cap B')$ is • *Understanding* [1]
(a) 0.36 (b) 0.48 (c) 0.88 (d) 0.036

(xii) The value of the determinant of a matrix A of order 3 is 3. If C is the matrix of co-factors of the matrix A, then what is the value of determinant of C^2? • *Analysis* [1]

(xiii) If a relation R on the set $\{a, b, c\}$ defined by $R = \{(b, b)\}$, then classify the relation.
• *Understanding* [1]

(xiv)

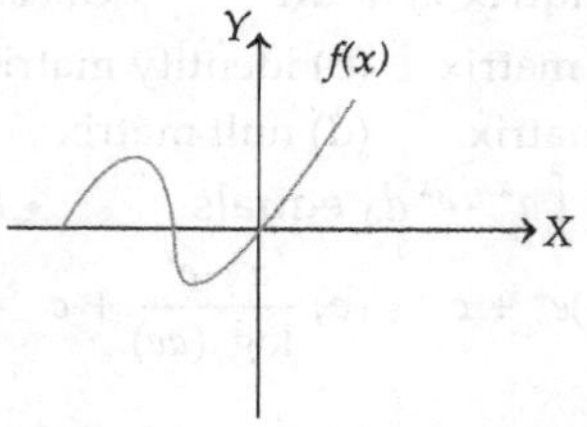

The given function $f: R \to R$ is not onto function. Give reason. • *Understanding* [1]

(xv) There are three machines and 2 of them are faulty. They are tested one by one in a random order till both the faulty machines are identified. What is the probability that only two tests are needed to identify the faulty machines? • *Application* [1]

2. (i) If $x^y = y^x$, then find $\frac{dy}{dx}$. • *Understanding* [2]

Or

(ii) Find the interval in which the function $f(x) = x^2 e^{-x}$ is strictly increasing or decreasing. • *Understanding* [2]

3. Evaluate $\int_0^{\sqrt{2}} [x^2] dx$ • *Evaluate* [2]

4. Find the equation to the tangent at (0, 0) on the curve $y = 4x^2 - 2x^3$. • *Analysis* [2]

5. (i) Evaluate $\int \frac{2x^3 - 1}{x^4 + x} dx$ • *Evaluate* [2]

Or

(ii) Evaluate $\int e^x \operatorname{cosec} x(1 - \cot x) dx$ • *Evaluate* [2]

6. Find the value of $\tan^{-1}\left(\frac{x}{y}\right) + \tan^{-1}\left(\frac{y-x}{y+x}\right)$ • *Application* [2]

7. Solve $\sin^{-1}(x) + \sin^{-1}(1-x) = \cos^{-1} x$. • *Application* [4]

8. Evaluate $\int \sqrt{\sec \frac{x}{2} - 1}\, dx$ • *Application* [4]

9. (i) A kite is being pulled down by a string that goes through a ring on the ground 8 m away from the person pulling it. If the string is pulled in at 1 m per second, how fast is the kite coming down when it is 15 m high? • *Application* [4]

Or

(ii) If $y = (x + \sqrt{a^2 + x^2})^m$, prove that

$$(a^2 + x^2)\frac{d^2y}{dx^2} + x\frac{dy}{dx} - m^2 y = 0$$ • *Analysis* [4]

10. (i) Three friends go to a restaurant to have pizza. They decide who will pay for the pizza by tossing a coin. It is decided that each one of them will toss a coin and if one person gets a different result (heads or tails) than the other two, that person would pay. If all three get the same result (all heads or all tails), they will toss again until they get a different result. • *Analysis* [4]

(a) What is the probability that all three friends will get the same result (all heads or all tails) in one round of tossing?

(b) What is the probability that they will get a different result in one round of tossing?

(c) What is the probability that they will need exactly four rounds of tossing to determine who would pay?

Or

(ii) Students of under graduation submitted a case study on 'Understanding the Probability of Left-Handedness in Children Based on Parental Handedness'.

Following recent studies suggest that roughly 12% of the world population is left-handed. Depending on the parents' handedness, the chances of having a left-handed child vary as follows:

Scenario A

Both parents are left-handed, with a 24% chance of the child being left-handed.

Scenario B

The father is right-handed and the mother is left-handed, with a 22% chance of child being left-handed.

Scenario C

The father is left-handed and the mother is right-handed, with a 17% chance of child being left-handed.

Scenario D

Both parents are right-handed, with a 9% chance of having a left-handed child.

Assuming that scenarios A, B, C and D are equally likely and L denotes the event that the child is left-handed, answer the following questions.

(a) What is the overall probability that a randomly selected child is left-handed?

(b) Given that exactly one parent is left-handed, what is the probability that a randomly selected child is left-handed?

(c) If a child is left-handed, what is the probability that both parents are left-handed?

11. To raise money for an orphanage, students of three schools *A*, *B* and *C* organised an exhibition in their residential colony, where they sold paper bags, scrap books and pastel sheets made by using recycled paper. Students of school *A* sold 30 paper bags, 20 scrap books and 10 pastel sheets and raised ₹ 410. Students of school *B* sold 20 paper bags, 10 scrap books and 20 pastel sheets and raised ₹ 290.

Students of school C sold 20 paper bags, 20 scrap books and 20 pastel sheets and raised ₹ 440.

Answer the following question.

(i) Translate the problem into a system of equations.

(ii) Solve the system of equation by using matrix method.

(iii) Hence, find the cost of one paper bag, one scrap book and one pastel sheet. • *Application* [6]

12. (i) Solve the differential equation.

$$(xdy - ydx)y\sin\left(\frac{y}{x}\right) = (ydx + xdy)\,x\cos\left(\frac{y}{x}\right).$$

Find the particular solution satisfying the condition that $y = \pi$ when $x = 1$. • *Application* [6]

Or

(ii) Evaluate $\int_0^{\pi} (\sin^4 x + \cos^4 x)dx$ and hence evaluate $\int_{-2\pi}^{2\pi} \frac{\sin^4 x + \cos^4 x}{1 + e^x}\,dx.$ • *Evaluate*

13. (i) A cone of maximum volume is inscribed in a given sphere. Then, prove that ratio of the height of the cone to the diameter of the sphere is equal to 2 / 3. • *Application*

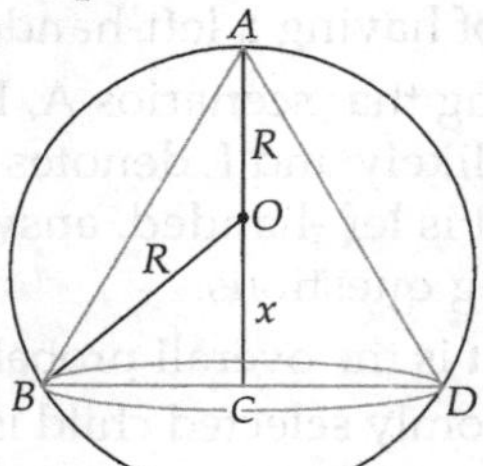

Or

(ii) A given quantity of metal is to be cast into a solid half circular cylinder with a rectangular base and semi-circular ends. If the total surface area is minimum, then prove that the ratio of the length of cylinder to the diameter of semi-circular ends is $\pi : \pi + 2$. • *Application*

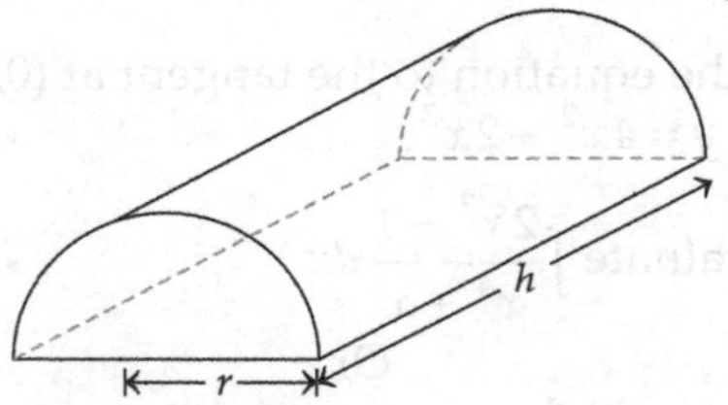

14. Kiran plays a game of throwing a fair die 3 times but to quit as and when she gets a six. Kiran gets + 1 point for a six and − 1 for any other number. • *Analysis* [6]

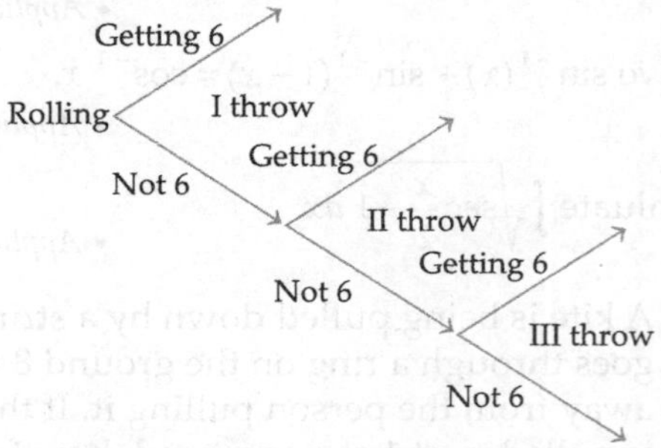

(i) If X denotes the random variable 'points earned' then what are the possible values X can take?

(ii) Find the probability distribution of this random variable X.

(iii) Find the expected value of the points she gets.

Section B (15 Marks)

15. In subparts (i) and (iii) choose the correct options and in subparts (iv) to (v), answer the questions as instructed.

(i) Consider the following statements and choose the correct option.

Statement I If $\vec{a}$ and $\vec{b}$ represent two adjacent sides of a parallelogram, then the diagonals are represented by $\vec{a} + \vec{b}$ and F$\vec{a} - \vec{b}$.

Statement II If $\vec{a}$ and $\vec{b}$ represents two diagonals of a parallelogram, then the adjacent sides are represented by $2(\vec{a} + \vec{b})$ and $2(\vec{a} - \vec{b})$. • *Recall*

Which of the following is correct?

(a) Only Statement I

(b) Only Statement II

(c) Both Statements I and II

(d) Neither Statement I nor Statement II

(ii) The distance of the plane through (1, 1, 1) and perpendicular to the line $\frac{x-1}{3} = \frac{y-1}{0} = \frac{z-1}{4}$ from the origin is • *Application*

(a) $\frac{3}{4}$ (b) $\frac{4}{3}$

(c) $\frac{7}{5}$ (d) 1

(iii) If the direction cosines of a line are $<\frac{1}{c}, \frac{1}{c}, \frac{1}{c}>$, then • *Understanding*

(a) $c > 0$
(b) $0 < c < 1$
(c) $c = \pm\sqrt{3}$
(d) $c > 2$

(iv) If $\hat{a}$ is a unit vector perpendicular to $\vec{b}$ and $(\vec{a} + 2\vec{b}) \cdot (3\vec{a} - \vec{b}) = -5$, find $|\vec{b}|$. • *Understanding*

(v) Shown below is a cuboid. Find $\overrightarrow{BA} \cdot \overrightarrow{BC}$

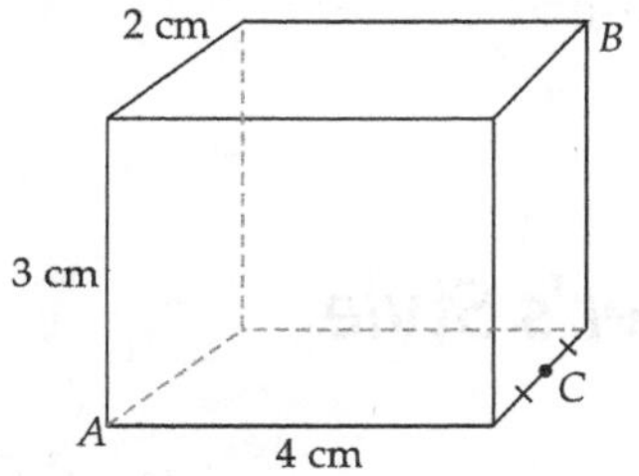

16. (i) Find a vector of magnitude 9 units and perpendicular to the vectors $\vec{a} = 4\hat{i} - \hat{j} + \hat{k}$ and $\vec{b} = -2\hat{i} + \hat{j} - 2\hat{k}$. • *Application*

Or

(ii) What are the values of x for which the angle between the vectors? $2x^2\hat{i} + 3x\hat{j} + \hat{k}$ and $\hat{i} - 2\hat{j} + x^2\hat{k}$ is obtuse? • *Application*

17. (i) Show that the line whose vector equation is $\vec{r} = (2\hat{i} - 2\hat{j} + 3\hat{k}) + \lambda(\hat{i} - \hat{j} + 4\hat{k})$ is parallel to the plane whose vector equation is $\vec{r} \cdot (\hat{i} + 5\hat{j} + \hat{k}) = 5$. Also, find the distance between them. • *Application*

Or

(ii) Find the equation of the plane containing the line $\frac{x}{-2} = \frac{y-1}{3} = \frac{1-z}{1}$ and the point $(-1, 0, 2)$. • *Application*

18. (i) Sketch the region enclosed bounded by the curve, $y = x|x|$ and the coordinates $x = -1$ and $x = 1$.

(ii) Evaluate $\int_0^1 x^2 dx$.

(iii) Hence, find the area bounded by the curve, $y = x|x|$ and the coordinates $x = -1$ and $x = 1$.

Section C (15 Marks)

19. In subparts (i) and (ii) choose the correct options and in subparts (iii) to (v), answer the questions as instructed.

(i) Which condition is true if Average Cost (AC) is constant at all levels of out put • *Recall*

(a) $MC > AC$
(b) $MC = AC$
(c) $MC < AC$
(d) $MC = \frac{1}{2}AC$

(ii) Read the following statements and choose the correct option.

(I) If $r = 0$, then regression lines are not defined.
(II) If $r = 0$, then regression lines are parallel.
(III) If $r = 0$, then regression lines are perpendicular.
(IV) If $r = \pm 1$, then regression lines coincide. • *Recall*

Which of the following is correct?
(a) Only IV is correct.
(b) Only I and II are correct.
(c) Only I and IV are correct.
(d) Only III and IV are correct.

(iii) Mean of $x = 53$, mean of $y = 28$, regression coefficient of y on $x = -1 \cdot 2$, regression coefficient of x on $y = -0.3$. Find coefficient of correlation (r). • *Understanding*

(iv) The total revenue received from the sale of x unit of a product is given by $R(x) = 3x^2 + 36x + 5$. Find the marginal revenue when $x = 5$. • *Understanding*

(v) A manufacturing company finds that the daily cost of producing x item of product is given by $C(x) = 210x + 7000$. Find the minimum number that must be produced and sold daily, if each item is sold for ₹ 280. • *Understanding*

20. (i) The cost function of a commodity is $C(x) = 200 + 20x - \frac{1}{2}x^2$ (in rupees). Find the range where AC falls. • *Application* [2]

Or

(ii) The demand function of a monopoly is given by $x = 100 - 4p$. Find the quantity at which the MR will be zero. • *Application*

21. (i) A survey of 50 families to study the relationships between expenditure on accommodation in (₹ x) and expenditure on food and entertainment (₹ y) gave the following results.
$\Sigma x = 8500, \Sigma y = 9600, \sigma_x = 60, \sigma_y = 20, r = 0.6$
Estimate the expenditure on food and entertainment when expenditure on accommodation is ₹ 200. • *Application*

Or

(ii) The random variables have regression lines $3x + 2y - 26 = 0$ and $6x + y - 31 = 0$
Calculate
(a) Mean value of x and y.
(b) Coefficient of correlations. • *Application*

22. A linear programming problem is given by $Z = px + qy$ where $p, q > 0$ subject to the constraints: • *Analysis* [4]

$x + y \le 60,\ 5x + y \le 100,\ x \ge 0$ and $y \ge 0$

(i) Solve graphically to find the corner points of the feasible region.

(ii) If $Z = px + qy$ is maximum at (0, 60) and (10, 50), find the relation of p and q.

Also mention the number of optimal solution(s) in this case.

Solutions *in Topper's Style*

1. (i) (d) Let A be a matrix.
$\because$ A is symmetric,

$\Rightarrow \quad A = A^T \quad$ ...(i)

and A is skew-symmetric

$\Rightarrow \quad A = -A^T \quad$ ...(ii)

On adding Eqs. (i) and (ii), we get

$\Rightarrow \quad A + A = A^T - A^T$

$\Rightarrow \quad 2A = O \Rightarrow A = O$

which is null matrix.

(ii) (b) Let $I = \int \underset{\text{I}}{a^x} \cdot \underset{\text{II}}{e^x}\, dx \quad$ ...(i)

On integrating by parts, we get

$$I = a^x \int e^x dx - \int \left(\frac{d}{dx} a^x \cdot \int e^x dx \right) dx + C$$

$$= a^x \cdot e^x - \int a^x \log_e a \cdot e^x \cdot dx + C$$

$$= a^x e^x - \log_e a \cdot \int a^x \cdot e^x\, dx + C$$

From Eq. (i), we get

$$I = a^x e^x - \log_e a \cdot I + C$$

$$(1 + \log_e a) I = a^x e^x + C$$

$$\therefore \quad I = \frac{a^x e^x}{1 + \log_e a} + C$$

$$= \frac{a^x e^x}{\log_e e + \log_e a} + C \quad [\because \log_e e = 1]$$

$$= \frac{a^x e^x}{\log_e (ae)} + C$$

$[\because \log m + \log n = \log mn]$

(iii) (c) We have, $\tan^{-1} x = 3 \tan^{-1} a$

We know that

$$3 \tan^{-1} \theta = \tan^{-1} \left(\frac{3\theta - \theta^3}{1 - 3\theta^2} \right)$$

$$\therefore \quad \tan^{-1} x = \tan^{-1} \left(\frac{3a - a^3}{1 - 3a^2} \right)$$

$$\Rightarrow \quad x = \frac{3a - a^3}{1 - 3a^2}$$

For the tangent inverse function to be defined, the argument must be real.

So, $\quad 1 - 3a^2 \ne 0$

$\Rightarrow \quad 1 \ne 3a^2$

$\Rightarrow \quad a^2 \ne \frac{1}{3}$

$\Rightarrow \quad |a| \ne \frac{1}{\sqrt{3}}$

So, the solution is valid for $|a| < \frac{1}{\sqrt{3}}$.

(iv) (d) **Assertion** (A) The given differential equation

$$a\left(\frac{dy}{dx}\right)^2 + b\left(\frac{dy}{dx}\right) = C$$

The power of the heighest order derivative = 2

$\therefore$ The degree of the given differential equation is 2.

So, Assertion is false and reason is true.

(v) (c) Given, five numbers x_1, x_2, x_3, x_4 and x_5 randomly selected from the numbers 1, 2, 3, ..., 18.

$\therefore$ Total number of ways to choose 5 numbers out of $18 = {}^{18}C_5$

$$= \frac{18!}{5!\,13!}$$

$$= \frac{18 \times 17 \times 16 \times 15 \times 14}{5 \times 4 \times 3 \times 2}$$

$$= 18 \times 17 \times 2 \times 14$$

These number arranged in the increasing pattern $x_1 < x_2 < x_3 < x_4 < x_5$,
On fixing $x_2 = 7$ and $x_4 = 11$
Then, number of ways of choosing x_1 from (1, 2, ..., 6) = 6 ways.
Number of ways choosing x_3 from {8, 9, 10} = 3 ways.
and number of ways of choosing x_5 from {12, 13, ..., 18} = 7 ways
Now, the number of favourable outcomes

$$= 6 \times 3 \times 7$$
$$= 126 \text{ ways}$$

∴ Required probability

$$= \frac{\text{Number of favourable outcomes}}{\text{Total number of outcomes}}$$
$$= \frac{126}{18 \times 17 \times 2 \times 14} = \frac{1}{17 \times 2 \times 2} = \frac{1}{68}$$

Hence, the probability that $x_2 = 7$ and $x_4 = 11$ is $\frac{1}{68}$.

(vi) (d) Given, $\begin{vmatrix} a & b & c \\ m & n & p \\ x & y & z \end{vmatrix} = k$ ...(i)

Then, $\Delta = \begin{vmatrix} 6a & 2b & 2c \\ 3m & n & p \\ 3x & y & z \end{vmatrix}$

On taking 2 as common from first row, we get

$$\Delta = 2\begin{vmatrix} 3a & b & c \\ 3m & n & p \\ 3x & y & z \end{vmatrix}$$

Now, taking 3 as common from first "Column" we get

$$\Delta = 2 \times 3\begin{vmatrix} a & b & c \\ m & n & p \\ x & y & z \end{vmatrix}$$

$\Delta = 6k$ [using Eq. (i)]

Hence, $\begin{vmatrix} 6a & 2b & 2c \\ 3m & n & p \\ 3x & y & z \end{vmatrix} = 6k$

(vii) (a) Given, $y = x^{\frac{1}{3}}$

To check the continuity at $x = 0$, we find

$$\text{LHL} = \lim_{x \to 0^-} f(x) = \lim_{h \to 0} f(0-h)$$
$$= \lim_{h \to 0} (-h)^{1/3} = 0$$
$$\text{RHL} = \lim_{x \to 0^+} f(x) = \lim_{h \to 0} f(0+h)$$
$$= \lim_{h \to 0} h^{1/3} = 0$$
$$f(0) = 0$$

Here, LHL = RHL = $f(0)$

Hence, $f(x) = x^{\frac{1}{3}}$ is continuous at $x = 0$.

Now, $y = x^{\frac{1}{3}}$

On differentiating w.r.t. x, we get

$$\frac{dy}{dx} = \frac{1}{3}x^{-\frac{2}{3}}$$

at $x = 0$,

$$\left.\frac{dy}{dx}\right|_{x=0} = \left.\frac{1}{3x^{\frac{2}{3}}}\right|_{x=0}$$

which is not define.

Hence, the function is not differentiable at $x = 0$.

(viii) (b) We have, $y = |x-1| + |x-4|$
for $x = 3$, $y = (x-1) - (x-4)$

$$y = x - 1 - x + 4$$
$$\Rightarrow \quad y = 3$$

On differentiating w.r.t. x, we get

$$\frac{dy}{dx} = \frac{d}{dx}(3) = 0 \qquad \left[\because \frac{d}{dx}(\text{constant}) = 0\right]$$

(ix) (c) **Statement I** An equivalence relation on a set is a relation which is reflexive, symmetric and transitive.

Reflexivity Let R and S be two equivalence relations on set A, then for any $a \in A$, $(a, a) \in R$ and $(a, a) \in S$. Thus, $(a, a) \in R \cap S$. Therefore, $R \cap S$ is reflexive.

Symmetry If $(a, b) \in R \cap S \Rightarrow (a, b) \in R$ and $(a, b) \in S$.
Since, R and S are symmetric, therefore $(b, a) \in R$ and $(b, a) \in S$.

$$\Rightarrow \quad (b, a) \in R \cap S$$

Therefore, $R \cap S$ is symmetric.

Transitivity If $(a, b) \in R \cap S$ and $(b, c) \in R \cap S$, then $(a, b) \in R$, $(a, b) \in S$ and $(b, c) \in R$, $(b, c) \in S$
$\Rightarrow (a, c) \in R$ and $(a, c) \in S$
$\Rightarrow (a, c) \in R \cap S$
Therefore, $R \cap S$ is transitive.

Thus, the intersection of two equivalence relation is also an equivalence relation. So, Statement I is true.
The union of two equivalence relations is not necessarily an equivalence relation.
If the union of two equivalence relations is an equivalence relation, then intersection also will be an equivalence relation.
So, Statement I is true only if Statement II is true.

(x) (a) Given a_{ij} denotes the elements of ith row and j^{th} column.

and $A = a_{ij} = \begin{cases} 0 & \text{for } i = j \\ 1 & \text{for } i > j \\ -1 & \text{for } i < j \end{cases}$

Let $A=\begin{bmatrix} a_{11} & a_{12} & a_{13} \\ a_{21} & a_{22} & a_{23} \\ a_{31} & a_{32} & a_{33} \end{bmatrix}$

Then, $A=\begin{bmatrix} 0 & -1 & -1 \\ 1 & 0 & -1 \\ 1 & 1 & 0 \end{bmatrix}$

$\because \quad |A|=\begin{vmatrix} 0 & -1 & -1 \\ 1 & 0 & -1 \\ 1 & 1 & 0 \end{vmatrix}$

$= 0(0+1)+1(0+1)-1(1-0)$

$= 0+1-1=0$

So, A is not invertible.

and Reason is the correct explanation of A.

(xi) (a) Given, $P\left(\frac{A}{B}\right)=0.25$ and $P(A\cap B)=0.12$

$\because \quad P\left(\frac{A}{B}\right)=\frac{P(A\cap B)}{P(A)}$

$\Rightarrow \quad P(A)=\frac{P(A\cap B)}{P\left(\frac{A}{B}\right)}=\frac{0.12}{0.25}=0.48$

Now, we know that

$P(A)=P(A\cap B)+P(A\cap B')$

$\Rightarrow P(A\cap B')=P(A)-P(A\cap B)$

$=0.48-0.12=0.36$

Hence, $P(A\cap B')=0.36$

(xii) Given, $|A|=3$

$\because \quad C=(\text{adj } A)^T$

$\Rightarrow \quad |C|=|(\text{adj } A)^T|=|\text{adj } A|=|A|^{3-1}$

[$\because |\text{adj } A|=|A|^{n-1}$, where n is the order of A]

$=3^{3-1}=3^2=9$

Hence, $|C^2|=|C|\cdot|C|=9\times 9=81$

(xiii) Given, R is a relation on set $\{a, b, c\}$ and $R=\{(b, b)\}$

Reflexivity Since, $(a,a)\notin R$ and $(c,c)\notin R$, therefore the relation R is not reflexive.

Symmetry If a relation is symmetric, then $(a,b)\in R \Rightarrow (b,a)\in R$.

Here, $(b,b)\in R$, so it is symmetric.

Transitivity R is not transitive.

Hence, the relation R is symmetric but not reflexive and transitive.

(xiv) Given function, $f: R\to R$.

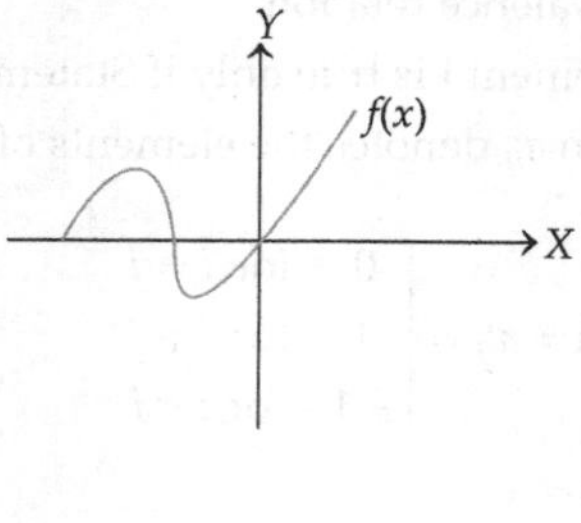

Since, each line in co-domain of the function parallel to X-axis, does not cuts the graph of function at least one point, therefore $f(x)$ is not an onto function.

(xv) Given, total number of machines = 3

Number of faulty machines = 2

Number of good machines = 3 − 2 = 1

Two test will be required and outcome will be first machine is faulty and second is good or both machines are faulty.

$\therefore$ Probability that only two tests are needed

$=\frac{2}{3}\times\frac{1}{2}+\frac{2}{3}\times\frac{1}{2}$

$=\frac{1}{3}+\frac{1}{3}$

$=\frac{2}{3}$

2. (i) We have, $x^y=y^x$

On taking log both sides, we get

$y\log x = x\log y$

On differentiating both sides, we get

$\frac{d}{dx}(y\log x)=\frac{d}{dx}(x\log y)$

$\Rightarrow \quad y\cdot\frac{1}{x}+\log x\frac{dy}{dx}=x\cdot\frac{1}{y}\frac{dy}{dx}+\log y$

$\Rightarrow \quad \frac{dy}{dx}\left(\log x-\frac{x}{y}\right)=\log y-\frac{y}{x}$

$\therefore \quad \frac{dy}{dx}=\frac{\log y-\frac{y}{x}}{\log x-\frac{x}{y}}$

Or

(ii) We have, $f(x)=x^2e^{-x}$

On differentiating both sides, we get

$f'(x)=-x^2e^{-x}+e^{-x}\cdot 2x$

$=e^{-x}(-x)[x-2]=-e^{-x}[x(x-2)]$

$\because e^x$ is always positive.

$\therefore \quad x(x-2)=0\Rightarrow x=0$ or $x=2$

For strictly decreasing function, $f'(x)<0$

$\Rightarrow x<0$ or $x>2$

$\therefore x\in(-\infty, 0)\cup(2,\infty)$

For strictly increasing function,

$f'(x)>0\Rightarrow 0<x<2\Rightarrow x\in(0, 2)$

$\therefore f(x)$ is strictly increasing in (0, 2) and strictly decreasing in $(-\infty, 0)\cup(2,\infty)$.

3. Let $I=\int_0^{\sqrt{2}}[x^2]\,dx$

We know that if $n\le x<n+1$ for any integer n, then $[x]=n$

$\therefore \int_0^{\sqrt{2}}[x^2]\,dx=\int_0^1 0\,dx+\int_1^{\sqrt{2}}1\,dx=(x)_1^{\sqrt{2}}=\sqrt{2}-1$

4. Given, the equation of the curve is

$$y = 4x^2 - 2x^3$$

On differentiating w.r.t. x, we get

$$\frac{dy}{dx} = 8x - 6x^2$$

$$= 2x(4 - 3x)$$

Slope of the tangent to the curve at origin.

$$m = \left(\frac{dy}{dx}\right)_{(0,0)} = 0$$

Now, the equation of tangent to the curve at $(0, 0)$ is

$$y - y_1 = m(x - x_1)$$

$$\Rightarrow \quad y - 0 = 0(x - 0) \Rightarrow y = 0$$

Hence, X-axis is the tangent to the curve.

5. (i) Let $I = \int \frac{2x^3 - 1}{x^4 + x}\,dx$

On dividing both numerator and denominator by x^2, we get

$$= \int \frac{\left(2x - \frac{1}{x^2}\right)}{x^2 + \frac{1}{x}}\,dx$$

On putting $x^2 + \frac{1}{x} = t, \Rightarrow \left(2x - \frac{1}{x^2}\right)dx = dt$

We get, $\quad I = \int \frac{1}{t}\,dt = \ln|t| + C$

$$\therefore \quad I = \ln\left|x^2 + \frac{1}{x}\right| + C$$

Or

(ii) Let $I = \int e^x \operatorname{cosec} x\,(1 - \cot x)\,dx$

$$= \int e^x(\operatorname{cosec} x - \operatorname{cosec} x \cdot \cot x)\,dx$$

$$= \int e^x(\operatorname{cosec} x + (-\operatorname{cosec} x \cdot \cot x))\,dx$$

$$\therefore \quad I = e^x \operatorname{cosec} x + C$$

$$\left[\because \int e^x(f(x) + f'(x))\,dx = e^x f(x) + C\right]$$

6. We have, $\tan^{-1}\left(\frac{x}{y}\right) + \tan^{-1}\left(\frac{y - x}{y + x}\right)$

$$= \tan^{-1}\left(\frac{x}{y}\right) + \tan^{-1}\left(\frac{1 - \frac{x}{y}}{1 + \frac{x}{y}}\right)$$

$$= \tan^{-1}\left(\frac{x}{y}\right) + \tan^{-1}(1) - \tan^{-1}\left(\frac{x}{y}\right)$$

$$\left[\because \tan^{-1} a - \tan^{-1} b = \tan^{-1}\left(\frac{a - b}{1 + ab}\right)\right]$$

$$= \tan^{-1}(1) = \frac{\pi}{4}$$

7. We have, $\sin^{-1}(x) + \sin^{-1}(1 - x) = \cos^{-1} x$

$$\Rightarrow \sin^{-1}(x) + \sin^{-1}(1 - x) = \frac{\pi}{2} - \sin^{-1} x,$$

$$\left[\because \cos^{-1} a + \sin^{-1} a = \frac{\pi}{2}\right]$$

$$\Rightarrow \quad \sin^{-1}(1 - x) = \frac{\pi}{2} - 2\sin^{-1} x$$

$$\Rightarrow \quad (1 - x) = \sin\left(\frac{\pi}{2} - 2\sin^{-1} x\right)$$

$$\Rightarrow \quad (1 - x) = \cos(2\sin^{-1} x)$$

$$\left[\because \sin\left(\frac{\pi}{2} - \theta\right) = \cos\theta\right]$$

$$\Rightarrow \quad (1 - x) = \cos(\cos^{-1}(1 - 2x^2))$$

$$[\because 2\sin^{-1} a = \cos^{-1}(1 - 2a^2)]$$

$$\Rightarrow \quad (1 - x) = 1 - 2x^2$$

$$\Rightarrow \quad 2x^2 - x = 0 \Rightarrow x(2x - 1) = 0$$

$$\therefore \quad x = 0, \frac{1}{2}$$

8. Let $I = \int \sqrt{\sec\frac{x}{2} - 1}\,dx$

$$= \int \sqrt{\frac{1 - \cos\frac{x}{2}}{\cos\frac{x}{2}}}\,dx$$

$$= \int \sqrt{\frac{\left(1 - \cos\frac{x}{2}\right)\left(1 + \cos\frac{x}{2}\right)}{\cos\frac{x}{2}\left(1 + \cos\frac{x}{2}\right)}}\,dx$$

$$= \int \frac{\sin\frac{x}{2}}{\sqrt{\cos^2\frac{x}{2} + \cos\frac{x}{2}}}\,dx$$

Put $\cos\frac{x}{2} = t$

$$\Rightarrow \quad -\sin\frac{x}{2} \cdot \frac{1}{2}\,dx = dt$$

$$\Rightarrow \quad \sin\frac{x}{2} \cdot dx = -2dt$$

Then, $\quad I = -2\int \frac{dt}{\sqrt{t^2 + t}} = -2\int \frac{dt}{\sqrt{\left(t + \frac{1}{2}\right)^2 - \left(\frac{1}{2}\right)^2}}$

$$= -2\log_e\left|\left(t + \frac{1}{2}\right) + \sqrt{t^2 + t}\right| + C$$

$$= -2\log_e\left|\left(\cos\frac{x}{2} + \frac{1}{2}\right) + \sqrt{\cos^2\frac{x}{2} + \cos\frac{x}{2}}\right| + C$$

$$\left[\because t = \cos\frac{x}{2}\right]$$

9. (i) Let $y(t)$ be the height of the kite at time t, x be the horizontal distance between the person and the ring on the ground, which is given as 8 m and $s(t)$ be the length of the string between the kite and the ring at time t.

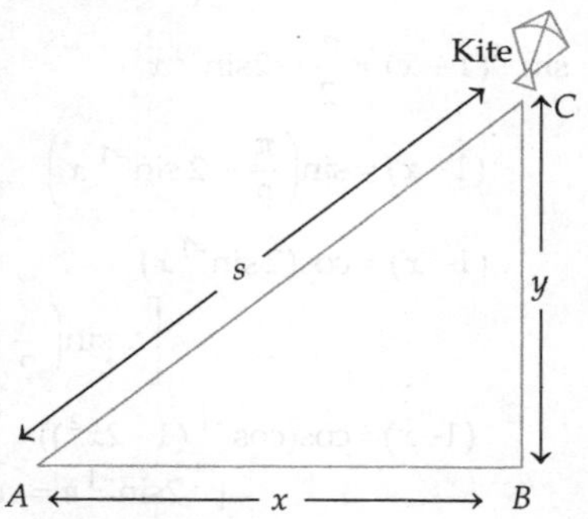

Given, $\frac{ds}{dt} = -1\,\text{m/sec}$

In ΔABC, using Pythagoras theorem,

$$s^2 = x^2 + y^2$$

$$\Rightarrow \quad s^2 = 8^2 + y^2 \quad \text{...(i)}$$

On differentiating w.r.t t, we get

$$2s\frac{ds}{dt} = 2y\frac{dy}{dt}$$

$$\Rightarrow \quad s\frac{ds}{dt} = y\frac{dy}{dt} \quad \text{...(ii)}$$

From Eq. (i), when $y = 15$, we get

$$s^2 = 8^2 + 15^2$$

$$= 64 + 225 = 289$$

$$\Rightarrow \quad s = 17\,\text{m}$$

Now, from Eq. (ii), putting $\frac{ds}{dt} = -1\,\text{m/sec}$,

$s = 17$ m and $y = 15$, we get

$$17(-1) = 15\frac{dy}{dt}$$

$$\therefore \quad \frac{dy}{dt} = -\frac{17}{15}\,\text{m/sec}$$

Hence, the kite is coming down at $\frac{17}{15}$ m/sec.

Or

(ii) We have,

$$y = (x + \sqrt{a^2 + x^2})^m \quad \text{...(i)}$$

On differentiating w.r.t. x, we get

$$\frac{dy}{dx} = m(x + \sqrt{a^2 + x^2})^{m-1}\cdot\left(1 + \frac{2x}{2\sqrt{a^2 + x^2}}\right)$$

$$\Rightarrow \frac{dy}{dx} = m(x + \sqrt{a^2 + x^2})^{m-1}\cdot\left(\frac{x + \sqrt{a^2 + x^2}}{\sqrt{a^2 + x^2}}\right) \quad \text{...(ii)}$$

$$\frac{dy}{dx} = \frac{m(x + \sqrt{a^2 + x^2})^m}{\sqrt{a^2 + x^2}}$$

$$\Rightarrow \quad \sqrt{a^2 + x^2}\cdot\frac{dy}{dx} = my$$

On squaring both sides, we get

$$\Rightarrow \quad (a^2 + x^2)\left(\frac{dy}{dx}\right)^2 = m^2y^2$$

Again, differentiating w.r.t. x, we get

$$2x\cdot\left(\frac{dy}{dx}\right)^2 + (a^2 + x^2)\cdot 2\cdot\frac{dy}{dx}\frac{d^2y}{dx^2} = 2m^2y\cdot\frac{dy}{dx}$$

On dividing by $2\cdot\frac{dy}{dx}$ both sides, we get

$$x\cdot\frac{dy}{dx} + (a^2 + x^2)\cdot\frac{d^2y}{dx^2} = m^2y$$

$$\therefore \quad (a^2 + x^2)\frac{d^2y}{dx^2} + x\frac{dy}{dx} - m^2y = 0$$ **Hence proved.**

10. Total number of possible outcomes, when a coin tossed three times $= 2^3 = 8$.

$S = \{HHH, HHT, HTT, HTH, TTH, THT, THH, TTT\}$

(a) If all three friends will get the same result, then

$S_1 = \{HHH, TTT\}$

Number of favourable outcomes = 2

$\therefore$ Probability that all three friends will get same result.

i.e. P(no odd person)

$$= \frac{\text{Number of favourable outcomes}}{\text{Total number of outcomes}}$$

$$= \frac{2}{8} = \frac{1}{4}$$

(b) Probability that they will get a different result in one round of tossing $= 1 - P$(no odd person)

$$= 1 - \frac{1}{4} = \frac{3}{4}$$

(c) Probability that they will need exactly four rounds of tossing to determine who would pay

$= P(\text{no odd person}) \times P(\text{no odd person})$

$\times P(\text{no odd person}) \times P(\text{odd person})$

$$= \frac{1}{4}\times\frac{1}{4}\times\frac{1}{4}\times\frac{3}{4} = \frac{3}{256}$$

Or

(ii) Let us define the events,

L = The event that the child is left-handed.

A = If both parents are left-handed with a 24% chance of the child being left handed.

B = If father is right-handed and the mother is left-handed with a 22% chance of child being left handed.

C = If father is left-handed and mother is right-handed with a 17% chance of child being left-handed.

D = Both parents are right-handed with a 9% chance of having a left handed-child.

Given that the events A, B, C and D are equally likely.

Therefore, $P(A) = P(B) = P(C) = P(D) = \frac{1}{4}$.

Now, $P\left(\frac{L}{A}\right) = \frac{24}{100} = 0.24$, $P\left(\frac{L}{B}\right) = \frac{22}{100} = 0.22$,

$P\left(\frac{L}{C}\right) = \frac{17}{100} = 0.17$ and $P\left(\frac{L}{D}\right) = \frac{9}{100} = 0.09$

(a) Probability that a randomly selected child is left-handed

$$= P(A) \times P\left(\frac{L}{A}\right) + P(B) \times P\left(\frac{L}{B}\right) + P(C) \times P\left(\frac{L}{C}\right) + P(D) \times P\left(\frac{L}{D}\right)$$

$$= \frac{1}{4} \times \frac{24}{100} + \frac{1}{4} \times \frac{22}{100} + \frac{1}{4} \times \frac{17}{100} + \frac{1}{4} \times \frac{9}{100}$$

$$= \frac{1}{4} \times \frac{72}{100} = \frac{18}{100} = 0.18$$

(b) The probability that a randomly selected child is left-handed given that exactly one of the parents is left handed $= P\left(\frac{L}{B}\right) + P\left(\frac{L}{C}\right)$

$$= \frac{22}{100} + \frac{17}{100}$$

$$= \frac{39}{100} = 0.39$$

(c) If a child is left handed, then the probability that both parents are left handed

$$P\left(\frac{A}{L}\right) = \frac{P(A) \times P\left(\frac{L}{A}\right)}{P(A) \times P\left(\frac{L}{A}\right) + P(B) \times P\left(\frac{L}{B}\right) + P(C) \times P\left(\frac{L}{C}\right) + P(D) \times P\left(\frac{L}{D}\right)}$$

$$= \frac{\frac{1}{4} \times \frac{24}{100}}{\frac{1}{4} \times \frac{72}{100}} \quad \text{[using part (i)]}$$

$$= \frac{24}{72} = \frac{1}{3}$$

11. Let x, y and z be the cost of one paper bag, one scrapbook and one pastel sheet respectively.

	Paper bags	**Scrap books**	**Pastel sheets**	**Fund raised**
School A	30	20	10	₹ 410
School B	20	10	20	₹ 290
School C	20	20	20	₹ 440

(i) Now, setting up the above information into a system of equations.

$$30x + 20y + 10z = 410$$
$$20x + 10y + 20z = 290$$
$$20x + 20y + 20z = 440$$

(ii) We have, $30x + 20y + 10z = 410$

$$20x + 10y + 20z = 290$$
$$20x + 20y + 20z = 440$$

Rewrite the system in matrix form $MX = N$ ...(i)

where $M = \begin{bmatrix} 30 & 20 & 10 \\ 20 & 10 & 20 \\ 20 & 20 & 20 \end{bmatrix}$, $X = \begin{bmatrix} x \\ y \\ z \end{bmatrix}$ and $N = \begin{bmatrix} 410 \\ 290 \\ 440 \end{bmatrix}$

$$\because |M| = \begin{vmatrix} 30 & 20 & 10 \\ 20 & 10 & 20 \\ 20 & 20 & 20 \end{vmatrix}$$

$$= 30(200 - 400) - 20(400 - 400) + 10(400 - 200)$$
$$= 30 \times (-200) + 10 \times 200$$
$$= -6000 + 2000 = -4000 \neq 0$$

$\therefore M^{-1}$ exists.

The cofactors of matrix M are

$M_{11} = -200$, $M_{12} = 0$, $M_{13} = 200$

$M_{21} = -200$, $M_{22} = 400$, $M_{23} = -200$

$M_{31} = 300$, $M_{32} = -400$, $M_{33} = -100$

$$\because \text{adj}(M) = \begin{bmatrix} -200 & 0 & 200 \\ -200 & 400 & -200 \\ 300 & -400 & -100 \end{bmatrix}^T$$

$$= \begin{bmatrix} -200 & -200 & 300 \\ 0 & 400 & -400 \\ 200 & -200 & -100 \end{bmatrix}$$

$$\therefore \quad M^{-1} = \frac{1}{|M|} \text{adj}(M)$$

$$= \frac{-1}{4000} \begin{bmatrix} -200 & -200 & 300 \\ 0 & 400 & -400 \\ 200 & -200 & -100 \end{bmatrix}$$

Now, from Eq. (i), we get $X = M^{-1}N$

$$= -\frac{1}{4000} \begin{bmatrix} -200 & -200 & 300 \\ 0 & 400 & -400 \\ 200 & -200 & -100 \end{bmatrix} \begin{bmatrix} 410 \\ 290 \\ 440 \end{bmatrix}$$

$$= -\frac{1}{40} \begin{bmatrix} -2 & -2 & 3 \\ 0 & 4 & -4 \\ 2 & -2 & -1 \end{bmatrix} \begin{bmatrix} 410 \\ 290 \\ 440 \end{bmatrix}$$

$$= -\frac{1}{4} \begin{bmatrix} -2 & -2 & 3 \\ 0 & 4 & -4 \\ 2 & -2 & -1 \end{bmatrix} \begin{bmatrix} 41 \\ 29 \\ 44 \end{bmatrix}$$

$$= -\frac{1}{4} \begin{bmatrix} -82 - 58 + 132 \\ 0 + 116 - 176 \\ 82 - 58 - 44 \end{bmatrix} = -\frac{1}{4} \begin{bmatrix} -8 \\ -60 \\ -20 \end{bmatrix} = \begin{bmatrix} 2 \\ 15 \\ 5 \end{bmatrix}$$

Hence, $x = 2$, $y = 15$ and $z = 5$

(iii) The cost of one paper bag is ₹ 2, the cost of one scrap book is ₹ 15, and the cost of one pastel sheet is ₹ 5.

12. (i) **Method 1**

We have,

$$(xdy - ydx)y\sin\left(\frac{y}{x}\right) = (ydx + xdy)x\cos\left(\frac{y}{x}\right)$$

$$\Rightarrow \frac{dy}{dx} = \frac{(xy)\cos\left(\frac{y}{x}\right) + y^2\sin\left(\frac{y}{x}\right)}{(xy)\sin\left(\frac{y}{x}\right) - x^2\cos\left(\frac{y}{x}\right)}$$

$$\Rightarrow \frac{dy}{dx} = \frac{1+\left(\frac{y}{x}\right)\tan\left(\frac{y}{x}\right)}{\tan\left(\frac{y}{x}\right) - \frac{1}{\left(\frac{y}{x}\right)}},$$

which is homogenous differential equation of type $\frac{dy}{dx} = f\left(\frac{y}{x}\right)$.

Let $y = vx \Rightarrow \frac{dy}{dx} = v + x\frac{dv}{dx}$

$$\Rightarrow \quad v + x\frac{dv}{dx} = \frac{1 + v\tan v}{\tan v - \frac{1}{v}}$$

$$\Rightarrow \left(\tan v - \frac{1}{v}\right)dv = 2\frac{dx}{x},$$

which is variable separable form where variables are v and x.

On integrating both sides, we get

$$\Rightarrow \quad \int\left(\tan v - \frac{1}{v}\right)dv = 2\int\frac{dx}{x}$$

$$\Rightarrow \log|\sec v| - \log|v| = 2\log|x| + \log c$$

$$\Rightarrow \quad \log|\sec v| = \log|v \cdot x^2 \cdot c|$$

$$\Rightarrow \quad \sec v = cx^2 v$$

$$\Rightarrow \quad \sec\left(\frac{y}{x}\right) = c(xy)$$

Given that $y = \pi$ when $x = 1$

Then, $\sec\pi = c\pi$

$$\Rightarrow \quad c = -\frac{1}{\pi}$$

Hence, required particular solution is

$$\sec\left(\frac{y}{x}\right) = -\frac{1}{\pi}(xy)$$

Alternate

The given differential equation is

$$(xdy - ydx)\,y\sin\left(\frac{y}{x}\right) = (ydx + xdy)\,x\cos\left(\frac{y}{x}\right).$$

$$\Rightarrow (xdy - ydx)\frac{\sin\left(\frac{y}{x}\right)}{\cos\left(\frac{y}{x}\right)} = \frac{(ydx + xdy)x}{y}$$

On dividing both sides by x^2, we get

$$\Rightarrow \frac{(xdy - ydx)}{x^2}\tan\left(\frac{y}{x}\right) = \frac{(ydx + xdy)x}{x^2 y}$$

$$\Rightarrow \frac{(xdy - ydx)}{x^2}\tan\left(\frac{y}{x}\right) = \frac{(ydx + xdy)}{xy}$$

$$\Rightarrow \tan\left(\frac{y}{x}\right)d\left(\frac{y}{x}\right) = \frac{d(xy)}{xy}$$

which is variable separable form where variables are $\frac{y}{x}$ and xy.

On integrating both sides, we get

$$\Rightarrow \quad \int\tan\frac{y}{x}\cdot d\left(\frac{y}{x}\right) = \int\frac{d(xy)}{xy}$$

$$\Rightarrow \quad \log\left|\sec\left(\frac{y}{x}\right)\right| = \log(xy) + \log c$$

$$\Rightarrow \quad \sec\left(\frac{y}{x}\right) = c(xy)$$

Given that $y = \pi$ when $x = 1$

So that $c = -\frac{1}{\pi}$.

Hence, required particular solution is

$$\sec\left(\frac{y}{x}\right) = -\frac{1}{\pi}(xy).$$

Or

(ii) We have, $\int_0^{\pi}(\sin^4 x + \cos^4 x)dx$

$$\left[\because \sin^4 x + \cos^4 x = 1 - \frac{1}{2}\sin^2 2x = \frac{1}{4}(3 + \cos 4x)\right]$$

$$\therefore \int_0^{\pi}(\sin^4 x + \cos^4 x)dx = \frac{1}{4}\int_0^{\pi}(3 + \cos 4x)dx$$

$$= \frac{1}{4}\left[3x + \frac{\sin 4x}{4}\right]_0^{\pi} = \frac{3\pi}{4}$$

Let $I = \int_{-2\pi}^{2\pi}\frac{\sin^4 x + \cos^4 x}{1 + e^x}dx$ ...(i)

$$= \int_{-2\pi}^{2\pi}\frac{\sin^4(-x) + \cos^4(-x)}{1 + e^{-x}}dx$$

$$\left[\because \int_a^b f(x)dx = \int_a^b f(a + b - x)dx\right]$$

$$= \int_{-2\pi}^{2\pi}\frac{\sin^4 x + \cos^4 x}{1 + e^{-x}}dx$$

$I = \int_{-2\pi}^{2\pi}\frac{e^x(\sin^4 x + \cos^4 x)}{1 + e^x}dx$ ...(ii)

On adding Eqs. (i) and (ii), we get

$$I + I = \int_{-2\pi}^{2\pi}\frac{\sin^4 x + \cos^4 x}{1 + e^x}dx + \int_{-2\pi}^{2\pi}\frac{e^x(\sin^4 x + \cos^4 x)}{1 + e^x}dx$$

$$\therefore 2I = \int_{-2\pi}^{2\pi}(\sin^4 x + \cos^4 x)dx$$

$$= 2\int_0^{2\pi}(\sin^4 x + \cos^4 x)dx$$

$$\left[\because \int_{-a}^{a} f(x)dx = 2\int_0^a f(x)dx, \text{ if } f(-x) = f(x)\right]$$

$$\therefore I = \int_0^{2\pi}(\sin^4 x + \cos^4 x)dx = 2\int_0^{\pi}(\sin^4 x + \cos^4 x)dx$$

$$\left[\because \int_0^{2a} f(x)dx = 2\int_0^a f(x)dx, \text{ if } f(2a - x) = f(x)\right]$$

$$= 2 \cdot \frac{3\pi}{4} = \frac{3\pi}{2} \quad \left[\because \int_0^{\pi}(\sin^4 x + \cos^4 x)\, dx = \frac{3\pi}{4}\right]$$

13. (i) Given radius of sphere be R.

Let radius and height of cone be r and h.

Then, height of cone, $h = R + x$

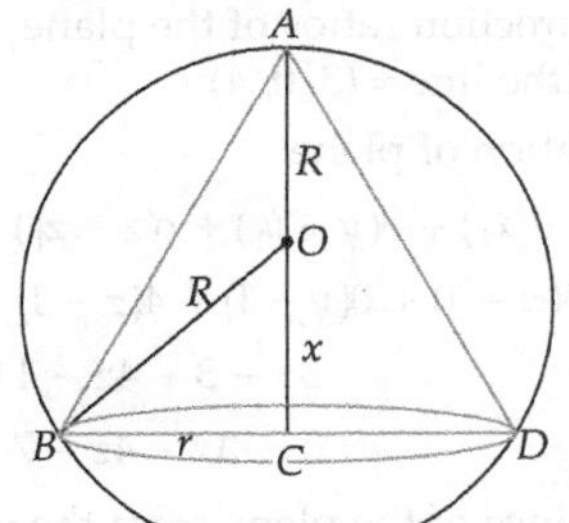

From the diagram

In ΔOCB,

$$r^2 + x^2 = R^2 \quad \ldots\text{(i) [using Pythagoras theorem]}$$

Volume of cone, $V = \frac{1}{3}\pi r^2 h = \frac{1}{3}\pi r^2(R + x)$

$$= \frac{1}{3}\pi(R + x)(R^2 - x^2)$$

[from Eq. (i)]

$$\frac{dV}{dx} = \frac{1}{3}\pi[(R^2 - x^2)(1) + (R + x)(-2x)]$$

$$\frac{dV}{dx} = \frac{1}{3}\pi(R + x)(R - 3x)$$

and $\frac{d^2V}{dx^2} = \frac{1}{3}\pi\,[1(R - 3x) + (R + x)(-3)]$

$$= \frac{1}{3}\pi\,(-2R - 6x)$$

For maxima and minima, $\frac{dV}{dx} = 0$

$$\Rightarrow \quad \frac{1}{3}\pi\,(R + x)(R - 3x) = 0$$

$$\Rightarrow R = 3x \text{ or } x = \frac{R}{3}$$

Now, applying the second derivative test, we have

$$\frac{d^2V}{dx^2} = \frac{1}{3}\pi[-2R - 6x] < 0, \text{ at } x = \frac{R}{3}$$

Volume is maximum at $x = \frac{R}{3}$

Height of cone, $h = R + x = R + \frac{R}{3} = \frac{4R}{3}$

$\therefore$ Ratio of height of cone to diameter of sphere

$$= \frac{h}{2R} = \frac{\frac{4R}{3}}{2R} = \frac{2}{3}$$

Or

(ii) Given r and h be the radius and height of the cylinder, respectively. (from figure)

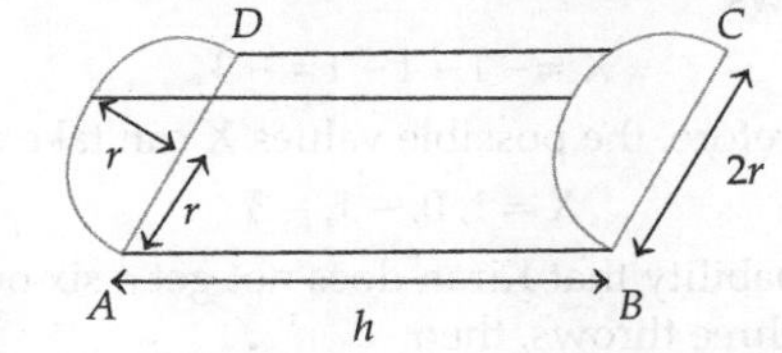

Volume of half cylinder $= \frac{1}{2}\pi r^2 h = V$

$$\Rightarrow \quad h = \frac{2V}{\pi r^2}$$

and total surface area $S = \pi r^2 + \pi r h + 2rh$

$$= \pi r^2 + \pi r \cdot \frac{2V}{\pi r^2} + 2r \cdot \frac{2V}{\pi r^2}$$

$$= \pi r^2 + \frac{1}{r}\left(2V + \frac{4V}{\pi}\right)$$

On differentiating two times w.r.t. r, we get

$$\frac{dS}{dr} = 2\pi r - \frac{1}{r^2}\left(2V + \frac{4V}{\pi}\right)$$

and $\frac{d^2S}{dr^2} = 2\pi + \frac{2}{r^3}\left(2V + \frac{4V}{\pi}\right)$

For maximum and minimum, $\frac{dS}{dr} = 0$

$$\Rightarrow \quad 2\pi r - \frac{1}{r^2}\left(2V + \frac{4V}{\pi}\right) = 0$$

$$\Rightarrow \quad 2\pi r = \frac{1}{r^2}\left(2V + \frac{4V}{\pi}\right)$$

$$\Rightarrow \quad \pi r^3 = V\left(\frac{\pi + 2}{\pi}\right) \Rightarrow r^3 = \frac{V}{\pi}\left(\frac{\pi + 2}{\pi}\right)$$

At $r^3 = \frac{V}{\pi}\left(\frac{\pi + 2}{\pi}\right)$

$$\frac{d^2S}{dr^2} = 2\pi + \frac{2}{r^3}\left(2V + \frac{4}{\pi}\right) > 0$$

$\therefore$ Surface area is minimum.

Now, on putting the value of V in Eq. (i), we get

$$\pi r^3 = \frac{1}{2}\pi r^2 h \cdot \frac{\pi + 2}{\pi} \Rightarrow \frac{2r}{h} = \frac{\pi + 2}{\pi}$$

Hence, ratio of the length of cylinder to the diameter of semi-circular ends is $\pi : \pi + 2$.

14. The random variable X denotes the points earned by Kiran. The possible values of X depends on the outcomes of the die rolls.

(i) If Kiran get a six on the first throw, then

$X = 1$ [$\because$ she gets + 1 for the six]

If Kiran does not get a six on the first throw but get a six on the second throw, then

$X = -1 + 1 = 0$

If Kiran does not get a six on the first two throws but gets a six on the third throw, then

$$X = -1 - 1 + 1 = -1$$

If Kiran does not get a six on any of the three throws.

$$X = -1 - 1 - 1 = -3$$

Therefore, the possible values X can take are

$$X = 1, 0, -1, -3$$

(ii) Probability that Kiran does not get a six on any of the three throws, then

$$P(X = -3) = \frac{5}{6} \times \frac{5}{6} \times \frac{5}{6} = \frac{125}{216}$$

Probability that Kiran gets a six on the third thrown, then

$$P(X = -1) = \frac{5}{6} \times \frac{5}{6} \times \frac{1}{6} = \frac{25}{216}$$

Probability that Kiran gets a six on the second thrown, then

$$P(X = 0) = \frac{5}{6} \times \frac{1}{6} = \frac{5}{36}$$

Probability that Kiran gets a six on the first throw, then

$$P(X = 1) = \frac{1}{6}$$

Hence, required probability distribution

X	-3	-1	0	1
$P(X)$	$\frac{125}{216}$	$\frac{25}{216}$	$\frac{5}{36}$	$\frac{1}{6}$

(iii) Required expected value $= \Sigma P_i X_i = (-3)\left(\frac{125}{216}\right)$

$$+ (-1)\left(\frac{25}{216}\right) + 0 + \left(\frac{1}{6}\right)$$

$$= -\frac{91}{54} = -1\frac{37}{54} \approx -1.69$$

15. (i) (a) **Statement I** If $\vec{a}$ and $\vec{b}$ represent two adjacent sides of a parallelogram, then the diagonals are represented as

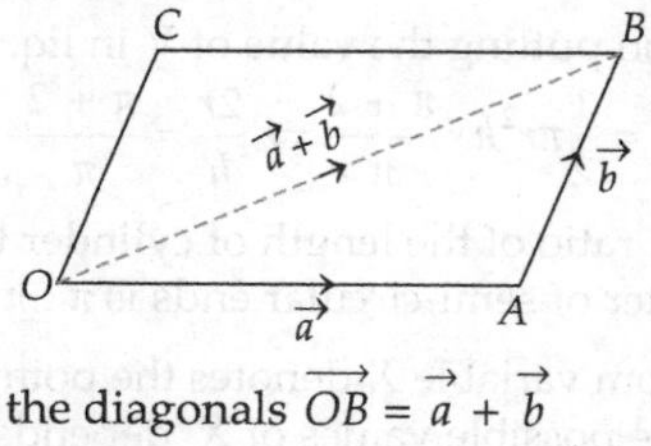

Here, the diagonals $\overrightarrow{OB} = \vec{a} + \vec{b}$

and diagonal $\overrightarrow{AC} = \vec{a} - \vec{b}$

So, Statement I is correct.

Statement II We know that the diagonals of a parallelogram intersects each other at the mid point.

Therefore, the sides of the parallelogram are actually represented by $\frac{1}{2}(\vec{a} + \vec{b})$ and $\frac{1}{2}(\vec{a} - \vec{b})$.

So, Statement II is incorrect.

(ii) (c) Given, plane passes through the point $P \equiv (1, 1, 1)$ and the equation of line is

$$\frac{x-1}{3} = \frac{y-1}{0} = \frac{z-1}{4}$$

Since, the line is perpendicular to the plane, therefore the normal of the plane is parallel to the line.

$\Rightarrow$ The direction ratios of the plane = The direction ratios of the line = (3, 0, 4)

The equation of plane

$$a(x - x_1) + b(y - y_1) + c(z - z_1) = 0$$

$$\Rightarrow \quad 3(x-1) + 0(y-1) + 4(z-1) = 0$$

$$\Rightarrow \quad 3x - 3 + 4z - 4 = 0$$

$$\Rightarrow \quad 3x - 4z - 7 = 0$$

The distance of the plane from the origin

$$d = \left|\frac{3 \times 0 + 4 \times 0 - 7}{\sqrt{3^2 + 4^2}}\right|$$

$$d = \left|\frac{-7}{\sqrt{25}}\right| = \left|\frac{-7}{5}\right| = \frac{7}{5} \text{ units}$$

(iii) (c) Given, the direction cosines of the line are $< \frac{1}{c}, \frac{1}{c}, \frac{1}{c} >$.

We know that

$$l^2 + m^2 + n^2 = 1$$

$$\Rightarrow \quad \left(\frac{1}{c}\right)^2 + \left(\frac{1}{c}\right)^2 + \left(\frac{1}{c}\right)^2 = 1$$

$$\Rightarrow \quad \frac{3}{c^2} = 1$$

$$\Rightarrow \quad c^2 = 3$$

$$\therefore \quad c = |\sqrt{3}|$$

$$\Rightarrow \quad c = \pm\sqrt{3}$$

(iv) Given, $\hat{a}$ is a unit vector

$$\Rightarrow \quad |\hat{a}| = 1$$

and $\vec{a}$ is perpendicular to $\vec{b}$

$$\Rightarrow \quad \vec{a} \cdot \vec{b} = 0$$

$$\because \quad (\vec{a} + 2\vec{b}) \cdot (3\vec{a} - \vec{b}) = -5$$

$$\because 3|\vec{a}|^2 - \vec{a} \cdot \vec{b} + 6\vec{b} \cdot \vec{a} - 2|\vec{b}|^2 = -5$$

$$\Rightarrow \quad 3 - 2|\vec{b}|^2 = -5 \quad [\because \vec{a} \cdot \vec{b} = \vec{b} \cdot \vec{a} = 0]$$

$$\Rightarrow \quad 8 = 2|\vec{b}|^2 \Rightarrow |\vec{b}|^2 = 4$$

$$\therefore \quad |\vec{b}| = 2$$

(v) Placing the coordinate axes as illustrated, coordinates of A are (2, 0, 0), B are (0, 4, 3) and C are (1, 4, 0).

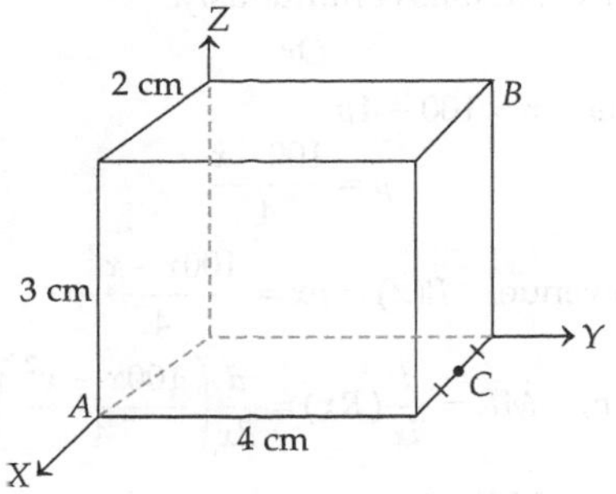

$\therefore \quad \overrightarrow{BA} = \overrightarrow{OA} - \overrightarrow{OB} = 2\hat{i} - 4\hat{j} - 3\hat{k}$

and $\overrightarrow{BC} = \overrightarrow{OC} - \overrightarrow{OB} = \hat{i} - 3\hat{k}$

Now, $\overrightarrow{BA} \cdot \overrightarrow{BC} = (2\hat{i} - 4\hat{j} - 3\hat{k}) \cdot (\hat{i} - 3\hat{k}) = 2 + 9 = 11$

16. (i) Given, $\vec{a} = 4\hat{i} - \hat{j} + \hat{k}$ and $\vec{b} = -2\hat{i} + \hat{j} - 2\hat{k}$

$$\vec{a} \times \vec{b} = \begin{vmatrix} \hat{i} & \hat{j} & \hat{k} \\ 4 & -1 & 1 \\ -2 & 1 & -2 \end{vmatrix}$$

$$= \hat{i}(2-1) - \hat{j}(-8+2) + \hat{k}(4-2)$$
$$= \hat{i} + 6\hat{j} + 2\hat{k}$$

and $|\vec{a} \times \vec{b}|$

$$= \sqrt{(1)^2 + 6^2 + 2^2} = \sqrt{41}$$

A vector of magnitude 9 units and perpendicular to the vectors $\vec{a}$ and $\vec{b}$ is $9\left(\dfrac{\vec{a} \times \vec{b}}{|\vec{a} \times \vec{b}|}\right)$

Hence, required vector is $\dfrac{9}{\sqrt{41}}(\hat{i} + 6\hat{j} + 2\hat{k})$.

Or

(ii) Let $\vec{a} = 2x^2\hat{i} + 3x\hat{j} + \hat{k}$ and $\vec{b} = \hat{i} - 2\hat{j} + x^2\hat{k}$

$\because$ Angle between the vectors is obtuse

$\Rightarrow \quad \cos\theta < 0$

$\Rightarrow \quad \dfrac{\vec{a} \cdot \vec{b}}{|\vec{a}||\vec{b}|} < 0$

$\Rightarrow \quad \vec{a} \cdot \vec{b} < 0$

$\Rightarrow \quad 2x^2 - 6x + x^2 < 0 \Rightarrow 3x(x-2) < 0$

$\therefore 0 < x < 2$ i.e. $x \in (0, 2)$

17. Given equation of line is

$\vec{r} = (2\hat{i} - 2\hat{j} + 3\hat{k}) + \lambda(\hat{i} - \hat{j} + 4\hat{k})$.

Position vector of the point on the line is $2\hat{i} - 2\hat{j} + 3\hat{k}$

and direction vector, $\vec{d} = \hat{i} - \hat{j} + 4\hat{k}$

Given plane is $\vec{r} \cdot (\hat{i} + 5\hat{j} + \hat{k}) - 5 = 0$.

$\therefore$ Normal vector of the plane is $\vec{n} = \hat{i} + 5\hat{j} + \hat{k}$

If straight line and plane are parallel to each other, then direction vector of line and normal vector of the plane are perpendicular to each other.

Now, $\vec{n} \cdot \vec{d} = (\hat{i} - \hat{j} + 4\hat{k})(\hat{i} + 5\hat{j} + \hat{k}) = 1 - 5 + 4 = 0$

$\Rightarrow$ They are perpendicular to each other.

$\therefore$ Straight line and plane are parallel to each other.

$\therefore$ Required distance $= \dfrac{(2\hat{i} - 2\hat{j} + 3\hat{k}) \cdot (\hat{i} + 5\hat{j} + \hat{k}) - 5}{\sqrt{1 + 25 + 1}}$

$$= \frac{10}{\sqrt{27}} = \frac{10}{3\sqrt{3}} \text{ units}$$

Or

(ii) Let the equation of the plane be $a(x - x_1) + b(y - y_1) + c(z - z_1) = 0$, which is passing through $(-1, 0, 2)$.

$\therefore \quad a(x + 1) + b(y - 0) + c(z - 2) = 0 \quad$ ...(i)

Given line $\dfrac{x - 0}{-2} = \dfrac{y - 1}{3} = \dfrac{z - 1}{-1}$ is passing through the point (0, 1, 1) and having direction ratios $<-2, 3, -1>$

Since, the plane contains the line and the point, then

$$a(1) + b(1) + c(1 - 2) = 0$$

$\Rightarrow \quad a + b - c = 0 \quad$ ...(ii)

Also, the line and normal to the plane are perpendicular

$\therefore \quad -2a + 3b - c = 0 \quad$ ...(iii)

On solving Eqs. (ii) and (iii), we get

$$\frac{a}{\begin{vmatrix} 1 & -1 \\ 3 & -1 \end{vmatrix}} = \frac{b}{\begin{vmatrix} -1 & 1 \\ -1 & -2 \end{vmatrix}} = \frac{c}{\begin{vmatrix} 1 & 1 \\ -2 & 3 \end{vmatrix}}$$

$$\frac{a}{2} = \frac{b}{3} = \frac{c}{5} = k \text{ (say)}$$

Hence, required equation of the plane is

$2(x + 1) + 3(y - 0) + 5(z - 2) = 0$

or $\quad 2x + 3y + 5z - 8 = 0$

18. (i) Given, the equation of the curve is $y = x|x|$.

$$\therefore \begin{cases} -x^2, & x < 0 \\ x^2, & x \geq 0 \end{cases}$$

Hence, sketch of the region enclosed bounded by the curve, $y = x|x|$ and the ordinates $x = -1$ and $x = 1$ is as follows.

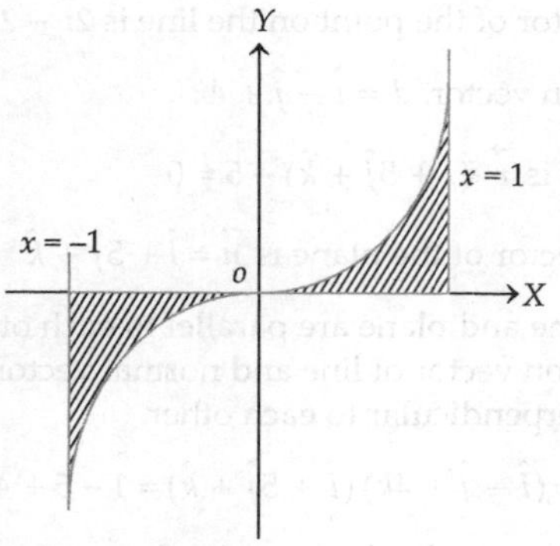

(ii) $\int_0^1 x^2 dx = \left[\frac{x^3}{3}\right]_0^1 = \frac{1}{3}$

(iii) Area of the shaded region = 2× Area of shaded region is Ist quadratnt $= 2\int_0^1 x^2 dx = \frac{2}{3}$ sq units

19. (i) (b) If the average cost (AC) is constant at all level of output, it means that the marginal cost (MC) is equal to the average cost (AC).
So, MC = AC

(ii) (d) If $r = 0$, then the regression lines are perpendicular to each other and if $r = \pm 1$, then regression lines are coincide.
Hence, only III and IV statements are correct.

(iii) Given, $\bar{x} = 53$, $\bar{y} = 28$, $b_{yx} = -1.2$ and $b_{xy} = -0.3$
We know that $r^2 = b_{yx} \times b_{xy} = (-1.2) \times (-0.3) = 0.36$
$\Rightarrow \quad r = -0.6$
[b_{xy} and b_{yx} both are negative]

(iv) Given, $R(x) = 36x + 3x^2 + 5$
$\Rightarrow \quad MR = \frac{d}{dx}(36x + 3x^2 + 5) = 36 + 6x$
$\therefore \; MR(x = 5) = 66$

(v) Given, $C(x) = 210x + 7000$ and $R(x) = 280x$
Minimum number must be produced and sold daily when $R(x) = C(x)$
$\Rightarrow \quad 210x + 7000 = 280x$
$\Rightarrow \quad 70x = 7000$
$\Rightarrow \quad x = 100$
Hence, minimum number that must be produced and sold is 100.

20. (i) Given, $C(x) = 200 + 20x - \frac{1}{2}x^2$
We know that average cost
$$AC = \frac{C(x)}{x}$$
$$\Rightarrow \quad AC = \frac{200}{x} + 20 - \frac{1}{2}x$$
To find AC falls,
$$\frac{d}{dx}(AC) = \frac{d}{dx}\left(\frac{200}{x} + 20 - \frac{1}{2}x\right)$$
$$= -\frac{200}{x^2} - \frac{1}{2} = -\left(\frac{200}{x^2} + \frac{1}{2}\right) < 0, \forall \, x > 0.$$
Hence, AC falls continuously.

Or

(ii) Given, $x = 100 - 4p$
$$\Rightarrow \quad p = \frac{100 - x}{4}$$
$$\therefore \text{Revenue,} \quad R(x) = px = \frac{100x - x^2}{4}$$
$$\text{Then,} \quad MR = \frac{d}{dx}(Rx) = \frac{d}{dx}\left(\frac{100x - x^2}{4}\right) = \frac{100 - 2x}{4}$$
$\because \quad MR = 0$
$$\frac{100 - 2x}{4} = 0 \Rightarrow 100 = 2x$$
$\therefore \quad x = 50$

21. (i) Given,
Number of families, $n = 50$
Expenditure on accommodation = ₹ x
Expenditure on food and entertainment = ₹ y
$\Sigma x = 8500$, $\Sigma y = 9600$
$\sigma_x = 60$, $\sigma_y = 20$ and $r = 0.6$.
$$\text{Now,} \quad \bar{x} = \frac{\Sigma x}{n} = \frac{8500}{50} = 170,$$
$$\bar{y} = \frac{\Sigma y}{n} = \frac{9600}{50} = 192,$$
$$\text{and } b_{yx} = r\frac{\sigma_y}{\sigma_x} = 0.6 \times \frac{20}{60} = 0.2$$
Regression equation y on x is
$$y - \bar{y} = b_{yx}(x - \bar{x})$$
$$y - 192 = 0.2(x - 170)$$
$\Rightarrow \quad y - 192 = 0.2x - 34$
$\Rightarrow \quad y = 0.2x + 158$
When $\quad x = 200$
Then, $\quad y = 0.2(200) + 158 = 198$
$\therefore$ Expenditure on food and entertainment is ₹ 198.

Or

(ii) (a) Given, linear regression $3x + 2y - 26 = 0$ ...(i)
and $6x + y - 31 = 0$ ...(ii)
Let $\bar{x}$ and $\bar{y}$ be the mean value of x and y.
Then, $(\bar{x}, \bar{y})$ satisfies the Eqs. (i) and (ii), we get
$3\bar{x} + 2\bar{y} - 26 = 0$ ...(iii)
$6\bar{x} + \bar{y} - 31 = 0$ ...(iv)
By cross-multiplication method, we get
$$\frac{\bar{x}}{\begin{matrix} 2 & -26 \\ 1 & -31 \end{matrix}} = \frac{\bar{y}}{\begin{matrix} -26 & 3 \\ -31 & 6 \end{matrix}} = \frac{1}{\begin{matrix} 3 & 2 \\ 6 & 1 \end{matrix}}$$
$$\Rightarrow \quad \frac{\bar{x}}{-36} = \frac{\bar{y}}{-63} = \frac{1}{-9}$$

or $\frac{\overline{x}}{4} = \frac{\overline{y}}{7} = \frac{1}{1}$

$\Rightarrow \overline{x} = 4$ and $\overline{y} = 7$

Hence, the mean values of x and y are 4 and 7.

(b) We have,

$$3x + 2y - 26 = 0 \quad \text{...(i)}$$
$$6x + y - 31 = 0 \quad \text{...(ii)}$$

From Eq. (i)

$$2y = -3x + 26$$
$$y = -\frac{3}{2}x + 13$$
$$\therefore \quad b_{xy} = -\frac{3}{2}$$

From Eq. (ii), we get

$$6x = -y + 31$$
$$\Rightarrow \quad x = \frac{-1}{6}y + \frac{31}{6}$$
$$\Rightarrow \quad x = \frac{-1}{6}y + \frac{31}{6}$$
$$\therefore \quad b_{yx} = \frac{-1}{6}$$

Now, $r^2 = b_{yx} \times b_{xy}$

$$= \left(-\frac{3}{2}\right) \times \left(\frac{-1}{6}\right) = \frac{1}{4}$$
$$\therefore \quad r^2 = \frac{1}{4} \Rightarrow r = \frac{\pm 1}{2}$$

We know that b_{yx}, b_{xy} and r have same sign,

therefore $r = -\frac{1}{2}$.

22. Given, $Z = px + qy$, $p, q > 0$

Subject to constraints $x + y \leq 60$

$5x + y \leq 100$

and $x, y \geq 0$

Table for $x + y = 60$ is ...(i)

x	0	60
y	60	0

The line passes through the points (0, 60) and (60, 0).

At (0, 0),

$$0 + 0 \leq 60$$
$$\Rightarrow \quad 0 \leq 6 \text{ (true)}$$

So, the half plane lies towards the origin.

Table for $5x + y = 100$ is ...(ii)

x	0	20
y	100	0

The line passes through the points (0, 100) and (20, 0).

At (0, 0),

$$0 + 0 \leq 100$$
$$\Rightarrow \quad 0 \leq 100 \text{ (true)}$$

So, the half plane lies towards the origin.

On solving Eqs. (i) and (ii), we get

$$x = 10 \text{ and } y = 50$$

On plating the graph, we get the feasible region $ABCD$ as shown below

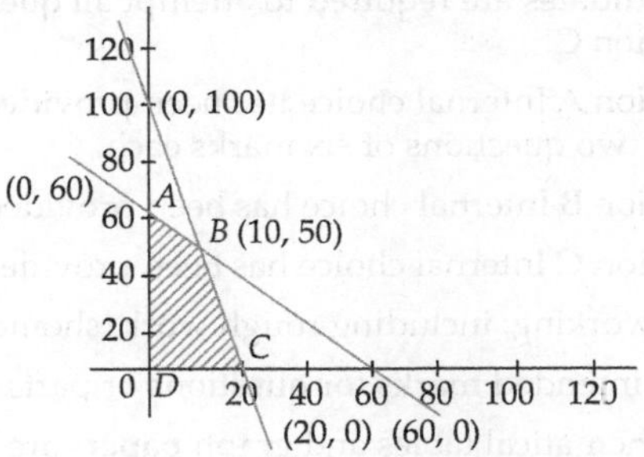

Thus, the corner points of the feasible region are $A(0, 60)$, $B(10, 50)$, $C(20, 0)$ and $D(0, 0)$.

(ii) We have, $Z = px + qy$

Given, Z is maximum at (0, 60) and (10, 50)

$$\therefore \quad 0 \cdot p + 60 \cdot q = 10 \cdot p + 50 \cdot q$$
$$\Rightarrow \quad 10p = 10q$$
$$\Rightarrow \quad p = q$$

which is the required relation. Also, there can be infinite number of optimal solutions.

Write your Roll No.

Board Exam Paper 2024

Mathematics 12th (Code 860)

No. of Ques : 22 **No. of Sections :** 3 **Time :** 3 Hrs. **Max. Marks :** 80

General Instructions

1. Candidates are allowed additional 15 minutes for only reading the paper. They must not start writing during this time.
2. This question paper consists of three sections A, B and C.
3. Candidates are required to attempt all questions from Section A and all questions Either from Section B or Section C.
4. Section A Internal choice has been provided in two questions of two marks each, two questions of four marks each and two questions of six marks each.
5. Section B Internal choice has been provided in one question of two marks and one question of four marks.
6. Section C Internal choice has been provided in one question of two marks and one question of four marks.
2. All working, including rough work, should be done on the same sheet as, and adjacent to the rest of the answer.
8. The intended marks for questions or parts of questions are given in bracket [ ].
9. Mathematical tables and graph papers are provided.

Section A (65 Marks)

1. In subparts (i) to (x) choose the correct options and in subparts (xi) to (xv), answer the questions as instructed. [$15 \times 1 = 15$]

(i) Let L be a set of all straight lines in a plane. The relation R on L defined as 'perpendicular to' is

(a) Symmetric and Transitive
(b) Transitive
(c) Symmetric (d) Equivalence

(ii) The order and the degree of differential equation $1+\left(\frac{dy}{dx}\right)^2 = \frac{d^2y}{dx^2}$ are

(a) 2 and $\frac{3}{2}$ (b) 2 and 3
(c) 3 and 4 (d) 2 and 1

(iii) Let A be a non-empty set.

Statement I Identity relation on A is reflexive.

Statement II Every reflexive relation on A is an identity relation.

(a) Both the statements are true.
(b) Both the statements are false.
(c) Statement I is true and Statement II is false.
(d) Statement I is false and Statement II is true.

(iv) The graph of the function f is shown below

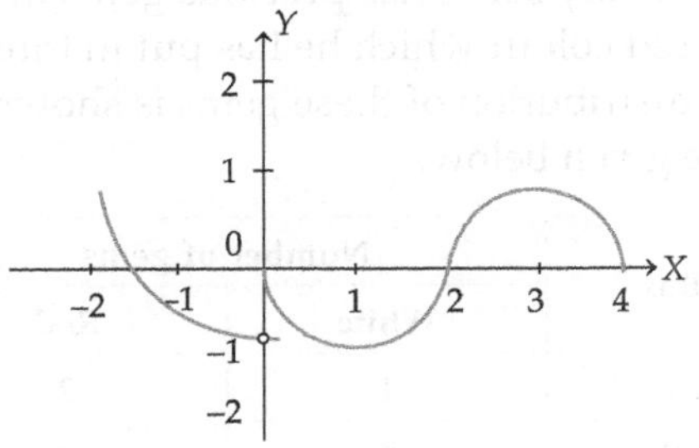

Of the following options, at what values of x is the function f not differentiable?

(a) At $x = 0$ and $x = 2$
(b) At $x = 1$ and $x = 3$
(c) At $x = -1$ and $x = 1$
(d) At $x = -1.5$ and $x = 1.5$

(v) The value of $\text{cosec}\left(\sin^{-1}\left(\frac{-1}{2}\right)\right) - \sec\left(\cos^{-1}\left(\frac{-1}{2}\right)\right)$ is equal to

(a) – 4 (b) 0 (c) – 1 (d) 4

(vi) The value $\int_1^{\sqrt{3}} \frac{dx}{1+x^2}$ is

(a) $\frac{\pi}{2}$ (b) $\frac{2\pi}{3}$ (c) $\frac{\pi}{6}$ (d) $\frac{\pi}{12}$

(vii) **Assertion** (A) Let the matrices $A = \begin{pmatrix} -3 & 2 \\ -5 & 4 \end{pmatrix}$ and $B = \begin{pmatrix} 4 & -2 \\ 5 & -3 \end{pmatrix}$ be such that $A^{100} B = BA^{100}$.

Reason (R) $AB = BA$ implies $A^n B = BA^n$ for all positive integers n.

(a) Both Assertion and Reason are true and Reason is the correct explanation for Assertion.
(b) Both Assertion and Reason are true but Reason is not the correct explanation for Assertion.
(c) Assertion is true and Reason is false.
(d) Assertion is false and Reason is true.

(viii) If $\int (\cot x - \text{cosec}^2 x) e^x \, dx = e^x f(x) + C$, then $f(x)$ will be

(a) $\cot x + \text{cosec } x$ (b) $\cot^2 x$
(c) $\cot x$ (d) $\text{cosec } x$

(ix) In which one of the following intervals is the function $f(x) = x^3 - 12x$ increasing?

(a) $(-2, 2)$ (b) $(-\infty, -2) \cup (2, \infty)$
(c) $(-2, \infty)$ (d) $(-\infty, 2)$

(x) If A and B are symmetric matrices of the same order, then $AB - BA$ is

(a) Skew-symmetric matrix
(b) Symmetric matrix
(c) Diagonal matrix
(d) Identity matrix

(xi) Find the derivative of $y = \log x + \frac{1}{x}$ with respect to x.

(xii) Teena is practising for an upcoming Rifle Shooting tournament. The probability of her shooting the target in the 1st, 2nd, 3rd and 4th shots are 0.4, 0.3, 0.2 and 0.1, respectively. Find the probability of atleast one shot of Teena hitting the target.

(xiii) Which one of the following graphs is a function of x?

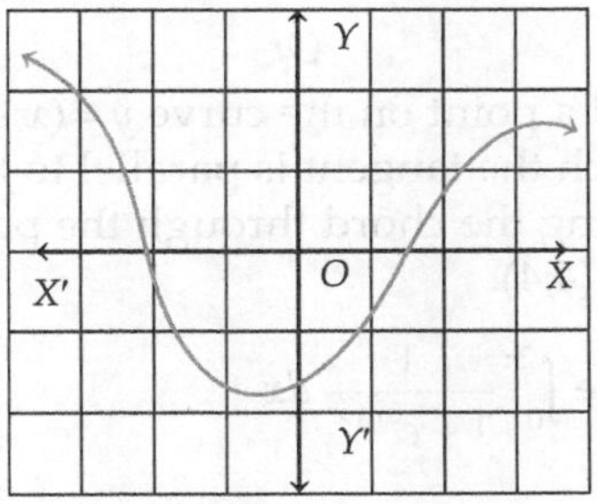

Graph A

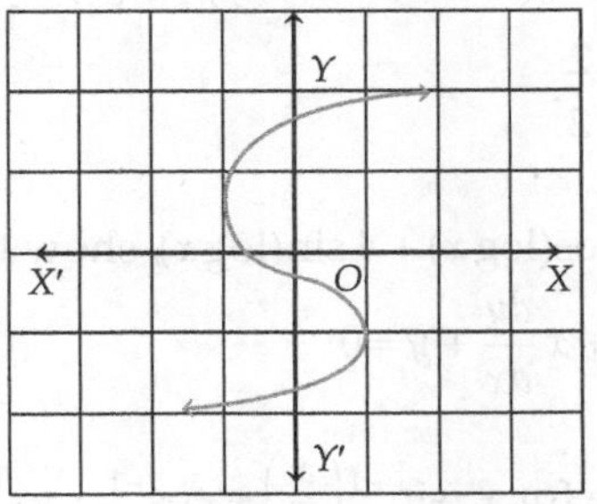

Graph B

(xiv) Evaluate $\int_0^6 |x+3| \, dx$

(xv) Given that $\frac{1}{y} + \frac{1}{x} = \frac{1}{12}$ and y decreases at a rate of 1 cms^{-1}, find the rate of change of x when $x = 5$ cm and $y = 1$ cm.

2. (i) Let $f : R - \left\{\frac{-1}{3}\right\} \to R - \{0\}$ be defined as $f(x) = \frac{5}{3x+1}$ is invertible. Find $f^{-1}(x)$. [2]

Or

(ii) If $f: R \rightarrow R$ is defined by $f(x)=\frac{2x-7}{4}$, show that $f(x)$ is one-one and onto. [2]

3. Find the value of the determinant given below, without expanding it at any stage.

$$\begin{vmatrix} \beta\gamma & 1 & \alpha(\beta+\gamma) \\ \gamma\alpha & 1 & \beta(\gamma+\alpha) \\ \alpha\beta & 1 & \gamma(\alpha+\beta) \end{vmatrix}$$ [2]

4. (i) Determine the value of k for which the following function is continuous at $x=3$.

$$f(x)=\begin{cases} \frac{(x+3)^2-36}{x-3}; & x \neq 3 \\ k; & x=3 \end{cases}$$ [2]

Or

(ii) Find a point on the curve $y=(x-2)^2$ at which the tangent is parallel to the line joining the chord through the points (2,0) and (4,4). [2]

5. Evaluate $\int_0^{2\pi} \frac{1}{1+e^{\sin x}}\, dx$ [2]

6. Evaluate $P(A \cup B)$, if $2P(A)=P(B)=\frac{5}{13}$ and $P\left(\frac{A}{B}\right)=\frac{2}{3}$. [2]

7. If $y=3\cos(\log x)+4\sin(\log x)$, show that

$$x^2\frac{d^2y}{dx^2}+x\frac{dy}{dx}+y=0$$ [4]

8. (i) Solve for x: $\sin^{-1}\left(\frac{x}{2}\right)+\cos^{-1} x=\frac{\pi}{6}$ [4]

Or

(ii) If $\sin^{-1} x+\sin^{-1} y+\sin^{-1} z=\pi$, show that $x^2-y^2-z^2+2yz\sqrt{1-x^2}=0$. [4]

9. (i) Evaluate $\int x^2 \cos x\, dx$ [4]

Or

(ii) Evaluate $\int \frac{x+7}{x^2+4x+7}\, dx$ [4]

10. A jewellery seller has precious gems in white and red colour which he has put in three boxes. The distribution of these gems is shown in the table given below:

Box	Number of gems	
	White	Red
I	1	2
II	2	3
III	3	1

He wants to gift two gems to his mother. So, he asks her to select one box at random and pick out any two gems one after the other without replacement from the selected box. The mother selects one white and one red gem.

Calculate the probability that the gems drawn are from Box II. [4]

11. A furniture factory uses three types of wood namely, teakwood, rosewood and satinwood for manufacturing three types of furniture, that are table, chair and cot.

The wood requirements (in tonnes) for each type of furniture are given below

	Table	Chair	Cot
Teakwood	2	3	4
Rosewood	1	1	2
Satinwood	3	2	1

It is found that 29 tonnes of teakwood, 13 tonnes of rosewood and 16 tonnes of satinwood are available to make all three types of furniture.

Using the above information, answer the following questions:

(i) Express the data given in the table above in the form of a set of simultaneous equations.

(ii) Solve the set of simultaneous equations formed in subpart (i) by matrix method.

(iii) Hence, find the number of table(s), chair(s) and cot(s) produced. [6]

12. (i) Mrs. Roy designs a window in her son's study room, so that the room gets maximum sunlight. She designs the window in the shape of a rectangle surmounted by an equilateral triangle.
If the perimeter of the window is 12 m, find the dimensions of the window that will admit maximum sunlight into the room.

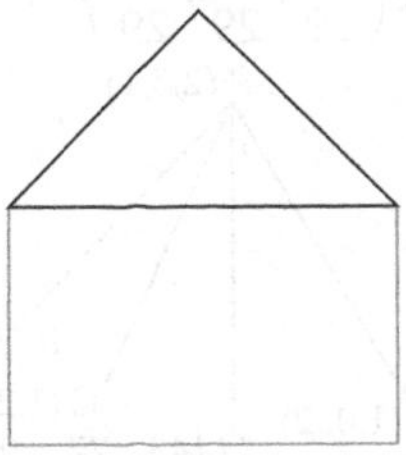

[6]

Or

(ii) Sumit has bought a closed cylindrical dustbin. The radius of the dustbin is r cm and height is h cm. It has a volume of $20\pi\, \text{cm}^3$.

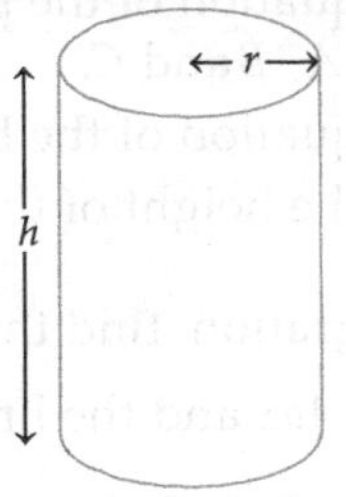

(a) Express h in terms of r, using the given volume.

(b) Prove that the total surface area of the dustbin is $2\pi r^2 + \frac{40\pi}{r}$.

(c) Sumit wants to paint the dustbin. The cost of painting the base and top of the dustbin is ₹ 2 per cm^2 and the cost of painting the curved side is ₹ 25 per cm^2. Find the total cost in terms of r, for painting the outer surface of the dustbin including the base and top.

(d) Calculate the minimum cost for painting the dustbin. [6]

13. (i) Solve the following differential equation
$2ye^{\frac{x}{y}}dx + \left(y - 2xe^{\frac{x}{y}}\right)dy = 0$, given $x = 0$ and $y = 1$. [6]

Or

(ii) Solve the following differential equation
$x(x^2 - 1)\frac{dy}{dx} = 1$, $y = 0$, given $x = 2$. [6]

14. A primary school teacher wants to teach the concept of 'larger number' to the students of Class II.

To teach this concept, he conducts an activity in his class. He asks the children to select two numbers from a set of numbers given as 2, 3, 4, 5 one after the other without replacement.

All the outcomes of this activity are tabulated in the form of ordered pairs given below.

	2	3	4	5
2	(2, 2)	(2, 3)	(2, 4)	
3	(3, 2)	(3, 3)		(3, 5)
4	(4, 2)		(4, 4)	(4, 5)
5		(5, 3)	(5, 4)	(5, 5)

(i) Complete the table given above.

(ii) Find the total number of ordered pairs having one larger number.

(iii) Let the random variable X denote the larger of two numbers in the ordered pair.
Now, complete the probability distribution table for X given below

X	3	4	5
$P(X = x)$			

(iv) Find the value of $P(X < 5)$.

(v) Calculate the expected value of the probability distribution. [6]

Section B (15 Marks)

15. In subparts (i) and (ii) choose the correct options and in subparts (iii) to (v), answer the questions as instructed. [5×1 = 5]

(i) If $\vec{a} = 3\hat{i} - 2\hat{j} + \hat{k}$ and $\vec{b} = 2\hat{i} - 4\hat{j} - 3\hat{k}$, then the value of $|\vec{a} - 2\vec{b}|$ will be

(a) $\sqrt{85}$ (b) $\sqrt{86}$ (c) $\sqrt{87}$ (d) $\sqrt{88}$

(ii) If a line makes an angle α, β and γ with positive direction of the coordinate axes, then the value of $\sin^2\alpha + \sin^2\beta + \sin^2\gamma$ will be

(a) 1 (b) 3 (c) – 2 (d) 2

(iii) In the figure given below, if the coordinates of the point P are (a, b, c), then what are the perpendicular distances of P from XY, YZ and ZX planes respectively?

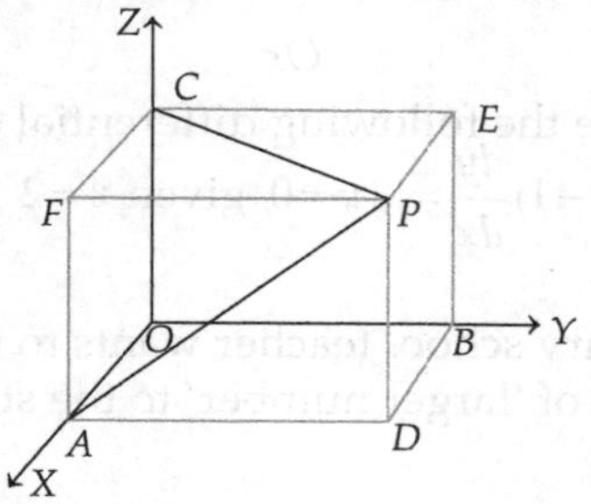

(iv) If $\vec{a} = 2\hat{i} + \hat{j} + 2\hat{k}$ and $\vec{b} = 5\hat{i} - 3\hat{j} + \hat{k}$, find the projection of $\vec{b}$ on $\vec{a}$.

(v) Find a vector of magnitude 20 units parallel to the vector $2\hat{i} + 5\hat{j} + 4\hat{k}$.

16. (i) If $\vec{a} \times \vec{b} = \vec{a} \times \vec{c}$ where $\vec{a}$, $\vec{b}$ and $\vec{c}$ are non-zero vectors, then prove that either $\vec{b} = \vec{c}$ or $\vec{a}$ and $(\vec{b} - \vec{c})$ are parallel. [2]

Or

(ii) If $\vec{a}$ and $\vec{b}$ are two non-zero vectors such that $|\vec{a} \times \vec{b}| = \vec{a} \cdot \vec{b}$, find the angle between $\vec{a}$ and $\vec{b}$. [2]

17. A mobile tower is situated at the top of a hill. Consider the surface on which the tower stands as a plane having points $A(1, 0, 2)$, $B(3, -1, 1)$ and $C(1, 2, 1)$ on it. The mobile tower is tied with three cables from the points A, B and C such that it stands vertically on the ground. The top of the tower is at point $P(2, 3, 1)$ as shown in the figure below. The foot of the perpendicular from the point P on the plane is at the point $Q\left(\frac{43}{29}, \frac{77}{29}, \frac{9}{29}\right)$.

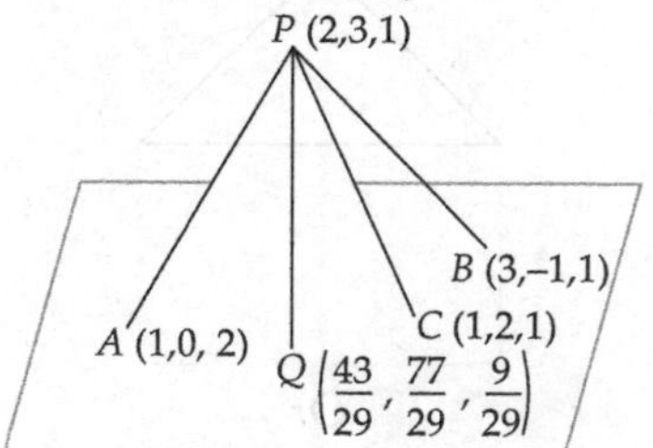

Answer the following questions.

(i) Find the equation of the plane containing the points A, B and C.

(ii) Find the equation of the line PQ.

(iii) Calculate the height of the tower. [4]

18. (i) Using integration, find the area bounded by the curve $y^2 = 4ax$ and the line $x = a$. [4]

Or

(ii) Using integration, find the area of the region bounded by the curve $y^2 = 4x$ and $x^2 = 4y$. [4]

Section C (15 Marks)

19. In subparts (i) and (ii) choose the correct options and in subparts (iii) to (v), answer the questions as instructed. [5×1 = 5]

(i) A company sells hand towels at ₹100 per unit. The fixed cost for the company to manufacture hand towels is ₹ 35000 and variable cost is estimated to be 30% of total revenue. What will be the total cost function for manufacturing hand towels?

(a) 35000 + 3x

(b) 35000 + 30x

(c) 35000 + 100x

(d) 35000 + 10x

(ii) If the correlation coefficient of two sets of variables (X, Y) is $\frac{-3}{4}$, which one of the following statements is true for the same set of variables?

(a) Only one of the two regression lines has a negative coefficient.

(b) Both regression coefficients are positive.

(c) Both regression coefficients are negative.

(d) One of the lines of regression is parallel to the X-axis.

(iii) If the total cost function is given by $C = x + 2x^3 - \frac{7}{2}x^2$, find the Marginal Average Cost function (MAC).

(iv) The equations of two lines of regression are $4x+3y+7=0$ and $3x+4y+8=0$. Find the mean value of x and y.

(v) The manufacturer of a pen fixes its selling price at ₹ 45, and the cost function is $C(x)=30x+240$. The manufacturer will begin to earn profit, if he sells more than 16 pens. Why? Give one reason.

20. (i) The average cost function associated with producing and marketing x units of an item is given by $AC=x+5+\frac{36}{x}$.

(a) Find the total cost function.

(b) Find the range of values of x for which average cost is increasing. [2]

Or

(ii) A monopolist's demand function is $x=60-\frac{p}{5}$. At what level of output will marginal revenue be zero? [2]

21. (i) *XYZ* company plans to advertise some vacancies. The Manager is asked to suggest the monthly salary for these vacancies based on the years of experience. To do so, the Manager studies the years of service and the monthly salary drawn by the existing employees in the company.

Following is the data that the Manager refers to

Years of service (X)	11	7	9	5	8	6	10
Monthly salary (in ₹ 1000) (Y)	10	8	6	5	9	7	11

(a) Find the regression equation of monthly salary on the years of service.

(b) If a person with 13 years of experience applies for a job in this company, what monthly salary will be suggested by the Manager? [4]

Or

(ii) The line of regression of marks in Statistics (X) and marks in Accountancy (Y) for a class of 50 students is $3y-5x+180=0$. The average score in Accountancy is 44 and the variance of marks in Statistics is $\left(\frac{9}{16}\right)$th of variance of marks in Accountancy.

(a) Find the average score in Statistics

(b) Find the coefficient of correlation between marks in Statistics and marks in Accountancy. [4]

22. Aman has ₹ 1500 to purchase rice and wheat for his grocery shop. Each sack of rice and wheat costs ₹ 180 and ₹ 120 respectively. He can store a maximum number of 10 bags in his shop. He will earn a profit of ₹ 11 per bag of rice and ₹ 9 per bag of wheat. [4]

(i) Formulate a linear programming problem to maximise Aman's profit.

(ii) Calculate the maximum profit.

Solutions *in Topper's Style*

1. (i) (c) Given, the relation R is defined as

$$R = \{(L_1, L_2) : L_1 \perp L_2\}$$

Now, R is not reflexive as every line is not perpendicular to itself.

Since, $L_1 \perp L_2$, therefore L_2 is also perpendicular to L_1.

Thus, relation is symmetric.

Also, $L_1 \perp L_2$ and $L_2 \perp L_3$.

Then, L_1 may or may not be perpendicular to L_3.

So, R is not transitive.

(ii) (d) Given, $1 + \left(\frac{dy}{dx}\right)^2 = \frac{d^2y}{dx^2}$

Here, the highest order derivative is $\frac{d^2y}{dx^2}$.

So, the order of given differential equation = 2

and the degree of given differential equation = 1

(iii) (c) Let A be a non-empty set.

Statement I Identity relation on A is reflexive.

Consider an example.

Let $A = \{1, 2, 3\}$

Now, a relation R defined as

$R = \{(1, 1), (2,2), (3, 3)\}$ is an identity relation which is reflexive.

But $R' = \{(1, 1), (1, 3), (3, 3), (2, 2), (2, 3)\}$ is a reflexive relation but not identity relation.

So, Statement II is not necessarily true.

(iv) (a) Given, graph of the function f is

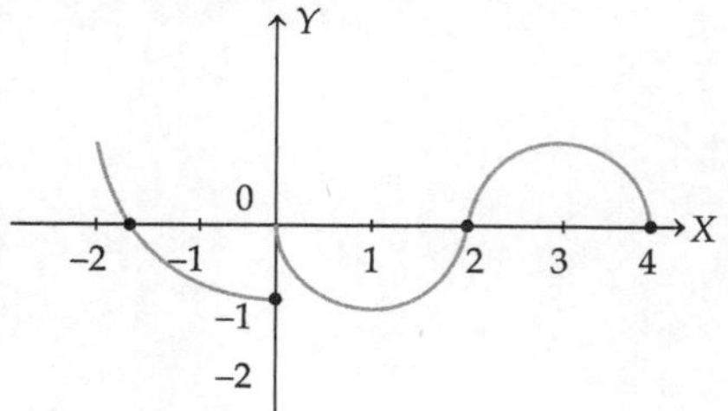

At $x = 0$, we cannot draw a tangent, therefore the function is not differentiable at $x = 0$.

Similarly, at $x = 2$, we cannot draw a tangent. Therefore, function is not differentiable at $x = 2$.

(v) (b) We have,

$$\text{cosec}\left[\sin^{-1}\left(\frac{-1}{2}\right) - \sec\left[\cos^{-1}\left(\frac{-1}{2}\right)\right]\right]$$

$$= \text{cosec}\left[\sin^{-1}\left\{\sin\left(\frac{-\pi}{6}\right)\right\}\right] - \sec\left[\cos^{-1}\left\{\cos\left(\frac{2\pi}{3}\right)\right\}\right]$$

$$\left[\because -\sin\frac{\pi}{6} = \sin\left(\frac{-\pi}{6}\right) = \frac{-1}{2} \text{ and } \cos\left(\frac{2\pi}{3}\right) = \frac{-1}{2}\right]$$

$$= \text{cosec}\left[\frac{\pi}{6}\right] - \sec\left[\frac{2\pi}{3}\right] = -2 - (-2) = 0$$

(vi) (d) Let

$$I = \int_1^{\sqrt{3}} \frac{dx}{1 + x^2}$$

$$= [\tan^{-1} x]_1^{\sqrt{3}}$$

$$\left[\because \int \frac{1}{x^2 + a^2}\, dx = \frac{1}{a} \tan^{-1}\left(\frac{x}{a}\right)\right]$$

$$= \tan^{-1}(\sqrt{3}) - \tan^{-1}(1)$$

$$= \frac{\pi}{3} - \frac{\pi}{4} = \frac{\pi}{12}$$

(vii) (a) We have,

$$A = \begin{bmatrix} -3 & 2 \\ -5 & 4 \end{bmatrix} \text{ and } B = \begin{bmatrix} 4 & -2 \\ 5 & -3 \end{bmatrix}$$

Here, $AB = \begin{bmatrix} -3 & 2 \\ -5 & 4 \end{bmatrix} \begin{bmatrix} 4 & -2 \\ 5 & -3 \end{bmatrix} = \begin{bmatrix} -2 & 0 \\ 0 & -2 \end{bmatrix}$

and $BA = \begin{bmatrix} 4 & -2 \\ 5 & -3 \end{bmatrix} \begin{bmatrix} -3 & 2 \\ -5 & 4 \end{bmatrix} = \begin{bmatrix} -2 & 0 \\ 0 & -2 \end{bmatrix}$

We know that if $AB = BA$, then by mathematical induction $A^n B = BA^n$, n is positive integers.

For $n = 100$, we get

$$A^{100} B = BA^{100}$$

Hence, both Assertion (A) and Reason (R) are true and Reason (R) is the correct explanation of Assertion (A).

(viii) (c) We have,

$$\int (\cot x - \text{cosec}^2 x) e^x \, dx = e^x f(x) + C$$

Taking LHS

$$\int (\cot x - \text{cosec}^2 x) e^x \, dx$$

$$= \int e^x \cot x \, dx - \int e^x \text{cosec}^2 x \, dx$$

$= e^x \cot x + \int \operatorname{cosec}^2 x \cdot e^x dx - \int e^x \operatorname{cosec}^2 x \, dx$ [integrating by part]

$= e^x \cot x + C$

On comparing with RHS, we get

$f(x) = \cot x$

(ix) (b) We have,

$$f(x) = x^3 - 12x$$

$$\Rightarrow \quad f'(x) = 3x^2 - 12$$

For increasing,

$$f'(x) > 0$$

$$\Rightarrow \quad 3x^2 - 12 > 0$$

$$\Rightarrow \quad 3(x^2 - 4) > 0$$

$$\Rightarrow \quad 3(x - 2)(x + 2) > 0$$

Now, sign of $f'(x)$

$-\infty$ —— + ve —— -2 —— − ve —— 2 —— + ve —— ∞

Function is increasing on $(-\infty, -2)$ and $(2, \infty)$.

Hence, the function is increasing in the interval $(-\infty, -2) \cup (2, \infty)$.

(x) (a) Given, A and B are two symmetric matrices.

Then, $A' = A$ and $B' = B$

Now, $(AB - BA)' = (AB)' - (BA)'$

$= (B'A' - A'B')$

$= (BA - AB)$

$= -(AB - BA)$

Hence, $(AB - BA)$ is skew-symmetric matrix.

(xi) We have,

$$y = \log x + \frac{1}{x}$$

On differentiating w.r.t. x, we get

$$\frac{dy}{dx} = \frac{d}{dx}(\log x) + \frac{d}{dx}\left(\frac{1}{x}\right)$$

$$= \frac{1}{x} - \frac{1}{x^2}$$

(xii) Given, probability of her shooting the target in

$P(\text{1st shot}) = 0.4$

$P(\text{2nd shot}) = 0.3$

$P(\text{3rd shot}) = 0.2$

and $P(\text{4th shot}) = 0.1$

$\therefore$ The probability of atleast one shot of Teena hit the target

$= 1 -$ Probability of none of the shot hitting the target

$= 1 - [(1 - 0.4)(1 - 0.3)(1 - 0.2)(1 - 0.1)]$

$= 1 - (0.6 \times 0.7 \times 0.8 \times 0.9)$

$= 1 - 0.3024 = 0.6976$

(xiii) By the definition of function

If A and B are any two sets, then a function $f : A \to B$ is a rule that assigns to each element of A exactly one element of B.

So, Graph A represents a function of x but Graph B is not a function because at $x = 0$, we get three values of y.

(xiv) We have,

$$\int_0^6 |x + 3| \, dx$$

Here, $f(x) = \begin{cases} x + 3, & x \geq -3 \\ -(x + 3) & x < -3 \end{cases}$

By the property of definite integral, we know

$$\int_a^b f(x)\,dx = \int_a^c f(x)\,dx + \int_c^b f(x)\,dx$$

where, $a < c < b$

Now, $\int_0^6 |x + 3| \, dx = \int_0^{-3} -(x + 3)\,dx + \int_{-3}^6 (x + 3)\,dx$

$$= -\left[\frac{x^2}{2} + 3x\right]_0^{-3} + \left[\frac{x^2}{2} + 3x\right]_{-3}^{6}$$

$$= -\left[\frac{9}{2} - 9\right] + \left[18 + 18 - \frac{9}{2} + 9\right]$$

$$= \frac{9}{2} + 45 - \frac{9}{2} = 45$$

(xv) We have, $\frac{1}{y} + \frac{1}{x} = \frac{1}{12}$ ...(i)

and $\frac{dy}{dt} = -1 \text{ cm/s}$

On differentiating Eq. (i) w.r.t. t, we get

$$-\frac{1}{y^2}\frac{dy}{dt} - \frac{1}{x^2}\frac{dx}{dt} = 0$$

$$\Rightarrow \quad \frac{1}{y^2} - \frac{1}{x^2}\frac{dx}{dt} = 0 \quad \left[\because \frac{dy}{dt} = -1\right]$$

$$\Rightarrow \quad \frac{dx}{dt} = \frac{x^2}{y^2}$$

When $x = 5$ cm and $y = 1$ cm, then

$$\frac{dx}{dt} = \frac{5^2}{1^2} = 25 \text{ cm/s}$$

Hence, the rate of change of x i.e. $\frac{dx}{dt}$ is 25 cm/s.

2. (i) Given that $f : R - \left\{\frac{-1}{3}\right\} \longrightarrow R - \{0\}$ be defined as

$$f(x) = \frac{5}{3x + 1}$$

Assume that $y = \frac{5}{3x + 1}$

$$\Rightarrow \quad 3xy + y = 5$$

$$\Rightarrow \quad 3xy = 5 - y$$

$\Rightarrow \quad x = \dfrac{5-y}{3y} = f(y)$

Thus, $f^{-1}(x) = \left(\dfrac{5-x}{3x}\right)$

which is the required solution.

Or

(ii) A mapping $f : R \longrightarrow R$ is defined by $f(x) = \dfrac{2x-7}{4}$

Let $x_1, x_2 \in R$, then for one-one,

$$f(x_1) = f(x_2)$$

$$\Rightarrow \quad \frac{2x_1 - 7}{4} = \frac{2x_2 - 7}{4}$$

$$\Rightarrow \quad 2x_1 - 7 = 2x_2 - 7 \Rightarrow x_1 = x_2$$

Thus, f is one-one.

Now, let $\quad y = \dfrac{2x-7}{4}$

Then, $\quad 4y = 2x - 7$

$\Rightarrow \quad 2x = 4y + 7$

$$x = \frac{4y+7}{2} = f(y)$$

Clearly, for each $y \in R$, there exists

$x = \dfrac{4y+7}{2} \in R$ such that

$$f(x) = f\left(\frac{4y+7}{2}\right) = \frac{1}{4}\left[2\left(\frac{4y+7}{2}\right) - 7\right]$$

$$= \frac{1}{4}[4y + 7 - 7] = y$$

Thus, f is onto.

Hence, f is one-one and onto i.e. f is bijective.

3. We have,

$$\begin{vmatrix} \beta\gamma & 1 & \alpha(\beta+\gamma) \\ \gamma\alpha & 1 & \beta(\gamma+\alpha) \\ \alpha\beta & 1 & \gamma(\alpha+\beta) \end{vmatrix}$$

On applying $C_1 \to C_1 + C_3$, we get

$$\begin{vmatrix} \alpha\beta+\beta\gamma+\gamma\alpha & 1 & \alpha(\beta+\gamma) \\ \alpha\beta+\beta\gamma+\gamma\alpha & 1 & \beta(\gamma+\alpha) \\ \alpha\beta+\beta\gamma+\gamma\alpha & 1 & \gamma(\alpha+\beta) \end{vmatrix}$$

Taking $(\alpha\beta+\beta\gamma+\gamma\alpha)$ common from C_1, we get

$$(\alpha\beta+\beta\gamma+\gamma\alpha)\begin{vmatrix} 1 & 1 & \alpha(\beta+\alpha) \\ 1 & 1 & \beta(\gamma+\alpha) \\ 1 & 1 & \gamma(\alpha+\beta) \end{vmatrix}$$

$= 0 \quad$ [$\because$ determinant will be zero, if two rows or columns are identical]

4. (i) Given, $f(x) = \begin{cases} \dfrac{(x+3)^2 - 36}{x-3}; & x \neq 3 \\ k; & x = 3 \end{cases}$

$$\text{LHL} = \lim_{x \to 3^-} f(x) = \lim_{h \to 0} f(3-h)$$

$$= \lim_{h \to 0} \frac{(3-h+3)^2 - 36}{3-h-3}$$

$$= \lim_{h \to 0} \frac{(6-h)^2 - 36}{-h}$$

$$= \lim_{h \to 0} \frac{36 + h^2 - 12h - 36}{-h}$$

$$= \lim_{h \to 0} \frac{h^2 - 12h}{-h} = \lim_{h \to 0}(12 - h) = 12$$

$$\text{RHL} = \lim_{x \to 3^+} f(x) = \lim_{h \to 0} f(3+h)$$

$$= \lim_{h \to 0} \frac{(3+h+3)^2 - 36}{3+h-3}$$

$$= \lim_{h \to 0} \frac{36 + h^2 + 12h - 36}{h}$$

$$= \lim_{h \to 0}(h + 12) = 12 \text{ and } f(3) = k$$

Since, f is continuous at $x = 3$.

Therefore, LHL = RHL = $f(3)$

$\Rightarrow \quad 12 = 12 = k$

Hence, $\quad k = 12$

Or

(ii) Given equation of curve is $y = (x-2)^2$ ...(i)

Let (h, k) be the point at which the tangent is parallel to the line joining the chord through the points (2, 0) and (4, 4).

Then, $y' = 2(x-2)$

At point (h, k)

$$\left.\frac{dy}{dx}\right|_{(h,k)} = 2(h-2)$$

Also, slope of the chord joining the points (2, 0) and (4, 4)

$$= \frac{4-0}{4-2} = \frac{4}{2} = 2$$

Since, tangent line is parallel to chord, therefore,

$$2(h-2) = 2 \Rightarrow h = 3$$

Also, the point (h, k) will lie on the curve (i), then

$$k = (h-2)^2 = (3-2)^2 \quad [\because h = 3]$$

$\therefore \quad k = 1$

Hence, the required point is (3, 1).

5. Let $$I = \int_0^{2\pi} \frac{1}{1+e^{\sin x}}\,dx \quad \text{...(i)}$$

We know that
$$\int_0^a f(x)\,dx = \int_0^a f(a-x)\,dx$$

$$\therefore \quad I = \int_0^{2\pi} \frac{1}{1+e^{\sin(2\pi - x)}}\,dx$$

$$= \int_0^{2\pi} \frac{1}{1+e^{-\sin x}}\,dx$$

$$\Rightarrow \quad I = \int_0^{2\pi} \frac{e^{\sin x}}{1+e^{\sin x}}\,dx \quad \text{...(ii)}$$

On adding Eqs. (i) and (ii), we get
$$2I = \int_0^{2\pi} \frac{1+e^{\sin x}}{1+e^{\sin x}}\,dx$$

$$= \int_0^{2\pi} 1 \cdot dx = [x]_0^{2\pi} = 2\pi$$

$$\Rightarrow \quad I = \pi$$

Hence, $\int_0^{2\pi} \frac{1}{1+e^{\sin x}}\,dx = \pi$

6. Given,
$$2P(A) = P(B) = \frac{5}{13}$$

and $$P\left(\frac{A}{B}\right) = \frac{2}{5}$$

We know that
$$P\left(\frac{A}{B}\right) = \frac{P(A \cap B)}{P(B)}$$

$$\Rightarrow \quad \frac{2}{5} = \frac{P(A \cap B)}{5/13}$$

$$\Rightarrow \quad P(A \cap B) = \frac{2}{13}$$

$$\therefore \quad P(A \cup B) = P(A) + P(B) - P(A \cap B)$$
$$= P(A) + 2P(A) - P(A \cap B)$$
$$= 3P(A) - P(A \cap B)$$
$$= \frac{15}{26} - \frac{2}{13} = \frac{11}{26}$$

Hence, $P(A \cup B) = \frac{11}{26}$

7. We have, $y = 3\cos(\log x) + 4\sin(\log x)$ ...(i)

On differentiating w.r.t x, we get
$$\frac{dy}{dx} = \frac{-3}{x}\sin(\log x) + \frac{4}{x}\cos(\log x) \quad \text{...(ii)}$$

On multiplying by x both sides, we get
$$x\frac{dy}{dx} = -3\sin(\log x) + 4\cos(\log x) \quad \text{...(iii)}$$

Again, on differentiating Eq. (ii) w.r.t x, we get
$$\frac{d^2y}{dx^2} = \frac{3}{x^2}\sin(\log x) - \frac{3}{x^2}\cos(\log x) - \frac{4}{x^2}\cos(\log x) - \frac{4}{x^2}\sin(\log x)$$

On multiplying by x^2 both sides, we get
$$x^2\frac{d^2y}{dx^2} = 3\sin(\log x) - 3\cos(\log x) - 4\cos(\log x) - 4\sin(\log x)$$
$$= -[-3\sin(\log x) + 4\cos(\log x)] - [3\cos(\log x) + 4\sin(\log x)]$$

$$\Rightarrow \quad x^2\frac{d^2y}{dx^2} = -x\frac{dy}{dx} - y \quad \text{[using Eqs. (i) and (iii)]}$$

$$\therefore \quad x^2\frac{d^2y}{dx^2} + x\frac{dy}{dx} + y = 0$$

Hence proved.

8. (i) We have, $\sin^{-1}\frac{x}{2} + \cos^{-1}x = \frac{\pi}{6}$

$$\Rightarrow \cos^{-1}x = \frac{\pi}{6} - \sin^{-1}\frac{x}{2}$$

$$\Rightarrow \quad x = \cos\left(\frac{\pi}{6} - \sin^{-1}\frac{x}{2}\right)$$

$$\Rightarrow \quad x = \cos\frac{\pi}{6}\cos\left(\sin^{-1}\frac{x}{2}\right) + \sin\frac{\pi}{6}\sin\left(\sin^{-1}\frac{x}{2}\right)$$

$$\Rightarrow \quad x = \frac{\sqrt{3}}{2}\cos\left(\sin^{-1}\frac{x}{2}\right) + \frac{1}{2}\cdot\frac{x}{2}$$

Let $\sin^{-1}\frac{x}{2} = \theta \Rightarrow \frac{x}{2} = \sin\theta$

$$\Rightarrow \quad \cos\theta = \sqrt{1 - \frac{x^2}{4}}$$

$$\Rightarrow \quad \theta = \cos^{-1}\sqrt{1 - \frac{x^2}{4}}$$

$$\therefore \quad x = \frac{\sqrt{3}}{2}\cos\left(\cos^{-1}\sqrt{1-\frac{x^2}{4}}\right) + \frac{x}{4}$$

$$= \frac{\sqrt{3}}{2}\sqrt{1-\frac{x^2}{4}} + \frac{x}{4}$$

$$\Rightarrow \quad x - \frac{x}{4} = \frac{\sqrt{3}}{2}\sqrt{1-\frac{x^2}{4}}$$

$$\Rightarrow \quad \frac{3x}{4} = \frac{\sqrt{3}}{2}\sqrt{1-\frac{x^2}{4}}$$

$$\Rightarrow \quad \frac{9x^2}{16} = \frac{3}{4}\left(1-\frac{x^2}{4}\right)$$

$$\Rightarrow \quad \frac{9x^2}{16} + \frac{3x^2}{16} = \frac{3}{4} \Rightarrow \frac{3}{4}x^2 = \frac{3}{4}$$

$$\Rightarrow \quad x^2 = 1$$

$$\Rightarrow \quad x = \pm 1$$

But $x = -1$, does not satisfy the given equation.

Henec, $x = 1$ is the required solution.

Or

(ii) We have, $\sin^{-1}x + \sin^{-1}y + \sin^{-1}z = \pi$

$\Rightarrow \quad \sin^{-1}x + \sin^{-1}y = \pi - \sin^{-1}z$

$\Rightarrow \sin^{-1}(x\sqrt{1-y^2} + y\sqrt{1-x^2}) = \pi - \sin^{-1}z$

$\Rightarrow \quad x\sqrt{1-y^2} + y\sqrt{1-x^2} = \sin(\pi - \sin^{-1}z)$

$\Rightarrow \quad x\sqrt{1-y^2} + y\sqrt{1-x^2} = \sin\pi\cos(\sin^{-1}z)$

$\quad -\cos\pi\sin(\sin^{-1}z)$

$\Rightarrow \quad x\sqrt{1-y^2} + y\sqrt{1-x^2} = 0 + z$

$\Rightarrow \quad x\sqrt{1-y^2} = z - y\sqrt{1-x^2}$

On squaring both sides, we get

$x^2(1-y^2) = z^2 + y^2(1-x^2) - 2yz\sqrt{1-x^2}$

$\Rightarrow x^2 - x^2y^2 = z^2 + y^2 - x^2y^2 - 2yz\sqrt{1-x^2}$

$\Rightarrow x^2 - y^2 - z^2 + 2yz\sqrt{1-x^2} = 0$ **Hence proved.**

9. (i) Let $I = \int x^2 \cos x \, dx$

On integrating by parts, we get

$= x^2\sin x - \int 2x\sin x \, dx$

$= x^2\sin x - 2[-x\cos x + \int \cos x \, dx]$

$= x^2\sin x + 2x\cos x - 2\sin x + C$

Hence, $\int x^2 \cos x \, dx$

$= x^2\sin x + 2x\cos x - 2\sin x + C$

where, C is an integrating constant.

Or

(ii) Let $I = \int \frac{x+7}{x^2+4x+7} dx$

Let us assume that

$x + 7 = A\frac{d}{dx}(x^2 + 4x + 7) + B = A(2x + 4) + B$

On comparing the coefficients of x and constant terms both sides, we get

$2A = 1 \Rightarrow A = \frac{1}{2}$

and $4A + B = 7$

$\Rightarrow \quad B = 5$

So, $\quad x + 7 = \frac{1}{2}(2x + 4) + 5$

$\therefore \quad I = \int \frac{\frac{1}{2}(2x+4)+5}{x^2+4x+7} dx$

$= \frac{1}{2}\int \frac{2x+4}{x^2+4x+7} dx + 5\int \frac{1}{x^2+4x+7} dx$

$= \frac{1}{2}\ln|x^2 + 4x + 7| + 5\int \frac{1}{(x+2)^2+3} dx$

$= \frac{1}{2}\ln|x^2 + 4x + 7| + \frac{5}{\sqrt{3}}\tan^{-1}\left(\frac{x+2}{\sqrt{3}}\right) + C$

Hence, $\int \frac{x+7}{x^2+4x+7} dx$

$= \frac{1}{2}\ln|x^2 + 4x + 7| + \frac{5}{\sqrt{3}}\tan^{-1}\left(\frac{x+2}{\sqrt{3}}\right) + C$

where, C is an integrating constant.

10. Let A : one gem is white and other is red

E_1 : both gems are from Box I

E_2 : both gems are from Box II

E_3 : both gems are from Box III

Probability of selection of each box

$= P(E_1) = P(E_2) = P(E_3) = \frac{1}{3}$

Required probability $P\left(\frac{E_2}{A}\right)$

$= \frac{P(A/E_2)\cdot P(E_2)}{P\left(\frac{A}{E_1}\right)\cdot P(E_1) + P\left(\frac{A}{E_2}\right)\cdot P(E_2) + P\left(\frac{A}{E_3}\right)\cdot P(E_3)}$,

[using Baye's theorem]

$= \frac{\frac{^2C_1 \times {^3C_1}}{^5C_2} \times \frac{1}{3}}{\frac{^1C_1 \times {^2C_1}}{^3C_2} \times \frac{1}{3} + \frac{^2C_1 \times {^3C_1}}{^5C_2} \times \frac{1}{3} + \frac{^3C_1 \times {^1C_1}}{^4C_2} \times \frac{1}{3}}$

$= \frac{\left(\frac{6}{10}\right)}{\left(\frac{2}{3} + \frac{6}{10} + \frac{3}{6}\right)} = \frac{6}{10} \times \frac{30}{53} = \frac{18}{53}$

Hence, the probability that the gems drawn are from Box II is $\frac{18}{53}$.

11. (i) Let x, y and z be the number of tables, chairs and cots, respectively produced by factory.

The wood requirements (in tonnes) for each type of furniture are given below.

	Table	Chair	Cot	Availability
Teakwood	2	3	4	29
Rosewood	1	1	2	13
Satinwood	3	2	1	16
	x	y	z	

Mathematical formulation of the above data is

$2x + 3y + 4z = 29$

$x + y + 2z = 13$

$3x + 2y + z = 16$

which is the required set of simultaneous equations.

(ii) The obtained set of equations

$$2x + 3y + 4z = 29$$
$$x + y + 2z = 13$$
$$3x + 2y + z = 16$$

Re-write the system of equations into matrix form $AX = B$.

$$\begin{bmatrix} 2 & 3 & 4 \\ 1 & 1 & 2 \\ 3 & 2 & 1 \end{bmatrix}\begin{bmatrix} x \\ y \\ z \end{bmatrix} = \begin{bmatrix} 29 \\ 13 \\ 16 \end{bmatrix}$$

where, $A = \begin{bmatrix} 2 & 3 & 4 \\ 1 & 1 & 2 \\ 3 & 2 & 1 \end{bmatrix}, X = \begin{bmatrix} x \\ y \\ z \end{bmatrix}, B = \begin{bmatrix} 29 \\ 13 \\ 16 \end{bmatrix}$

Now, $|A| = \begin{vmatrix} 2 & 3 & 4 \\ 1 & 1 & 2 \\ 3 & 2 & 1 \end{vmatrix}$

$$= 2(1 - 4) - 3(1 - 6) + 4(2 - 3)$$
$$= - 6 + 15 - 4 = 5 \neq 0$$

Cofactors of the elements of matrix A are

$C_{11} = - 3, C_{12} = 5, C_{13} = - 1$
$C_{21} = 5, C_{22} = - 10, C_{23} = 5$
$C_{31} = 2, C_{32} = 0, C_{33} = - 1$

Now, we find the adjoint of matrix A.

$$\therefore \text{adj}(A) = \begin{bmatrix} -3 & 5 & -1 \\ 5 & -10 & 5 \\ 2 & 0 & -1 \end{bmatrix}^T = \begin{bmatrix} -3 & 5 & 2 \\ 5 & -10 & 0 \\ -1 & 5 & -1 \end{bmatrix}$$

So, $A^{-1} = \frac{1}{|A|}\text{adj}(A)$

$$= \frac{1}{5}\begin{bmatrix} -3 & 5 & 2 \\ 5 & -10 & 0 \\ -1 & 5 & -1 \end{bmatrix}$$

Thus, $X = A^{-1}B$

$$= \frac{1}{5}\begin{bmatrix} -3 & 5 & 2 \\ 5 & -10 & 0 \\ -1 & 5 & -1 \end{bmatrix}\begin{bmatrix} 29 \\ 13 \\ 16 \end{bmatrix}$$

$$= \frac{1}{5}\begin{bmatrix} -87 + 65 + 32 \\ 145 - 130 + 0 \\ -29 + 65 - 16 \end{bmatrix}$$

$$\Rightarrow \begin{bmatrix} x \\ y \\ z \end{bmatrix} = \frac{1}{5}\begin{bmatrix} 10 \\ 15 \\ 20 \end{bmatrix} = \begin{bmatrix} 2 \\ 3 \\ 4 \end{bmatrix}$$

Hence, $x = 2, y = 3$ and $z = 4$.

(iii) The number of tables is 2, number of chairs is 3 and the number of cots is 4.

12. (i) Let x be the length and y be the width of the rectangular portion of the window as shown in the figure.

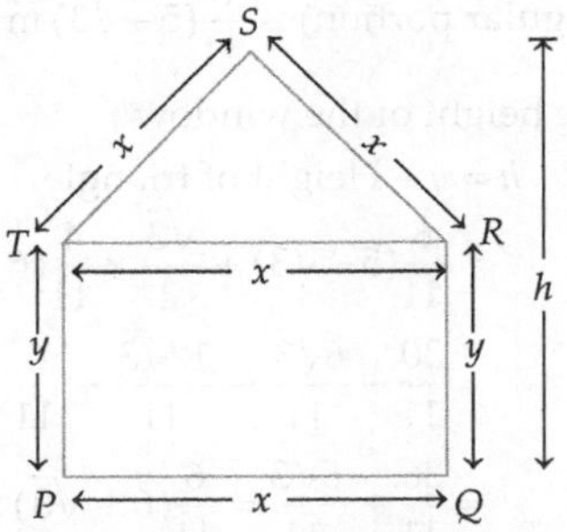

An equilateral triangle with side x placed on the rectangular shape.

$\because$ Perimeter of window $= PQ + QR + RS + ST + TP$

$\Rightarrow \quad 12 = x + y + x + x + y$

$\Rightarrow \quad 12 = 3x + 2y \quad$ ...(i)

Now, the area of the window,

A = Area of rectangle + Area of equilateral triangle

$$= xy + \frac{\sqrt{3}}{4}x^2 = x\left[\frac{12 - 3x}{2}\right] + \frac{\sqrt{3}}{4}x^2$$

[using Eq. (i)]

$$= 6x - \frac{3}{2}x^2 + \frac{\sqrt{3}}{4}x^2 = x^2\left(\frac{\sqrt{3}}{4} - \frac{3}{2}\right) + 6x$$

For maximum sunlight, area of window should be maximum.

Now, $\frac{dA}{dx} = 2x\left(\frac{\sqrt{3}}{4} - \frac{3}{2}\right) + 6 = x\left(\frac{\sqrt{3}}{2} - 3\right) + 6$

For maximum, $\frac{dA}{dx} = 0$

$$\Rightarrow x\left(\frac{\sqrt{3}}{2} - 3\right) + 6 = 0$$

$$\Rightarrow \quad x = \frac{6}{\left(3 - \frac{\sqrt{3}}{2}\right)} = \left(\frac{12}{6 - \sqrt{3}}\right) \times \frac{6 + \sqrt{3}}{6 + \sqrt{3}}$$

$$= \frac{4}{11}(6 + \sqrt{3})\text{ m}$$

Also, $\frac{d^2A}{dx^2} = \left(\frac{\sqrt{3}}{2} - 3\right) < 0$

Hence, the area is maximum at $x = \frac{4}{11}(6 + \sqrt{3})$.

So, from Eq. (i), $y = \frac{12 - 3x}{2} = 6 - \frac{3}{2} \times \frac{4}{11}(6 + \sqrt{3})$

$$= 6 - \frac{6}{11}(6 + \sqrt{3}) = \frac{66 - 36 - 6\sqrt{3}}{11}$$

$$= \frac{30 - 6\sqrt{3}}{11} = \frac{6}{11}(5 - \sqrt{3})$$

Hence, the length of window (rectangular portion) is $\frac{4}{11}(6+\sqrt{3})$ m and the width of window (rectangular portion) is $\frac{6}{11}(5-\sqrt{3})$ m

and the height of the window

$$h = y + \text{Height of triangle}$$
$$= \frac{6}{11}(5-\sqrt{3}) + \frac{\sqrt{3}}{2} \times \frac{4}{11}(6+\sqrt{3})$$
$$= \frac{30}{11} - \frac{6\sqrt{3}}{11} + \frac{12\sqrt{3}}{11} + \frac{6}{11}$$
$$= \frac{36}{11} + \frac{6\sqrt{3}}{11} = \frac{6}{11}(6+\sqrt{3})\text{ m}$$

Or

(ii) Given, volume of closed cylindrical dustbin $= 20\pi \text{ cm}^3$

Also, given r and h are the radius and height of the dustbin, respectively.

(a) We have, $V = 20\pi \text{ cm}^3 \Rightarrow \pi r^2 h = 20\pi$

$$\Rightarrow r^2 h = 20 \Rightarrow h = \frac{20}{r^2}$$

(b) Total surface area of closed dustbin,

S = Area of top and bottom + Curved surface area

$$= 2\pi r^2 + 2\pi rh$$
$$= 2\pi r^2 + 2\pi r \times \frac{20}{r^2} \qquad \left[\because h = \frac{20}{r^2}\right]$$
$$= 2\pi r^2 + \frac{40\pi}{r}$$
$$S = 2\pi r^2 + \frac{40\pi}{r}$$

Hence proved.

(c) Given, the cost of painting the base and top of the dustbin = ₹ 2/cm^2

and the cost of painting the curved surface area of dustbin = ₹ 25/cm^2

$$\therefore \text{Total cost of painting} = 2 \times 2\pi r^2 + 25 \times \frac{40\pi}{r}$$
$$= ₹4\pi r^2 + ₹\frac{1000\pi}{r}$$
$$= ₹\left(4\pi r^2 + \frac{1000\pi}{r}\right)$$

(d) We have, the total cost of painting

$$C(r) = 4\pi r^2 + \frac{1000\pi}{r} \qquad \text{[from Part (c)]}$$
$$\Rightarrow C'(r) = 8\pi r - \frac{1000\pi}{r^2}$$

For minimum and maximum cost,

$$C'(r) = 0$$
$$\Rightarrow 8\pi r - \frac{1000\pi}{r^2} = 0$$
$$\Rightarrow 8r^3 - 1000 = 0 \Rightarrow (2r)^3 = (10)^3$$
$$\Rightarrow 2r = 10 \Rightarrow r = 5$$

Again, $C''(r) = 8\pi + \frac{2000\pi}{r^3}$

At $r = 5$, $C''(5) = \left(8\pi + \frac{2000\pi}{125}\right) > 0$

Hence, the cost is minimum at $r = 5$ cm.

$$\therefore C(5) = 4\pi(5)^2 + \frac{1000\pi}{5}$$
$$= 100\pi + 200\pi = 300\pi = 300 \times \frac{22}{7}$$
$$= ₹\,942.85 \text{ (approx)}$$

Thus, the minimum cost of painting is ₹ 942.85 (approx).

13. (i) The given differential equation is

$2ye^{x/y}dx + (y - 2xe^{x/y})\,dy = 0$, with $y(0) = 1$

$$\Rightarrow \frac{dx}{dy} = \frac{2xe^{x/y} - y}{2ye^{x/y}}$$

On putting $x = vy$ and $\frac{dx}{dy} = v + y\frac{dv}{dy}$, we get

$$v + y\frac{dv}{dy} = \frac{2vye^v - y}{2ye^v} = \frac{2ve^v - 1}{2e^v}$$
$$\Rightarrow y\frac{dv}{dy} = \frac{2ve^v - 1}{2e^v} - v = \frac{-1}{2e^v}$$
$$\Rightarrow \frac{dy}{y} = -2e^v dv$$

On integrating both sides, we get

$$\int \frac{dy}{y} = \int -2e^v dv$$
$$\Rightarrow \log y = -2e^v + C \Rightarrow \log y + 2e^v = C$$
$$\Rightarrow \log y + 2e^{x/y} = C \qquad [\because x = vy]$$

On applying the given condition, $y(0) = 1$, we get

$$0 + 2e^0 = C \Rightarrow C = 2$$
$$\therefore \log y + 2e^{x/y} - 2 = 0$$

which is the required solution.

Or

(ii) The given differential equation is

$$x(x^2 - 1)\frac{dy}{dx} = 1, \text{ with } y(2) = 0$$
$$\Rightarrow \frac{dx}{x(x^2 - 1)} = dy$$
$$\Rightarrow \frac{dx}{x(x-1)(x+1)} = dy$$

By partial fraction, we get

$$\left[\frac{-1}{x} + \frac{1}{2(x-1)} + \frac{1}{2(x+1)}\right]dx = dy$$

On integrating, we get

$$\int\left(\frac{-1}{x}\right)dx + \frac{1}{2}\int\frac{1}{x-1}dx + \frac{1}{2}\int\frac{1}{x+1}dx = \int dy + K$$

$$\Rightarrow -\ln|x| + \frac{1}{2}\ln|x-1| + \frac{1}{2}\ln|x+1| = y + K \quad \ldots(i)$$

On applying the initial condition $y(2) = 0$, we get

$$-\ln|2| + \frac{1}{2}\ln|1| + \frac{1}{2}\ln|3| = K$$

$$\Rightarrow \quad K = \ln(\sqrt{3}) - \ln|2|$$

$$K = \ln\left|\frac{\sqrt{3}}{2}\right|$$

On substituting the value of K in Eq. (i), we get

$$-\ln|x| + \frac{1}{2}\ln|x-1| + \frac{1}{2}\ln|x+1| = y + \ln\left|\frac{\sqrt{3}}{2}\right|$$

$$\Rightarrow \quad y = -\ln|x| + \ln\left|\sqrt{x^2-1}\right| - \ln\left|\frac{\sqrt{3}}{2}\right|$$

$$= \ln\left|\frac{\sqrt{(x^2-1)}}{x}\right| - \ln\left|\frac{\sqrt{3}}{2}\right|$$

$$\because \quad y = \ln\left|\frac{2}{x}\sqrt{\left(\frac{x^2-1}{3}\right)}\right|$$

which is the required solution.

14. Given, set of numbers is

$$A = \{2, 3, 4, 5\}$$

Total number of ordered pairs $= 2^{|A|} = 2^4 = 16$

(i) All outcomes of this cutting are tabulated in the form of ordered pairs given below

	2	3	4	5
2	(2, 2)	(2, 3)	(2, 4)	(2, 5)
3	(3, 2)	(3, 3)	(3, 4)	(3, 5)
4	(4, 2)	(4, 3)	(4, 4)	(4, 5)
5	(5, 2)	(5, 3)	(5, 4)	(5, 5)

(ii) The total number of pairs having one larger number

= Total number of ordered pair
− Number of ordered pair having same number
= 16 − 4 = 12

(iii) Let X be a random variable denotes the larger of two numbers in ordered pair.

Total number of ordered pair = 12

Number of ordered pair having 3 as a larger number = 2

$$P(X = 3) = \frac{2}{12} = \frac{1}{6}$$

Number of ordered pair having 4 as a larger number = 4

$$P(X = 4) = \frac{4}{12} = \frac{1}{3}$$

Also, number of ordered pair having 5 as a larger number = 6

$$P(X = 5) = \frac{6}{12} = \frac{1}{2}$$

Hence, the complete probability distribution are

X	3	4	5
$P(X = x)$	$\frac{1}{6}$	$\frac{1}{3}$	$\frac{1}{2}$

(iv) Here, $P(X < 5) = P(X = 2) + P(X = 3) + P(X = 4)$

$$= 0 + \frac{1}{6} + \frac{1}{3} = \frac{1}{2}$$

(v) Excepted value of probability distribution

$$E(X) = \sum_{i=1}^{n} x_i p_i$$

$$= 2\cdot P(X = 2) + 3\cdot P(X = 3) + 4\cdot P(X = 4) + 5\cdot P(X = 5)$$

$$= 0 + 3 \times \frac{1}{6} + 4 \times \frac{1}{3} + 5 \times \frac{1}{2}$$

$$= \frac{1}{2} + \frac{4}{3} + \frac{5}{2} = \frac{3 + 8 + 15}{6} = \frac{26}{6} = \frac{13}{3}$$

Hence, the expected value of probability distribution is $\frac{13}{3}$.

15. (i) (b) We have, $\vec{a} = 3\hat{i} - 2\hat{j} + \hat{k}$ ...(i)

and $\vec{b} = 2\hat{i} - 4\hat{j} - 3\hat{k}$

$\Rightarrow \quad 2\vec{b} = 2(2\hat{i} - 4\hat{j} - 3\hat{k})$

[multiplying by 2 on both sides]

$= 4\hat{i} - 8\hat{j} - 6\hat{k}$ ...(ii)

On subtracting Eq. (ii) from Eq. (i), we get

$$\vec{a} - 2\vec{b} = (3\hat{i} - 2\hat{j} + \hat{k}) - (4\hat{i} - 8\hat{j} - 6\hat{k})$$

$$= (3-4)\hat{i} + (-2+8)\hat{j} + (1+6)\hat{k}$$

$$= -\hat{i} + 6\hat{j} + 7\hat{k}$$

Now, $|\vec{a} - 2\vec{b}| = |-\hat{i} + 6\hat{j} + 7\hat{k}|$

$$= \sqrt{(-1)^2 + (6)^2 + 7^2}$$

$$= \sqrt{1 + 36 + 49} = \sqrt{86}$$

(ii) (d) We have, $\sin^2\alpha + \sin^2\beta + \sin^2\gamma$

$$= (1 - \cos^2\alpha) + (1 - \cos^2\beta) + (1 - \cos^2\gamma)$$

$$= 3 - (\cos^2\alpha + \cos^2\beta + \cos^2\gamma) = 3 - 1$$

[$\because \cos\alpha, \cos\beta$ and $\cos\gamma$ are the direction cosines of the line]

$= 2$

(iii) Let PD, PE and PF are the perpendicular distance of P from XY, YZ and ZX-planes respectively.

Now, for any point P(a, b, c), a is perpendicular distance of P from YZ-plane, b is perpendicular distance of P from XZ-plane and c is perpendicular distance of P from XY-plane.

Hence, the perpendicular distances of P(a, b, c) fromXY, YZ and ZX-planes are c, a and b, respectively.

(iv) We have,

$$\vec{a} = 2\hat{i} + \hat{j} + 2\hat{k} \text{ and } \vec{b} = 5\hat{i} - 3\hat{j} + \hat{k}$$

The projection of $\vec{b}$ on $\vec{a}$

$$= \frac{\vec{b}\cdot\vec{a}}{|\vec{a}|} = \frac{(5\hat{i} - 3\hat{j} + \hat{k})\cdot(2\hat{i} + \hat{j} + 2\hat{k})}{\sqrt{2^2 + 1^2 + 2^2}}$$

$$= \frac{10 - 3 + 2}{\sqrt{4+1+4}} = \frac{9}{\sqrt{9}} = \frac{9}{3} = 3$$

$\therefore$ The projection of $\vec{b}$ on $\vec{a}$ is 3.

(v) We have, $\vec{a} = 2\hat{i} + 5\hat{j} + 4\hat{k}$

$$\therefore \quad |\vec{a}| = \sqrt{2^2 + 5^2 + 4^2} = \sqrt{4 + 25 + 16}$$

$$= \sqrt{45} = 3\sqrt{5}$$

Now, unit vector in direction of $\hat{a} = \dfrac{\vec{a}}{|\vec{a}|}$

$$\Rightarrow \quad \hat{a} = \frac{1}{3\sqrt{5}}[2\hat{i} + 5\hat{j} + 4\hat{k}]$$

$$= \frac{2}{3\sqrt{5}}\hat{i} + \frac{5}{3\sqrt{5}}\hat{j} + \frac{4}{3\sqrt{5}}\hat{k}$$

Thus, the vector with magnitude 1

$$= \frac{2}{3\sqrt{5}}\hat{i} + \frac{5}{3\sqrt{5}}\hat{j} + \frac{4}{3\sqrt{5}}\hat{k}$$

$\therefore$ Vector with magnitude 20

$$= 20 \times \left[\frac{2}{3\sqrt{5}}\hat{i} + \frac{5}{3\sqrt{5}}\hat{j} + \frac{4}{3\sqrt{5}}\hat{k}\right]$$

$$= \frac{40}{3\sqrt{5}}\hat{i} + \frac{100}{3\sqrt{5}}\hat{j} + \frac{80}{3\sqrt{5}}\hat{k}$$

$$= \frac{8\sqrt{5}}{3}\hat{i} + \frac{20\sqrt{5}}{3}\hat{j} + \frac{16\sqrt{5}}{3}\hat{k}$$

16. (i) Given, $\vec{a} \times \vec{b} = \vec{a} \times \vec{c}$, where $\vec{a}$, $\vec{b}$ and $\vec{c}$ are non-zero vectors.

Since, $\quad \vec{a} \times \vec{b} = \vec{a} \times \vec{c}$

$$\Rightarrow \quad \vec{a} \times \vec{b} - \vec{a} \times \vec{c} = 0$$

$$\Rightarrow \quad \vec{a} \times (\vec{b} - \vec{c}) = 0$$

$$\Rightarrow \quad \vec{a} \parallel (\vec{b} - \vec{c}) \text{ or } \vec{b} - \vec{c} = 0 \qquad [\because \vec{a} \neq 0]$$

$$\Rightarrow \quad \vec{a} \parallel (\vec{b} - \vec{c}) \text{ or } \vec{b} = \vec{c}$$

Hence proved.

Or

(ii) Given, $\vec{a}$ and $\vec{b}$ two non-zero vectors such that

$$|\vec{a} \times \vec{b}| = \vec{a}\cdot\vec{b}$$

$$\Rightarrow \quad |\vec{a}|\cdot|\vec{b}|\sin\theta = |\vec{a}|\cdot|\vec{b}|\cos\theta$$

$$\Rightarrow \quad \sin\theta = \cos\theta$$

$$\Rightarrow \quad \frac{\sin\theta}{\cos\theta} = 1$$

$$\Rightarrow \quad \tan\theta = 1$$

$$\Rightarrow \quad \theta = \tan^{-1}(1) = \frac{\pi}{4}$$

Thus, the angle between $\vec{a}$ and $\vec{b}$ is $\frac{\pi}{4}$.

17. (i) Given points are A(1, 0, 2), B(3, – 1, 1) and C(1, 2, 1).

Then, the equation of plane is

$$\begin{vmatrix} x - x_1 & y - y_1 & z - z_1 \\ x_2 - x_1 & y_2 - y_1 & z_2 - z_1 \\ x_3 - x_1 & y_3 - y_1 & z_3 - z_1 \end{vmatrix} = 0$$

$$\Rightarrow \quad \begin{vmatrix} x - 1 & y - 0 & z - 2 \\ 3 - 1 & -1 - 0 & 1 - 2 \\ 1 - 1 & 2 - 0 & 1 - 2 \end{vmatrix} = 0$$

$$\Rightarrow \quad \begin{vmatrix} x - 1 & y & z - 2 \\ 2 & -1 & -1 \\ 0 & 2 & -1 \end{vmatrix} = 0$$

$$\Rightarrow \quad (x - 1)[1 + 2] - 2[-y - 2(z - 2)] = 0$$

$$\Rightarrow \quad (x - 1)\cdot[3] - 2[-y - 2z + 4] = 0$$

$$\Rightarrow \quad 3x - 3 + 2y + 4z - 8 = 0$$

$$\Rightarrow \quad 3x + 2y + 4z - 11 = 0$$

$$\Rightarrow \quad 3x + 2y + 4z = 11$$

(ii) The point P(2, 3, 1) and the equation of the plane containing the points A, B and C is

$3x + 2y + 4z = 11$

Since, PQ is perpendicular to the plane.

We know that equation of line perpendicular to the plane $ax + by + cz = \lambda$ and passing through the point (x_1, y_1, z_1) is given by

$$\frac{x - x_1}{a} = \frac{y - y_1}{b} = \frac{z - z_1}{c}$$

Thus, the equation of the line PQ is

$$\frac{x - 2}{3} = \frac{y - 3}{2} = \frac{z - 1}{4}$$

(iii) The equation of plane is $3x + 2y + 4z = 11$

i.e. $3x + 2y + 4z - 11 = 0$

Now, the height of the top of tower $P(2, 3, 1)$ is perpendicular from the ground.

$$= \left| \frac{ax_1 + by_1 + cz_1 - k}{\sqrt{a^2 + b^2 + c^2}} \right|$$

$$= \left| \frac{3(2) + 2(3) + 4(1) - 11}{\sqrt{3^2 + 2^2 + 4^2}} \right|$$

$$= \left| \frac{6 + 6 + 4 - 11}{\sqrt{9 + 4 + 16}} \right| = \frac{5}{\sqrt{29}}$$

Thus, the height of the tower is $\frac{5}{\sqrt{29}}$ units.

18. (i) Shaded part of the following figure shows area enclosed by curve $y^2 = 4ax$ and the line $x = a$.

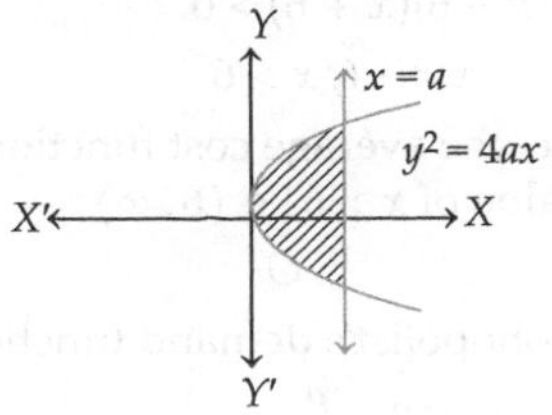

Thus, the required area $= 2\int_{x=0}^{x=a} y\,dx = 2\int_0^a \sqrt{4ax}\,dx$

$$= 4\sqrt{a}\int_0^a \sqrt{x}\,dx = 4\sqrt{a} \cdot \left[\frac{x^{3/2}}{3/2}\right]_0^a$$

$$= 4\sqrt{a} \times \frac{2}{3}[a^{3/2} - 0^{3/2}]$$

$$= \frac{8\sqrt{a}}{3} \cdot a^{3/2} = \frac{8}{3}a^2 \text{ sq units}$$

Or

(ii) We have two parabolas,

$$y^2 = 4x \text{ and } x^2 = 4y$$

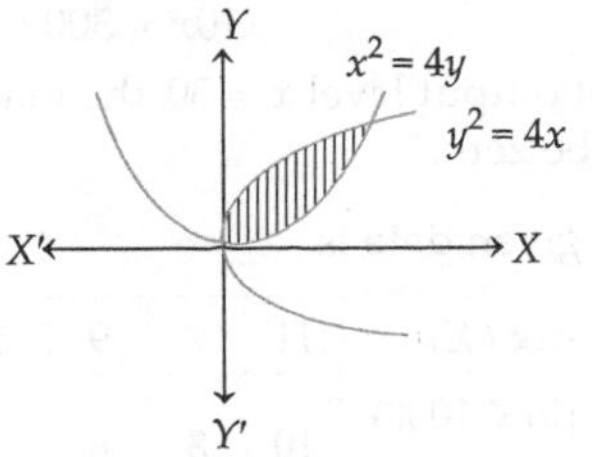

Since, $\quad y^2 = 4x$

$\Rightarrow \quad \left(\frac{x^2}{4}\right)^2 = 4x \quad \left[\because \frac{x^2}{4} = y\right]$

$\Rightarrow \quad \frac{x^4}{16} = 4x \Rightarrow x^4 - 64x = 0$

$\Rightarrow \quad x(x^3 - 64) = 0$

$\Rightarrow \quad x = 0, x^3 = 64$

$\Rightarrow \quad x = 0, x = 4$

When $x = 0$, then $y = 0$

When $x = 4$, then $y = 4$

$\therefore$ Required area $= \int_{x=0}^{x=4} [y(\text{parabola } y^2 = 4x)$

$$- y(\text{parabola } 4y = x^2)]\,dx$$

$$= \int_0^4 \left[\sqrt{4x} - \frac{x^2}{4}\right] dx$$

$$= \int_0^4 \left[2\sqrt{x} - \frac{x^2}{4}\right] dx$$

$$= \left[2 \cdot \frac{2}{3} \cdot x^{3/2}\right]_0^4 - \frac{1}{4}\left[\frac{x^3}{3}\right]_0^4$$

$$= \frac{4}{3}[4^{3/2} - 0] - \frac{1}{12}[4^3 - 0]$$

$$= \frac{4}{3}[8 - 0] - \frac{1}{12}[64 - 0]$$

$$= \frac{32}{3} - \frac{64}{12} = \frac{16}{3} \text{ sq units}$$

19. (i) (b) Let the number of units of manufacturing hand towels be x and selling price per unit = ₹ 100

Thus, the revenue generated on selling particular number of units is

$$R(x) = 100 \times x = 100x$$

Also, variable cost = 30% of total revenue

$$= \frac{30}{100} \text{ of } R(x) = \frac{30}{100} \times 100x = 30x$$

$\therefore$ Total cost = Fixed cost + Variable cost

$$= 35000 + 30x$$

$\therefore$ The total cost function for manufacturing hand towels is $35000 + 30x$.

(ii) (c) The value of correlation coefficient r lies between -1 and 1 where, -1 indicates a perfect negative linear relationship and 1 indicates a perfect positive linear relationship. Since, the correlation coefficient of two sets of variables (X, Y) is $\frac{-3}{4}$, which is negative linear relationship between the variables X and Y.

Thus, both regression coefficients are negative.

(iii) Given, total cost function is

$$C(x) = x + 2x^3 - \frac{7}{2}x^2$$

Thus, the average cost is

$$AC = \frac{C(x)}{x} = \frac{x + 2x^3 - \frac{7}{2}x^2}{x}$$

$$= 1 + 2x^2 - \frac{7}{2}x$$

Here, the marginal average cost function is

$$\text{MAC} = \frac{d}{dx}(\text{AC}) = \frac{d}{dx}\left(1 + 2x^2 - \frac{7}{2}x\right)$$

$$= 0 + 2(2x) - \frac{7}{2} = 4x - \frac{7}{2}$$

Thus, the Marginal Average Cost function (MAC) is $4x - \frac{7}{2}$.

(iv) Given two lines of regression are $4x + 3y + 7 = 0$ and $3x + 4y + 8 = 0$

Now, to find the mean value of x and y, we solve the system of equations formed by the two given lines of regression.

$$3x + 4y + 8 = 0 \quad \ldots\text{(i)}$$

$$4x + 3y + 7 = 0 \quad \ldots\text{(ii)}$$

On multiplying Eq. (i) by 4 and Eq. (ii) by 3, we get

$$12x + 16y + 32 = 0 \quad \ldots\text{(iii)}$$

$$12x + 9y + 21 = 0 \quad \ldots\text{(iv)}$$

Now, subtract Eq. (iv) from Eq. (iii), we get

$$x = \frac{-4}{7} \text{ and } y = \frac{-11}{7}$$

So, the mean value of x is $\frac{-4}{7}$ and the mean value of y is $\frac{-11}{7}$.

(v) Selling price of pen fixed at ₹ 45.

The cost function is $C(x) = 30x + 240$

and the revenue function is $R(x) = 45x$

So, the profit is

$$P(x) = R(x) - C(x) = 45x - (30x + 240)$$

$$= 45x - 30x - 240 = 15x - 240$$

For break even point, we put $P(x) = 0$

$$P(x) = 0 \Rightarrow 15x - 240 = 0$$

$$\Rightarrow 15x = 240 \Rightarrow x = \frac{240}{15} = 16$$

Since, the break even point is 16.

Therefore, the manufacturer will begin to earn profit, if he sells more than 16 pens..

20. (i) Given, average cost function is

$$\text{AC} = x + 5 + \frac{36}{x}$$

(a) We know that

$$\text{Average cost} = \frac{\text{Total cost}}{x}$$

$$\Rightarrow \quad \text{AC} = \frac{C(x)}{x}$$

$$\Rightarrow x + 5 + \frac{36}{x} = \frac{C(x)}{x}$$

$$\Rightarrow \quad C(x) = x\left(x + 5 + \frac{36}{x}\right)$$

$$= x^2 + 5x + 36$$

Thus, the total cost function is $x^2 + 5x + 36$.

(b) Since, $\text{AC} = x + 5 + \frac{36}{x}$

$$\frac{d}{dx}(\text{AC}) = \frac{d}{dx}\left(x + 5 + \frac{36}{x}\right)$$

$$= 1 + 0 - \frac{36}{x^2}$$

$$= 1 - \frac{36}{x^2}$$

For AC to be increasing,

$$\frac{d}{dx}(\text{AC}) > 0$$

$$\Rightarrow \quad 1 - \frac{36}{x^2} > 0$$

$$\Rightarrow \quad x^2 - 36 > 0$$

$$\Rightarrow \quad (x - 6)(x + 6) > 0$$

$$\Rightarrow \quad x < -6, x > 6$$

Hence, the average cost function increases, if the value of $x > 6$ i.e. $(6, \infty)$

Or

(ii) Given monopolist's demand function is

$$x = 60 - \frac{p}{5}$$

$$\Rightarrow \quad 5x = 300 - p$$

$$\Rightarrow \quad p = 300 - 5x$$

Thus, the revenue function = Profit function × x

$$\Rightarrow \quad R(x) = p \times x$$

$$= (300 - 5x)x = 300x - 5x^2$$

Now, marginal revenue $= \frac{dR}{dx} = \frac{d}{dx}[300x - 5x^2]$

$$= 300 - 10x$$

Then, the marginal revenue = 0

$$\Rightarrow \quad 300 - 10x = 0$$

$$\Rightarrow \quad 10x = 300 \Rightarrow x = 30$$

Thus, at output level $x = 30$, the marginal revenue would be zero.

21. (i) (a) The given data is

Years of service (X)	11	7	9	5	8	6	10
Monthly salary (in ₹ 1000) (Y)	10	8	6	5	9	7	11

Sum of $X = 56$

Sum of $Y = 56$

So, Mean $(\overline{X}) = \frac{\Sigma X}{n} = \frac{56}{7} = 8 = M_X$

and Mean $(\overline{Y}) = \frac{\Sigma Y}{n} = \frac{56}{7} = 8 = M_Y$

X	Y	$X - M_x$	$Y - M_Y$	$(X - M_x)^2$	$(X - M_x)(Y - M_Y)$
11	10	3	+ 2	9	6
7	8	− 1	0	1	0
9	6	1	− 2	1	− 2
5	5	− 3	− 3	9	9
8	9	0	1	0	0
6	7	− 2	− 1	4	2
10	11	2	3	4	6

Thus, using the above table,

Sum of squares, $SS_x = \Sigma(X - M_x)^2 = 28$

Sum of products, $SP = \Sigma(X - M_x)(Y - M_y) = 21$

$\therefore \quad b = \frac{SP}{SS_x} = \frac{21}{28} = 0.75$

and $a = M_y - bM_x = 8 - 0.75 \times 8 = 2$

Since, regression equation $\hat{y} = bX + a$

$\therefore \quad \hat{y} = 0.75X + 2$

(b) Using part (a)

$\hat{y} = 0.75X + 2$

Since, $X = 13$

Thus, $\hat{y} = 0.75 \times 13 + 2 = 11.75$

∴ If a person with 13 years of experience applies for a job in the company, then the monthly salary will be suggested by the manager is ₹ 11750.

Or

(ii) Given, $n = 50$, $x =$ Marks in Statistics,

$y =$ Marks in Accountancy

Regression equation of X on Y is

$3y - 5x + 180 = 0$

Also given, $\bar{y} = 44$, $\sigma_X^2 = \frac{9}{14}\sigma_Y^2$

(a) Since, regression equation is

$3y - 5x + 180 = 0$

$\Rightarrow \quad 5x = 3y + 180 \Rightarrow x = \frac{3}{5}y + 36$

On comparing it with $x = b_{XY}y + a$, we get

$b_{XY} = \frac{3}{5}, a = 36$

So, $\quad a = \bar{x} - b_{XY}\bar{y}$

$\Rightarrow \quad 36 = \bar{x} - \frac{3}{5} \times 44 \Rightarrow \bar{x} = 62.4$

Thus, $\bar{x} =$ Average score in Statistics $= 62.4$

(b) Since, $\sigma_X^2 = \frac{9}{16}\sigma_Y^2$

$\Rightarrow \quad \frac{\sigma_X^2}{\sigma_Y^2} = \frac{9}{16} \Rightarrow \frac{\sigma_X}{\sigma_Y} = \frac{3}{4}$

and we know that

$b_{XY} = r \times \frac{\sigma_X}{\sigma_Y}$

$\Rightarrow \quad \frac{3}{5} = r \times \frac{3}{4} \Rightarrow r = \frac{4}{5} = 0.8$

Thus, the correlation coefficient (r) between marks in Statistics and Accountancy is 0.8.

22. (i) Let the number of wheat and rice bags be x and y. Since, each sack of rice and wheat cost ₹ 180 and ₹ 120, Aman has total ₹ 1500.

Therefore, $120x + 180y \le 1500$ ...(i)

Also, he can store maximum number of 10 bags.

$\therefore \quad x + y \le 10$ ...(ii)

Thus, the linear programming to maximise Aman's profit is

Maximise, $Z = 9x + 11y$

Subject to the constraints

$120x + 180y \le 1500$

$x + y \le 10$

$x \ge 0, y \ge 0$

(ii) To calculate the maximum profit, we draw the feasible region using given constraints.

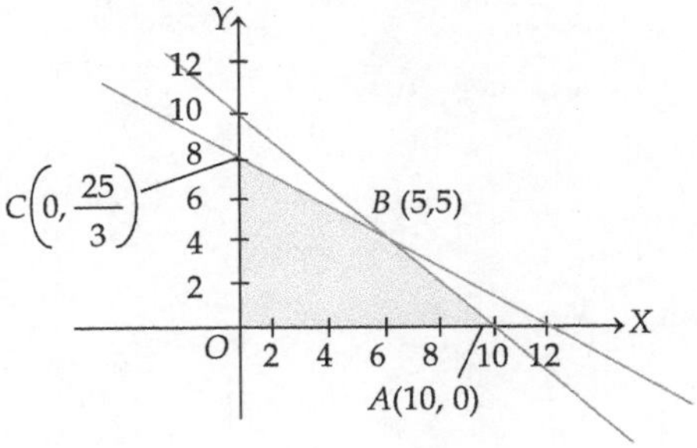

Feasible region is $OABCO$.

Thus, the corner points of feasible region are $O(0, 0)$, $A(10, 0)$, $B(5, 5)$ and $C\left(0, \frac{25}{3}\right)$.

The value of Z at corner point is

Corner points	$Z = 9x + 11y$
$O(0, 0)$	0
$A(10, 0)$	90
$B(5, 5)$	100 (Maximum)
$C\left(0, \frac{25}{3}\right)$	91.67

The maximum value of Z is 100 at point $B(5, 5)$.

∴ The maximum profit is ₹ 100.

Proficiency Building Zone

Welcome to the Proficiency Building Zone !

This section contains **15 Sample Question Papers** designed to enhance your problem-solving skills and proficiency. Use these papers to practice regularly and track your progress. Remember, consistent practice is key to mastering Maths.

Progress Tracker Tick the papers as you complete them.

- ☐ Sample Paper 1 _____ (Fill your score)
- ☐ Sample Paper 2 _____ (Fill your score)
- ☐ Sample Paper 3 _____ (Fill your score)
- ☐ Sample Paper 4 _____ (Fill your score)
- ☐ Sample Paper 5 _____ (Fill your score)
- ☐ Sample Paper 6 _____ (Fill your score)
- ☐ Sample Paper 7 _____ (Fill your score)
- ☐ Sample Paper 8 _____ (Fill your score)
- ☐ Sample Paper 9 _____ (Fill your score)
- ☐ Sample Paper 10 _____ (Fill your score)
- ☐ Sample Paper 11 _____ (Fill your score)
- ☐ Sample Paper 12 _____ (Fill your score)
- ☐ Sample Paper 13 _____ (Fill your score)
- ☐ Sample Paper 14 _____ (Fill your score)
- ☐ Sample Paper 15 _____ (Fill your score)

SQP Code : **PB-1/15** Series **i-Succeed 1-25/15** Roll No. | | | | | | | | |

Sample Question Paper 01

Mathematics 12th (Code 860)

General Instructions

1. The Question Paper consists of three sections A, B and C.
2. Candidates are required to attempt all questions from Section A and all questions either from Section B Or Section C.
3. Section A Internal choice has been provided in two questions of two marks each, two questions of four marks each and two questions of six marks each.
4. Section B Internal choice has been provided in one questions of two marks and one question of four marks.
5. Section C Internal choice has been provided in one question of two marks and one question of four marks.
6. All working, including rough work, should be done on the same sheet as, and adjacent to the rest of the answer.
7. The intended marks for questions or parts of questions are given in brackets [].
8. Mathematical tables and graph papers are provided.

Time : 3 Hrs.

Max. Marks : 80

Section A (65 Marks)

1. In subparts (i) to (x) choose the correct options and in subparts (xi) to (xv), answer the questions as instructed.

(i) If $y = \sec(\tan^{-1} x)$, then $\frac{dy}{dx}$ is equal to

• *Understanding* [1]

(a) $xy/(1+x)$ (b) $xy\sqrt{(1+x^2)}$

(c) $y/\sqrt{(1+x^2)}$ (d) $xy/(1+x^2)$

(ii) **Statement I** The value of

$$\tan^{-1}\left(\frac{-1}{\sqrt{3}}\right) + \cot^{-1}\left(\frac{1}{\sqrt{3}}\right) + \tan^{-1}\left[\sin\left(-\frac{\pi}{2}\right)\right] \text{ is } -\frac{\pi}{12}$$ [1]

Statement II The value of $\tan^{-1}\left(-\frac{1}{\sqrt{3}}\right) = \frac{\pi}{6}$ and $\cot^{-1}\left(\frac{1}{\sqrt{3}}\right) = -\frac{\pi}{3}$.

• *Recall*

(a) Statement I is true.

(b) Statement II is true.

(c) Both statements are true.

(d) Both statements are false.

(iii) Given below are the graphs of $f(x)$ along with the statement. Which of the following is true?

• *Analysis*

(a)

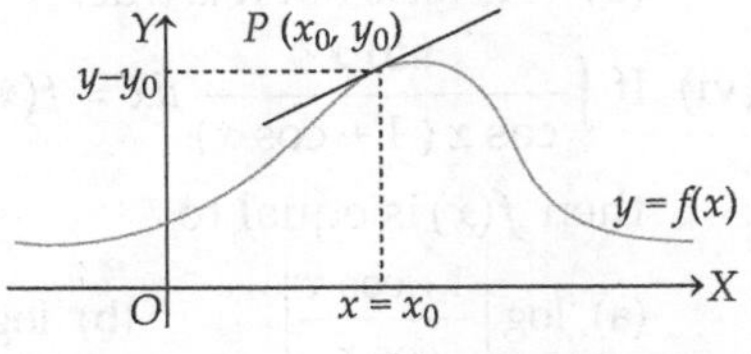

The function $y = f(x)$ is not differentiable at $x = x_0$.

(b)

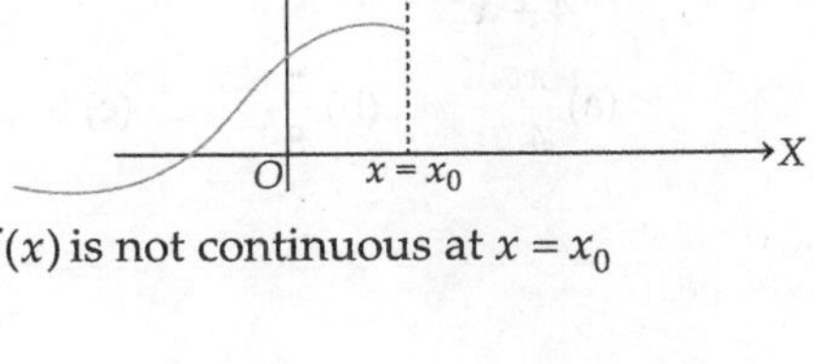

$f(x)$ is not continuous at $x = x_0$

(c)

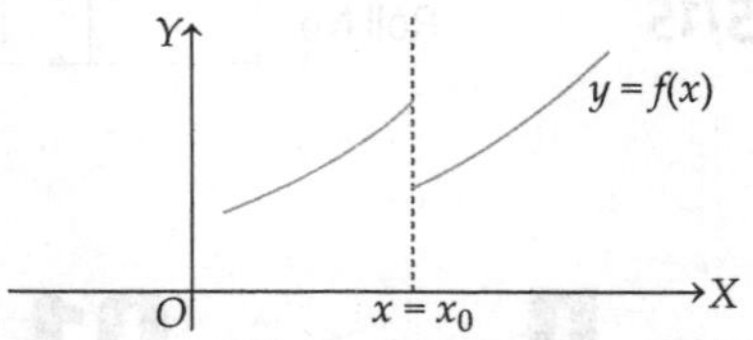

$f(x)$ is continuous at $x = x_0$

(d)

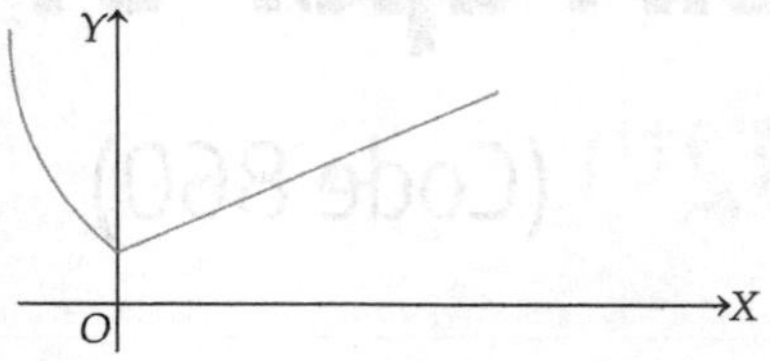

The function is differentiable at 0.

(iv) Let T be the set of all triangles in a plane with R be the relation in T given by

$R = \{(T_1, T_2) : T_1 \text{ is congruent to } T_2\}$.

Then, R is • *Understanding* [1]

(a) reflexive only.
(b) not transitive.
(c) an equivalence relation.
(d) symmetric only.

(v) **Assertion** The function

$f(x) = \tan x - x$ is always increase. [1]

Reason Let f be continuous on $[a, b]$ and differentiable on the open interval (a, b). Then, f is increasing in $[a, b]$, if $f'(x) > 0$, for each $x \in (a, b)$. • *Analysis*

(a) Both A and R are correct and R is the correct explanation of A.
(b) Both A and R are correct but R is not the correct explanation of A.
(c) A is true but R is false.
(d) A is false but R is true.

(vi) If $\int \frac{\sin x}{\cos x\,(1 + \cos x)}\, dx = f(x) + C,$

then $f(x)$ is equal to • *Evaluate* [1]

(a) $\log \left| \frac{1 + \cos x}{\cos x} \right|$ (b) $\log \left| \frac{\cos x}{1 + \cos x} \right|$

(c) $\log \left| \frac{\sin x}{1 + \sin x} \right|$ (d) $\log \left| \frac{1 + \sin x}{\sin x} \right|$

(vii) $\int_0^2 \frac{dx}{4 + x^2}$ is equal to • *Evaluate* [1]

(a) $\frac{\pi}{4}$ (b) $\frac{\pi}{8}$ (c) 0 (d) – 1

(viii) Shown below in the graph of a function $f(x)$.

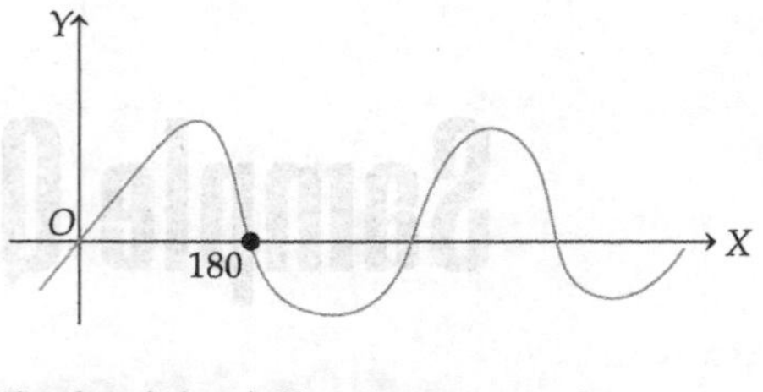

Which of the following is true? • *Analysis*

(a) $f(x)$ is onto when $\left[\frac{-\pi}{2}, \frac{\pi}{2}\right] \to R$
(b) $f(x)$ is not one-one.
(c) $f(x)$ is one-one.
(d) $f(x)$ is bijective.

(ix) **Assertion** (A) If $P(A) = 0.60$, $P(B) = 0.30$ and $P(A \cap B) = 0.18$, then the event A and event B are independent events.

Reason (R) Two events A and B are said to be independent if the occurance of one event does not effect the occurance of the other. Therefore, $P(A \cap B) = P(A) \cdot P(B)$. • *Analysis*

(a) Both A and R are correct and R is the correct explanation of A.
(b) Both A and R are correct but R is not the correct explanation of A.
(c) A is true, R is false.
(d) A is false, R is true.

(x) Consider the following statements. [1]

Statement I Let E and F be events associated with the sample space S of an experiment. Then, we have $P(S/F) = P(F/F) = 1$.

Statement II If A and B are any two events associated with the sample space S and F is an event associated with S such that $P(F) \neq 0$, then

$$P((A \cup B)/F) = P(A/F) + P(B/F) - P((A \cap B)/F)$$

• *Application*

Choose the correct option.

(a) Statement I is true.
(b) Statement II is true.
(c) Both statements are true.
(d) Both statements are false.

(xi) The graph of the function is given below.

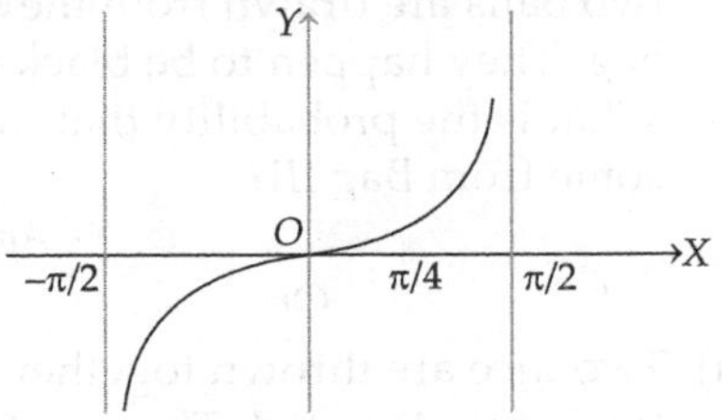

Which is greater, tan 1 or $\tan^{-1} 1$? • *Recall*

(xii) Prove that
$\sec^2(\tan^{-1} 2) + \text{cosec}^2(\cot^{-1} 3) = 15$
• *Understanding* [1]

(xiii) Find the local maximum and local minimum values of the function $2x^3 - 15x^2 + 36x + 11$. • *Application* [1]

(xiv) If matrix $A = [1 \quad 4 \quad 5]$, then find AA', where A' is the transpose of matrix A.
• *Application* [1]

(xv) A pharmaceutical company is conducting a clinical trial for a new drug intended to reduce blood pressure (BP).

The trial involves 200 participants divided into two groups.

Group A (treatment group) consists of 120 participants who receive the new drug.

Group (B) (control group) consists of 80 participants who receive a placebo.

At the end of the trial, the company finds that 90 participants in Group A experienced a significant reduction in BP, where as only 20 participants in Group B experienced the same effect.

Given that a participant experienced a significant reduction in BP, what is the probability that they were from Group A?
• *Application*

2. (i) The table below shown some of the values of differentiable function u and v and their derivatives.

x	$u(x)$	$u'(x)$	$v(x)$	$v'(x)$
0	−1	2	4	6
2	0	−1	1	2
3	2	1.5	2	2.5

If $g(x) = v[u(x)]$, find $g'(3)$.
• *Understanding* [2]

Or

(ii) If $f(x) = 3x^2 - 24x + 5$, find the interval where $f: R \to R$ is increasing.
• *Analysis* [2]

3. Examine the continuity of the function
$$f(x) = \begin{cases} 2, & x < 0 \\ x-3, & x \geq 0 \end{cases} \text{ at } x = 0.$$
• *Analysis* [2]

4. If $A = \begin{bmatrix} -1 & 3 \\ 4 & -2 \end{bmatrix}$ and $B = \begin{bmatrix} 2 & -3 \\ 4 & -5 \end{bmatrix}$, then find AB.
• *Evaluate* [2]

5. (i) The side of an equilateral triangle is increasing at the rate of 3 cm/s. At what rate, its area is increasing when the side of the triangle is 30 cm? • *Application* [2]

Or

(ii) The volume of a cube is increasing at a rate of 9 cm^3/s. How fast is the surface area increasing when the length of an edge is 10 cm? • *Application* [2]

6. What is the range of the function
$$f(x) = \frac{|x-1|}{x-1}, x \neq 1?$$
• *Recall* [2]

7. If $A = \begin{bmatrix} 1 & 2 & 0 \\ -2 & -1 & -2 \\ 0 & -1 & 1 \end{bmatrix}$, then find A^{-1}. Hence solve the system of equations
$x - 2y = 10, 2x - y - z = 8, -2y + z = 7$.
• *Application* [4]

8. Show that $\tan\left(\frac{1}{2}\sin^{-1}\frac{3}{4}\right) = \frac{4-\sqrt{7}}{3}$.
• *Recall* [4]

9. (i) Evaluate $\int \frac{1+\sin x}{\sin x(1+\cos x)} dx$.
• *Evaluate* [4]

Or

(ii) Evaluate $\int_0^{\pi/2} \frac{(\sin x + \cos x)dx}{9 + 16\sin 2x}$.
• *Evaluate* [4]

10. (i) Consider the initial value problem $e^{\frac{dy}{dx}} = x + 1, y(0) = 5$. Then, answer the following questions. • *Analysis*

(a) Write the given Initial value problem into the standard form of linear differntial equation.

(b) Find the general solution.

(c) Find the particular solution at $y(0) = 5$.

(d) Solve the initial value problem for $y(0) = 0$. [4]

Or

(ii) Consider the differential equation $y\,dx + (x - y^2)\,dy = 0$. Then, answer the following questions. • *Application*

(a) Find particular integral for given differential equation.

(b) Find the general solution.

(c) Find the particular solution for $y(0) = 0$. [4]

11. Consider the following function defined by

$$f(x) = \begin{cases} 3, & \text{if } 0 \le x \le 1 \\ 4, & \text{if } 1 < x < 3 \\ 5, & \text{if } 3 \le x \le 10 \end{cases}$$

Answer the following questions. • *Application*

(i) Show that the function is discontinuous at $x = 3$.

(ii) Discuss the differentiability of the function at $x = 1$.

(iii) Write the interval in which the given function is continuous. [6]

12. (i) Coloured balls are distributed in three bags as shown in the following table.

Bags	Colour		
	Black	White	Red
I	1	2	3
II	2	4	1
III	4	5	3

A bag is selected at random and then two balls are drawn from the selected bag. They happen to be black and red. What is the probability that they have come from Bag III?

• *Application* [6]

Or

(ii) Two dice are thrown together and the total score is noted. The events E, F and G are 'a total of 4', 'a total of 9 or more' and 'a total divisible by 5', respectively. Calculate $P(E)$, $P(F)$ and $P(G)$ and decide which pairs of events, if any are independent? • *Application* [6]

13. (i) Find the intervals in which the function f given by $f(x) = \sin x - \cos x, 0 \le x \le 2\pi$ is strictly increasing or strictly decreasing.

• *Understanding* [6]

Or

(ii) Find the angle of intersection of the curves $y^2 = 4ax$ and $x^2 = 4by$. • *Evaluate* [6]

14. There are two matrices:

$$A = \begin{bmatrix} 1 & p & 0 \\ 0 & 1 & p \\ 0 & 0 & 1 \end{bmatrix} \text{ and } B = \begin{bmatrix} 1 & 0 & 0 \\ q & 1 & 0 \\ 0 & q & 1 \end{bmatrix}$$

Answer the following questions.

• *Application*

(i) Find the inverse of matrix A.

(ii) Find the inverse of matrix B.

(iii) Find the product of the matrices A and B.

(iv) Find $(AB)^{-1}$. [6]

Section B (15 Marks)

15. In subparts (i) and (ii) choose the correct options and in subparts (iii) to (v), answer the questions as instructed. [5]

(i) Observe the vector diagram shown below and the expression that follows.

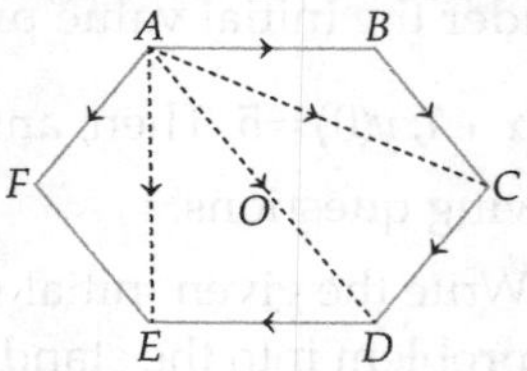

• *Application*

Statement I (1) $\overrightarrow{AC} + \overrightarrow{CD} = \overrightarrow{AD}$ (2) $\overrightarrow{ED}$

Statement II (3) $-\overrightarrow{EA}$ (4) $\overrightarrow{AB}$

(a) Statement I is true

(b) Statement II is true.

(c) Both Statements are true.

(d) Both Statements are false.

(ii) The cartesian equation of the plane $\vec{r} \cdot (2\hat{i} + 3\hat{j} + 4\hat{k}) = 5$ is • *Understanding*

(a) $2x + 3y + 4z = 5$ (b) $2x + 3y + z = 5$

(c) $x + 3y + z = 5$ (d) None of these

(iii) The projection of the vector $\hat{i} - \hat{j}$ on the vector $\hat{i} + \hat{j}$ is • *Understanding*

(a) 0 (b) 1 (c) −1 (d) $\frac{1}{\sqrt{2}}$

(iv) Find the coordinates of the point where the line through the points (5, 1, 6) and (3, 4, 1) crosses the *YZ*-plane. • *Understanding*

(v) The figure is shown below.

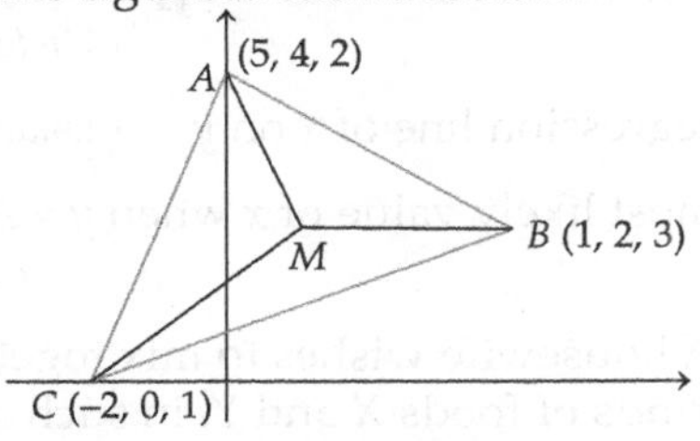

Find the equation of *CM*, which passes through the centroid of the triangular prism. • *Application*

16. (i) If *O*, *G* and *H* are respectively the circumcentre, centroid and orthocentre of a ΔABC, then prove that *O*, *G* and *H* are collinear and *G* divides *OH* in the ratio 1 : 2. • *Recall* [2]

Or (ii) Write the direction ratios of the vector $\vec{a} = \hat{i} + \hat{j} - 2\hat{k}$ and hence find its direction cosines. • *Recall* [2]

17. (i) Find the equation of the plane passing through the points (−1, 2, 0), (2, 2, −1) and parallel to the line $\frac{x-1}{1} = \frac{2y+1}{2} = \frac{z+1}{-1}$.

• *Application* [4]

Or (ii) Find the equation of the planes parallel to the plane $2x - 4y + 4z = 7$ and which are at a distance of 5 units from the point (3, −1, 2). • *Application* [4]

18. Find the area bounded by the curves $y = 6x - x^2$ and $y = x^2 - 2x$. • *Application* [4]

Section C (15 Marks)

19. In subparts (i) and (ii) choose the correct options and in subparts (iii) to (v), answer the questions as instructed. [5]

(i) A firm has the cost function $C = 2x^3 + \frac{x^2}{2} - 5$ and demand function $x = 100 - p$, then the total profit function in term of *x* is • *Recall*

(a) $100x - \frac{3x^2}{2} - 2x^3 + 5$

(b) $\frac{x^3}{3} - 5x^2 - 50x + 5$

(c) $\frac{x^3}{3} - 5x^2 - 50x + 5$ (d) None of these

(ii) The scatter plot below shows the relationship between games played and tickets won.

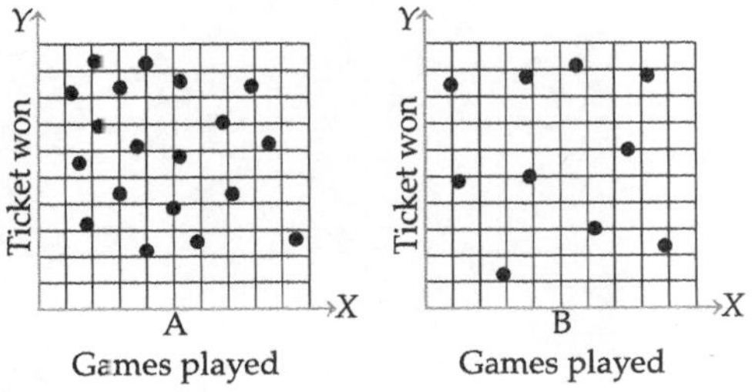

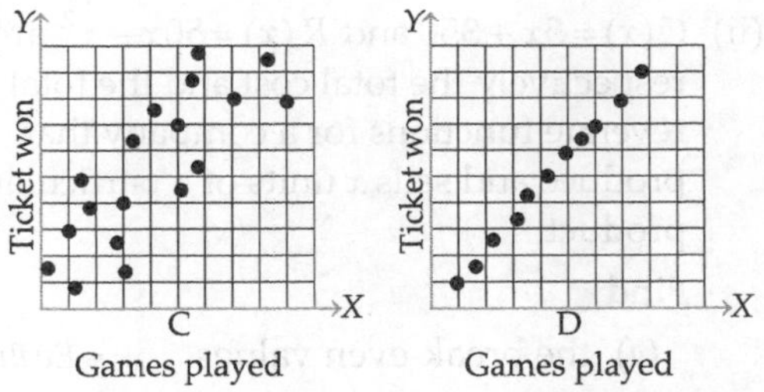

Which one of the given graphs could a line of best fit be drawn for? • *Analysis*

(a) Only A

(b) Only C and D

(c) Only D

(d) Only B and D

(iii) If the total cost function is given by $C = a + bx + cx^2$, where *x* is the quantity of output.

Show that $\frac{d}{dx}(\text{AC}) = \frac{1}{x}(\text{MC} - \text{AC})$, where MC is the marginal cost and AC is the average cost. • *Application*

SP-01

(iv) The average cost function associated with producing and marketing x units of an item is given by $AC = 2x - 11 + \frac{50}{x}$.

Find the range of values of the output x, for which AC is increasing. • *Application*

(v) If x and y are a pair of correlated variables, then 10 observations of their values (x_i, y_i) have the following results

$\Sigma x_i = 55$, $\Sigma y_i = 55$, $\Sigma x_i y_i = 350$ and $\Sigma x_i^2 = 385$

Predict the value of y when the value of x is 6. • *Understanding*

20. (i) The demand function of a monopolist is given by $p = 3x^2 + 5x - 50$.

Find

(*a*) the revenue function • *Application*

(*b*) the marginal revenue function. • *Understanding* [2]

Or

(ii) $C(x) = 5x + 350$ and $R(x) = 50x - x^2$ are respectively the total cost and the total revenue functions for a company that produce and sells x units of a particular product.

Find [2]

(*a*) the break-even values. • *Evaluate*

(*b*) the values of x that produce a profit. • *Evaluate*

21. From the given data

Variable	x	y
Mean	6	8
Standard Deviation	4	6

and correlation coefficient is $\frac{2}{3}$. Find

(i) regression coefficients b_{yx} and b_{xy}. • *Understanding*

(ii) regression line of x on y. • *Understanding*

(iii) most likely value of x when $y = 20$. • *Recall* [4]

22. (i) A housewife wishes to mix together two kinds of foods X and Y, in such a way that the mixture contains atleast 10 units of vitamin *A*, 12 units of vitamin *B* and 8 units of vitamin C.

The vitamin contents of 1 kg of food are given below

	Vitamin A	Vitamin B	Vitamin C
Food *X*	1	2	3
Food *Y*	2	2	1

1 kg of food X costs ₹ 6 and 1 kg of food *Y* costs ₹ 10. Find the least cost of the mixture which will produce the diet. • *Application* [4]

Or

(ii) Solve the following LPP graphically:

Minimise $Z = 5x + 10y$, subject to the constraints are $x + 2y \le 120$, $x + y \ge 60$, $x - 2y \ge 0$ and $x, y \ge 0$ • *Application* [4]

SP-01

Solutions in Topper's Style

My Commitment *I affirm that I am reviewing these solutions only after I have solved the Sample Question Paper 1 on my own. My purpose of looking the solutions is solely to verify whether my answers/solutions were correct or not and to identify my mistakes in case my solutions were wrong or I could not solve that.*

1. (i) (d) Given, $y = \sec(\tan^{-1} x)$

On differentiating both sides w.r.t. x, we get

$$\frac{dy}{dx} = \sec(\tan^{-1} x) \cdot \tan(\tan^{-1} x) \cdot \frac{1}{1+x^2}$$

$$= y \cdot x \cdot \frac{1}{1+x^2} = \frac{xy}{1+x^2}$$

(ii) (a) We know that

$$\tan^{-1}\left(\frac{-1}{\sqrt{3}}\right) = \frac{-\pi}{6}, \cot^{-1}\left(\frac{1}{\sqrt{3}}\right) = \frac{\pi}{3} \text{ and } \sin\left(\frac{-\pi}{2}\right) = -1$$

We have, $\tan^{-1}\left(\frac{-1}{\sqrt{3}}\right) + \cot^{-1}\left(\frac{1}{\sqrt{3}}\right) + \tan^{-1}\left[\sin\left(-\frac{\pi}{2}\right)\right]$

$$= \frac{-\pi}{6} + \frac{\pi}{3} + \tan^{-1}(-1) = \frac{-\pi}{6} + \frac{\pi}{3} - \frac{\pi}{4} = \frac{-\pi}{12}$$

Hence, statement I is true and II is false.

(iii) (b) From the figure (b),

we have

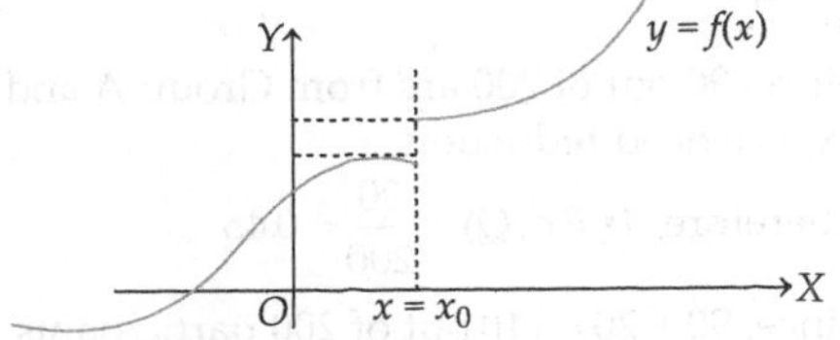

We see that the function breaks at $x = x_0$, so the function is not continuous at $x = x_0$.

(iv) (c) R is reflexive, since every triangle is congruent to itself.

Further $(T_1, T_2) \in R$

$\Rightarrow$ T_1 is congruent to T_2

$\Rightarrow$ T_2 is congruent to T_1

$\Rightarrow$ $(T_2, T_1) \in R$.

Therefore, R is symmetric.

Moreover, $(T_1, T_2), (T_2, T_3) \in R$

$\Rightarrow$ T_1 is congruent to T_2 and T_2 is congruent to T_3

$\Rightarrow$ T_1 is congruent to T_3

$\Rightarrow$ $(T_1, T_3) \in R$.

Therefore, R is transitive. Hence, R is an equivalence relation.

(v) (a) We have, $f(x) = \tan x - x$

$\therefore$ $f'(x) = \sec^2 x - 1$,

Here, $f'(x) \geq 0, \forall\, x \in R$

So, $f(x)$ always increases.

Reason is also correct and R is the correct explanation of A.

(vi) (a) Let $I = \int \frac{\sin x}{\cos x(1+\cos x)} dx$

Put $\cos x = t \Rightarrow -\sin x\, dx = dt$

$$\therefore \quad I = \int \frac{-dt}{t(1+t)}$$

$$= \int -\left[\frac{1}{t} - \frac{1}{t+1}\right] dt$$

$$= -[\log|t| - \log|t+1|] + C$$

$$= \left[\log \frac{t+1}{t} + C\right]$$

$$\left[\because \log m - \log n = \log \frac{m}{n}\right]$$

$$= \log\left|\frac{\cos x + 1}{\cos x}\right| + C$$

(vii) (b) Let $I = \int_0^2 \frac{dx}{4+x^2} = \int_0^2 \frac{dx}{(2)^2 + x^2} = \frac{1}{2}\left[\tan^{-1}\left(\frac{x}{2}\right)\right]_0^2$

$$\left[\because \int \frac{dx}{x^2+a^2} = \frac{1}{a}\tan^{-1}\left(\frac{x}{a}\right) + C\right]$$

$$= \frac{1}{2}[\tan^{-1}(1) - \tan^{-1}(0)]$$

$$= \frac{1}{2}\left[\frac{\pi}{4} - 0\right] = \frac{\pi}{8}$$

(viii) (b) The given graph is of the function $f(x) = \sin x$.

By horizontal line test, if the graph of the function intersects the horizontal line more than one point, then the function is not one-one.

Hence, the function is not one-one.

(ix) (a) Given,

$P(A) = 0.6$, $P(B) = 0.3$ and $P(A \cap B) = 0.18$

If the events are independent, then

$$P(A \cap B) = P(A) \cdot P(B)$$

$$\Rightarrow \quad 0.18 = 0.6 \times 0.3$$

$$\Rightarrow \quad 0.18 = 0.18$$

Hence, the events are independent. So, Assertion is correct.

Also, R is the correct explanation of A.

(x) (c) I. We know that,

$$P\left(\frac{S}{F}\right) = \frac{P(S \cap F)}{P(F)} = \frac{P(F)}{P(F)} = 1$$

Also, $$P\left(\frac{F}{F}\right) = \frac{P(F \cap F)}{P(F)} = \frac{P(F)}{P(F)} = 1$$

Thus, $$P\left(\frac{S}{F}\right) = P\left(\frac{F}{F}\right) = 1$$

II. We have, $P\left(\frac{(A \cup B)}{F}\right) = \frac{P[(A \cup B) \cap F]}{P(F)}$

$$= \frac{P[(A \cap F) \cup (B \cap F)]}{P(F)}$$

[by distributive law of union of sets over intersection]

$$= \frac{P(A \cap F) + P(B \cap F) - P(A \cap B \cap F)}{P(F)}$$

$$= \frac{P(A \cap F)}{P(F)} + \frac{P(B \cap F)}{P(F)} - \frac{P[(A \cap B) \cap F]}{P(F)}$$

$$= P\left(\frac{A}{F}\right) + P\left(\frac{B}{F}\right) - P\left(\frac{(A \cap B)}{F}\right)$$

Hence, both statements are true.

Note When A and B are disjoint events, then $P\left(\frac{(A \cap B)}{F}\right) = 0$

$$\Rightarrow \quad P\left(\frac{(A \cup B)}{F}\right) = P\left(\frac{A}{F}\right) + P\left(\frac{B}{F}\right)$$

(xi) From the given graph,

The function $y = \tan x$ is an increasing function in the interval $\left(\frac{-\pi}{2}, \frac{\pi}{2}\right)$.

Since, $1 > \frac{\pi}{4}$

Therefore, $\tan 1 > \tan \frac{\pi}{4}$

$\Rightarrow \tan 1 > 1 \Rightarrow \tan 1 > 1 > \frac{\pi}{4}$

$\Rightarrow \tan 1 > 1 > \tan^{-1}(1)$

Hence, $\tan(1) > \tan^{-1}(1)$.

(xii) Consider LHS

$= \sec^2(\tan^{-1} 2) + \text{cosec}^2(\cot^{-1} 3)$

$= \{\sec(\tan^{-1} 2)\}^2 + \{\text{cosec}(\cot^{-1} 3)\}^2$

$= \{\sec(\sec^{-1}\sqrt{5})\}^2 + \{\text{cosec}(\text{cosec}^{-1}\sqrt{10})\}^2$

$[\because \tan^{-1} x = \text{cosec}^{-1}\sqrt{1+x^2}$ and $\cot^{-1} x = \text{cosec}^{-1}\sqrt{1+x^2}]$

$= (\sqrt{5})^2 + (\sqrt{10})^2$

$= 5 + 10 = 15 = \text{RHS}$ **Hence proved.**

(xiii) Let $y = 2x^3 - 15x^2 + 36x + 11$ ...(i)

$\therefore \frac{dy}{dx} = 6x^2 - 30x + 36$

$= 6(x^2 - 5x + 6)$

$= 6(x-2)(x-3)$ ...(ii)

Sign scheme for $\frac{dy}{dx}$ i.e. for $(x-2)(x-3)$ is

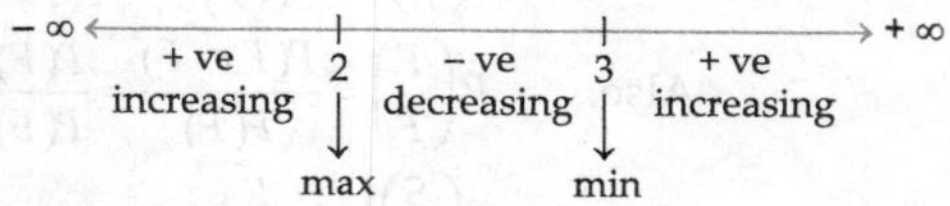

y has local maximum value at $x = 2$.

From Eq. (i), the corresponding local maximum value of

$y = 2(2)^3 - 15(2)^2 + 36(2) + 11$

$= 16 - 60 + 72 + 11 = 39$

y has local minimum value at $x = 3$.

From Eq. (i), the corresponding local minimum value of

$y = 2(3)^3 - 15(3)^2 + 36(3) + 11$

$\Rightarrow \quad y = 54 - 135 + 108 + 11 = 38$

(xiv) We have, $A = [1 \quad 4 \quad 5]$

Now, $A' = [1 \quad 4 \quad 5]' = \begin{bmatrix} 1 \\ 4 \\ 5 \end{bmatrix}$

[in transpose matrix, change row into column]

Now, $AA' = [1 \quad 4 \quad 5]\begin{bmatrix} 1 \\ 4 \\ 5 \end{bmatrix} = [1 \cdot 1 + 4 \cdot 4 + 5 \cdot 5]$

$= [1 + 16 + 25] = 42$

(xv) Let's define the events

P : Participant from Group A

Q : Participant experienced a significant reduction in BP.

Since, 90 out of 200 are from Group A and experienced reduction.

Therefore, $P(P \cap Q) = \frac{90}{200} = 0.45$

Since, $90 + 20 = 110$ out of 200 participants experienced the reduction in both groups.

Therefore,

$$P(Q) = \frac{90 + 20}{200} = \frac{110}{200} = 0.55$$

Thus, the probability that a participant is from Group A experienced a significant reduction in BP.

$$P(P/Q) = \frac{P(P \cap Q)}{P(Q)} = \frac{0.45}{0.55} = \frac{9}{11}$$

2. (i) We have,

$g(x) = v[u(x)]$

On differentiating w.r.t. x, we get

$g'(x) = v'[u(x)]\, u'(x)$

At $x = 3$,

$g'(3) = v'[u(3)] \cdot u'(3)$

$= v'(2) \times 1.5 \quad [\because u(3) = 2,\ u'(3) = 1.5]$

$= 2 \times 1.5 \quad [\because v'(2) = 2]$

$= 3$

Or

(ii) We have,

$f(x) = 3x^2 - 24x + 5$

On differentiating both sides w.r.t. x, we get

$f'(x) = 6x - 24$

For increasing, put

$$f'(x)=0 \Rightarrow 6x-24=0 \Rightarrow x=4$$

Sign for $f'(x)$,

$-\infty$ ——(−ve)—— 0 ——(−ve)—— 4 ——(+ve)—— $+\infty$

Hence, $(4, \infty)$ is the interval at which the function is increasing.

3. We have, $f(x)=\begin{cases} 2, & x<0 \\ x-3, & x \geq 0 \end{cases}$

$$\text{LHL}=\lim_{x \to 0^-} f(x)=\lim_{h \to 0} f(0-h)=2$$

$$\text{RHL}=\lim_{x \to 0^+} f(x)=\lim_{h \to 0} f(0+h)=\lim_{h \to 0}(h-3)=-3$$

Hence, LHL $\neq$ RHL

Hence, $f(x)$ is discontinuous at $x=0$.

4. We have, $A=\begin{bmatrix} -1 & 3 \\ 4 & -2 \end{bmatrix}$ and $B=\begin{bmatrix} 2 & -3 \\ 4 & -5 \end{bmatrix}$

$$AB=\begin{bmatrix} -1 & 3 \\ 4 & -2 \end{bmatrix}\begin{bmatrix} 2 & -3 \\ 4 & -5 \end{bmatrix}$$

$$=\begin{bmatrix} -2+12 & 3-15 \\ 8-8 & -12+10 \end{bmatrix}=\begin{bmatrix} 10 & -12 \\ 0 & -2 \end{bmatrix}$$

5. (i) Let a cm be the side of an equilateral triangle and A be its area at any time t s.

We know that $\quad A=\frac{\sqrt{3}}{4}a^2 \quad$ ...(i)

On differentiating Eq. (i) w.r.t. t, we get

$$\frac{dA}{dt}=\frac{\sqrt{3}}{4}2a\left(\frac{da}{dt}\right)$$

$$\Rightarrow \quad \frac{dA}{dt}=\frac{\sqrt{3}}{4}2a\cdot(3)=\frac{3\sqrt{3}a}{2} \quad \left[\text{given, } \frac{da}{dt}=3 \text{ cm/s}\right]$$

When $a=30$, then $\frac{dA}{dt}=\frac{3\sqrt{3}}{2}\times 30=45\sqrt{3}\text{ cm}^2/\text{s}$

Common Mistake

In case of increasing, we take the value with '+' ve sign, in case of decreasing, we take the value with '–' ve sign.

Or

(ii) Let the volume of a cube be V cm^3.

Then, we have $\frac{dV}{dt}=9\text{ cm}^3/\text{s}$

and edge of cube, $x=10$ cm

$\because \quad V=x^3$

On differentiating both sides w.r.t. t, we get

$$\frac{dV}{dt}=3x^2\frac{dx}{dt}$$

$$\Rightarrow \quad 9=3x^2\frac{dx}{dt}$$

$$\Rightarrow \quad \frac{dx}{dt}=\frac{3}{x^2} \quad \text{...(i)}$$

Also, surface area of a cube, $S=6x^2$

On differentiating both sides w.r.t. t, we get

$$\frac{dS}{dt}=12x\frac{dx}{dt}=12\times 10\times\frac{3}{x^2} \quad \text{[using Eq. (i)]}$$

At $x=10$ cm,

$$\frac{ds}{dt}=12\times 10\times\frac{3}{10\times 10}=3.6\text{ cm}^2/\text{s}$$

6. Given function is

$$f(x)=\frac{|x-1|}{x-1}, x\neq 1$$

The above function can be written as

$$f(x)=\begin{cases} \frac{x-1}{x-1}, & \text{if } x>1 \\ -\frac{(x-1)}{x-1}, & \text{if } x<1 \end{cases}$$

$$\Rightarrow \quad f(x)=\begin{cases} 1, \text{ if } x>1 \\ -1, \text{ if } x<1 \end{cases}$$

Hence, the range of $f(x)$ is $\{-1, 1\}$.

7. We have, $A=\begin{bmatrix} 1 & 2 & 0 \\ -2 & -1 & -2 \\ 0 & -1 & 1 \end{bmatrix}$ ...(i)

$$=1(-1-2)-2(-2-0)+0$$

$$\therefore \quad |A|=\begin{vmatrix} 1 & 2 & 0 \\ -2 & -1 & -2 \\ 0 & -1 & 1 \end{vmatrix}=1(-3)-2(-2)+0=1\neq 0$$

So, A is invertible.

Now, cofoctors of matrix A are

$A_{11}=-3, A_{12}=2, A_{13}=2, \; A_{21}=-2, A_{22}=1, A_{23}=1,$
$A_{31}=-4, A_{32}=2$ and $A_{33}=3$

$$\text{Then, adj}(A)=\begin{bmatrix} -3 & 2 & 2 \\ -2 & 1 & 1 \\ -4 & 2 & 3 \end{bmatrix}^T=\begin{bmatrix} -3 & -2 & -4 \\ 2 & 1 & 2 \\ 2 & 1 & 3 \end{bmatrix}$$

$$\therefore \quad A^{-1}=\frac{\text{adj } A}{|A|}=\frac{1}{1}\begin{bmatrix} -3 & -2 & -4 \\ 2 & 1 & 2 \\ 2 & 1 & 3 \end{bmatrix}$$

$$\Rightarrow \quad A^{-1}=\begin{bmatrix} -3 & -2 & -4 \\ 2 & 1 & 2 \\ 2 & 1 & 3 \end{bmatrix} \quad \text{...(ii) (2)}$$

Also, we have the system of linear equations as

$$x-2y=10,$$

$$2x-y-z=8 \text{ and } -2y+z=7$$

In the form of $CX=D$, it can be written as

$$\begin{bmatrix} 1 & -2 & 0 \\ 2 & -1 & -1 \\ 0 & -2 & 1 \end{bmatrix}\begin{bmatrix} x \\ y \\ z \end{bmatrix}=\begin{bmatrix} 10 \\ 8 \\ 7 \end{bmatrix}$$

where, $C=\begin{bmatrix} 1 & -2 & 0 \\ 2 & -1 & -1 \\ 0 & -2 & 1 \end{bmatrix}, X=\begin{bmatrix} x \\ y \\ z \end{bmatrix}$ and $D=\begin{bmatrix} 10 \\ 8 \\ 7 \end{bmatrix}$

$\therefore \quad C^T = \begin{bmatrix} 1 & 2 & 0 \\ -2 & -1 & -2 \\ 0 & -1 & 1 \end{bmatrix} = A$ [using Eq. (i)]

We know that $(A^T)^{-1} = (A^{-1})^T$ (1)

$\therefore \quad X = C^{-1} D = (A^{-1})^T D$

$\Rightarrow \begin{bmatrix} x \\ y \\ z \end{bmatrix} = \begin{bmatrix} -3 & 2 & 2 \\ -2 & 1 & 1 \\ -4 & 2 & 3 \end{bmatrix} \begin{bmatrix} 10 \\ 8 \\ 7 \end{bmatrix}$ [using Eq. (ii)]

$= \begin{bmatrix} -30+16+14 \\ -20+8+7 \\ -40+16+21 \end{bmatrix} = \begin{bmatrix} 0 \\ -5 \\ -3 \end{bmatrix}$

$\therefore x = 0, y = -5$ and $z = -3$ (2)

8. We have, $\tan\left(\frac{1}{2}\sin^{-1}\frac{3}{4}\right) = \frac{4-\sqrt{7}}{3}$

$\text{LHS} = \tan\left[\frac{1}{2}\sin^{-1}\left(\frac{3}{4}\right)\right] = \tan\theta,$ ...(i)

where $\frac{1}{2}\sin^{-1}\frac{3}{4} = \theta$ let $\Rightarrow \sin^{-1}\frac{3}{4} = 2\theta$

$\Rightarrow \quad \sin 2\theta = \frac{3}{4} \Rightarrow \frac{2\tan\theta}{1+\tan^2\theta} = \frac{3}{4}$

$\Rightarrow \quad 3 + 3\tan^2\theta = 8\tan\theta$

$\Rightarrow \quad 3\tan^2\theta - 8\tan\theta + 3 = 0$

Again, let $\tan\theta = y$

Then, $3y^2 - 8y + 3 = 0$

On comparing with $ay^2 + by + c = 0$, we get

$a = 3, b = -8$ and $c = 3$

Using quadratic formula, we get

$y = \frac{-b \pm \sqrt{b^2 - 4ac}}{2a}$

$= \frac{-(-8) \pm \sqrt{(-8)^2 - 4\times3\times3}}{2\times3}$

$\Rightarrow \quad y = \frac{8 \pm \sqrt{64-36}}{2\times3}$

$= \frac{8\pm\sqrt{28}}{6} = \frac{2[4\pm\sqrt{7}]}{6}$

$\Rightarrow \tan\theta = \frac{4\pm\sqrt{7}}{3} \Rightarrow \theta = \tan^{-1}\left[\frac{4\pm\sqrt{7}}{3}\right]$

Take '–' ve sign and then put the value in eq^n (i), we get

$\text{LHS} = \tan\left[\tan^{-1}\left(\frac{4-\sqrt{7}}{3}\right)\right] = \frac{4-\sqrt{7}}{3} = \text{RHS}$

Hence proved.

9. (i) Let $I = \int \frac{1+\sin x}{\sin x(1+\cos x)} dx$

Again, let $\tan\frac{x}{2} = t \Rightarrow \frac{1}{2}\sec^2\frac{x}{2} dx = dt$

$\Rightarrow \quad dx = \frac{2dt}{1+\tan^2\frac{x}{2}} \Rightarrow dx = \frac{2dt}{1+t^2}$

By trigonometric identity, we get

$\sin x = \frac{2\tan\frac{x}{2}}{1+\tan^2\frac{x}{2}} = \frac{2t}{1+t^2},$

and $\cos x = \frac{1-\tan^2\frac{x}{2}}{1+\tan^2\frac{x}{2}} = \frac{1-t^2}{1+t^2}$

On putting the above values in Eq. (i), we get

$I = \int \frac{1+\frac{2t}{1+t^2}}{\frac{2t}{1+t^2}\left(1+\frac{1-t^2}{1+t^2}\right)} \times \frac{2dt}{1+t^2}$

$= \int \frac{1+t^2+2t}{t(1+t^2+1-t^2)} dt = \frac{1}{2}\int \frac{1+t^2+2t}{t} dt$

$= \frac{1}{2}\int\left(\frac{1}{t}+t+2\right) dt = \frac{1}{2}\left(\log|t| + \frac{t^2}{2} + 2t\right) + C$

$= \frac{1}{2}\log\left|\tan\frac{x}{2}\right| + \frac{1}{4}\tan^2\frac{x}{2} + \tan\frac{x}{2} + C$

$\left[\because t = \tan\frac{x}{2}\right]$

Value Point

Do express the process by which you are converting sinx and cosx in terms of t.

Or

(ii) Let $I = \int_0^{\pi/2} \frac{(\sin x + \cos x)dx}{9 + 16\sin 2x}$ ...(i)

Again, let $\sin x - \cos x = t$

$\Rightarrow (\cos x + \sin x)dx = dt$

Also, on squaring both sides, we get

$(\sin x - \cos x)^2 = t^2$

$\Rightarrow \quad \sin^2 x + \cos^2 x - 2\sin x\cos x = t^2$

$\Rightarrow 1 - \sin 2x = t^2 \Rightarrow \sin 2x = 1 - t^2$

When $x = 0$, then $t = \sin 0 - \cos 0 = -1$

When $x = \frac{\pi}{2}$, then $t = \sin\frac{\pi}{2} - \cos\frac{\pi}{2} = 1$

On putting the above values in Eq. (i), we get

$\therefore \quad I = \int_{-1}^{1} \frac{dt}{9+16(1-t^2)} = \int_{-1}^{1}\frac{dt}{25-16t^2}$

$= \frac{1}{16}\int_{-1}^{1}\frac{dt}{\left(\frac{5}{4}\right)^2 - t^2} = \frac{1}{40}\left[\log\left|\frac{5+4t}{5-4t}\right|\right]_{-1}^{1}$

$\left[\because \int\frac{1}{a^2-x^2}dx = \frac{1}{2a}\log\left|\frac{a+x}{a-x}\right| + C\right]$

$= \frac{1}{40}\left[\log 9 - \log\frac{1}{9}\right] = \frac{1}{40}2\log 9$

$= \frac{1}{20}\log 9 = \frac{1}{20}\log 3^2 = \frac{1}{10}\log 3$

10. (i) (a) Given differential equation is $e^{\frac{dy}{dx}} = x + 1$

Now, taking log on both sides, we get

$$\frac{dy}{dx} = \log|x+1|,$$

which is the required form of linear differential equation.

(b) We have, $\frac{dy}{dx} = \log|x+1|$

On separating the variables, we get

$$dy = \log|x+1|\,dx$$

On integrating both sides, we get

$$\int dy = \int \log|x+1|\,dx$$

$$\Rightarrow \quad y = \int \underset{\text{II}}{1} \cdot \underset{\text{I}}{\log|x+1|}\,dx$$

$$\Rightarrow \quad y = \log|x+1| \cdot x - \int \frac{1}{x+1} \cdot x\,dx$$

$$\Rightarrow \quad y = x\log|x+1| - \int \frac{(x+1-1)}{(x+1)}\,dx$$

$$\Rightarrow \quad y = x\log|x+1| - \left\{\int \frac{(x+1)}{(x+1)}\,dx - \int \frac{1}{x+1}\,dx\right\}$$

$$\Rightarrow \quad y = x\log|x+1| - \int dx + \int \frac{dx}{x+1}$$

$$\Rightarrow \quad y = x\log|x+1| - x + \log|x+1| + C,$$

which is the required general solution.

(c) We have,

$$y = x\log|x+1| - x + \log|x+1| + C \quad \ldots\text{(i) [from part (b)]}$$

$\because$ It is given that $y = 5$, when $x = 0$.

$$\therefore \quad 5 = 0 \cdot \log(0+1) - 0 + \log|0+1| + C$$

$$\Rightarrow \quad C = 5$$

Now, substituting the value of C in Eq. (i), we get

$$y = x\log(x+1) - x + \log|x+1| + 5,$$

which is the required particular solution.

(d) The general solution of the given initial value problem is

$$y = x\log|x+1| - x + \log|x+1| + C,$$

where C is an arbitrary constant.

Now, on applying the initial condition $y(0) = 0$, we get

$$0 = 0 - 0 + 0 + C \Rightarrow C = 0$$

On substituting, $C = 0$ in the general solution, we get

$$y = x\log|x+1| - x + \log|x+1|,$$

which is the required particular solution for $y(0) = 0$.

(ii) (a) Given differential equation is

$$y\,dx + (x - y^2)\,dy = 0$$

$$\Rightarrow \quad \frac{dx}{dy} = -\frac{x}{y} + \frac{y^2}{y} \Rightarrow \frac{dx}{dy} + \frac{1}{y} \cdot x = y$$

This is a linear differential equation of the form $\frac{dx}{dy} + Px = Q$, where P and Q are the functions of y.

Here, $P = \frac{1}{y}$ and $Q = y$

$\therefore$ Particular integral =

$$\text{IF} = e^{\int P\,dy} = e^{\int \frac{1}{y} dy} = e^{\log|y|} = y$$

(b) The given differential equation is

$$\frac{dx}{dy} + \frac{1}{y}x = y$$

and IF $= y$

Then, general solution is

$$x\,(\text{IF}) = \int Q \cdot \text{IF}\,dy + C$$

$$\Rightarrow \quad xy = \int y^2\,dy + C$$

$$\Rightarrow \quad xy = \frac{y^3}{3} + C,$$

this is the required general solution.

(c) The general solution is given by

$$xy = \frac{y^3}{3} + C,$$

where C is an arbitrary constant.

On applying the initial condition $y(0) = 0$, we get

$$0 = \frac{0}{3} + C \Rightarrow C = 0$$

Hence, $\quad xy = \frac{y^3}{3}$

$$\Rightarrow \quad 3x = y^2 \text{ or } y = \pm\sqrt{3x}$$

11. (i) We have, $f(x) = \begin{cases} 3, & \text{if } 0 \le x \le 1 \\ 4, & \text{if } 1 < x < 3 \\ 5, & \text{if } 3 \le x \le 10 \end{cases}$

Now, LHL at $x = 3$,

$$\lim_{x \to 3^-} f(x) = \lim_{h \to 0} f(3-h) = \lim_{h \to 0} 4 = 4$$

RHL at $x = 3$,

$$\lim_{x \to 3^+} f(x) = \lim_{h \to 0} f(3+h) = \lim_{h \to 0} 5 = 5$$

Here, we see that LHL $\ne$ RHL, which shows that the given function is discontinuous at $x = 3$.

(ii) We have, $f(x) = \begin{cases} 3, & \text{if } 0 \le x \le 1 \\ 4, & \text{if } 1 < x < 3 \\ 5, & \text{if } 3 \le x \le 10 \end{cases}$

First we check the continuity of the function at $x = 1$.

LHL at $x = 1$

$$\lim_{x \to 1^-} f(x) = \lim_{h \to 0} f(1-h) = \lim_{h \to 0} 3 = 3$$

RHL at $x = 1$,

$$\lim_{x \to 1^+} f(x) = \lim_{h \to 0} f(1+h) = \lim_{h \to 0} 4 = 4$$

Here, we see that LHL $\neq$ RHL, therefore the function is not continuous at $x=1$.

Also, we know that a function is differentiable iff it is continuous.

So, the given function is not differentiable at $x=1$.

(iii) From, part (i) and (ii), we see that the function is discontinuous at $x=1$ and $x=3$.

The points of discontinuity are $x=1$ and 3 or $\{1,3\}$.

Thus, the interval in which the function is continuous is $R-\{1,3\}$

i.e. the function is continuous for all x except $x=1$ and $x=3$.

12. (i) Let E_1, E_2, E_3 and A be the events defined as follows

E_1 : Bag I is selected,

E_2 : Bag II is selected, E_3 : Bag III is selected,

A: one black and one red ball has been drawn from the selected bag.

As the bag is selected at random,

$$P(E_1)=P(E_2)=P(E_3)=\frac{1}{3}$$

Since, the balls are drawn randomly from the selected bag.

$\therefore$ Total number of balls in Bag I $=1+2+3=6$

$P(A/E_1)=$ Probability of drawing one black and one red ball when Bag I has been selected

$$=\frac{{}^1C_1\times{}^3C_1}{{}^6C_2}=\frac{1\times3}{15}=\frac{1}{5}$$

Total number of balls in Bag II $=2+4+1=7$

$P(A/E_2)=$ Probability of drawing one black and one red ball when Bag II has been selected

$$=\frac{{}^2C_1\times{}^1C_1}{{}^7C_2}=\frac{2\times1}{21}=\frac{2}{21}$$

Total number of balls in Bag III $=4+5+3=12$

$P(A/E_3)=$ Probability of drawing one black and one red ball when Bag III has been selected

$$=\frac{{}^4C_1\times{}^3C_1}{{}^{12}C_2}=\frac{4\times3}{66}=\frac{2}{11}$$

Now, by Baye's theorem,

$$P(E_3/A)=\frac{P(E_3)P(A/E_3)}{P(E_1)P(A/E_1)+P(E_2)P(A/E_2)+P(E_3)P(A/E_3)}$$

$$=\frac{\frac{1}{3}\times\frac{2}{11}}{\frac{1}{3}\times\frac{1}{5}+\frac{1}{3}\times\frac{2}{21}+\frac{1}{3}\times\frac{2}{11}}$$

$$=\frac{\frac{2}{11}}{\frac{1}{5}+\frac{2}{21}+\frac{2}{11}}=\frac{\frac{2}{11}}{\frac{231+110+210}{1155}}$$

$$=\frac{2}{11}\times\frac{1155}{551}=\frac{2\times105}{551}=\frac{210}{551}$$

Or

(ii) Two dice are thrown together, so number of outcomes in the sample space is 36

$\Rightarrow \quad n(S)=36$

$E=$ Total of $4=\{(2,2),(3,1),(1,3)\}$

$\Rightarrow \quad n(E)=3$

$F=$ Total of 9 or more

$$=\begin{Bmatrix}(3,6),(6,3),(4,5),(5,4),(4,6),\\(6,4),(5,5),(5,6),(6,5),(6,6)\end{Bmatrix}$$

$\Rightarrow \quad n(F)=10$

and $\quad G=$ Total divisible by 5

$=\{(1,4),(4,1),(2,3),(3,2),(4,6),(6,4),(5,5)\}$

$\Rightarrow \quad n(G)=7$

Here, $(E\cap F)=\phi$ and $(E\cap G)=\phi$

Also, $(F\cap G)=\{(4,6),(6,4),(5,5)\}$

$\Rightarrow \quad n(F\cap G)=3$ and $(E\cap F\cap G)=\phi$

$$\therefore \quad P(E)=\frac{n(E)}{n(S)}=\frac{3}{36}=\frac{1}{12}$$

$$P(F)=\frac{n(F)}{n(S)}=\frac{10}{36}=\frac{5}{18}$$

$$\text{and } P(G)=\frac{n(G)}{n(S)}=\frac{7}{36}$$

$$\therefore \quad P(F\cap G)=\frac{3}{36}=\frac{1}{12}$$

$$\text{and } P(F)\cdot P(G)=\frac{5}{18}\times\frac{7}{36}=\frac{35}{648}$$

Here, we see that $P(F\cap G)\neq P(F)\cdot P(G)$

[$\because$ only F and G have common events, so only F and G are used here]

Hence, there is no pair which is independent.

13. (i) Given function is $f(x)=\sin x-\cos x, 0\le x\le 2\pi$

On differentiating both sides w.r.t. x, we get

$f'(x)=\cos x+\sin x$

On putting $f'(x)=0$, we get

$\cos x+\sin x=0$

$\Rightarrow \quad \sin x=-\cos x$

$\Rightarrow \quad \dfrac{\sin x}{\cos x}=-1 \Rightarrow \tan x=-1$

For $x\in[0,2\pi]$, $\tan x=\tan\dfrac{3\pi}{4}\Rightarrow x=\dfrac{3\pi}{4}$

or $\quad \tan x=\tan\dfrac{7\pi}{4}$

$\Rightarrow \quad x=\dfrac{7\pi}{4}$

$\therefore \quad x=\dfrac{3\pi}{4},\dfrac{7\pi}{4}$

[$\because$ tan θ is negative in IInd quadrant and IVth quadrant]

Now, we find the intervals in which $f(x)$ is strictly increasing or strictly decreasing.

Interval	Test value	$f'(x) = \cos x + \sin x$	Sign of $f'(x)$
$0 < x < \frac{3\pi}{4}$	At $x = \frac{\pi}{2}$	$f'\left(\frac{\pi}{2}\right) = \cos\frac{\pi}{2} + \sin\frac{\pi}{2} = 0 + 1 = 1$	+ ve
$\frac{3\pi}{4} < x < \frac{7\pi}{4}$	At $x = \frac{5\pi}{6}$	$f'\left(\frac{5\pi}{6}\right) = \cos\frac{5\pi}{6} + \sin\frac{5\pi}{6}$ $= \cos\left(\pi - \frac{\pi}{6}\right) + \sin\left(\pi - \frac{\pi}{6}\right)$ $= -\cos\frac{\pi}{6} + \sin\frac{\pi}{6} = \frac{-\sqrt{3}}{2} + \frac{1}{2} = \frac{-\sqrt{3}+1}{2}$	− ve
$\frac{7\pi}{4} < x < 2\pi$	At $x = \frac{23\pi}{12}$	$f'\left(\frac{23\pi}{12}\right) = \cos\frac{23\pi}{12} + \sin\frac{23\pi}{12}$ $= \cos\left(2\pi - \frac{\pi}{12}\right) + \sin\left(2\pi - \frac{\pi}{12}\right) = \cos\frac{\pi}{12} - \sin\frac{\pi}{12} > 0$	+ ve

We know that a function $f(x)$ is said to be strictly increasing in an interval when $f'(x) > 0$ and it is said to be strictly decreasing when $f'(x) < 0$. So, the given function $f(x)$ is strictly increasing in intervals $\left(0, \frac{3\pi}{4}\right)$ and $\left(\frac{7\pi}{4}, 2\pi\right)$ and it is strictly decreasing in the interval $\left(\frac{3\pi}{4}, \frac{7\pi}{4}\right)$.

Or

(ii) Given, equations of curves are

$$y^2 = 4ax \quad \ldots(\text{i})$$

and
$$x^2 = 4by \quad \ldots(\text{ii})$$

Clearly, the angle of intersection of curves (i) and (ii) is the angle between the tangents to the curves at the point of intersection.

So, let us first find the intersection point of given curves.

On substituting the value of y from Eq. (ii) in Eq. (i), we get

$$\left(\frac{x^2}{4b}\right)^2 = 4ax \Rightarrow \frac{x^4}{16b^2} = 4ax$$

$$\Rightarrow \quad x^4 = 64ab^2x$$

$$\Rightarrow \quad x^4 - 64ab^2x = 0$$

$$\Rightarrow \quad x(x^3 - 64ab^2) = 0$$

$$\Rightarrow \quad x = 0 \text{ or } x = 4a^{1/3}b^{2/3}$$

Clearly, when $x = 0$, then from Eq. (i), $y = 0$ and when $x = 4a^{1/3}b^{2/3}$, then from Eq. (i), we get

$$y^2 = 16a^{4/3}b^{2/3} \Rightarrow y = 4a^{2/3}b^{1/3}$$

Thus, the points of intersection are (0, 0) and $(4a^{1/3}b^{2/3}, 4a^{2/3}b^{1/3})$.

Now, let us find the angle of intersection at (0, 0) and $(4a^{1/3}b^{2/3}, 4a^{2/3}b^{1/3})$.

Let m_1 be the slope of tangent to the curve (i) and m_2 be the slope of tangent to the curve (ii).

For angle of intersection at (0, 0),

$$m_1 = \left(\frac{dy}{dx}\right)_{\text{at}(0,0)} = \left(\frac{2a}{y}\right)_{\text{at}(0,0)} = \infty$$

$$\left[\because \text{from Eq. (i), } 2y\frac{dy}{dx} = 4a \Rightarrow \frac{dy}{dx} = \frac{2a}{y}\right]$$

and
$$m_2 = \left(\frac{dy}{dx}\right)_{\text{at}(0,0)} = \left(\frac{x}{2b}\right)_{\text{at}(0,0)} = 0$$

$$\left[\because \text{from Eq. (ii), } 2x = 4b\frac{dy}{dx} \Rightarrow \frac{dy}{dx} = \frac{x}{2b}\right]$$

$\Rightarrow$ tangent to the curve (i) is parallel to Y-axis and tangent to the curve (ii) is parallel to X-axis.

$\therefore$ Angle between these two curves is $\frac{\pi}{2}$.

$\Rightarrow$ The angle of intersection of the curves is $\frac{\pi}{2}$.

For angle of intersection at $(4a^{1/3}b^{2/3}, 4a^{2/3}b^{1/3})$.

Here,
$$m_1 = \frac{2a}{4a^{2/3}b^{1/3}} = \frac{1}{2}\cdot\frac{a^{1/3}}{b^{1/3}} = \frac{1}{2}\left(\frac{a}{b}\right)^{1/3}$$

and
$$m_2 = \frac{4a^{1/3}b^{2/3}}{2b} = 2\left(\frac{a}{b}\right)^{1/3}$$

Let θ be the angle between the tangents.

Then,
$$\tan\theta = \left|\frac{m_2 - m_1}{1 + m_1 m_2}\right| = \left|\frac{2\left(\frac{a}{b}\right)^{1/3} - \frac{1}{2}\left(\frac{a}{b}\right)^{1/3}}{1 + 2\left(\frac{a}{b}\right)^{1/3}\frac{1}{2}\left(\frac{a}{b}\right)^{1/3}}\right|$$

$$= \left|\frac{\frac{3}{2}\left(\frac{a}{b}\right)^{1/3}}{1 + \left(\frac{a}{b}\right)^{2/3}}\right| = \left|\frac{\frac{3}{2}\left(\frac{a}{b}\right)^{1/3}\cdot b^{2/3}}{b^{2/3} + a^{2/3}}\right| = \left|\frac{3(ab)^{1/3}}{2(a^{2/3} + b^{2/3})}\right|$$

$$\Rightarrow \quad \theta = \tan^{-1}\left\{\frac{3(ab)^{1/3}}{2(a^{2/3} + b^{2/3})}\right\}$$

Hence, the angles of intersection of the curves are $\frac{\pi}{2}$ and $\tan^{-1}\left\{\frac{3(ab)^{1/3}}{2(a^{2/3} + b^{2/3})}\right\}$

14. (i) Let $A=\begin{bmatrix}1 & p & 0\\0 & 1 & p\\0 & 0 & 1\end{bmatrix}$

$\therefore\ |A|=1(1-0)-p(0-0)+0=1\neq 0$

So, A^{-1} exists.

Cofactors of matrix A are

$A_{11}=1-0=1,\ A_{12}=-(0-0)=0,\ A_{13}=0-0=0,$
$A_{21}=-(p-0)=-p,\ A_{22}=1-0=1,\ A_{23}=-(0-0)=0,$
$A_{31}=(p^2-0)=p^2,\ A_{32}=-(p-0)=-p,$
$A_{33}=(1-0)=1$

$$\therefore\quad \text{adj}(A)=\begin{bmatrix}A_{11} & A_{21} & A_{31}\\A_{12} & A_{22} & A_{32}\\A_{13} & A_{23} & A_{33}\end{bmatrix}=\begin{bmatrix}1 & -p & p^2\\0 & 1 & -p\\0 & 0 & 1\end{bmatrix}$$

$$\text{Now, } A^{-1}=\frac{1}{|A|}\cdot\text{adj}(A)=\begin{bmatrix}1 & -p & p^2\\0 & 1 & -p\\0 & 0 & 1\end{bmatrix}\quad \ldots\text{(i)}$$

(ii) We have, $B=\begin{bmatrix}1 & 0 & 0\\q & 1 & 0\\0 & q & 1\end{bmatrix}$

$\therefore\quad |B|=1(1-0)=1\neq 0$

So, B^{-1} exists.

Cofactors of matrix B are

$B_{11}=1,\ B_{12}=-q,\ B_{13}=q^2$
$B_{21}=0,\ B_{22}=1,\ B_{23}=-q$
$B_{31}=0,\ B_{32}=0,\ B_{33}=1$

$$\therefore\ \text{adj}(B)=\begin{bmatrix}1 & -q & q^2\\0 & 1 & -q\\0 & 0 & 1\end{bmatrix}'=\begin{bmatrix}1 & 0 & 0\\-q & 1 & 0\\q^2 & -q & 1\end{bmatrix}$$

$$\text{Now, } B^{-1}=\frac{1}{|B|}\text{adj}(B)=\begin{bmatrix}1 & 0 & 0\\-q & 1 & 0\\q^2 & -q & 1\end{bmatrix}\quad \ldots\text{(ii)}$$

(iii) We have, $A=\begin{bmatrix}1 & p & 0\\0 & 1 & p\\0 & 0 & 1\end{bmatrix}$ and $B=\begin{bmatrix}1 & 0 & 0\\q & 1 & 0\\0 & q & 1\end{bmatrix}$

$$\text{Now, } AB=\begin{bmatrix}1 & p & 0\\0 & 1 & p\\0 & 0 & 1\end{bmatrix}\begin{bmatrix}1 & 0 & 0\\q & 1 & 0\\0 & q & 1\end{bmatrix}$$

$$=\begin{bmatrix}1+pq & p & 0\\q & 1+pq & p\\0 & q & 1\end{bmatrix}$$

(iv) We have to find the inverse of the matrix

$$AB=\begin{bmatrix}1+pq & p & 0\\q & 1+pq & p\\0 & q & 1\end{bmatrix}\text{ i.e. }(AB)^{-1}$$

Now, $(AB)^{-1}=B^{-1}A^{-1}$

$$=\begin{bmatrix}1 & 0 & 0\\-q & 1 & 0\\q^2 & -q & 1\end{bmatrix}\begin{bmatrix}1 & -p & p^2\\0 & 1 & -p\\0 & 0 & 1\end{bmatrix}$$

[using Eq. (i) and Eq. (ii)]

$$=\begin{bmatrix}1 & -p & p^2\\-q & pq+1 & -p^2q-p\\q^2 & -pq^2-q & p^2q^2+pq+1\end{bmatrix}$$

15. (i) (b) (1) Using triangle law of addition,

$\overrightarrow{AC}+\overrightarrow{CD}=\overrightarrow{AD}$ [which is true]

(2) $\overrightarrow{ED}$ does not follow because from figure D is initial point and E is terminal point.

(3) $-\overrightarrow{EA}$ follows, because $-\overrightarrow{EA}$ is negative vector of $\overrightarrow{AE}$

(4) $\overrightarrow{AB}$ follows.

Hence, statement is true.

(ii) (a) We have, $\vec{r}\cdot(2\hat{i}+3\hat{j}+4\hat{k})=5$

$\Rightarrow (x\hat{i}+y\hat{j}+z\hat{k})\cdot(2\hat{i}+3\hat{j}+4\hat{k})=5$

$\Rightarrow\quad 2x+3y+4z=5$

(iii) (a) Let $\vec{a}=\hat{i}-\hat{j}$ and $\vec{b}=\hat{i}+\hat{j}$

We know that projection of $\vec{a}$ on $\vec{b}$ is $\dfrac{\vec{a}\cdot\vec{b}}{|\vec{b}|}$.

$$\therefore\text{Required projection}=\frac{(\hat{i}-\hat{j})\cdot(\hat{i}+\hat{j})}{|\hat{i}+\hat{j}|}=\frac{1-1}{\sqrt{2}}=0$$

(iv) Here, direction ratios of the line passing through the points (5, 1, 6) and (3, 4, 1) are

$<3-5, 4-1, 1-6>$

or $<-2, 3, -5>$

or $<2, -3, 5>$

$\therefore$ The equation of the line through the given points having direction ratios $<2, -3, 5>$ is

$$\frac{x-5}{2}=\frac{y-1}{-3}=\frac{z-6}{5}=\lambda\text{ (say)}\ \ldots\text{(i)}$$

or $\quad x=2\lambda+5,\ y=-3\lambda+1,\ z=5\lambda+6$

Any point on the line (i) is $(5+2\lambda, 1-3\lambda, 6+5\lambda)$.

If the point lies on YZ-plane, then its x-coordinate is zero

$$\Rightarrow\quad 5+2\lambda=0\ \Rightarrow\ \lambda=-\frac{5}{2}$$

Hence, the required point is $\left(0, 1+3\times\dfrac{5}{2}, 6-5\times\dfrac{5}{2}\right)$

i.e. $\left(0, \dfrac{17}{2}, -\dfrac{13}{2}\right)$.

(v) Given, $A\equiv(5,4,2)$, $B\equiv(1,2,3)$ and $C\equiv(-2,0,1)$

The coordinates of centroid of triangular prism,

$$M=\left(\frac{5+1-2}{3}, \frac{4+2+0}{3}, \frac{3+2+1}{3}\right)$$

$$=\left(\frac{4}{3}, 2, 2\right)$$

Now, the direction ratios of line CM are

$\left(\frac{4}{3}+2, 2-0, 2-1\right)$ i.e. $\left(\frac{10}{3}, 2, 1\right)$

Hence, the equation of line CM is

$$\frac{x+2}{10/3}=\frac{y-0}{2}=\frac{z-1}{1}$$

16. (i) Let O be the circumcentre of ΔABC and $\overrightarrow{OA}=\vec{a}$, $\overrightarrow{OB}=\vec{b}$ and $\overrightarrow{OC}=\vec{c}$.

Since, G is centroid, then position vector of G is $\frac{\vec{a}+\vec{b}+\vec{c}}{3}$ i.e. $\overrightarrow{OG}=\frac{\vec{a}+\vec{b}+\vec{c}}{3}$.

Let P be the point whose position vector is $(\vec{a}+\vec{b}+\vec{c})$ i.e. $\overrightarrow{OP}=\vec{a}+\vec{b}+\vec{c}$.

As O is the circumcentre, therefore $\overrightarrow{OA}=\overrightarrow{OB}=\overrightarrow{OC}$

$\Rightarrow \quad |\vec{a}|=|\vec{b}|=|\vec{c}|$

Now, $\quad |\vec{a}|^2-|\vec{b}|^2=0$

$\Rightarrow \quad (\vec{a})^2-(\vec{b})^2=0$

$\Rightarrow \quad (\vec{a}+\vec{b})\cdot(\vec{a}-\vec{b})=0$

$\Rightarrow \quad (\vec{a}+\vec{b}+\vec{c}-\vec{c})\cdot(\vec{a}-\vec{b})=0$

$\Rightarrow \quad (\overrightarrow{OP}-\overrightarrow{OC})\cdot(\overrightarrow{OA}-\overrightarrow{OB})=0$

$\Rightarrow \quad \overrightarrow{CP}\cdot\overrightarrow{BA}=0 \Rightarrow \overrightarrow{CP}\perp\overrightarrow{BA}$

Similarly, we can show that $\overrightarrow{BP}\perp\overrightarrow{CA}$ and $\overrightarrow{AP}\perp\overrightarrow{BC}$.

So, P is the orthocentre of ΔABC and the point P is same as H.

$\therefore \quad \overrightarrow{OH}=\overrightarrow{OP}=\vec{a}+\vec{b}+\vec{c}=3\overrightarrow{OG}$

Hence, O, G and H are collinear and G divides OH in ratio $1:2$. **Hence proved.**

Or

(ii) We have, vector $\vec{a}=\hat{i}+\hat{j}-2\hat{k}$

We know that direction ratios of a vector $\vec{r}=x\hat{i}+y\hat{j}+z\hat{k}$ are the scalar components x, y and z of the vector.

So, required direction ratios are 1, 1 and -2.

Now, $|\vec{a}|=|\hat{i}+\hat{j}-2\hat{k}|$

$=\sqrt{(1)^2+(1)^2+(-2)^2}$

$=\sqrt{1+1+4}=\sqrt{6}$

Suppose l, m and n are the direction cosines of given vector $\vec{a}$.

Then, $\quad l=\frac{x}{|\vec{a}|}, m=\frac{y}{|\vec{a}|}$ and $n=\frac{z}{|\vec{a}|}$

$\Rightarrow \quad l=\frac{1}{\sqrt{6}}, m=\frac{1}{\sqrt{6}}$ and $n=\frac{-2}{\sqrt{6}}$

Hence, the required direction cosines are $\left(\frac{1}{\sqrt{6}}, \frac{1}{\sqrt{6}}, \frac{-2}{\sqrt{6}}\right)$.

17. (i) Let the equation of plane passing through the point $(-1, 2, 0)$ be $a(x+1)+b(y-2)+c(z-0)=0$ ...(i)

where, a, b and c are direction ratios of normal to the plane.

Since, the plane also passes through $(2, 2, -1)$. Therefore, we have

$a(2+1)+b(2-2)+c(-1-0)=0$

$\Rightarrow \quad 3a+0\cdot b-c=0$ ...(ii)

Also, the plane is parallel to the line

$$\frac{x-1}{1}=\frac{2y+1}{2}=\frac{z+1}{-1}$$

or $\quad \frac{x-1}{1}=\frac{y+\frac{1}{2}}{1}=\frac{z+1}{-1}$

Therefore, we have

$a+b-c=0$ ...(iii)

[$\because$ the normal to the plane will be perpendicular to the line i.e. $a_1a_2+b_1b_2+c_1c_2=0$]

On solving Eqs. (ii) and (iii), we get

$$\frac{a}{0+1}=\frac{-b}{-3+1}=\frac{c}{3-0}$$

$\Rightarrow \quad \frac{a}{1}=\frac{-b}{-2}=\frac{c}{3}$

$\Rightarrow \quad \frac{a}{1}=\frac{b}{2}=\frac{c}{3}=\lambda$ (say)

On substituting the values of a, b and c in Eq. (i), we get the required equation of plane as

$1(x+1)+2(y-2)+3z=0$

$\Rightarrow \quad x+1+2y-4+3z=0$

$\Rightarrow \quad x+2y+3z=3,$

which is the required equation of plane.

Common Mistake

Make sure that equation of line should be in proper symmetrical form.

Or

(ii) The equation of the plane parallel to the plane $2x-4y+4z=7$ is given by

$2x-4y+4z+k=0$ ...(i)

Given that the required plane is at a distance of 5 units from the point $(3, -1, 2)$.

$$\left|\frac{2(3)-4(-1)+4(2)+k}{\sqrt{4+16+16}}\right|=5$$

$\left[\because \text{perpendicular distance from } (x_1, y_1, z_1) \text{ to the plane } ax+by+cz=0 \text{ is } d=\left|\frac{ax_1+by_1+cz_1}{\sqrt{a^2+b^2+c^2}}\right|\right]$

$\Rightarrow \quad \left|\frac{6+4+8+k}{\sqrt{36}}\right|=5$

$$\Rightarrow \quad \frac{18+k}{6} = \pm 5$$

$$\Rightarrow \quad k = \pm 30 - 18$$

$$\Rightarrow \quad k = 12 \text{ or } -48$$

Hence, the possible equations of required planes are $2x - 4y + 4z + 12 = 0$

and $2x - 4y + 4z - 48 = 0$

[put $k = 12$ and $k = -48$ in Eq. (i)]

18. The given curves are $y = 6x - x^2$ ...(i)

and $y = x^2 - 2x$ ...(ii)

Eq. (i) can be written as

$$x^2 - 6x + 9 = -y + 9$$

$$\Rightarrow \quad (x-3)^2 = -(y-9)$$

which represents a downward parabola with vertex at (3, 9).

Now, Eq. (ii) can be written as

$$x^2 - 2x + 1 = y + 1 \Rightarrow (x-1)^2 = y + 1$$

which represents an upward parabola with vertex at (1, −1).

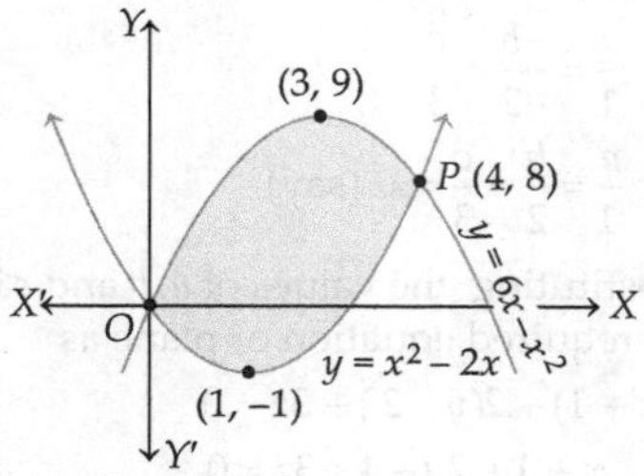

On solving Eqs. (i) and (ii), we get

$$6x - x^2 = x^2 - 2x$$

$$\Rightarrow \quad 2x^2 - 8x = 0$$

$$\Rightarrow \quad 2x(x-4) = 0$$

$$\Rightarrow \quad x = 0 \text{ and } x = 4$$

Then, from Eq (i), we get

$$y = 0 \text{ and } y = 24 - (4)^2 = 8$$

Thus, the points of intersection of the curves are $O(0, 0)$ and $P(4, 8)$.

$$\therefore \text{ Required area} = \int_0^4 (y_2 - y_1)\, dx$$

$$= \int_0^4 [(6x - x^2) - (x^2 - 2x)]\, dx$$

$$= \int_0^4 (6x - x^2 - x^2 + 2x)\, dx$$

$$= \int_0^4 (8x - 2x^2)\, dx$$

$$= \left[8 \times \frac{x^2}{2} - \frac{2x^3}{3}\right]_0^4$$

$$= \frac{8 \times 16}{2} - 2 \times \frac{64}{3} = 64 - \frac{128}{3}$$

$$= \frac{192 - 128}{3} = \frac{64}{3} \text{ sq units}$$

19. (i) (a) Total revenue function $= px = x(100 - x)$

$\therefore$ Profit function

= Revenue function − cost function

$$= (100x - x^2) - \left(2x^3 + \frac{x^2}{2} - 5\right)$$

$$= 100x - \frac{3x^2}{2} - 2x^3 + 5$$

(ii) (c) A line of best fit is a straight line that minimise the distance between it and data points.

(iii) Given, cost function $(C) = a + bx + cx^2$

Then, average cost $(AC) = \frac{C}{x} = \frac{a}{x} + b + cx$

and marginal cost $(MC) = \frac{d}{dx}(C)$

$$= \frac{d}{dx}(a + bx + cx^2) = b + 2cx$$

Now, $\frac{d}{dx}(AC) = \frac{d}{dx}\left(\frac{a}{x} + b + cx\right) = -\frac{a}{x^2} + c$ ...(i)

and $\frac{1}{x}(MC - AC) = \frac{1}{x}\left(b + 2cx - \frac{a}{x} - b - cx\right)$

$$= \frac{1}{x}\left(cx - \frac{a}{x}\right)$$

$$= c - \frac{a}{x^2} = -\frac{a}{x^2} + c \quad \text{...(ii)}$$

From Eqs. (i) and (ii),

$$\frac{d}{dx}(AC) = \frac{1}{x}(MC - AC)$$ **Hence proved.**

(iv) Given, $AC = 2x - 11 + \frac{50}{x}$ ...(i)

On differentiating Eq. (i) w.r.t. x, we get

$$\frac{d}{dx}(AC) = 2 - \frac{50}{x^2}$$

For AC to be increasing,

$$\frac{d}{dx}(AC) > 0 \Rightarrow 2 - \frac{50}{x^2} > 0 \Rightarrow 2 > \frac{50}{x^2}$$

$$\Rightarrow \quad 2x^2 > 50 \Rightarrow x^2 > 25 \Rightarrow x < -5 \text{ and } x > 5$$

$$\Rightarrow \quad x \in (-\infty, -5) \cup (5, \infty)$$

(v) Given, $\Sigma x_i = 55, \Sigma y_i = 55, \Sigma x_i y_i = 350, \Sigma x_i^2 = 385$ and $n = 10$

$$\therefore \quad \bar{x} = \frac{\Sigma x_i}{n} = \frac{55}{10} = 5.5$$

and $$\bar{y} = \frac{\Sigma y_i}{n} = \frac{55}{10} = 5.5$$

Also, $$b_{yx} = \frac{\Sigma x_i y_i - \frac{(\Sigma x_i)(\Sigma y_i)}{n}}{\Sigma x_i^2 - \frac{(\Sigma x_i)^2}{n}} = \frac{350 - \frac{(55) \times (55)}{10}}{385 - \frac{(55)^2}{10}}$$

$$= \frac{350 - 302.5}{385 - 302.5} = \frac{47.5}{82.5} = 0.5758$$

Now, the equation of regression line of y on x is

$$y - \bar{y} = b_{yx}(x - \bar{x}).$$

$\Rightarrow \quad y - 5.5 = 0.5758(x - 5.5)$

$\Rightarrow \quad y = 0.5758x + 2.3331$

When $x = 6$, then the predicted value of y is $(0.5758)6 + 2.3331 = 5.7879 = 5.79$

20. (i) Given, $p(x) = 3x^2 + 5x - 50$

(a) The revenue function is given by

$$R(x) = px = (3x^2 + 5x - 50)x = 3x^3 + 5x^2 - 50x$$

(b) The marginal revenue function

$$= \frac{d}{dx}\{R(x)\} = \frac{d}{dx}(3x^3 + 5x^2 - 50x) = 9x^2 + 10x - 50$$

$\therefore$ MR $= 9x^2 + 10x - 50$

(ii) (a) For break-even values,

$$C(x) = R(x)$$

$\therefore \quad 5x + 350 = 50x - x^2$

$\Rightarrow x^2 - 45x + 350 = 0$

$$\therefore x = \frac{45 \pm \sqrt{(-45)^2 - 4 \times 350}}{2 \times 1} = \frac{45 \pm \sqrt{625}}{2} = \frac{45 \pm 25}{2} = 35 \text{ or } 10$$

Hence, for break-even, the company can produce and sell 35 units or 10 units.

(b) The values of x that will produce profit are given by $R(x) > C(x)$.

$\Rightarrow \quad 50x - x^2 > 5x + 350$

$\Rightarrow \quad 45x - x^2 - 350 > 0$

$\Rightarrow \quad x^2 - 45x + 350 < 0$

$\Rightarrow x^2 - 35x - 10x + 350 < 0$

$\Rightarrow x(x - 35) - 10(x - 35) < 0$

$\Rightarrow \quad (x - 10)(x - 35) < 0$

By the method of intervals,

we find that this inequality is satisfied only when x lies between 10 and 35 i.e. $10 < x < 35$.

Hence for profit, the number of units produced should be between 10 and 35.

21. Given, $\bar{x} = 6, \bar{y} = 8$

$\sigma_x = 4, \sigma_y = 6$ and $r = \frac{2}{3}$

(i) We know that $b_{yx} = r \cdot \frac{\sigma_y}{\sigma_x}$

$\therefore b_{yx} = \frac{2}{3} \times \frac{6}{4} = 1$ and $b_{xy} = r \cdot \frac{\sigma_x}{\sigma_y} = \frac{2}{3} \times \frac{4}{6} = \frac{4}{9}$

(ii) Regression line of x on y is

$$x - \bar{x} = b_{xy}(y - \bar{y})$$

$\Rightarrow \quad x - 6 = \frac{4}{9}(y - 8)$

$\Rightarrow \quad 9x - 54 = 4y - 32 \Rightarrow 9x - 4y - 22 = 0$

(iii) When $y = 20$, then from Eq. (i), we get

$$9x = 4 \times 20 + 22$$

$\Rightarrow \quad 9x = 80 + 22 \Rightarrow x = \frac{102}{9}$

22. (i) Let the mixture contains x kg of food X and y kg of food Y.

Given, 1 kg of food X contains 1 unit of vitamin A and 1 kg of food Y contains 2 units of vitamin A. Then, mixture of x kg of food X and y kg of food Y will contains $x + 2y$ units of vitamin A but the mixture must contain atleast 10 units of vitamin A.

$\therefore \quad x + 2y \geq 10$

Similarly, the constraints for vitamin B is $2x + 2y \geq 12$ and for vitamin C is $3x + y \geq 8$. Also, the quantities of food X and food Y cannot be negative, therefore $x, y \geq 0$.

Also, as per given rate, the cost of the mixture of x kg of food X and y kg of food Y will be ₹$(6x + 10y)$. This cost has to be minimum.

Hence, the given LPP is minimise $Z = 6x + 10y$

Subject to constraints are

$$x + 2y \geq 10, \; 2x + 2y \geq 12, \; 3x + y \geq 8$$

and $\quad x \geq 0, y \geq 0$

Table for line $x + 2y = 10$ or $y = \frac{10 - x}{2}$ is

x	0	10
y	5	0

So, the line passes through the points (0, 5) and (10, 0).

Put (0, 0) in the inequality $x + 2y \geq 10$, we get

$0 + 0 \geq 10$ [false]

So, the half plane is away from the origin.

Table for line $2x + 2y = 12$ or $y = 6 - x$ is

x	6	0
y	0	6

So, the line passes through the points (6, 0) and (0, 6).

Put (0, 0) in the inequality $2x + 2y \geq 12$, we get

$0 + 0 \geq 12$ [false]

So, the half plane is away from the origin.

Table for line $3x + y = 8$ or $y = 8 - 3x$ is

x	0	8/3
y	8	0

So, the line passes through the points (0, 8) and (8/3, 0).

Put (0, 0) in the inequality $3x + y \geq 8$, we get

$0 + 0 \geq 8$ [false]

So, the half plane is away from the origin.

Also, $x, y \geq 0$, so the feasible region lies in Ist quadrant.

The point of intersection of given inequalities are $B(2, 4)$ and $C(1, 5)$.

Now, plot all the inequalities on a graph paper as shown below.

The shaded region $ABCD$ is the unbounded feasible region.

The corner points of the feasible region are $A(10, 0)$, $B(2, 4)$, $C(1, 5)$ and $D(0, 8)$.

The values of Z at the corner points are given below.

Corner points	Value of $Z = 6x + 10y$
$A(10, 0)$	$Z = 6 \times 10 + 10 \times 0 = 60$
$B(2, 4)$	$Z = 6 \times 2 + 10 \times 4 = 52$ (Minimum)
$C(1, 5)$	$Z = 6 \times 1 + 10 \times 5 = 56$
$D(0, 8)$	$Z = 6 \times 0 + 10 \times 8 = 80$

From the above, we find that the minimum value of Z is 52 at $B(2, 4)$. Since, the feasible region is unbounded.

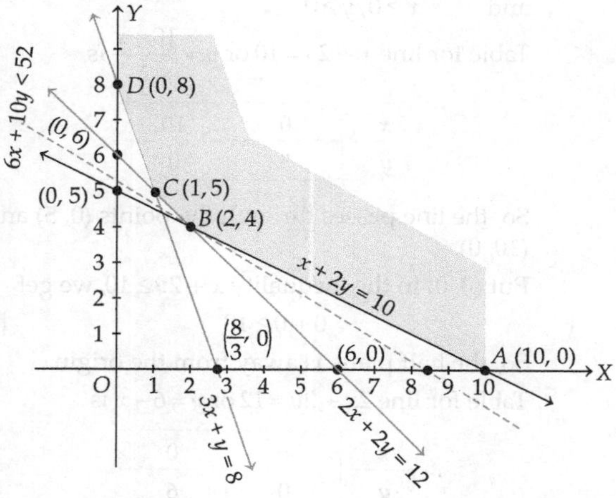

So, 52 may or may not be the minimum value of the LPP.

For this, we draw the open half plane $6x + 10y < 52$ and check whether the open half plane has common point with the feasible region or not.

From the graph, we see that the open half plane has no point in common with the feasible region.

Hence, the least cost of the mixture is ₹ 52.

Or

(ii) Our problem is to minimise

$$Z = 5x + 10y \qquad \text{...(i)}$$

Subject to constraints

$$x + 2y \leq 120 \qquad \text{...(ii)}$$

$$x + y \geq 60 \qquad \text{...(iii)}$$

$$x - 2y \geq 0 \qquad \text{...(iv)}$$

and $\quad x, y \geq 0$

Table for line $x + 2y = 120$ is

x	0	120
y	60	0

Put (0, 0) in the inequality $x + 2y \leq 120$, we get

$0 + 2 \times 0 \leq 120 \Rightarrow 0 \leq 120$ [which is true]

So, the half plane is towards the origin. Table for the line $x + y = 60$ is

x	0	60
y	60	0

On putting (0, 0) in the inequality $x + y \geq 60$, we get

$0 + 0 \geq 60 \Rightarrow 0 \geq 60$ [which is false]

So, the half plane is away from the origin.

Table for the line $x - 2y = 0$ is

x	0	10
y	0	5

On putting (5, 0) in the inequality $x - 2y \geq 0$, we get

$5 - 2 \times 0 \geq 0 \Rightarrow 5 \geq 0$ [which is true]

Thus, the half plane is towards the X-axis.

Also, $x, y \geq 0$

So, the feasible region lies in the Ist quadrant.

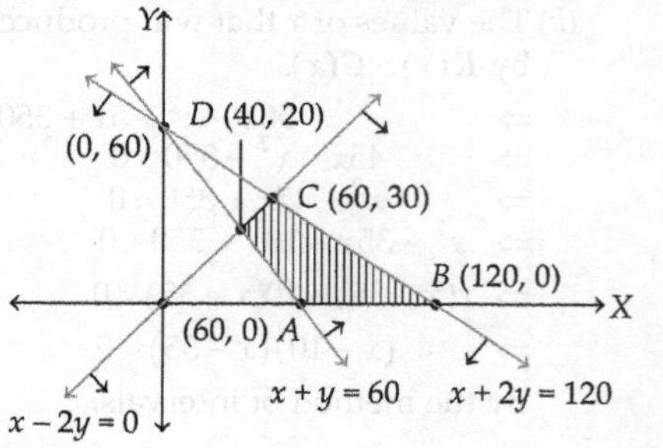

On solving equations $x - 2y = 0$ and $x + y = 60$, we get $D(40, 20)$

and on solving equations $x - 2y = 0$ and $x + 2y = 120$, we get $C(60, 30)$.

Now, plot all the in inequalities on a graph paper. The shaded region $ABCDA$ is the feasible region.

The corner points of the feasible region are $A(60, 0)$, $B(120, 0)$, $C(60, 30)$ and $D(40, 20)$.

The value of Z at these points are as follows

Corner point	Value of $Z = 5x + 10y$
$A(60, 0)$	300 (Minimum)
$B(120, 0)$	600
$C(60, 30)$	600
$D(40, 20)$	400

Clearly, the minimum value of Z is 300 at the point $A(60, 0)$.

SQP Code : **PB-2/15** Series **i-Succeed 2-25/15** Roll No. | | | | | | | |

Sample Question Paper 02

Mathematics 12th (Code 860)

General Instructions

1. The Question Paper consists of three sections A, B and C.
2. Candidates are required to attempt all questions from Section A and all questions either from Section B Or Section C.
3. Section A Internal choice has been provided in two questions of two marks each, two questions of four marks each and two questions of six marks each.
4. Section B Internal choice has been provided in one questions of two marks and one question of four marks.
5. Section C Internal choice has been provided in one question of two marks and one question of four marks.
6. All working, including rough work, should be done on the same sheet as, and adjacent to the rest of the answer.
7. The intended marks for questions or parts of questions are given in brackets [].
8. Mathematical tables and graph papers are provided.

Time : 3 Hrs.

Max. Marks : 80

Section A (65 Marks)

1. In subparts (i) to (xi) choose the correct options and in subparts (xii) to (xv), answer the questions as instructed.

(i) If the sides of an equilateral triangle are increasing at the rate of 2 cm/s, then the rate at which the area increases, when side is 10 cm, is • *Application* [1]

(a) $10 \text{ cm}^2/\text{s}$ (b) $\sqrt{3} \text{ cm}^2/\text{s}$

(c) $10\sqrt{3} \text{ cm}^2/\text{s}$ (d) $\frac{10}{3} \text{ cm}^2/\text{s}$

(ii) **Assertion** (A) If $y = \sqrt{\sin x + y}$, then $\frac{dy}{dx}$ is equal to $\frac{\cos x}{2y-1}$ [1]

Reason (R) If y is a function of u and u is a function of x, then $\frac{dy}{dx} = \frac{dy}{dx} \times \frac{du}{dx}$ • *Analysis*

(a) Both A and R are true and R is the correct explanation for A.

(b) Both A and R are true and R is not the correct explanation for A.

(c) A is true but R is false.

(d) A is false but R is true.

(iii) Which of the following is the principle value branch of $\cos^{-1} x$? (as shown in figure) • *Application* [1]

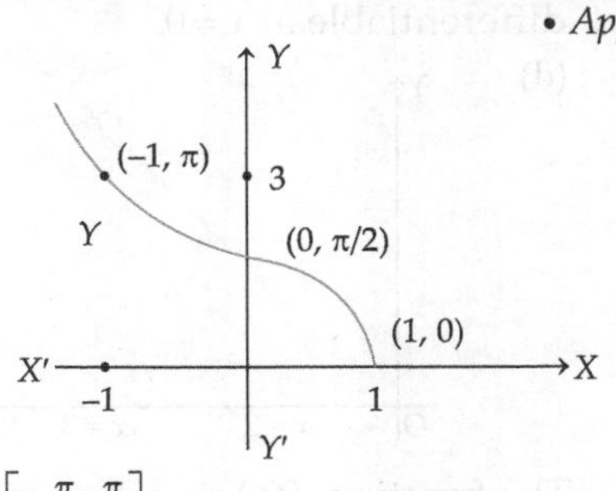

(a) $\left[-\frac{\pi}{2}, \frac{\pi}{2}\right]$ (b) $(0, \pi)$

(c) $[0, \pi]$ (d) $(0, \pi) - \left\{\frac{\pi}{2}\right\}$

(iv) The maximum number of equivalence relations on the set $A = \{1, 2, 3\}$ are • *Recall* [1]

(a) 1 (b) 2
(c) 3 (d) 5

(v) Given below are the graphs of $f(x)$ along with the statements. Which one of the following statements is not correct about the graphs? • *Application* [1]

(a)

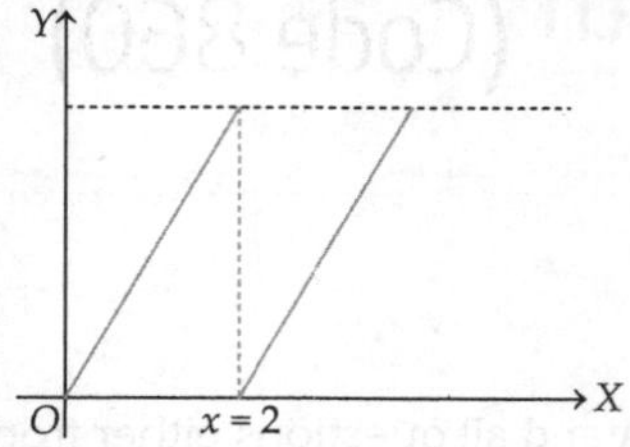

The function $f(x)$, has jump discontinuity at $x = 2$.

(b)

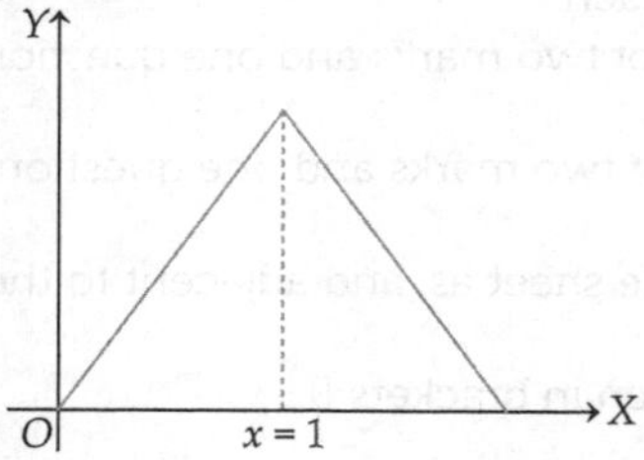

The function $f(x)$ is differentiable at $x = 1$.

(c)

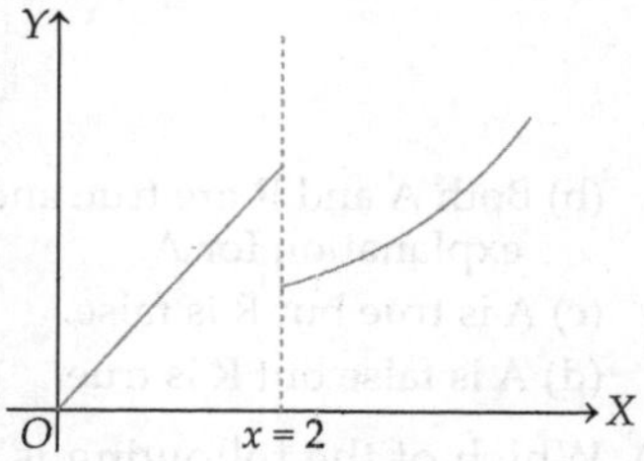

The function $f(x)$ is continuous but not differentiable at $x = 0$.

(d)

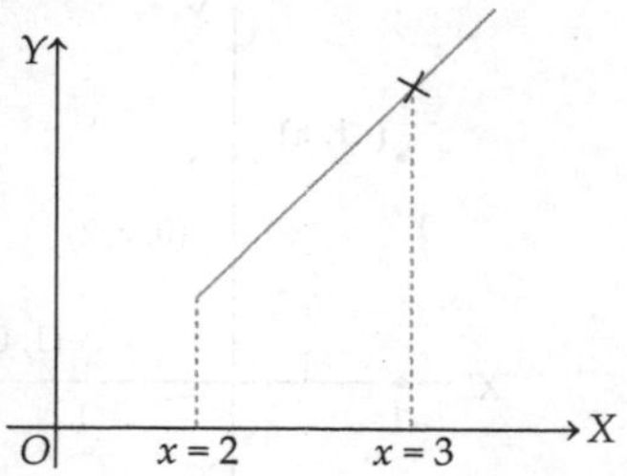

The function $f(x)$ shows a removable discontinuity at $x = 3$.

(vi) **Statement I** The degree of the differential equation

$$\frac{d^2y}{dx^2} + 3\left(\frac{dy}{dx}\right)^2 = x^2\left(\frac{d^2y}{dx^2}\right)^2, \text{ is 2.}$$

Statement II The degree of a differential equation is the order of the heighest derivative occurring in the equation. • *Understanding* [1]

Choose the correct option.

(a) Statement I is true.
(b) Statement II is true.
(c) Both statements are true.
(d) Both statements are false.

(vii) If a relation R on the set {1, 2, 3} be defined by $R = \{(1, 2)\}$, then R is • *Recall* [1]

(a) reflexive (b) transitive
(c) symmetric (d) None of these

(viii) If $A = \begin{bmatrix} 1 & -2 \\ 2 & 3 \end{bmatrix}$ and $B = \begin{bmatrix} 1 & 2 & 3 \\ 2 & 3 & 1 \end{bmatrix}$, then $|AB|$ is equal to • *Evaluate* [1]

(a) $\begin{bmatrix} 8 & 13 & 9 \\ -3 & -4 & 1 \end{bmatrix}$ (b) $\begin{bmatrix} 8 & -3 \\ 13 & -4 \\ 9 & 1 \end{bmatrix}$

(c) $\begin{bmatrix} -3 & 8 \\ -4 & 13 \\ 1 & 9 \end{bmatrix}$

(d) Cannot be determined.

(ix) **Assertion** (A) If A is a square matrix, then $A \cdot \text{adj}(A) = \text{adj}(A) \cdot A = \det(A) \cdot I$

Reason (R) The adjoint of matrix A, denoted as adj(A), is defined as the transpose of the cofactor matrix of A. • *Analysis* [1]

(a) Both A and R are true and R is the correct explanation of A.
(b) Both A and R are true but R is not the correct explanation of A.
(c) A is true, R is false.
(d) A is false, R is true.

(x) For any function f, if F is one of its anti-derivative. Then,

Statement I Family $\{F + C, C \in R\}$ provides all possible anti-derivatives of f.

Statement II Functions with same anti-derivatives differ by a constant. • *Understanding* [1]

Choose the correct option.
(a) Statement I is true.
(b) Statement II is true.
(c) Both statements are true.
(d) Both statements are false.

(xi) The probability that atleast one of the two events A and B occurs is 0.6. If A and B occur simultaneously with probability 0.3, then the value o

$P(\overline{A})+P(\overline{B})$ is • *Understanding* [1]
(a) 0.9 (b) 0.3
(c) 1.1 (d) None of these

(xii) Two events A and B are such that

$P(A)=0.7$, $P(B)=0.4$ and $P\left(\frac{A}{B}\right)=0.3$.

Determine the probability that neither A nor B occurs. • *Understanding* [1]

(xiii) Let $A=\{a, b, c\}$ and the relation R be defined on A as follows • *Analysis* [1]

$$R=\{(a,a),(b,c),(a,b)\}$$

Then, write minimum number of ordered pairs to be added in R to make R reflexive and transitive.

(xiv) Find the principal value of

$\sin^{-1}\left(\frac{-1}{2}\right)$. • *Evaluate* [1]

(xv) A medical test is used to diagnose a particular disease. The test results can be either positive (indicating the presence of the disease) or negative (indicating the absence of the disease).

The following probabilities are known.

The probability of a person having the disease (D) is 0.01.

The probability of testing positive given that the person has the disease ($P(T^+/D)$) is 0.99.

The probability of getting testing positive given that the person does not have the disease ($P(T^+/D^C)$) is 0.05.

Answer the following questions. • *Application* [2]

(i) What is the probability that a randomly selected person tests positive for the disease ($P(T^+)$)?

(ii) Given that a person tests positive, what is the probability that they actually have the disease ($P(D/T^+)$)?

2. Evaluate $\int_{-\pi}^{\pi}(1-x^2)\sin x\cdot\cos^2 x\,dx$. • *Evaluate* [2]

3. The volume of a cube increases at a constant rate. Prove that the increase in its surface area varies inversely as the length of the side. • *Application* [2]

4. (i) Solve the differential equation

$$\frac{dx}{dy}+\sqrt{\frac{1-x^2}{1-y^2}}=0.$$ • *Understanding* [2]

Or

(ii) Find $\int \frac{x^2+1}{(x^2+2)(x^2+3)}dx$ • *Evaluate* [2]

5. (i) Determine the value of k for which the following function is continuous at $x=3$.

$$f(x)=\begin{cases}\frac{(x+3)^2-36}{x-3}, & x\neq 3\\ k & , x=3\end{cases}$$ • *Recall* [2]

Or

(ii) Find the values of a and b such that the function f defined by

$$f(x)=\begin{cases}\frac{x-4}{|x-4|}+a, \text{ if } x \\ a+b, \quad \text{if } x=4 \\ \frac{x-4}{|x-4|}+b, \text{ if } x\end{cases}$$

is a continuous function at $x=4$. • *Analysis* [2]

6. If $A=\begin{bmatrix}\cos\alpha & \sin\alpha\\ -\sin\alpha & \cos\alpha\end{bmatrix}$, then find α satisfying $0<\alpha<\frac{\pi}{2}$ when $A+A^T=\sqrt{2}\,I_2$; where A^T is transpose of A. • *Understanding* [2]

SP-02

7. If $\cos^{-1}\frac{x}{a}+\cos^{-1}\frac{y}{b}=\alpha$, then prove that
$\frac{x^2}{a^2}-\frac{2xy}{ab}\cos\alpha+\frac{y^2}{b^2}=\sin^2\alpha.$ • *Recall* [4]

8. Solve the differential equation
$\left(x\sin\frac{y}{x}\right)dy=\left(y\sin\frac{y}{x}-x\right)dx.$ • *Application* [4]

9. (i) An integer is chosen at random from the first two hundred positive integers. What is the probability that the integer chosen is divisible by 4 or 6? • *Understanding* [4]

Or

(ii) Two balls are drawn from an urn containing 2 white, 3 red and 4 black balls one by one without replacement. What is the probability that • *Understanding* [4]

(a) both the balls are of same colour?
(b) atleast one ball is red?

10. (i) Consider the following parametric equations.
$x=\sqrt{a^{\sin^{-1}t}}$ and $y=\sqrt{a^{\cos^{-1}t}}$ • *Evaluate* [4]

Answer the following questions.

(a) Find $\frac{dx}{dt}$.
(b) Find $\frac{dy}{dt}$
(c) Evaluate $\frac{dy}{dx}$.
(d) Find $\left(\frac{dy}{dx}\right)$ at the point $(1,-2)$.

Or

(ii) Differentiate $(x^2-5x+8)(x^3+7x+9)$ in three ways mentioned below.

(a) By using product rule.
(b) By expanding the product to obtain a single polynomial.
(c) By logarithmic differentiation.

Do they all given the same answer? • *Application* [4]

11. If $A=\begin{bmatrix}1 & 2\\ 3 & 4\end{bmatrix}$, then verify the following results.

(i) $|\text{adj } A|=|A|$
(ii) $\text{adj}(A^T)=(\text{adj } A)^T$
(iii) $|\text{adj}(\text{adj } A)|=|A|$ • *Analysis* [6]

12. There are three urns having the following composition of black and white balls

Urn I 7 white and 3 black balls
Urn II 4 white and 6 black balls
Urn III 2 white and 8 black balls

One of these urns is chosen at random with probabilities 0.2, 0.6 and 0.2, respectively. From the chosen urn, two balls are drawn at random without replacement. Both the balls happen to be white. Calculate the probability that the balls drawn were from Urn III. • *Understanding* [6]

13. (i) Find the intervals in which the function $f(x)=\sin 3x-\cos 3x$, $0<x<\pi$, is strictly increasing or strictly decreasing. • *Application* [6]

Or

(ii) Find the equations of tangent and normal to the curve $x=1-\cos\theta$, $y=\theta-\sin\theta$ at $\theta=\frac{\pi}{4}$. • *Application* [6]

14. (i) If $f(x)$ be a continuous function defined by $f(x)=\frac{5x}{(x+1)(x^2+9)}$ • *Evaluate* [6]

Answer the following questions.

(a) Decompose the function using partial fraction.
(b) Differentiate the function $f(x)$.
(c) Evaluate $\int f(x)\,dx$.
(d) Evaluate $\int_0^1 f(x)\,dx$.

Or (ii) Prove that $\int_0^{\pi/4}(\sqrt{\tan x}+\sqrt{\cot x})dx=\sqrt{2}\cdot\frac{\pi}{2}$

Section B (15 Marks)

15. In subparts (i) and (iii) choose the correct options and in subparts (iv) to (v), answer the questions as instructed. • *Recall* [5]

(i) Observe the diagram show below. What are the intercepts made on the coordinate axes by the plane.

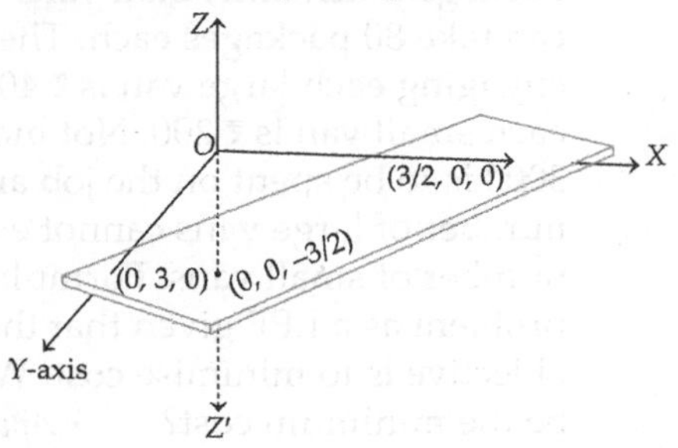

(a) $\frac{-3}{2}, -3, \frac{-3}{2}$ (b) $\frac{3}{2}, 3, \frac{-3}{2}$

(c) $\frac{3}{2}, -3, \frac{-3}{2}$ (d) $\frac{3}{2}, 3, \frac{3}{2}$

(ii) **Statement I** The vector of length 3 units along the vector $\hat{i} - 2\hat{j} - 2\hat{k}$ is $\hat{j} + 2\hat{k}$. • *Recall*

Statement II A vector that has a magnitude of 1 is a unit vector.

Which is the following is correct

(a) Only Statement I.

(b) Only Statement II.

(c) Both Statements I and II.

(d) Neither Statement I nor Statement II.

(iii) If $\vec{a} = 3\hat{i} - 2\hat{j} + \hat{k}$ and $\vec{b} = 2\hat{i} - 4\hat{j} - 3\hat{k}$, then $|\vec{a} - 2\vec{b}|$ is equal to • *Recall*

(a) $\hat{i} + 6\hat{j} + 7\hat{k}$ (b) $-\hat{i} + 6\hat{j} + 7\hat{k}$

(c) $-\hat{i} - 6\hat{j} + 7\hat{k}$ (d) $\hat{i} - 6\hat{j} + 7\hat{k}$

(iv) Find the equation of the plane passing through the point (1, 1, 1) and is perpendicular to the line $\frac{x-1}{3} = \frac{y-2}{0} = \frac{z-3}{4}$. Also, find the distance of this plane from the origin. • *Application*

(v) The position vectors of two points A and B are $\overrightarrow{OA} = 2\hat{i} - \hat{j} - \hat{k}$ and $\overrightarrow{OB} = 2\hat{i} - \hat{j} + 2\hat{k}$, respectively. Find the position vector of a point P which divides the line segment joining A and B in the ratio 2 : 1. • *Application*

16. (i) If $|\vec{a}| = 8$, $|\vec{b}| = 3$ and $|\vec{a} \times \vec{b}| = 12$, then find the angle between $\vec{a}$ and $\vec{b}$. • *Evaluate* [2]

Or

(ii) Find the angle between two vectors $\vec{a}$ and $\vec{b}$ with magnitude 2 and 1 respectively, such that $\vec{a} \cdot \vec{b} = \sqrt{3}$. • *Evaluate* [2]

17. (i) Find the length and foot of the perpendicular from the point $P(1, 1, 2)$ to the plane $\vec{r} \cdot (2\hat{i} - 2\hat{j} + 4\hat{k}) + 5 = 0$. • *Understanding* [4]

Or

(ii) Show that lines $\vec{r} = (\hat{i} + \hat{j} - \hat{k}) + \lambda(3\hat{i} - \hat{j})$ and $\vec{r} = (4\hat{i} - \hat{k}) + \mu(2\hat{i} + 3\hat{k})$ intersect each other. Find their point of intersection. • *Understanding* [4]

18. Draw a rough sketch and find the area enclosed by the parabola $y^2 = x$ and the line $y + x = 2$. • *Application* [4]

SP-02

Section C (15 Marks)

19. In subparts (i) and (ii) choose the correct options and in subparts (iii) to (v), answer the questions as instructed. [5]

(i) The cost function of a firm is given by $C = \frac{3}{2}x^3 - 6x^2 + 9x + 2$, then the average cost is • *Understanding*

(a) 17 (b) 15

(c) 4 (d) None of these

(ii) If the regression line of x on y is, $9x + 3y - 46 = 0$ and y on x is, $3x + 12y - 7 = 0$, then the correlation coefficient r is equal to • *Recall*

(a) $\frac{-1}{12}$ (b) $\frac{1}{12}$

(c) $\frac{-1}{2\sqrt{3}}$ (d) $\frac{1}{2\sqrt{3}}$

(iii) A computer software manufacturer wants to start the production of floppy disks. He observes that he will have to spend ₹ 2 lakh for technical knowledge. The cost of setting up the machine is ₹ 88000 and the cost of producing each unit is ₹ 30. He can sell each floppy at ₹ 45. Determine the total cost function for producing x floppies. • *Application*

(iv) The cost function of a firm is given by $C = 2x^2 + x - 5$. Find the marginal cost, when $x = 4$ and interpret it. • *Evaluate*

(v) For 5 observation of pairs (x, y) of variables x and y, the following results are obtained $\Sigma x = 15$, $\Sigma y = 25$, $\Sigma x^2 = 55$, $\Sigma y^2 = 135$ and $\Sigma xy = 83$. Calculate the value of b_{xy}. • *Evaluate*

20. (i) A company produces a commodity with ₹ 28000 as fixed cost. The variable cost, estimated to be 20% of the total revenue received on selling the product, at the rate of ₹10 per unit. Find the break-even point. • *Application* [2]

Or (ii) If the cost function of a product is given by $C(x) = \frac{x^3}{3} - 45x^2 - 900x$, where x is the number of units produced, then how many units of the product must be produced to minimise the marginal cost? • *Application* [2]

21. Find the equations of the lines of regression on the basis of the data. • *Understanding* [4]

x	4	2	3	4	2
y	2	3	2	4	4

22. (i) A firm has to transport 1200 packages using large vans which can carry 200 packages each and small vans which can take 80 packages each. The cost for engaging each large van is ₹ 400 and each small van is ₹ 200. Not more than ₹ 3000 is to be spent on the job and the number of large vans cannot exceed the number of small vans. Formulate this problem as a LPP given that the objective is to minimise cost. What will be the minimum cost? • *Application* [4]

Or

(ii) A manufacturer makes two types of calculators. Deluxe sells for ₹ 120 and standard sells for ₹ 100. It costs ₹ 90 to produce a deluxe and ₹ 80 to produce a standard calculator. In one week, manufacturer can produce from 200 to 300 deluxe calculators and from 100 to 250 standard calculators but not more than 500 total calculators. How many of each type should be produced per week to maximise the profit? • *Application* [4]

Solutions *in Topper's Style*

My Commitment *I affirm that I am reviewing these solutions only after I have solved the Sample Question Paper 2 on my own. My purpose of looking the solutions is solely to verify whether my answers/solutions were correct or not and to identify my mistakes in case my solutions were wrong or I could not solve that.*

1. (i) (c) Let the side of an equilateral triangle be x cm.

$\therefore$ Area of equilateral triangle,

$$A = \frac{\sqrt{3}}{4}x^2 \quad \ldots(i)$$

Also, given $\frac{dx}{dt} = 2\,\text{cm/s}$

On differentiating Eq. (i) w.r.t. t, we get

$$\frac{dA}{dt} = \frac{\sqrt{3}}{4} \cdot 2x \cdot \frac{dx}{dt}$$

At $x = 10$ and $\frac{dx}{dt} = 2$

$$\frac{dA}{dt} = \frac{\sqrt{3}}{4} \cdot 2 \cdot 10 \cdot 2$$

$$= 10\sqrt{3}\,\text{cm}^2/\text{s}$$

(ii) (a) Given, $y = (\sin x + y)^{1/2}$

$$\therefore \frac{dy}{dx} = \frac{1}{2}(\sin x + y)^{\frac{-1}{2}} \cdot \frac{d}{dx}(\sin x + y)$$

$$\Rightarrow \frac{dy}{dx} = \frac{1}{2} \cdot \frac{1}{(\sin x + y)^{1/2}} \cdot \left(\cos x + \frac{dy}{dx}\right)$$

$$\Rightarrow \frac{dy}{dx} = \frac{1}{2y}\left(\cos x + \frac{dy}{dx}\right) \quad [\because (\sin x + y)^{1/2} = y]$$

$$\Rightarrow \quad \frac{dy}{dx}\left(1-\frac{1}{2y}\right)=\frac{\cos x}{2y}$$

$$\therefore \quad \frac{dy}{dx}=\frac{\cos x}{2y}\cdot\frac{2y}{2y-1}=\frac{\cos x}{2y-1}$$

Thus, Assertion is true.

Reason is also true and correct explanation of A.

(iii) (c) We know that the principle value branch of $\cos^{-1} x$ is $[0, \pi]$.

(iv) (d) Given that $A=\{1, 2, 3\}$

Now, number of equivalence relations are as follows

$R_1=\{(1, 1), (2, 2), (3, 3)\}$

$R_2=\{(1, 1), (2, 2), (3, 3), (1, 2), (2,1)\}$

$R_3=\{(1, 1), (2, 2), (3, 3), (1, 3), (3,1)\}$

$R_4=\{(1, 1), (2, 2), (3, 3), (2, 3), (3, 2)\}$

$R_5=\{(1, 2, 3) \Leftrightarrow A\times A=A^2\}$

$\therefore$ Maximum number of equivalence relation on the set $A=\{1,2,3\}=5$

(v) (b) From the graph (b),

We observe that the function is not differentiable at $x=1$.

Hence, option (b) is incorrect.

(vi) (c) Given, $\frac{d^2y}{dx^2}+3\left(\frac{dy}{dx}\right)^2=x^2\left(\frac{d^2y}{dx^2}\right)^2$ ...(i)

Here, differential equation has highest order derivative of order 2 and its power is 2.

$\therefore$ Degree of given differential equation is 2.

(vii) (b) R on the set $\{1, 2, 3\}$ be defined by $R=\{(1, 2)\}$.

Since, $(1, 1) \notin R$, so it is not reflexive,

Since, $(1, 2) \in R$, but $(2, 1) \notin R$. So, it is use symmetric.

Hence, no counter examples to disapprove transitive condition. Therefore, R is transitive.

(viii) (d) Given, $A=\begin{bmatrix}1 & -2\\ 2 & 3\end{bmatrix}$ and $B=\begin{bmatrix}1 & 2 & 3\\ 2 & 3 & 1\end{bmatrix}$

Now, $AB=\begin{bmatrix}1 & -2\\ 2 & 3\end{bmatrix}\begin{bmatrix}1 & 2 & 3\\ 2 & 3 & 1\end{bmatrix}=\begin{bmatrix}1-4 & 2-6 & 3-2\\ 2+6 & 4+9 & 6+3\end{bmatrix}$

[multiplying rows by columns]

$=\begin{bmatrix}-3 & -4 & 1\\ 8 & 13 & 9\end{bmatrix}$

Also, $|AB|=\begin{vmatrix}-3 & -4 & 1\\ 8 & 139 & 9\end{vmatrix}$

which is not a square matrix.

Hence, $|AB|$ cannot be determined.

(ix) (b) Let $A=\begin{bmatrix}1 & 2\\ 3 & 4\end{bmatrix}$ be a square matrix.

Then, $|A|=4-6=-2$

and $\text{adj}(A)=\begin{bmatrix}4 & -2\\ -3 & 1\end{bmatrix}$

Now, $\text{adj}(A)\cdot A=\begin{bmatrix}4 & -2\\ -3 & 1\end{bmatrix}\begin{bmatrix}1 & 2\\ 3 & 4\end{bmatrix}=\begin{bmatrix}-2 & 0\\ 0 & -2\end{bmatrix}$

$=-2\begin{bmatrix}1 & 0\\ 0 & 1\end{bmatrix}=\det(A)\cdot I$ $[\because |A|=-2]$

Thus, A is correct and R is also correct.

Hence, A and R are correct but R is not the correct explanation of A.

(x) (a) Functions with same derivatives differ by a constant. To show this, let g and h be two functions having the same derivatives on an interval I.

Consider the function $f=g-h$ defined by $f(x)=g(x)-h(x), \forall x\in I$.

Then, $\frac{df}{dx}=f'=g'-h'$

$\Rightarrow \quad f'(x)=g'(x)-h'(x), \forall x\in I.$

or $f'(x)=0, \forall x \in I$ by hypothesis,

i.e. the rate of change of f with respect to x is zero on I and hence f is constant.

Thus, the family $\{F+C, C\in R\}$ provides all possible anti-derivatives of f.

(xi) (c) We know that $A\cup B$ denotes the occurrence of atleast one of A and B and $A\cap B$ denotes the occurrence of both A and B, simultaneously.

Thus, given $P(A\cup B)=0.6$ and $P(A\cap B)=0.3$

Also, $P(A\cup B)=P(A)+P(B)-P(A\cap B)$

$\Rightarrow \quad 0.6=P(A)+P(B)-0.3$

$\Rightarrow \quad P(A)+P(B)=0.9$

$\Rightarrow \quad [1-P(\overline{A})]+[1-P(\overline{B})]=0.9$

$[\because P(A)=1-P(\overline{A})$ and $P(B)=1-P(\overline{B})]$

$\Rightarrow \quad P(\overline{A})+P(\overline{B})=2-0.9=1.1$

(xii) Given, $P(A)=0.7$, $P(B)=0.4$ and $P\left(\frac{A}{B}\right)=0.3$

Now, $P(A\cap B)=P(B)\times P(A/B)$

$=0.4\times 0.3=0.12$

and $P(A\cup B)=P(A)+P(B)-P(A\cap B)$

$=0.7+0.4-0.12=0.98$

$\therefore$ P(neither A nor B occurs) $=1-P(A\cup B)$

$=1-0.98=0.02$

(xiii) Given relation, $R=\{(a,a),(b,c),(a,b)\}$

To make R reflexive we must add (b,b) and (c,c) to R. Also, to make R transitive we must add (a,c) to R.

So, the minimum number of ordered pairs to be added are (b,b), (c,c), (a,c) i.e. 3.

(xiv) Let $\sin^{-1}\left(\frac{-1}{2}\right)=\theta$

$\Rightarrow \sin\theta=\frac{-1}{2}=-\sin\frac{\pi}{6}=\sin\left(-\frac{\pi}{6}\right)$

$[\because \sin(-\theta)=-\sin\theta]$

We know that the principal value branch of $\sin^{-1}$ is

$\left[-\frac{\pi}{2},\frac{\pi}{2}\right]$ and $\theta=-\frac{\pi}{6}\in\left[-\frac{\pi}{2},\frac{\pi}{2}\right]$

$\therefore$ The principal value of $\sin^{-1}\left(\frac{-1}{2}\right)$ is $-\frac{\pi}{6}$.

(xv) (i) Given, $P(D)=0.01$, then $P(D^C)=1-0.01=0.99$, $P(T^+/D)=0.99$ and $P(T^+/D^C)=0.05$

Using the law of total probability, we get

$P(T^+)=P(T^+/D)P(D)+P(T^+/D^C)P(D^C)$

Therefore,

$P(T^+)=0.99\times0.01+0.05\times0.99$
$=0.0099+0.0495=0.0594$

(ii) From part (i), we have

$P(T^+)=0.0594$

Using Baye's theorem

$P(D/T^+)=\frac{P(T^+/D)P(D)}{P(T^+)}$

$=\frac{(0.99)\times0.01}{0.0594}=\frac{0.0099}{0.0594}\simeq0.1667$

Hence, the probability that a person actually has the disease given that they tested positive is approximately 0.1667 or 16.67%.

2. Let $I=\int_{-\pi}^{\pi}(1-x^2)\sin x\cos^2 x\,dx$

Again, let $f(x)=(1-x^2)\sin x\cos^2 x$

$\Rightarrow f(-x)=[1-(-x)^2]\sin(-x)\cos^2(-x)$
$=(1-x^2)(-\sin x)\cos^2 x\;[\because \sin(-\theta)=-\sin\theta]$
$=-(1-x^2)\sin x\cos^2 x=-f(x)$ (1)

$\Rightarrow f(x)$ is an odd function.

$\therefore\quad I=0$

$[\because \int_{-a}^{a} f(x)\,dx=0$, if $f(x)$ is an odd function] (1)

3. Let the side of a cube be x unit.

$\therefore$ Volume of cube, $V=x^3$

On differentiating both sides w.r.t. t, we get

$\frac{dV}{dt}=3x^2\frac{dx}{dt}=k$ [constant]

$\Rightarrow \frac{dx}{dt}=\frac{k}{3x^2}$ ...(i)

Also, surface area of cube, $S=6x^2$

On differentiating w.r.t. t, we get

$\frac{dS}{dt}=12x\cdot\frac{dx}{dt}$

$\Rightarrow \frac{dS}{dt}=12x\cdot\frac{k}{3x^2}$ [using Eq. (i)]

$\Rightarrow \frac{dS}{dt}=\frac{12k}{3x}=4\left(\frac{k}{x}\right)\Rightarrow\frac{dS}{dt}\propto\frac{1}{x}$

Hence, the surface area of the cube varies inversely as the length of the side. **Hence proved.**

4. (i) Given differential equation is

$\frac{dx}{dy}+\sqrt{\frac{1-x^2}{1-y^2}}=0\Rightarrow\frac{dx}{dy}=-\frac{\sqrt{1-x^2}}{\sqrt{1-y^2}}$

On separating the variables, we get

$\frac{1}{\sqrt{1-x^2}}dx=-\frac{1}{\sqrt{1-y^2}}dy$

On integrating both sides, we get

$\int\frac{1}{\sqrt{1-x^2}}dx=-\int\frac{1}{\sqrt{1-y^2}}dy$

$\Rightarrow \sin^{-1}x=-\sin^{-1}y+C$

$\Rightarrow \sin^{-1}x+\sin^{-1}y=C$

which is the required general solution.

Or

(ii) Let $I=\int\frac{x^2+1}{(x^2+2)(x^2+3)}dx$

Again, let $x^2=y$

Then, $\frac{x^2+1}{(x^2+2)(x^2+3)}=\frac{y+1}{(y+2)(y+3)}$

Also, $\frac{y+1}{(y+2)(y+3)}=\frac{A}{y+2}+\frac{B}{y+3}$ ...(i)

$\Rightarrow y+1=A(y+3)+B(y+2)$ ...(ii) (1)

On putting $y=-2$ and $y=-3$ successively in Eq. (ii), we get

$A=-1$ and $B=2$

On substituting the values of A and B in Eq. (i), we get

$\frac{y+1}{(y+2)(y+3)}=\frac{-1}{y+2}+\frac{2}{y+3}$

$\therefore I=\int\frac{x^2+1}{(x^2+2)(x^2+3)}dx=\int\frac{-1}{x^2+2}dx+\int\frac{2}{x^2+3}dx$

$=-\frac{1}{\sqrt{2}}\tan^{-1}\left(\frac{x}{\sqrt{2}}\right)+\frac{2}{\sqrt{3}}\tan^{-1}\left(\frac{x}{\sqrt{3}}\right)+C$ (2)

5. (i) Given, $f(x)=\begin{cases}\frac{(x+3)^2-36}{x-3}, & x\neq3\\ k, & x=3\end{cases}$

Since, $f(x)$ is continuous at $x=3$.

$\therefore \lim_{x\to3}f(x)=f(3)$

$\Rightarrow \lim_{x\to3}\frac{(x+3)^2-36}{x-3}=k$

$$\Rightarrow \lim_{x\to 3}\frac{(x+3)^2-6^2}{x-3}=k$$

$$\Rightarrow \lim_{x\to 3}\frac{(x+3-6)(x+3+6)}{x-3}=k$$

$$[\because a^2-b^2=(a-b)(a+b)]$$

$$\Rightarrow \lim_{x\to 3}\frac{(x-3)(x+9)}{(x-3)}=k$$

$$\Rightarrow \lim_{x\to 3}(x+9)=k$$

$$\Rightarrow 3+9=k \Rightarrow k=12$$

Or

(ii) We have, $f(x)=\begin{cases}\dfrac{x-4}{|x-4|}+a, \text{if } x \\ a+b, \quad \text{if } x=4 \\ \dfrac{x-4}{|x-4|}+b, \text{if } x\end{cases}$

At $x=4$, LHL $=\lim_{x\to 4^-}\dfrac{x-4}{|x-4|}+a$

$$=\lim_{h\to 0}\frac{4-h-4}{|4-h-4|}+a=\lim_{h\to 0}\frac{-h}{h}+a$$

$$=-1+a$$

$$\text{RHL}=\lim_{x\to 4^+}\frac{x-4}{|x-4|}+b$$

$$=\lim_{h\to 0}\frac{4+h-4}{|4+h-4|}+b=\lim_{h\to 0}\frac{h}{h}+b$$

$$=1+b$$

and $f(4)=a+b$

Since, f is continuous at $x=4$, therefore

$$\text{LHL}=\text{RHL}=f(4)$$

$$\Rightarrow -1+a=1+b=a+b$$

$$\Rightarrow -1+a=a+b \text{ and } 1+b=a+b$$

$$\therefore b=-1 \text{ and } a=1$$

6. Given, $A=\begin{bmatrix}\cos\alpha & \sin\alpha \\ -\sin\alpha & \cos\alpha\end{bmatrix}$

Also, given $A+A^T=\sqrt{2}\,I_2$

$$\therefore \begin{bmatrix}\cos\alpha & \sin\alpha \\ -\sin\alpha & \cos\alpha\end{bmatrix}+\begin{bmatrix}\cos\alpha & \sin\alpha \\ -\sin\alpha & \cos\alpha\end{bmatrix}^T=\sqrt{2}\begin{bmatrix}1 & 0 \\ 0 & 1\end{bmatrix}$$

$$\Rightarrow \begin{bmatrix}\cos\alpha & \sin\alpha \\ -\sin\alpha & \cos\alpha\end{bmatrix}+\begin{bmatrix}\cos\alpha & -\sin\alpha \\ \sin\alpha & \cos\alpha\end{bmatrix}=\begin{bmatrix}\sqrt{2} & 0 \\ 0 & \sqrt{2}\end{bmatrix}$$

$$\Rightarrow \begin{bmatrix}\cos\alpha+\cos\alpha & \sin\alpha-\sin\alpha \\ -\sin\alpha+\sin\alpha & \cos\alpha+\cos\alpha\end{bmatrix}=\begin{bmatrix}\sqrt{2} & 0 \\ 0 & \sqrt{2}\end{bmatrix}$$

$$\Rightarrow \begin{bmatrix}2\cos\alpha & 0 \\ 0 & 2\cos\alpha\end{bmatrix}=\begin{bmatrix}\sqrt{2} & 0 \\ 0 & \sqrt{2}\end{bmatrix}$$

On equating the corresponding elements from both sides, we get

$$2\cos\alpha=\sqrt{2} \Rightarrow \cos\alpha=\frac{\sqrt{2}}{2}$$

$$\Rightarrow \cos\alpha=\frac{1}{\sqrt{2}}=\cos\frac{\pi}{4}$$

$\therefore \alpha=\dfrac{\pi}{4}$, which is satisfying $0<\alpha<\dfrac{\pi}{2}$.

7. Given, $\cos^{-1}\dfrac{x}{a}+\cos^{-1}\dfrac{y}{b}=\alpha$

$$\Rightarrow \cos^{-1}\left\{\frac{xy}{ab}-\sqrt{1-\frac{x^2}{a^2}}\sqrt{1-\frac{y^2}{b^2}}\right\}=\alpha$$

$$[\because \cos^{-1}a+\cos^{-1}b=\cos^{-1}\{ab-\sqrt{1-a^2}\sqrt{1-b^2}\}]$$

$$\Rightarrow \frac{xy}{ab}-\sqrt{1-\frac{x^2}{a^2}}\sqrt{1-\frac{y^2}{b^2}}=\cos\alpha$$

$$\Rightarrow \frac{xy}{ab}-\cos\alpha=\sqrt{1-\frac{x^2}{a^2}}\sqrt{1-\frac{y^2}{b^2}}$$

$$\Rightarrow \left(\frac{xy}{ab}-\cos\alpha\right)^2=\left(1-\frac{x^2}{a^2}\right)\left(1-\frac{y^2}{b^2}\right)$$

[squaring both sides]

$$\Rightarrow \frac{x^2y^2}{a^2b^2}+\cos^2\alpha-\frac{2xy\cos\alpha}{ab}=1-\frac{y^2}{b^2}-\frac{x^2}{a^2}+\frac{x^2y^2}{a^2b^2}$$

$$\Rightarrow \frac{x^2}{a^2}+\frac{y^2}{b^2}-\frac{2xy\cos\alpha}{ab}=1-\cos^2\alpha$$

$$\Rightarrow \frac{x^2}{a^2}+\frac{y^2}{b^2}-\frac{2xy}{ab}\cos\alpha=\sin^2\alpha$$ **Hence proved.**

8. Given, $\left(x\sin\dfrac{y}{x}\right)dy=\left(y\sin\dfrac{y}{x}-x\right)dx$

$$\Rightarrow \frac{dy}{dx}=\frac{y\sin\frac{y}{x}-x}{x\sin\frac{y}{x}}$$

$$\Rightarrow \frac{dy}{dx}=\frac{\frac{y}{x}\sin\frac{y}{x}-1}{\sin\frac{y}{x}} \quad \ldots\text{(i)}$$

which is a homogeneous differential equation.

Let $y=vx \Rightarrow \dfrac{dy}{dx}=v+x\dfrac{dv}{dx}$

On substituting the values of y and $\dfrac{dy}{dx}$ in Eq. (i), we get

$$v+x\frac{dv}{dx}=\frac{v\sin v-1}{\sin v}$$

$$\Rightarrow x\frac{dv}{dx}=\frac{v\sin v-1}{\sin v}-v$$

$$\Rightarrow x\frac{dv}{dx}=\frac{v\sin v-1-v\sin v}{\sin v}$$

$$\Rightarrow x\frac{dv}{dx}=\frac{-1}{\sin v} \Rightarrow -\sin v\,dv=\frac{dx}{x}$$

On integrating both sides, we get

$$\int(-\sin v)\,dv=\int\frac{dx}{x}$$

$\Rightarrow \quad \cos v=\log|x|+C$

$\therefore \quad \cos\frac{y}{x}=\log|x|+C, \quad \left[\text{putting } v=\frac{y}{x}\right]$

where C is an arbitrary constant.

9. (i) Total number of exhaustive, mutually exclusive and equally likely cases i.e. $n(S)=200$

Integers from 1 to 200 and divisible by 4 are 4, 8, 12, 16, ..., 200. Their number $=\frac{200}{4}=50$

Integers from 1 to 200 and divisible by 6 are 6, 12, 18, 24, ..., 198. Their number $=\frac{198}{6}=33$

Integers from 1 to 200 and divisible by both 4 and 6 (i.e. divisible by their LCM 12)

are 12, 24, 36, 48, ..., 192. Their number $=\frac{192}{12}=16$

These 16 numbers have been counted twice, in multiples of 4 and in multiples of 6.

$\therefore$ Favourable number of cases $=50+33-16=67$

Hence, required probability $=\frac{67}{200}$

Or

(ii) Given an urn containing 2 white balls (2W), 3 red balls (3R) and 4 black balls (4B).

Total number of balls $=4+2+3=9$

(a) P (both the balls are of same colour)

$= P(WW \text{ or } RR \text{ or } BB)$

$= P(W)P(W)+P(R)P(R)+P(B)P(B)$

$=\frac{2}{9}\times\frac{1}{8}+\frac{3}{9}\times\frac{2}{8}+\frac{4}{9}\times\frac{3}{8}=\frac{2}{72}+\frac{6}{72}+\frac{12}{72}$

$=\frac{20}{72}=\frac{5}{18}$

(b) P (atleast one ball is red)

$=1-P$ (neither of the two balls is red)

$=1-P[WW \text{ or } WB \text{ or } BW \text{ or } BB]$

$=1-[P(WW)+P(WB)+P(BW)+P(BB)]$

$=1-[P(W)P(W)+P(W)P(B)+P(B)P(W)+P(B)P(B)]$

$=1-\left(\frac{2}{9}\times\frac{1}{8}+\frac{2}{9}\times\frac{4}{8}+\frac{4}{9}\times\frac{2}{8}+\frac{4}{9}\times\frac{3}{8}\right)$

$=1-\left(\frac{2+8+8+12}{72}\right)=1-\frac{30}{72}$

$=\frac{72-30}{72}=\frac{42}{72}=\frac{7}{12}$

10. (i) (a) We have, $x=\sqrt{a^{\sin^{-1}t}}$

Taking log on both sides, we get

$$\log x=\log(a^{\sin^{-1}t})^{1/2}$$

$\Rightarrow \log x=\frac{1}{2}\log a^{\sin^{-1}t} \Rightarrow \log x=\frac{1}{2}\sin^{-1}t\log a$

On differentiating w.r.t. t, we get

$$\frac{1}{x}\cdot\frac{dx}{dt}=\frac{1}{2}\log a\frac{d}{dt}(\sin^{-1}t)=\frac{1}{2}\log a\frac{1}{\sqrt{1-t^2}}$$

$\Rightarrow \quad \frac{dx}{dt}=\frac{x\log a}{2}\times\frac{1}{\sqrt{1-t^2}}$

(b) We have, $y=\sqrt{a^{\cos^{-1}t}}$

On taking log both sides, we get

$\log y=\log(a^{\cos^{-1}t})^{1/2}$

$\Rightarrow \quad \log y=\frac{1}{2}\log a^{\cos^{-1}t}$

$\Rightarrow \quad \log y=\frac{1}{2}\cos^{-1}t\log a$

On differentiating w.r.t. t, we get

$$\frac{1}{y}\cdot\frac{dy}{dt}=\frac{1}{2}\log a\times\left[\frac{-1}{\sqrt{1-t^2}}\right]$$

$\Rightarrow \quad \frac{dy}{dt}=-\frac{y\log a}{2}\times\frac{1}{\sqrt{1-t^2}}$

(c) We have, $\frac{dx}{dt}=\frac{x\log a}{2}\times\frac{1}{\sqrt{1-t^2}}$

and $\quad \frac{dy}{dt}=-\frac{1}{2}y\log a\times\frac{1}{\sqrt{1-t^2}}$

Then, we know that

$$\frac{dy}{dx}=\frac{dy}{dt}\times\frac{dt}{dx}$$

$\Rightarrow \quad \frac{dy}{dx}=\frac{-y\log a}{2}\times\frac{1}{\sqrt{1-t^2}}\times\frac{2\times\sqrt{1-t^2}}{x\log a}$

$\Rightarrow \quad \frac{dy}{dx}=\frac{-y}{x}$

(d) We have, $\frac{dy}{dx}=\frac{-y}{x}$

At point $(1,-2)$, we get

$$\left[\frac{dy}{dx}\right]_{(1,-2)}=-\left(\frac{-2}{1}\right)=2$$

Or

(ii) Let $y=(x^2-5x+8)(x^3+7x+9)$ ...(i)

(a) On differentiating both sides by using product rule, we get

$$\frac{dy}{dx}=(x^2-5x+8)\frac{d}{dx}(x^3+7x+9)+(x^3+7x+9)\frac{d}{dx}(x^2-5x+8)$$

$=(x^2-5x+8)(3x^2+7)+(x^3+7x+9)(2x-5)$

$=3x^4-15x^3+24x^2+7x^2-35x+56+2x^4+14x^2+18x-5x^3-35x-45$

$=5x^4-20x^3+45x^2-52x+11$ ...(ii)

(b) Writing y as a single polynomial, we get

$$y=(x^2-5x+8)(x^3+7x+9)$$
$$=x^5-5x^4+15x^3-26x^2+11x+72$$

On differentiating both sides w.r.t. x, we get

$$\frac{dy}{dx}=\frac{d}{dx}(x^5-5x^4+15x^3-26x^2+11x+72)$$
$$=5x^4-20x^3+45x^2-52x+11 \quad \text{...(iii)}$$

(c) Taking logarithms on both sides of Eq. (i), we get

$$\log y=\log\{(x^2-5x+8)(x^3+7x+9)\}$$
$$\Rightarrow \log y=\log(x^2-5x+8)+\log(x^3+7x+9)$$

On differentiating both sides w.r.t. x, we get

$$\frac{1}{y}\frac{dy}{dx}=\frac{1}{x^2-5x+8}\frac{d}{dx}(x^2-5x+8)+\frac{1}{x^3+7x+9}\frac{d}{dx}(x^3+7x+9) \text{ [using chain rule]}$$

$$\Rightarrow \frac{1}{y}\frac{dy}{dx}=\frac{2x-5}{x^2-5x+8}+\frac{3x^2+7}{x^3+7x+9}$$

$$\Rightarrow \frac{dy}{dx}=y\left(\frac{2x-5}{x^2-5x+8}+\frac{3x^2+7}{x^3+7x+9}\right)$$

$$=(x^2-5x+8)(x^3+7x+9)\left(\frac{2x-5}{x^2-5x+8}+\frac{3x^2+7}{x^3+7x+9}\right)$$

$$=(2x-5)(x^3+7x+9)+(3x^2+7)(x^2-5x+8)$$
$$=2x^4+14x^2+18x-5x^3-35x-45+3x^4-15x^3+24x^2+7x^2-35x+56$$
$$=5x^4-20x^3+45x^2-52x+11 \quad \text{...(iv)}$$

From Eqs. (ii), (iii) and (iv), we find that result is same in every case.

11. Let $A=\begin{bmatrix}1&2\\3&4\end{bmatrix}$, then $|A|=\begin{vmatrix}1&2\\3&4\end{vmatrix}$.

Now, cofactors of elements of $|A|$ are

$A_{11}=4, A_{12}=-3, A_{21}=-2$ and $A_{22}=1$

$$\therefore \text{adj } A=\begin{bmatrix}A_{11}&A_{12}\\A_{21}&A_{22}\end{bmatrix}^T=\begin{bmatrix}4&-3\\-2&1\end{bmatrix}^T=\begin{bmatrix}4&-2\\-3&1\end{bmatrix} \quad \text{...(i)}$$

(i) Now, $|A|=\begin{vmatrix}1&2\\3&4\end{vmatrix}=4-6=-2$ ...(ii)

and $|\text{adj}(A)|=\begin{vmatrix}4&-2\\-3&1\end{vmatrix}=4-6=-2$ ...(iii)

$\therefore$ $|\text{adj}(A)|=|A|$ [from Eqs. (ii) and (iii)]

(ii) We have, $A=\begin{bmatrix}1&2\\3&4\end{bmatrix}$

$\therefore$ $A^T=\begin{bmatrix}1&3\\2&4\end{bmatrix}$ and $|A^T|=\begin{vmatrix}1&3\\2&4\end{vmatrix}$

Now, cofactors of elements of $|A^T|$ are

$C_{11}=4, C_{12}=-2, C_{21}=-3, C_{22}=1.$

$$\therefore \text{adj}(A^T)=\begin{bmatrix}C_{11}&C_{12}\\C_{21}&C_{22}\end{bmatrix}^T$$

$$=\begin{bmatrix}4&-2\\-3&1\end{bmatrix}^T=\begin{bmatrix}4&-3\\-2&1\end{bmatrix} \quad \text{...(iv)}$$

From Eq. (i), we get

$$(\text{adj } A)^T=\begin{bmatrix}4&-2\\-3&1\end{bmatrix}^T=\begin{bmatrix}4&-3\\-2&1\end{bmatrix}$$

$\Rightarrow (\text{adj } A)^T=\text{adj}(A^T)$ [from Eq. (iv)]

(iii) We have, $(\text{adj } A)=\begin{bmatrix}4&-2\\-3&1\end{bmatrix}$

$\therefore$ $|\text{adj } A|=\begin{vmatrix}4&-2\\-3&1\end{vmatrix}$

Now, cofactors of elements of $|\text{adj } A|$ are

$C_{11}=1, C_{12}=3, C_{21}=2$ and $C_{22}=4.$

$$\therefore \text{adj}(\text{adj } A)=\begin{bmatrix}C_{11}&C_{12}\\C_{21}&C_{22}\end{bmatrix}^T=\begin{bmatrix}1&3\\2&4\end{bmatrix}^T=\begin{bmatrix}1&2\\3&4\end{bmatrix}$$

$$\Rightarrow |\text{adj}(\text{adj } A)|=\begin{vmatrix}1&2\\3&4\end{vmatrix}=4-6=-2=|A|$$

[from Eq. (ii)]

Hence proved.

12.

Urn I	Urn II	Urn III
7 White 3 Black	4 White 6 Black	2 White 8 Black

Let E_1, E_2 and E_3 be the events of choosing Urn I, Urn II and Urn III, respectively.

$\therefore$ $P(E_1)=0.2, P(E_2)=0.6$ and $P(E_3)=0.2$

Let A be the event of drawing 2 white balls from an urn.

$\therefore$ $P(A/E_1)=$ Probability that 2 white balls are drawn when Urn I is chosen without replacement

$$=\frac{{}^7C_2}{{}^{10}C_2}=\frac{21}{45}=\frac{7}{15}$$

Similarly,

$$P(A/E_2)=\frac{{}^4C_2}{{}^{10}C_2}=\frac{6}{45}=\frac{2}{15} \text{ and } P(A/E_3)=\frac{{}^2C_2}{{}^{10}C_2}=\frac{1}{45}$$

$\therefore$ Required probability

= probability that 2 white balls were drawn from Urn III

$= P(E_3/A)$

Using Baye's theorem, we have

$$P(E_3/A)=\frac{P(E_3)P(A/E_3)}{P(E_1)P(A/E_1)+P(E_2)P(A/E_2)+P(E_3)P(A/E_3)}$$

$$=\frac{(0.2)\frac{1}{45}}{(0.2)\frac{7}{15}+(0.6)\frac{2}{15}+(0.2)\frac{1}{45}}$$

$$=\frac{\frac{0.2}{45}}{\frac{4.2+3.6+0.2}{45}}=\frac{0.2}{8}=\frac{1}{40}$$

13. (i) Given, $f(x)=\sin 3x-\cos 3x,\ 0<x<\pi$

On differentiating both sides w.r.t. x, we get $f'(x)=3\cos 3x+3\sin 3x$

On putting $f'(x)=0$, we get

$\sin 3x=-\cos 3x \Rightarrow \tan 3x=-1$

$$\Rightarrow \quad 3x=\frac{3\pi}{4},\frac{7\pi}{4},\frac{11\pi}{4} \qquad [\because \tan\theta \text{ is negative in IInd and IVth quadrant}]$$

$$\Rightarrow \quad x=\frac{\pi}{4},\frac{7\pi}{12},\frac{11\pi}{12}$$

Now, we find intervals and check in which intervals $f(x)$ is strictly increasing or strictly decreasing.

Interval	Test value	$f'(x)=3(\cos 3x+\sin 3x)$	Sign of $f'(x)$
$0<x<\frac{\pi}{4}$	At $x=\frac{\pi}{6}$	$3\left(\cos\frac{\pi}{2}+\sin\frac{\pi}{2}\right)=3(0+1)=3$	+ ve
$\frac{\pi}{4}<x<\frac{7\pi}{12}$	At $x=\frac{\pi}{3}$	$3(\cos\pi+\sin\pi)=3(-1+0)=-3$	− ve
$\frac{7\pi}{12}<x<\frac{11\pi}{12}$	At $x=\frac{3\pi}{4}$	$3\left(\cos\frac{9\pi}{4}+\sin\frac{9\pi}{4}\right)=3\left(\frac{1}{\sqrt2}+\frac{1}{\sqrt2}\right)=3\sqrt2$	+ ve
$\frac{11\pi}{12}<x<\pi$	At $x=\frac{23\pi}{24}$	$3\left(\cos\frac{23\pi}{8}+\sin\frac{23}{8}\pi\right)=3\left[\cos\left(3\pi-\frac{\pi}{8}\right)+\sin\left(3\pi-\frac{\pi}{8}\right)\right]$ $=3\left(-\cos\frac{\pi}{8}+\sin\frac{\pi}{8}\right)=3\left(\sin\frac{\pi}{8}-\cos\frac{\pi}{8}\right)<0$	− ve

Here, we see that $f'(x)>0$, for $0<x<\frac{\pi}{4}$ and $\frac{7\pi}{12}<x<\frac{11\pi}{12}$, so $f(x)$ is strictly increasing in the intervals $\left(0,\frac{\pi}{4}\right)$ and $\left(\frac{7\pi}{12},\frac{11\pi}{12}\right)$. While, $f'(x)<0$ for $\frac{\pi}{4}<x<\frac{7\pi}{12}$ and $\frac{11\pi}{12}<x<\pi$.

So, $f(x)$ is strictly decreasing in the intervals $\left(\frac{\pi}{4},\frac{7\pi}{12}\right)$ and $\left(\frac{11\pi}{12},\pi\right)$.

Common Mistake

Be careful in observing the sign of $f'(x)$ in the interval before deciding the nature of function.

Or

(ii) Given curves are $x=1-\cos\theta$ and $y=\theta-\sin\theta$.

On differentiating both sides w.r.t. θ, we get

$$\frac{dx}{d\theta}=\frac{d}{d\theta}(1-\cos\theta)=\sin\theta$$

and $$\frac{dy}{d\theta}=\frac{d}{d\theta}(\theta-\sin\theta)=1-\cos\theta$$

$$\therefore \quad \frac{dy}{dx}=\frac{dy/d\theta}{dx/d\theta}=\frac{1-\cos\theta}{\sin\theta}$$

$$\text{At } \theta=\frac{\pi}{4}, \left(\frac{dy}{dx}\right)_{\theta=\frac{\pi}{4}}=\frac{1-\cos\frac{\pi}{4}}{\sin\frac{\pi}{4}}=\frac{1-\frac{1}{\sqrt2}}{\frac{1}{\sqrt2}}=\sqrt2-1$$

Also, at $\theta=\frac{\pi}{4}$,

$$x_1=1-\cos\frac{\pi}{4}=1-\frac{1}{\sqrt2}=\frac{\sqrt2-1}{\sqrt2}$$

and $$y_1=\frac{\pi}{4}-\sin\frac{\pi}{4}=\frac{\pi}{4}-\frac{1}{\sqrt2}$$

We know that equation of tangent at (x_1,y_1) having slope m, is given by

$$y-y_1=m(x-x_1)$$

$$\therefore \quad y-\left(\frac{\pi}{4}-\frac{1}{\sqrt2}\right)=(\sqrt2-1)\left[x-\left(\frac{\sqrt2-1}{\sqrt2}\right)\right]$$

$$\Rightarrow \quad y-\frac{\pi}{4}+\frac{1}{\sqrt2}=x(\sqrt2-1)-\frac{(\sqrt2-1)^2}{\sqrt2}$$

$$\Rightarrow \quad y-\frac{\pi}{4}+\frac{1}{\sqrt2}=x(\sqrt2-1)-\frac{(2+1-2\sqrt2)}{\sqrt2}$$

$$[\because (a-b)^2=a^2+b^2-2ab]$$

$$\Rightarrow \left(y-\frac{\pi}{4}+\frac{1}{\sqrt2}\right)=x(\sqrt2-1)-\frac{(3-2\sqrt2)}{\sqrt2}$$

$$\Rightarrow \ x(\sqrt2-1)-y=\frac{3-2\sqrt2}{\sqrt2}-\frac{\pi}{4}+\frac{1}{\sqrt2}$$

$$x(\sqrt2-1)-y=\frac{12-8\sqrt2-\sqrt2\pi+4}{4\sqrt2}$$

$$\Rightarrow x(8-4\sqrt2)-4\sqrt2y=(16-\sqrt2\pi-8\sqrt2)$$

which is the required equation of tangent.

Also, the equation of normal at (x_1,y_1) having slope $-\frac{1}{m}$ is given by

$$y-y_1=-\frac{1}{m}(x-x_1)$$

$$\therefore y-\left(\frac{\pi}{4}-\frac{1}{\sqrt{2}}\right)=\frac{-1}{\sqrt{2}-1}\left(x-\frac{\sqrt{2}-1}{\sqrt{2}}\right)$$

$$\Rightarrow y(\sqrt{2}-1)-\left(\frac{\sqrt{2}\pi-4}{4\sqrt{2}}\right)(\sqrt{2}-1)=-x+\frac{\sqrt{2}-1}{\sqrt{2}}$$

$$\Rightarrow y(\sqrt{2}-1)-\left(\frac{2\pi-\sqrt{2}\pi-4\sqrt{2}+4}{4\sqrt{2}}\right)=\frac{-\sqrt{2}x+\sqrt{2}-1}{\sqrt{2}}$$

$$\Rightarrow 4\sqrt{2}y(\sqrt{2}-1)-2\pi+\sqrt{2}\pi+4\sqrt{2}-4$$
$$=-4\sqrt{2}x+4\sqrt{2}-4$$
$$\Rightarrow 4\sqrt{2}x+4\sqrt{2}y(\sqrt{2}-1)=2\pi-\sqrt{2}\pi$$
$$\Rightarrow 4\sqrt{2}x+y(8-4\sqrt{2})=2\pi-\sqrt{2}\pi$$
$$\Rightarrow 4\sqrt{2}x+(8-4\sqrt{2})y=\pi(2-\sqrt{2})$$

which is the required equation of normal.

14. (i) (a) Let $\frac{5x}{(x-1)(x^2+9)}=\frac{A}{x+1}+\frac{Bx+C}{x^2+9}$

$$\Rightarrow 5x=A(x^2+9)+(Bx+C)(x+1)$$
$$\Rightarrow 5x=Ax^2+9A+Bx^2+Bx+Cx+C$$

On equating the coefficients of x^2, x and constant term from both sides, we get

$$A+B=0,\ B+C=5,\ 9A+C=0$$

On solving these equations, we get

$$A=-\frac{1}{2},\ B=\frac{1}{2} \text{ and } C=\frac{9}{2}$$

$$\therefore \frac{5x}{(x+1)(x^2+9)}=-\left(\frac{1}{2(x+1)}\right)+\frac{1}{2}\left(\frac{x+9}{x^2+9}\right) \quad \ldots\text{(i)}$$

which is the required partial decomposition.

(b) We have, $f(x)=\frac{5x}{(x+1)(x^2+9)}$

Using partial fraction, we get

$$f(x)=-\frac{1}{2(x+1)}+\frac{1}{2}\left(\frac{x+9}{x^2+9}\right) \quad \text{[using Eq. (i)]}$$

On differentiating w.r.t. x, we get

$$f'(x)=-\frac{1}{2}\frac{d}{dx}\left(\frac{1}{x+1}\right)+\frac{1}{2}\frac{d}{dx}\left(\frac{x+9}{x^2+9}\right)$$
$$=\frac{1}{2}\frac{1}{(x+1)^2}+\frac{1}{2}\left[\frac{(x^2+9)-(x+9)(2x)}{(x^2+9)^2}\right].$$
$$\Rightarrow f'(x)=\frac{1}{2}\frac{1}{(x+1)^2}-\frac{1}{2}\left[\frac{x^2+18x-9}{(x^2+9)^2}\right]$$

which is the required result.

(c) We have, $f(x)=\frac{5x}{(x+1)(x^2+9)}$

From part (a), we have

$$f(x)=-\frac{1}{2(x+1)}+\frac{1}{2}\left(\frac{x+9}{x^2+9}\right)$$

$$\therefore \int\frac{5x}{(x+1)(x^2+9)}dx$$
$$=-\frac{1}{2}\int\frac{1}{x+1}dx+\frac{1}{2}\int\left(\frac{x+9}{x^2+9}\right)dx$$
$$=\int\frac{\left(-\frac{1}{2}\right)}{(x+1)}dx+\int\frac{\frac{1}{2}x+\frac{9}{2}}{x^2+9}dx$$
$$=-\frac{1}{2}\log|x+1|+\frac{1}{2}\cdot\frac{1}{2}\int\frac{2x}{x^2+9}dx+\frac{9}{2}\int\frac{1}{x^2+9}dx$$
$$=-\frac{1}{2}\log|x+1|+\frac{1}{4}\log|x^2+9|+\frac{9}{2}\cdot\frac{1}{3}\tan^{-1}\left(\frac{x}{3}\right)+C$$
$$\left[\because \int\frac{dx}{a^2+x^2}=\frac{1}{a}\tan^{-1}\left(\frac{x}{a}\right)\right]$$
$$=-\frac{1}{2}\log|x+1|+\frac{1}{4}\log|x^2+9|+\frac{3}{2}\tan^{-1}\left(\frac{x}{3}\right)+C$$

(d) From part (c), we have

$$\int f(x)dx=-\frac{1}{2}\log|x+1|+\frac{1}{4}\log|x^2+9|+\frac{3}{2}\tan^{-1}\left(\frac{x}{3}\right)+C$$

Now,
$$\int_0^1 f(x)\,dx=\left[-\frac{1}{2}\log|x+1|+\frac{1}{4}\log|x^2+9|+\frac{3}{2}\tan^{-1}\left(\frac{x}{3}\right)\right]_0^1$$
$$=\frac{-1}{2}\log 2+\frac{1}{4}\log 10-\frac{1}{4}\log 9+\frac{3}{2}\tan^{-1}\left(\frac{1}{3}\right)$$
$$=\frac{-1}{2}\log 2+\frac{1}{4}\log\left(\frac{10}{9}\right)+\frac{3}{2}\tan^{1}\left(\frac{1}{3}\right)$$
$$=-\frac{1}{4}\log 4+\frac{1}{4}\log\left(\frac{10}{9}\right)+\frac{3}{2}\tan^{-1}\left(\frac{1}{3}\right)$$
$$=\frac{1}{4}\log\left(\frac{5}{18}\right)+\frac{3}{2}\tan^{-1}\left(\frac{1}{3}\right)$$
$$\left[\because \log m-\log n=\log\frac{m}{n}\right]$$
$$\therefore \int_0^1 f(x)dx=\frac{1}{4}\log\left(\frac{5}{18}\right)+\frac{3}{2}\tan^{-1}\left(\frac{1}{3}\right)$$

Or

(ii) We have, $\int_0^{\pi/4}(\sqrt{\tan x}+\sqrt{\cot x})\,dx=\sqrt{2}\cdot\frac{\pi}{2}$

$$\text{LHS}=\int_0^{\pi/4}(\sqrt{\tan x}+\sqrt{\cot x})\,dx$$
$$=\int_0^{\pi/4}\left[\frac{\sqrt{\sin x}}{\sqrt{\cos x}}+\frac{\sqrt{\cos x}}{\sqrt{\sin x}}\right]dx$$
$$=\sqrt{2}\int_0^{\pi/4}\frac{(\sin x+\cos x)}{\sqrt{2\sin x\cos x}}dx$$
$$=\sqrt{2}\int_0^{\pi/4}\frac{(\sin x+\cos x)}{\sqrt{1-(\sin x-\cos x)^2}}dx$$
$$[\because (a-b)^2=a^2+b^2-2ab]$$

Let $\sin x-\cos x=t \Rightarrow (\cos x+\sin x)\,dx=dt$

Lower limit when $x=0 \Rightarrow t=-1$

Upper Limit when $x=\frac{\pi}{4} \Rightarrow t=0$

$\therefore \int_0^{\pi/4}(\sqrt{\tan x}+\sqrt{\cot x})\,dx=\sqrt{2}\int_{-1}^{0}\frac{dt}{\sqrt{1-t^2}}$

$=\sqrt{2}\,[\sin^{-1}t]_{-1}^{0}=\sqrt{2}\,[0-\sin^{-1}(-1)]$

$=\sqrt{2}\,[\sin^{-1}1]=\sqrt{2}\times\frac{\pi}{2}$

$=\sqrt{2}\cdot\frac{\pi}{2}=\text{RHS}$ **Hence proved.**

15. (i) (b) From the figure,

intercept on X-axis $=3/2$

intercept on Y-axis $=3$

and intercept on Z-axis $=-3/2$

(ii) (b) We know that a vector that has a magnitude of 1 is a unit vector.

The vector of length 3 units in the direction of $\hat{i}-2\hat{j}+2\hat{k}$

$$=3\cdot\frac{\hat{i}-2\hat{j}+2\hat{k}}{|\hat{i}-2\hat{j}+2\hat{k}|}=3\cdot\frac{\hat{i}-2\hat{j}+2\hat{k}}{\sqrt{(1)^2+(-2)^2+(2)^2}}$$

$$=3\cdot\frac{\hat{i}-2\hat{j}+2\hat{k}}{\sqrt{1+4+4}}=3\cdot\frac{\hat{i}-2\hat{j}+2\hat{k}}{\sqrt{9}}$$

$$=3\cdot\frac{(\hat{i}-2\hat{j}+2\hat{k})}{3}=(\hat{i}-2\hat{j}+2\hat{k})$$

Hence, only Statement II is correct.

(iii) (b) We have, $\vec{a}=3\hat{i}-2\hat{j}+\hat{k}$ ...(i)

and $\vec{b}=2\hat{i}-4\hat{j}-3\hat{k}$

$\Rightarrow$ $2\vec{b}=2(2\hat{i}-4\hat{j}-3\hat{k})$

[multiplying by 2 on both sides]

$\Rightarrow$ $2\vec{b}=4\hat{i}-8\hat{j}-6\hat{k}$ ...(ii)

On subtracting Eq. (ii) from Eq. (i), we get

$\vec{a}-2\vec{b}=(3\hat{i}-2\hat{j}+\hat{k})-(4\hat{i}-8\hat{j}-6\hat{k})$

$=(3-4)\hat{i}+(-2+8)\hat{j}+(1+6)\hat{k}$

[subtracting corresponding terms]

$=-\hat{i}+6\hat{j}+7\hat{k}$

(iv) The required plane is perpendicular to the line $\frac{x-1}{3}=\frac{y-2}{0}=\frac{z-3}{4}$.

$\therefore$ Its direction ratios are 3, 0, 4.

Now, equation of plane passing through the point (1, 1, 1) and having direction ratios 3, 0, 4 is given by

$3(x-1)+0(y-1)+4(z-1)=0$

$\Rightarrow$ $3x-3+4z-4=0$

$\Rightarrow$ $3x+4z-7=0$

Now, distance of this plane from the origin is

$=\left|\frac{3(0)+4(0)-7}{\sqrt{9+16}}\right|=\frac{7}{5}$ units

(v) We have,

Position vector of A, $\overrightarrow{OA}=2\hat{i}-\hat{j}-\hat{k}$

and position vector of B, $\overrightarrow{OB}=2\hat{i}-\hat{j}+2\hat{k}$

Since, P divides AB in the ratio 2 : 1, then

Position vector of $P=\frac{2(2\hat{i}-\hat{j}+2\hat{k})+1(2\hat{i}-\hat{j}-\hat{k})}{2+1}$

$=\frac{4\hat{i}-2\hat{j}+4\hat{k}+2\hat{i}-\hat{j}-\hat{k}}{3}$

$=\frac{6\hat{i}-3\hat{j}+3\hat{k}}{3}=2\hat{i}-\hat{j}+\hat{k}$

16. (i) Let θ be the angle between $\vec{a}$ and $\vec{b}$.

Given, $|\vec{a}|=8, |\vec{b}|=3$ and $|\vec{a}\times\vec{b}|=12$

We know that $|\vec{a}\times\vec{b}|=|\vec{a}||\vec{b}|\sin\theta$

$\therefore$ $|\vec{a}||\vec{b}|\sin\theta=12$

$\Rightarrow$ $\sin\theta=\frac{12}{|\vec{a}||\vec{b}|}$

$\Rightarrow$ $\sin\theta=\frac{12}{8\times3}$

$\Rightarrow$ $\sin\theta=\frac{1}{2}\Rightarrow\theta=\frac{\pi}{6}$

Hence, the required angle between $\vec{a}$ and $\vec{b}$ is $\frac{\pi}{6}$.

Or

(ii) Given, $|\vec{a}|=2, |\vec{b}|=1$ and $\vec{a}\cdot\vec{b}=\sqrt{3}$.

Let θ be the angle between $\vec{a}$ and $\vec{b}$.

Then, $\cos\theta=\frac{\vec{a}\cdot\vec{b}}{|\vec{a}||\vec{b}|}\Rightarrow\cos\theta=\frac{\sqrt{3}}{2\times1}$ [given]

$\Rightarrow$ $\cos\theta=\frac{\sqrt{3}}{2}\Rightarrow\cos\theta=\cos\frac{\pi}{6}$ $\left[\because\cos\frac{\pi}{6}=\frac{\sqrt{3}}{2}\right]$

$\Rightarrow$ $\theta=\frac{\pi}{6}$

Hence, the angle between $\vec{a}$ and $\vec{b}$ is $\frac{\pi}{6}$.

17. (i) Given plane is $\vec{r}\cdot(2\hat{i}-2\hat{j}+4\hat{k})+5=0$ ...(i)

Clearly, the position vector of P (1, 1, 2) is $\hat{i}+\hat{j}+2\hat{k}$ and perpendicular distance from (1, 1, 2) to the plane (i) is given by

$$\frac{|\vec{a}\cdot\vec{n}-d|}{|\vec{n}|}$$

where, $\vec{a} = \hat{i} + \hat{j} + 2\hat{k}$, $\vec{n} = 2\hat{i} - 2\hat{j} + 4\hat{k}$ and $d = -5$

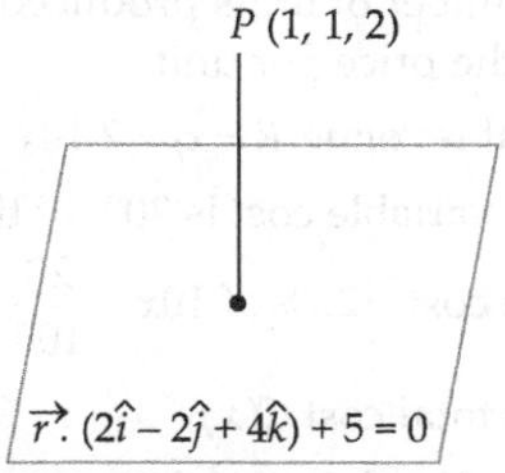

∴ Required perpendicular distance

$$= \frac{|(\hat{i} + \hat{j} + 2\hat{k})\cdot(2\hat{i} - 2\hat{j} + 4\hat{k}) - (-5)|}{\sqrt{4+4+16}}$$

$$= \frac{|2-2+8+5|}{\sqrt{24}}$$

$$= \frac{13}{\sqrt{24}} = \frac{13}{2\sqrt{6}} = \frac{13\sqrt{6}}{12}$$

Now, foot of the perpendicular

$$= \vec{a} - \frac{(\vec{a}\cdot\vec{n} - d)\vec{n}}{\vec{n}\cdot\vec{n}}$$

$$= (\hat{i} + \hat{j} + 2\hat{k}) - \frac{[(\hat{i} + \hat{j} + 2\hat{k})\cdot(2\hat{i} - 2\hat{j} + 4\hat{k}) - (-5)](2\hat{i} - 2\hat{j} + 4\hat{k})}{(2\hat{i} - 2\hat{j} + 4\hat{k})\cdot(2\hat{i} - 2\hat{j} + 4\hat{k})}$$

$$= (\hat{i} + \hat{j} + 2\hat{k}) - \frac{(2-2+8+5)(2\hat{i} - 2\hat{j} + 4\hat{k})}{4+4+16}$$

$$= (\hat{i} + \hat{j} + 2\hat{k}) - \frac{13}{24}(2\hat{i} - 2\hat{j} + 4\hat{k})$$

$$= (\hat{i} + \hat{j} + 2\hat{k}) - \frac{13}{12}(\hat{i} - \hat{j} + 2\hat{k})$$

$$= \left(1 - \frac{13}{12}\right)\hat{i} + \left(1 + \frac{13}{12}\right)\hat{j} + \left(2 - \frac{26}{12}\right)\hat{k}$$

$$= \frac{-1}{12}\hat{i} + \frac{25}{12}\hat{j} - \frac{2}{12}\hat{k}$$

Thus, the coordinates of foot of perpendicular are $\left(-\frac{1}{12}, \frac{25}{12}, -\frac{2}{12}\right)$.

Or

(ii) Given lines are $\vec{r} = (\hat{i} + \hat{j} - \hat{k}) + \lambda(3\hat{i} - \hat{j})$ ...(i)

and $\vec{r} = (4\hat{i} - \hat{k}) + \mu(2\hat{i} + 3\hat{k})$ ...(ii)

Clearly, these lines will intersect, if $(\hat{i} + \hat{j} - \hat{k}) + \lambda(3\hat{i} - \hat{j}) = (4\hat{i} - \hat{k}) + \mu(2\hat{i} + 3\hat{k})$, for some particular values of λ and μ.

Collecting the like terms, we get

$(1 + 3\lambda)\hat{i} + (1 - \lambda)\hat{j} - \hat{k} = (4 + 2\mu)\hat{i} + (-1 + 3\mu)\hat{k}$

On equating the coefficients of $\hat{i}$ from both sides, we get

$$1 + 3\lambda = 4 + 2\mu \Rightarrow 3\lambda - 2\mu = 3$$

On equating the coefficients of $\hat{j}$ from both sides, we get

$$1 - \lambda = 0 \Rightarrow \lambda = 1$$

On equating the coefficients of $\hat{k}$ from both sides, we get

$$-1 = -1 + 3\mu$$

$\Rightarrow \quad \mu = 0$

$\therefore \quad \mu = 0$ and $\lambda = 1$

Also, these values satisfy $3\lambda - 2\mu = 3$, therefore the given lines intersect.

On putting $\lambda = 1$ in Eq. (i), we get

$$\vec{r} = (\hat{i} + \hat{j} - \hat{k}) + 1(3\hat{i} - \hat{j}) = 4\hat{i} + 0\hat{j} - \hat{k}$$

Hence, the point of intersection of given lines is $(4, 0, -1)$.

18. Given, equation of the parabola is

$$y^2 = x \quad \text{...(i)}$$

It represents a right hand parabola with vertex at (0, 0).

The given line is $y + x = 2$

i.e. $x = 2 - y$ ...(ii)

On solving Eqs. (i) and (ii), we get

$$y^2 = 2 - y \Rightarrow y^2 + y - 2 = 0$$

$\Rightarrow (y-1)(y+2) = 0 \Rightarrow y = 1$ or -2

When $y = 1$, then $x = 1$ and when $y = -2$, then $x = 4$.

Thus, the points of intersection are $P(1, 1)$ and $Q(4, -2)$.

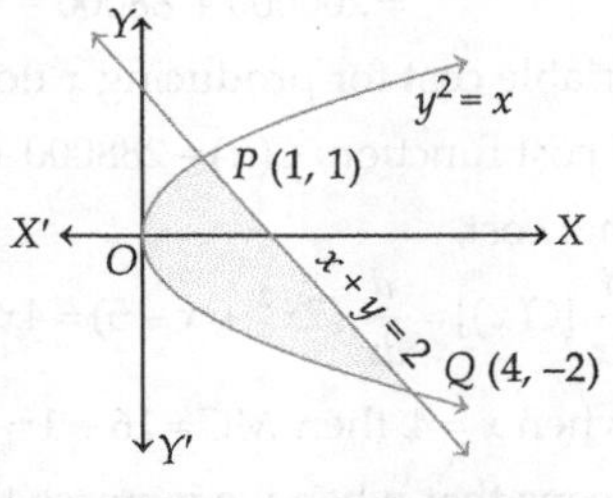

∴ Required area = Area of the shaded region

$$= \int_{-2}^{1} [x_2\,(\text{line}) - x_1\,(\text{parabola})]\,dy$$

$$= \int_{-2}^{1} [(2 - y) - y^2]\,dy$$

$$= \left[2y - \frac{y^2}{2} - \frac{y^3}{3}\right]_{-2}^{1}$$

$$= \left(2 - \frac{1}{2} - \frac{1}{3}\right) - \left(-4 - 2 + \frac{8}{3}\right)$$

$$= 2 - \frac{1}{2} - \frac{1}{3} + 6 - \frac{8}{3} = 8 - \frac{1}{2} - \frac{9}{3}$$

$$= \frac{9}{2} = 4\frac{1}{2} \text{ sq units}$$

19. (i) (d) We have, $C(x)=\frac{3}{2}x^3-6x^2+9x+2$

Then, average cost,

$$AC=\frac{C(x)}{x}=\frac{\frac{3}{2}x^3-6x^2+9x+2}{x}$$

$$=\frac{3}{2}x^2-6x+9+\frac{2}{x}$$

(ii) (c) Given, regression line of x on y is

$$9x+3y-46=0 \Rightarrow x=\frac{-3}{9}y+\frac{46}{9}$$

$$\therefore \quad b_{xy}=\frac{-3}{9}=\frac{-1}{3}$$

and the regression line of y on x is

$$3x+12y-7=0 \Rightarrow y=\frac{-3}{12}x+\frac{7}{12}$$

$$\therefore \quad b_{yx}=-\frac{3}{12}=-\frac{1}{4}$$

Hence, correlation coefficient $r=-\sqrt{b_{yx}\times b_{xy}}$

$$=-\sqrt{\left(\frac{-1}{4}\right)\times\left(\frac{-1}{3}\right)}$$

$$=-\sqrt{\frac{1}{12}}$$

$$\Rightarrow \quad r=-\frac{1}{2\sqrt{3}}$$

(iii) Here, Fixed cost = Cost of technical knowledge + Cost of setting up machine

$= 200000 + 88000 =$ ₹ 288000

and variable cost for producing x floppies $= 30x$

$\therefore$ Total cost function, $C(x)=288000+30x$

(iv) Marginal cost,

$$MC=\frac{d}{dx}[C(x)]=\frac{d}{dx}(2x^2+x-5)=4x+1$$

Now, when $x=4$, then $MC=16+1=17$

This means that when we increase the output from units, the additional cost incurred is ₹ 17.

(v) Given for 5 observations,

$\Sigma x=15, \Sigma y=25, \Sigma x^2=55, \Sigma y^2=135,$

$\Sigma xy=83$ and $n=5$

$$\therefore \quad \bar{x}=\frac{\Sigma x}{n}=\frac{15}{5}=3, \bar{y}=\frac{\Sigma y}{n}=\frac{25}{5}=5$$

$$\text{Now, } b_{xy}=\frac{\Sigma xy-\frac{\Sigma x\cdot\Sigma y}{n}}{\Sigma y^2-\frac{(\Sigma y)^2}{n}}=\frac{83-\frac{1}{5}(15)(25)}{135-\frac{1}{5}(25)^2}$$

$$=\frac{83-75}{135-125}=\frac{8}{10}=0.8$$

20. (i) Given, fixed cost of the commodity = ₹ 28000

Let the number of units produced by company be x and p be the price per unit.

Then, total revenue $R=xp=$ ₹ $10x$

Since, the variable cost is 20% of the total revenue.

$$\therefore \text{Variable cost} = 20\% \text{ of } 10x=\frac{20}{100}\times 10x=2x$$

Now, the total cost $C(x)$

= Fixed cost of the commodity + Variable cost of the commodity

$= 28000 + 2x$

For break-even point, $R(x)=C(x)$

$$\Rightarrow \quad 10x=28000+2x \Rightarrow 8x=28000$$

$$\Rightarrow \quad x=\frac{28000}{8} \Rightarrow x=3500$$

Hence, break-even point is 3500.

Or

(ii) Given cost function, $C(x)=\frac{x^3}{3}-45x^2-900x$

$$\therefore \quad \text{Marginal Cost }(MC)=\frac{d}{dx}[C(x)]$$

$$\Rightarrow \quad MC=\frac{1}{3}\cdot 3x^2-45\cdot 2x-900\cdot 1$$

$$=x^2-90x-900$$

To find value(s) of x so that MC is minimum, we should find value(s) of x, where $\frac{d}{dx}(MC)=0$ and $\frac{d^2}{dx^2}(MC)$.

Here, $\frac{d}{dx}(MC)=2x-90$ and $\frac{d^2}{dx^2}(MC)=2$

Now, $\frac{d}{dx}(MC)=0 \Rightarrow 2x-90=0 \Rightarrow x=45$

When $x=45$, then $\frac{d^2}{dx^2}(MC)=2>0$

So, marginal cost (MC) is minimum, when $x=45$.

Hence, the required units of product = 45.

21. Let us consider the following table

x	y	x^2	y^2	xy
4	2	16	4	8
2	3	4	9	6
3	2	9	4	6
4	4	16	16	16
2	4	4	16	8
$\Sigma x=15$	$\Sigma y=15$	$\Sigma x^2=49$	$\Sigma y^2=49$	$\Sigma xy=44$

Here, $n=5, \bar{x}=\frac{\Sigma x}{n}=\frac{15}{5}=3, \bar{y}=\frac{\Sigma y}{n}=\frac{15}{5}=3$

$$\therefore \quad b_{yx}=\frac{\Sigma xy-\frac{\Sigma x \cdot \Sigma y}{n}}{\Sigma x^2-\frac{(\Sigma x)^2}{n}}=\frac{44-\frac{15\times 15}{5}}{49-\frac{(15)^2}{5}}=\frac{44-45}{49-45}=\frac{-1}{4}$$

$\therefore$ The equation of line of regression of y on x having mean (3, 3) is

$$y-3=\frac{-1}{4}(x-3) \quad [\because y-\bar{y}=b_{yx}(x-\bar{x})]$$

$\Rightarrow \quad x+4y=15$

$$\text{and } b_{xy}=\frac{\Sigma xy-\frac{\Sigma x \cdot \Sigma y}{n}}{\Sigma y^2-\frac{(\Sigma y)^2}{n}}=\frac{44-\frac{15\times 15}{5}}{49-\frac{(15)^2}{5}}=\frac{44-45}{49-45}=\frac{-1}{4}$$

$\therefore$ The equation of line of regression of x on y having mean (3, 3) is

$$x-3=\frac{-1}{4}(y-3) \quad [\because x-\bar{x}=b_{xy}(y-\bar{y})]$$

$\Rightarrow \quad 4x-12=-y+3$

$\Rightarrow \quad 4x+y=15$

Hence, the equations of lines of regression are $x+4y=15$ and $4x+y=15$.

22. (i) Let the firm has x number of large vans and y number of small vans. From the given information, we have following corresponding constraint table.

	Large vans (x)	**Small vans** (y)	**Maximum / Minimum**
Packages	200	80	1200
Cost	400	200	3000

Thus, we see that objective function for minimum cost is $Z=400x+200y$.

Subject to constraints

$200x+80y \geq 1200$ [package constraint]

$\Rightarrow \quad 5x+2y \geq 30$ ...(i)

and $400x+200y \leq 3000$ [cost constraint]

$\Rightarrow \quad 2x+y \leq 15$ ...(ii)

and $x \leq y$ ...(iii)

[van constraint]

and $x \geq 0, y \geq 0$ ...(iv)

[non-negative constraints]

Thus, required LPP to minimise cost is minimise $Z=400x+200y$

Subject to constraints,

$5x+2y \geq 30,\ 2x+y \leq 15,\ x \leq y,$

and $x \geq 0,\ y \geq 0$

Table for line $5x+2y=30$ is

x	0	6
y	15	0

On putting (0, 0) in the inequality $5x+2y \geq 30$, we get $0+0 \geq 30$ (false)

So, the half plane is away from the origin.

Table for line $2x+y=15$, is

x	0	7.5
y	15	0

On putting (0, 0) in the inequality $2x+y \leq 15$, we get $0+0 \leq 15$ (true)

So, the half plane is towards the origin.

Table for line $x=y$ is

x	1	0
y	1	0

On putting (0, 0) in the inequality $x \leq y$, we get $0 \leq 0$ (true)

So, the half plane is towards the origin.

The intersection point of $2x+y=15$ and $5x+2y=30$ is (0, 15), intersection point of $2x+y=15$ and $y=x$ is (5, 5) and intersection point of $5x+2y=30$ and $y=x$ is $\left(\frac{30}{7}, \frac{30}{7}\right)$.

Now, on plotting these points on a graph paper we get the feasible region ABC. Whose corner points are $A\left(\frac{30}{7}, \frac{30}{7}\right)$, $B(5, 5)$ and $C(0, 15)$.

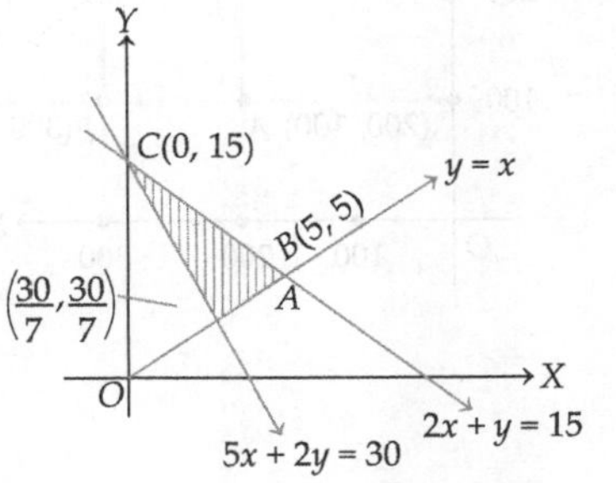

The values of Z at these points are as follows.

Corner points	$Z=400x+200y$
$A\left(\frac{30}{7}, \frac{30}{7}\right)$	$Z=\frac{18000}{7}=2571.4$
B (5, 5)	$B=3000$
C (0, 15)	$Z=3000$

Hence, the minimum cost is ₹ 2571.4.

Or

(ii) Let x be the number of deluxe calculators and y be the number of standard calculators produced per week. The profit per deluxe calculator is ₹(120 − 90) = ₹30 and per standard calculator is ₹(100 − 80) = ₹20. Thus, the problem can be formulated as,

Maximise $Z = 30x + 20y$

Subject to the constraints, $200 \le x \le 300$,

$100 \le y \le 250, x + y \le 500, x \ge 0, y \ge 0$

Here, lines $x = 200$ and $x = 300$ are perpendicular on X-axis.

Lines $y = 100$ and $y = 250$ are perpendicular on Y-axis.

Table for line $x + y = 500$ is

x	0	500	200	300
y	500	0	300	200

On putting (0, 0) in the equality $x + y \le 500$, we get

$0 + 0 \le 500$ (true)

So, the half plane is towards the origin.

Also, $x, y \ge 0$, so the feasible region lies in the first quadrant.

The point of intersection of these lines are $A(200,100)$, $B(300, 100)$, $C(300, 200)$, $D(250,250)$ and $E(200, 250)$.

Now, plot all the inequalities on a graph paper and the feasible region $ABCDE$ is bounded.

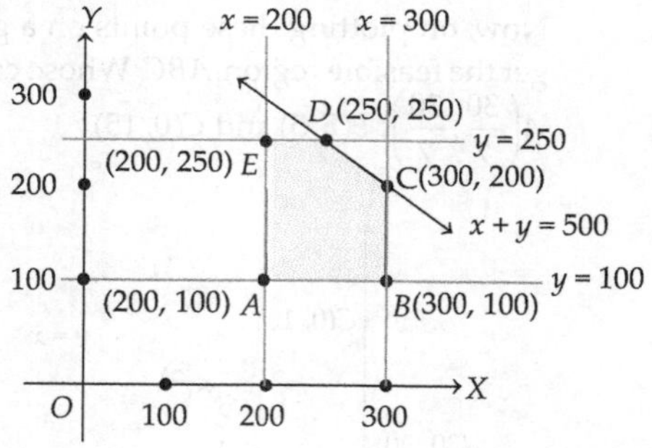

The corner points of the feasible region are $A(200, 100)$, $B(300, 100)$, $C(300, 200)$, $D(250, 250)$ and $E(200, 250)$.

Now, the values of Z at these points are as follows

Corner points	$Z = 30x + 20y$
A (200, 100)	$Z = 30 \times 200 + 20 \times 100$ $= 6000 + 2000$ $= 8000$
B (300, 100)	$Z = 30 \times 300 + 20 \times 100$ $= 9000 + 2000$ $= 11000$
C (300, 200)	$Z = 30 \times 300 + 20 \times 200$ $= 9000 + 4000$ $= 13000$ (maximum)
D (250, 250)	$Z = 30 \times 250 + 20 \times 250$ $= 7500 + 5000$ $= 12500$
E (200, 250)	$Z = 30 \times 200 + 20 \times 250$ $= 6000 + 5000$ $= 11000$

Hence, for maximum profit, ₹13000 per week, 300 deluxe calculators and 200 standard calculators should be produced per week.

Common Mistake

Be careful to find the half plane is towards the origin or away from the origin.

SQP Code **PB-3/15** Series **i-Succeed 3-25/15** Roll No.

Sample Question Paper 03

Mathematics 12th (Code 860)

General Instructions

1. The Question Paper consists of three sections A, B and C.
2. Candidates are required to attempt all questions from Section A and all questions either from Section B Or Section C.
3. Section A Internal choice has been provided in two questions of two marks each, two questions of four marks each and two questions of six marks each.
4. Section B Internal choice has been provided in one questions of two marks and one question of four marks.
5. Section C Internal choice has been provided in one question of two marks and one question of four marks.
6. All working, including rough work, should be done on the same sheet as, and adjacent to the rest of the answer.
7. The intended marks for questions or parts of questions are given in brackets [].
8. Mathematical tables and graph papers are provided.

Time : 3 Hrs.

Max. Marks : 80

Section A (65 Marks)

1. In subparts (i) to (xi) choose the correct options and in subparts (xii) to (xv), answer the questions as instructed.

(i) **Assertion** (A) The function f, where f is defined by $f(x)=\begin{cases}-2, & x\le -1\\ 2x, & -1<x<\infty\end{cases}$ is continuous at R

Reason (R) A function f is said to be continuous if it is continuous at every point of its domain. • *Analysis* [1]

(a) Both A and R are correct and R is the correct explanation of A.
(b) Both A and R are correct and R is not the correct explanation of A.
(c) A is correct but R is incorrect.
(d) A is incorrect but R is correct.

(ii) If $P(A)=0.4$, $P(B)=0.8$ and $P(B/A)=0.6$, then

Statement I $P(A\cup B)$ is equal to 0.96

Statement II $P(A\cap B)$ is equal to 0.96 • *Application* [1]

(a) Statement I is true and II is false.
(b) Statement II is true and I is false.
(c) Both Statements are true.
(d) Both Statements are false.

(iii) $\int_0^1 (x^2+x)\,dx$ is equal to • *Evaluate* [1]

(a) $\frac{2}{3}$ (b) $\frac{3}{2}$
(c) $\frac{6}{5}$ (d) $\frac{5}{6}$

(iv) The relation R in the set $\{1,2,3\}$ given by $R=\{(1,1),(2,2),(3,3),(1,2),(2,3)\}$ is • *Analysis* [1]

(a) reflexive but neither symmetric nor transitive.
(b) reflexive, symmetric but not transitive.
(c) symmetric but neither reflexive nor transitive.
(d) an equivalence relation.

(v) $\int \frac{x + \sin x}{1 + \cos x} dx$ is equal to • *Understanding* [1]

(a) $\log|1 + \cos x| + C$ (b) $\log|x + \sin x| + C$
(c) $x - \tan\frac{x}{2} + C$ (d) $x \cdot \tan\frac{x}{2} + C$

(vi) If $f : R \to R$ be defined by $f(x) = 2x + \cos x$, then f • *Understanding* [1]

(a) has a minimum at $x = \pi$.
(b) has a maximum at $x = 0$.
(c) is an decreasing function.
(d) is an increasing function.

(vii) The differential coefficient of $\sin[\cos(x^2)]$ with respect to x is • *Analysis* [1]

(a) $-2x\sin x^2 \cos(\cos x^2)$
(b) $2x\sin(x^2)\cos(x^2)$
(c) $2x\sin(x^2)\cos(x^2)\cos x$
(d) None of the above

(viii) Shown below is the graph of a function $h(x)$. • *Application* [1]

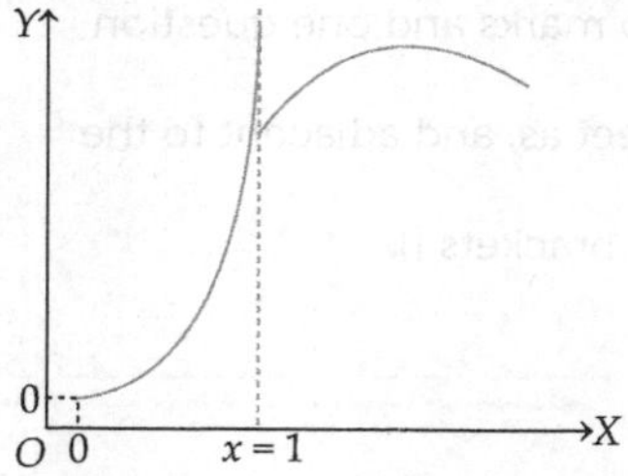

(a) $h(x)$ is continuous and differentiable at $x = 1$.
(b) $h(x)$ is continuous but not differentiable at $x = 1$.
(c) $h(x)$ is not continuous but differentiable at $x = 1$.
(d) $h(x)$ is neither continuous nor differentiable at $x = 1$.

SP-03

(ix) Consider the following statements

Statement I $\sec^{-1} x$ can be defined as a function, if the domain is R and range is $[0, \pi] - \left\{\frac{\pi}{2}\right\}$.

Statement II The principal value branch of the $\sec^{-1} x$ is $[0, \pi] - \left\{\frac{\pi}{2}\right\}$.

Choose the correct option. • *Recall* [1]

(a) Only Statement I is true.
(b) Only Statement II is true.
(c) Both statements I and II are true.
(d) Neither statements I nor II is true.

(x) **Assertion** (A) The degree of the differential equation $\frac{d^3y}{dx^3} + 2\left(\frac{d^2y}{dx^2}\right)^2 - \frac{dy}{dx} + y = 0$ can be defined.

Reason (R) The degree of a differential equation can be defined, if it is a polynomial equation in derivatives.

Choose the correct option. • *Analysis* [1]

(a) Both A and R are correct; R is the correct explanation of A
(b) Both A and R are correct; R is not the correct explanation of A
(c) A is correct but R is incorrect
(d) R is correct but A is incorrect

(xi) Write the number of all possible matrices of order 2×2 with each entry 1, 2 or 3 is • *Evaluate* [1]

(a) 3 (b) 9 (c) 27 (d) 81

(xii) A die, whose faces are marked 1, 2 and 3 in red and 4, 5 and 6 in green, is tossed. Let A be the event 'number obtained is even' and B be the event 'number obtained is odd'. Check whether A and B are independent events or not. • *Application* [1]

(xiii) Let D be the domain of the real valued function f defined by $f(x) = \sqrt{25 - x^2}$. Then, write D. • *Understanding* [1]

(xiv) Evaluate $\begin{vmatrix} x^2 - x + 1 & x - 1 \\ x + 1 & x + 1 \end{vmatrix}$ • *Evaluate* [1]

(xv) *XYZ* corporation has implemented a new email filtering system designed to identify and categorise incoming emails into 'spam' and 'not spam'. The system uses a variety of indicators to classify emails but It's not perfect. • *Application*

- Probability that any given email is spam, $P(\text{spam}) = 0.2$
- Probability that an email is identified as given that it is actually spam $P[\text{identified as spam/spam}] = 0.9$
- Probability that an email is identified as spam given that it is not actually spam $P[\text{identified as spam/not spam}] = 0.1$

If an email is identified as spam, what is the probability that it actually is spam?

2. (i) The table below shows some of the values of differentiable functions u and v and their derivatives.

x	$u(x)$	$u'(x)$	$v(x)$	$v'(x)$
1	3	2	4	1
2	5	–1	0	3
3	2	4	1	–2
4	7	0	3	2

If $r(x) = u[v(x)]$, then find $r'(3)$.

• *Application*

Or

(ii) If the area of a circle increase at a uniform rate, then prove that perimeter varies inversely as the radius.

• *Application* [2]

3. Solve the differential equation $y - x\frac{dy}{dx} = a\left(y^2 + \frac{dy}{dx}\right)$.

• *Understanding* [2]

4. Prove that $2\tan^{-1}\frac{1}{2} + \tan^{-1}\frac{1}{7} = \tan^{-1}\frac{31}{17}$.

• *Recall* [2]

5. (i) Show that the function $f(x) = 4x^3 - 18x^2 + 27x - 7$ is always increasing on R.

• *Analysis* [2]

Or

(ii) Find the interval, where the function is increasing $f(x) = x^3 - 6x^2 + 9x + 15$.

• *Evaluate* [2]

6. If matrix $\begin{bmatrix} 0 & a & 3 \\ 2 & b & -1 \\ c & 1 & 0 \end{bmatrix}$ is a skew-symmetric matrix, then find the values of a, b and c.

• *Evaluate* [2]

7. Evaluate $\int_2^5 [|x-2| + |x-3| + |x-5|]\, dx$.

• *Evaluate* [4]

8. Find the adjoint of the matrix

$A = \begin{bmatrix} -1 & -2 & -2 \\ 2 & 1 & -2 \\ 2 & -2 & 1 \end{bmatrix}$ and hence show that

$A(\text{adj } A) = |A| I_3$.

• *Understanding* [4]

9. (i) An instructor has a question bank consisting of 300 easy true/false questions, 200 difficult true/false questions, 500 easy multiple choice questions and 400 difficult multiple choice questions. If a question is selected at random from the question bank, then what is the probability that it will be an easy question, given that it is a multiple choice question?

• *Application* [4]

Or

(ii) A box contains 4 oranges and 4 green balls, another box contains 3 oranges and 5 green balls, one of the two box is selected at random and a ball is drawn from the box, which is found to be orange. Find the probability that the ball is drawn from the first box.

• *Application* [4]

10. (i) In a school, teacher ask a question to three students Ravi, Mohit, Sonia. The probability of solving the question by Ravi, Mohit, Sonia are 30%, 25% and 45%, respectively. The probability of making error by Ravi, Mohit and Sonia are 1%, 1.2% and 2%, respectively.

On the basis of above information, answer the following questions.

• *Application*

(a) Find the conditional probability that an error is committed in solving question given that question is solved by Sonia.

(b) Find the probability that Sonia solved the question and committed an error.

(c) Find the total probability of committing an error in solving the question.

(d) If the solution of question is checked by teacher and has some error, then find the probability that the question is not solved by Ravi. [4]

Or

(ii) A doctor is to visit a patient. From the post experience, it is known that the probabilities that he will come by train, bus, scooter or by other means of transport are respectively $\frac{3}{10}, \frac{1}{5}, \frac{1}{10}$ and $\frac{2}{5}$. The probability that he will be late are $\frac{1}{4}, \frac{1}{3}$ and $\frac{1}{12}$, if he comes by train, bus and scooter respectively, but if he comes by other means of transport, then he will not be late.

On the basis of above information, answer the following questions.
• *Application*

(a) Find the probability, that doctor is late given that he come by bus.

(b) Find the probability that doctor come by train and he is late.

(c) Find the probability that he is late. [4]

11. The sum of three numbers x, y and z is 6. If we multiply third number by 3 and add second number to it, we get 11. By adding first and third numbers, we get double of the second number. • *Analysis*

On the basis of above information, answer the following questions.

(i) Form a simultaneous set of equations for the above information.

(ii) Find the inverse of matrix $\begin{bmatrix} 1 & 1 & 1 \\ 0 & 1 & 3 \\ 1 & -2 & 1 \end{bmatrix}$.

(iii) Find the values of x, y and z. [6]

12. (i) Find $\int \dfrac{\sin^{-1}\sqrt{x} - \cos^{-1}\sqrt{x}}{\sin^{-1}\sqrt{x} + \cos^{-1}\sqrt{x}}\, dx,\ x \in [0, 1].$
• *Evaluate* [6]

Or

(ii) Evaluate $\int \dfrac{1}{x^4 + 1}\, dx.$
• *Evaluate* [6]

13. (i) Evaluate $\int_0^{\pi} \dfrac{x \tan x}{\sec x \cdot \operatorname{cosec} x}\, dx.$
• *Evaluate* [6]

Or

(ii) Evaluate $\int \dfrac{x^2}{(x^2+1)(2x^2+1)}\, dx.$
• *Evaluate* [6]

14. A point on the hypotenuse of a right triangle is at distances a and b from the sides of the triangle. Show that the minimum length of the hypotenuse is $(a^{2/3} + b^{2/3})^{3/2}$.
• *Application* [6]

Section B (15 Marks)

15. In subparts (i) to (iii) choose the correct options and in subparts (iv) and (v), answer the questions as instructed. [5]

(i) Observe the vector diagram shown below and the expression that follows :

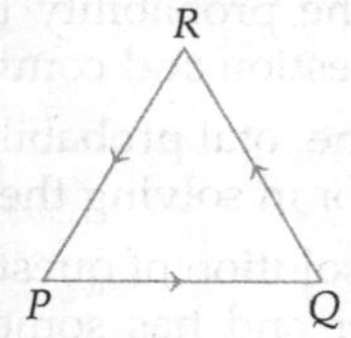

The value of $\overrightarrow{PQ} + \overrightarrow{QR} - \overrightarrow{RP}$ is
• *Application*

(a) $2\overrightarrow{PR}$ (b) $2\overrightarrow{QR}$

(c) $\vec{0}$ (d) $2\overrightarrow{QP}$

(ii) **Statement I** The cartesian equation of the plane $\vec{r} \cdot (\hat{i} + \hat{j} - \hat{k}) = 2$ is $x + y - z = 2$.

Statement II The cartesian equation of the plane $\vec{r} \cdot (3\hat{i} - 5\hat{j} + 3k) = 3$ is $3x - 5y + 3z = 3$. • *Understanding*

Which of the following is correct?

(a) Only statement I

(b) Only statement II

(c) Both statements I and II

(d) Neither statement I nor II

(iii) The value of λ, such that the line $\dfrac{x-2}{6} = \dfrac{y-1}{\lambda} = \dfrac{z+5}{-4}$ is perpendicular to the plane $3x - y - 2z = 7$ is
• *Understanding*

(a) 2 (b) -2 (c) 1 (d) -1

(iv) Shown below is a cube of side a.
• *Understanding*

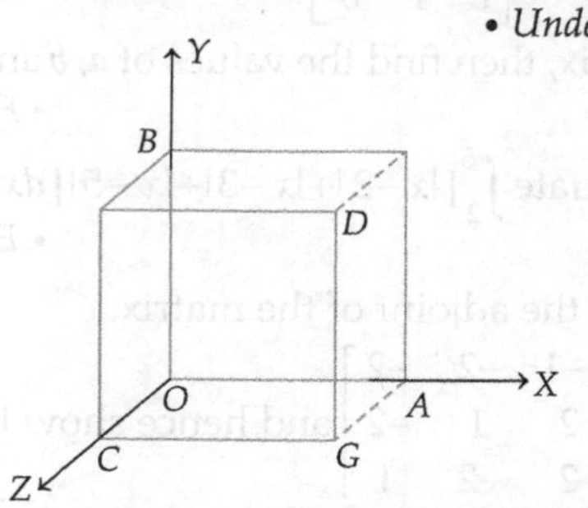

Find the angle between two diagonals of a cube.

(v) Find $|\vec{x}|$, if for a unit vector $\hat{a}$, $(\vec{x} - \hat{a}) \cdot (\vec{x} + \hat{a}) = 15$.
• *Recall*

16. (i) Find a vector $\vec{a}$ of magnitude $5\sqrt{2}$, making an angle of $\frac{\pi}{4}$ with X-axis, $\frac{\pi}{2}$ with Y-axis and an acute angle θ with Z-axis. • *Application* [2]

Or

(ii) Find the position vectors of the point which divide the line joining the two points $3\vec{a}-2\vec{b}$ and $2\vec{a}-5\vec{b}$ internally and externally in the ratio 3 : 2. • *Application* [2]

17. (i) Find the angle between the lines whose direction cosines are given by the equations $3l+m+5n=0$, $6mn-2nl+5lm=0$. • *Recall* [4]

Or (ii) Show that lines $\vec{r}=(-2\hat{i}+2\hat{j}-2\hat{k})+\lambda(3\hat{i}-\hat{j})$ and $\vec{r}=(4\hat{i}-2\hat{k})+\mu(2\hat{i}+3\hat{k})$ intersect each other. Find their point of intersection. • *Analysis* [4]

18. Draw the rough sketch and find the area of the region enclosed between the two circles $x^2+y^2=9$ and $(x-3)^2+y^2=9$. • *Application* [4]

Section C (15 Marks)

19. In subparts (i) and (ii) choose the correct options and in subparts (iii) to (v), answer the questions as instructed. [5]

(i) A company produces a commodity with ₹ 28000 fixed cost. The variable cost is estimated to be 40% of the total revenue recovered on selling the product at a rate of ₹ 10 per unit. Then, the cost function is • *Application*

(a) $28000+2x$ (b) $28000+4x$
(c) $4x$ (d) None of these

(ii) Which line best fits the trend of the data shown? • *Application*

(a)
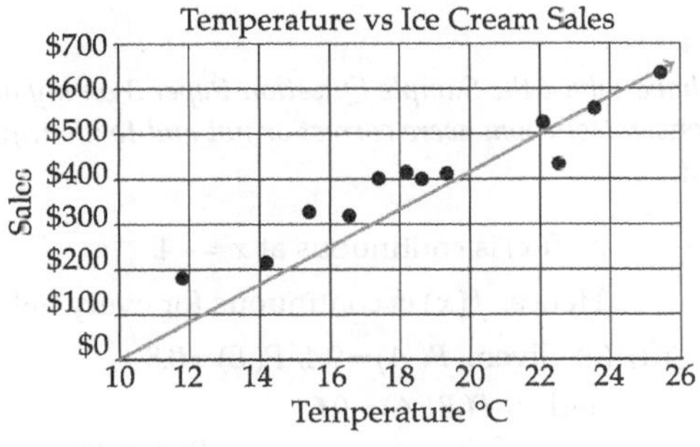

(b)
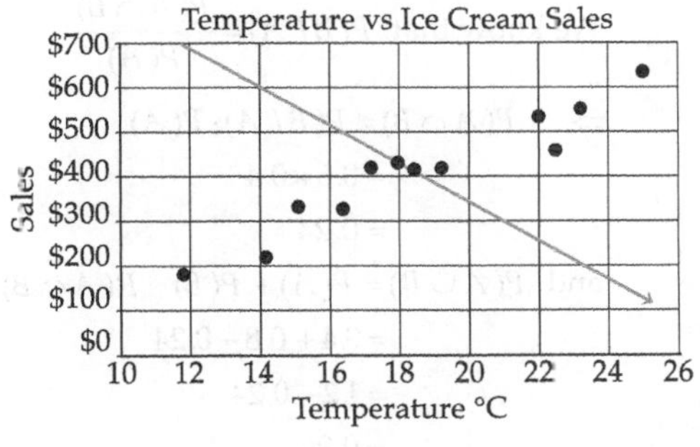

(c)
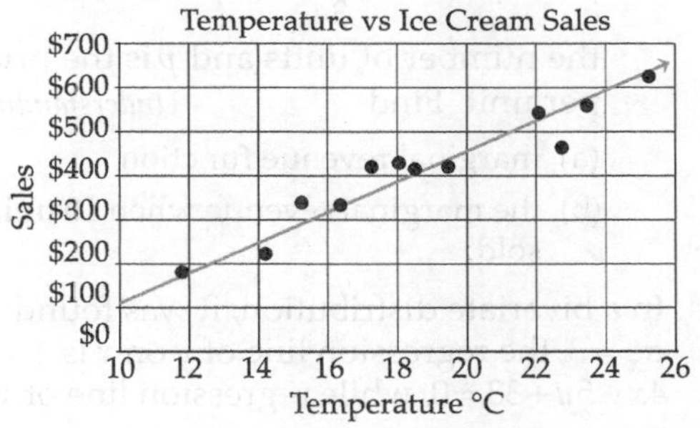

(d)
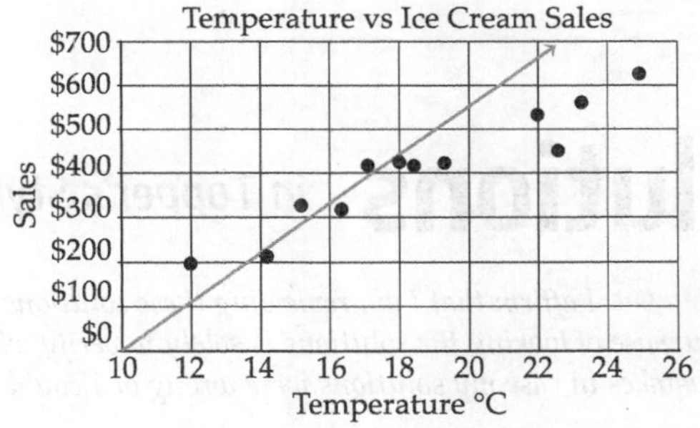

(iii) In a bivariate distribution, it was found $\sigma_x=3$, the regression line of Y on X is $8x-10y+66=0$ while regression line of X on Y is $40x-18y-214=0$. Calculate $\bar{x}$ and $\bar{y}$. • *Evaluate*

(iv) The demand function for TV sets is $p=$ ₹ $(8000-5x)$. Find the total revenue and average revenue by selling 20 sets. • *Understanding*

(v) It is known that cost of producing 100 units of commodity is ₹ 250 and cost of producing 200 units is ₹ 300. Assuming that AVC is constant, find the cost function. • *Application*

20. (i) The rate of change of total cost (y) of a commodity per unit change of output (x) is called the marginal cost of the commodity. If there exists a relation between y and x in the form $y = 3x\left(\frac{x+7}{x+5}\right) + 5$, then • *Application* [2]

(a) find the marginal cost of the commodity.

(b) prove that marginal cost falls continuously as the output increases.

Or

(ii) The demand for a certain product is represented by the equation $p = 400 + 20x - \frac{x^2}{3}$ in rupees, where x is the number of units and p is the price per unit. Find • *Understanding* [2]

(a) marginal revenue function.

(b) the marginal revenue when 10 units are sold.

21. In a bivariate distribution, it was found $\sigma_x = 3$, the regression line of y on x is $4x - 5y + 33 = 0$, while regression line of x on y is $20x - 9y - 107 = 0$.

Calculate $\bar{x}, \bar{y}, \rho(x, y), \text{Cov}(x, y)$ and σ_y. • *Analysis* [4]

22. (i) A gardener has a supply of fertilizer of Type I which consists of 10% nitrogen and 6% phosphoric acid and Type II fertilizer which consists of 5% nitrogen and 10% phosphoric acid. After testing the soil conditions, he finds that he needs atleast 14 kg of nitrogen and 14 kg of phosphoric acid for his crop. If the Type I fertilizer costs 60 paise per kg and Type II fertilizer costs 40 paise per kg, how many kilograms of each fertilizer should be used, so that nutrient requirements are met at a minimum cost and what is the minimum cost? • *Application* [4]

Or

(ii) Solve the following LPP graphically.

Maximise $Z = 3x + 2y$, subject to constraints are $x + 2y \le 10, 3x + y \le 15$ and $x \ge 0, y \ge 0$. • *Application* [4]

Solutions *in Topper's Style*

My Commitment *I affirm that I am reviewing these solutions only after I have solved the Sample Question Paper 3 on my own. My purpose of looking the solutions is solely to verify whether my answers/solutions were correct or not and to identify my mistakes in case my solutions were wrong or I could not solve that.*

1. (i) (d) We have, $f(x) = \begin{cases} -2, & \text{if } x \le -1 \\ 2x, & \text{if } -1 < x < \infty \end{cases}$

Since, $f(x)$ is a polynomial function, so it is continuous everywhere except at $x = -1$.

So, we have to check the continuity at $x = -1$ only.

At $x = -1$, $f(-1) = -2$

$\text{LHL} = \lim_{x \to -1^-} f(x) = \lim_{x \to -1^-} (-2) = -2$

$\text{RHL} = \lim_{x \to -1^+} f(x)$

$= \lim_{x \to -1^+} 2x = \lim_{h \to 0} 2(-1 + h)$

[put $x = -1 + h$; when $x \to -1^+$, then $h \to 0$]

$= \lim_{h \to 0} (-2 + 2h) = -2$

Thus, $f(-1) = \text{LHL} = \text{RHL}$

$\therefore$ $f(x)$ is continuous at $x = -1$.

Hence, $f(x)$ is continuous for every value of x.

(ii) (a) Given, $P(A) = 0.4$, $P(B) = 0.8$ and $P(B/A) = 0.6$

We know that, $P(B/A) = \frac{P(A \cap B)}{P(A)}$

$\Rightarrow \quad P(A \cap B) = P(B/A) \cdot P(A)$

$= 0.6 \times 0.4$

$= 0.24$

and $P(A \cup B) = P(A) + P(B) - P(A \cap B)$

$= 0.4 + 0.8 - 0.24$

$= 1.2 - 0.24$

$= 0.96$

Hence, Statement I is true and II is false.

(iii) (d) Let $I=\int_0^1 (x^2+x)dx$

$$=\left[\frac{x^3}{3}+\frac{x^2}{2}\right]_0^1=\frac{1}{3}+\frac{1}{2}=\frac{5}{6}$$

(iv) (a) Let the given set be $A=\{1,2,3\}$

and $R=\{(1,1),(2,2),(3,3),(1,2),(2,3)\}$

Reflexive Here, $1, 2, 3 \in A$

and $(1, 1), (2, 2), (3, 3) \in R$

i.e. $\forall\, a \in A, (a, a) \in R$.

So, R is reflexive.

Symmetric Here, $(1, 2) \in R$ but $(2, 1) \notin R$.

So, R is not symmetric.

Transitive Here, $(1, 2) \in R$ and $(2, 3) \in R$

but $(1, 3) \notin R$.

So, R is not transitive.

(v) (d) Let $I=\int \frac{x+\sin x}{1+\cos x}dx$

$$=\int \frac{x}{1+\cos x}dx+\int \frac{\sin x}{1+\cos x}dx$$

$$=\int \frac{x}{2\cos^2 x/2}dx+\int \frac{2\sin x/2\cos x/2}{2\cos^2 x/2}dx$$

$[\because \sin 2\theta=2\sin\theta\cos\theta \text{ and } \cos 2\theta=2\cos^2\theta-1]$

$$=\frac{1}{2}\int x\sec^2 x/2\,dx+\int \tan x/2\,dx$$

$$=\frac{1}{2}\left[x\cdot\tan x/2\cdot 2-\int \tan\frac{x}{2}\cdot 2\,dx\right]+\int \tan\frac{x}{2}dx$$

$$=x\cdot\tan\frac{x}{2}+C$$

(vi) (d) We have, $f(x)=2x+\cos x$

$\therefore \quad f'(x)=2+(-\sin x)=2-\sin x$

Since, $f'(x)>0, \forall\, x$

Hence, $f(x)$ is an increasing function.

(vii) (a) Let $y=\sin(\cos x^2)$

Therefore, $\frac{dy}{dx}=\frac{d}{dx}\sin(\cos x^2)$

$$=\cos(\cos x^2)\frac{d}{dx}(\cos x^2)$$

$$=\cos(\cos x^2)(-\sin x^2)\frac{d}{dx}(x^2)$$

$$=-\sin x^2\cos(\cos x^2)(2x)$$

$$=-2x\sin x^2\cos(\cos x^2)$$

(viii) (b) From the graph,

we observe that $h(x)$ is continuous but not differentiable at $x=1$.

(ix) (b) $\sec^{-1}x$ can be defined as a function whose domain is $R-(-1, 1)$ and range could be any of the intervals $[-\pi, 0]-\left\{\frac{-\pi}{2}\right\}, [0, \pi]-\left\{\frac{\pi}{2}\right\}, [\pi, 2\pi]-\left\{\frac{3\pi}{2}\right\}$ etc.

Corresponding to each of these intervals, we get different branches of the function $\sec^{-1}x$.

The branch with range $[0, \pi]-\left\{\frac{\pi}{2}\right\}$ is called the principal value branch of the function $\sec^{-1}x$.

(x) (a) To study the degree of a differential equation the key point is that the differential equation must be a polynomial equation in derivatives, i.e. y', y'', y''' etc. The given differential equation is

$$\frac{d^3y}{dx^3}+2\left(\frac{d^2y}{dx^2}\right)^2-\frac{dy}{dx}+y=0$$

This is a polynomial equation in y''', y'' and y'.

$\therefore$ Its degree can be defined.

(xi) (d) We know that a matrix of order 2×2 has 4 entries. Since, each entry has 3 choices, namely 1, 2 or 3, therefore number of required matrices

$$=3\times3\times3\times3=3^4=81$$

(xii) Here, a die is thrown, therefore the sample space is

$$S=\{1,2,3,4,5,6\} \Rightarrow n(S)=6$$

Also, event A : Number is even

and event B : Number is odd.

$\therefore$ $A=\{2,4,6\}$ and $B=\{1,3,5\}$ and $A\cap B=\{\phi\}$

$\Rightarrow$ $n(A)=3, n(B)=3$ and $n(A\cap B)=0$

Now, $P(A)=\frac{n(A)}{n(S)}=\frac{3}{6}=\frac{1}{2}$

$P(B)=\frac{n(B)}{n(S)}=\frac{2}{6}=\frac{1}{3}$

and $P(A\cap B)=\frac{n(A\cap B)}{n(S)}=\frac{0}{6}=0$

$$P(A)\times P(B)=\frac{1}{2}\times\frac{1}{3}=\frac{1}{6}\neq 0=P(A\cap B)$$

$\Rightarrow \quad P(A\cap B)\neq P(A)\times P(B)$

Hence, A and B are not independent events.

(xiii) Given function is,

$$f(x)=\sqrt{25-x^2}$$

For real value of $f(x)$,

$25-x^2\geq 0$

$\Rightarrow \quad x^2\leq 25$

$\Rightarrow \quad -5\leq x\leq +5$

$\therefore \quad D=[-5, 5]$

(xiv) We have, $\begin{vmatrix} x^2-x+1 & x-1 \\ x+1 & x+1 \end{vmatrix}$

$$=\begin{vmatrix} x^2-2x+2 & x-1 \\ 0 & x+1 \end{vmatrix} \quad [\text{apply } C_1\to C_1-C_2]$$

$$=[(x^2-2x+2)\cdot(x+1)-(x-1)\cdot 0]$$

$$=x^3-2x^2+2x+x^2-2x+2$$

$$=x^3-x^2+2$$

(xv) Given, $P(\text{identified as spam/spam}) = 0.9$

$P(\text{spam}) = 0.2$

and $P(\text{identified as spam/not spam}) = 0.1$

$\because P(\text{not spam}) = 1 - P(\text{spam})$

$= 1 - 0.2 = 0.8$

Now, $P(\text{identified as spam}) = P(\text{identified as spam/spam}) \times P(\text{spam}) + P(\text{identified as spam/not spam}) \times P(\text{not spam})$

$= 0.9 \times 0.2 + 0.1 \times 0.8$

$= 0.18 + 0.08$

$= 0.26$

Therefore, $P(\text{spam/identified as spam})$

$$= \frac{P(\text{identified as spam / spam}) \times P(\text{spam})}{P(\text{identified as spam})}$$

$$= \frac{0.9 \times 0.2}{0.26} = \frac{0.18}{0.26} = \frac{9}{13}$$

Hence, the probability that identified spam email is actually spam is $\frac{9}{13}$.

2. (i) We have, $r(x) = u[v(x)]$

On differentiating w.r.t x, we get

$$r'(x) = u'[v(x)] \cdot v'(x)$$

At $x = 3$,

$$r'(3) = u'[v(3)] \cdot v'(3) = u'[1] \cdot v'(3) \quad [\because v(3) = 1]$$

$$= 2 \times (-2) \quad [\because v'(3) = -2, u'(1) = 2]$$

$$= -4$$

Or

(ii) Let r be the radius, A be the area and P be the perimeter.

Then, we have $\frac{dA}{dt} = \text{constant} = k$ (say)

$$\Rightarrow \frac{d}{dt}(\pi r^2) = k \quad [\because A = \pi r^2]$$

$$\Rightarrow 2\pi r \frac{dr}{dt} = k \Rightarrow \frac{dr}{dt} = \frac{k}{2\pi r} \quad \ldots\text{(i)}$$

Now, $\frac{dP}{dt} = \frac{d}{dt}(2\pi r) = 2\pi \frac{dr}{dt} \quad [\therefore P = 2\pi r]$

$$= 2\pi \times \frac{k}{2\pi r} = \frac{k}{r} \quad \text{[from Eq. (i)]}$$

Hence, $\frac{dP}{dt} \propto \frac{1}{r}$ **Hence proved.**

3. Given, $y - x\frac{dy}{dx} = a\left(y^2 + \frac{dy}{dx}\right)$

$$\Rightarrow y - ay^2 = (x + a)\frac{dy}{dx} \Rightarrow \frac{dy}{y - ay^2} = \frac{dx}{x + a}$$

$$\Rightarrow \left(\frac{1}{y} + \frac{a}{1 - ay}\right)dy = \frac{dx}{x + a}$$

$$\left[\because \frac{1}{y - ay^2} = \frac{1}{y(1 - ay)} = \frac{1}{y} + \frac{a}{1 - ay}\right]$$

On integrating both sides, we get

$$\int\left(\frac{1}{y} + \frac{a}{1 - ay}\right)dy = \int \frac{dx}{x + a}$$

$$\Rightarrow \log|y| + a\frac{\log|1 - ay|}{-a} = \log|x + a| + C$$

$$\Rightarrow \log|y| - \log|1 - ay| - \log|x + a| = C$$

$$\Rightarrow \log|y| - (\log|1 - ay| + \log|x + a|) = C$$

$$\Rightarrow \log|y| - \log|(1 - ay)(x + a)| = C$$

$$\Rightarrow \log\left|\frac{y}{(1 - ay)(x + a)}\right| = C$$

$$\Rightarrow \left|\frac{y}{(1 - ay)(x + a)}\right| = e^C$$

$$\Rightarrow y = \pm e^C(1 - ay)(x + a)$$

$$\Rightarrow y = A(1 - ay)(x + a)$$

where, $A = \pm e^C$ is an arbitrary constant.

Common Mistake

$\int \frac{1}{1 - ay}dy \neq \log|1 - ay|$ instead of $\int \frac{1}{1 - ay}dy = \frac{\log|1 - ay|}{(-a)}$

4. We have, $2\tan^{-1}\frac{1}{2} + \tan^{-1}\frac{1}{7} = \tan^{-1}\frac{31}{17}$

$$\text{LHS} = 2\tan^{-1}\frac{1}{2} + \tan^{-1}\frac{1}{7}$$

$$= \tan^{-1}\left[\frac{2 \times \frac{1}{2}}{1 - \left(\frac{1}{2}\right)^2}\right] + \tan^{-1}\frac{1}{7}$$

$$\left[\because 2\tan^{-1}x = \tan^{-1}\left(\frac{2x}{1 - x^2}\right), \text{if } -1 < x < 1\right]$$

$$= \tan^{-1}\left(\frac{1}{1 - \frac{1}{4}}\right) + \tan^{-1}\frac{1}{7}$$

$$= \tan^{-1}\left(\frac{1}{\frac{4 - 1}{4}}\right) + \tan^{-1}\frac{1}{7}$$

$$= \tan^{-1}\frac{4}{3} + \tan^{-1}\frac{1}{7} = \tan^{-1}\left(\frac{\frac{4}{3} + \frac{1}{7}}{1 - \frac{4}{3} \times \frac{1}{7}}\right)$$

$$\left[\because \tan^{-1}x + \tan^{-1}y = \tan^{-1}\left(\frac{x + y}{1 - xy}\right), \text{if } xy < 1\right]$$

$$= \tan^{-1}\left(\frac{\frac{28 + 3}{21}}{\frac{21 - 4}{21}}\right) = \tan^{-1}\left(\frac{31}{17}\right) = \text{RHS}$$

Hence proved.

5. (i) We have, $f(x)=4x^3-18x^2+27x-7$

On differentiating both sides w.r.t. x, we get

$$f'(x)=12x^2-36x+27$$
$$\Rightarrow \quad f'(x)=3(4x^2-12x+9)$$
$$\Rightarrow \quad f'(x)=3(2x-3)^2$$

$\Rightarrow$ For any $x\in R, (2x-3)^2>0$

Since, a perfect square number cannot be negative.

$\therefore f'(x)>0$

Hence, function $f(x)$ is an increasing function on R.

Or

(ii) We have,

$f(x)=x^3-6x^2+9x+15$

On differentiating w.r.t x, we get

$f'(x)=3x^2-12x+9$

For increasing, $f'(x)\geq 0$

$$\Rightarrow \quad 3x^2-12x+9=0$$
$$\Rightarrow \quad x^2-4x+3=0$$
$$\Rightarrow \quad (x-3)(x-1)=0$$
$$\Rightarrow \quad x=1,3$$

Now, signs of $f'(x)$

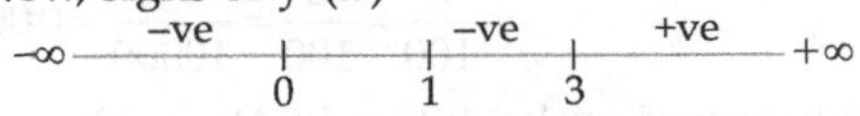

Hence, the function is increasing on $(-\infty,1)\cup(3,\infty)$.

6. Let $A=\begin{bmatrix}0 & a & 3\\ 2 & b & -1\\ c & 1 & 0\end{bmatrix}$

Since, A is a skew-symmetric matrix.

$$\therefore \quad A'=-A$$

$$\Rightarrow \quad \begin{bmatrix}0 & a & 3\\ 2 & b & -1\\ c & 1 & 0\end{bmatrix}'=-\begin{bmatrix}0 & a & 3\\ 2 & b & -1\\ c & 1 & 0\end{bmatrix}$$

$$\Rightarrow \quad \begin{bmatrix}0 & 2 & c\\ a & b & 1\\ 3 & -1 & 0\end{bmatrix}=\begin{bmatrix}0 & -a & -3\\ -2 & -b & 1\\ -c & -1 & 0\end{bmatrix}$$

Using definition of equality of two matrices, we get

$$a=-2,\ c=-3 \text{ and } b=-b$$
$$\Rightarrow \quad a=-2,\ b=0 \text{ and } c=-3$$

7. Let $I=\int_2^5 [|x-2|+|x-3|+|x-5|]\,dx$

Here, $f(x)=|x-2|+|x-3|+|x-5|$.

We describe the function in different intervals as

$$f(x)=\begin{cases}x-2-x+3-x+5, & 2\leq x<3\\ x-2+x-3-x+5, & 3\leq x<5\end{cases}$$

$$\Rightarrow \quad f(x)=\begin{cases}6-x, & 2\leq x<3\\ x, & 3\leq x<5\end{cases}$$

$$\therefore \quad I=\int_2^5 f(x)dx=\int_2^3 f(x)dx+\int_3^5 f(x)dx$$

$$=\int_2^3(6-x)dx+\int_3^5 x\,dx=\left(6x-\frac{x^2}{2}\right)_2^3+\left(\frac{x^2}{2}\right)_3^5$$

$$=\left(18-\frac{9}{2}-12+2+\frac{25}{2}-\frac{9}{2}\right)=\frac{23}{2}$$

8. Given, $A=\begin{bmatrix}-1 & -2 & -2\\ 2 & 1 & -2\\ 2 & -2 & 1\end{bmatrix}$

Let A_{ij} be the cofactor of an element a_{ij} of matrix A.

Then, cofactors of elements of matrix A are

$$A_{11}=(-1)^{1+1}\begin{vmatrix}1 & -2\\ 2 & 1\end{vmatrix}=(1-4)=-3$$

$$A_{12}=(-1)^{1+2}\begin{vmatrix}2 & -2\\ 2 & 1\end{vmatrix}=-(2+4)=-6$$

$$A_{13}=(-1)^{1+3}\begin{vmatrix}2 & 1\\ 2 & -2\end{vmatrix}=(-4-2)=-6$$

$$A_{21}=(-1)^{2+1}\begin{vmatrix}-2 & -2\\ -2 & 1\end{vmatrix}=-(-2-4)=6$$

$$A_{22}=(-1)^{2+2}\begin{vmatrix}-1 & -2\\ 2 & 1\end{vmatrix}=(-1+4)=3$$

$$A_{23}=(-1)^{2+3}\begin{vmatrix}-1 & -2\\ 2 & -2\end{vmatrix}=-(2+4)=-6$$

$$A_{31}=(-1)^{3+1}\begin{vmatrix}-2 & -2\\ 1 & -2\end{vmatrix}=(4+2)=6$$

$$A_{32}=(-1)^{3+2}\begin{vmatrix}-1 & -2\\ 2 & -2\end{vmatrix}=-(2+4)=-6$$

$$A_{33}=(-1)^{3+3}\begin{vmatrix}-1 & -2\\ 2 & 1\end{vmatrix}=(-1+4)=3$$

Clearly, the adjoint of the matrix A is given by

$$\text{adj } A=\begin{bmatrix}A_{11} & A_{21} & A_{31}\\ A_{12} & A_{22} & A_{32}\\ A_{13} & A_{23} & A_{33}\end{bmatrix}=\begin{bmatrix}-3 & 6 & 6\\ -6 & 3 & -6\\ -6 & -6 & 3\end{bmatrix}$$

Now, $|A|=\begin{vmatrix}-1 & -2 & -2\\ 2 & 1 & -2\\ 2 & -2 & 1\end{vmatrix}$

$$=-1(1-4)+2(2+4)-2(-4-2)$$
$$=-1(-3)+2(6)-2(-6)=3+12+12=27$$

and $A\cdot(\text{adj } A)=\begin{bmatrix}-1 & -2 & -2\\ 2 & 1 & -2\\ 2 & -2 & 1\end{bmatrix}\begin{bmatrix}-3 & 6 & 6\\ -6 & 3 & -6\\ -6 & -6 & 3\end{bmatrix}$

$$=\begin{bmatrix}3+12+12 & -6-6+12 & -6+12-6\\ -6-6+12 & 12+3+12 & 12-6-6\\ -6+12-6 & 12-6-6 & 12+12+3\end{bmatrix}$$

$$=\begin{bmatrix}27 & 0 & 0\\ 0 & 27 & 0\\ 0 & 0 & 27\end{bmatrix}=27\begin{bmatrix}1 & 0 & 0\\ 0 & 1 & 0\\ 0 & 0 & 1\end{bmatrix}$$

$=27I_3=|A|I_3$ **Hence proved.**

9. (i) Total number of questions,

$n(S) = 300 + 200 + 500 + 400 = 1400$

Let E be the event that question is easy and F be the event that question is a multiple choice question.

Then, $n(E) = 500 + 300 = 800$

$\therefore P(E) = \dfrac{\text{Number of easy questions}}{\text{Total number of questions}}$

$= \dfrac{n(E)}{n(S)} = \dfrac{800}{1400} = \dfrac{4}{7}$

Also, $n(F) = 500 + 400 = 900$

$\therefore P(F) = \dfrac{\text{Number of multiple choice questions}}{\text{Total number of questions}}$

$= \dfrac{n(F)}{n(S)} = \dfrac{900}{1400} = \dfrac{9}{14}$

and $P(E \cap F)$

$= \dfrac{\text{Total number of easy multiple choice questions}}{\text{Total number of questions}}$

$= \dfrac{500}{1400} = \dfrac{5}{14}$

$\therefore P\left(\dfrac{E}{F}\right) = \dfrac{P(E \cap F)}{P(F)} = \dfrac{5/14}{9/14} = \dfrac{5}{9}$

Hence, required probability is $\dfrac{5}{9}$.

Or

(ii) Let E_1 = Event of selecting Box I

and E_2 = Event of selecting Box II.

Let A = Event of drawing an orange ball.

Now, $P(E_1) = \dfrac{1}{2}$ and $P(E_2) = \dfrac{1}{2}$

$P(A/E_1)$ = Probability of selecting an orange ball from Box I

$= \dfrac{4}{8} = \dfrac{1}{2}$

[$\because$ total balls = 8 and orange balls = 4]

and $P(A/E_2)$ = Probability of selecting an orange ball from Box II

$= \dfrac{3}{8}$

[$\because$ total balls = 8 and orange balls = 3]

Now, $P(E_1/A)$ = Probability that drawn ball is from the first box

$= \dfrac{P(E_1) \cdot P(A/E_1)}{P(E_1) \cdot P(A/E_1) + P(E_2) \cdot P(A/E_2)}$

$= \dfrac{\frac{1}{2} \times \frac{1}{2}}{\left(\frac{1}{2} \times \frac{1}{2}\right) + \left(\frac{1}{2} \times \frac{3}{8}\right)} = \dfrac{\frac{1}{4}}{\frac{1}{4} + \frac{3}{16}}$

$= \dfrac{1/4}{\frac{4+3}{16}} = \dfrac{1}{4} \times \dfrac{16}{7} = \dfrac{4}{7}$

Hence, the probability that the ball is drawn from the first box is $\dfrac{4}{7}$.

10. (i) Let

A : The event that question has some error

E_1 : The event that question is solved by Ravi

E_2 : The event that question is solved by Mohit

E_3 : The event that question is solved by Sonia

Then, we have

$P(E_1) = \dfrac{30}{100}, \; P(E_2) = \dfrac{25}{100}, \; P(E_3) = \dfrac{45}{100}$

$P(A/E_1) = \dfrac{1}{100}, \; P(A/E_2) = \dfrac{1.2}{100}, \; P(A/E_3) = \dfrac{2}{100}$

(a) Required probability $= P(A/E_3) = \dfrac{2}{100} = 0.02$

(b) Required probability

$= P(E_3 \cap A) = P(A \cap E_3)$

$= P(E_3)\, P(A/E_3)$

$= \dfrac{45}{100} \times \dfrac{2}{100} = \dfrac{90}{10000} = 0.009$

(c) Required probability $= P(A)$

$= \sum_{i=1}^{3} P(E_i)\, P(A/E_i)$

$= P(E_1)\, P(A/E_1) + P(E_2) P(A/E_2) + P(E_3)\, P(A/E_3)$

$= \dfrac{30}{100} \times \dfrac{1}{100} + \dfrac{25}{100} \times \dfrac{1.2}{100} + \dfrac{45}{100} \times \dfrac{2}{100}$

$= 0.003 + 0.003 + 0.009 = 0.015$

(d) Required probability $= P(\bar{E_1}/A)$

$= 1 - P(E_1/A)$

$= 1 - \left[\dfrac{P(E_1) P(A/E_1)}{P(E_1) P(A/E_1) + P(E_2) P(A/E_2) + P(E_3) P(A/E_3)}\right]$

$= 1 - \left[\dfrac{\frac{30}{100} \times \frac{1}{100}}{\frac{30}{100} \times \frac{1}{100} + \frac{25}{100} \times \frac{1.2}{100} + \frac{45}{100} \times \frac{2}{100}}\right]$

$= 1 - \dfrac{0.003}{0.015} = 1 - 0.2 = 0.8$

Or

(ii) Let E_1, E_2, E_3 and E_4 be the events that the doctor comes by train, bus, scooter and other means of transport, respectively. It is given that

$P(E_1) = \dfrac{3}{10}, \; P(E_2) = \dfrac{1}{5}, \; P(E_3) = \dfrac{1}{10}, \; P(E_4) = \dfrac{2}{5}$

Let A denote the event that the doctor visits the patient late. It is given that

$$P\left(\frac{A}{E_1}\right)=\frac{1}{4},\ P\left(\frac{A}{E_2}\right)=\frac{1}{3},\ P\left(\frac{A}{E_3}\right)=\frac{1}{12},\ P\left(\frac{A}{E_4}\right)=0$$

(a) Required probability $= P\left(\frac{A}{E_2}\right)=\frac{1}{3}$

(b) Required probability $= P(E_1 \cap A) = P(A \cap E_1)$

$$= P(E_1)\,P\left(\frac{A}{E_1}\right)$$

$$= \frac{3}{10}\times\frac{1}{4}=\frac{3}{40}$$

(c) Required probability $= P(A)=\sum_{i=1}^{4} P(E_i)\,P\left(\frac{A}{E_i}\right)$

$$= P(E_1)\,P\left(\frac{A}{E_1}\right)+P(E_2)\,P\left(\frac{A}{E_2}\right)+P(E_3)\,P\left(\frac{A}{E_3}\right)+P(E_4)\,P(A/E_4)$$

$$=\frac{3}{10}\times\frac{1}{4}+\frac{1}{5}\times\frac{1}{3}+\frac{1}{10}\times\frac{1}{12}+\frac{2}{5}\times 0$$

$$=\frac{3}{40}+\frac{1}{15}+\frac{1}{120}=\frac{9+8+1}{120}=\frac{18}{120}=\frac{3}{20}$$

11. (i) According to the given information, we get

$$x+y+z=6,\ y+3z=11$$

and $\quad x+z=2y \Rightarrow x-2y+z=0$

In matrix form, this system of equations can be written as

$$AX=B \qquad \ldots\text{(i)}$$

where, $A=\begin{bmatrix}1&1&1\\0&1&3\\1&-2&1\end{bmatrix}$, $X=\begin{bmatrix}x\\y\\z\end{bmatrix}$ and $B=\begin{bmatrix}6\\11\\0\end{bmatrix}$

(ii) Here, $|A|=\begin{vmatrix}1&1&1\\0&1&3\\1&-2&1\end{vmatrix}=1(1+6)-1(0-3)+1(0-1)$

[expanding along R_1]

$$=7+3-1=9\neq 0$$

Since, $|A|\neq 0$, so the inverse of A exists.

Now, cofactors corresponding to each element of $|A|$ are

$$C_{11}=(-1)^{1+1}\begin{vmatrix}1&3\\-2&1\end{vmatrix}=1+6=7$$

$$C_{12}=(-1)^{1+2}\begin{vmatrix}0&3\\1&1\end{vmatrix}=-(0-3)=3$$

$$C_{13}=(-1)^{1+3}\begin{vmatrix}0&1\\1&-2\end{vmatrix}=0-1=-1$$

$$C_{21}=(-1)^{2+1}\begin{vmatrix}1&1\\-2&1\end{vmatrix}=-(1+2)=-3$$

$$C_{22}=(-1)^{2+2}\begin{vmatrix}1&1\\1&1\end{vmatrix}=0$$

$$C_{23}=(-1)^{2+3}\begin{vmatrix}1&1\\1&-2\end{vmatrix}=-(-2-1)=3$$

$$C_{31}=(-1)^{3+1}\begin{vmatrix}1&1\\1&3\end{vmatrix}=3-1=2$$

$$C_{32}=(-1)^{3+2}\begin{vmatrix}1&1\\0&3\end{vmatrix}=-(3-0)=-3$$

$$C_{33}=(-1)^{3+3}\begin{vmatrix}1&1\\0&1\end{vmatrix}=1-0=1$$

Then, $\text{adj}(A)=\begin{bmatrix}7&3&-1\\-3&0&3\\2&-3&1\end{bmatrix}^T=\begin{bmatrix}7&-3&2\\3&0&-3\\-1&3&1\end{bmatrix}$

Hence, $A^{-1}=\frac{1}{|A|}\text{adj}(A)=\frac{1}{9}\begin{bmatrix}7&-3&2\\3&0&-3\\-1&3&1\end{bmatrix}$

(iii) Now, the solution of Eq. (i) is given by

$$X=A^{-1}B \qquad \ldots\text{(ii)}$$

On putting the values of A^{-1} and B in RHS of Eq. (ii), we get

$$X=\frac{1}{9}\begin{bmatrix}7&-3&2\\3&0&-3\\-1&3&1\end{bmatrix}\begin{bmatrix}6\\11\\0\end{bmatrix}$$

$$=\frac{1}{9}\begin{bmatrix}7\times6-3\times11+2\times0\\3\times6+0\times11-3\times0\\-1\times6+3\times11+1\times0\end{bmatrix}$$

$$=\frac{1}{9}\begin{bmatrix}42-33+0\\18+0-0\\-6+33+0\end{bmatrix}=\frac{1}{9}\begin{bmatrix}9\\18\\27\end{bmatrix}=\begin{bmatrix}9/9\\18/9\\27/9\end{bmatrix}=\begin{bmatrix}1\\2\\3\end{bmatrix}$$

$$\Rightarrow \begin{bmatrix}x\\y\\z\end{bmatrix}=\begin{bmatrix}1\\2\\3\end{bmatrix}$$

On comparing both sides, we get

$$x=1,\ y=2 \text{ and } z=3$$

12. (i) Let $I=\int\frac{\sin^{-1}\sqrt{x}-\cos^{-1}\sqrt{x}}{\sin^{-1}\sqrt{x}+\cos^{-1}\sqrt{x}}\,dx$

We know that $\sin^{-1}\sqrt{x}+\cos^{-1}\sqrt{x}=\pi/2$

$$\Rightarrow \cos^{-1}\sqrt{x}=\frac{\pi}{2}-\sin^{-1}\sqrt{x}$$

$$\therefore I=\int\frac{\sin^{-1}\sqrt{x}-\left(\frac{\pi}{2}-\sin^{-1}\sqrt{x}\right)}{\pi/2}\,dx$$

$$=\int\frac{2\sin^{-1}\sqrt{x}-\frac{\pi}{2}}{\frac{\pi}{2}}\,dx=\frac{2}{\pi}\int\left(2\sin^{-1}\sqrt{x}-\frac{\pi}{2}\right)dx$$

$$=\frac{4}{\pi}\int\sin^{-1}\sqrt{x}\,dx-\int 1dx=\frac{4}{\pi}\int\sin^{-1}\sqrt{x}\,dx-x$$

$$\Rightarrow I=\frac{4}{\pi}I_1-x \qquad \ldots\text{(i) } \mathbf{(1)}$$

where $I_1=\int\sin^{-1}\sqrt{x}\,dx$

Put $\sqrt{x}=t \Rightarrow x=t^2$ and $dx=2t\,dt$

$\therefore\quad I_1=\int \sin^{-1} t\, 2t\,dt = 2\int \sin^{-1} t \cdot t\,dt$

$$=2\left[\sin^{-1} t\int t\,dt-\int\left\{\frac{d}{dt}(\sin^{-1} t)\int t\,dt\right\}dt\right]$$

[using integration by parts]

$$=2\left[\sin^{-1} t\cdot\frac{t^2}{2}-\int\frac{1}{\sqrt{1-t^2}}\cdot\frac{t^2}{2}dt\right] \quad (1)$$

$$=t^2\sin^{-1} t+\int\frac{(1-t^2)-1}{\sqrt{1-t^2}}dt$$

$$=t^2\sin^{-1} t+\int\sqrt{1-t^2}\,dt-\int\frac{1}{\sqrt{1-t^2}}dt \quad (1)$$

$$=t^2\sin^{-1} t+\frac{t\sqrt{1-t^2}}{2}+\frac{1}{2}\sin^{-1} t-\sin^{-1} t+C_1$$

$$\left[\because \int\sqrt{a^2-x^2}\,dx=\frac{x}{2}\sqrt{a^2-x^2}+\frac{a^2}{2}\sin^{-1}\frac{x}{a}+C \text{ and } \int\frac{1\,dx}{\sqrt{1-x^2}}=\sin^{-1} x+C\right]$$

$$=\left(t^2-\frac{1}{2}\right)\sin^{-1} t+\frac{1}{2}t\sqrt{1-t^2}+C_1 \quad (1)$$

$$=\frac{1}{2}[(2x-1)\sin^{-1}\sqrt{x}+\sqrt{x}\sqrt{1-x}]+C_1$$

$[\because t=\sqrt{x}]$

$$\Rightarrow I_1=\frac{1}{2}[(2x-1)\sin^{-1}\sqrt{x}+\sqrt{x-x^2}]+C_1 \quad (1)$$

On putting the value of I_1 in Eq. (i), we get

$$I=\frac{2}{\pi}[(2x-1)\sin^{-1}\sqrt{x}+\sqrt{x-x^2}]-x+C,$$

where $C=\frac{4}{\pi}C_1$ (1)

Or

(ii) Let $I=\int\frac{1}{x^4+1}dx=\frac{1}{2}\int\frac{2}{1+x^4}dx$

$$=\frac{1}{2}\int\frac{(x^2+1)-(x^2-1)}{x^4+1}dx$$

$$=\frac{1}{2}\int\frac{x^2+1}{x^4+1}dx-\frac{1}{2}\int\frac{x^2-1}{x^4+1}dx$$

$\Rightarrow I=\frac{1}{2}I_1-\frac{1}{2}I_2$ (say) ...(i)

Where, $I_1=\int\frac{x^2+1}{x^4+1}dx$ and $I_2=\int\frac{x^2-1}{x^4+1}dx$

Now, $I_1=\int\frac{x^2+1}{x^4+1}dx=\int\frac{x^2\left(1+\frac{1}{x^2}\right)}{x^2\left(x^2+\frac{1}{x^2}\right)}dx$

$$=\int\frac{\left(1+\frac{1}{x^2}\right)}{x^2+\frac{1}{x^2}}dx$$

$$=\int\frac{1+\frac{1}{x^2}}{x^2+\frac{1}{x^2}+2-2}dx=\int\frac{1+\frac{1}{x^2}}{\left(x-\frac{1}{x}\right)^2+2}dx$$

Put $x-\frac{1}{x}=t\Rightarrow\left(1+\frac{1}{x^2}\right)dx=dt$

Then, $I_1=\int\frac{dt}{t^2+(\sqrt{2})^2}=\frac{1}{\sqrt{2}}\tan^{-1}\left(\frac{t}{\sqrt{2}}\right)+C_1$

$$\left[\because\int\frac{dx}{x^2+a^2}=\frac{1}{a}\tan^{-1}\left(\frac{x}{a}\right)+C\right]$$

$$=\frac{1}{\sqrt{2}}\tan^{-1}\left(\frac{x^2-1}{\sqrt{2}x}\right)+C_1 \quad \text{...(ii)}$$

$$\left[\because t=\frac{x^2-1}{x}\right]$$

and $I_2=\int\frac{x^2-1}{x^4+1}dx=\int\frac{x^2\left(1-\frac{1}{x^2}\right)}{x^2\left(x^2+\frac{1}{x^2}\right)}dx$

$$=\int\frac{\left(1-\frac{1}{x^2}\right)}{x^2+\frac{1}{x^2}+2x^2}dx=\int\frac{\left(1-\frac{1}{x^2}\right)}{\left(x+\frac{1}{x}\right)^2-2}dx$$

Put $x+\frac{1}{x}=t\Rightarrow\left(1-\frac{1}{x^2}\right)dx=dt$

Then, $I_2=\int\frac{dt}{t^2-(\sqrt{2})^2}$

$$=\frac{1}{2\sqrt{2}}\log\left|\frac{t-\sqrt{2}}{t+\sqrt{2}}\right|+C_2$$

$$\left[\because\int\frac{dx}{x^2-a^2}=\frac{1}{2a}\log\left|\frac{x-a}{x+a}\right|+C\right]$$

$$=\frac{1}{2\sqrt{2}}\log\left|\frac{x^2+1-\sqrt{2}x}{x^2+1+\sqrt{2}x}\right|+C_2 \quad \text{...(ii)}$$

$$\left[\because t=\frac{x^2+1}{x}\right]$$

On putting the values I_1 and I_2 from Eqs. (ii) and (iii), in Eq. (i), we get

$$I=\frac{1}{2}\left[\frac{1}{\sqrt{2}}\tan^{-1}\left(\frac{x^2-1}{\sqrt{2}x}\right)+C_1\right]-\frac{1}{2}\left[\frac{1}{2\sqrt{2}}\log\left|\frac{x^2+1-\sqrt{2}x}{x^2+1+\sqrt{2}x}\right|+C_2\right]$$

$$\Rightarrow I=\frac{1}{2\sqrt{2}}\tan^{-1}\left(\frac{x^2-1}{\sqrt{2}x}\right)-\frac{1}{4\sqrt{2}}\log\left|\frac{x^2+1-\sqrt{2}x}{x^2+1+\sqrt{2}x}\right|+C,$$

where $C=\frac{1}{2}C_1-\frac{1}{2}C_2$

13. (i) Let $I=\int_0^{\pi}\frac{x\tan x}{\sec x\cdot\operatorname{cosec} x}\,dx$ ...(i)

Using the property $\int_0^a f(x)\,dx=\int_0^a f(a-x)\,dx$, we get

$$I=\int_0^{\pi}\frac{(\pi-x)\tan(\pi-x)}{\sec(\pi-x)\operatorname{cosec}(\pi-x)}\,dx$$

$$\Rightarrow \quad I=\int_0^{\pi}\frac{(\pi-x)(-\tan x)}{-\sec x\operatorname{cosec} x}\,dx$$

$[\because \tan(\pi-\theta)=-\tan\theta,\ \sec(\pi-\theta)=-\sec\theta$ and $\operatorname{cosec}(\pi-\theta)=\operatorname{cosec}\theta]$

$$\Rightarrow \quad I=\int_0^{\pi}\frac{(\pi-x)\tan x}{\sec x\operatorname{cosec} x}\,dx \quad ...(ii)$$

On adding Eqs. (i) and (ii), we get

$$2I=\int_0^{\pi}\frac{\pi\tan x}{\sec x\operatorname{cosec} x}\,dx$$

$$\Rightarrow \quad I=\frac{\pi}{2}\int_0^{\pi}\frac{\sin^2 x(\cos x)}{(\cos x)}\,dx=\frac{\pi}{2}\int_0^{\pi}\sin^2 x\,dx$$

$$=\frac{\pi}{2}\int_0^{\pi}\left(\frac{1-\cos 2x}{2}\right)dx \quad [\because \cos 2\theta=1-2\sin^2\theta]$$

$$=\frac{\pi}{4}\left[x-\frac{\sin 2x}{2}\right]_0^{\pi}$$

$$\Rightarrow \quad I=\frac{\pi}{4}\left[\pi-\frac{\sin 2\pi}{2}-0+\frac{\sin 0}{2}\right]$$

$$\Rightarrow \quad I=\frac{\pi}{4}[\pi-0]$$

$$\Rightarrow \quad I=\frac{\pi^2}{4}$$

Or

(ii) Let $I=\int\frac{x^2}{(x^2+1)(2x^2+1)}\,dx$

On putting $x^2=y$ (only for partial fractions), then

$$\frac{x^2}{(x^2+1)(2x^2+1)}=\frac{y}{(y+1)(2y+1)}$$

$$=\frac{A}{y+1}+\frac{B}{2y+1} \quad ...(i)$$

$$\Rightarrow \quad y=A(2y+1)+B(y+1)$$

$$\Rightarrow \quad y=y(2A+B)+A+B$$

On equating the coefficients of y and constant term from both sides, we get

$$2A+B=1$$

and $\quad A+B=0$

On solving, we get

$$A=1 \text{ and } B=-1$$

On substituting the values of A and B in Eq. (i), we get

$$\frac{x^2}{(x^2+1)(2x^2+1)}=\frac{1}{y+1}-\frac{1}{(2y+1)}$$

$$=\frac{1}{x^2+1}-\frac{1}{2x^2+1}$$

$$\therefore \quad I=\int\frac{x^2}{(x^2+1)(2x^2+1)}\,dx=\int\frac{dx}{x^2+1}-\int\frac{dx}{2x^2+1}$$

$$=\int\frac{dx}{x^2+1^2}-\frac{1}{2}\int\frac{dx}{x^2+\left(\frac{1}{\sqrt{2}}\right)^2}$$

$$=\tan^{-1}x-\frac{1}{2}\cdot\sqrt{2}\tan^{-1}\left(\frac{x}{1/\sqrt{2}}\right)+C$$

$$=\tan^{-1}x-\frac{1}{\sqrt{2}}\tan^{-1}(\sqrt{2}x)+C$$

14. Let P be a point on the hypotenuse AC of right angled ΔABC, such that $PL\perp AB$ and $PL=a$ and $PM\perp BC$ and $PM=b$.

Let $\quad \angle APL=\angle ACB=\theta$ [say]

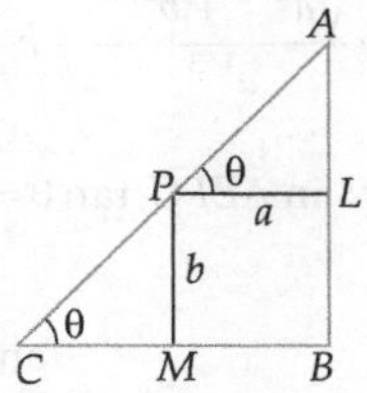

In ΔALP, $\cos\theta=\frac{PL}{AP}=\frac{a}{AP}\Rightarrow AP=a\sec\theta$

In ΔPMC, $\sin\theta=\frac{PM}{PC}=\frac{b}{PC}$

$\Rightarrow PC=b\operatorname{cosec}\theta$

Let l be the length of the hypotenuse, then

$$l=AP+PC$$

$$\Rightarrow \quad l=a\sec\theta+b\operatorname{cosec}\theta,\ 0<\theta<\frac{\pi}{2}$$

On differentiating both sides w.r.t. θ, we get

$$\frac{dl}{d\theta}=a\sec\theta\tan\theta-b\operatorname{cosec}\theta\cot\theta \quad ...(i)$$

For maxima or minima, put $\frac{dl}{d\theta}=0$ (1)

$\Rightarrow a\sec\theta\tan\theta=b\operatorname{cosec}\theta\cot\theta$

$$\Rightarrow \quad \frac{a\sin\theta}{\cos^2\theta}=\frac{b\cos\theta}{\sin^2\theta}\Rightarrow\frac{\sin^3\theta}{\cos^3\theta}=\frac{b}{a}$$

$$\Rightarrow \quad \tan\theta=\left(\frac{b}{a}\right)^{1/3}$$ (1)

Again, on differentiating both sides of Eq. (i) w.r.t. θ, we get

$$\frac{d^2l}{d\theta^2}=a(\sec\theta\times\sec^2\theta+\tan\theta\times\sec\theta\tan\theta)$$
$$-b[\operatorname{cosec}\theta(-\operatorname{cosec}^2\theta)+\cot\theta(-\operatorname{cosec}\theta\cot\theta)]$$

$$=a\sec\theta(\sec^2\theta+\tan^2\theta)$$
$$+b\operatorname{cosec}\theta(\operatorname{cosec}^2\theta+\cot^2\theta)$$

For $0<\theta<\frac{\pi}{2}$, all trigonometric ratios are positive. (1)
Also, $a>0$ and $b>0$.

$\therefore \quad \frac{d^2 l}{d\theta^2}$ is positive.

$\Rightarrow l$ is least when $\tan\theta=\left(\frac{b}{a}\right)^{\frac{1}{3}}$

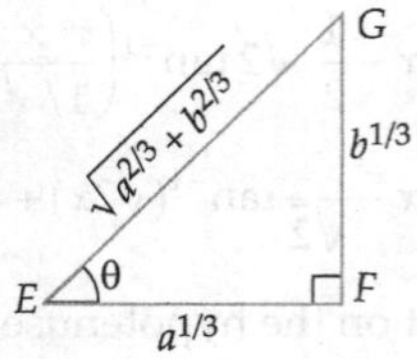

$\therefore$ Least value of,

$$l=a\sec\theta+b\,\text{cosec}\,\theta$$
$$=a\frac{\sqrt{a^{2/3}+b^{2/3}}}{a^{1/3}}+b\frac{\sqrt{a^{2/3}+b^{2/3}}}{b^{1/3}}$$

$\left[\because \text{ in } \Delta EFG, \tan\theta=\frac{b^{1/3}}{a^{1/3}}, \sec\theta=\frac{\sqrt{a^{2/3}+b^{2/3}}}{a^{1/3}} \text{ and cosec}\,\theta=\frac{\sqrt{a^{2/3}+b^{2/3}}}{b^{1/3}}\right]$

$$=\sqrt{a^{2/3}+b^{2/3}}(a^{2/3}+b^{2/3})$$
$$=(a^{2/3}+b^{2/3})^{3/2}$$ **Hence proved.**

15. (i) (a) By triangle law of vector addition, we get

$$\overrightarrow{PQ}+\overrightarrow{QR}=\overrightarrow{PR} \quad \ldots(i)$$

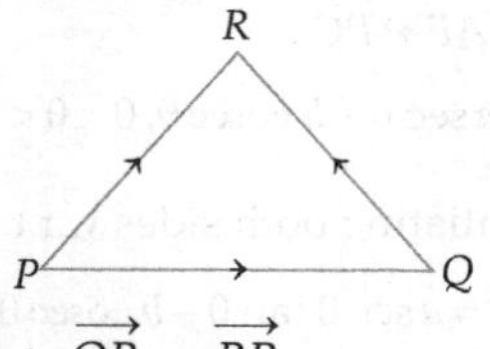

Now, $\overrightarrow{PQ}+\overrightarrow{QR}-\overrightarrow{RP}$

$=\overrightarrow{PR}-\overrightarrow{RP}$ [using Eq. (i)]

$=\overrightarrow{PR}+\overrightarrow{PR}$ $[\because \overrightarrow{PR}=-\overrightarrow{RP}]$

$=2\overrightarrow{PR}$

(ii) (c) **Statement I** We have, $\vec{r}\cdot(\hat{i}+\hat{j}-\hat{k})=2$

$\Rightarrow (x\hat{i}+y\hat{j}+z\hat{k})\cdot(\hat{i}+\hat{j}-\hat{k})=2$

$\Rightarrow \quad x+y-z=2,$

which is the required form of plane.

Statement II We have, $\vec{r}\cdot(3\hat{i}-5\hat{j}+3\hat{k})=3$

$\Rightarrow (x\hat{i}+y\hat{j}+z\hat{k})\cdot(3\hat{i}-5\hat{j}+3\hat{k})=3$

$\Rightarrow 3x-5y+3z=3$

which is the required form of plane.

Hence, both Statements I and II are correct.

(iii) Given, line $\frac{x-2}{6}=\frac{y-1}{\lambda}=\frac{z+5}{-4}$ is perpendicular to plane $3x-y-2z=7$.

Therefore, DR's of the line are proportional to the direction ratias of normal to the plane.

$\therefore \quad \frac{6}{3}=\frac{\lambda}{-1}=\frac{-4}{-2}$

$\Rightarrow \quad 2=-\lambda=2 \Rightarrow \; 2=-\lambda$

$\Rightarrow \quad \lambda=-2$

Common Mistake

Make sure that equation of line should be in proper symmetrical form.

(iv) Let a be the side of the cube and $O=(0,0,0)$, $D=(a,a,a)$, $B=(0,a,0)$, $G=(a,0,a)$.

$\because$ The equation of OD is

$$\frac{x}{a}=\frac{y}{a}=\frac{z}{a}$$

and the equation of BG is

$$\frac{x}{a}=\frac{y-a}{-a}=\frac{z}{a}$$

Let the angle between the diagonals OD and BG is θ.

Then, $\cos\theta=\frac{a^2-a^2+a^2}{\sqrt{3a^2}\sqrt{3a^2}}=\frac{a^2}{3a^2}$

$\left[\because \cos\theta=\frac{|a_1a_2+b_1b_2+c_1c_2|}{\sqrt{a_1^2+b_1^2+c_1^2}\sqrt{a_2^2+b_2^2+c_2^2}}\right]$

$\Rightarrow \quad \cos\theta=\frac{1}{3}$

$\Rightarrow \quad \theta=\cos^{-1}\left(\frac{1}{3}\right)$

Hence, the angle between the diagonals OD and BG is $\cos^{-1}\left(\frac{1}{3}\right)$.

(v) Given, $\hat{a}$ is a unit vector. Then, $|\hat{a}|=1$.

Now, we have $\quad (\vec{x}-\hat{a})\cdot(\vec{x}+\hat{a})=15$

$\Rightarrow \quad \vec{x}\cdot\vec{x}-\hat{a}\cdot\vec{x}+\vec{x}\cdot\hat{a}-\hat{a}\cdot\hat{a}=15$

$\Rightarrow \quad \vec{x}\cdot\vec{x}-\hat{a}\cdot\vec{x}+\hat{a}\cdot\vec{x}-\hat{a}\cdot\hat{a}=15$

[$\because$ scalar product is commutative, i.e. $\vec{a}\cdot\vec{b}=\vec{b}\cdot\vec{a}$]

$\Rightarrow \quad |\vec{x}|^2-|\hat{a}|^2=15 \quad [\because \vec{z}\cdot\vec{z}=|\vec{z}|^2]$

$\Rightarrow \quad |\vec{x}|^2-1=15$

$\Rightarrow \quad |\vec{x}|^2=16$

$\therefore \quad |\vec{x}|=4$

16. (i) Given, vector $\vec{a}$ makes an angle $\frac{\pi}{4}$ with X-axis and $\frac{\pi}{2}$ with Y-axis.

So, $l = \cos\frac{\pi}{4}$ and $m = \cos\frac{\pi}{2}$

$\Rightarrow$ $l = \frac{1}{\sqrt{2}}$ and $m = 0$

We know that $l^2 + m^2 + n^2 = 1$

$\therefore \left(\frac{1}{\sqrt{2}}\right)^2 + (0)^2 + n^2 = 1 \Rightarrow \frac{1}{2} + n^2 = 1$

$\Rightarrow$ $n^2 = 1 - \frac{1}{2} \Rightarrow n = \pm\frac{1}{\sqrt{2}} \Rightarrow n = \frac{1}{\sqrt{2}}$

[$\because \vec{a}$ makes acute angle with Z-axis, so we take a positive sign]

$\therefore$ $\cos\theta = \frac{1}{\sqrt{2}}$

[$\because \theta$ is an acute angle with Z-axis]

Thus, the direction cosines of $\vec{a}$ are $\left(\frac{1}{\sqrt{2}}, 0, \frac{1}{\sqrt{2}}\right)$.

Now, vector $\vec{a}$

$= |\vec{a}|\left(\cos\frac{\pi}{4}\hat{i} + \cos\frac{\pi}{2}\hat{j} + \cos\theta\hat{k}\right)$

$= 5\sqrt{2}\left(\frac{1}{\sqrt{2}}\hat{i} + 0\hat{j} + \frac{1}{\sqrt{2}}\hat{k}\right)$ [given, $|\vec{a}| = 5\sqrt{2}$]

$= 5\hat{i} + 5\hat{k}$

Or

(ii) Let A and B be the given points whose position vectors are $3\vec{a} - 2\vec{b}$ and $2\vec{a} - 5\vec{b}$, respectively with respect to the origin O i.e. $\overrightarrow{OA} = 3\vec{a} - 2\vec{b}$ and $\overrightarrow{OB} = 2\vec{a} - 5\vec{b}$.

Let P be the point, which divides the line joining A and B internally and Q be the point, which divides the line AB externally, respectively in the ratio 3 : 2.

Then, by using section formula of internal division, we get

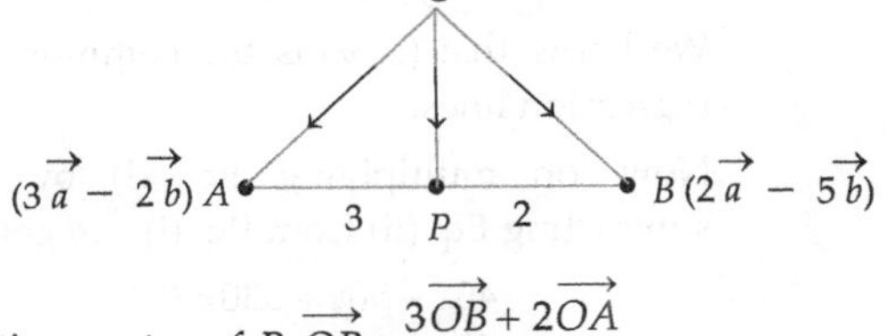

Position vector of P, $\overrightarrow{OP} = \frac{3\overrightarrow{OB} + 2\overrightarrow{OA}}{3+2}$

$= \frac{3(2\vec{a} - 5\vec{b}) + 2(3\vec{a} - 2\vec{b})}{5}$

$= \frac{6\vec{a} - 15\vec{b} + 6\vec{a} - 4\vec{b}}{5} = \frac{12\vec{a} - 19\vec{b}}{5}$

$= \frac{12}{5}\vec{a} - \frac{19}{5}\vec{b}$

Now, using section formula of external division, we get

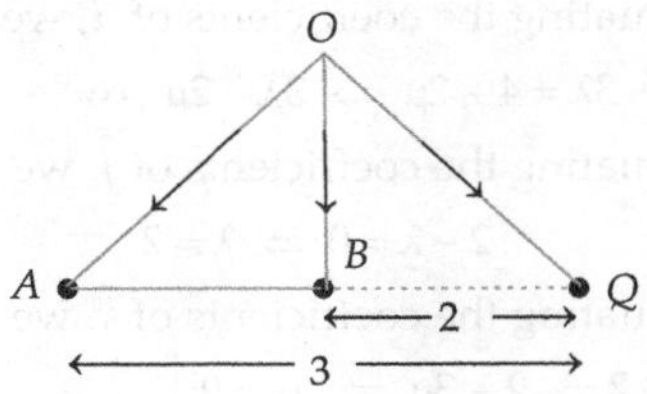

Position vector of Q, $\overrightarrow{OQ} = \frac{3\overrightarrow{OB} - 2\overrightarrow{OA}}{3-2}$

$= \frac{3(2\vec{a} - 5\vec{b}) - 2(3\vec{a} - 2\vec{b})}{1}$

$= \frac{6\vec{a} - 15\vec{b} - 6\vec{a} + 4\vec{b}}{1} = -11\vec{b}$

17. (i) The given equations are

$3l + m + 5n = 0$ ...(i)

and $6mn - 2nl + 5lm = 0$ ...(ii)

Now, from Eq. (i), we get

$m = -3l - 5n$ ...(iii)

On substituting $m = -3l - 5n$ in Eq. (ii), we get

$6(-3l - 5n)n - 2nl + 5l(-3l - 5n) = 0$

$\Rightarrow$ $30n^2 + 45ln + 15l^2 = 0$

$\Rightarrow$ $2n^2 + 3ln + l^2 = 0$

$\Rightarrow$ $2n^2 + 2nl + nl + l^2 = 0$

$\Rightarrow$ $2n(n + l) + l(n + l) = 0$

$\Rightarrow$ $(n + l)(2n + l) = 0$

$\Rightarrow$ Either $l = -n$ or $l = -2n$

If $l = -n$, then $m = -2n$ [using Eq. (iii)]

and if $l = -2n$, then $m = n$. [using Eq. (iii)]

Thus, the direction ratios of two lines are proportional to $(-n, -2n, n)$ and $(-2n, n, n)$ i.e. $(-1, -2, 1)$ and $(-2, 1, 1)$, respectively.

Now, let θ be the acute angle between the lines, then

$\cos\theta = \frac{|a_1a_2 + b_1b_2 + c_1c_2|}{\sqrt{a_1^2 + b_1^2 + c_1^2}\sqrt{a_2^2 + b_2^2 + c_2^2}}$

$= \frac{|2 - 2 + 1|}{\sqrt{1 + 4 + 1}\sqrt{4 + 1 + 1}} = \frac{1}{6}$

$\Rightarrow$ $\theta = \cos^{-1}\left(\frac{1}{6}\right)$

Or

(ii) Given lines are $\vec{r} = (-2\hat{i} + 2\hat{j} - 2\hat{k}) + \lambda(3\hat{i} - \hat{j})$ ...(i)

and $\vec{r} = (4\hat{i} - 2\hat{k}) + \mu(2\hat{i} + 3\hat{k})$ ...(ii)

Clearly, these lines will intersect, if $(-2\hat{i} + 2\hat{j} - 2\hat{k}) + \lambda(3\hat{i} - \hat{j}) = (4\hat{i} - 2\hat{k}) + \mu(2\hat{i} + 3\hat{k})$, for some particular values of λ and μ.

Collecting the like terms, we get

$$(-2+3\lambda)\hat{i}+(2-\lambda)\hat{j}-2\hat{k}=(4+2\mu)\hat{i}+(-2+3\mu)\hat{k}$$

On equating the coefficients of $\hat{i}$, we get

$$-2+3\lambda=4+2\mu \Rightarrow 3\lambda-2\mu=6$$

On equating the coefficients of $\hat{j}$, we get

$$2-\lambda=0 \Rightarrow \lambda=2$$

On equating the coefficients of $\hat{k}$, we get

$$-2=-2+3\mu \Rightarrow \mu=0$$

$\therefore$ $\mu=0$ and $\lambda=2$

Also, these values satisfy $3\lambda-2\mu=6$, therefore the given lines intersect.

On putting $\lambda=1$ in Eq. (i), we get

$$\vec{r}=(-2\hat{i}+2\hat{j}-2\hat{k})+1(3\hat{i}-\hat{j})$$
$$=\hat{i}+\hat{j}-2\hat{k}$$

Hence, the point of intersection of given lines is $(1, 1, -2)$.

18. Given circles are, $x^2+y^2=9$ ...(i)

and $(x-3)^2+y^2=9$ ...(ii)

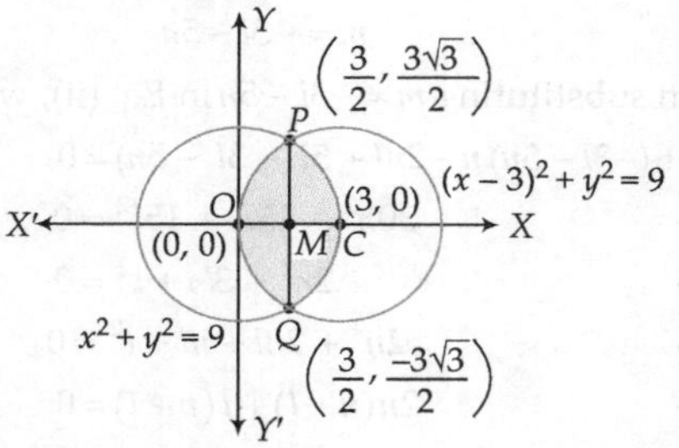

Here, Eq. (i) represents circle with centre (0, 0) and radius 3 units and Eq. (ii) represents circle with centre (3, 0) and radius 3 units.

On solving Eqs. (i) and (ii), we get

$$x^2-(x-3)^2=0$$
$$\Rightarrow x^2-x^2+6x-9=0$$
$$\Rightarrow 6x-9=0$$
$$\Rightarrow 3(2x-3)=0$$
$$\Rightarrow 2x-3=0 \Rightarrow x=\frac{3}{2}$$

When $x=\frac{3}{2}$, then from Eq. (i), we get

$$\left(\frac{3}{2}\right)^2+y^2=9 \Rightarrow y^2=9-\frac{9}{4}$$
$$\Rightarrow y^2=\frac{36-9}{4} \Rightarrow y^2=\frac{27}{4}$$
$$\Rightarrow y=\pm\frac{3\sqrt{3}}{2}$$

So, the points of intersection of Eqs. (i) and (ii) are $P\left(\frac{3}{2}, \frac{3\sqrt{3}}{2}\right)$ and $Q\left(\frac{3}{2}, \frac{-3\sqrt{3}}{2}\right)$.

$\therefore$ Required area

$$= \text{Area of the shaded region}$$
$$= 2\times(\text{Area of the region } OMCPO)$$
$$= 2\times2\times(\text{Area of region } MCPM)$$
$$= 4\times\int_{3/2}^{3} y\,dx = 4\times\int_{3/2}^{3}\sqrt{9-x^2}\,dx \quad [\text{using Eq. (i)}]$$
$$= 4\left[\frac{x\sqrt{9-x^2}}{2}+\frac{3^2}{2}\sin^{-1}\frac{x}{3}\right]_{3/2}^{3}$$
$$= 4\left(\frac{3\times0}{2}+\frac{9}{2}\sin^{-1}\frac{3}{3}-\frac{3}{4}\sqrt{9-\frac{9}{4}}-\frac{9}{2}\sin^{-1}\frac{1}{2}\right)$$
$$= 4\left(\frac{9}{2}\times\frac{\pi}{2}-\frac{3}{4}\sqrt{\frac{36-9}{4}}-\frac{9}{2}\times\frac{\pi}{6}\right)$$
$$= \left(9\pi-3\times\frac{\sqrt{27}}{2}-\frac{9\pi}{3}\right)$$
$$= \left(9\pi-3\pi-\frac{3\times3\sqrt{3}}{2}\right)=\left(6\pi-\frac{9\sqrt{3}}{2}\right)$$

Hence, the required area is $\left(6\pi-\frac{9\sqrt{3}}{2}\right)$ sq units.

19. (i) (b) Let the x number of units be produced and sold. As, each unit's variable cost is 40% of revenue.

$\therefore$ The variable cost of x units = 40% of $10x$

$$=\frac{40}{100}\times10x=₹\,4x$$

$\therefore$ Total cost of producing x units

$C(x)$ = Fixed cost commodity + Variable cost of commodity

$$\Rightarrow C(x)=₹(28000+4x)$$

$\therefore$ The cost function is $C(x)=28000+4x$

(ii) (c) From the data shown in figure (c), we observe that the distance between the data points to line is minimum. So, the line in option (c) best fits.

(iii) We have, $8x-10y+66=0$ ...(i)

and $40x-18y-214=0$ ...(ii)

We know that $(\bar{x}, \bar{y})$ is the common point of two regression lines.

Now, on multiplying Eq. (i) by 5 and then subtracting Eq. (ii) from Eq. (i), we get

$$40x-50y+330=0$$
$$40x-18y-214=0$$
$$-\quad+\quad+$$
$$-32y+544=0$$

$$\Rightarrow y=17$$

On putting $y=17$ in Eq. (i), we get

$$8x-170+66=0$$
$$\Rightarrow 8x=104 \Rightarrow x=13$$

$\therefore$ Common point $(\bar{x}, \bar{y}) = (x, y) = (13, 17)$

Hence, $\bar{x} = 13$ and $\bar{y} = 17$

(iv) Given, price $p = ₹(8000 - 5x)$ per item

$\therefore$ Total revenue by selling x sets

$$= ₹\, px = ₹(8000 - 5x)x$$

Hence, total revenue by selling 20 sets

$$= ₹(8000 - 5 \times 20) \times 20 = ₹\ 158000$$

and average revenue by selling 20 items

$$= \frac{\text{Total revenue}}{\text{Number of selling sets}}$$

$$= ₹\frac{158000}{20} = ₹\,7900$$

(v) Let the total fixed cost (TFC) be ₹ a.

Let AVC = ₹ b

Then, total value cost (TVC) = (AVC)x = ₹ bx

$\therefore$ TC = TFC + TVC = ₹$(a + bx)$

Given that when $x = 100$, TC = ₹ 250

Then, $a + 100b = 250$ ...(i)

and when $x = 200$, TC = ₹ 300

Then, $a + 200b = 300$ ...(ii)

On subtracting Eq. (i) from Eq. (ii), we get

$$100b = 50 \Rightarrow b = \frac{1}{2}$$

On putting the value of b in Eq. (i), we get

$$a + 100 \cdot \frac{1}{2} = 250$$

$$\Rightarrow a = 200$$

Hence, the cost function is $C(x) = 200 + \frac{1}{2}x$.

20. (i) (a) Given, total cost

$$y = 3x\left(\frac{x+7}{x+5}\right) + 5 = 3\left(\frac{x^2 + 7x}{x+5}\right) + 5$$

$\therefore$ Marginal Cost (MC)

$$= \frac{dy}{dx} = 3\left[\frac{(x+5)(2x+7) - (x^2 + 7x)}{(x+5)^2}\right]$$

$$= 3\left[\frac{x^2 + 10x + 35}{(x+5)^2}\right]$$

$$= 3\left[\frac{(x+5)^2 + 10}{(x+5)^2}\right] = 3\left[1 + \frac{10}{(x+5)^2}\right]$$

(b) To show that MC falls continuously with increase in x, we should show that $\frac{d}{dx}(\text{MC}) < 0$ for all values of x.

Here, $\frac{d}{dx}(\text{MC}) = \frac{d}{dx}\left(3 + \frac{30}{(x+5)^2}\right) = \frac{-60}{(x+5)^3} < 0,$

for all (positive) values of x.

Hence, the marginal cost falls continuously as the output increases. **Hence proved.**

Or

(ii) Given, $p = 400 + 20x - \frac{x^2}{3}$

Clearly, total revenue

$$R(x) = px = \left(400 + 20x - \frac{x^2}{3}\right)x = 400x + 20x^2 - \frac{x^3}{3}$$

(a) We know that

$$\text{Marginal revenue} = \frac{dR}{dx}$$

$$= \frac{d}{dx}\left(400x + 20x^2 - \frac{x^3}{3}\right) = ₹(400 + 40x - x^2)$$

(b) Marginal revenue at $x = 10$, is given by

$$\left(\frac{dR}{dx}\right)_{x=10} = 400 + 40(10) - (10)^2$$

$$= 400 + 400 - 100 = ₹\,700$$

21. Given, regression line of y on x is

$$4x - 5y + 33 = 0 \quad \text{...(i)}$$

and regression line of x on y is

$$20x - 9y - 107 = 0 \quad \text{...(ii)}$$

On solving Eqs. (i) and (ii), we get

$\therefore$ $x = 13$ and $y = 17$

We know that two lines of regression intersect each other at mean $(\bar{x}, \bar{y})$

$$\bar{x} = 13 \text{ and } \bar{y} = 17$$

From Eq. (i), we get $4x - 5y + 33 = 0$, y on x

$$\Rightarrow y = \frac{4}{5}x + \frac{33}{5} = 0.8x + 6.6$$

$\therefore$ Regression coefficient of y on x is $b_{yx} = 0.8$

From Eq. (ii), we get

$20x - 9y - 107 = 0$, x on y

$$x = \frac{9}{20}y + \frac{107}{20} = 0.45y + 5.35$$

$\therefore$ Regression coefficient of x on y is $b_{xy} = 0.45$

Now, $r^2 = b_{xy} \cdot b_{yx} = (0.45)(0.8) = 0.36$

$\therefore$ $r = \rho(x, y) = \sqrt{0.36} = 0.6$

[since, r has positive sign as b_{yx} and b_{xy} have same sign]

We know that $b_{yx} = \frac{\text{Cov}(x, y)}{\sigma_x^2}$

$\Rightarrow \text{Cov}(x, y) = b_{yx} \cdot \sigma_x^2 = (0.8)(3)^2 = 7.2$ [$\because \sigma_x = 3$, given]

For finding σ_y, we use

$$b_{xy} = \frac{\text{Cov}(x, y)}{\sigma_y^2} \Rightarrow 0.45 = \frac{7.2}{\sigma_y^2}$$

$$\Rightarrow \sigma_y^2 = \frac{7.2}{0.45} = 16 \Rightarrow \sigma_y = 4$$

Value Point

Write the relation being used to find the unknown.

22. (i) Let the fertilizers of Type I and Type II be x kg and y kg, respectively.

Then, $x \geq 0$ ...(i)

and $y \geq 0$ ...(ii)

Type I Fertilizer contains 10% nitrogen and 6% of phosphoric acid.

Type II Fertilizer contains 5% of nitrogen and 10% of phosphoric acid and he needs atleast 14 kg of nitrogen and 14 kg of phosphoric acid.

Then, we have $\frac{10}{100}x + \frac{5}{100}y \geq 14$

$\Rightarrow \quad 2x + y \geq 280$ ...(iii)

and $\frac{6}{100}x + \frac{10}{100}y \geq 14$

$\Rightarrow \quad 3x + 5y \geq 700$ ...(iv)

Also, cost of Type I fertilizer per kg is ₹ 0.6 and cost of Type II fertilizer per kg is ₹ 0.4

$\therefore$ We have to minimise $Z = 0.6x + 0.4y$, subject to the constraints Eqs. (i) to (iv).

Table for line $2x + y = 280$ or $y = 280 - 2x$ is

x	0	100	140
y	280	80	0

So, line passes through the points (0, 280), (100, 80) and (140, 0).

On putting (0, 0) in the inequality $2x + y \geq 280$, we get $0 + 0 \geq 280 \Rightarrow 0 \geq 280$ (false)

So, the half plane is away from the origin.

Table for line $3x + 5y = 700$ or $y = \frac{700 - 3x}{5}$ is

x	0	100	700/3
y	140	80	0

So, line passes through the points (0, 140), (100, 80) and (700/3, 0).

On putting (0, 0) in the inequality $3x + 5y \geq 700$, we get

$0 + 0 \geq 700 \Rightarrow 0 \geq 700$ (false)

So, the half plane is away from the origin.

Also, $x \geq 0$ and $y \geq 0$, so the feasible region lies in Ist quadrant.

The intersection point of the lines $2x + y = 280$ and $3x + 5y = 700$ is $B(100, 80)$.

Now, plot all the inequalities on a graph paper as shown below

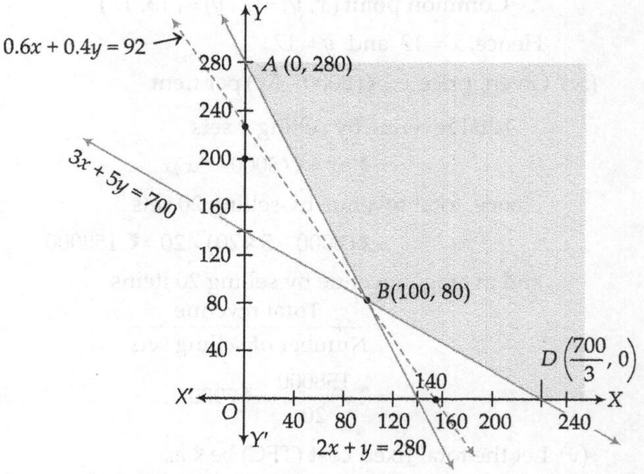

It can be seen that the feasible region is unbounded. The corner points of the boundary of the region are $A(0, 280)$, $B(100, 80)$ and $D\left(\frac{700}{3}, 0\right)$.

The value of Z at corner points is given below.

Corner points	$Z = 0.6x + 0.4y$
$A(0, 280)$	$Z = 0.6 \times 0 + 0.4 \times 280 = 112$
$B(100, 80)$	$Z = 0.6 \times 100 + 0.4 \times 80 = 92$ (minimum)
$D\left(\frac{700}{3}, 0\right)$	$Z = 0.6 \times \frac{700}{3} + 0.4 \times 0 = 140$

As the feasible region is unbounded, therefore 92 may or may not be the minimum value of Z. For this, we draw a graph of the inequality $0.6x + 0.4y < 92$ and check whether the resulting half plane has points in common with the feasible region. It can be seen that the feasible region has no common points with $0.6x + 0.4y < 92$.

Therefore, the gardener should use 100 kg of Type I fertilizer and 80 kg of Type II fertilizer to meet nutrient requirements at a minimum cost and the minimum cost is ₹ 92.

Or

(ii) Given problem is to maximise $Z = 3x + 2y$ ...(i)

Subject to constraints,

$x + 2y \leq 10$ ...(ii)

$3x + y \leq 15$ ...(iii)

and $x \geq 0, y \geq 0$ ...(iv)

Table for line $x + 2y = 10$ is

x	0	4
y	5	3

So, the line passes through the points (0, 5) and (4, 3).

On putting (0, 0) in the inequality $x + 2y \le 10$, we get

$$0 + 2\times0 \le 10 \Rightarrow 0 \le 10 \text{ (true)}$$

So, the half plane is towards the origin.

Table for line $3x + y = 15$ is

x	4	5
y	3	0

So, the line passes through the points (4, 3) and (5, 0).

On putting (0, 0) in the inequality $3x + y \le 15$, we get

$$3\times0 + 0 \le 15 \Rightarrow 0 \le 15 \quad \text{(true)}$$

So, the half plane is towards the origin.

Also, $x, y \ge 0$, so the region lies in the I quadrant.

On solving equations $x + 2y = 10$ and $3x + y = 15$, we get

$$x = 4 \text{ and } y = 3$$

So, the intersection point is $B(4, 3)$.

Now, plot all the inequalities on a graph paper as shown below. From the graph, the feasible region $OABCO$ is bounded.

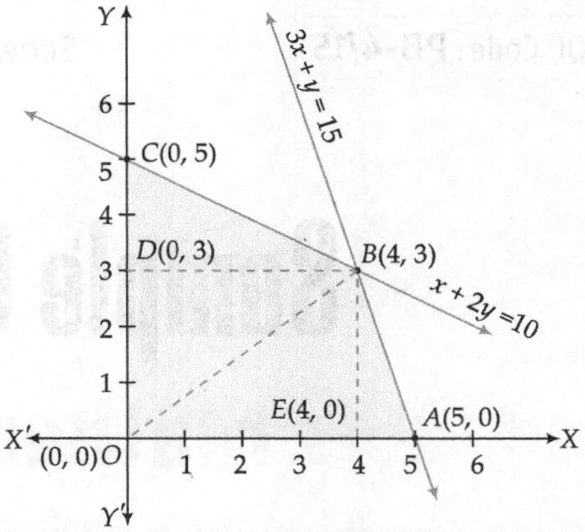

The corner points of the feasible region are $O(0, 0)$, $A(5, 0)$, $B(4, 3)$ and $C(0, 5)$.

The values of Z at the corner points are given below

Corner points	$Z = 3x + 2y$
$O(0, 0)$	$Z = 3\times0 + 2\times0 = 0$
$A(5, 0)$	$Z = 3\times5 + 2\times0 = 15$
$B(4, 3)$	$Z = 3\times4 + 2\times3 = 18$ (Maximum)
$C(0, 5)$	$Z = 3\times0 + 2\times5 = 10$

Therefore, the maximum value of Z is 18 at the point $B(4, 3)$.

SQP Code : **PB-4/15**	Series **i-Succeed 4-25/15**	Roll No.

Sample Question Paper 04

Mathematics 12th (Code 860)

General Instructions

1. The Question Paper consists of three sections A, B and C.
2. Candidates are required to attempt all questions from Section A and all questions either from Section B Or Section C.
3. Section A Internal choice has been provided in two questions of two marks each, two questions of four marks each and two questions of six marks each.
4. Section B Internal choice has been provided in one questions of two marks and one question of four marks.
5. Section C Internal choice has been provided in one question of two marks and one question of four marks.
6. All working, including rough work, should be done on the same sheet as, and adjacent to the rest of the answer.
7. The intended marks for questions or parts of questions are given in brackets [].
8. Mathematical tables and graph papers are provided.

Time : 3 Hrs.

Max. Marks : 80

Section A (65 Marks)

1. In subparts (i) to (xi) choose the correct options and in subparts (xii) to (xv), answer the questions as instructed.

(i) **Assertion** (A) $y = x(x-3)^2$ decreases for the values of x given by $1 < x < 3$.

Reason (R) A function f is strictly decreasing in (a, b) if $f'(x) > 0$ for each $x \in (a, b)$.

• *Analysis* [1]

(a) Both A and R are true but R is the correct explanation of A.

(b) Both A and R are true and R is not the correct explanation of A.

(c) A is true but R is false.

(d) A is false but R is true.

(ii) An integrating factor of the differential equation $x\dfrac{dy}{dx} + y \log x = xe^x x^{-\frac{1}{2}\log x}$, $(x > 0)$ is

• *Understanding* [1]

(a) $x^{\log x}$ (b) $(\sqrt{x})^{\log x}$

(c) $(\sqrt{e})^{(\log x)^2}$ (d) e^{x^2}

(iii) **Statement I** If $A = \begin{bmatrix} 1 & 1 \\ 2 & 2 \\ 3 & 4 \end{bmatrix}$, then order of the matrix A is 3×2.

Statement II If a matrix have m rows and n columns, then order of matrix is written as $n \times m$.

• *Analysis* [1]

(a) Statement I is true and II is false.

(b) Statement I is false and II is true.

(c) Both the statements are true.

(d) Both the statements are false.

(iv) The graph of the function $f(x) = \dfrac{1}{x - [x]}$, where $[x]$ is greatest integer function is shown below.

• *Application* [1]

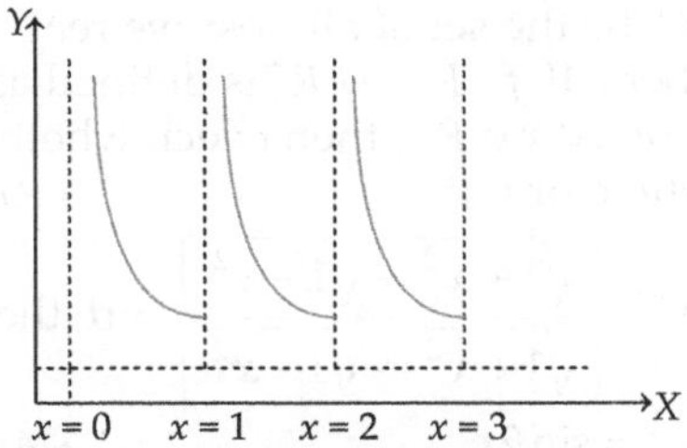

(a) $f(x)$ is continuous at $x = 1$.
(b) $f(x)$ is differentiable at $x = 2$.
(c) $f(x)$ is differentiable at $x = 3$.
(d) $f(x)$ is not differentiable for all integers $x \in I$.

(v) The relation R in the set of natural numbers N defined as $R = \{(x, y) : y = x + 5 \text{ and } x < 4\}$ is • *Analysis* [1]

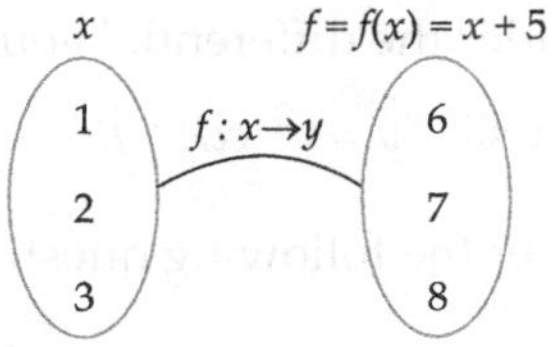

(a) reflexive
(b) symmetric
(c) transitive
(d) an equivalence relation

(vi) The events E and F are independent. If $P(E) = 0.3$ and $P(E \cup F) = 0.5$, then $P(E/F) - P(F/E)$ is equal to • *Application* [1]

(a) $\frac{1}{7}$ (b) $\frac{2}{7}$ (c) $\frac{3}{35}$ (d) $\frac{1}{70}$

(vii) For two events A and B, if $P(A) = 0.5$, $P(B) = 0.8$ and $P(B/A) = 0.8$, then $P(A \cup B)$ is equal to • *Application* [1]

(a) 0.24 (b) 0.3 (c) 0.80 (d) 0.90

(viii) $\int_0^{\pi/2} \left| \cos \frac{x}{2} \right| dx$ is equal to • *Evaluate* [1]

(a) $\sqrt{2}$ (b) -2 (c) $\sqrt{2}/2$ (d) 0

(ix) **Assertion** (A) $\tan^{-1} x + \cot^{-1}(x + 1) = \tan^{-1}(x^2 + x)$.

Reason (R) $\cot^{-1} \frac{xy + 1}{x - y} + \cot^{-1} \frac{yz + 1}{y - z} + \cot^{-1} \frac{zx + 1}{z - x} = \pi$.

Choose the correct option. • *Recall* [1]

(a) Both A and R are correct, R is the correct explanation of A.
(b) Both A and R are correct, R is not the correct explanation of A.
(c) A is correct, R is incorrect.
(d) R is correct, A is incorrect.

(x) Consider the two events E and F which are associated with the sample space of a random experiment.

Statement I $P(E/F) = \frac{n(E \cap F)}{n(F)}$.

Statement II $P(E/F) = \frac{P(E \cap F)}{P(F)}$.

Choose the correct option. • *Recall* [1]

(a) Statement I is true; Statement II is true; Statement II is a correct explanation for Statement I.
(b) Statement I is true; Statement II is true; Statement II is not a correct explanation for Statement I.
(c) Statement I is true; Statement II is false.
(d) Statement I is false; Statement II is true.

(xi) The sum of the order and degree of the differential equation $\frac{d}{dx}\left\{\left(\frac{dy}{dx}\right)^3\right\} = 0$ is • *Understanding* [1]

(a) 1 (b) 2 (c) 3 (d) 4

(xii) Prove that $\tan^{-1}(x) + \tan^{-1}\left(\frac{2x}{1-x^2}\right) = \tan^{-1}\left(\frac{3x - x^3}{1 - 3x^2}\right)$, where $|x| < \frac{1}{3}$. • *Analysis* [1]

(xiii) Evaluate $\int \sin^3 x \, dx$. • *Evaluate* [1]

(xiv) A retail store categorises its customers into two groups based upon on their shopping behaviour.
Regular customer and occasional customers. The probabilities associated with these groups are

- The probability that a customer is a regular customer (R) is 0.60.
- The probability that a customer is an occasional customer (O) is 0.40.
- The probability that a regular customer will make a purchase (P) is 0.75.
- The probability that an occasional customer will make a purchase (P) is 0.30.

Answer the following questions.

What is the probability that a randomly selected customer will make a purchase $P(P)$? • *Application* [1]

(xv) Let $f(x)=\begin{bmatrix}\cos x & -\sin x & 0\\ \sin x & \cos x & 0\\ 0 & 0 & 1\end{bmatrix}$,

show that $f(x)\cdot f(y)=f(x+y)$. • *Analysis* [1]

2. If the function f defined by

$$f(x)=\begin{cases}\dfrac{\log(1+ax)-\log(1-bx)}{x}, & x\neq 0\\ k, & x=0\end{cases}$$

is continuous at $x=0$, find the value of k. • *Understanding* [2]

3. (i) Find $\dfrac{dy}{dx}$, when $y=\dfrac{e^x+\log x}{\sin 3x}$ • *Recall* [2]

Or

(ii) The table below shows some of the values of differentiable functions u and v and their derivatives.

x	$u(x)$	$u'(x)$	$v(x)$	$v'(x)$
1	3	2	4	1
2	5	−1	0	3
3	2	4	1	−2
5	7	0	3	−9

If $r(x)=v[u(x)]$, then find $r'(2)$. • *Application* [2]

4. Solve the differential equation

$$(e^x+e^{-x})\frac{dy}{dx}=e^x-e^{-x}.$$

• *Application* [2]

5. (i) Divide 20 into two parts, so that the product of the square of the one and the cube of the other may be the greatest possible. • *Understanding* [2]

Or

(ii) A cylindrical vessel of radius 0.6 m is filled with oil at the rate of 0.30 cm^3/min. Find the rate at which the oil in the vessel rises. • *Application* [2]

6. Without expanding, show that

$$\begin{vmatrix}a & b & c\\ b & c & a\\ c & a & b\end{vmatrix}=\begin{vmatrix}c & b & a\\ b & a & c\\ a & c & b\end{vmatrix}$$

• *Analysis* [2]

7. Let R^+ be the set of all positive real numbers. If $f: R^+\to R^+$ is defined as $f(x)=e^x, \forall\, x\in R^+$, then check whether f is invertible or not. • *Analysis* [4]

8. If $\tan^{-1}\left\{\dfrac{\sqrt{1+x^2}-\sqrt{1-x^2}}{\sqrt{1+x^2}+\sqrt{1-x^2}}\right\}=\alpha$, then prove that $x^2=\sin 2\alpha$. • *Analysis* [4]

9. Prove that

$$\int_0^{\pi/2}\frac{\sin^2 x}{\sin x+\cos x}\,dx=\frac{1}{\sqrt{2}}\log(\sqrt{2}+1)$$

• *Analysis* [4]

10. (i) Find $\displaystyle\int\frac{\sec x}{1+\operatorname{cosec} x}\,dx.$ • *Evaluate* [2]

(ii) Evaluate $\displaystyle\int\frac{1}{\cos^4 x+\sin^4 x}\,dx.$ • *Evaluate* [2]

11. Consider the differential equation

$$\frac{dy}{dx}+x\sin 2y=x^3\cos^2 y.$$

Answer the following questions. • *Application* [6]

(i) Write the given differential equation into standard form of linear differential equation.

(ii) Find the integrating factor of the given differential equation.

(iii) Find the solution of the given differential equation.

12. (i) An open box with a square base is to be made out of a given quantity of cardboard of area C^2 sq units. Show that the maximum volume of box is $\dfrac{C^3}{6\sqrt{3}}$ cu units. • *Application* [6]

Or (ii) (a) Find the point on the curve $y=x^3-11x+5$ at which the tangent has the equation $y=x-11$. • *Understanding*

(b) Show that the function f given by $f(x)=x^3-3x^2+3x$ is strictly increasing on R except at $x=1$. • *Analysis* [6]

13. (i) A card from a pack of 52 cards is lost. From the remaining cards of the pack, two cards are drawn and are found to be both clubs.

Find the probability of the lost card being a club. • *Application* [6]

SP-04

Or

(ii) In answering a question on a multiple choice test, a student either knows the answer or guesses. Let 3/4 be the probability that he knows the answers and 1/4 be the probability that he guesses. Assuming that a student who guesses the answer will be correct with probability 1/4. What is the probability that the student knows the answer, given that he answered it correctly?

• *Application* [6]

14. In a legislative assembly election, a political group hired a public relations firm to promote its candidate in three ways: telephone, house calls and letters. The cost per contact (in paise) is given in the matrix A as

Cost per contact

$$A = \begin{bmatrix} 40 \\ 100 \\ 50 \end{bmatrix} \begin{matrix} \text{Telephone} \\ \text{House call} \\ \text{Letter} \end{matrix}$$

The number of contacts of each type made in two cities X and Y is given by

$$\begin{matrix} & \text{Telephone} & \text{House call} & \text{Letter} & \\ B = & \begin{bmatrix} 1000 & 500 & 5000 \\ 3000 & 1000 & 10000 \end{bmatrix} & & & \begin{matrix} \to X \\ \to Y \end{matrix} \end{matrix}$$

On the basis of above information, answer the following questions . • *Application* [6]

(i) Find the order of the matrix A.

(ii) Find the order of the matrix B.

(iii) Find A' and B' (iv) Find BA.

(v) Find $(BA)'$. (vi) Find AB.

Section B (15 Marks)

15. In subparts (i) to (iii) choose the correct options and in subparts (iv) and (v), answer the questions as instructed. [5]

(i) The vector in the direction of the vector $\hat{i} - 2\hat{j} + 2\hat{k}$ that has magnitude 9, is • *Recall*

(a) $\hat{i} - 2\hat{j} + 2\hat{k}$ (b) $\dfrac{\hat{i} - 2\hat{j} + 2\hat{k}}{3}$

(c) $3(\hat{i} - 2\hat{j} + 2\hat{k})$ (d) $9(\hat{i} - 2\hat{j} + 2\hat{k})$

(ii) The cartesian equation of the plane $\vec{r} \cdot (6\hat{i} - 3\hat{j} + \hat{k}) = 5$ is • *Recall*

(a) $5x + 6y + z = 5$ (b) $6x - 3y + z = 5$

(c) $x + 6y + 2z = 5$ (d) None of these

(iii) **Statement I** If $A(-3, 2, 4)$, $B(2, 5, -2)$, $C(1, -2, 2)$ and $D(4, 2, 3)$ are four given points, then the angle θ between AB and CD is $21/\sqrt{1820}$.

Statement II If $l_1 m_1 n_1$ and $l_2 m_2 n_2$ are the direction cosines of two lines then, the angle θ between them is given by $\cos\theta = l_1 l_2 + m_1 m_2 + n_1 n_2$. Which of the following is correct? • *Analysis*

(a) Only Statement I. (b) Only Statement II.

(c) Both Statements I and II.

(d) Neither Statement I nor Statement II.

(iv) Shown below is a plane. Which is parallel to X-axis.

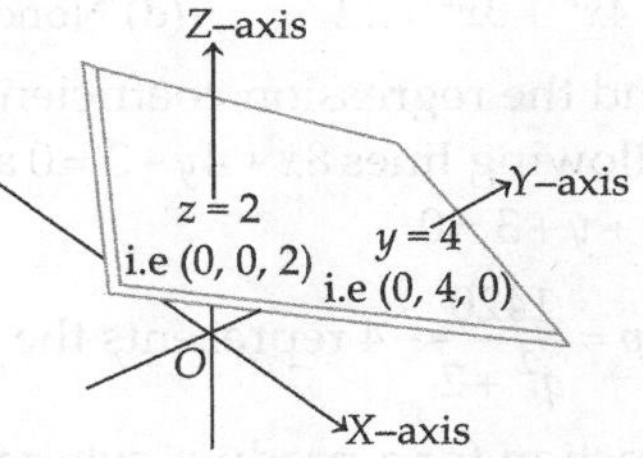

Find the equation of the plane.

• *Application*

(v) If $\vec{a} + \vec{b} + \vec{c} = 0$, show that the angle θ between the vectors $\vec{b}$ and $\vec{c}$ is given by $\cos\theta = \dfrac{|\vec{a}|^2 - |\vec{b}|^2 - |\vec{c}|^2}{2|\vec{b}||\vec{c}|}$.

• *Analysis*

16. (i) If two medians of a triangle are equal, then prove that (using vectors) the triangle is isosceles. • *Analysis* [2]

Or (ii) If $\vec{a}$, $\vec{b}$ and $\vec{c}$ are three mutually perpendicular vectors of equal magnitude, then find the angle between $\vec{a}$ and $(\vec{a} + \vec{b} + \vec{c})$.

• *Recall* [2]

17. (i) Find the shortest distance between the lines $\vec{r} = (4\hat{i} - \hat{j}) + \lambda(\hat{i} + 2\hat{j} - 3\hat{k})$ and $\vec{r} = (\hat{i} - \hat{j} + 2\hat{k}) + \mu(2\hat{i} + 4\hat{j} - 5\hat{k})$.

• *Understanding* [4]

Or (ii) Show that the points $\hat{i} - \hat{j} + 3\hat{k}$ and $3(\hat{i} + \hat{j} + \hat{k})$ are equidistant from the plane $\vec{r} \cdot (5\hat{i} + 2\hat{j} - 7\hat{k}) + 9 = 0$. • *Analysis* [4]

Section C (15 Marks)

19. In subparts (i) to (ii) choose the correct options and in subparts (iii) to (v), answer the questions as instructed. [5]

(i) If $b_{xy} = \frac{-3}{4}$ and $b_{yx} = \frac{-3}{4}$, then the coefficient of correlation is • *Understanding*

(a) $-\frac{3}{4}$ (b) $\frac{3}{4}$ (c) $\frac{5}{4}$ (d) $\frac{8}{5}$

(ii) If the total cost function for x units of a commodity is $C(x) = 3x^5 + 2x^2 + x$, then the marginal cost is • *Understanding*

(a) $15x^4 + 4x + 1$ (b) $15x^4 - 4x + 1$

(c) $4x^3 + 3x^2 + 12$ (d) None of these

(iii) Find the regression coefficients of following lines $8x + 4y - 3 = 0$ and $5x + y + 3 = 0$. • *Analysis*

(iv) If $p = \frac{1420}{q^2 + 2} - 4$ represents the demand function for a product, where p is the price per unit for q units. Determine the marginal revenue function. • *Application*

(v) Given, the total cost function for x units of a commodity is $C(x) = \frac{x^5}{5} + 4x^3 + 2x$, find the marginal and average cost. • *Analysis*

20. (i) The fixed cost of a new product is ₹ 30000 and the variable cost per unit is ₹ 800. If the demand function is $p(x) = 4500 - 100x$. • *Application* [2]

(a) Find the cost function $C(x)$.

(b) Find the revenue function.

Or

(ii) The cost of manufacturing of certain items consists of ₹ 1600 as overheads, ₹ 30 per item as the cost of the material and the labour cost ₹ $\frac{x^2}{100}$ for x items produced.

How many items must be produced to have a minimum average cost? • *Application* [2]

21. The personnel manager of the factory wants to find a measure which he can use to fix the monthly income of persons applying for a job in production department. As an experiment project, he collected data on 7 persons from that department referring to years of service and their monthly income.

Years of service (x)	11	7	9	5	8	6	10
Income in ₹ 100 (y)	10	8	6	5	9	7	11

(i) Find $\bar{x}$ and $\bar{y}$.

(ii) Find the regression equation of (y) on (x).

(iii) Using it what initial start would you recommend for a person applying for a job after having served in similar capacity in another factory for 13 yr? • *Application* [4]

22. (i) A manufacturer wishes to produce two commodities A and B. The number of units of material, labour and equipment needed to produce one unit of each commodity is shown in the following table.

	A	B	Available
Material	1	2	8
Labour	3	2	12
Equipment	1	1	10

Also, show the available number of units of each of the items, material, labour and equipment.

Find the maximum profit, if each of commodity A earns a profit of ₹ 2 and each unit of B earns ₹ 3. • *Analysis* [4]

Or (ii) Solve the following linear programming problems graphically.

Maximise $Z = -x + 2y$,
subject to constraints are $x \geq 3$, $x + y \geq 5$, $x + 2y \geq 6$ and $x, y \geq 0$. • *Analysis* [4]

SP-04

Solutions in Topper's Style

My Commitment *I affirm that I am reviewing these solutions only after I have solved the Sample Question Paper 4 on my own. My purpose of looking the solutions is solely to verify whether my answers/solutions were correct or not and to identify my mistakes in case my solutions were wrong or I could not solve that.*

1. (i) (c) We have, $y = x(x-3)^2$

$$\therefore \quad \frac{dy}{dx} = x \cdot 2(x-3) \cdot 1 + (x-3)^2 \cdot 1$$
$$= 2x^2 - 6x + x^2 + 9 - 6x$$
$$= 3x^2 - 12x + 9$$
$$= 3(x^2 - 3x - x + 3)$$
$$= 3(x-3)(x-1)$$

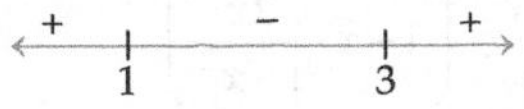

So, $y = x(x-3)^2$ decreases for (1, 3).

[$\because y' < 0$ for all $x \in (1, 3)$, hence y is decreasing in (1, 3)]

Hence, Assertion is true and Reason is false.

(ii) (c) Given, $x\dfrac{dy}{dx} + y\dfrac{1}{x}\log x = e^x x^{-(1/2)\log x}$,

which is a linear differential equation.

Here, $P = \dfrac{1}{x}\log x$ and $Q = e^x x^{-(1/2)\log x}$

$$\therefore \quad \text{IF} = e^{\int P\,dx} = e^{\int \frac{1}{x}\log x\,dx} = e^{\frac{(\log x)^2}{2}} = (\sqrt{e})^{(\log x)^2}$$

(iii) (a) If a matrix has m rows and n columns, then order of matrix is given by $m \times n$.

$\therefore$ Order of matrix A is 3×2.

(iv) (d) Given, $f(x) = \dfrac{1}{x - [x]}$

When x is an integer, $x - [x] = 0$

$\therefore$ For all $x \in I$, function is not defined.

Hence, for all $x \in I$, function is not continuous, so not differentiable.

(v) (c) Given, $R = \{(x, y) : y = x + 5, x < 4 \text{ and } x \in N\}$
$$= \{(x, x+5), x < 4 \text{ and } x \in N\}$$
$$= \{(1, 6), (2, 7), (3, 8)\}$$

Now, if $y = x$, then $x \neq x + 5$

$\Rightarrow (x, x) \notin R$ e.g. $(1, 1) \notin R$.

So, R is not reflexive.

Now, if $y = x + 5$, then $x \neq y + 5$

e.g. $(1, 6) \in R$ but $(6, 1) \notin R$.

So, R is not symmetric.

Since, here $(1, 6) \in R$ and there is no order pair in R which has 6 as the first element, same in the case for $(2, 7)$ and $(3, 8)$.

So, R is transitive.

(vi) (d) Given, $P(E) = 0.3$ and $P(E \cup F) = 0.5$

Let $P(F) = x$

We know that

$$P(E \cup F) = P(E) + P(F) - P(E \cap F)$$
$$= P(E) + P(F) - P(E) \cdot P(F)$$

[$\because$ E and F are independent events]

$$\Rightarrow \quad 0.5 = 0.3 + x - 0.3x$$
$$\Rightarrow \quad 0.7x = 0.5 - 0.3$$
$$\Rightarrow \quad x = \frac{0.2}{0.7} = \frac{2}{7}$$
$$\Rightarrow \quad P(F) = \frac{2}{7}$$

Now, $P(E/F) - P(F/E) = \dfrac{P(E \cap F)}{P(F)} - \dfrac{P(F \cap E)}{P(E)}$

$$= \frac{P(E \cap F)\,P(E) - P(F \cap E) \cdot P(F)}{P(E) \cdot P(F)}$$
$$= \frac{P(E \cap F)[P(E) - P(F)]}{P(E \cap F)} = P(E) - P(F)$$
$$= \frac{3}{10} - \frac{2}{7} = \frac{21 - 20}{70} = \frac{1}{70}$$

(vii) (d) Given, $P(A) = 0.5$, $P(B) = 0.8$ and $P(B/A) = 0.8$

We know that

$$P\left(\frac{B}{A}\right) = \frac{P(B \cap A)}{P(A)}$$
$$= \frac{P(A \cap B)}{P(A)}$$
$$\Rightarrow \quad 0.8 = \frac{P(A \cap B)}{0.5}$$
$$\Rightarrow P(A \cap B) = 0.40$$

Now, $P(A \cup B) = P(A) + P(B) - P(A \cap B)$
$$= 0.5 + 0.8 - 0.40 = 0.90$$

(viii) (a) $\displaystyle\int_0^{\pi/2} \left|\cos\frac{x}{2}\right| dx = \int_0^{\pi/2} \cos\frac{x}{2}\,dx$

$$\left[\because 0 < x < \frac{\pi}{2}, \left|\cos\frac{x}{2}\right| = \cos\frac{x}{2}\right]$$
$$= 2\left[\sin\frac{x}{2}\right]_0^{\pi/2}$$
$$= 2\left[\sin\frac{\pi}{4} - \sin 0\right]$$
$$= \frac{2}{\sqrt{2}} = \sqrt{2}$$

(ix) (d) We have, $\tan^{-1} x + \cot^{-1}(x + 1)$

$$= \tan^{-1} x + \tan^{-1} \frac{1}{x+1} = \tan^{-1}\left(\frac{x + \frac{1}{x+1}}{1 - x\left(\frac{1}{x+1}\right)}\right)$$

$$\left[\because \tan^{-1} A + \tan^{-1} B = \tan^{-1}\left(\frac{A+B}{1-AB}\right)\right]$$

$$= \tan^{-1}\left(\frac{x^2+x+1}{x+1-x}\right) = \tan^{-1}(x^2+x+1)$$

Hence, A is incorrect.

Now, $\cot^{-1}\frac{xy+1}{x-y} + \cot^{-1}\frac{yz+1}{y-z} + \cot^{-1}\frac{zx+1}{z-x}$

$$= \tan^{-1}\frac{x-y}{1+xy} + \tan^{-1}\frac{y-z}{1+yz} + \tan^{-1}\frac{z-x}{1+zx} + \pi$$

$$= \tan^{-1}x - \tan^{-1}y + \tan^{-1}y - \tan^{-1}z + \tan^{-1}z - \tan^{-1}x + \pi = \pi$$

In this, we can consider

$$x > y \text{ and } y > z$$

$$\Rightarrow \quad x > z$$

$$\Rightarrow \quad z - x < 0$$

$\cot^{-1} x = \pi + \tan^{-1}\frac{1}{x}$ when, $x < 0$

$\therefore$ R is correct.

(x) (a) I. The conditional probability of E given that F has occurred is

$$P\left(\frac{E}{F}\right) = \frac{\text{Number of elementary events favourable to } E \cap F}{\text{Number of elementary events which are favourable } F}$$

$$= \frac{n(E \cap F)}{n(F)}$$

Dividing the numerator and the denominator by total number of elementary events of the sample space, we see that $P\left(\frac{E}{F}\right)$ can also be written as

$$P\left(\frac{E}{F}\right) = \frac{\frac{n(E \cap F)}{n(S)}}{\frac{n(F)}{n(S)}} = \frac{P(E \cap F)}{P(F)} \quad \text{...(i)}$$

Note that I is valid only when $P(F) \neq 0$ i.e. $F \neq \phi$.

II. If E and F are two events associated with the same sample space of a random experiment, then conditional probability of the event E given that F has occurred i.e. $P\left(\frac{E}{F}\right)$ is given by

$$P\left(\frac{E}{F}\right) = \frac{P(E \cap F)}{P(F)} \text{ provided } P(F) \neq 0$$

(xi) (c) Given differential equation is $\frac{d}{dx}\left\{\left(\frac{dy}{dx}\right)^3\right\} = 0$

$$\Rightarrow \quad 3\left(\frac{dy}{dx}\right)^{3-1} \frac{d}{dx}\left(\frac{dy}{dx}\right) = 0$$

$$\Rightarrow \quad 3\left(\frac{dy}{dx}\right)^2 \frac{d^2y}{dx^2} = 0$$

Here, order = 2 and degree = 1

$\therefore$ Sum of the order and degree = 2 + 1 = 3

(xii) LHS $= \tan^{-1}(x) + \tan^{-1}\left(\frac{2x}{1-x^2}\right)$

$$= \tan^{-1}\left(\frac{x + \frac{2x}{1-x^2}}{1 - x \cdot \frac{2x}{1-x^2}}\right)$$

$$\left[\because \tan^{-1}x + \tan^{-1}y = \tan^{-1}\frac{x+y}{1-xy}\right]$$

$$= \tan^{-1}\left(\frac{\frac{x - x^3 + 2x}{1-x^2}}{\frac{1 - x^2 - 2x^2}{1-x^2}}\right) = \tan^{-1}\left(\frac{3x - x^3}{1 - 3x^2}\right)$$

= RHS **Hence proved.**

(xiii) Let $I = \int \sin^3 x \, dx = \int \frac{3\sin x - \sin 3x}{4} dx$

$$[\because \sin 3\theta = 3\sin\theta - 4\sin^3\theta]$$

$$= \frac{1}{4}\int 3\sin x \, dx - \frac{1}{4}\int \sin 3x \, dx$$

$$= \frac{1}{4}\left(-3\cos x + \frac{\cos 3x}{3}\right) + C$$

(xiv) Given,

$$P(R) = 0.60,\ P(O) = 0.40$$

$$P(P/R) = 0.75 \text{ and } P(P/O) = 0.30$$

Using the law of total probability, we get

$$P(P) = P(P/R)\,P(R) + P(P/O)\,P(O)$$

$$= 0.75 \times 0.6 + 0.3 \times 0.4$$

$$= 0.45 + 0.12 = 0.57$$

(xv) We have, $f(x) = \begin{bmatrix} \cos x & -\sin x & 0 \\ \sin x & \cos x & 0 \\ 0 & 0 & 1 \end{bmatrix}$

Now,

$$f(x) \cdot f(y) = \begin{bmatrix} \cos x & -\sin x & 0 \\ \sin x & \cos x & 0 \\ 0 & 0 & 1 \end{bmatrix} \begin{bmatrix} \cos y & -\sin y & 0 \\ \sin y & \cos y & 0 \\ 0 & 0 & 1 \end{bmatrix}$$

$$= \begin{bmatrix} \cos x\cos y - \sin x \sin y & -\sin y \cos x - \sin x \cos y & 0 \\ \sin x \cos y + \cos x \sin y & -\sin x \sin y + \cos x \cos y & 0 \\ 0 & 0 & 1 \end{bmatrix}$$

$$= \begin{bmatrix} \cos(x+y) & -\sin(x+y) & 0 \\ \sin(x+y) & \cos(x+y) & 0 \\ 0 & 0 & 1 \end{bmatrix}$$

$[\because \cos A \cos B - \sin A \sin B = \cos(A+B),$
$\sin A \cos B - \cos A \sin B = \sin(A+B)]$

$= f(x+y)$ **Hence proved.**

2. We have, $f(x) = \begin{cases} \dfrac{\log(1+ax) - \log(1-bx)}{x}, & x \neq 0 \\ k, & x = 0 \end{cases}$

Now, $\lim_{x\to 0} f(x) = \lim_{x\to 0} \dfrac{\log(1+ax) - \log(1-bx)}{x}$

$= \lim_{x\to 0} \dfrac{\log(1+ax)}{x} - \lim_{x\to 0} \dfrac{\log(1-bx)}{x}$

$= \lim_{ax\to 0} \dfrac{\log(1+ax)}{ax} \cdot a - \lim_{-bx\to 0} \dfrac{\log(1-bx)}{-bx} \cdot (-b)$

[as $x \to 0, ax \to 0, -bx \to 0$]

$= 1 \cdot a - 1 \cdot (-b)$ $\left[\because \lim_{x\to 0} \dfrac{\log(1+x)}{x} = 1\right]$

$= a + b$

Also, $f(0) = k$

Since, the function f is continuous at $x = 0$,

$\therefore$ $\lim_{x\to 0} f(x) = f(0)$

$\Rightarrow$ $a + b = k$

Hence, the function f is continuous at $x = 0$, if $k = a + b$.

Common Mistake

$\lim_{x\to 0} \dfrac{\log(1+ax)}{x} \neq 1$ instead $\lim_{ax\to 0} \dfrac{a(\log(1+ax))}{ax} = a$

3. (i) We have, $y = \dfrac{e^x + \log x}{\sin 3x}$

$\therefore$ $\dfrac{dy}{dx} = \dfrac{\sin 3x\left(e^x + \dfrac{1}{x}\right) - 3\cos 3x(e^x + \log x)}{(\sin 3x)^2}$

On differentiating w.r.t x, we get

$\dfrac{dy}{dx} = \dfrac{e^x \sin 3x + \dfrac{\sin 3x}{x} - 3e^x \cos 3x - 3\cos 3x \log x}{(\sin 3x)^2}$

$\Rightarrow$ $\dfrac{dy}{dx} = \dfrac{e^x(\sin 3x - 3\cos 3x) + \dfrac{\sin 3x}{x} - 3\cos 3x \log x}{(\sin 3x)^2}$

$\Rightarrow$ $\dfrac{dy}{dx} = \dfrac{e^x}{\sin 3x}\left(\dfrac{\sin 3x}{\sin 3x} - \dfrac{3\cos 3x}{\sin 3x}\right) + \dfrac{\sin 3x}{x(\sin 3x)^2} - \dfrac{3\cos 3x \log x}{(\sin 3x)^2}$

$\Rightarrow$ $\dfrac{dy}{dx} = e^x \operatorname{cosec} 3x(1 - 3\cot 3x) + \dfrac{\operatorname{cosec} 3x}{x}$

$-3\cot 3x \operatorname{cosec} 3x \log x$

Or

(ii) We have,

$r(x) = v[u(x)]$

On differentiating w.r.t x, we get

$r'(x) = v'[u(x)]u'(x)$

On putting $x = 2$,

$r'(2) = v'[u(2)]u'(2)$

$= v'(5) \times (-1)$

[$\because u(2) = 5, u'(2) = -1$ from the table]

$= -9 \times (-1) = 9$ [$\because v'(5) = 9$]

4. Given differential equation is

$(e^x + e^{-x})\dfrac{dy}{dx} = e^x - e^{-x}$

$\Rightarrow$ $dy = \left(\dfrac{e^x - e^{-x}}{e^x + e^{-x}}\right)dx$

On integrating both sides, we get

$\int dy = \int \left(\dfrac{e^x - e^{-x}}{e^x + e^{-x}}\right)dx$ ...(i)

Let $e^x + e^{-x} = t \Rightarrow (e^x - e^{-x})dx = dt$

$\therefore$ From Eq. (i), we get

$\int dy = \int \dfrac{1}{t} dt$

$\Rightarrow$ $y = \log|t| + C$

$\Rightarrow$ $y = \log(e^x + e^{-x}) + C$ [$\because t = e^x + e^{-x}$]

5. (i) Let the two parts be x and y, then

$x + y = 20$ ...(i)

According to the question,

$z = y^2x^3 \Rightarrow z = (20 - x)^2 \cdot x^3$ [$\because$ from Eq. (i)]

$\Rightarrow$ $z = (400 - 40x + x^2)x^3$

$\Rightarrow$ $z = 400x^3 - 40x^4 + x^5$

On differentiating both sides w.r.t. x, we get

$\dfrac{dz}{dx} = 1200x^2 - 160x^3 + 5x^4$ ...(ii)

For maxima or minima, put $\dfrac{dz}{dx} = 0$

$\Rightarrow$ $1200x^2 - 160x^3 + 5x^4 = 0$

$\Rightarrow$ $5x^2(240 - 32x + x^2) = 0$

$\Rightarrow$ $5x^2(x - 20)(x - 12) = 0$

$\Rightarrow$ $x = 0, 12$ and 20

Since, x cannot be 0 or 20, therefore $x = 12$.

On differentiating Eq. (ii) w.r.t. x, we get

$\dfrac{d^2z}{dx^2} = 2400x - 480x^2 + 20x^3 = 20x(120 - 24x + x^2)$

At $x = 12$, $\dfrac{d^2z}{dx^2} = 240(120 - 288 + 144) = -5760 < 0$

So, at $x = 12$, z is maxima i.e. y^2x^3 is maximum. Then, from Eq. (i), we get $y = 20 - x = 20 - 12 = 8$

Hence, the two parts into which 20 can be divided are 12 and 8.

Or

(ii) We know that volume of cylinder, $V = \pi r^2 h$

Given, $r = 0.6$ m, $\frac{dV}{dt} = 0.30 \text{ cm}^3/\text{min}$

$= \frac{0.3}{10^6} \text{m}^3/\text{min}$ ...(i)

Now, $V = \pi \times (0.6)^2 \times h \Rightarrow V = 0.36\pi h$

On differentiating both sides w.r.t. t, we get

$$\frac{dV}{dt} = 0.36\pi \frac{dh}{dt} \Rightarrow \frac{0.3}{10^6} = 0.36\pi \frac{dh}{dt}$$

$$\Rightarrow \frac{dh}{dt} = \frac{0.3}{10^6 \times 0.36\pi} = \frac{30}{10^6 \times 36\pi} \quad \text{[from Eq. (i)]}$$

$$= \frac{1}{12\pi \times 10^5} \text{ m/min}$$

Hence, the required rate is $\frac{1}{12\pi \times 10^5}$ m/min.

6. $\text{LHS} = \begin{vmatrix} a & b & c \\ b & c & a \\ c & a & b \end{vmatrix}$

Interchanging C_1 and C_3, we get

$$\text{LHS} = (-)\begin{vmatrix} c & b & a \\ a & c & b \\ b & a & c \end{vmatrix}$$

Interchanging R_2 and R_3, we get

$$\text{LHS} = (-)(-)\begin{vmatrix} c & b & a \\ b & a & c \\ a & c & b \end{vmatrix} = \begin{vmatrix} c & b & a \\ b & a & c \\ a & c & b \end{vmatrix} = \text{RHS}$$

Common Mistake

After interchanging the rows or columns, do consider the negative sign.

7. We have a function $f: R^+ \to R^+$, defined as $f(x) = e^x$

For one-one Let $x_1, x_2 \in R^+$ such that

$f(x_1) = f(x_2) \Rightarrow e^{x_1} = e^{x_2}$

On taking log both sides, we get

$\log e^{x_1} = \log e^{x_2} \Rightarrow x_1 = x_2$ $[\because \log e = 1]$

So, f is one-one.

For onto Let $y \in R^+$ be any arbitrary element.

Now, let $y = f(x)$

$\Rightarrow y = e^x \Rightarrow \log y = \log e^x$ [taking log on both sides]

$\Rightarrow x = \log y \in R^+, \forall\, y \in R^+ - (0, 1]$

Thus, for $y \in (0, 1]$, there does not exist any $x \in R^+$ such that $f(x) = y$.

So, f is not onto.

Hence, f is not invertible.

8. We have, $\tan^{-1}\left\{\frac{\sqrt{1+x^2} - \sqrt{1-x^2}}{\sqrt{1+x^2} + \sqrt{1-x^2}}\right\} = \alpha$

$$\Rightarrow \frac{\sqrt{1+x^2} - \sqrt{1-x^2}}{\sqrt{1+x^2} + \sqrt{1-x^2}} = \tan\alpha$$

On applying componendo and dividendo rule, we get

$$\frac{(\sqrt{1+x^2} - \sqrt{1-x^2}) + (\sqrt{1+x^2} + \sqrt{1-x^2})}{(\sqrt{1+x^2} - \sqrt{1-x^2}) - (\sqrt{1+x^2} + \sqrt{1-x^2})} = \frac{\tan\alpha + 1}{\tan\alpha - 1}$$

$$\Rightarrow \frac{2\sqrt{1+x^2}}{-2\sqrt{1-x^2}} = \frac{\tan\alpha + 1}{\tan\alpha - 1}$$

$$\Rightarrow \frac{\sqrt{1-x^2}}{\sqrt{1+x^2}} = \frac{1 - \tan\alpha}{1 + \tan\alpha}$$

$$\Rightarrow \sqrt{\frac{1-x^2}{1+x^2}} = \frac{\cos\alpha - \sin\alpha}{\cos\alpha + \sin\alpha} \quad \left[\because \tan\theta = \frac{\sin\theta}{\cos\theta}\right]$$

On squaring both sides, we get

$$\frac{1-x^2}{1+x^2} = \left(\frac{\cos\alpha - \sin\alpha}{\cos\alpha + \sin\alpha}\right)^2$$

$$\Rightarrow \frac{1-x^2}{1+x^2} = \frac{\cos^2\alpha + \sin^2\alpha - 2\sin\alpha\cos\alpha}{\cos^2\alpha + \sin^2\alpha + 2\cos\alpha\sin\alpha}$$

$$\Rightarrow \frac{1-x^2}{1+x^2} = \frac{1 - \sin 2\alpha}{1 + \sin 2\alpha}$$

$[\because \cos^2\theta + \sin^2\theta = 1$ and $\sin 2\theta = 2\sin\theta\cos\theta]$

Again, applying componendo and dividendo rule, we get

$$\frac{(1-x^2) + (1+x^2)}{(1-x^2) - (1+x^2)} = \frac{(1 - \sin 2\alpha) + (1 + \sin 2\alpha)}{(1 - \sin 2\alpha) - (1 + \sin 2\alpha)}$$

$$\Rightarrow \frac{2}{-2x^2} = \frac{2}{-2\sin 2\alpha}$$

$$\Rightarrow x^2 = \sin 2\alpha$$ **Hence proved.**

9. Let $I = \int_0^{\pi/2} \frac{\sin^2 x}{\sin x + \cos x} dx$ ...(i)

$$\Rightarrow I = \int_0^{\pi/2} \frac{\sin^2\left(\frac{\pi}{2} - x\right)}{\sin\left(\frac{\pi}{2} - x\right) + \cos\left(\frac{\pi}{2} - x\right)} dx$$

$$\left[\because \int_0^a f(x)dx = \int_0^a f(a-x)dx\right]$$

$$\Rightarrow I = \int_0^{\pi/2} \frac{\cos^2 x}{\cos x + \sin x} dx \quad \text{...(ii)}$$

On adding Eqs. (i) and (ii), we get

$$2I = \int_0^{\pi/2} \frac{\sin^2 x + \cos^2 x}{\sin x + \cos x} dx$$

$$\Rightarrow 2I = \int_0^{\pi/2} \frac{1}{\sin x + \cos x} dx \quad [\because \sin^2\theta + \cos^2\theta = 1]$$

$$\Rightarrow 2I=\int_0^{\pi/2}\frac{1}{\dfrac{2\tan(x/2)}{1+\tan^2(x/2)}+\dfrac{1-\tan^2(x/2)}{1+\tan^2(x/2)}}dx$$

$$\left[\because \sin\theta=\frac{2\tan\frac{\theta}{2}}{1+\tan^2\frac{\theta}{2}} \text{ and } \cos\theta=\frac{1-\tan^2\frac{\theta}{2}}{1+\tan^2\frac{\theta}{2}}\right]$$

$$\Rightarrow 2I=\int_0^{\pi/2}\frac{\sec^2(x/2)}{2\tan(x/2)+1-\tan^2(x/2)}dx$$

$[\because 1+\tan^2\theta=\sec^2\theta]$

Put $\tan\frac{x}{2}=t \Rightarrow \sec^2\frac{x}{2}\cdot\frac{1}{2}dx=dt$

$\Rightarrow \sec^2\frac{x}{2}dx=2dt$

Lower limit When $x=0$, then $t=\tan 0=0$

Upper limit When $x=\frac{\pi}{2}$, then $t=\tan\frac{\pi}{4}=1.$ (1)

$$\therefore\ 2I=\int_0^1\frac{2dt}{2t+1-t^2}=2\int_0^1\frac{dt}{-[t^2-2t-1]}$$

$$=2\int_0^1\frac{dt}{-[(t-1)^2-1-1]}=2\int_0^1\frac{dt}{(\sqrt{2})^2-(t-1)^2}$$

$$=\left[\frac{2}{2\sqrt{2}}\log\left|\frac{\sqrt{2}+t-1}{\sqrt{2}-t+1}\right|\right]_0^1$$

$$\left[\because\int\frac{dx}{a^2-x^2}=\frac{1}{2a}\log\left|\frac{a+x}{a-x}\right|+C\right]$$

$$=\frac{1}{\sqrt{2}}\left[\log\frac{\sqrt{2}+1-1}{\sqrt{2}-1+1}-\log\frac{\sqrt{2}+0-1}{\sqrt{2}-0+1}\right]$$

$$=\frac{1}{\sqrt{2}}\left[\log 1-\log\frac{\sqrt{2}-1}{\sqrt{2}+1}\right] \quad (1)$$

$$=-\frac{1}{\sqrt{2}}\log\left[\frac{\sqrt{2}-1}{\sqrt{2}+1}\times\frac{\sqrt{2}+1}{\sqrt{2}+1}\right] \quad [\because \log 1=0]$$

$$=\frac{-1}{\sqrt{2}}\log\frac{2-1}{(\sqrt{2}+1)^2} \quad [\because (a-b)(a+b)=a^2-b^2]$$

$$=\frac{-1}{\sqrt{2}}\log\frac{1}{(\sqrt{2}+1)^2}$$

$$=\frac{-1}{\sqrt{2}}[\log 1-\log(\sqrt{2}+1)]^2$$

$$=\frac{1}{\sqrt{2}}\log(\sqrt{2}+1)^2 \Rightarrow 2I=\frac{2}{\sqrt{2}}\log(\sqrt{2}+1)$$

$\Rightarrow I=\frac{1}{\sqrt{2}}\log(\sqrt{2}+1)$ **Hence proved.** (1)

10. (i) Let $I=\int\frac{\sec x\,dx}{1+\operatorname{cosec} x}=\int\frac{\dfrac{1}{\cos x}}{1+\dfrac{1}{\sin x}}dx$

$$=\int\frac{\sin x\,dx}{\cos x(1+\sin x)}=\int\frac{\sin x\cos x\,dx}{\cos^2 x(1+\sin x)}$$

$$=\int\frac{\sin x\cos dx}{(1-\sin^2 x)(1+\sin x)} \quad [\because \sin^2\theta+\cos^2\theta=1]$$

$$\Rightarrow\quad I=\int\frac{\sin x\cos x\,dx}{(1-\sin x)(1+\sin x)^2}$$

$[\because a^2-b^2=(a+b)(a-b)]$

On putting $\sin x=t \Rightarrow \cos x\,dx=dt$, we get

$$I=\int\frac{t}{(1+t)^2(1-t)}dt$$

Now, $\frac{t}{(1+t)^2(1-t)}=\frac{A}{1+t}+\frac{B}{(1+t)^2}+\frac{C}{1-t}$

$\Rightarrow t=A(1+t)(1-t)+B(1-t)+C(1+t)^2$

On putting $t=-1$, then we get $-1=2B \Rightarrow B=\frac{-1}{2}$

On putting $t=1$, then we get

$\therefore\quad 1=4C \Rightarrow\quad C=1/4$

On putting $t=0$, then we get

$\therefore\quad 0=A+B+C$

$\Rightarrow\quad 0=A+\left(\frac{-1}{2}\right)+\left(\frac{1}{4}\right)$

$\Rightarrow\quad A=\frac{1}{2}-\frac{1}{4}=\frac{2-1}{4}=\frac{1}{4}$

Then, $\frac{1}{(1+t)^2(1-t)}=\frac{1}{4(1+t)}-\frac{1}{2(1+t)^2}+\frac{1}{4(1+t)}$

$$\therefore\ I=\int\left[\frac{1}{4(1+t)}-\frac{1}{2(1+t)^2}+\frac{1}{4(1-t)}\right]dt$$

$$\Rightarrow I=\frac{1}{4}\int\frac{1}{1+t}dt+\left(\frac{-1}{2}\right)\int\frac{1}{(1+t)^2}dt+\frac{1}{4}\int\frac{1}{(1-t)}dt$$

$$=\frac{1}{4}\log|1+t|+\frac{-1}{2}\times\frac{-1}{1+t}-\frac{1}{4}\log|1-t|+C$$

$$=\frac{1}{4}\log|1+\sin x|+\frac{1}{2(1+\sin x)}-\frac{1}{4}\log|1-\sin x|+C$$

$[\because t=\sin x]$

(ii) Let $I=\int\frac{1}{\cos^4 x+\sin^4 x}dx$

On dividing numerator and denominator by $\cos^4 x$ in RHS, we get

$$I=\int\frac{\sec^4 x}{1+\tan^4 x}dx$$

$$\Rightarrow\quad I=\int\frac{(\sec^2 x)(\sec^2 x)}{1+(\tan^2 x)^2}dx$$

$$\Rightarrow\quad I=\int\frac{\sec^2 x(1+\tan^2 x)}{1+(\tan^2 x)^2}dx \quad [\because 1+\tan^2\theta=\sec^2\theta]$$

Put $\tan x=t \Rightarrow \sec^2 x\,dx=dt$

Then, $I=\int\frac{1+t^2}{1+t^4}dt$

Again, on dividing numerator and denominator by t^2 in RHS, we get

$$I=\int\frac{1+\frac{1}{t^2}}{t^2+\frac{1}{t^2}+2-2}\,dt=\int\frac{1+\frac{1}{t^2}}{\left(t-\frac{1}{t}\right)^2+2}\,dt$$

Again, let $t-\frac{1}{t}=u \Rightarrow \left(1+\frac{1}{t^2}\right)dt=du$

Then, $I=\int\frac{du}{u^2+(\sqrt{2})^2} \Rightarrow I=\frac{1}{\sqrt{2}}\tan^{-1}\left(\frac{u}{\sqrt{2}}\right)+C$

$$\left[\because \int\frac{dx}{x^2+a^2}=\frac{1}{a}\tan^{-1}\left(\frac{x}{a}\right)+C\right]$$

$$\Rightarrow \quad I=\frac{1}{\sqrt{2}}\tan^{-1}\left(\frac{t-\frac{1}{t}}{\sqrt{2}}\right)+C \quad \left[\because u=t-\frac{1}{t}\right]$$

$$\Rightarrow \quad I=\frac{1}{\sqrt{2}}\tan^{-1}\left(\frac{t^2-1}{\sqrt{2}t}\right)+C$$

$$\Rightarrow \quad I=\frac{1}{\sqrt{2}}\tan^{-1}\left(\frac{\tan^2 x-1}{\sqrt{2}\tan x}\right)+C \quad (1)$$

$[\because t=\tan x]$

11. (i) Given differential equation is,

$$\frac{dy}{dx}+x\cdot\sin 2y=x^3\cos^2 y$$

$$\Rightarrow \quad \frac{dy}{dx}+x\cdot 2\sin y\cos y=x^3\cos^2 y$$

$[\because \sin 2\theta=2\sin\theta\cos\theta]$

$$\Rightarrow \quad \sec^2 y\frac{dy}{dx}+2x\tan y=x^3 \quad \text{...(i)}$$

[divide both sides by $\cos^2 y$]

Let $\tan y=z$

$$\Rightarrow \quad \sec^2 y\frac{dy}{dx}=\frac{dz}{dx}$$

Then, Eq. (i) becomes $\frac{dz}{dx}+(2x)z=x^3$ ...(ii)

which is a linear differential equation of the form

$$\frac{dz}{dx}+Pz=Q,$$

where $P=2x$ and $Q=x^3$.

(ii) Integrating factor, $\text{IF}=e^{\int P dx}=e^{\int 2x\,dx}=e^{x^2}$

(iii) The general solution is

$$z\cdot\text{IF}=\int Q\cdot\text{IF}\,dx+C$$

$$\Rightarrow \quad ze^{x^2}=\int x^3 e^{x^2}\,dx+C$$

$$=\int x^2 e^{x^2}\cdot x\,dx+C$$

In RHS put $t=x^2 \Rightarrow dt=2x\,dx$, then we get

$$ze^{x^2}=\frac{1}{2}\int \underset{\text{I}}{t}\,\underset{\text{II}}{e^t}\,dt+C$$

$$\Rightarrow \quad ze^{x^2}=\frac{1}{2}\left[t\int e^t\,dt-\int\left(\frac{d}{dt}(t)\int e^t\,dt\right)dt\right]+C$$

[using integration by parts]

$$\Rightarrow \quad ze^{x^2}=\frac{1}{2}\left[t\,e^t-\int e^t\,dt\right]+C$$

$$\Rightarrow \quad ze^{x^2}=\frac{1}{2}(t-1)e^t+C$$

$$\Rightarrow \quad e^{x^2}\tan y=\frac{1}{2}(x^2-1)e^{x^2}+C$$

[put $t=x^2$ and $z=\tan y$]

which is the required solution.

12. (i) Let the dimensions of the box be x and y. Also, let V denotes its volume and S denotes its total surface area.

Now, $S=x^2+4xy$ $\quad$ [$\because S=$ area of square base + area of the four walls]

Given, $x^2+4xy=C^2$

$$\Rightarrow \quad y=\frac{C^2-x^2}{4x} \quad \text{...(i)}$$

Also, volume of the box is given by

$$V=x^2y \Rightarrow V=x^2\left(\frac{C^2-x^2}{4x}\right) \quad \text{[from Eq. (i)]}$$

$$\Rightarrow \quad V=\frac{xC^2-x^3}{4}$$

On differentiating both sides w.r.t. x, we get

$$\frac{dV}{dx}=\frac{C^2-3x^2}{4} \quad \text{...(ii)}$$

For maxima or minima, put $dV/dx=0$

$$\Rightarrow \quad \frac{C^2-3x^2}{4}=0$$

$$\Rightarrow \quad C^2=3x^2$$

$$\Rightarrow \quad x=C/\sqrt{3}$$

On differentiating Eq. (ii), w.r.t x, we get

$$\frac{d^2V}{dx^2}=\frac{d}{dx}\left(\frac{dV}{dx}\right)=\frac{d}{dx}\left(\frac{C^2-3x^2}{4}\right)=\frac{-6x}{4}=\frac{-3x}{2}<0$$

At $x=\frac{C}{\sqrt{3}}, \frac{d^2V}{dx^2}<0$

$\Rightarrow V$ is maximum.

Now, maximum volume at $x=\frac{C}{\sqrt{3}}$ is

$$V=\frac{xC^2-x^3}{4}$$

$$=\frac{1}{4}\left[\frac{C}{\sqrt{3}}\cdot C^2-\left(\frac{C}{\sqrt{3}}\right)^3\right] \quad \left[\text{putting } x=\frac{C}{\sqrt{3}}\right]$$

$$=\frac{1}{4}\left[\frac{C^3}{\sqrt{3}}-\frac{C^3}{3\sqrt{3}}\right]$$

$$=\frac{1}{4}\left[\frac{3C^3-C^3}{3\sqrt{3}}\right]=\frac{1}{4}\times\frac{2C^3}{3\sqrt{3}}=\frac{C^3}{6\sqrt{3}}$$

Hence, the maximum volume of box is $\frac{C^3}{6\sqrt{3}}$ cu units. **Hence proved.**

Or

(ii) (*a*) The given curve is $y=x^3-11x+5$ ...(i)

Let $P(x_1, y_1)$ be the required point, then P lies on Eq. (i),

$\therefore \quad y_1=x_1^3-11x_1+5$ ...(ii)

On differentiating Eq. (i) w.r.t. x, we get

$$\frac{dy}{dx}=3x^2-11$$

$\therefore$ The slope of tangent to the curve (i) at $P(x_1, y_1)$ $=3x_1^2-11$

But the tangent at P is the line $y=x-11$ (given)

Then, Slope of tangent at $P=$ Slope of the line $y=x-11$

$\Rightarrow \quad 3x_1^2-11=1$

$\Rightarrow \quad 3x_1^2=12 \Rightarrow x_1^2=4$

$\Rightarrow \quad x_1=2,-2$

On putting $x_1=2$ in Eq. (ii), we get

$y_1=2^3-11\cdot 2+5=-9$ and

On putting $x_1=-2$ in Eq. (ii), we get

$y_1=(-2)^3-11\cdot(-2)+5=19.$

Thus, two points on given curve are $(2,-9)$ and $(-2,19)$.

But when we put the coordinate of the point $(-2,19)$ in the tangent line $y=x-11$, we see that $19\neq -2-11$.

Therefore, this point does not satisfy the equation of tangent line.

Hence, the required point on the curve is $(2,-9)$.

Common Mistake

Obtained points must satisfy the equation of tangent line.

(*b*) Given, $f(x)=x^3-3x^2+3x$

On differentiating w.r.t. x, we get

$$\frac{df}{dx}=3x^2-6x+3$$

$$=3(x^2-2x+1)=3(x-1)^2\geq 0\,\forall\, x\in R$$

Here, we see that at $x=1$,

$$\frac{df}{dx}=0$$

Hence, $f(x)$ is strictly increasing in $R-\{1\}$.

13. (i) Let E_1, E_2 and A be the events defined as follows

$E_1=$ lost card is of clubs,

$E_2=$ lost card is not of clubs and

$A=$ two cards drawn are both of clubs.

Then, $P(E_1)=\frac{\text{Number of clubs cards}}{\text{Total number of cards}}$

$=\frac{13}{52}=\frac{1}{4}$ and

$P(E_2)=\frac{\text{Number of other than clubs cards}}{\text{Total number of cards}}$

$=\frac{39}{52}=\frac{3}{4}$

When one card is lost, number of remaining card in the pack $=51$

When E_1 has occurred i.e. when a card of clubs is lost, then the probability of drawing 2 cards of clubs from remaining pack $=\frac{^{12}C_2}{^{51}C_2}$

$$\Rightarrow P(A/E_1)=\frac{^{12}C_2}{^{51}C_2}=\frac{12\cdot 11}{1\cdot 2}\times\frac{1\cdot 2}{51\cdot 50}=\frac{22}{425}$$

When E_2 has occurred i.e. card of club is not lost, then the probability of drawing 2 cards of clubs from remaining pack $=\frac{^{13}C_2}{^{51}C_2}$

$$\Rightarrow P(A/E_2)=\frac{^{13}C_2}{^{51}C_2}=\frac{13\cdot 12}{1\cdot 2}\times\frac{1\cdot 2}{51\cdot 50}=\frac{26}{425}$$

We want to find $P(E_1/A)$.

By using Baye's theorem, we get

$$P(E_1/A)=\frac{P(E_1)\,P(A/E_1)}{P(E_1)\,P(A/E_1)+P(E_2)\,P(A/E_2)}$$

$$=\frac{\frac{1}{4}\cdot\frac{22}{425}}{\frac{1}{4}\cdot\frac{22}{425}+\frac{3}{4}\cdot\frac{26}{425}}$$

$$=\frac{22}{22+78}=\frac{22}{100}=\frac{11}{50}$$

Or

(ii) Let $E_1=$ Student knows the answer

$E_2=$ Student guesses the answer

and $A=$ Student answered correctly

$\therefore \quad P(E_1)=\frac{3}{4}$ and $P(E_2)=\frac{1}{4}$

Now, $P\left(\frac{A}{E_2}\right)=P$ (student answered correctly, when he guesses)

$=\frac{1}{4}$

and $P\left(\frac{A}{E_1}\right)=P$ (he answers correctly given that he knew the answer)

$=1$

$\therefore$ Required probability,

$$P\left(\frac{E_1}{A}\right)=\frac{P(E_1)\cdot P\left(\frac{A}{E_1}\right)}{\left[P(E_1)\cdot P\left(\frac{A}{E_1}\right)+P(E_2)\cdot P\left(\frac{A}{E_2}\right)\right]}$$

[using Baye's theorem]

$$=\frac{\frac{3}{4}\times 1}{\left(\frac{3}{4}\times 1\right)+\left(\frac{1}{4}\times\frac{1}{4}\right)}=\frac{\frac{3}{4}}{\frac{3}{4}+\frac{1}{16}}=\frac{\frac{3}{4}}{\frac{12+1}{16}}$$

$$=\frac{3}{4}\times\frac{16}{13}=\frac{12}{13}$$

Hence, the probability that the student knows the answer, given that he answered it correctly, is $\frac{12}{13}$.

14. (i) We have, $A=\begin{bmatrix}40\\100\\50\end{bmatrix}$

$\therefore$ Order of $A=3\times 1$

(ii) We have, $B=\begin{bmatrix}1000 & 500 & 5000\\3000 & 1000 & 10000\end{bmatrix}$

$\therefore$ Order of $B=2\times 3$

(iii) $A'=\begin{bmatrix}40\\100\\50\end{bmatrix}'=[40\quad 100\quad 50]$

and $B'=\begin{bmatrix}1000 & 500 & 5000\\3000 & 1000 & 10000\end{bmatrix}'=\begin{bmatrix}1000 & 3000\\500 & 1000\\5000 & 10000\end{bmatrix}$

(iv) $BA=\begin{bmatrix}1000 & 500 & 5000\\3000 & 1000 & 10000\end{bmatrix}\begin{bmatrix}40\\100\\50\end{bmatrix}$

$$=\begin{bmatrix}40000+50000+250000\\120000+100000+500000\end{bmatrix}=\begin{bmatrix}340000\\720000\end{bmatrix}$$

(v) $(BA)'=\begin{bmatrix}340000\\720000\end{bmatrix}'$

$=[340000\quad 720000]$

Hence order of $A=3\times 1$ and order of $B=2\times 3$

Since, number of columns of A $\neq$ number of rows of B.

So, AB cannot be find.

15. (i) (c) Let $\vec{a}=\hat{i}-2\hat{j}+2\hat{k}$

Any vector in the direction of a vector $\vec{a}$ is given by

$$\frac{\vec{a}}{|\vec{a}|}=\frac{\hat{i}-2\hat{j}+2\hat{k}}{\sqrt{(1)^2+(-2)^2+(2)^2}}=\frac{\hat{i}-2\hat{j}+2\hat{k}}{3}$$

Now, vector in the direction of $\vec{a}$ with magnitude 9

$$=9\cdot\frac{\hat{i}-2\hat{j}+2\hat{k}}{3}=3(\hat{i}-2\hat{j}+2\hat{k})$$

(ii) (b) We have, $\vec{r}\cdot(6\hat{i}-3\hat{j}+\hat{k})=5$

$\Rightarrow\quad (x\hat{i}+y\hat{j}+z\hat{k})\cdot(6\hat{i}-3\hat{j}+\hat{k})=5$

$\Rightarrow\quad 6x-3y+z=5,$

which is the required cartesian form.

(iii) (c) Given four points are

$A(-3,2,4)$, $B(2,5,-2)$, $C(1,-2,2)$ and $D(4,2,3)$.

Now, direction ratios of AB are $<2+3,5-2,-2-4>$ i.e. $<5,3,-6>$.

and $\sqrt{(5)^2+(3)^2+(-6)^2}=\sqrt{25+9+36}=\sqrt{70}$

Therefore, direction cosines of AB are

$$l_1=\frac{5}{\sqrt{70}},\ m_1=\frac{3}{\sqrt{70}},\ n_1=\frac{-6}{\sqrt{70}}$$

Also, direction ratios of CD are

$<4-1,2+2,3-2>$ i.e. $<3,4,1>$

and $\sqrt{(3)^2+(4)^2+(1)^2}=\sqrt{9+16+1}=\sqrt{26}$

Therefore, direction cosines of CD are

$$l_2=\frac{3}{\sqrt{26}},\ m_2=\frac{4}{\sqrt{26}},\ n_2=\frac{1}{\sqrt{26}}$$

Let θ be the angle between AB and CD, then

$$\cos\theta=|l_1l_2+m_1m_2+n_1n_2|$$

$$=\left|\frac{5}{\sqrt{70}}\times\frac{3}{\sqrt{26}}+\frac{3}{\sqrt{70}}\times\frac{4}{\sqrt{26}}+\frac{-6}{\sqrt{70}}\times\frac{1}{\sqrt{26}}\right|$$

$$=\left|\frac{15}{\sqrt{1820}}+\frac{12}{\sqrt{1820}}-\frac{6}{\sqrt{1820}}\right|$$

$$=\frac{21}{\sqrt{1820}}$$

Hence, both statements are correct.

(iv) From the figure, we have

Plane passes through Y and Z-axes from the points (0, 4, 0) and (0, 0, 2) respectively.

Let a, b and c be the direction ratios of the plane.

Then, equation of plane passing through (0, 4, 0).

$$a(x-0)+b(y-4)+c(z-0)=0 \quad \ldots\text{(i)}$$

Also, plane (i) passes through the points (0, 0, 2), then

$$a(0-0)+b(0-4)+c(2-0)=0$$

$\Rightarrow\quad -4b+2c=0$

$\Rightarrow\quad c=2b \quad \ldots\text{(ii)}$

Also, given that plane is parallel to X-axis, therefore normal to the plane are perpendicular to X-axis.

$\therefore\quad 1\times a+b\times 0+c\times 0=0\Rightarrow a=0$

and from Eq. (ii), we get $\frac{b}{1}=\frac{c}{2}$, so $\frac{a}{0}=\frac{b}{1}=\frac{c}{2}$ ....(iii)

Hence, the equation of plane is

$$y-4+2z=0 \quad \text{[from Eq. (i) and (ii)]}$$

$\Rightarrow\quad y+2z=4$

(v) Given, $\vec{a}+\vec{b}+\vec{c}=\vec{0} \Rightarrow \vec{a}=-(\vec{b}+\vec{c})$

Now, $|\vec{a}|^2=\vec{a}\cdot\vec{a}=[-(\vec{b}+\vec{c})]\cdot[-(\vec{b}+\vec{c})]$

$\Rightarrow \quad |\vec{a}|^2=(\vec{b}+\vec{c})\cdot(\vec{b}+\vec{c})$

$\Rightarrow \quad |\vec{a}|^2=\vec{b}\cdot\vec{b}+\vec{b}\cdot\vec{c}+\vec{c}\cdot\vec{b}+\vec{c}\cdot\vec{c}$

$\Rightarrow \quad |\vec{a}|^2=|\vec{b}|^2+2\vec{b}\cdot\vec{c}+|\vec{c}|^2$

$\Rightarrow \quad 2\vec{b}\cdot\vec{c}=|\vec{a}|^2-|\vec{b}|^2-|\vec{c}|^2$

$\Rightarrow \quad 2[|\vec{b}||\vec{c}|\cos\theta]=|\vec{a}|^2-|\vec{b}|^2-|\vec{c}|^2$

$$\Rightarrow \quad \cos\theta=\frac{|\vec{a}|^2-|\vec{b}|^2-|\vec{c}|^2}{2|\vec{b}||\vec{c}|}$$

16. (i) Let BF and CE be two equal medians of a ΔABC. Take A as origin and $\vec{b}, \vec{c}$ be the position vectors of the points B, C respectively.

Then, position vector of $E=\frac{1}{2}\vec{b}$ and

position vector of $F=\frac{1}{2}\vec{c}$

$\therefore \overrightarrow{BF}=$ Position vector of F – Position vector of B

$=\frac{1}{2}\vec{c}-\vec{b}$

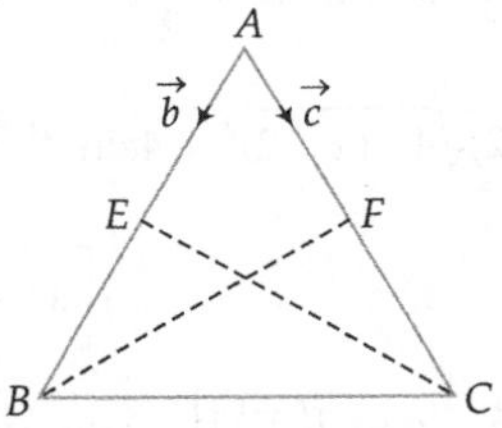

and $\overrightarrow{CE}=$ Position vector of E – Position vector of C

$=\frac{1}{2}\vec{b}-\vec{c}$

Since, both medians are equal

$\therefore \quad BF=CE \Rightarrow BF^2=CE^2$

$\Rightarrow \quad |\overrightarrow{BF}|^2=|\overrightarrow{CE}|^2$

$\Rightarrow \quad \overrightarrow{BF}\cdot\overrightarrow{BF}=\overrightarrow{CE}\cdot\overrightarrow{CE}$

$\Rightarrow \quad \left(\frac{1}{2}\vec{c}-\vec{b}\right)\cdot\left(\frac{1}{2}\vec{c}-\vec{b}\right)=\left(\frac{1}{2}\vec{b}-\vec{c}\right)\cdot\left(\frac{1}{2}\vec{b}-\vec{c}\right)$

$\Rightarrow \quad \frac{1}{4}|\vec{c}|^2-\vec{c}\cdot\vec{b}+|\vec{b}|^2=\frac{1}{4}|\vec{b}|^2-\vec{c}\cdot\vec{b}+|\vec{c}|^2$

$\Rightarrow \quad \frac{-1}{4}|\vec{c}|^2+|\vec{c}|^2=\frac{-1}{4}|\vec{b}|^2+|\vec{b}|^2$

$\Rightarrow \quad \frac{3}{4}|\vec{c}|^2=\frac{3}{4}|\vec{b}|^2 \Rightarrow |\vec{c}|=|\vec{b}|$

Hence, the triangle is isosceles. **Hence proved.**

Or

(ii) Given, $\vec{a}, \vec{b}$ and $\vec{c}$ are mutually perpendicular vectors with equal magnitude.

$\therefore$ We have, $\vec{a}\cdot\vec{b}=\vec{b}\cdot\vec{c}=\vec{c}\cdot\vec{a}=0$

and $\quad |\vec{a}|=|\vec{b}|=|\vec{c}|$ ...(i)

Let θ be the angle between $\vec{a}$ and $(\vec{a}+\vec{b}+\vec{c})$.

Then, $\cos\theta=\frac{\vec{a}\cdot(\vec{a}+\vec{b}+\vec{c})}{|\vec{a}||\vec{a}+\vec{b}+\vec{c}|}=\frac{\vec{a}\cdot\vec{a}+\vec{a}\cdot\vec{b}+\vec{a}\cdot\vec{c}}{|\vec{a}||\vec{a}+\vec{b}+\vec{c}|}$

$=\frac{|\vec{a}|^2+0+0}{|\vec{a}||\vec{a}+\vec{b}+\vec{c}|}$ [from Eq. (i)]

$=\frac{|\vec{a}|}{|\vec{a}+\vec{b}+\vec{c}|}$ ...(ii)

Now, $|\vec{a}+\vec{b}+\vec{c}|^2=(\vec{a}+\vec{b}+\vec{c})\cdot(\vec{a}+\vec{b}+\vec{c})$

$=|\vec{a}|^2+|\vec{b}|^2+|\vec{c}|^2+2\vec{a}\cdot\vec{b}+2\vec{c}\cdot\vec{a}+2\vec{b}\cdot\vec{c}$

$\Rightarrow \quad |\vec{a}+\vec{b}+\vec{c}|^2=|\vec{a}|^2+|\vec{b}|^2+|\vec{c}|^2+0+0+0$

$=|\vec{a}|^2+|\vec{a}|^2+|\vec{a}|^2$ [from Eq. (i)]

$=3|\vec{a}|^2$

$\Rightarrow \quad |\vec{a}+\vec{b}+\vec{c}|=\sqrt{3}|\vec{a}|$

On putting the above value in Eq. (ii), we get

$\cos\theta=\frac{|\vec{a}|}{\sqrt{3}|\vec{a}|}=\frac{1}{\sqrt{3}}$

$\Rightarrow \quad \theta=\cos^{-1}\left(\frac{1}{\sqrt{3}}\right)$

17. (i) Given equation of lines are

$\vec{r}=(4\hat{i}-\hat{j})+\lambda(\hat{i}+2\hat{j}-3\hat{k})$ ...(i)

and $\quad \vec{r}=(\hat{i}-\hat{j}+2\hat{k})+\mu(2\hat{i}+4\hat{j}-5\hat{k})$ ...(ii)

On comparing Eqs. (i) and (ii) with $\vec{r}=\vec{a}_1+\lambda\vec{b}_1$ and $\vec{r}=\vec{a}_2+\mu\vec{b}_2$ respectively, we get

$\vec{a}_1=4\hat{i}-\hat{j}, \vec{b}_1=\hat{i}+2\hat{j}-3\hat{k}$

and $\quad \vec{a}_2=\hat{i}-\hat{j}+2\hat{k}, \vec{b}_2=2\hat{i}+4\hat{j}-5\hat{k}$

Here, $\quad \vec{a}_2-\vec{a}_1=(\hat{i}-\hat{j}+2\hat{k})-(4\hat{i}-\hat{j})=-3\hat{i}+2\hat{k}$

and $\quad \vec{b}_1\times\vec{b}_2=\begin{vmatrix}\hat{i} & \hat{j} & \hat{k}\\ 1 & 2 & -3\\ 2 & 4 & -5\end{vmatrix}$

$=\hat{i}(-10+12)-\hat{j}(-5+6)+\hat{k}(4-4)$

$=2\hat{i}-\hat{j}$

$\Rightarrow \quad |\vec{b}_1\times\vec{b}_2|=\sqrt{2^2+(-1)^2}=\sqrt{4+1}=\sqrt{5}$

Now, the shortest distance between the given lines is given by

$$d=\frac{|(\vec{b_1}\times\vec{b_2})\cdot(\vec{a_2}-\vec{a_1})|}{|\vec{b_1}\times\vec{b_2}|}=\frac{|(2\hat{i}-\hat{j})\cdot(-3\hat{i}+2\hat{k})|}{\sqrt{5}}$$

$$=\frac{|-6|}{\sqrt{5}}=\frac{6}{\sqrt{5}}\text{ units}$$

Or

(ii) The given plane is $\vec{r}\cdot(5\hat{i}+2\hat{j}-7\hat{k})+9=0$

or $\quad \vec{r}\cdot(5\hat{i}+2\hat{j}-7\hat{k})=-9 \quad \ldots(\text{i})$

On comparing Eq. (i) with $\vec{r}\cdot\vec{n}=d$, we get

$$\vec{n}=5\hat{i}+2\hat{j}-7\hat{k} \text{ and } d=-9$$

Let $\vec{a}=\hat{i}-\hat{j}+3\hat{k}$ and $\vec{b}=3(\hat{i}+\hat{j}+\hat{k})$

Let A and B be the points whose position vectors are $\vec{a}$ and $\vec{b}$.

$\therefore$ Distance of A from the plane $=\dfrac{|d-\vec{a}\cdot\vec{n}|}{|\vec{n}|}$

$$=\frac{|-9-(\hat{i}-\hat{j}+3\hat{k})\cdot(5\hat{i}+2\hat{j}-7\hat{k})|}{|5\hat{i}+2\hat{j}-7\hat{k}|}$$

$$=\frac{|-9-(5-2-21)|}{\sqrt{25+4+49}}=\frac{|-9+18|}{\sqrt{78}}=\frac{9}{\sqrt{78}}\text{ units}$$

Also, the distance of B from the plane $=\dfrac{|d-\vec{b}\cdot\vec{n}|}{|\vec{n}|}$

$$=\frac{|-9-(3\hat{i}+3\hat{j}+3\hat{k})\cdot(5\hat{i}+2\hat{j}-7\hat{k})|}{|5\hat{i}+2\hat{j}-7\hat{k}|}$$

$$=\frac{|-9-(15+6-21)|}{\sqrt{78}}=\frac{|-9|}{\sqrt{78}}=\frac{9}{\sqrt{78}}\text{ units}$$

Hence, the points A and B are equidistant from the plane. **Hence proved.**

18. Given equation of circles are

$$x^2+y^2=4 \quad \ldots(\text{i})$$

and $\quad (x-2)^2+y^2=4 \quad \ldots(\text{ii})$

Eq. (i) is a circle with centre at origin and radius 2.
Eq. (ii) is a circle with centre at $C(2,0)$ and radius 2.

On solving Eqs. (i) and (ii), we get

$$(x-2)^2+y^2=x^2+y^2$$

$\Rightarrow \quad x^2-4x+4+y^2=x^2+y^2$

$\Rightarrow \quad x=1$

On putting $x=1$ in Eq. (i), we get

$1+y^2=4 \Rightarrow y^2=3$

$\Rightarrow \quad y=\pm\sqrt{3}$

Thus, the points of intersection of the given circles are $A(1,\sqrt{3})$ and $A'(1,-\sqrt{3})$ as shown in the figure given below

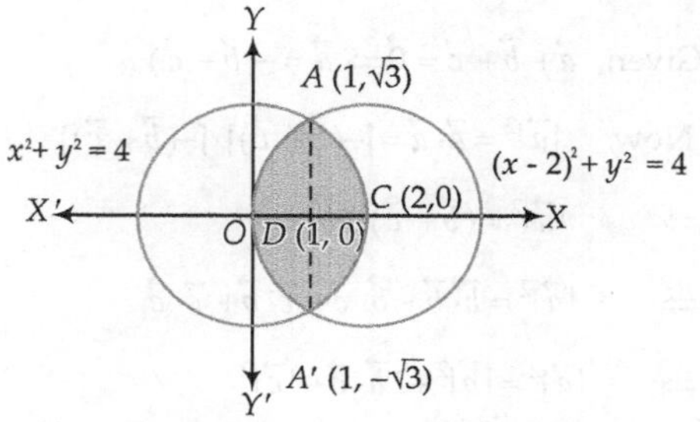

$\therefore$ Required area of the enclosed region $OACA'O$ between circles

$=2\,[\text{Area of the region } ODCAO]$

$=2\,[\text{Area of the region } ODAO + \text{Area of the region } DCAD]$

$$=2\left[\int_0^1 y_2\,dx+\int_1^2 y_1\,dx\right]$$

[where, $y_1=\sqrt{4-x^2}$ and $y_2=\sqrt{4-(x-2)^2}$]

$$=2\left[\int_0^1\sqrt{4-(x-2)^2}\,dx+\int_1^2\sqrt{4-x^2}\,dx\right]$$

$$=2\left[\frac{1}{2}(x-2)\sqrt{4-(x-2)^2}+\frac{1}{2}\times 4\sin^{-1}\left(\frac{x-2}{2}\right)\right]_0^1$$

$$+2\left[\frac{1}{2}x\sqrt{4-x^2}+\frac{1}{2}\times 4\sin^{-1}\frac{x}{2}\right]_1^2$$

$$\left[\because \int\sqrt{a^2-x^2}\,dx=\frac{x}{2}\sqrt{a^2-x^2}+\frac{a^2}{2}\sin^{-1}\frac{x}{a}+C\right]$$

$$=\left[(x-2)\sqrt{4-(x-2)^2}+4\sin^{-1}\left(\frac{x-2}{2}\right)\right]_0^1$$

$$+\left[x\sqrt{4-x^2}+4\sin^{-1}\frac{x}{2}\right]_1^2$$

$$=\left[\left\{-\sqrt{3}+4\sin^{-1}\left(\frac{-1}{2}\right)\right\}-4\sin^{-1}(-1)\right]$$

$$+\left[4\sin^{-1}1-\sqrt{3}-4\sin^{-1}\frac{1}{2}\right]$$

$$=\left[\left(-\sqrt{3}-4\times\frac{\pi}{6}\right)+4\times\frac{\pi}{2}\right]+\left[4\times\frac{\pi}{2}-\sqrt{3}-4\times\frac{\pi}{6}\right]$$

$$=\left(-\sqrt{3}-\frac{2\pi}{3}+2\pi\right)+\left(2\pi-\sqrt{3}-\frac{2\pi}{3}\right)$$

$$=\frac{8\pi}{3}-2\sqrt{3}\text{ sq units}$$

Value Point

Precisely shade the required region and do mention the intersection points.

19. (i) (a) We know that coefficient of correlation,

$$r=\sqrt{b_{yx}\times b_{xy}}$$

$\therefore$ Required coefficient of correlation

$$=-\sqrt{\left(-\frac{3}{4}\right)\left(-\frac{3}{4}\right)}=-\frac{3}{4}$$

[$\because$ both regression coefficients are negative, so we take negative sign outside the root]

(ii) (a) Given, $C(x) = 3x^5 + 2x^2 + x$

Then, $MC = \frac{d}{dx}C(x) = 15x^4 + 4x + 1$

(iii) Given regression of lines are

$$8x + 4y - 3 = 0 \text{ and } 5x + y + 3 = 0$$

Let us consider regression line of y on x is

$$8x + 4y - 3 = 0 \Rightarrow 4y = 3 - 8x$$

$$\Rightarrow \quad y = \frac{3}{4} - 2x$$

$\therefore$ Regression coefficient of y on x is

$$b_{yx} = -2$$

And consider regression line of x on y is

$$5x + y + 3 = 0 \Rightarrow 5x = -y - 3 \Rightarrow x = -\frac{y}{5} - \frac{3}{5}$$

$\therefore$ Regression coefficient of x on y is

$$b_{xy} = -\frac{1}{5}$$

Now, $b_{xy} \cdot b_{yx} = -\frac{1}{5} \times (-2) = \frac{2}{5} < 1$

Thus, our assumption is correct.

Hence, required regression coefficients are

$$b_{xy} = -\frac{1}{5} \text{ and } b_{yx} = -2$$

(iv) Given demand function,

$$p = \frac{1420}{q^2 + 2} - 4$$

$$\therefore \text{ Marginal revenue (MR)} = \frac{dp}{dq} = \frac{d}{dq}\left(\frac{1420}{q^2 + 2} - 4\right)$$

$$= 1420(-1)(q^2 + 2)^{-2} \times 2q$$

$$= \frac{-1420}{(q^2 + 2)^2} \times 2q = -\frac{2840q}{(q^2 + 2)^2}$$

(v) Given, cost function, $C(x) = \frac{x^5}{5} + 4x^3 + 2x$

$$\text{Marginal cost (MC)} = \frac{dC}{dx} = \frac{d}{dx}\left(\frac{x^5}{5} + 4x^3 + 2x\right)$$

$$= x^4 + 12x^2 + 2$$

$$\text{and average cost} = \frac{C(x)}{x} = \frac{\left(\frac{x^5}{5} + 4x^3 + 2x\right)}{x}$$

$$= \frac{x^4}{5} + 4x^2 + 2$$

20. (i) Given, fixed cost = ₹ 30000

and variable cost = ₹ 800 per unit

Suppose x units of the new product are produced,

(a) The cost function $C(x)$ is given by

$$C(x) = \text{Fixed cost} + \text{Variable cost}$$

$$= 30000 + 800x$$

(b) The revenue function $R(x)$ is given by

$$R(x) = x\,p(x) = x(4500 - 100x) = 4500x - 100x^2$$

Or

(ii) Given cost function, $C(x) = \frac{x^2}{100} + 30x + 1600$

$$\therefore \text{ Average cost, (AC)} = \frac{C(x)}{x} = \frac{\frac{x^2}{100} + 30x + 1600}{x}$$

$$= \frac{x}{100} + 30 + \frac{1600}{x}$$

On differentiating w.r.t x, two times, we get

$$\frac{d(AC)}{dx} = \frac{d}{dx}\left(\frac{x}{100} + 30 + \frac{1600}{x}\right)$$

$$= \frac{1}{100} + 0 - \frac{1600}{x^2} = \frac{1}{100} - \frac{1600}{x^2}$$

$$\text{and } \frac{d^2(AC)}{dx^2} = \frac{d}{dx}\left(\frac{1}{100} - \frac{1600}{x^2}\right) = \frac{3200}{x^3}$$

For maximum or minimum average cost, put

$$\frac{d}{dx}(AC) = 0 \Rightarrow \frac{1}{100} - \frac{1600}{x^2} = 0$$

$$\Rightarrow \quad \frac{1600}{x^2} = \frac{1}{100}$$

$$\Rightarrow \quad x^2 = 160000$$

$$\Rightarrow \quad x = \pm 400$$

$$\text{Now, } \frac{d^2}{dx^2}(AC) = 0 + \frac{1600 \times 2}{x^3} = \frac{3200}{x^3}$$

$$\text{At } x = 400, \quad \frac{d^2(AC)}{dx^2} = \frac{3200}{(400)^3} > 0,$$

so average cost is minimum.

Hence, minimum 400 items must be produced.

21. (i) Here, $\bar{x} = \frac{\Sigma x}{7} = \frac{11+7+9+5+8+6+10}{7} = \frac{56}{7} = 8$

and $\bar{y} = \frac{\Sigma y}{7} = \frac{10+8+6+5+9+7+11}{7} = \frac{56}{7} = 8$

To make a table for correlation coefficient

x	y	$d_x = x - 8$, $\bar{x} = 8$	$d_y = y - 8$, $\bar{y} = 8$	d_x^2	$d_x \cdot d_y$
11	10	3	2	9	6
7	8	− 1	0	1	0
9	6	1	− 2	1	− 2
5	5	− 3	− 3	9	9
8	9	0	1	0	0
6	7	− 2	− 1	4	2
10	11	2	3	4	6
$\Sigma x = 56$	$\Sigma y = 56$			$\Sigma d_x^2 = 28$	$\Sigma d_x d_y = 21$

(ii) The regression equation of y on x is

$$y - \bar{y} = \frac{\Sigma d_x d_y}{\Sigma d_x^2}(x - \bar{x})$$

$$\Rightarrow \quad y - 8 = \frac{21}{28}(x - 8)$$

$\Rightarrow \quad y-8=\frac{3}{4}(x-8)$

$\Rightarrow \quad 4y-32=3x-24$

$\Rightarrow \quad 4y=3x+8$

(iii) When $x=13$, $4y=39+8$

$\Rightarrow \quad y=\frac{47}{4}=11.75$

Hence, the initial start should be ₹ 11.75×100 i.e. ₹ 1175.

22. (i) Let x be the number of units of commodity A produced and y be the number of units of commodity B produced. The values of x and y must satisfy the following constraints

$x\geq 0;\ y\geq 0;$

$x+2y\leq 8$ [material constraint]

$3x+2y\leq 12$ [labour constraint]

$x+y\leq 10$ [equipment constraint]

Let P be the profit, then $P=2x+3y$.

The table for line $x+2y=8$ or $y=\frac{8-x}{2}$ is

x	0	8
y	4	0

So, this line passes through the points (0, 4) and (8, 0).

Put (0, 0) is the inequality $x+2y\leq 8$, we get

$0+0\leq 8$ [true]

So, the half plane is towards the origin.

The table for line $3x+2y=12$ or $y=\frac{12-3x}{2}$ is

x	0	4
y	6	0

So, this line passes through the points (0, 6) and (4, 0).

Put (0, 0) in the inequality $3x+2y\leq 12$, we get

$0+0\leq 12$ [true]

So, the half plane is towards the origin.

The table for line $x+y=10$ or $y=10-x$ is

x	0	10
y	10	0

So, this line passes through the points (0, 10) and (10, 0).

Put (0, 0) in the inequality $x+y\leq 10$, we get

$0+0\leq 10$ [true]

So, the half plane is towards the origin.

The intersection point of lines $3x+2y=12$ and $x+2y=8$ is $A(2,3)$.

Now, plot all the constraints on a graph paper.

The solution set of this system is the feasible (shaded) region $OBAC$ in the diagram.

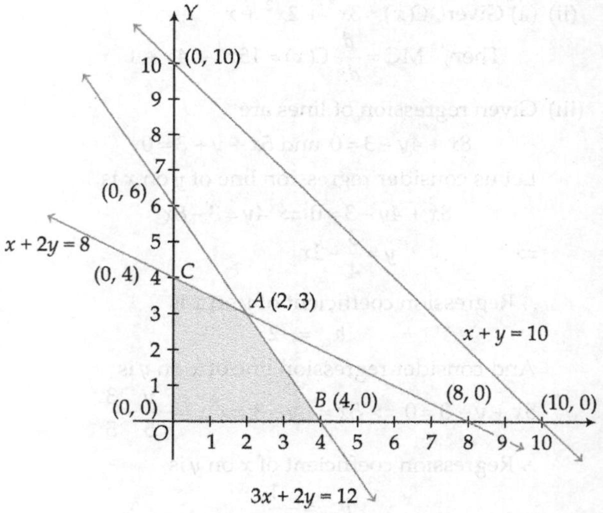

The corner points of the feasible region are $O(0,0)$, $A(2,3)$, $B(4,0)$ and $C(0,4)$.

The values of P at these corner points are given below

Corner points	$P=2x+3y$
$O(0,0)$	$0\times 2+0\times 3=$ ₹ 0
$A(2,3)$	$2\times 2+3\times 3=$ ₹ 13 (maximum)
$B(4,0)$	$4\times 2+0\times 3=$ ₹ 8
$C(0,4)$	$0\times 2+4\times 3=$ ₹ 12

Hence, the maximum profit is ₹ 13.

Or

(ii) Given problem is to maximise $Z=-x+2y$ ...(i)

Subject to constraints,

$x\geq 3$ ...(ii)

$x+y\geq 5$ ...(iii)

$x+2y\geq 6$ ...(iv)

and $x\geq 0,\ y\geq 0$ ...(v)

Table for line $x+y=5$ is

x	0	5
y	5	0

So, this line passes through the points (0, 5) and (5, 0).

On putting (0, 0) in the inequality $x+y\geq 5$, we get

$0+0\geq 5$

$\Rightarrow \quad 0\geq 5$, which is not true.

So, the half plane is away from the origin.

Table for line $x+2y=6$ is

x	0	6
y	3	0

So, this line passes through the points (0,3) and (6,0).

On putting (0, 0) in the inequality $x + 2y \geq 6$, we get

$$0 + 2 \times 0 \geq 6$$

$\Rightarrow$ $0 \geq 6$, which is not true.

So, the half plane is away from the origin.

Also, $x \geq 3$, so the region is away from the origin.

Since, $x \geq 0, y \geq 0$. So, the region lies in the I quadrant.

The points of intersection of lines $x = 3$ and $x + y = 5$ is $C(3, 2)$ and lines $x + 2y = 6$ and $x + y = 5$ is $B(4, 1)$.

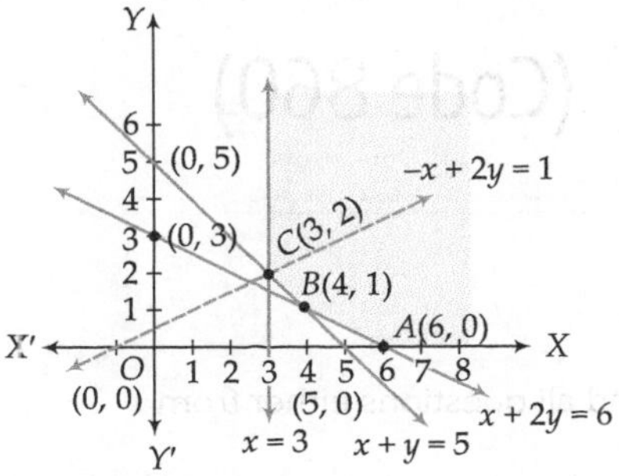

Now, plot all the inequalities on the graph paper as show below. It can be seen that the feasible region *CBA* is unbounded.

The corner points of the feasible region are $A(6, 0)$, $B(4, 1)$ and $C(3, 2)$.

The values of Z at corner points are given below

Corner points	$Z = -x + 2y$
$A(6, 0)$	$Z = -6 + 2 \times 0 = -6$
$B(4, 1)$	$Z = -4 + 2 \times 1 = -2$
$C(3, 2)$	$Z = -3 + 2 \times 2 = 1$

As the feasible region is unbounded, therefore $Z = 1$ may or may not be the maximum value. For this, we draw the graph of the inequality $-x + 2y > 1$ and check whether the resulting half plane has points in common with the feasible region or not. The feasible region have points in common with the $-x + 2y > 1$. Therefore, $Z = 1$ is not the maximum value.

Hence, Z has no maximum value.

SQP Code : **PB-5/15** Series **i-Succeed 5-25/15** Roll No.

Sample Question Paper 05

Mathematics 12th (Code 860)

Time : 3 Hrs.

Max. Marks : 80

General Instructions

1. The Question Paper consists of three sections A, B and C.
2. Candidates are required to attempt all questions from Section A and all questions either from Section B Or Section C.
3. Section A Internal choice has been provided in two questions of two marks each, two questions of four marks each and two questions of six marks each.
4. Section B Internal choice has been provided in one questions of two marks and one question of four marks.
5. Section C Internal choice has been provided in one question of two marks and one question of four marks.
6. All working, including rough work, should be done on the same sheet as, and adjacent to the rest of the answer.
7. The intended marks for questions or parts of questions are given in brackets [].
8. Mathematical tables and graph papers are provided.

Section A (65 Marks)

1. In subparts (i) to (xi) choose the correct options and in subparts (xii) to (xv), answer the questions as instructed.

(i) If $e^x + e^y = e^{x+y}$, then $\frac{dy}{dx}$ is

• *Understanding* [1]

(a) e^{y-x} (b) e^{x+y} (c) $-e^{y-x}$ (d) $2e^{x-y}$

(ii) $\int \frac{\sin^2 x - \cos^2 x}{\sin^2 x \cos^2 x} dx$ is equal to

(a) $\tan x + \cot x + C$ (b) $\tan x - \cot x + C$
(c) $-\tan x + \cot x + C$ (d) None of these

(iii) **Assertion** (A) For the set $A = \{1, 2, 3\}$, define a relation R in the set A as follows

$$R = \{(1, 1), (2, 2), (3, 3), (1, 3)\}$$

Then, the ordered pair to be added to R to make it the smallest equivalence relation is $(3, 1)$.

• *Recall* [1]

Reason (R) A relation R on a set A is said to be an equivalence relation iff it is reflexive, symmetric and transitive. [1]

(a) Both A and R are true and R is the correct explanation of A.

(b) Both A and R are true and R is not the correct explanation of A.

(c) A is true but R is false.

(d) A is false but R is true.

(iv) The degree of the differential equation

$$x = 1 + \left(\frac{dy}{dx}\right) + \frac{1}{2!}\left(\frac{dy}{dx}\right)^2 + \frac{1}{3!}\left(\frac{dy}{dx}\right)^3 + \cdots, \text{ is}$$

• *Understanding* [1]

(a) 3
(b) 2
(c) 1
(d) not defined

(v) Interval(s) in which the function $f(x) = \sin x + \cos x,\ x \in \left(0, \frac{\pi}{2}\right)$ is strictly increasing. • *Analysis* [1]

(a) $\left(\frac{\pi}{4}, \frac{\pi}{2}\right)$ (b) $\left(0, \frac{\pi}{2}\right)$

(c) $\left(0, \frac{\pi}{4}\right)$ (d) None of these

(vi) **Statement I** If $\sin^{-1} x = y$, then $-\frac{\pi}{2} \le y \le \frac{\pi}{2}$.

Statement II If $\operatorname{cosec}^{-1} x = y$, then $-\frac{\pi}{2} \le y \le \frac{\pi}{2}$ which of the following is correct? • *Recall* [1]

(a) Only Statement I.

(b) Only Statement II.

(c) Both Statements I and II.

(d) Neither Statement I nor Statement II.

(vii) The value of k for which $f(x) = \begin{cases} \frac{\sin 5x}{3x}, & \text{if } x \ne 0 \\ k, & \text{if } x = 0 \end{cases}$ is continuous at $x = 0$, is • *Analysis* [1]

(a) $\frac{1}{3}$ (b) 0

(c) $\frac{3}{5}$ (d) $\frac{5}{3}$

(viii) The graph of the function $g(x)$ is shown below. • *Understanding* [1]

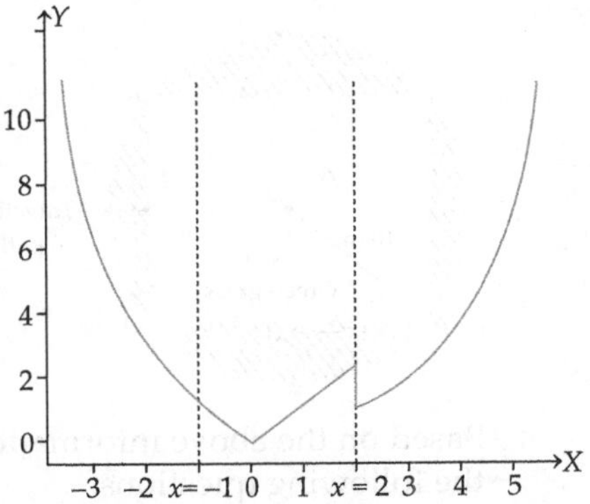

(a) The function $g(x)$ is continuous at $x = -1$ and differentiable at $x = 2$

(b) $g(x)$ is differentiable at $x = -1$ and $x = 2$

(c) $g(x)$ is not differentiable at $x = -1$ and $x = 2$

(d) $g(x)$ is differentiable at $x = -1$ and not differentiable at $x = 2$

(ix) Consider the following statements.

Statement I For multiplication of two matrices A and B, the number of columns in A should be less than the number of rows in B.

Statement II For getting the elements of the product matrix, we take rows of A and column of B, multiply them elementwise and take the sum.

Choose the correct option. • *Recall* [1]

(a) Only I is true

(b) Only II is true

(c) Both I and II are true

(d) Neither I nor II is true

(x) **Assertion** (A) $f(x) = 2x^3 - 9x^2 + 12x - 3$ is increasing outside the interval $(1, 2)$.

Reason (R) $f'(x) < 0$ for $x \in (1, 2)$.

Then, which of the following is true? • *Application* [1]

(a) Both A and R are true and R is the correct explanation for A

(b) Both A and R are true and R is not the correct explanation for A

(c) A is true but R is false

(d) A is false but R is true

(xi) Two balls are drawn from an urn containing 2 white, 3 red and 4 black balls one-by-one without replacement. The probability that atleast one ball is red, is • *Application* [1]

(a) $\frac{2}{3}$ (b) $\frac{5}{8}$ (c) $\frac{7}{12}$ (d) $\frac{3}{8}$

(xii) If $\sin\left(\sin^{-1}\frac{1}{5} + \cos^{-1} x\right) = 1$, then find the value of x. • *Application* [1]

(xiii) A relation A in the set of real numbers R defined as $A = \{(a, b) : \sqrt{a} = b\}$ is a function or not. Justify. • *Understanding* [1]

(xiv) Evaluate $\int_1^2 \frac{2}{4x^2 - 1}\, dx$. • *Evaluate* [1]

(xv) If $A = \begin{bmatrix} 2 & 3 & 1 \\ 1 & -1 & 2 \\ 4 & 1 & 2 \end{bmatrix}$, then determine $\frac{A + A'}{2}$. • *Application* [1]

2. (i) One card is drawn from a pack of 52 cards, so that each card is equally likely to be selected. Show that the events E_1 and E_2 are independent or not?

E_1 : The card drawn is a spade,

E_2 : The card drawn is an ace.

• *Analysis* [2]

Or

(ii) Evaluate $P(A \cap B)$, if $2P(A) = P(B) = \frac{7}{13}$ and $P\left(\frac{A}{B}\right) = \frac{4}{5}$.

• *Evaluate* [2]

3. If $A = \begin{bmatrix} -1 & a \\ b & 7 \end{bmatrix}$ and A is symmetric matrix, then show that $a = b$.

• *Analysis* [2]

4. Check whether the relation R in the set Z of integers defined as $R = \{(a,b) : a + b$ is "divisible by 2"$\}$ is reflexive, symmetric or transitive.

• *Undestanding* [2]

5. (i) A given rectangular area is to be fenced off in a field whose length lies along a straight river. If no fencing is needed along the river, show that the least amount of fencing will be required when the length of the field is twice its breadth.

• *Application* [2]

Or

(ii) Find the rate of change of the area of a circle with respect to its radius r when $r = 4$ cm.

• *Application* [2]

6. Show that the determinant $\begin{vmatrix} x & \sin\theta & \cos\theta \\ -\sin\theta & -x & 1 \\ \cos\theta & 1 & x \end{vmatrix}$ is independent of θ.

• *Understanding* [2]

7. If $a \neq p, b \neq q, c \neq r$ and $\begin{vmatrix} p & b & c \\ a & q & c \\ a & b & r \end{vmatrix} = 0$, then find the value of $\frac{p}{p-a} + \frac{q}{q-b} + \frac{r}{r-c}$

• *Application* [4]

8. If $a > b > c > 0$, then prove that

$$\cot^{-1}\left(\frac{ab+1}{a-b}\right) + \cot^{-1}\left(\frac{bc+1}{b-c}\right) + \cot^{-1}\left(\frac{ac+1}{c-a}\right) = \pi.$$

• *Application* [4]

9. (i) Two horses are considered for a race. The probability of selection of the first horse is $\frac{1}{3}$ and that of the second is $\frac{1}{2}$. What is the probability that

(a) both of them will be selected?

(b) only one of them will be selected?

(c) None of them will be selected?

• *Analysis* [4]

Or (ii) Find a and b, if the function given by $f(x) = \begin{cases} ax^2 + b, & \text{if } x < 1 \\ 2x + 1, & \text{if } x \geq 1 \end{cases}$ is differentiable at $x = 1$.

• *Application* [4]

10. (i) Consider the following values

$$x = a\cos^3\theta,\ y = a\sin^3\theta$$

On the basis of above information, answer the following questions.

(a) Find $\left.\frac{dx}{d\theta}\right|_{\theta=\frac{\pi}{4}}$.

(b) Find $\left.\frac{dy}{d\theta}\right|_{\theta=\frac{\pi}{4}}$.

(c) Find $\frac{dy}{dx}$.

(d) Find $\left.\frac{dy}{dx}\right|_{\theta=\frac{\pi}{6}}$.

• *Evaluate* [4]

Or

(ii) An architect designs a garden in a society. The garden is in the shape of a rectangle inscribed in a circle of radius 10m as shown in given figure.

• *Evaluate* [4]

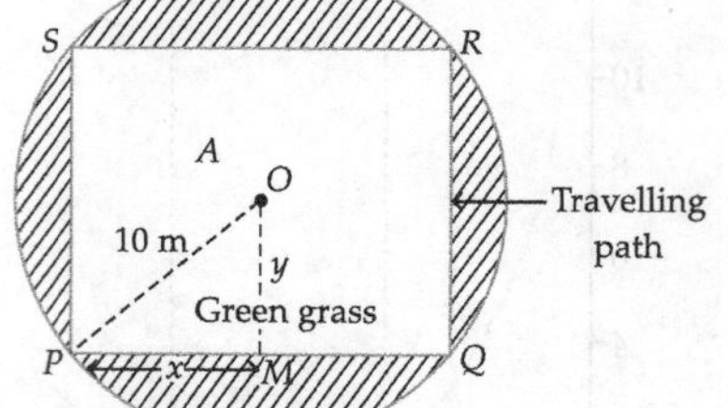

Based on the above information, answer the following questions.

(a) $2x$ and $2y$ represents the length and breadth of the rectangular part, then find the relation between the variables.

(b) The area of the green grass A expressed as a function of x. Find the function.

(c) Find the maximum value of area A.

11. Find the intervals in which the function $f(x) = (x-1)^3 (x-2)^2$ is
(a) increasing.
(b) decreasing. • *Analysis* [6]

12. A manufacturing firm produces steel pipes in three plants *A*, *B* and *C* with daily production of 500, 1000 and 2000 units, respectively. The fractions of defective steel pipes output produced by the plants *A*, *B* and *C* are, respectively 0.005, 0.008 and 0.010.
If a pipe is selected from a day's total production and found to be defective, then find out the probability that it came from the first plant. • *Application* [6]

13. (i) Evaluate $\int \frac{x^2}{(x\sin x + \cos x)^2} dx$ • *Evaluate* [6]

Or

(ii) Evaluate $\int \frac{2x}{(x^2+1)(x^2+2)^2} dx$ • *Evaluate* [6]

14. (i) For a function $f(x)$, if $f(-x) = f(x)$, then $f(x)$ is an even function and if $f(-x) = -f(x)$, then $f(x)$ is an odd function.
Again, we have
$$\int_{-1}^{a} f(x)\,dx = \begin{cases} 2\int_0^a f(x)dx, & \text{if } f(x) \text{ is even} \\ 0, & \text{if } f(x) \text{ is odd} \end{cases}$$
On the basis of above information, answer the following questions.
(a) Check the following function is even or odd.
$$f(x) = x^2 \sin x$$
(b) Evaluate $\int_{-\pi}^{\pi} f(x)\,dx$.
(c) If $g(x) = x \sin x$, then find $\int_{-\pi}^{\pi} x \sin x\, dx$.
(d) Evaluate $\int_{-\pi/2}^{\pi/2} |\sin x|\, dx$. • *Analysis* [6]

Or

(ii) Consider the given equation
$$\frac{dy}{dx} + Py = Q$$
The above equation is known as linear differential equation.
Here, $= e^{\int P dx}$ and solution is given by
$$y\cdot \quad = \int Q\cdot \quad dx + C$$
Now, consider the given equation
$$(1+\sin x)\frac{dy}{dx} + y\cos x + x = 0$$
On the basis of above information, answer the following questions.
(a) Find the value of *P* and *Q*.
(b) Find the value of IF.
(c) Find the solution of the given equation. • *Analysis* [6]

Section B (15 Marks)

15. In subparts (i) to (iii) choose the correct options and in subparts (iv) and (v), answer the questions as instructed. • *Understanding* [5]
(i) The magnitude of each of the two vectors $\vec{a}$ and $\vec{b}$, having the same magnitude such that the angle between them is 60º and their scalar product is $\frac{9}{2}$ is
(a) 4 (b) 7
(c) 3 (d) 6
(ii) Consider the following statements and choose the correct option.
Statement I The plane is shown in the figure passes through the points (8, 0, 0), (0, 3, 0) and (0, 0, 7). Then,

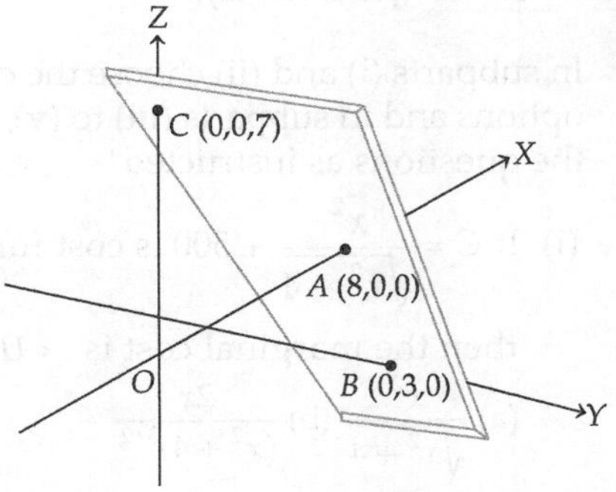

The equation of the plane is $\frac{x}{8} + \frac{y}{3} + \frac{z}{7} = 1$

Statement II The equation of the plane having intercepts of length *a*, *b* and *c* with coordinate areas *x*, *y* and *z*, respectively is $\frac{x}{a} + \frac{y}{b} + \frac{z}{c} = 1$. • *Recall* [4]

SP-05

Which of the following is correct?

(a) Only Statement I.
(b) Only Statement II.
(c) Both Statements I and II.
(d) Neither Statement I nor Statement II.

(iii) The acute angle between the lines $\frac{x-4}{3}=\frac{y+3}{4}=\frac{z+1}{5}$ and $\frac{x-1}{4}=\frac{y+1}{-3}=\frac{z+10}{5}$ is • *Application* [4]

(a) $\frac{\pi}{3}$
(b) $\frac{\pi}{4}$
(c) $\frac{\pi}{6}$
(d) $\frac{\pi}{2}$

(iv) If $\overrightarrow{AO}+\overrightarrow{OB}=\overrightarrow{BO}+\overrightarrow{OC}$, then prove that the points A, B and C are collinear. • *Understanding* [4]

(v) If $\vec{a}=4\hat{i}+6\hat{j}+2\hat{k}$ and $\vec{b}=3\hat{i}+2\hat{j}-3\hat{k}$, then find the value of $\vec{b}\cdot\vec{a}$.

16. (i) Show that the points A, B, C with position vectors $2\hat{i}-\hat{j}+\hat{k}$, $\hat{i}-3\hat{j}-5\hat{k}$ and $3\hat{i}-4\hat{j}-4\hat{k}$ respectively, are the vertices of a right angled triangle. Hence, find the area of the triangle. • *Application* [2]

Or

(ii) If $\vec{a}$, $\vec{b}$ and $\vec{c}$ determine the vertices of a triangle, then show that $\frac{1}{2}[\vec{b}\times\vec{c}+\vec{c}\times\vec{a}+\vec{a}\times\vec{b}]$ gives the vector area of the triangle. Hence, deduce the condition that the three points $\vec{a}$, $\vec{b}$ and $\vec{c}$ are collinear. • *Application* [2]

17. (i) Find the equation of the perpendicular from point (3, –1, 11) to line $\frac{x}{2}=\frac{y-2}{3}=\frac{z-3}{4}$. Also, find the coordinates of foot of perpendicular and the length of perpendicular. • *Application* [4]

Or

(ii) Find the equation of plane passing through the point (1, –1, –1) and perpendicular to each of the planes $2(x-2y)+2(y-z)-(6z+x)=0$ and $2(y-x)+3(y+z)+4(x-z)=0$. • *Application* [2]

18. Find the area of the smaller region bounded by the ellipse $\frac{x^2}{a^2}+\frac{y^2}{b^2}=1$ and the straight line $\frac{x}{a}+\frac{y}{b}=1$. • *Evaluate* [4]

Section C (15 Marks)

SP-05

19. In subparts (i) and (ii) choose the correct options and in subparts (iii) to (v), answer the questions as instructed. [5]

(i) If $C=\frac{x^2}{\sqrt{x^2+4}}+500$ is cost function, then the marginal cost is • *Understanding*

(a) $\frac{x^2}{\sqrt{x^2+4}}$ (b) $\frac{2x}{(x^2+4)^{3/2}}$
(c) $\frac{8x}{(x^2+4)^{3/2}}$ (d) $\frac{2x}{(x^2+4)}$

(ii) If $b_{yx}=2$ and $b_{xy}=0.18$, then the coefficient of correlation between x and y is • *Recall*

(a) 0.5 (b) 0.6
(c) 0.8 (d) 3

(iii) The cost function of a firm is given by $C(x)=6x^3-5x+4$. Find the average cost when $x=4$. • *Evaluate*

(iv) The demand function of a monopolist is given by $p=1400-4x+8x^2$. Find the marginal revenue for any level of output x. Also, find marginal revenue (MR), when $x=12$. • *Understanding*

(v) Compute b_{yx} for the data {(x, y):(5, 2), (7, 4), (8, 3), (4, 2), (6, 4)}. • *Evaluate*

20. (i) The manufacturing cost of an item is ₹ 3 per item, fixed cost is ₹ 900 and the labour cost is ₹ $\frac{x^2}{100}$ for x items produced. How many items must be produced to have average cost minimum? • *Application* [2]

Or

(ii) The cost function for a commodity is

$C(x) = 200 + 20x - \frac{x^2}{2}$ (in ₹).

Find the marginal cost function and calculate the marginal cost, when $x = 4$ and interpret it.

• *Application* [2]

21. For observations of pairs (x, y) of the variables X and Y, the following results are obtained. $\Sigma x = 30$, $\Sigma y = 42$, $\Sigma x^2 = 184$, $\Sigma y^2 = 318$, $\Sigma xy = 199$ and $n = 6$. Find the equation of the line of regression of x on y. Estimate the value of x, if $y = 10$. • *Application* [4]

22. (i) A company produces two types of items, P and Q. Manufacturing of both items requires the metals gold and copper. Each unit of item P requires 3 gm of gold and 1 gm of copper while that of item Q requires 1 gm of gold and 2 gm of copper. The company has 9 gm of gold and 8 gm of copper in its store. If each unit of item P makes a profit of ₹ 50 and each unit of item Q makes a profit of ₹ 60, then determine the number of units of each item that the company should produce to maximise profit. What is the maximum profit? • *Analysis* [4]

Or

(ii) If a young man rides his motorcycle at the speed of 25 km/h, he has to spend ₹ 2 per kilometre on petrol; if he rides at a faster speed of 40 km/h, the petrol cost increases to ₹ 5 per kilometre. He has ₹ 100 to spend on petrol and wishes to find the maximum distance he can travel within one hour. Express this as a linear programming problem and hence solve it.

• *Analysis* [4]

Solutions *in Topper's Style*

My Commitment *I affirm that I am reviewing these solutions only after I have solved the Sample Question Paper 5 on my own. My purpose of looking the solutions is solely to verify whether my answers/solutions were correct or not and to identify my mistakes in case my solutions were wrong or I could not solve that.*

1. (i) (c) We have, $e^x + e^y = e^{x+y}$

$$\Rightarrow \quad e^x + e^y = e^x \cdot e^y$$

On dividing both sides by $e^x . e^y$, we get

$$\frac{e^x}{e^x \cdot e^y} + \frac{e^y}{e^x e^y} = \frac{e^x \cdot e^y}{e^x \cdot e^y}$$

$$\Rightarrow \quad e^{-y} + e^{-x} = 1$$

On differentiating w.r.t. x, we get

$$-e^{-y} \cdot \frac{dy}{dx} - e^{-x} = 0$$

$$\Rightarrow \quad \frac{dy}{dx} = -\frac{e^{-x}}{e^{-y}}$$

$$\Rightarrow \quad \frac{dy}{dx} = -\frac{e^y}{e^x} = -e^{y-x}$$

(ii) (a) Let $I = \int \frac{\sin^2 x - \cos^2 x}{\sin^2 x \cos^2 x} dx$

$$= \int \frac{\sin^2 x}{\sin^2 x \cos^2 x} dx - \int \frac{\cos^2 x}{\sin^2 x \cos^2 x} dx$$

$$= \int \sec^2 x \, dx - \int \text{cosec}^2 x \, dx = \tan x + \cot x + C$$

(iii) (a) Clearly R is reflexive and transitive. For R to be symmetric we should add (3, 1) in R.

Hence, A and R both are true and R is the correct explanation of A.

(iv) (c) Given, differential equation is

$$x = 1 + \frac{dy}{dx} + \frac{1}{2!}\left(\frac{dy}{dx}\right)^2 + \frac{1}{3!}\left(\frac{dy}{dx}\right)^3 + \cdots$$

$$\Rightarrow \quad x = e^{\frac{dy}{dx}} \quad \left[\because e^x = 1 + x + \frac{x^2}{2!} + \frac{x^3}{3!} + \ldots\right]$$

On taking log both sides, we get $\log_e x = \frac{dy}{dx} \cdot \log_e e$

$$\Rightarrow \frac{dy}{dx} = \log_e x$$

Hence, degree of differential equation is 1.

(v) (c) Given function is $f(x) = \sin x + \cos x$

On differentiating both sides w.r.t. x, we get

$$f'(x) = \cos x - \sin x$$

Put $f'(x) = 0 \Rightarrow \cos x - \sin x = 0$

$\Rightarrow \tan x = 1 \Rightarrow x = \frac{\pi}{4} \in \left(0, \frac{\pi}{2}\right)$

Now, $\frac{\pi}{4}$ divides the interval $\left(0, \frac{\pi}{2}\right)$ into two sub intervals $\left(0, \frac{\pi}{4}\right)$ and $\left(\frac{\pi}{4}, \frac{\pi}{2}\right)$.

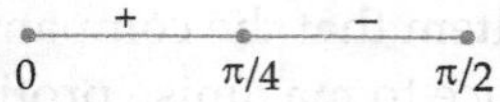

In interval $\left(0, \frac{\pi}{4}\right)$, $\cos x > \sin x$

$\therefore \quad \cos x - \sin x > 0 \Rightarrow f'(x) > 0$

So, $f(x)$ is strictly increasing function in $\left(0, \frac{\pi}{4}\right)$.

(vi) (a) The range of $\sin^{-1} x$ is $\left[-\frac{\pi}{2}, \frac{\pi}{2}\right]$

So, $\sin^{-1} x = y \Rightarrow -\frac{\pi}{2} \le y < \frac{\pi}{2}$.

The range of $\text{cosec}^{-1} x$ is $\left[-\frac{\pi}{2}, \frac{\pi}{2}\right] - \{0\}$

Hence, Statement I is true and Statement II is false.

(vii) (d) For continuity at $x = 0$, we must have

$\lim_{x \to 0} f(x) = f(0)$.

Now, $\lim_{x \to 0} f(x) = \lim_{x \to 0} \frac{\sin 5x}{3x}$

$= \lim_{x \to 0} \frac{\sin 5x}{5x} \times \frac{5}{3} = \frac{5}{3} \quad \left[\because \lim_{x \to 0} \frac{\sin x}{x} = 1\right]$

So, we must have $f(0) = \frac{5}{3}$.

Hence, $k = \left(\frac{5}{3}\right)$

(viii) (c) From the given figure,

At $x = -1$, and $x = 2$ the graph changes direction abruptly.

So, $\lim_{h \to 0^-} \frac{g(x-h) - g(x)}{-h} \ne \lim_{h \to 0^+} \frac{g(x+h) - g(x)}{h}$

Thus, $g(x)$ is not differentiable at $x = -1$ and $x = 2$.

(ix) (b) For multiplication of two matrices A and B, the number of columns in A should be equal to the number of rows in B. Furthermore, for getting the elements of the product matrix, we take rows of A and columns of B, multiply them elementwise and take the sum. Hence, only Statement II is true.

(x) (b) Given, $f(x) = 2x^3 - 9x^2 + 12x - 3$

On differentiating w.r.t to x, we get

$f'(x) = 6x^2 - 18x + 12 = 6(x^2 - 3x + 2)$

For increasing function, $f'(x) \ge 0$

$\therefore \quad 6(x^2 - 3x + 2) \ge 0$

$\Rightarrow \quad 6(x-2)(x-1) \ge 0$

$\Rightarrow \quad x \le 1$ and $x \ge 2$

$\therefore$ $f(x)$ is increasing outside the interval (1, 2), therefore Assertion is true.

Now, $\quad f'(x) < 0$

$\Rightarrow \quad 6(x-2)(x-1) < 0$

$\Rightarrow \quad 1 < x < 2$

Hence, A and R are both true but R is not the correct explanation of A.

(xi) (c) Let A: not getting a red ball in first draw and B: not getting a red ball in second draw too

Now, $P(A)$ = Probability of not getting a red ball in first draw

= Probability of getting a white or a black ball

$= \frac{{}^6C_1}{{}^9C_1} = \frac{6}{9} = \frac{2}{3}$

Again, for getting a ball which is not red in second draw too, there are 3 red and 5 balls of other colour.

Then, $P(B) = \frac{{}^5C_1}{{}^8C_1} = \frac{5}{8}$

Hence, required probability $= 1 - P(A) \times P(B)$

$= 1 - \frac{2}{3} \times \frac{5}{8} = 1 - \frac{5}{12} = \frac{7}{12}$

(xii) We have,

$$\sin\left(\sin^{-1}\frac{1}{5} + \cos^{-1} x\right) = 1$$

$$\Rightarrow \quad \sin^{-1}\frac{1}{5} + \cos^{-1} x = \sin^{-1} 1$$

$$\Rightarrow \quad \sin^{-1}\frac{1}{5} + \cos^{-1} x = \frac{\pi}{2} \quad \left[\because \sin\frac{\pi}{2} = 1\right]$$

$$\Rightarrow \quad \cos^{-1} x = \frac{\pi}{2} - \sin^{-1}\frac{1}{5}$$

$$\cos^{-1} x = \cos^{-1}\frac{1}{5}$$

$$\left[\because \sin^{-1}\theta + \cos^{-1}\theta = \frac{\pi}{2}\right]$$

$$\therefore \quad x = \frac{1}{5}$$

(xiii) We know that $\sqrt{a}$ is not defined for $a \in (-\infty, 0)$.

$\therefore$ $A = \{(a, b) : \sqrt{a} = b\}$ is not a function.

(xiv) $\int_1^2 \frac{2}{4x^2 - 1} dx = 2 \cdot \frac{1}{4} \int_1^2 \frac{dx}{x^2 - \left(\frac{1}{2}\right)^2}$

$$= \frac{1}{2} \cdot \frac{1}{2 \cdot \frac{1}{2}} \left[\log\left|\frac{x - \frac{1}{2}}{x + \frac{1}{2}}\right|\right]_1^2$$

$$\left[\because \int \frac{1}{x^2 - a^2} dx = \frac{1}{2a} \log\left|\frac{x-a}{x+a}\right|\right]$$

$$= \frac{1}{2}\left[\log\left|\frac{2x-1}{2x+1}\right|\right]_1^2$$

$$= \frac{1}{2}\left(\log\frac{3}{5} - \log\frac{1}{3}\right)$$

$$=\frac{1}{2}\log\left(\frac{3}{5}\times\frac{3}{1}\right)\left[\because \log m-\log n=\log\frac{m}{n}\right]$$

$$=\frac{1}{2}\log\frac{9}{5}$$

(xv) We have, $A=\begin{bmatrix}2 & 3 & 1\\ 1 & -1 & 2\\ 4 & 1 & 2\end{bmatrix}$

$$\therefore\quad A'=\begin{bmatrix}2 & 3 & 1\\ 1 & -1 & 2\\ 4 & 1 & 2\end{bmatrix}'=\begin{bmatrix}2 & 1 & 4\\ 3 & -1 & 1\\ 1 & 2 & 2\end{bmatrix}$$

Now, $\dfrac{A+A'}{2}=\dfrac{1}{2}\left\{\begin{bmatrix}2 & 3 & 1\\ 1 & -1 & 2\\ 4 & 1 & 2\end{bmatrix}+\begin{bmatrix}2 & 1 & 4\\ 3 & -1 & 1\\ 1 & 2 & 2\end{bmatrix}\right\}$

$$=\frac{1}{2}\begin{bmatrix}4 & 4 & 5\\ 4 & -2 & 3\\ 5 & 3 & 4\end{bmatrix}=\begin{bmatrix}2 & 2 & \frac{5}{2}\\ 2 & -1 & \frac{3}{2}\\ \frac{5}{2} & \frac{3}{2} & 2\end{bmatrix}$$

2. (i) The sample space consists of simple events of drawing one card of one type from 52 cards.

$\therefore\quad n(S)=52$

E_1: The card drawn is a spade.

$\therefore\quad P(E_1)=\dfrac{13}{52}=\dfrac{1}{4}$

E_2: The card drawn is an ace.

$\therefore\quad P(E_2)=\dfrac{4}{52}=\dfrac{1}{13}$

$E_1\cap E_2$: The card drawn is an ace of spade.

$\therefore\quad P(E_1\cap E_2)=\dfrac{1}{52}$

Now, $P(E_1)\times P(E_2)=\dfrac{1}{4}\times\dfrac{1}{13}=\dfrac{1}{52}=P(E_1\cap E_2)$

Therefore, E_1 and E_2 are independent events.

Or

(ii) Given, $P(B)=\dfrac{7}{13}, 2P(A)=\dfrac{7}{13}\Rightarrow P(A)=\dfrac{7}{26}$

and $P\left(\dfrac{A}{B}\right)=\dfrac{4}{5}$

Now, $P\left(\dfrac{A}{B}\right)=\dfrac{P(A\cap B)}{P(B)}\Rightarrow\dfrac{4}{5}=\dfrac{P(A\cap B)}{7/13}$

$\Rightarrow\quad P(A\cap B)=\dfrac{4\times 7}{5\times 13}=\dfrac{28}{65}$

3. Given, $A=\begin{bmatrix}-1 & a\\ b & 7\end{bmatrix}$

Then, $A'=\begin{bmatrix}-1 & b\\ a & 7\end{bmatrix}$

$\because$ A is a symmetric matrix.

$\therefore\ A=A'\Rightarrow\begin{bmatrix}-1 & a\\ b & 7\end{bmatrix}=\begin{bmatrix}-1 & b\\ a & 7\end{bmatrix}$

On comparing the corresponding element, we get

$a=b$ **Hence proved.**

4. We have, $R=\{(a,b): a+b$ is "divisible by 2"$\}$

Reflexivity

For any $a\in Z$, we have

$a+a=2a$, which is divisible by 2.

$\Rightarrow\quad (a,a)\in R$

So, R is reflexive. (1)

Symmetry

Let $(a,b)\in R$. Then,

$\Rightarrow$ $(a+b)$ is divisible by 2.

$\Rightarrow$ $(b+a)$ is divisible by 2.

$\Rightarrow$ $(b,a)\in R$

So, R is symmetric. (1)

Transitivity

Let $(a,b)\in R$ and $(b,c)\in R$. Then,

$(a+b)$ is divisible by 2 and $(b+c)$ is divisible by 2.

$\Rightarrow\quad a+b=2\lambda$ ...(i)

and $\quad b+c=2\mu$ ...(ii)

On adding Eqs. (i) and (ii), we get

$$a+2b+c=2(\lambda+\mu)$$

$\Rightarrow\quad a+c=2(\lambda+\mu-b)$

$\Rightarrow\quad a+c=2k$, where $k=\lambda+\mu-b$

$\Rightarrow$ $a+c$ is divisible by 2.

$\Rightarrow$ $(a,c)\in R$

So, R is transitive.

Hence, R is reflexive, symmetric and transitive, so R is an equivalence relation.

5. (i) Let A (positive constant) be the area of the given rectangular field and $x(>0)$ be the length of the field, then its breadth $=\dfrac{A}{x}$. $[\because A=xy]$

Let l be the length of the fencing required, then

$$l=x+2\cdot\frac{A}{x}\quad\text{...(i)}$$

On differentiating both sides of Eq. (i) w.r.t. x, we get

$$\frac{dl}{dx}=1-\frac{2A}{x^2}$$

Again, differentiating both sides w.r.t. x, we get

$$\frac{d^2l}{dx^2}=\frac{4A}{x^3}$$

For maxima or minima, put

$$\frac{dl}{dx}=0\Rightarrow 1-\frac{2A}{x^2}=0$$

$\Rightarrow\quad x^2=2A$

$\Rightarrow\quad x=\sqrt{2A}\quad[\because x>0]$

Also, at $x=\sqrt{2A}$, $\left(\dfrac{d^2l}{dx^2}\right)_{x=\sqrt{2A}}=\dfrac{4A}{2A\cdot\sqrt{2A}}\geq 0$

So, l is minimum at $x=\sqrt{2A}$.

Therefore, fencing required is least when length of field $=\sqrt{2A}$ and breadth $=\dfrac{A}{\sqrt{2A}}=\dfrac{\sqrt{2A}}{2}=\dfrac{1}{2}$ of length of field.

Hence, the fencing is least when the length of the field is twice its breadth. **Hence proved.**

Or

(ii) Let A be the area of a circle of radius r, then $A=\pi r^2$.

$\therefore$ The rate of change of area A with respect to its radius $r=\dfrac{dA}{dr}=\pi\cdot 2r=2\pi r$

When $r=4$ cm, then $\dfrac{dA}{dr}=2\pi\times 4=8\pi$

Hence, the area of the circle is changing at the rate of 8π cm^2/cm, when $r=4$ cm.

6. Let $\Delta=\begin{vmatrix} x & \sin\theta & \cos\theta \\ -\sin\theta & -x & 1 \\ \cos\theta & 1 & x\end{vmatrix}$ (1)

On expanding along R_1, we get

$$\Delta=x(-x^2-1)-\sin\theta(-x\sin\theta-\cos\theta)+\cos\theta(-\sin\theta+x\cos\theta)$$

$$=-x^3-x+x(\sin^2\theta+\cos^2\theta)+\sin\theta\cos\theta-\cos\theta\sin\theta$$

$$=-x^3-x+x$$

$=-x^3$, which is independent of θ. **Hence proved.** (2)

Common Mistake

Sometime students expand the determinant without taking proper sign. For expanding a determinant we must use signs as follow $\begin{vmatrix} + & - & + \\ - & + & - \\ + & - & + \end{vmatrix}$.

7. Given, $\begin{vmatrix} p & b & c \\ a & q & c \\ a & b & r\end{vmatrix}=0$

On applying $R_1\to R_1-R_2$ and $R_2\to R_2-R_3$, we get

$$\begin{vmatrix} p-a & b-q & 0 \\ 0 & q-b & c-r \\ a & b & r\end{vmatrix}=0$$

On taking $p-a$ common from C_1, $q-b$ common from C_2

and $r-c$ common from C_3, we get

$$(p-a)(q-b)(r-c)\begin{vmatrix} 1 & -1 & 0 \\ 0 & 1 & -1 \\ \dfrac{a}{p-a} & \dfrac{b}{q-b} & \dfrac{r}{r-c}\end{vmatrix}=0$$

On applying $C_1\to C_1+C_2+C_3$, we get

$$\begin{vmatrix} 0 & -1 & 0 \\ 0 & 1 & -1 \\ \dfrac{a}{p-a}+\dfrac{b}{q-b}+\dfrac{r}{r-c} & \dfrac{b}{q-b} & \dfrac{r}{r-c}\end{vmatrix}=0$$

On expanding along C_1, we get

$$0+0+\left(\frac{a}{p-a}+\frac{b}{q-b}+\frac{r}{r-c}\right)(1-0)=0$$

$$\Rightarrow \left(\frac{a}{p-a}+1\right)+\left(\frac{b}{q-b}+1\right)+\frac{r}{r-c}=1+1$$

[adding 1 + 1 on both sides]

$$\Rightarrow \frac{a+p-q}{p-a}+\frac{b+q-b}{q-b}+\frac{r}{r-c}=2 \quad \frac{p}{p-a}+\frac{q}{q-b}+\frac{r}{r-c}=2$$

8. We know that

$$\tan^{-1}\left(\frac{1}{x}\right)=\begin{cases}\cot^{-1}x, & \text{for } x>0\\ -\pi+\cot^{-1}x, & \text{for } x<0\end{cases}$$

and $$\cot^{-1}(x)=\begin{cases}\tan^{-1}\dfrac{1}{x}, & \text{for } x>0\\ \pi+\tan^{-1}\dfrac{1}{x} & \text{for } x<0\end{cases}$$

$$\therefore \cot^{-1}\left(\frac{ab+1}{a-b}\right)+\cot^{-1}\left(\frac{bc+1}{b-c}\right)+\cot^{-1}\left(\frac{ac+1}{c-a}\right)$$

$$=\tan^{-1}\left(\frac{a-b}{1+ab}\right)+\tan^{-1}\left(\frac{b-c}{1+bc}\right)+\pi+\tan^{-1}\left(\frac{c-a}{1+ac}\right)$$

$[\because a>b>c>0]$

$$=\tan^{-1}a-\tan^{-1}b+\tan^{-1}b-\tan^{-1}c+\pi+\tan^{-1}c-\tan^{-1}a$$

$$\left[\because \tan^{-1}x-\tan^{-1}y=\tan^{-1}\left(\frac{x-y}{1+xy}\right)\right]$$

$=\pi$ **Hence proved.**

9. (i) Let A : Selection of Ist horse

B : Selection of IInd horse

$\therefore P(A)=P$ (Ist horse select) $=\dfrac{1}{3}$

and $P(B)=P$ (IInd horse select) $=\dfrac{1}{2}$

(a) P (both of them will be selected) $=P(AB)$

$=P(A)\cdot P(B)$

[since, A and B are independent events]

$$=\frac{1}{3}\times\frac{1}{2}=\frac{1}{6}$$

(b) P (only one of them will be selected)

$$=P(A\bar{B}+\bar{A}B)=P(A)\,P(\bar{B})+P(\bar{A})P(B)$$

$$=\frac{1}{3}\times\left(1-\frac{1}{2}\right)+\left(1-\frac{1}{3}\right)\times\frac{1}{2}=\frac{1}{3}\times\frac{1}{2}+\frac{2}{3}\times\frac{1}{2}$$

$$=\frac{1}{6}+\frac{2}{6}=\frac{1+2}{6}=\frac{3}{6}=\frac{1}{2}$$

(c) P (none of them will be selected)

$= P(\bar{A}\bar{B}) = P(\bar{A})\,P(\bar{B})$

$= \left(1-\frac{1}{3}\right)\left(1-\frac{1}{2}\right) = \frac{2}{3}\times\frac{1}{2} = \frac{1}{3}$

Or

(ii) We have, $f(x) = \begin{cases} ax^2+b, & \text{if } x<1 \\ 2x+1, & \text{if } x\ge 1 \end{cases}$ is differentiable at $x=1$.

$\therefore$ $f(x)$ is also continuous at $x=1$.

Now, $\lim_{x\to 1^+} f(x) = \lim_{x\to 1^+} (2x+1) = 2(1)+1 = 3$

$\lim_{x\to 1^-} f(x) = \lim_{x\to 1^-} (ax^2+b) = a(-1)^2 + b = a+b$

and $f(1) = 2(1)+1$, $f(1) = 3$

As, $f(x)$ is continuous at $x=1$.

$\therefore \quad a+b=3 \quad \ldots$(i)

Now, $Lf'(1) = \lim_{h\to 0^-} \frac{f(1-h)-f(1)}{-h}$

$= \lim_{h\to 0^-} \frac{a(1-h)^2+b-3}{-h}$

$= \lim_{h\to 0^-} \frac{a+ah^2-2ah+b-3}{-h}$

$= \lim_{h\to 0^-} (-ah+2a) = 2a$ [from Eq. (i)]

$Rf'(1) = \lim_{h\to 0^+} \frac{f(1+h)-f(1)}{h}$

$= \lim_{h\to 0^+} \frac{2(1+h)+1-3}{h}$

$= \lim_{h\to 0} \frac{2(1+h)-2}{h}$

$= \lim_{h\to 0} \frac{2(1+h-1)}{h} = \lim_{h\to 0} \frac{2h}{h} = 2$

As, $f(x)$ is differentiable at $x=1$, so $Lf'(1) = Rf'(1)$.

So, we have, $2a = 2 \Rightarrow a = 1$.

$\therefore$ Then, from Eq. (i), we get $1+b=3 \Rightarrow b=2$

Hence, $a=1$ and $b=2$

10. (i) (a) Given, $x = a\cos^3\theta$

On differentiating w.r.t. θ, we get

$\frac{dx}{d\theta} = a(3\cos^2\theta(-\sin\theta)) = -3a\cos^2\theta\sin\theta$

At $\theta = \frac{\pi}{4}$, $\left.\frac{dx}{d\theta}\right|_{\theta=\frac{\pi}{4}} = -3a\cos^2\frac{\pi}{4}\sin\frac{\pi}{4}$

$= -3a\left(\frac{1}{\sqrt{2}}\right)^2\left(\frac{1}{\sqrt{2}}\right) = \frac{-3a}{2\sqrt{2}}$

(b) Given, $y = a\sin^3\theta$

On differentiating w.r.t. θ, we get

$\frac{dy}{d\theta} = a(3\sin^2\theta\cos\theta) = 3a\sin^2\theta\cos\theta$

$\therefore$ At $\theta = \frac{\pi}{4}$, $\left.\frac{dy}{d\theta}\right|_{\theta=\frac{\pi}{4}} = 3a\sin^2\frac{\pi}{4}\cos\frac{\pi}{4}$

$= 3a\left(\frac{1}{\sqrt{2}}\right)^2\left(\frac{1}{\sqrt{2}}\right) = \frac{3a}{2\sqrt{2}}$

(c) $\frac{dy}{dx} = \frac{\frac{dy}{d\theta}}{\frac{dx}{d\theta}} = \frac{3a\sin^2\theta\cos\theta}{-3a\cos^2\theta\sin\theta}$ [from part (a) and (b)]

$= -\tan\theta$

(d) At $\theta = \frac{\pi}{6}$, $\left.\frac{dy}{dx}\right|_{\theta=\frac{\pi}{6}} = -\tan\frac{\pi}{6} = \frac{-1}{\sqrt{3}}$

Or

(ii) Given, radius of circle $OP = 10$ m

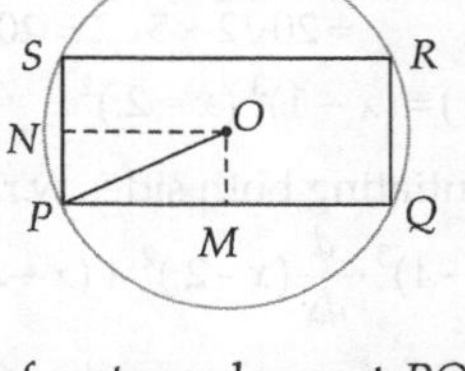

(a) Length of rectangular part $PQ = 2x$ and breadth $PS = 2y$

Draw $OM \perp PQ$ and $ON \perp PS$ then M and N are mid-points of PQ and PS, respectively.

$\therefore PM = MQ = \frac{PQ}{2} = \frac{2x}{2} = x$

and $PN = NS = \frac{PS}{2} = \frac{2y}{2} = y$

In ΔOMP, we have

$OP^2 = PM^2 + OM^2 \Rightarrow (10)^2 = x^2 + y^2$

$[\because PN = OM = y]$

$\Rightarrow x^2 + y^2 = 100 \quad \ldots$(i)

(b) The area of green grass, A = Area of rectangle

= Length $\times$ breadth $= (2x)(2y)$

$= 4xy = 4x\sqrt{100-x^2}$

[$\because$ from Eq. (i), we have $y = \sqrt{100-x^2}$]

(c) We have, $A = 4x\sqrt{100-x^2}$

On differentiating w.r.t. x, we get

$\frac{dA}{dx} = 4\left[\sqrt{100-x^2} + \frac{x}{2\sqrt{100-x^2}}(-2x)\right]$

$= 4\left[\frac{(100-x^2)-x^2}{\sqrt{100-x^2}}\right] = 4\left[\frac{100-2x^2}{\sqrt{100-x^2}}\right]$

Now, again on differentiating w.r.t. x, we get

$$\frac{d^2A}{dx^2} = \frac{4\left[-4x\sqrt{100-x^2} - (100-2x^2)\frac{1}{2\sqrt{100-x^2}}(-2x)\right]}{(100-x^2)}$$

$$= 4\frac{[-4x(100-x^2)+(100x-2x^3)]}{(100-x^2)^{3/2}}$$

$$= 4\frac{[-300x+2x^3]}{(100-x^2)^{3/2}}$$

For maximum or minimum, put $\frac{dA}{dx}=0$

$$\Rightarrow 4\left[\frac{100-2x^2}{\sqrt{100-x^2}}\right]=0 \Rightarrow 100=2x^2 \Rightarrow x=5\sqrt{2}$$

[$\because x$ cannot be negative]

At $x=5\sqrt{2}$, $\left(\frac{d^2A}{dx^2}\right)_{x=5\sqrt{2}} = -$ ve

Thus, A is maximum when $x=5\sqrt{2}$ m

Hence, $A_{max}=4\times5\sqrt{2}\sqrt{100-50}$

$$=20\sqrt{2}\times5\sqrt{2}=200\text{ m}^2$$

11. Given, $f(x)=(x-1)^3(x-2)^2$

On differentiating both sides w.r.t. x, we get

$$f'(x)=(x-1)^3\cdot\frac{d}{dx}(x-2)^2+(x-2)^2\cdot\frac{d}{dx}(x-1)^3$$

$$\left[\because \frac{d}{dx}(uv)=u\frac{dv}{dx}+v\frac{du}{dx}\right]$$

$$\Rightarrow f'(x)=(x-1)^3\cdot2(x-2)+(x-2)^2\cdot3(x-1)^2$$

$$=(x-1)^2(x-2)[2(x-1)+3(x-2)]$$

$$=(x-1)^2(x-2)(2x-2+3x-6)$$

$$\Rightarrow f'(x)=(x-1)^2(x-2)(5x-8)$$

Now, put $f'(x)=0$

$\Rightarrow (x-1)^2(x-2)(5x-8)=0$

$\Rightarrow$ Either $(x-1)^2=0$ or $x-2=0$ or $5x-8=0$

$\Rightarrow x=1,\frac{8}{5},2$

Now, we find intervals and check in which interval $f(x)$ is strictly increasing and strictly decreasing.

Interval	$f'(x)=(x-1)^2(x-2)(5x-8)$	Sign of $f'(x)$
$x<1$	$(+)(-)(-)$	+ve
$1<x<\frac{8}{5}$	$(+)(-)(-)$	+ve
$\frac{8}{5}<x<2$	$(+)(-)(+)$	−ve
$x>2$	$(+)(+)(+)$	+ve

We know that a function $f(x)$ is said to be strictly increasing, if $f'(x)>0$ and strictly decreasing, if $f'(x)<0$.

So, the given function $f(x)$ is increasing on the intervals $(-\infty,1)$, $\left(1,\frac{8}{5}\right)$ and $(2,\infty)$ and decreasing on $\left(\frac{8}{5},2\right)$.

Since, $f(x)$ is a polynomial function, so it is continuous at $x=1,\frac{8}{5}$ and 2 also.

Hence, $f(x)$ is

(a) increasing on intervals $\left(-\infty,\frac{8}{5}\right]$ and $[2,\infty)$.

(b) decreasing on interval $\left[\frac{8}{5},2\right]$.

12. Given, per day production from plant $A=500$ units, per day production from plant $B=1000$ units and per day production from plant $C=2000$ units

Let the events be

$E_1=$ Selecting the pipe from (plant) A

$E_2=$ Selecting the pipe from (plant) B

$E_3=$ Selecting the pipe from (plant) C.

Let D be the event of selecting defective pipe.

Now, $P(E_1)=\frac{500}{500+1000+2000}=\frac{500}{3500}=\frac{1}{7}$

$P(E_2)=\frac{1000}{3500}=\frac{2}{7}$ and $P(E_3)=\frac{2000}{3500}=\frac{4}{7}$

The probability that defective pipe produce from plant A, $P(D/E_1)=0.005$

The probability that defective pipe produce from plant B, $P(D/E_2)=0.008$

The probability that the defective pipe produce from plant C, $P(D/E_3)=0.010$

$\therefore$ The probability that the selected pipe produce from plant A is defective is

$$P(E_1/D)=\frac{P(E_1)\cdot P(D/E_1)}{P(E_1)\cdot P(D/E_1)+P(E_2)\cdot P(D/E_2)+P(E_3)\cdot P(D/E_3)}$$

[by using Baye's theorem]

$$=\frac{\frac{1}{7}\times0.005}{\frac{1}{7}\times0.005+\frac{2}{7}\times0.008+\frac{4}{7}\times0.010}$$

$$=\frac{\frac{1}{7}\times0.005}{\frac{1}{7}(0.005+2\times0.008+4\times0.010)}$$

$$=\frac{0.005}{0.005+0.016+0.04}=\frac{0.005}{0.061}=\frac{5}{61}$$

13. (i) Let $I=\int\frac{x^2}{(x\sin x+\cos x)^2}dx$

$$\Rightarrow I=\int\frac{x\cos x}{(x\sin x+\cos x)^2}\cdot x\sec x\,dx \quad \text{...(i)}$$

Let $I_1=\int\frac{x\cos x}{(x\sin x+\cos x)^2}dx$

Put $x \sin x + \cos x = t$

$\Rightarrow (x\cos x + \sin x - \sin x)\,dx = dt$

$\Rightarrow \quad x\cos x\,dx = dt$

$$\therefore \quad I_1 = \int \frac{x\cos x}{(x\sin x + \cos x)^2}dx$$

$$= \int \frac{dt}{t^2} = \frac{-1}{t} = \frac{-1}{x\sin x + \cos x}$$

$$\therefore \quad \int \frac{x\cos x\,dx}{(x\sin x + \cos x)^2} = \frac{-1}{x\sin x + \cos x} \quad \text{...(ii)}$$

$[\because t = x\sin x + \cos x]$

Now, from Eq. (i), we get

$$I = \int \underset{\text{I}}{x\sec x} \cdot \underset{\text{II}}{\frac{x\cos x}{(x\sin x + \cos x)^2}}dx$$

$$= x\sec x \int \frac{x\cos x}{(x\sin x + \cos x)^2}dx - \int \left[\frac{d}{dx}(x\sec x)\int \frac{x\cos x\,dx}{(x\sin x + \cos x)^2}\right]dx$$

[integrating by parts]

$$= x\sec x \cdot \frac{(-1)}{x\sin x + \cos x} - \int (1\cdot \sec x + x\sec x\tan x)\cdot \frac{-dx}{x\sin x + \cos x}$$

[using Eq. (ii)]

$$= \frac{-x\sec x}{x\sin x + \cos x} + \int \sec x\left(1 + \frac{x\sin x}{\cos x}\right)\frac{dx}{x\sin x + \cos x}$$

$$= \frac{-x\sec x}{x\sin x + \cos x} + \int \sec^2 x\,dx$$

$$= \frac{-x\sec x}{x\sin x + \cos x} + \tan x + C$$

Or

(ii) Let $I = \int \frac{2x}{(x^2+1)(x^2+2)^2}dx$

Put $x^2 = t \Rightarrow 2x\,dx = dt$

$$\therefore \quad I = \int \frac{dt}{(t+1)(t+2)^2}$$

Again, let $\frac{1}{(t+1)(t+2)^2} = \frac{A}{t+1} + \frac{B}{t+2} + \frac{C}{(t+2)^2}$

$$\Rightarrow \frac{1}{(t+1)(t+2)^2} = \frac{A(t+2)^2 + B(t+1)(t+2) + C(t+1)}{(t+1)(t+2)^2}$$

$\Rightarrow 1 = A(t+2)^2 + B(t+1)(t+2) + C(t+1)$

$\Rightarrow 1 = A(t^2+4+4t) + B(t^2+2t+t+2) + C(t+1)$

$\Rightarrow 1 = A(t^2+4t+4) + B(t^2+3t+2) + C(t+1)$

$\Rightarrow 1 = t^2(A+B) + t(4A+3B+C) + 4A+2B+C$

On comparing the coefficients of t^2, t and constant terms on both sides, we get

$$A + B = 0 \quad \text{...(i)}$$

$$4A + 3B + C = 0 \quad \text{... (ii)}$$

and $$4A + 2B + C = 1 \quad \text{... (iii)}$$

From Eq. (i), $A = -B$

On putting the value of A in Eqs. (ii) and (iii), we get

$$-4B + 3B + C = 0 \Rightarrow -B + C = 0$$

$$\Rightarrow \quad B - C = 0 \quad \text{...(iv)}$$

and $$-4B + 2B + C = 1 \Rightarrow -2B + C = 1$$

$$\Rightarrow \quad 2B - C = -1 \quad \text{...(v)}$$

On solving Eqs. (i), (iv) and (v), we get

$A = 1$, $B = -1$ and $C = -1$

Then, $\frac{1}{(t+1)(t+2)^2} = \frac{1}{t+1} + \frac{(-1)}{(t+2)} + \frac{(-1)}{(t+2)^2}$

$$\therefore \quad I = \int \frac{1}{t+1}dt + \int \frac{(-1)}{t+2}dt + \int \frac{(-1)}{(t+2)^2}dt$$

$$= \log|t+1| - \log|t+2| - \frac{(t+2)^{-1}}{-1} + C$$

$$= \log|t+1| - \log|t+2| + \frac{1}{(t+2)} + C$$

$$\therefore \quad I = \log|x^2+1| - \log|x^2+2| + \frac{1}{(x^2+2)} + C$$

$[\because t = x^2]$

14. (i) (a) We have, $f(x) = x^2 \sin x$

$\therefore \quad f(-x) = (-x)^2 \sin(-x)$

$= -x^2 \sin x = -f(x)$

Hence $f(x)$ is an odd function.

(b) Since, $f(x)$ is an odd function, then therefore

$$\int_{-\pi}^{\pi} f(x)\,dx = 0$$

(c) We have, $g(x) = x\sin x$

$\therefore \; g(-x) = (-x)\sin(-x) = x\sin x = g(x)$

$\Rightarrow \; g(x)$ is an even function.

Now, $$\int_{-\pi}^{\pi} x\sin x\,dx = 2\int_0^{\pi} x\sin x\,dx$$

$$= 2\left[[x(-\cos x)]_0^{\pi} - \int_0^{\pi}(-\cos x)\cdot 1\,dx\right]$$

$$= 2[[-x\cos x]_0^{\pi} + [\sin x]_0^{\pi}]$$

$$= 2[-\pi\cos\pi] = 2\pi$$

(d) Let $h(x) = |\sin x|$

$h(-x) = |\sin(-x)| = |-\sin x| = |\sin x| = h(x)$

$\Rightarrow h(x)$ is an even function.

$$\therefore \int_{-\pi/2}^{\pi/2} |\sin x|\,dx = 2\int_0^{\pi/2} |\sin x|\,dx$$

$$= 2\int_0^{\pi/2} \sin x\,dx = 2[-\cos x]_0^{\pi/2}$$

$$= 2\left[-\cos\frac{\pi}{2} + \cos 0\right] = 2$$

(ii) We have, $(1+\sin x)\dfrac{dy}{dx} + y\cos x + x = 0$

$$\Rightarrow \frac{dy}{dx} + \frac{\cos x}{1+\sin x}y = \frac{-x}{1+\sin x} \quad \text{...(i)}$$

(a) On comparing Eq. (i) with $\dfrac{dy}{dx} + Py = Q$, we get

$$P = \frac{\cos x}{1+\sin x} \text{ and } Q = \frac{-x}{1+\sin x}$$

(b) $= e^{\int P dx} = e^{\int \frac{\cos x}{1+\sin x}dx}$

$$= e^{\log(1+\sin x)}$$

$$= 1 + \sin x$$

(c) The solution of the given differential equation is

$$y \cdot \text{IF} = \int Q \cdot \text{IF}\,dx + c$$

$$\Rightarrow y(1+\sin x) = \int \frac{-x}{1+\sin x}\cdot(1+\sin x)\,dx + C$$

$$\Rightarrow y(1+\sin x) = -\frac{x^2}{2} + C$$

15. (i) (c) Given, two vectors $\vec{a}$ and $\vec{b}$ such that $|\vec{a}| = |\vec{b}|$, $\vec{a}\cdot\vec{b} = \dfrac{9}{2}$ and angle between them is 60º.

We know that

$\vec{a}\cdot\vec{b} = |\vec{a}||\vec{b}|\cos\theta$, where θ is the angle between $\vec{a}$ and $\vec{b}$.

$$\therefore \quad \frac{9}{2} = |\vec{a}|\cdot|\vec{a}|\cos 60º$$

$$\Rightarrow \quad \frac{1}{2}\cdot|\vec{a}|^2 = \frac{9}{2} \quad \left[\because \cos 60° = \frac{1}{2}\right]$$

$$\Rightarrow \quad |\vec{a}|^2 = 9 \Rightarrow |\vec{a}| = 3$$

[$\because$ magnitude cannot be negative]

Thus, $\quad |\vec{a}| = |\vec{b}| = 3$

(ii) (c) Equation of a plane that cut the coordinate axes at (8, 0, 0), (0, 3, 0) and (0, 0, 7) i.e, cut the intercepts of length 8, 3 and 7 with coordinate axes *x*, *y* and *z*, respectively is given by

$$\frac{x}{8} + \frac{y}{3} + \frac{z}{7} = 1.$$

(iii) (a) Given, lines are

$$\frac{x-4}{3} = \frac{y+3}{4} = \frac{z+1}{5} \quad \text{...(i)}$$

and $\quad \dfrac{x-1}{4} = \dfrac{y+1}{-3} = \dfrac{z+10}{5} \quad \text{...(ii)}$

Direction ratios of line (i) are 3, 4, 5 and direction ratios of line (ii) are 4, –3, 5.

Let the angle between the line is θ.

Then, $\cos\theta = \dfrac{|a_1a_2 + b_1b_2 + c_1c_2|}{\sqrt{a_1^2+b_1^2+c_1^2}\sqrt{a_2^2+b_2^2+c_2^2}}$

$$= \frac{(3\times4 + 4\times(-3) + 5\times5)}{\sqrt{(3)^2+(4)^2+(5)^2}\sqrt{(4)^2+(-3)^2+(5)^2}}$$

$$\Rightarrow \quad \cos\theta = \frac{|12-12+25|}{\sqrt{9+16+25}\sqrt{16+9+25}}$$

$$\Rightarrow \quad \cos\theta = \frac{25}{\sqrt{50}\sqrt{50}} \quad (1/2)$$

$$\Rightarrow \quad \cos\theta = \frac{1}{2} \Rightarrow \theta = \frac{\pi}{3} \quad (1/2)$$

(iv) Given, $\quad \overrightarrow{AO} + \overrightarrow{OB} = \overrightarrow{BO} + \overrightarrow{OC} \Rightarrow \overrightarrow{AB} = \overrightarrow{BC}$

[by triangle law of vector addition]

$\Rightarrow \overrightarrow{AB}$ and $\overrightarrow{BC}$ have same or parallel supports.

But $\overrightarrow{AB}$ and $\overrightarrow{BC}$ have point *B* in common, therefore $\overrightarrow{AB}$ and $\overrightarrow{BC}$ have same support.

Hence, the points *A*, *B* and *C* are collinear.

(v) Given, $\vec{a} = 4\hat{i} + 6\hat{j} + 2\hat{k}$ and $\vec{b} = 3\hat{i} + 2\hat{j} - 3\hat{k}$

$$\therefore \vec{b}\cdot\vec{a} = (3\hat{i} + 2\hat{j} - 3\hat{k}).(4\hat{j} + 6\hat{j} + 2\hat{k})$$

$$= 12 + 12 - 6 = 18$$

16. (i) Given, the position vectors of points *A*, *B* and *C* are $\overrightarrow{OA} = 2\hat{i} - \hat{j} + \hat{k}$, $\overrightarrow{OB} = \hat{i} - 3\hat{j} - 5\hat{k}$

and $\quad \overrightarrow{OC} = 3\hat{i} - 4\hat{j} - 4\hat{k}$

Now, $\overrightarrow{AB} = \overrightarrow{OB} - \overrightarrow{OA}$

$$= (\hat{i} - 3\hat{j} - 5\hat{k}) - (2\hat{i} - \hat{j} + \hat{k}) = -\hat{i} - 2\hat{j} - 6\hat{k},$$

$$\overrightarrow{AC} = \overrightarrow{OC} - \overrightarrow{OA}$$

$$= (3\hat{i} - 4\hat{j} - 4\hat{k}) - (2\hat{i} - \hat{j} + \hat{k}) = \hat{i} - 3\hat{j} - 5\hat{k}$$

and $\quad \overrightarrow{BC} = \overrightarrow{OC} - \overrightarrow{OB}$

$$= (3\hat{i} - 4\hat{j} - 4\hat{k}) - (\hat{i} - 3\hat{j} - 5\hat{k}) = 2\hat{i} - \hat{j} + \hat{k}$$

We know that if vectors $\vec{a} = a_1\hat{i} + a_2\hat{j} + a_3\hat{k}$ and $\vec{b} = b_1\hat{i} + b_2\hat{j} + b_3\hat{k}$ are perpendicular to each other, then $\vec{a}\cdot\vec{b} = a_1b_1 + a_2b_2 + a_3b_3 = 0$

Now, $\overrightarrow{AB}\cdot\overrightarrow{AC} = (-\hat{i} - 2\hat{j} - 6\hat{k})\cdot(\hat{i} - 3\hat{j} - 5\hat{k})$

$$= (-1)(1) + (-2)(-3) + (-6)(-5)$$

$$= -1 + 6 + 30 = 35 \neq 0,$$

$$\overrightarrow{AB}\cdot\overrightarrow{BC} = (-\hat{i} - 2\hat{j} - 6\hat{k})\cdot(2\hat{i} - \hat{j} + \hat{k})$$

$$= (-1)(2) + (-2)(-1) + (-6)(1)$$

$$= -2 + 2 - 6 = -6 \neq 0$$

and $\quad \overrightarrow{AC}\cdot\overrightarrow{BC} = (\hat{i} - 3\hat{j} - 5\hat{k})\cdot(2\hat{i} - \hat{j} + \hat{k})$

$$= (1)(2) + (-3)(-1) + (-5)(1)$$

$$= 2 + 3 - 5 = 5 - 5 = 0$$

This shows that *A*, *B* and *C* are the vertices of right angled Δ*ABC*, right angled at *C*.

Hence proved.

Now, area of $\Delta ABC = \frac{1}{2}|AC \times BC|$

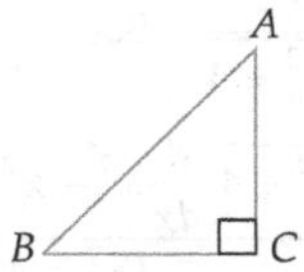

$$= \frac{1}{2}|(\hat{i} - 3\hat{j} - 5\hat{k}) \times (2\hat{i} - \hat{j} + \hat{k})|$$

$$= \frac{1}{2}\begin{vmatrix} \hat{i} & \hat{j} & \hat{k} \\ 1 & -3 & -5 \\ 2 & -1 & 1 \end{vmatrix}$$

$$= \frac{1}{2}|\hat{i}(-3-5) - \hat{j}(1+10) + \hat{k}(-1+6)|$$

$$= \frac{1}{2}|-8\hat{i} - 11\hat{j} + 5\hat{k}|$$

$$= \frac{1}{2}\sqrt{64+121+25} = \frac{1}{2}\sqrt{210} \text{ sq units}$$

Or

(ii) Given, $\vec{a}, \vec{b}$ and $\vec{c}$ are the vertices of a ΔABC as shown.

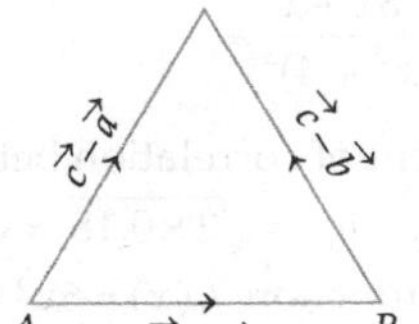

Then, $\vec{AB} = \vec{b} - \vec{a}$ and $\vec{AC} = \vec{c} - \vec{a}$, $\vec{BC} = \vec{c} - \vec{b}$,

Now, area of $\Delta ABC = \frac{1}{2}|\vec{AB} \times \vec{AC}|$

$\therefore$ Area of $\Delta ABC = \frac{1}{2}|(\vec{b} - \vec{a}) \times (\vec{c} - \vec{a})|$

$$= \frac{1}{2}|\vec{b} \times \vec{c} - \vec{b} \times \vec{a} - \vec{a} \times \vec{c} + \vec{a} \times \vec{a}|$$

$$= \frac{1}{2}|\vec{b} \times \vec{c} + \vec{a} \times \vec{b} + \vec{c} \times \vec{a} + \vec{0}|$$

$$= \frac{1}{2}|\vec{b} \times \vec{c} + \vec{a} \times \vec{b} + \vec{c} \times \vec{a}| \quad \ldots\text{(i)}$$

For three points to be collinear, area of the ΔABC should be equal to zero.

$$\therefore \quad \frac{1}{2}[\vec{b} \times \vec{c} + \vec{c} \times \vec{a} + \vec{a} \times \vec{b}] = 0$$

$$\Rightarrow \quad \vec{b} \times \vec{c} + \vec{c} \times \vec{a} + \vec{a} \times \vec{b} = 0 \quad \ldots\text{(ii)}$$

Hence proved.

17. (i) Given, equation of line AB is

$$\frac{x}{2} = \frac{y-2}{3} = \frac{z-3}{4} = \lambda \quad \text{[say]}$$

$$\Rightarrow \quad \frac{x}{2} = \lambda, \frac{y-2}{3} = \lambda \text{ and } \frac{z-3}{4} = \lambda$$

$$\Rightarrow \quad x = 2\lambda, y = 3\lambda + 2 \text{ and } z = 4\lambda + 3$$

$\therefore$ Any point P on the given line

$$= (2\lambda, 3\lambda + 2, 4\lambda + 3)$$

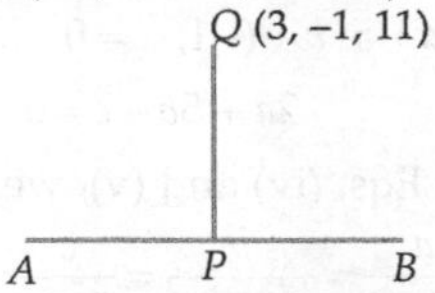

Let P be the foot of perpendicular drawn from point $Q(3, -1, 11)$ on line AB. Then, DR's of line

$$QP = (2\lambda - 3, 3\lambda + 2 + 1, 4\lambda + 3 - 11)$$

$$= (2\lambda - 3, 3\lambda + 3, 4\lambda - 8)$$

Here, $a_1 = 2\lambda - 3, b_1 = 3\lambda + 3, c_1 = 4\lambda - 8,$

and $a_2 = 2, b_2 = 3, c_2 = 4$

Since, $QP \perp AB$

$$\therefore \quad a_1a_2 + b_1b_2 + c_1c_2 = 0 \quad \ldots\text{(i)}$$

$$\Rightarrow \quad 2(2\lambda - 3) + 3(3\lambda + 3) + 4(4\lambda - 8) = 0$$

$$\Rightarrow \quad 4\lambda - 6 + 9\lambda + 9 + 16\lambda - 32 = 0$$

$$\Rightarrow \quad 29\lambda - 29 = 0 \Rightarrow 29\lambda = 29 \Rightarrow \lambda = 1$$

$\therefore$ Foot of perpendicular $P = (2, 3+2, 4+3) = (2, 5, 7)$

Now, equation of perpendicular QP, where $Q(3, -1, 11)$ and $P(2, 5, 7)$, is

$$\frac{x-3}{2-3} = \frac{y+1}{5+1} = \frac{z-11}{7-11}$$

$$\left[\text{using two points form of equation of line i.e. } \frac{x-x_1}{x_2-x_1} = \frac{y-y_1}{y_2-y_1} = \frac{z-z_1}{z_2-z_1}\right]$$

$$\Rightarrow \quad \frac{x-3}{-1} = \frac{y+1}{6} = \frac{z-11}{-4}$$

Now, length of perpendicular QP

= Distance between points $Q(3, -1, 11)$ and $P(2, 5, 7)$

$$= \sqrt{(2-3)^2 + (5+1)^2 + (7-11)^2}$$

$$\left[\because \text{distance} = \sqrt{(x_2-x_1)^2 + (y_2-y_1)^2 + (z_2-z_1)^2}\right]$$

$$= \sqrt{1+36+16} = \sqrt{53}$$

Hence, length of perpendicular is $\sqrt{53}$ units.

Or

(ii) Equation of any plane passing through the point $(1, -1, -1)$ is

$$a(x-1) + b(y+1) + c(z+1) = 0 \quad \ldots\text{(i)}$$

Given two planes are

$$2(x - 2y) + 2(y - z) - (6z + x) = 0$$

$$\Rightarrow \quad 2x - 4y + 2y - 2z - 6z - x = 0$$

$$\Rightarrow \quad x - 2y - 8z = 0 \quad \ldots\text{(ii)}$$

and $2(y - x) + 3(y + z) + 4(x - z) = 0$

$$\Rightarrow \quad 2y - 2x + 3y + 3z + 4x - 4z = 0$$

$$\Rightarrow \quad 2x + 5y - z = 0 \quad \ldots\text{(iii)}$$

As the plane (i) is perpendicular to both the planes (ii) and (iii), we get

$$1 \cdot a + (-2) \cdot b + (-8) \cdot c = 0$$

$\Rightarrow \quad a-2b-8c=0 \quad \ldots\text{(iv)}$

$[\because a_1a_2+b_1b_2+c_1c_2=0]$

$\Rightarrow \quad 2\cdot a+5\cdot b+(-1)\cdot c=0$

i.e. $\quad 2a+5b-c=0 \quad \ldots\text{(v)}$

On solving Eqs. (iv) and (v), we get

$$\frac{a}{2+40}=\frac{b}{-16+1}=\frac{c}{5+4}$$

$$\Rightarrow \quad \frac{a}{42}=\frac{b}{-15}=\frac{c}{9}$$

$$\Rightarrow \quad \frac{a}{14}=\frac{b}{-5}=\frac{c}{3}$$

$$\Rightarrow \quad a:b:c=14:-5:3$$

On substituting these values in Eq. (i), we get

$$14(x-1)-5(y+1)+3(z+1)=0$$

$$\Rightarrow \quad 14x-5y+3z-16=0,$$

which is the equation of the required plane.

18. The given ellipse is $\dfrac{x^2}{a^2}+\dfrac{y^2}{b^2}=1$

$$\Rightarrow \frac{y^2}{b^2}=1-\frac{x^2}{a^2} \Rightarrow y^2=\frac{b^2}{a^2}(a^2-x^2) \Rightarrow y=\frac{b}{a}\sqrt{a^2-x^2}$$

$[\because \text{in first quadrant}, y\ge 0]$

The given line is $\dfrac{x}{a}+\dfrac{y}{b}=1$

$$\Rightarrow \quad \frac{y}{b}=1-\frac{x}{a}=\frac{a-x}{a} \Rightarrow y=\frac{b}{a}(a-x)$$

The area of the smaller region bounded by the given ellipse and the given line is shown shaded in the figure.

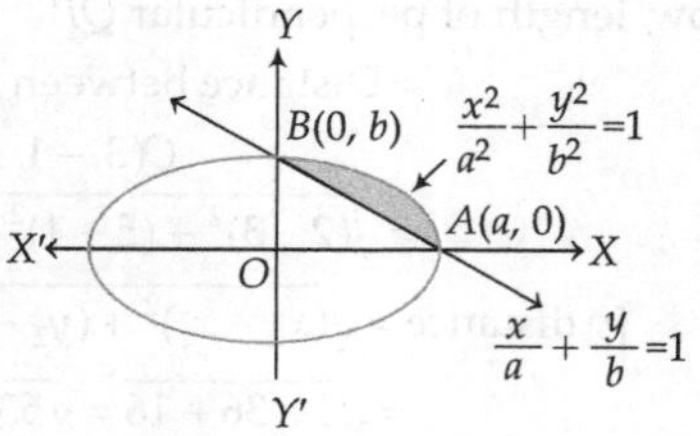

$\therefore$ Required area $=\displaystyle\int_0^a (y_2-y_1)\,dx$

$$=\int_0^a\left(\frac{b}{a}\sqrt{a^2-x^2}-\frac{b}{a}(a-x)\right)dx$$

$$=\frac{b}{a}\left[\frac{x\sqrt{a^2-x^2}}{2}+\frac{a^2}{2}\sin^{-1}\frac{x}{a}-ax+\frac{x^2}{2}\right]_0^a$$

$$\left[\because \int\sqrt{a^2-x^2}=\frac{x}{2}\sqrt{a^2-x^2}+\frac{a^2}{2}\sin^{-1}\frac{x}{a}\right]$$

$$=\frac{b}{a}\left[\left(0+\frac{a^2}{2}\sin^{-1}1-a^2+\frac{a^2}{2}\right)-\left(0+\frac{a^2}{2}\sin^{-1}0-0+0\right)\right]$$

$$=\frac{b}{a}\left[\left(\frac{a^2}{2}\cdot\frac{\pi}{2}-\frac{a^2}{2}\right)-0\right]=\frac{1}{4}(\pi-2)ab \text{ sq units}$$

19. (i) (c) We know that marginal cost, $MC=\dfrac{dC}{dx}$

Here, $\quad C=\dfrac{x^2}{\sqrt{x^2+4}}+500$ (given)

$$\therefore \quad MC=\left[\frac{\sqrt{x^2+4}\dfrac{d}{dx}x^2-x^2\dfrac{d}{dx}\sqrt{x^2+4}}{(x^2+4)}\right]$$

$$\left[\because \frac{d}{dx}\left(\frac{u(x)}{v(x)}\right)=\frac{v(x)\dfrac{d}{dx}u(x)-u(x)\dfrac{d}{dx}v(x)}{v^2(x)}\right]$$

$$=\left[\frac{2x\sqrt{x^2+4}-\dfrac{x^2\times 2x}{2\sqrt{x^2+4}}}{(x^2+4)}\right]$$

$$=\frac{2x(x^2+4)-x^3}{(x^2+4)\sqrt{x^2+4}}$$

$$=\frac{2x^3+8x-x^3}{(x^2+4)^{3/2}}$$

$$=\frac{8x+x^3}{(x^2+4)^{3/2}}$$

(ii) (b) Coefficient of correlation between x and $y=\sqrt{b_{yx}\times b_{xy}}=\sqrt{2\times 0.18}=\sqrt{0.36}=0.6$

(iii) Given, cost function, $C(x)=6x^3-5x+4$

Average Cost (AC) $=\dfrac{C(x)}{x}=\dfrac{6x^3-5x+4}{x}$

$$=6x^2-5+\frac{4}{x}$$

When $x=4$, then AC $=6(4)^2-5+\dfrac{4}{4}$

$$=96-5+1=92$$

(iv) Given, $p=1400-4x+8x^2$

Let R be the revenue function, then

$$R=px=(1400-4x+8x^2)x$$

$$=1400x-4x^2+8x^3$$

$\therefore$ Marginal Revenue (MR) $=\dfrac{d(R)}{dx}$

$$=\frac{d}{dx}(1400x-4x^2+8x^3)$$

$$=1400-8x+24x^2$$

When $x=12$, then

$$\text{MR}=1400-8\times 12+24(12)^2$$

$$=1400-96+3456=4760$$

(v) Make a table for regression coefficient

x	5	7	8	4	6	$\Sigma x=30$
y	2	4	3	2	4	$\Sigma y=15$
xy	10	28	24	8	24	$\Sigma xy=94$
x^2	25	49	64	16	36	$\Sigma x^2=190$

Here, $n=5$

$$\therefore\ b_{yx}=\frac{\Sigma xy-\frac{(\Sigma x)(\Sigma y)}{n}}{\Sigma x^2-\frac{(\Sigma x)^2}{n}}=\frac{94-\frac{30\times 15}{5}}{190-\frac{(30)^2}{5}}$$

$$=\frac{470-450}{950-900}=\frac{20}{50}=0.4$$

20. (i) Given, $C(x)=900+3x+\frac{x^2}{100}$

$\therefore$ Average Cost, $(AC)=\frac{C(x)}{x}=\frac{900}{x}+3+\frac{x}{100}$

On differentiating w.r.t. x, we get

$$\frac{d}{dx}(AC)=-\frac{900}{x^2}+\frac{1}{100}$$

For maximum or minimum, put

$$\frac{d}{dx}(AC)=0$$

$$\Rightarrow\quad -\frac{900}{x^2}+\frac{1}{100}=0\Rightarrow\frac{900}{x^2}=\frac{1}{100}$$

$$\Rightarrow\quad x^2=90000\Rightarrow x=300$$

Now, $\frac{d^2}{dx^2}(AC)=\frac{d}{dx}\left(\frac{-900}{x^2}+\frac{1}{100}\right)=\frac{1800}{x^3}$

For, $x=300$, $\quad \frac{d^2}{dx^2}(AC)=\frac{1800}{(300)^3}>0$

Hence, AC is minimum when $x=300$ items are produced.

Or

(ii) Given, $C(x)=200+20x-\frac{1}{2}x^2$

On differentiating both sides w.r.t. x, we get Marginal Cost (MC)

$$=\frac{dC}{dx}=\frac{d}{dx}\left(200+20x-\frac{1}{2}x^2\right)=20-x$$

At $x=4$, MC $=20-4=$ ₹16

This means that when we increase the output from 4 to 5 units, the additional cost incurred is ₹16.

21. Given, $\Sigma x=30, \Sigma y=42, \Sigma x^2=184, \Sigma y^2=318$,

$\Sigma xy=199$ and $n=6$

$$\therefore\ \bar{x}=\frac{\Sigma x}{n}=\frac{30}{6}=5,\ \bar{y}=\frac{\Sigma y}{n}=\frac{42}{6}=7$$

$$\therefore\ b_{xy}=\frac{n\Sigma xy-\Sigma x\Sigma y}{n\Sigma y^2-(\Sigma y)^2}=\frac{6(199)-30\times 42}{6(318)-(42)^2}$$

$$=\frac{1194-1260}{1908-1764}=-\frac{66}{144}=-\frac{33}{72}=-\frac{11}{24}$$

The regression equation of x on y is given by

$$x-\bar{x}=b_{xy}(y-\bar{y})$$

$$\Rightarrow\quad x-5=-\frac{11}{24}(y-7)$$

$$\Rightarrow\quad 24x-120=-11y+77$$

$$\Rightarrow\quad 24x+11y-197=0$$

Which is the required equation of the line of regression of x on y.

When $y=10$, then $24x+11\times 10-197=0$

$$\Rightarrow\quad 24x=197-110$$

$$\therefore\quad x=\frac{87}{24}=\frac{29}{8}$$

22. (i) Let the number of unit of stem P be x and the item Q be y.

Then, according to the question, the profit is to be maximised.

$\therefore$ Maximise, $\quad Z=50x+60y$ ...(i)

Subject to the constraints are

$3x+y\le 9$ ...(ii)

$x+2y\le 8$ ...(iii)

and $\quad x, y\ge 0$

Table for graph of the line $3x+y=9$

x	0	3
y	9	0

So, the line passes through the points (0, 9) and (3, 0).

On putting (0,0) in the inequality $3x+y\le 9$, we get

$0+0\le 9\Rightarrow 0\le 9$ [which is true]

So, the half plane is towards the origin.

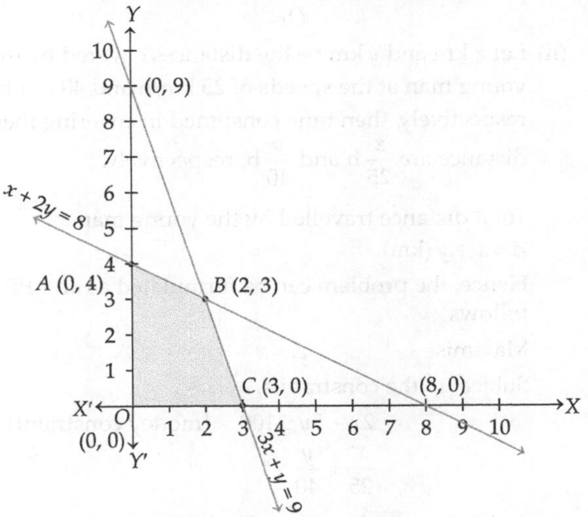

Table for graph of the line $x+2y=8$ is

x	0	8	4
y	4	0	2

So, the line passes through the points (0, 4), (8, 0) and (4, 2).

On putting (0,0) in the inequality $x+2y\le 8$, we get

$$0+0\le 8$$

$\Rightarrow\quad 0\le 8$ [which is true]

So, the half plane is towards the origin.

The intersection point of lines $3x + y = 9$ and $x + 2y = 8$ is $B(2, 3)$. Also, $x \geq 0, y \geq 0$ so the feasible region lies in Ist quadrant.

Now, plot all the inequalities on the graph paper. The shaded region represents feasible region *OCBAO*.

The corner points are $O(0,0)$, $A(0,4)$, $B(2,3)$ and $C(3,0)$.

The values of z at the corner points are as follows.

Corner points	Value of $Z = 50x + 60y$
$O(0,0)$	$50 \times 0 + 60 \times 0 = 0$
$A(0,4)$	$50 \times 0 + 60 \times 4 = 240$
$B(2,3)$	$50 \times 2 + 60 \times 3 = 100 + 180 = 280$ (Maximum)
$C(3,0)$	$50 \times 3 + 60 \times 0 = 150$

Hence, the maximum profit of the company is ₹280 when company produces 2 units of item P and 3 units of item Q.

Common Mistake

Be careful in finding the half plane is towards the origin or away from the origin.

Or

(ii) Let x km and y km be the distances covered by the young man at the speeds of 25 km/h and 40 km/h respectively, then time consumed in covering these distance are $\frac{x}{25}$ h and $\frac{y}{40}$ h, respectively.

Total distance travelled by the young man $Z = x + y$ (km).

Hence, the problem can be formulated as an LPP as follows

Maximise $Z = x + y$

Subject to the constraints,

$2x + 5y \leq 100$ [money constraint]

$\frac{x}{25} + \frac{y}{40} \leq 1$

i.e. $8x + 5y \leq 200$ [time constraint]

$x \geq 0, y \geq 0$

[non-negative constraints]

The table for line $2x + 5y = 100$ or $y = \frac{100 - 2x}{5}$ is

x	0	50
y	20	0

So, the line passes through the points (0, 20) and (50, 0).

On putting (0, 0) in the inequality $2x + 5y \leq 100$, we get

$$0 + 0 \leq 100 \quad \text{(which is true)}$$

So, the half plane is towards the origin.

The table for line $8x + 5y = 200$ or $y = \frac{200 - 8x}{5}$ is

x	0	25
y	40	0

So, the line passes through the points (0, 40) and (25, 0).

On putting (0, 0) in the inequality $8x + 5y \leq 200$, we get

$$0 + 0 \leq 200 \quad \text{(which is true)}$$

So, the half plane is towards the origin.

The point of intersection of the lines $2x + 5y = 100$ and $8x + 5y = 200$ is $B\left(\frac{50}{3}, \frac{40}{3}\right)$.

Also, $x \geq 0$, $y \geq 0$, so the feasible region lies in Ist quadrant. Now, plot all the constraints on the graph paper which is shown below.

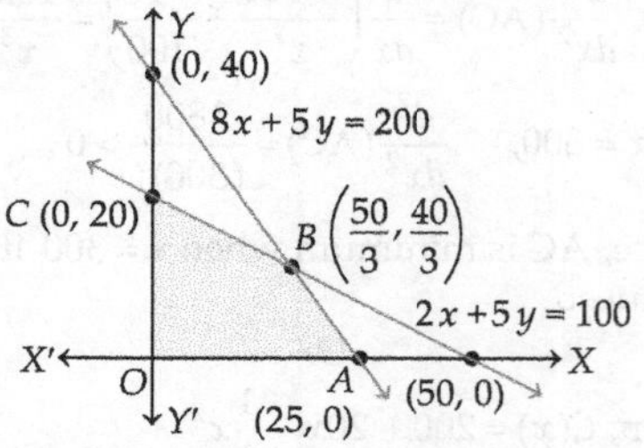

The shaded region represents the feasible region *OABC* which is bounded.

The corner points of the feasible region *OABC* are $O(0, 0)$, $A(25, 0)$, $B\left(\frac{50}{3}, \frac{40}{3}\right)$ and $C(0, 20)$.

The values of Z at corner points are as follows.

Corner points	$Z = x + y$
$O(0, 0)$	$Z = 0 + 0 = 0$
$A(25, 0)$	$Z = 25 + 0 = 25$
$B\left(\frac{50}{3}, \frac{40}{3}\right)$	$Z = \frac{50}{3} + \frac{40}{3} = 30$ (maximum)
$C(0, 20)$	$Z = 0 + 20 = 20$

From the table the value of Z is maximum at $B\left(\frac{50}{3}, \frac{40}{3}\right)$.

Hence, the young man covers a total distance of 30 km, if he rides his motorcycle $\frac{50}{3}$ km at the speed of 25 km/h and $\frac{40}{3}$ km at the speed of 40 km/h.

SQP Code : **PB-6/15** Series **i-Succeed 6-25/15** Roll No. | | | | | | | |

Sample Question Paper 06

Mathematics 12th (Code 860)

General Instructions

1. The Question Paper consists of three sections A, B and C.
2. Candidates are required to attempt all questions from Section A and all questions either from Section B Or Section C.
3. Section A Internal choice has been provided in two questions of two marks each, two questions of four marks each and two questions of six marks each.
4. Section B Internal choice has been provided in one questions of two marks and one question of four marks.
5. Section C Internal choice has been provided in one question of two marks and one question of four marks.
6. All working, including rough work, should be done on the same sheet as, and adjacent to the rest of the answer.
7. The intended marks for questions or parts of questions are given in brackets [].
8. Mathematical tables and graph papers are provided.

Time : 3 Hrs.

Max. Marks : 80

Section A (65 Marks)

1. In subparts (i) to (xi) choose the correct options and in subparts (xii) to (xv), answer the questions as instructed.

(i) The relation R defined in the set $A = \{1, 2, 3, 4, 5, 6\}$ as $R = \{(x, y) : y \text{ is divisible by } x\}$ is • *Recall* [1]

(a) reflexive, transitive but not symmetric
(b) reflexive, symmetric but not transitive
(c) an equivalence relation
(d) None of the above

(ii) The solution of differential equation $\cos x \sin y \, dx + \sin x \cos y \, dy = 0$ is • *Understanding* [1]

(a) $\dfrac{\sin x}{\sin y} = C$
(b) $\sin x \sin y = C$
(c) $\sin x + \sin y = C$
(d) $\cos x \cos y = C$

(iii) **Statement I** $\int \dfrac{\sec^2(\sin^{-1} x)}{\sqrt{1-x^2}} dx$ is equal to

Statement II $\int \dfrac{1}{\sqrt{a^2 - x^2}} dx$ is equal to $\cos^{-1} \dfrac{x}{a} + C.$ • *Application* [1]

Choose the correct option.
(a) Statement I is true.
(b) Statement II is true.
(c) Both Statements I and II are true.
(d) Both Statements I and II are false.

(iv) A matrix having m rows and n columns with $m \neq n$ is said to be a • *Recall* [1]

(a) rectangular matrix
(b) square matrix
(c) identity matrix
(d) scalar matrix

(v) A bag A contains 4 green and 3 red balls and bag B contains 4 red and 3 green balls. One bag is taken at random and a ball is drawn and noted to be green. The probability that it comes from bag B is • *Analysis* [1]

(a) $\frac{2}{7}$ (b) $\frac{2}{3}$ (c) $\frac{3}{7}$ (d) $\frac{1}{3}$

(vi) **Assertion** (A) The principal value of $\sec^{-1}\left(\frac{2}{\sqrt{3}}\right)$ is • *Understanding* [1]

Reason (R) The branch in which principal values of inverse trigonometric functions lie is called principal value branch.

Choose the correct option.

(a) A is true; R is true and R is the correct explanation of A.
(b) A is true; R is true but R is not the correct explanation of A.
(c) A is true but R is false.
(d) A is false but R is true.

(vii) The function f is given by $f(x)=2x^2-3x$, is • *Analysis [1]*

(a) strictly increasing in the interval $\left(\frac{3}{4},\infty\right)$
(b) strictly decreasing in the interval $\left(-\infty,\frac{3}{4}\right)$
(c) Both (a) and (b) are true
(d) Both (a) and (b) are false

(viii) If $\int\frac{x+2}{2x^2+6x+5}dx=P\int\frac{4x+6}{2x^2+6x+5}dx+\frac{1}{2}\int\frac{dx}{2x^2+6x+5}$, then the value of P is • *Evaluate* [1]

(a) $\frac{1}{3}$ (b) $\frac{1}{2}$ (c) $\frac{1}{4}$ (d) 2

(ix) **Assertion** (A) $f(x)=2x+\cot^{-1}x+\log(\sqrt{1+x^2}-x)$ is increasing in R. • *Understanding*

Reason (R) $f'(x)\geq 0$ for increasing function.

Choose the correct option. [1]

(a) A is true; R is true and R is the correct explanation of A.
(b) A is true; R is true and A is not the correct explanation of A.
(c) A is true but R is false.
(d) A is false but R is true.

(x) Consider the following statements.

Statement I. Scalar matrix $A=[a_{ij}]=\begin{cases}k; & i=j\\0; & i\neq j\end{cases}$ where k is a scalar, is an identity matrix when $k=1$.

Statement II. Every identity matrix is not a scalar matrix. • *Recall*

Choose the correct option. [1]

(a) Only I is true.
(b) Only II is true.
(c) Both I and II are true.
(d) Both I and II are false.

(xi) The value of determinant, $\begin{vmatrix}102 & 3 & 17\\18 & 6 & 3\\36 & 7 & 6\end{vmatrix}$ is • *Evaluate* [1]

(a) 0 (b) 1
(c) 6 (d) None of these

(xii) The volume v cm^3 of water is leaking from vessel in terms of the time t given by the formula $v=400-4t-t^2$. Find the rate at which the water is running out of the vessel when $t=12$. • *Application* [1]

(xiii) Given an example of relation, which is symmetric but neither reflexive nor transitive. • *Recall* [1]

(xiv) Evaluate $\int a^{3\log_a x}\,dx$. • *Evaluate* [1]

(xv) Prove that $\tan^{-1}\sqrt{x}=\frac{1}{2}\cos^{-1}\left(\frac{1-x}{1+x}\right)$, where $x\in[0,1]$. • *Application* [1]

2. (i) A pair of dice is thrown and the sum of the numbers appearing on the dice is observed to be 7. Find the probability that the number 5 has appeared on atleast one die. • *Analysis* [2]

Or

(ii) A die marked 1, 2, 3 in red and 4, 5, 6 in green is tossed. Let A be the event 'number is even' and B be the event 'number is marked red'. Find whether the events A and B are independent or not. • *Analysis* [2]

3. Solve the differential equation given by

$x\,dy - y\,dx - \sqrt{x^2 + y^2}\,dx = 0$ • *Application* [2]

4. Construct a matrix of order 2×3, whose elements are determined by $a_{ij} = \dfrac{2i - j}{3}$.

• *Understanding* [2]

5. (i) If $(\cos x)^y = (\cos y)^x$, then find $\dfrac{dy}{dx}$.

• *Application* [2]

Or

(ii) Differentiate the function x^x w.r.t x.

• *Application* [2]

6. If $A = \begin{bmatrix} 1 & 2 & 2 \\ 2 & 1 & 2 \\ 2 & 2 & 1 \end{bmatrix}$ and if $A^2 - 4A + 5I = O$, then find A^{-1}. • *Evaluate* [2]

7. Solve the differential equation

$y\,dx - (x + 2y^2)dy = 0.$ • *Application* [4]

8. Prove that

$\begin{vmatrix} b+c & c+a & a+b \\ q+r & r+p & p+q \\ y+z & z+x & x+y \end{vmatrix} = 2\begin{vmatrix} a & b & c \\ p & q & r \\ x & y & z \end{vmatrix}.$ • *Analysis* [4]

9. (i) Show that the function $f(x) = |x+1| + |x-1|$, for all $x \in R$, is not differentiable at the points $x = -1$ and $x = 1$. • *Application* [4]

Or

(ii) For what value of λ, function defined by $f(x) = \begin{cases} \lambda(x^2 + 2), & \text{if } x \le 0 \\ 4x + 6, & \text{if } x > 0 \end{cases}$ is continuous at $x = 0$? Hence, check the differentiability of $f(x)$ at $x = 0$.

• *Application* [4]

10. (i) Let a cone is inscribed in sphere of radius R. The height and radius of cone are h and r, respectively.

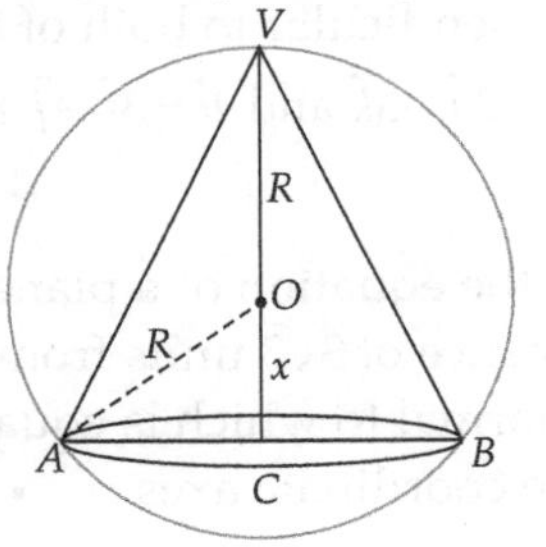

Based on above information, answer the following questions. • *Applications*

(a) Find the relation between r and R in terms of x.

(b) Find the volume V of the cone expressed as a function of x.

(c) Find the maximum value of volume V.

(d) Find the values of r, h when V is maximum. [4]

Or

(ii) Consider the function

$f(x) = (x-1)^{1/3}\,(x-2);\ 1 \le x \le 9.$

Answer the following questions.

(a) Differentiate the given function.

(b) Find the critical points.

(c) Find the points of absolute minima and maxima. • *Application* [4]

11. If $f(x)$ is a continuous function defined on $[0, a]$, then $\int_0^a f(x)\,dx = \int_0^a f(a-x)\,dx$.

On the above information, answer the following questions. • *Application*

(i) Evaluate $\displaystyle\int_0^a \frac{f(x)\,dx}{f(x) + f(a-x)}$.

(ii) If $f(x) = \dfrac{\sin x - \cos x}{1 + \sin x \cos x}$, then find the value of $f\left(\dfrac{\pi}{2} - x\right)$.

(iii) Evaluate $\displaystyle\int_0^{\pi/2} f(x)\,dx$. [6]

12. (i) The random variable X has the following probability distribution, where a and b are some constants

X	1	2	3	4	5
P(X)	0.2	a	a	0.2	b

If the mean $E(X) = 3$, then find the values of a and b and hence determine $P(X \ge 3)$. *Analysis* [6]

Or

(ii) Among the students in a college, it is known that 60% reside in hostel and 40% are day scholars (not residing in hostel). Previous year results report that 30% of all students who reside in hostel attain A grade and 20% of day scholars attain A grade in their annual exams. At the end of year, one student is chosen at random from the college and he has A grade, what is the probability that the student is a hosteler? • *Analysis* [6]

13. (i) Find the intervals in which the function f given by

$$f(x)=\frac{4\sin x-2x-x\cos x}{2+\cos x}, 0\le x\le 2\pi, \text{ is}$$

• *Evaluate*

(a) strictly increasing.

(b) strictly decreasing. [6]

Or

(ii) Evaluate $\int \frac{2\cos x}{(1-\sin x)(2-\cos^2 x)}\,dx.$

• *Evaluate* [6]

14. Consider the following formula

I. $\tan^{-1}x+\tan^{-1}y$

$$=\begin{cases}\tan^{-1}\left(\frac{x+y}{1-xy}\right), & xy<1\\ \pi+\tan^{-1}\left(\frac{x+y}{1-xy}\right), & xy>1\end{cases}$$

II. $\tan^{-1}x-\tan^{-1}y=\tan^{-1}\left(\frac{x-y}{1+xy}\right)$

On the basis of above information, answer the following questions.

(i) Find $\tan^{-1}2+\tan^{-1}3$.

(ii) Find $\tan^{-1}\frac{1}{7}+\tan^{-1}\frac{1}{13}$

(iii) Find $\tan^{-1}\frac{2}{11}+\tan^{-1}\frac{7}{24}$.

(iv) If $\tan^{-1}\frac{x}{2}+\tan^{-1}\frac{x}{3}=\frac{\pi}{4}, 0<x<\sqrt{6}$, then find x.

• *Analysis*

Section B (15 Marks)

15. In subparts (i) to (iii) choose the correct options and in subparts (iv) and (v), answer the questions as instructed. [5]

(i) If a plane passes through the points (8, 0, 0), (0, 5, 0) and (0, 0, 3), as shown in figure then the equation of plane is

• *Recall*

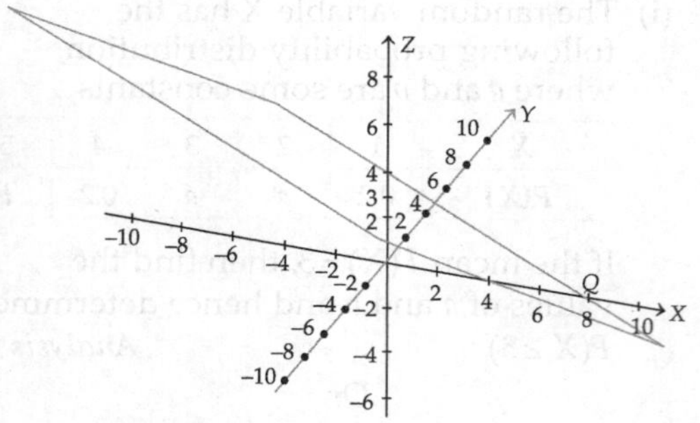

(a) $\frac{x}{8}+\frac{y}{5}+\frac{z}{3}=1$ (b) $\frac{x}{5}+\frac{y}{8}+\frac{z}{3}=1$

(c) $\frac{x}{5}+\frac{y}{6}+\frac{z}{10}=1$ (d) None of these

(ii) If $\vec{a}$ $x\hat{i}+2\hat{j}-z\hat{k}$ and $\vec{b}=3\hat{i}-y\hat{j}+\hat{k}$ are two equal vectors, then the value of $x+y+z$ is

• *Understanding*

(a) 1 (b) 2

(c) 3 (d) 0

(iii) **Statement I** The direction ratios of the line $\frac{4-x}{2}=\frac{y}{6}=\frac{1-z}{3}$ are 2, 6, 3.

• *Recall*

Statement II If a, b and c are direction ratios, then direction cosines are

$$\left(\frac{\pm a}{\sqrt{a^2+b^2+c^2}}, \frac{\pm b}{\sqrt{a^2+b^2+c^2}}, \frac{\pm c}{\sqrt{a^2+b^2+c^2}}\right)$$

Choose the correct options.

(a) Statement I is true.

(b) Statement II is true.

(c) Both Statements I and II are true.

(d) Both Statements I and II are false.

(iv) Find a vector of magnitude $\sqrt{171}$ which is perpendicular to both of the vectors $\vec{a}=\hat{i}+2\hat{j}-3\hat{k}$ and $\vec{b}=3\hat{i}-\hat{j}+2\hat{k}$.

• *Understanding*

(v) Find the equation of a plane which is at a distance of $3\sqrt{3}$ units from origin and the normal to which is equally inclined to the coordinate axes. • *Understanding*

16. (i) If the position vectors of the points A, B, C and D are $2\hat{i}+4\hat{k}, 5\hat{i}+3\sqrt{3}\hat{j}+4\hat{k}$, $-2\sqrt{3}\hat{j}+\hat{k}$ and $2\hat{i}+\hat{k}$ respectively, then prove that $\overrightarrow{CD}$ is parallel to $\overrightarrow{AB}$ and $\overrightarrow{CD}=\frac{2}{3}\overrightarrow{AB}$. • *Analysis* [2]

Or

(ii) If $\vec{a}=7\hat{i}+\hat{j}-4\hat{k}$ and $\vec{b}=2\hat{i}+6\hat{j}+3\hat{k}$, then find the projection of $\vec{a}$ on $\vec{b}$. • *Analysis* [2]

17. (i) Find the equation of the two planes passing through the points (0, 4, −3) and (6, −4, 3), if the sum of their intercepts on the three axes is zero. • *Application* [4]

Or

(ii) Find the foot of perpendicular drawn from the point $P(1,6,3)$ on the line $\frac{x}{1}=\frac{y-1}{2}=\frac{z-2}{3}$. Also, obtain the equation and the length of perpendicular. • *Application* [4]

18. Find the area of the region bounded by the curve $x^2+y^2=16$ and lines $y=1$ and $y=2$ in Ist quadrant. • *Application* [4]

Section C (15 Marks)

19. In subparts (i) and (ii) choose the correct options and in subparts (iii) to (v), answer the questions as instructed. [5]

(i) The total cost $C(x)$ of a firm is $C(x)=9x^3-4x^2+6x-100$, where x is the output, then the average cost is • *Understanding*

(a) $9x^3-4x^2+6x-\frac{100}{x}$

(b) $9x^2-4x+6-\frac{100}{x}$

(c) $9x^2-4x^2+6-\frac{100}{x}$

(d) None of the above

(ii) By using the data $\bar{x}=5, \bar{y}=7$ and $b_{yx}=\frac{-11}{34}$, the regression equation of y on x is • *Recall*

(a) $34x+11y=-293$ (b) $34y-11x=293$

(c) $11x+34y-293=0$ (d) $11x-34y-293=0$

(iii) The total cost $C(x)$ of a firm is $C(x)=0.005x^3-0.7x^2-30x+3000$, where x is the output. Determine marginal cost of function. • *Evaluate*

(iv) The equations $40x-18y=5$ and $8x-10y+6=0$ are respectively the regression equations of y on x and x on y. Is the given statement true? Give reasons. • *Analysis*

(v) The marginal cost of production of a commodity is $50+5x$. It is known that fixed costs are ₹ 150. Find the total cost of producing 50 units. • *Evaluate*

20. (i) The demand for a certain product is represented by the function $P=100+10x-x^2$ (in ₹) where x is the number of units demanded and P is the price per unit. • *Application*

(a) Find the marginal revenue.

(b) Obtain the marginal revenue when 5 units are sold and interpret it. [2]

Or

(ii) Suppose the demand per month for a commodity are 24 and 12, if the prices are ₹ 16 and ₹ 22, respectively assuming that the demand curve is linear, determine • *Application*

(a) the demand function.

(b) the total revenue function. [2]

21. Find the line of best fit to the following data using x as independent variable and y as dependent variable. • *Application* [4]

x	1	3	4	6	8	9	11	14
y	1	2	4	4	5	7	8	9

22. (i) A mill owner buys two types of machines A and B for his mill. Machine A occupies 1000 m^2 of area and requires 12 men to operate it, while machine B occupies 1200 m^2 of area and requires 8 men to operate it. The owner has 7600 m^2 of area available and 72 men to operate the machines. If machine A produces 50 units and machine B produces 40 units daily, how many machines of each type should he buy to maximise the daily output? Use linear programming to find the solution. • *Analysis* [4]

Or

(ii) A furniture dealer deals in two items : tables and chairs. He has ₹ 10000 to invest and a space to store atmost 60 pieces. A table costs him ₹ 500 and a chair costs him ₹ 100. He can sell a table at ₹ 550 and a chair at ₹ 115. Assume that he can sell the items that he buys. Formulate this problem as an LPP, so that he maximises his profit. Draw the feasible region on a graph and clearly mention the corner points and solve this problem using corner point method. • *Analysis* [4]

Solutions *in Topper's Style*

My Commitment *I affirm that I am reviewing these solutions only after I have solved the Sample Question Paper 6 on my own. My purpose of looking the solutions is solely to verify whether my answers/solutions were correct or not and to identify my mistakes in case my solutions were wrong or I could not solve that.*

1. (i) (a) Given, $R=\{(x,y): y \text{ is divisible by } x\}$

and $A=\{1,2,3,4,5,6\}$

Reflexive Let $x \in A$ be any arbitrary element.

We know that x is divisible by x.

[$\because$ every real number except zero is divisible by itself]

$\Rightarrow (x,x)\in R$

Since, $x\in A$ was arbitrary element, therefore $(x,x)\in R, \forall\, x\in A$. So, R is reflexive.

Symmetric Clearly, $2,4\in A$ and 4 is divisible by 2, but 2 is not divisible by 4.

$\therefore$ $(2,4)\in R$ but $(4,2)\notin R$

So, R is not symmetric.

Transitive Let $x,y,z\in A$ such that $(x,y)\in R$ and $(y,z)\in R$.

Now, as $(x,y)\in R$, therefore y is divisible by x.

i.e. $$\frac{y}{x}=k_1 \text{ (say)} \quad \ldots\text{(i)}$$

where, k_1 is a natural number

and as $(y,z)\in R$, therefore z is divisible by y

i.e. $$\frac{z}{y}=k_2 \quad \text{(say)} \quad \ldots\text{(ii)}$$

where, k_2 is a natural number.

On multiplying Eqs. (i) and (ii), we get

$$\frac{y}{x}\times\frac{z}{y}=k_1k_2 \Rightarrow \frac{z}{x}=k_1k_2$$

where, k_1k_2 is a natural number.

$\therefore$ z is divisible by x.

Thus, $(x,z)\in R$, for $(x,y),(y,z)\in R$

i.e. $(x,y)\in R, (y,z)\in R \Rightarrow (x,z)\in R$

Hence, R is transitive.

(ii) (b) Given differential equation is

$$\cos x\sin y\,dx+\sin x\cos y\,dy=0$$

$$\Rightarrow \cos x\sin y\,dx=-\sin x\cos y\,dy$$

$$\Rightarrow \frac{\cos x}{\sin x}dx=-\frac{\cos y}{\sin y}dy$$

$$\Rightarrow \cot x\,dx=-\cot y\,dy$$

On integrating both sides, we get

$$\int\cot x\,dx=-\int\cot y\,dy$$

$$\Rightarrow \log\sin x=-\log\sin y+\log C$$

$$\Rightarrow \log\sin x+\log\sin y=\log C$$

$$\Rightarrow \log(\sin x\sin y)=\log C \Rightarrow \sin x\cdot\sin y=C$$

(iii) (a) Let $I=\int\frac{\sec^2(\sin^{-1}x)}{\sqrt{1-x^2}}dx$

Put $\sin^{-1}x=t \Rightarrow \frac{dt}{dx}=\frac{1}{\sqrt{1-x^2}}$

$$\Rightarrow \quad dt = \frac{1}{\sqrt{1-x^2}}\, dx$$

$$\therefore \quad I = \int \sec^2 t\, dt = \tan t + C = \tan(\sin^{-1} x) + C$$

Also, we know that

$$\int \frac{1}{\sqrt{a^2 - x^2}}\, dx = \sin^{-1}\frac{x}{a} + C$$

Hence, only statement I is true.

(iv) (a) A matrix having m rows and n columns with $m \neq n$ is said to be a rectangular matrix.

(v) (c)

Bag A	Bag B
4 Green, 3 Red	3 Green, 4 Red

Let A = Event of taking bag A,
B = Event of taking bag B
and G = Event of taking green ball

$$\therefore P(A) = P(B) = \frac{1}{2}$$

$$P\left(\frac{G}{A}\right) = \frac{{}^4C_1}{{}^7C_1} = \frac{4}{7} \text{ and } P\left(\frac{G}{B}\right) = \frac{{}^3C_1}{{}^7C_1} = \frac{3}{7}$$

$$\text{Now, } P\left(\frac{B}{G}\right) = \frac{P(B)\cdot P\left(\frac{G}{B}\right)}{P(A)\cdot P\left(\frac{G}{A}\right) + P(B)\cdot P\left(\frac{G}{B}\right)}$$

$$= \frac{\frac{1}{2}\cdot\frac{3}{7}}{\frac{1}{2}\cdot\frac{4}{7} + \frac{1}{2}\cdot\frac{3}{7}} = \frac{3}{7}$$

(vi) (a) Let $\sec^{-1}\left(\frac{2}{\sqrt{3}}\right) = \theta \Rightarrow \sec\theta = \frac{2}{\sqrt{3}}$

We know that the range or principal value branch of $\sec^{-1}\theta$ is $[0, \pi] - \left\{\frac{\pi}{2}\right\}$

$$\therefore \quad \sec\theta = \frac{2}{\sqrt{3}} = \sec\frac{\pi}{6}$$

$$\Rightarrow \quad \theta = \frac{\pi}{6},$$

$$\Rightarrow \sec^{-1}\left(\frac{2}{\sqrt{3}}\right) = \frac{\pi}{6}$$

Hence, A and R both are true and R is correct explanation of A.

(vii) (c) Given, $f(x) = 2x^2 - 3x$

On differentiating w.r.t. x, we get

$$f'(x) = 4x - 3$$

On putting $f'(x) = 0$, we get

$$4x - 3 = 0$$

$$\Rightarrow \quad x = 3/4$$

The point $x = 3/4$ divides the real line into two disjoint intervals namely

$$\left(-\infty, \frac{3}{4}\right) \text{ and } \left(\frac{3}{4}, \infty\right).$$

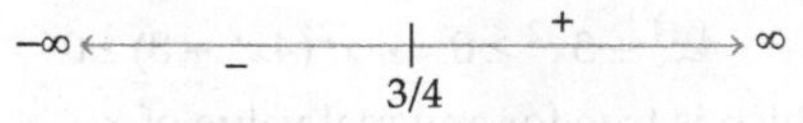

Intervals	Sign of $f'(x)$	Nature of $f(x)$
$\left(-\infty, \frac{3}{4}\right)$	(−) negative ($\because x < 3/4$)	Strictly decreasing
$\left(\frac{3}{4}, \infty\right)$	(+) positive ($\because x > 3/4$)	Strictly increasing

Hence, $f(x)$ is strictly increasing in $\left(\frac{3}{4}, \infty\right)$ and decreasing in $\left(-\infty, \frac{3}{4}\right)$.

(viii) (c) $\displaystyle\int \frac{x+2}{2x^2 + 6x + 5}\, dx = \frac{1}{4}\int \frac{4x + 6 + 2}{2x^2 + 6x + 5}\, dx$

[multiply and divide by 4]

$$= \frac{1}{4}\int \frac{4x + 6}{2x^2 + 6x + 5}\, dx + \frac{1}{2}\int \frac{dx}{2x^2 + 6x + 5}$$

$$\text{Given, } \int \frac{x+2}{2x^2 + 6x + 5}\, dx = P\int \frac{4x + 6}{2x^2 + 6x + 5}\, dx + \frac{1}{2}\int \frac{dx}{2x^2 + 6x + 5} \quad \ldots \text{(ii)}$$

On comparing Eqs. (i) and (ii), we get

$$P = \frac{1}{4}$$

(ix) (a) We have, $f(x) = 2x + \cot^{-1} x + \log(\sqrt{1 + x^2} - x)$

On differentiating both sides w.r.t. x, we get

$$f'(x) = 2 + \frac{-1}{1 + x^2} + \frac{1}{\sqrt{1 + x^2} - x} \times \left[\frac{1}{2\sqrt{1 + x^2}} \times 2x - 1\right]$$

$$= 2 - \frac{1}{1 + x^2} + \frac{1}{\sqrt{1 + x^2} - x}\left[\frac{x - \sqrt{1 + x^2}}{\sqrt{1 + x^2}}\right]$$

$$= 2 - \frac{1}{1 + x^2} + \frac{-1}{\sqrt{1 + x^2}}$$

$$= \frac{2 + 2x^2 - 1 - 1\sqrt{1 + x^2}}{1 + x^2}$$

$$\Rightarrow \quad f'(x) = \frac{1 + 2x^2 - \sqrt{1 + x^2}}{1 + x^2}$$

We know that $f'(x) \geq 0$ for increasing function.

$$\Rightarrow \quad 1 + 2x^2 - \sqrt{1 + x^2} \geq 0$$

$[\because 1 + x^2 \geq 0 \text{ for all } x \in R]$

$$\Rightarrow \quad 1 + 2x^2 \geq \sqrt{1 + x^2}$$

$$\Rightarrow \quad (1 + 2x^2)^2 \geq 1 + x^2 \quad \text{[squaring both sides]}$$

$$\Rightarrow \quad 1 + 4x^2 + 4x^4 \geq 1 + x^2$$

$\Rightarrow \quad 4x^4 + 3x^2 \geq 0 \Rightarrow x^2(4x^2+3) \geq 0$

which is true for any real value of x.

$\therefore f(x)$ is increasing in R.

So, both A and R are true and R is the correct explanation of A.

(x) (a) A scalar matrix $A = [a_{ij}] = \begin{cases} k, & i = j \\ 0, & i \neq j \end{cases}$ is an identity matrix when $k = 1$. But every identity matrix is clearly a scalar matrix.

(xi) (a) Let $\Delta = \begin{vmatrix} 102 & 3 & 17 \\ 18 & 6 & 3 \\ 36 & 7 & 6 \end{vmatrix}$

$$= \begin{vmatrix} 6(17) & 3 & 17 \\ 6(3) & 6 & 3 \\ 6(6) & 7 & 6 \end{vmatrix}$$

$$= 6\begin{vmatrix} 17 & 3 & 17 \\ 3 & 6 & 3 \\ 6 & 7 & 6 \end{vmatrix} \quad \text{[taking 6 common from } C_1]$$

$$= 6 \times 0 \quad [\because C_1 \text{ and } C_3 \text{ are identical}]$$

$$= 0$$

(xii) Given, $v = 400 - 4t - t^2$

On differentiating w.r.t. t, we get

$$\frac{dv}{dt} = -4 - 2t$$

At $t = 12$, the required rate,

$$\left(\frac{dv}{dt}\right)_{t=2} = -4 - 2(12) = -4 - 24 = -28 \text{ cm}^3/\text{s}$$

(xiii) Let A = Set of straight lines in a plane and $R = \{(a, b) : a \perp b\}$

Symmetric If a is perpendicular to b, then b is also perpendicular to a

i.e. $(a, b) \in R \Rightarrow (b, a) \in R$

So, R is symmetric.

Reflexive Since, line a is not perpendicular to itself i.e. $(a, a) \notin R$, so R is not reflexive.

Transitive If $a \perp b$ and $b \perp c$, then a is not perpendicular to c

i.e. $(a, b), (b, c) \in R \not\Rightarrow (a, c) \in R$, so R is not transitive.

(xiv) Let $I = \int a^{3\log_a x}\, dx$

$$= \int a^{\log_a x^3}\, dx \quad [\because m \log n = \log n^m]$$

$$= \int x^3 dx \quad [\because a^{\log_a f(x)} = f(x)]$$

$$= \frac{x^4}{4} + C \quad \left[\because \int x^n dx = \frac{x^{n+1}}{n+1} + C, \text{ if } n \neq -1\right]$$

Common Mistake

While solving an integral, constant of integration should be written, otherwise answer would be incomplete.

(xv) We have, RHS $= \frac{1}{2}\cos^{-1}\left(\frac{1-x}{1+x}\right)$

Put $x = \tan^2\theta \Rightarrow \theta = \tan^{-1}\sqrt{x}$

Then, RHS $= \frac{1}{2}\cos^{-1}\left[\frac{1-\tan^2\theta}{1+\tan^2\theta}\right]$

$$= \frac{1}{2}\cos^{-1}[\cos 2\theta] \quad \left[\because \cos 2\theta = \frac{1-\tan^2\theta}{1+\tan^2\theta}\right]$$

$$= \frac{1}{2} \times 2\theta = \theta = \tan^{-1}\sqrt{x} = \text{LHS}$$ **Hence proved.**

2. (i) We know that when a pair of dice is thrown, total possible outcomes $= 6 \times 6 = 36$

Let A be the event of getting sum as 7.

Possible outcomes = (1, 6), (2, 5), (3, 4), (4, 3), (5, 2), (6, 1)

Therefore, $P(A) = \frac{6}{36} = \frac{1}{6}$

Let B be the event of getting number 5 on atleast one dice.

Possible outcomes = (1, 5), (2, 5), (3, 5), (4, 5), (5, 1), (5, 2), (5, 3), (5, 4), (5, 5), (5, 6), (6, 5)

$\therefore P(B) = \frac{11}{36}$. (1)

Now, $(A \cap B)$ = (2, 5), (5, 2) = Getting sum as 7 with atleast one die showing 5

$\therefore P(A \cap B) = \frac{2}{36}$

Hence, $P\left(\frac{B}{A}\right) = \frac{P(A \cap B)}{P(A)} = \frac{2/36}{1/6} = \frac{1}{3}$

Or

(ii) We know that when a die is thrown, the sample space is

$S = \{1, 2, 3, 4, 5, 6\}$

$\Rightarrow \quad n(S) = 6$

Also, event A = number is even

and event B = number is marked red.

Then, $A = \{2, 4, 6\}$ and $B = \{1, 2, 3\}$ and $A \cap B = \{2\}$

$\therefore n(A) = 3, n(B) = 3$ and $n(A \cap B) = 1$

Now, $P(A) = \frac{n(A)}{n(S)} = \frac{3}{6} = \frac{1}{2}$

$$P(B) = \frac{n(B)}{n(S)} = \frac{3}{6} = \frac{1}{2}$$

and $$P(A \cap B) = \frac{n(A \cap B)}{n(S)} = \frac{1}{6}$$

Now, $P(A) \times P(B) = \frac{1}{2} \times \frac{1}{2} = \frac{1}{4} \neq \frac{1}{6} = P(A \cap B)$

$\Rightarrow \quad P(A \cap B) \neq P(A) \times P(B)$

Hence, A and B are not independent events.

3. Given differential equation is

$$xdy - ydx = \sqrt{x^2+y^2}\,dx$$

$$\Rightarrow \quad (y+\sqrt{x^2+y^2})dx = x\,dy$$

$$\Rightarrow \quad \frac{dy}{dx} = \frac{y}{x} + \sqrt{1+y^2/x^2} \qquad \ldots(i)$$

which is a homogeneous differential equation of the form $\frac{dy}{dx} = F\left(\frac{y}{x}\right)$

On putting $y = vx \Rightarrow \frac{dy}{dx} = v + x\frac{dv}{dx}$ in Eq. (i), we get

$$v + x\frac{dv}{dx} = v + \sqrt{1+v^2} \Rightarrow x\frac{dv}{dx} = \sqrt{1+v^2}$$

$$\Rightarrow \quad \frac{dv}{\sqrt{1+v^2}} = \frac{dx}{x}$$

On integrating both sides, we get

$$\int \frac{dv}{\sqrt{1+v^2}} = \int \frac{dx}{x}$$

$$\Rightarrow \quad \log\left|v+\sqrt{1+v^2}\right| = \log|x| + C$$

$$\left[\because \int \frac{dx}{\sqrt{a^2+x^2}} = \log\left|x+\sqrt{a^2+x^2}\right| + C\right]$$

$$\Rightarrow \quad \log\left|\frac{y}{x} + \sqrt{1+\frac{y^2}{x^2}}\right| = \log|x| + C \qquad [\because v = y/x]$$

$$\Rightarrow \quad \log\frac{y+\sqrt{x^2+y^2}}{x} - \log x = C$$

$$[\because \log m - \log n = \log(m/n)]$$

$$\Rightarrow \quad \log\frac{y+\sqrt{x^2+y^2}}{x^2} = C$$

$$\Rightarrow \quad \frac{y+\sqrt{x^2+y^2}}{x^2} = e^C \qquad [\text{if } \log y = z, \text{ then } y = e^z]$$

$$\Rightarrow \quad y+\sqrt{x^2+y^2} = x^2 \cdot e^C$$

$$\therefore \quad y+\sqrt{x^2+y^2} = Ax^2,$$

where, $A = e^C$

4. Let A be the matrix of order 2×3.

Then, $A = [a_{ij}]_{2\times 3} = \begin{bmatrix} a_{11} & a_{12} & a_{13} \\ a_{21} & a_{22} & a_{23} \end{bmatrix} \qquad \ldots(i)$

Given, $a_{ij} = \frac{2i-j}{3}$

$$\therefore \quad a_{11} = \frac{2(1)-1}{3} = \frac{1}{3},\; a_{12} = \frac{2(1)-2}{3} = 0,$$

$$a_{13} = \frac{2(1)-3}{3} = -\frac{1}{3}$$

$$a_{21} = \frac{2(2)-1}{3} = 1,\; a_{22} = \frac{2(2)-2}{3} = \frac{2}{3},$$

$$a_{23} = \frac{2(2)-3}{3} = \frac{1}{3}$$

On putting all values in Eq. (i), we get

$$A = \begin{bmatrix} \frac{1}{3} & 0 & -\frac{1}{3} \\ 1 & \frac{2}{3} & \frac{1}{3} \end{bmatrix}$$

which is the required 2×3 order matrix.

5. (i) Given, $(\cos x)^y = (\cos y)^x$

On taking log both sides, we get

$$\log(\cos x)^y = \log(\cos y)^x$$

$$\Rightarrow \quad y\log(\cos x) = x\log(\cos y) \quad [\because \log x^n = n\log x]$$

On differentiating both sides w.r.t. x, we get

$$y\cdot\frac{d}{dx}\log(\cos x) + \log\cos x\cdot\frac{d}{dx}(y)$$

$$= x\frac{d}{dx}\log(\cos y) + \log(\cos y)\frac{d}{dx}(x)$$

$$\left[\because \frac{d}{dx}(uv) = u\frac{dv}{dx} + v\frac{du}{dx}\right]$$

$$\Rightarrow \quad y\cdot\frac{1}{\cos x}\frac{d}{dx}(\cos x) + \log(\cos x)\frac{dy}{dx}$$

$$= x\cdot\frac{1}{\cos y}\frac{d}{dx}(\cos y) + \log\cos y$$

$$\Rightarrow \quad y\cdot\frac{1}{\cos x}(-\sin x) + \log(\cos x)\cdot\frac{dy}{dx}$$

$$= x\frac{1}{\cos y}(-\sin y)\cdot\frac{dy}{dx} + \log(\cos y)$$

$$\Rightarrow \quad -y\tan x + \log(\cos x)\frac{dy}{dx} = -x\tan y\frac{dy}{dx} + \log(\cos y)$$

$$\Rightarrow [x\tan y + \log(\cos x)]\frac{dy}{dx} = \log(\cos y) + y\tan x$$

$$\Rightarrow \quad \frac{dy}{dx} = \frac{\log(\cos y) + y\tan x}{x\tan y + \log(\cos x)}$$

Or

(ii) Let $y = x^x$

On taking log both sides, we get $\log y = x\log x$

On differentiating both sides w.r.t. x, we get

$$\frac{1}{y}\frac{dy}{dx} = x\frac{d}{dx}(\log x) + \log x\frac{d}{dx}(x)$$

[using product rule of derivative]

$$\therefore \quad \frac{dy}{dx} = y\left[x\times\frac{1}{x} + \log x\times(1)\right]$$

$$= x^x[1+\log x]$$

6. Given, $A = \begin{bmatrix} 1 & 2 & 2 \\ 2 & 1 & 2 \\ 2 & 2 & 1 \end{bmatrix}$ and $A^2 - 4A + 5I = O \qquad \ldots(i)$

Pre-multiplying on both sides by A^{-1} in Eq. (i), we get

$$A^{-1}\cdot A\cdot A - 4A^{-1}\cdot A + 5A^{-1}\cdot I = A^{-1}\cdot O$$

$\Rightarrow \quad I\cdot A - 4\cdot I + 5A^{-1} = O \qquad [\because A^{-1}A = I]$

$\Rightarrow \quad A - 4I + 5A^{-1} = O$

$\Rightarrow \quad 5A^{-1} = 4I - A$

$$\Rightarrow \quad 5A^{-1} = 4\begin{bmatrix}1 & 0 & 0\\ 0 & 1 & 0\\ 0 & 0 & 1\end{bmatrix} - \begin{bmatrix}1 & 2 & 2\\ 2 & 1 & 2\\ 2 & 2 & 1\end{bmatrix}$$

$$\Rightarrow \quad 5A^{-1} = \begin{bmatrix}4-1 & 0-2 & 0-2\\ 0-2 & 4-1 & 0-2\\ 0-2 & 0-2 & 4-1\end{bmatrix}$$

$$= \begin{bmatrix}3 & -2 & -2\\ -2 & 3 & -2\\ -2 & -2 & 3\end{bmatrix}$$

$$\therefore \quad A^{-1} = \begin{bmatrix}3/5 & -2/5 & -2/5\\ -2/5 & 3/5 & -2/5\\ -2/5 & -2/5 & 3/5\end{bmatrix}$$

7. Given, differential equation is $y\,dx - (x + 2y^2)\,dy = 0$

$\Rightarrow \quad y\,dx = (x + 2y^2)\,dy$

$\Rightarrow \quad \dfrac{dx}{dy} = \dfrac{x + 2y^2}{y}$

$\Rightarrow \quad \dfrac{dx}{dy} - \dfrac{x}{y} = 2y$

On comparing above equation with linear differential equation $\dfrac{dx}{dy} + Px = Q$, we get

$P = \dfrac{-1}{y}$ and $Q = 2y$

$\therefore \quad \text{IF} = e^{\int P dy} = e^{-\int \frac{1}{y} dy} = e^{-\log|y|} = e^{\log\frac{1}{|y|}} = \dfrac{1}{y}$

The solution is $x \times \text{IF} = \int (Q \times \text{IF})\,dy + C$

$\Rightarrow \quad \dfrac{x}{y} = \int \dfrac{2y}{y} dy + C = 2\int dy + C$

$\Rightarrow \quad \dfrac{x}{y} = 2y + C$

$\Rightarrow \quad x = 2y^2 + yC$

Common Mistake

In solving the linear differential equation of the form $\dfrac{dx}{dy} + Px = Q$ ensure that P and Q are constants or function of y only.

8. $\text{LHS} = \begin{vmatrix} b+c & c+a & a+b\\ q+r & r+p & p+q\\ y+z & z+x & x+y\end{vmatrix}$

On applying $C_3 \to C_3 - C_1 - C_2$, we get

$$\text{LHS} = \begin{vmatrix} b+c & c+a & -2c\\ q+r & r+p & -2r\\ y+z & z+x & -2z\end{vmatrix} = -2\begin{vmatrix} b+c & c+a & c\\ q+r & r+p & r\\ y+z & z+x & z\end{vmatrix}$$

[take common (-2) from C_3]

On applying $C_1 \to C_1 - C_3$ and $C_2 \to C_2 - C_3$, we get

$$\text{LHS} = -2\begin{vmatrix} b & a & c\\ q & p & r\\ y & x & z\end{vmatrix}$$

On applying $C_1 \leftrightarrow C_2$, we get

$$\text{LHS} = 2\begin{vmatrix} a & b & c\\ p & q & r\\ x & y & z\end{vmatrix} = \text{RHS}$$ **Hence proved.**

9. (i) Given, $f(x) = |x+1| + |x-1|, \forall x \in R$

It can be rewritten as

$$f(x) = \begin{cases} -(x+1) - (x-1), & x < -1\\ (x+1) - (x-1), & -1 \le x < 1\\ (x+1) + (x-1), & x \ge 1\end{cases}$$

$$= \begin{cases} -2x, & x < -1\\ 2, & -1 \le x < 1\\ 2x, & x \ge 1\end{cases}$$

Differentiability at $x = -1$

$Lf'(-1) = \lim\limits_{h\to 0} \dfrac{f(-1-h) - f(-1)}{-h}$

$= \lim\limits_{h\to 0} \dfrac{-2(-1-h) - 2}{-h}$

$= \lim\limits_{h\to 0} \dfrac{2 + 2h - 2}{-h} = \lim\limits_{h\to 0}(-2) = -2$

$Rf'(-1) = \lim\limits_{h\to 0} \dfrac{f(-1+h) - f(-1)}{h}$

$= \lim\limits_{h\to 0} \dfrac{2-2}{h} = \lim\limits_{h\to 0} \dfrac{0}{h} = 0$

$\because \quad Lf'(-1) \ne Rf'(-1)$

$\therefore \quad f$ is not differentiable at $x = -1$.

Differentiability at $x = 1$

$Lf'(1) = \lim\limits_{h\to 0} \dfrac{f(1-h) - f(1)}{-h}$

$= \lim\limits_{h\to 0} \dfrac{2-2}{-h} = \lim\limits_{h\to 0} \dfrac{0}{-h} = 0$

and $Rf'(1) = \lim\limits_{h\to 0} \dfrac{f(1+h) - f(1)}{h} = \lim\limits_{h\to 0} \dfrac{2(1+h) - 2}{h}$

$= \lim\limits_{h\to 0} \dfrac{2 + 2h - 2}{h} = \lim\limits_{h\to 0} \dfrac{2h}{h} = 2$

$\because \quad Lf'(1) \ne Rf'(1)$

$\therefore$ f is not differentiable at $x = 1$.

Hence, f is not differentiable at $x = 1$ and -1.

Or

(ii) Given, function is

$$f(x) = \begin{cases} \lambda(x^2 + 2), & \text{if } x \le 0\\ 4x + 6, & \text{if } x > 0\end{cases}.$$

Let $f(x)$ be continuous at $x = 0$.

Then, LHL = RHL = $f(0)$ ...(i)

Here, RHL = $\lim_{x\to 0^+} f(x) = \lim_{x\to 0^+} (4x+6)$

$= \lim_{h\to 0} [4(0+h)+6]$

[put $x = 0+h$; when $x \to 0^+$, then $h \to 0$]

$= \lim_{h\to 0} (4h+6) = 4\times 0 + 6 = 6$

and $f(0) = \lambda(0^2+2) = 2\lambda$

From Eq. (i), RHL = $f(0)$

$\Rightarrow 2\lambda = 6 \Rightarrow \lambda = 3$

Then, given function becomes

$$f(x) = \begin{cases} 3(x^2+2), & \text{if } x \le 0 \\ 4x+6, & \text{if } x > 0 \end{cases}$$

Now, let us check the differentiability at $x = 0$.

$$\text{LHD} = \lim_{h\to 0} \frac{f(0-h)-f(0)}{-h}$$

$$= \lim_{h\to 0} \frac{3[(0-h)^2+2]-3(0+2)}{-h}$$

$$= \lim_{h\to 0} \frac{3[h^2+2]-6}{-h} = \lim_{h\to 0}(-3h) = 0$$

and $$\text{RHD} = \lim_{h\to 0} \frac{f(0+h)-f(0)}{h}$$

$$= \lim_{h\to 0} \frac{[4(0+h)+6]-3(0+2)}{h} = \lim_{h\to 0} \frac{4h}{h} = 4$$

$\because$ LHD $\ne$ RHD

$\therefore f(x)$ is not differentiable at $x = 0$.

10. (i) (a) Given, radius of sphere, $OA = R$

height of cone, $VC = h = R + x$

radius of cone, AC (Or BC) $= r$

and $OC = x$

In ΔOCA, we have

$OC^2 + AC^2 = OA^2$

$\Rightarrow x^2 + r^2 = R^2$

$\Rightarrow r = \sqrt{R^2 - x^2}$

(b) Volume of cone, $V = \frac{1}{3}\pi r^2 h$

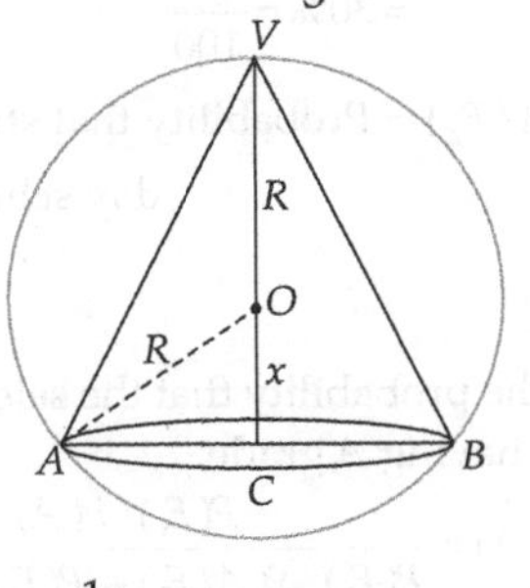

$= \frac{1}{3}\pi(R^2 - x^2)(R+x)$ [$\because h = R + x$]

$= \frac{1}{3}\pi(R+x)^2(R-x)$

(c) We have, $V = \frac{1}{3}\pi(R+x)^2(R-x)$

On differentiating w.r.t. x, we get

$$\frac{dV}{dx} = \frac{1}{3}\pi[2(R+x)(R-x) - (R+x)^2]$$

$$= \frac{1}{3}\pi[(R+x)(2R-2x-R-x)]$$

$$= \frac{1}{3}\pi[(R+x)(R-3x)]$$

Again on differentiating w.r.t. x, we get

$$\frac{d^2V}{dx^2} = \frac{1}{3}\pi[R-3x-3(R+x)]$$

$$= \frac{1}{3}\pi[R-3x-3R-3x]$$

$$= \frac{1}{3}\pi[-2R-6x]$$

For maximum value put $\frac{dV}{dx} = 0$

$\Rightarrow \frac{1}{3}\pi(R+x)(R-3x) = 0$

$\Rightarrow x = \frac{R}{3}$ [$\because R + x \ne 0$]

At $x = \frac{R}{3}$, $\left.\frac{d^2V}{dx^2}\right|_{x=\frac{R}{3}} < 0$

So, V is maximum at $x = \frac{R}{3}$

Hence, the maximum volume

$$= \frac{1}{3}\pi\left[R + \frac{R}{3}\right]^2\left[R - \frac{R}{3}\right]$$

$$= \frac{32\pi}{81}R^3$$

(d) When volume is maximum,

$$r = \sqrt{R^2 - x^2} = \sqrt{R^2 - \frac{R^2}{9}} = \frac{2\sqrt{2}}{3}R$$

and $h = R + x = R + \frac{R}{3} = \frac{4R}{3}$

Or

(ii) (a) We have, $f(x) = (x-1)^{1/3}(x-2)$ ...(i)

On differentiating both sides w.r.t. x, we get

$$f'(x) = (x-1)^{1/3}\cdot 1 + (x-2)\cdot\frac{1}{3}(x-1)^{-2/3}$$

[by product rule of derivative]

$$= (x-1)^{-2/3}\left[x - 1 + \frac{1}{3}(x-2)\right]$$

$$= (x-1)^{-2/3}\left[\frac{3x-3+x-2}{3}\right]$$

$$= (x-1)^{-2/3}\left(\frac{4x-5}{3}\right)$$

(b) We have, $f'(x) = (x-1)^{-2/3}\left(\frac{4x-5}{3}\right)$

Put $f'(x) = 0$

$\Rightarrow \frac{1}{3}(x-1)^{-2/3}(4x-5)=0$

$\Rightarrow \quad x=\frac{5}{4}, x=1$

Which are the required critical points.

(c) Now, on putting $x=1, \frac{5}{4}$ and 9 in Eq. (i)

respectively, we get

$f(1)=(1-1)^{1/3}(1-2)=0$

$$f\left(\frac{5}{4}\right)=\left(\frac{5}{4}-1\right)^{1/3}\left(\frac{5}{4}-2\right)$$

$$=\left(\frac{1}{4}\right)^{1/3}\left(\frac{-3}{4}\right)=\frac{-3}{4\cdot\sqrt[3]{4}}$$

and $f(9)=(9-1)^{1/3}(9-2)$

$=(8)^{1/3}\cdot 7=2\times 7=14$

Hence, $f(x)$ have absolute maximum at $x=9$ and absolute minimum at $x=\frac{5}{4}\cdot$

11. (i) Let $I=\int_0^a \frac{f(x)}{f(x)+f(a-x)}\,dx$ ...(i)

$$\Rightarrow \quad I=\int_0^a \frac{f(a-x)}{f(a-x)+f(a-(a-x))}\,dx$$

$\Rightarrow \quad I=\int_0^a \frac{f(a-x)}{f(a-x)+f(x)}\,dx$ ...(ii)

On adding Eqs. (i) and (ii), we get

$$2I=\int_0^a 1\,dx=[x]_0^a=a$$

$$\Rightarrow \quad I=\frac{1}{2}a$$

(ii) We have, $f(x)=\frac{\sin x-\cos x}{1+\sin x\cos x}$

$$\Rightarrow f\left(\frac{\pi}{2}-x\right)=\frac{\sin\left(\frac{\pi}{2}-x\right)-\cos\left(\frac{\pi}{2}-x\right)}{1+\sin\left(\frac{\pi}{2}-x\right)\cos\left(\frac{\pi}{2}-x\right)}$$

$$=\frac{\cos x-\sin x}{1+\cos x\sin x}=-\left[\frac{\sin x-\cos x}{1+\sin x\cos x}\right]$$

$$=-f(x)$$

(iii) From part (ii), we have

$$f\left(\frac{\pi}{2}-x\right)=-f(x)$$

$$f\left(\frac{\pi}{2}-x\right)+f(x)=0,$$

let $I=\int_0^{\pi/2} f(x)\,dx$ ...(i)

$\Rightarrow \quad I=\int_0^{\pi/2} f(\pi/2-x)\,dx$ ...(ii)

On adding Eqs. (i) and (ii), we get

$$2I=\int_0^{\pi/2}(f(\pi/2-x)+f(x))\,dx=\int_0^{\pi/2}0\,dx=0$$

$$\Rightarrow \quad I=0$$

12. (i) Given, mean $E(X)=3$ and probability distribution is

X	1	2	3	4	5
P(X)	0.2	a	a	0.2	b

Now, expected value,

$$E(X)=\Sigma x_i p_i=1\times 0.2+2\times a+3\times a+4\times 0.2+5\times b$$
$$=0.2+2a+3a+0.8+5b$$

$\Rightarrow \quad 3=5a+5b+1$

$\Rightarrow \quad 5a+5b=2$ ...(i)

We know that $\Sigma p_i=1$

$\Rightarrow \; 0.2+a+a+0.2+b=1 \Rightarrow 2a+b=0.6$ ...(ii)

On multiplying by 5 in Eq. (ii) and then subtracting from Eq. (i), we get

$$5a-10a=2-3$$

$$\Rightarrow -5a=-1 \Rightarrow a=\frac{1}{5}=0.2$$

On putting the value of a in Eq. (ii) we get

$2(0.2)+b=0.6 \Rightarrow b=0.6-0.4=0.2$

Now, $P(X\geq 3)=P(X=3)+P(X=4)+P(X=5)$

$=0.2+0.2+0.2=0.6$

Or

(ii) Let us define the events as

E_1 : Students reside in a hostel

E_2 : Students are day scholars

A : Students get A grade

Then,

$P(E_1)=$ Probability that student reside in a hostel

$=60\%=\frac{60}{100}$ (1)

and $P(E_2)=$ Probability that students are day scholars.

$=40\%=\frac{40}{100}$ (1)

Also, $P(A/E_1)=$ Probability that hostelers get A grade

$=30\%=\frac{30}{100}$

and $P(A/E_2)=$ Probability that students who are day scholars get A grade

$=20\%=\frac{20}{100}$ (1)

Hence, the probability that the selecting student is a hosteler having A grade,

$$P(E_1/A)=\frac{P(E_1)\cdot P(A/E_1)}{P(E_1)\cdot P(A/E_1)+P(E_2)\cdot P(A/E_2)}$$

[by Baye's theorem]

$$=\frac{\frac{60}{100}\times\frac{30}{100}}{\left(\frac{60}{100}\times\frac{30}{100}\right)+\left(\frac{40}{100}\times\frac{20}{100}\right)}$$

$$=\frac{1800}{1800+800}=\frac{1800}{2600}=\frac{18}{26}=\frac{9}{13}$$

13. (i) Given,

$$f(x)=\frac{4\sin x-2x-x\cos x}{2+\cos x}, 0\le x\le 2\pi$$

On differentiating w.r.t. x, we get

$$f'(x)=\frac{(2+\cos x)(4\cos x-2+x\sin x-\cos x)-(4\sin x-2x-x\cos x)(-\sin x)}{(2+\cos x)^2}$$

$$=\frac{(2+\cos x)(3\cos x-2+x\sin x)+(4\sin x-2x-x\cos x)\sin x}{(2+\cos x)^2}$$

$$=\frac{6\cos x-4+2x\sin x+3\cos^2 x-2\cos x+x\sin x\cos x+4\sin^2 x-2x\sin x-x\sin x\cos x}{(2+\cos x)^2}$$

$$=\frac{4\cos x-4+3\cos^2 x+4\sin^2 x}{(2+\cos x)^2}$$

$$=\frac{4\cos x-4(1-\sin^2 x)+3\cos^2 x}{(2+\cos x)^2}$$

$$=\frac{4\cos x-4\cos^2 x+3\cos^2 x}{(2+\cos x)^2} \quad [\because \sin^2\theta+\cos^2\theta=1]$$

$$=\frac{(4-\cos x)\cos x}{(2+\cos x)^2}$$

We know that $-1\le\cos x\le 1$, for all $x\in[0, 2\pi]$

$\Rightarrow$ $1\ge -\cos x\ge -1$ for all $x\in[0,2\pi]$

$\Rightarrow$ $5\ge 4-\cos x\ge 3$ for all $x\in[0,2\pi]$

$\Rightarrow$ $4-\cos x>0$ for all $x\in[0,2\pi]$

Also, $(2+\cos x)^2>0$ for all $x\in[0,2\pi]$

$\therefore$ $\frac{4-\cos x}{(2+\cos x)^2}>0$ for all $x\in[0,2\pi]$

(a) As we know that f is strictly increasing iff

$$f'(x)>0\Rightarrow\frac{\cos x(4-\cos x)}{(2+\cos x)^2}>0$$

$\Rightarrow$ $\cos x>0$ $\left[\because\frac{4-\cos x}{(2+\cos x)^2}>0\right]$

$\Rightarrow$ $x\in\left[0,\frac{\pi}{2}\right)\cup\left(\frac{3\pi}{2},2\pi\right]$

Hence, f is strictly increasing in $\left[0,\frac{\pi}{2}\right)\cup\left(\frac{3\pi}{2},2\pi\right]$.

(b) f is strictly decreasing iff $f'(x)<0$

$\Rightarrow$ $\frac{\cos x(4-\cos x)}{(2+\cos x)^2}<0$

$\Rightarrow$ $\cos x<0$ $\left[\because\frac{4-\cos x}{(2+\cos x)^2}>0\right]$

$\Rightarrow$ $x\in\left(\frac{\pi}{2},\frac{3\pi}{2}\right)$

Hence, f is strictly decreasing in $\left(\frac{\pi}{2},\frac{3\pi}{2}\right)$.

Or

(ii) Let $I=\int\frac{2\cos x}{(1-\sin x)(2-\cos^2 x)}dx$

$$=\int\frac{2\cos x}{(1-\sin x)(1+\sin^2 x)}dx$$

$[\because \sin^2\theta+\cos^2\theta=1\Rightarrow\cos^2\theta=1-\sin^2\theta]$

Put $\sin x=t\Rightarrow\cos x\,dx=dt$

$\therefore$ $I=\int\frac{2}{(1-t)(1+t^2)}dt$

Now, let $\frac{2}{(1-t)(1+t^2)}=\frac{A}{1-t}+\frac{Bt+C}{1+t^2}$

$\Rightarrow$ $2=A(1+t^2)+(Bt+C)(1-t)$ ...(i)

On putting $t=1$ in Eq. (i), we get

$2=2A\Rightarrow A=1$

On putting $t=0$ in Eq. (i), we get

$2=A+C\Rightarrow 2=1+C\Rightarrow C=1$

and putting $t=-1$ in Eq. (i), we get

$2=2A+(-B+C)(2)$

$\Rightarrow$ $2=2-2B+2\Rightarrow 2B=2\Rightarrow B=1$

Then, $\frac{2}{(1-t)(1+t^2)}=\frac{1}{1-t}+\frac{t+1}{1+t^2}$

$\therefore$ $I=1\int\frac{1}{1-t}dt+\int\frac{t+1}{1+t^2}dt$

$$=\int\frac{1}{1-t}dt+\frac{1}{2}\int\frac{2t}{1+t^2}dt+\int\frac{1}{1+t^2}dt$$

$$=-\log|1-t|+\frac{1}{2}\log|1+t^2|+\tan^{-1}t+C$$

$$=-\log|1-\sin x|+\frac{1}{2}\log|1+\sin^2 x|+\tan^{-1}(\sin x)+C \quad [\because t=\sin x]$$

$$=\tan^{-1}(\sin x)+\log\left|\frac{\sqrt{1+\sin^2 x}}{1-\sin x}\right|+C$$

$\left[\because \log m-\log n=\log\left(\frac{m}{n}\right)\text{ and } n\log m=\log m^n\right]$ (1)

14. (i) $\tan^{-1}2+\tan^{-1}3=\pi+\tan^{-1}\left(\frac{2+3}{1-2\times 3}\right)$

$[\because xy=2\times 3>1]$

$$=\pi+\tan^{-1}\left(\frac{5}{-5}\right)=\pi+\tan^{-1}(-1)$$

$$= \pi - \tan^{-1} 1$$

$$[\because \tan^{-1}(-\theta) = -\tan^{-1}\theta]$$

$$= \pi - \frac{\pi}{4} = \frac{3\pi}{4}$$

(ii) $\tan^{-1}\frac{1}{7} + \tan^{-1}\frac{1}{13} = \tan^{-1}\left(\frac{\frac{1}{7}+\frac{1}{13}}{1-\frac{1}{7}\times\frac{1}{13}}\right)$

$$\left[\because xy = \frac{1}{7}\times\frac{1}{13} < 1\right]$$

$$= \tan^{-1}\left(\frac{13+7}{91-1}\right)$$

$$= \tan^{-1}\frac{20}{90} = \tan^{-1}\frac{2}{9}$$

(iii) $\tan^{-1}\frac{2}{11} + \tan^{-1}\frac{7}{24} = \tan^{-1}\left(\frac{\frac{2}{11}+\frac{7}{24}}{1-\frac{2}{11}\times\frac{7}{24}}\right)$

$$\left[\because xy = \frac{2}{11}\times\frac{7}{24} < 1\right]$$

$$= \tan^{-1}\left(\frac{48+77}{264-14}\right)$$

$$= \tan^{-1}\frac{125}{250} = \tan^{-1}\frac{1}{2}$$

(iv) $\tan^{-1}\frac{x}{2} + \tan^{-1}\frac{x}{3} = \frac{\pi}{4}$

$\Rightarrow \tan^{-1}\left(\frac{\frac{x}{2}+\frac{x}{3}}{1-\frac{x}{2}\times\frac{x}{3}}\right) = \frac{\pi}{4}$ $\left[\because xy = \frac{x}{2}\times\frac{x}{3} = \frac{x^2}{6} < 1\right]$

$\Rightarrow \frac{5x}{6-x^2} = \tan\frac{\pi}{4} = 1$

$\Rightarrow 5x = 6 - x^2 \Rightarrow x^2 + 5x - 6 = 0$

$\Rightarrow (x-1)(x+6) = 0$

$\therefore x = 1, -6$

15. (i) (a) The equation of plane that cut the coordinate axes at (8, 0, 0), (0, 5, 0) and (0, 0, 3) is given by

$$\frac{x}{8} + \frac{y}{5} + \frac{z}{3} = 1$$

(ii) (d) We have, $\vec{a} = x\hat{i} + 2\hat{j} - z\hat{k}$ and $\vec{b} = 3\hat{i} - y\hat{j} + \hat{k}$ as equal vectors.

$\therefore x\hat{i} + 2\hat{j} - z\hat{k} = 3\hat{i} - y\hat{j} + \hat{k}$

On comparing the corresponding elements, we get

$$x = 3, y = -2 \text{ and } z = -1$$

Henc, $x + y + z = 3 - 2 - 1 = 0.$

(iii) (b) Given equation of line is

$$\frac{4-x}{2} = \frac{y}{6} = \frac{1-z}{3}$$

It can be rewritten in standard form as

$$\frac{x-4}{-2} = \frac{y}{6} = \frac{z-1}{-3}$$

Here, direction ratios of line are $-2, 6, -3$.

Hence, only Statement II is true.

Common Mistake

While finding the direction ratios of the line don't forget to convert the equation of line into standard form.

(iv) Given, $\vec{a} = \hat{i} + 2\hat{j} - 3\hat{k}$ and $\vec{b} = 3\hat{i} - \hat{j} + 2\hat{k}$

Now, $\vec{a}\times\vec{b} = \begin{vmatrix} \hat{i} & \hat{j} & \hat{k} \\ 1 & 2 & -3 \\ 3 & -1 & 2 \end{vmatrix}$

$$= \hat{i}(4-3) - \hat{j}(2+9) + \hat{k}(-1-6)$$

$$= \hat{i} - 11\hat{j} - 7\hat{k}$$

$\therefore |\vec{a}\times\vec{b}| = \sqrt{1^2 + (-11)^2 + (-7)^2}$

$$= \sqrt{1 + 121 + 49} = \sqrt{171}$$

Hence, Vectors of magnitude $\sqrt{171}$ that are perpendicular to both the vectors $\vec{a}$ and $\vec{b}$

$$= \sqrt{171}\left(\pm\frac{\vec{a}\times\vec{b}}{|\vec{a}\times\vec{b}|}\right)$$

$$= \sqrt{171}\left(\pm\frac{\hat{i} - 11\hat{j} - 7\hat{k}}{\sqrt{171}}\right)$$

$$= \pm(\hat{i} - 11\hat{j} - 7\hat{k})$$

(v) Let $<l, m, n>$ be the direction cosines of the perpendicular drawn from origin to the plane.

Given that the normal to the plane is equally inclined to the coordinate axes i.e. $l = m = n$

But $l^2 + m^2 + n^2 = 1$

$\Rightarrow 3l^2 = 1$

$\Rightarrow l = \pm\frac{1}{\sqrt{3}}$

Also given the length of perpendicular drawn from origin to the plane, $p = 3\sqrt{3}$.

Hence, the equation of the required plane is

$$\pm\frac{1}{\sqrt{3}}(x + y + z) = 3\sqrt{3} \quad [\because lx + my + nz = p]$$

$\Rightarrow x + y + z = \pm 9$

$\Rightarrow x + y + z = 9$

or $x + y + z + 9 = 0$

16. (i) Given position vectors of A, B, C and D are $\overrightarrow{OA} = 2\hat{i} + 4\hat{k}$, $\overrightarrow{OB} = 5\hat{i} + 3\sqrt{3}\,\hat{j} + 4\hat{k}$, $\overrightarrow{OC} = -2\sqrt{3}\,\hat{j} + \hat{k}$ and $\overrightarrow{OD} = 2\hat{i} + \hat{k}$

we have,

$\overrightarrow{AB}$ = Position vector of B − Position vector of A

$$= (5\hat{i} + 3\sqrt{3}\hat{j} + 4\hat{k}) - (2\hat{i} + 4\hat{k})$$
$$= 3\hat{i} + 3\sqrt{3}\hat{j} + 0\hat{k}$$
$$= 3(\hat{i} + \sqrt{3}\hat{j} + 0\hat{k})$$

and $\overrightarrow{CD}$ = Position vector of D − Position vector of C

$$= (2\hat{i} + \hat{k}) - (-2\sqrt{3}\hat{j} + \hat{k})$$
$$= 2\hat{i} + 2\sqrt{3}\hat{j} + 0\hat{k} = 2(\hat{i} + \sqrt{3}\hat{j} + 0\hat{k})$$
$$= \frac{2}{3}(3\hat{i} + 3\sqrt{3}\hat{j} + 0\hat{k}) = \frac{2}{3}\overrightarrow{AB}$$

Hence, $\overrightarrow{CD}$ is parallel to $\overrightarrow{AB}$ and $\overrightarrow{CD} = \frac{2}{3}\overrightarrow{AB}$.

Or

(ii) We have, $\vec{a} = 7\hat{i} + \hat{j} - 4\hat{k}$ and $\vec{b} = 2\hat{i} + 6\hat{j} + 3\hat{k}$

Then, $\vec{a}\cdot\vec{b} = (7\hat{i} + \hat{j} - 4\hat{k})\cdot(2\hat{i} + 6\hat{j} + 3\hat{k})$

$$= 7(2) + 1(6) - 4(3)$$
$$= 14 + 6 - 12 = 8$$

and $|\vec{b}| = \sqrt{2^2 + 6^2 + 3^2}$

$$= \sqrt{4 + 36 + 9} = \sqrt{49} = 7$$

Now, projection of $\vec{a}$ on $\vec{b} = \frac{\vec{a}\cdot\vec{b}}{|\vec{b}|} = \frac{8}{7}$

17. (i) Let the equation of the plane is

$$ax + by + cz + d = 0 \quad \ldots\text{(i)}$$

Since, plane passes through the points (0, 4, −3) and (6, −4, 3).

$\therefore$ $0 + 4b - 3c + d = 0$ ...(ii)

and $6a - 4b + 3c + d = 0$ ...(iii)

On adding Eqs. (ii) and (iii), we get

$$6a + 2d = 0$$

$\Rightarrow$ $a = \frac{-2d}{6} \Rightarrow a = \frac{-d}{3}$

On putting $a = \frac{-d}{3}$ in Eq. (iii), we get

$$6\times\left(\frac{-d}{3}\right) - 4b + 3c + d = 0$$

$\Rightarrow$ $-2d - 4b + 3c + d = 0$

$\Rightarrow$ $-4b + 3c - d = 0$

$\Rightarrow$ $4b - 3c = -d$

$\therefore$ $b = \frac{3c - d}{4}$

Considering equation $ax + by + cz + d = 0$ can be rewritten as $\frac{x}{-\frac{d}{a}} + \frac{y}{\frac{-d}{b}} + \frac{z}{\frac{-d}{c}} = 1$

According to the given condition, sum of their intercepts on the three axes is zero.

$$-\frac{d}{a} - \frac{d}{b} - \frac{d}{c} = 0$$

$\Rightarrow$ $-d\left[-\frac{3}{d} + \frac{4}{3c - d} + \frac{1}{c}\right] = 0$

$\Rightarrow$ $-d\left[\frac{-3c(3c - d) + 4cd + d(3c - d)}{d(3c - d)c}\right] = 0$

$\Rightarrow$ $-9c^2 + 3cd + 4cd + 3cd - d^2 = 0$

$\Rightarrow$ $9c^2 - 10cd + d^2 = 0$

$\Rightarrow$ $9c^2 - 9cd - cd + d^2 = 0$

$\Rightarrow$ $9c(c - d) - d(c - d) = 0$

$\Rightarrow$ $(9c - d)(c - d) = 0$

$\Rightarrow$ $c = \frac{d}{9}, d$

When $c = \frac{d}{9}$, then $b = \frac{3\times\frac{d}{9} - d}{4} = \left(\frac{d}{3} - d\right)\times\frac{1}{4}$

$$= \frac{d - 3d}{12} = \frac{-2d}{12} = \frac{-d}{6}$$

and when $c = d$, then $b = \frac{3\times d - d}{4} = \frac{2d}{4} = \frac{d}{2}$

On putting $a = \frac{-d}{3}, b = -\frac{d}{6}$ and $c = \frac{d}{9}$ in Eq. (i), we get

$$\frac{-d}{3}\times x + \left(\frac{-d}{6}\right)y + \frac{d}{9}z + d = 0$$

$\Rightarrow$ $\frac{-d(6x + 3y - 2z - 18)}{18} = 0$

i.e. $6x + 3y - 2z - 18 = 0$

and putting $a = \frac{-d}{3}, b = \frac{d}{2}$ and $c = d$ in Eq. (i), we get

$$\frac{-d}{3}\times x + \left(\frac{d}{2}\right)y + d\cdot z + d = 0$$

$\Rightarrow$ $\frac{-d(2x - 3y - 6z - 6)}{6} = 0$

$\Rightarrow$ $2x - 3y - 6z - 6 = 0$

Hence, the required equation of planes are $6x + 3y - 2z - 18 = 0$ and $2x - 3y - 6z - 6 = 0$.

(ii) The given line is $\frac{x - 0}{1} = \frac{y - 1}{2} = \frac{z - 2}{3} = t$ [say]...(i)

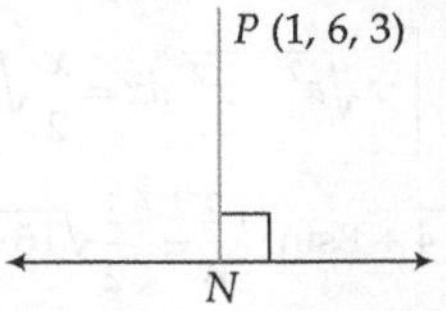

Let N be the foot of perpendicular drawn from the point $P(1, 6, 3)$ to the line (i). Any point on line (i) is in the form $(t, 1 + 2t, 2 + 3t)$.

Let the coordinates of N be $(t, 1 + 2t, 2 + 3t)$ for some t.

Then, direction ratios of the line NP are
$$<t-1, 1+2t-6, 2+3t-3>$$
i.e. $<t-1, 2t-5, 3t-1>$
and direction ratios of line (i) are $<1, 2, 3>$.
$\because$ NP is perpendicular to line of Eq. (i)
$$\therefore \quad 1\cdot(t-1)+2\cdot(2t-5)+3\cdot(3t-1)=0$$
$$[\because a_1a_2+b_1b_2+c_1c_2=0]$$
$$\Rightarrow \quad 14t-14=0 \Rightarrow t=1$$
On substituting $t=1$, the coordinates of the point N are $<1, 1+2\cdot(1), 2+3\cdot(1)>$, i.e. $<1, 3, 5>$
direction ratios of the line NP are
$$<1-1, 2-5, 3-1> \text{ i.e. } <0, -3, 2>$$
Hence, the equation of the line NP is
$$\frac{x-1}{0}=\frac{y-6}{-3}=\frac{z-3}{2}$$
and length of perpendicular from P to line (i)
$$=|NP|=\sqrt{(1-1)^2+(6-3)^2+(3-5)^2}$$
$$=\sqrt{0+9+4}=\sqrt{13} \text{ units}$$

18. The area of the region bounded by the curve $x^2+y^2=16$ and lines $y=1$ and $y=2$ in quadrant I is given by
$$A=\int_1^2 x\,dy$$
$$=\int_1^2 \sqrt{4^2-y^2}\,dy$$
[here, we take a horizontal strip]

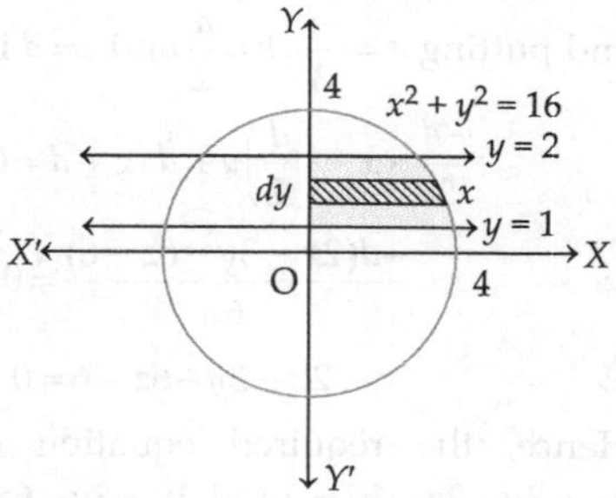

$$=\left[\frac{y}{2}\sqrt{16-y^2}+\frac{4^2}{2}\sin^{-1}\frac{y}{4}\right]_1^2$$
$$\left[\because \int\sqrt{a^2-x^2}\,dx=\frac{x}{2}\sqrt{a^2-x^2}+\frac{a^2}{2}\sin^{-1}\frac{x}{a}\right]$$
$$=\left[\frac{2}{2}\sqrt{16-4}+8\sin^{-1}\frac{2}{4}-\left(\frac{1}{2}\sqrt{16-1}+8\sin^{-1}\frac{1}{4}\right)\right]$$
$$=\left[2\sqrt{3}+8\times\frac{\pi}{6}-\left(\frac{1}{2}\sqrt{15}+8\sin^{-1}\frac{1}{4}\right)\right]$$
$$=\left[2\sqrt{3}+\frac{4\pi}{3}-\left(\frac{\sqrt{15}}{2}+8\sin^{-1}\frac{1}{4}\right)\right] \text{ sq units}$$

19. (i) (b) Given, $C(x)=9x^3-4x^2+6x-100$
$$\text{Average cost}=\frac{\text{Total cost}}{\text{Output}}=\frac{C(x)}{x}$$
$$=\frac{9x^3-4x^2+6x-100}{x}$$
$$=9x^2-4x+6-\frac{100}{x}$$

(ii) (c) We have, $\bar{x}=5, \bar{y}=7$ and $b_{yx}=\dfrac{-11}{34}$
$\therefore$ Regression equation of y on x is
$$y-\bar{y}=b_{yx}(x-\bar{x})$$
$$\Rightarrow \quad y-7=\frac{-11}{34}(x-5) \Rightarrow 11x+34y-293=0$$

(iii) Given,
Total cost, $C(x)=0.005x^3-0.7x^2-30x+3000$
Now,
$$\text{Marginal cost of function (MC)}=\frac{dC}{dx}$$
$$=\frac{d}{dx}(0.005x^3-0.7x^2-30x+3000)$$
$$\therefore MC=0.015x^2-1.4x^2-30 \quad \left[\because \frac{d}{dx}x^n=nx^{(n-1)}\right]$$

(iv) The regression equation of y on x is
$$40x-18y=5 \Rightarrow y=\frac{20}{9}x-\frac{5}{18} \quad \ldots\text{(i)}$$
$\therefore$ The regression coefficient of y on x is
$$b_{yx}=\text{Slope of the line of Eq. (i)}=\frac{20}{9}$$
The regression equation of x on y is
$$8x-10y+6=0 \Rightarrow x=\frac{5}{4}y-\frac{3}{4} \quad \ldots\text{(ii)}$$
$\therefore$ The regression coefficient of x on y is
$$b_{xy}=\text{Slope of the line of Eq. (ii)}=\frac{5}{4}$$
Now, $r^2=b_{yx}\cdot b_{xy}=\dfrac{20}{9}\times\dfrac{5}{4}=\dfrac{25}{9}>1$
But r^2 is always ≤ 1.
Hence, the given statement is false.

(v) Given, marginal cost, (MC) $=50+5x$
$\therefore$ Total cost function,
$$C(x)=\int(\text{MC})dx+k=\int(50+5x)dx+k$$
$$\Rightarrow \quad C(x)=50x+\frac{5x^2}{2}+k \quad \ldots\text{(i)}$$
Also, given when $x=0$, $C(x)=150$
$$\therefore \quad 150=50(0)+5(0)+k \quad \text{[using Eq. (i)]}$$
$$\Rightarrow \quad k=150$$
On putting $k=150$ in Eq. (i), we get
$$C(x)=50x+\frac{5}{2}x^2+150$$

When $x = 50$, then total cost

$$C(x) = 50(50) + \frac{5(50)^2}{2} + 150$$

$$= 2500 + 6250 + 150 = ₹8900$$

20. (i) Given, $P = 100 + 10x - x^2$

$\therefore$ Total revenue, $(R) = Px = (100 + 10x - x^2) \cdot x$

$$= 100x + 10x^2 - x^3$$

(a) Marginal revenue

$$(\text{MR}) = \frac{dR}{dx} = \frac{d}{dx}(100x + 10x^2 - x^3)$$

$$= 100 + 20x - 3x^2$$

(b) When $x = 5$, then

$$\text{MR} = 100 + 20 \times 5 - 3(5)^2 = 100 + 100 - 75 = 125$$

This means that when sales are increased from 5 to 6 units, additional revenue obtained is ₹ 125.

Or

(ii) (a) Let the linear demand function be

$$p = a + bx \quad \text{...(i)}$$

Given, $x = 24$ when $p = 16$

and $x = 12$ when $p = 22$

$\therefore$ Then, from Eq. (i), we get

$$a + 24b = 16 \text{ and } a + 12b = 22$$

On solving above equations, we get

$$a = 28 \text{ and } b = -1/2$$

Hence, the demand function is given by

$$p = 28 - \frac{1}{2}x$$

(b) Total revenue function, $R = px$

$$\Rightarrow R = \left(28 - \frac{1}{2}x\right)x \Rightarrow R = 28x - \frac{1}{2}x^2$$

Or

21. The lines of best fit are the regression lines.

Here, $\bar{x} = \frac{\Sigma x}{n} = \frac{56}{8} = 7$, $\bar{y} = \frac{\Sigma y}{n} = \frac{40}{8} = 5$

Make a table for regression coefficients

x	y	$d_x = x - \bar{x}$ $= x - 7$	$d_y = y - \bar{y}$ $= y - 5$	$d_x d_y$	d_x^2	d_y^2
1	1	−6	−4	24	36	16
3	2	−4	−3	12	16	9
4	4	−3	−1	3	9	1
6	4	−1	−1	1	1	1
8	5	1	0	0	1	0
9	7	2	2	4	4	4
11	8	4	3	12	16	9
14	9	7	4	28	49	16
Σx = 56	Σy = 40			$\Sigma d_x d_y$ = 84	Σd_x^2 = 132	Σd_y^2 = 56

$\therefore$ Regression coefficients,

$$b_{yx} = \frac{\Sigma d_x d_y}{\Sigma d_x^2} = \frac{84}{132} = \frac{7}{11} \text{ and } b_{xy} = \frac{\Sigma d_x d_y}{\Sigma d_y^2} = \frac{84}{56} = \frac{3}{2}$$

The regression equation of y on x (when x is independent variable) is

$$y - \bar{y} = b_{yx}(x - \bar{x}) \Rightarrow y - 5 = \frac{7}{11}(x - 7)$$

$$\Rightarrow 11y - 55 = 7x - 49 \Rightarrow 7x - 11y + 6 = 0$$

The regression equation of x on y (when x is dependent variable) is

$$x - \bar{x} = b_{xy}(y - \bar{y})$$

$$\Rightarrow \quad x - 7 = \frac{3}{2}(y - 5)$$

$$\Rightarrow \quad 2x - 14 = 3y - 15 \Rightarrow 2x - 3y + 1 = 0$$

22. (i) Let the number of type A machines be x and the number of type B machines be y.

Since, the profit is to be maximised.

$\therefore$ Maximise, $Z = 50x + 40y$

Subject to the constraints are

$1000x + 1200y \le 7600$ or $5x + 6y \le 38$ (area constraints)

$12x + 8y \le 72$ or $3x + 2y \le 18$ (men constraints)

$x \ge 0$ and $y \ge 0$ [non-negative constraints]

Table for the line $5x + 6y = 38$ is

x	0	38/5
y	19/3	0

So, the line passes through the points $\left(0, \frac{19}{3}\right)$ and $\left(\frac{38}{5}, 0\right)$.

On putting (0, 0) in the ineqality $5x + 6y \le 38$, we get

$$0 + 0 \le 38$$

$$\Rightarrow \quad 0 \le 38 \quad \text{[which is true]}$$

So, the half plane is towards the origin.

Table for the line $3x + 2y = 18$ is

x	0	6
y	9	0

So, the line passes through the points (0, 9) and (6, 0).

On putting (0, 0) in the inequality $3x + 2y \le 18$, we get

$$0 + 0 \le 18$$

$$\Rightarrow \quad 0 \le 18 \quad \text{[which is true]}$$

So, the half plane is towards the origin.

Also, $x \ge 0, y \ge 0$, so the feasible region lies in the first quadrant.

The point of intersection of lines $5x + 6y = 38$ and $3x + 2y = 13$ is $B(4,3)$.

Now, plot all the constraints on the graph paper as given below.

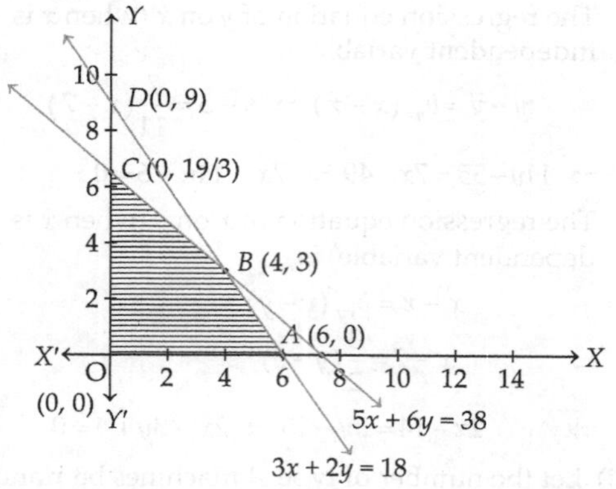

The shaded region $OABCO$ represents a bounded feasible region and its corner points are $O(0,0)$, $A(6,0)$, $B(4,3)$ and $C(0,19/3)$.

The values of Z at corner points are

Corner points	Value of $Z = 50x + 40y$
O (0,0)	$50 \times 0 + 40 \times 0 = 0$
$A(6,0)$	$50 \times 6 + 40 \times 0 = 300$
$B(4,3)$	$50 \times 4 + 40 \times 3 = 200 + 120 = 320$ (Maximum)
$C(0,19/3)$	$Z = 50 \times 0 + 40 \times 19/3 \approx 253$

Hence, the maximum daily output is 320, which will be achieved, when 4 machines of type A and 3 machines of type B are bought.

Or

(ii) Let x be the number of tables and y be the number of chairs that the dealer buys and sells. The profit on a table is $550 - 500 =$ ₹ 50 and the profit on a chair is $115 - 100 =$ ₹ 15.

So, the total profit $P = 50x + 15y$ (in ₹). Hence, the problem can be formulated as an LPP as follows.

Maximise $P = 50x + 15y$

Subject to the constraints,

$x + y \le 60$ [storage constraint]

$500x + 100y \le 10000$

i.e. $5x + y \le 100$ [investment constraint]

and $x \ge 0, y \ge 0$ [non-negative constraints]

The table for line $x + y = 60$ or $y = 60 - x$ is

x	0	60
y	60	0

So, the line passes through the points (0, 60) and (60, 0).

On putting (0, 0) in the inequality $x + y \le 60$, we get

$0 + 0 \le 60$ [true]

So, the half plane is towards the origin.

The table for line $5x + y = 100$ or $y = 100 - 5x$ is

x	0	20
y	100	0

So, the line passes through the points (0, 100) and (20, 0).

On putting (0, 0) in the inequality $5x + y \le 100$, we get

$0 + 0 \le 100$ [true]

So, the half plane is towards the origin.

Also, $x \ge 0$, $y \ge 0$, so the feasible region lies in Ist quardrant.

The point of intersection of lines $x + y = 60$ and $5x + y = 100$ is, $B(10, 50)$.

Now, plot all the constraints on a graph paper, as given below.

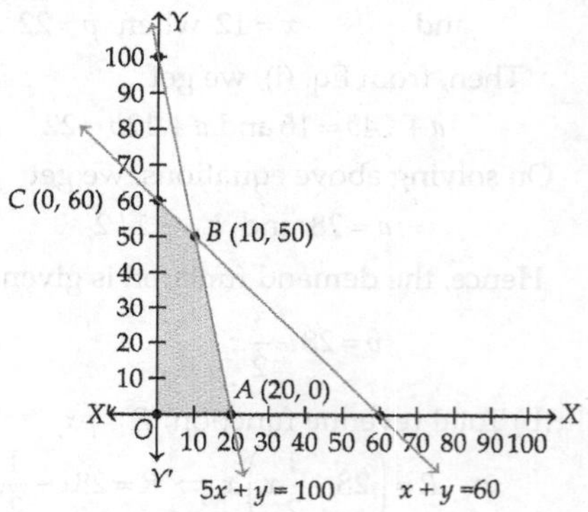

The shaded portion $OABCO$ shows the feasible region, which is bounded. The four corner points of the feasible region are $O(0,0)$, $A(20,0)$, $B(10,50)$ and $C(0,60)$.

The value of P at corner points are

Corner points	$P = 50x + 15y$
$O(0,0)$	$50 \times 0 + 15 \times 0 = 0$
$A(20,0)$	$50(20) + 15(0) = 1000$
$B(10,50)$	$50(10) + 15(50) = 1250$ (Maximum)
$C(0,60)$	$50(0) + 15(60) = 900$

Hence, P is maximum at $B(10,50)$.

Hence, the dealer gets a maximum profit of ₹ 1250 when he sells 10 tables and 50 chairs.

SQP Code : **PB-7/15** Series **i-Succeed 7-25/15** Roll No.

Sample Question Paper 07

Mathematics 12th (Code 860)

Time : 3 Hrs.

Max. Marks : 80

General Instructions

1. The Question Paper consists of three sections A, B and C.
2. Candidates are required to attempt all questions from Section A and all questions either from Section B Or Section C.
3. Section A Internal choice has been provided in two questions of two marks each, two questions of four marks each and two questions of six marks each.
4. Section B Internal choice has been provided in one questions of two marks and one question of four marks.
5. Section C Internal choice has been provided in one question of two marks and one question of four marks.
6. All working, including rough work, should be done on the same sheet as, and adjacent to the rest of the answer.
7. The intended marks for questions or parts of questions are given in brackets [].
8. Mathematical tables and graph papers are provided.

Section A (65 Marks)

1. In subparts (i) to (xi) choose the correct options and in subparts (xii) to (xv), answer the questions as instructed.

(i) The value of $\begin{vmatrix} \sin\theta & \cos\theta \\ -\cos\theta & \sin\theta \end{vmatrix}$ is • *Recall* [1]

(a) 1 (b) – 1
(c) 0 (d) None of these

(ii) **Assertion** (A) If $A=\begin{bmatrix} 2 & -2 \\ 0 & 3 \end{bmatrix}$ and $B=\begin{bmatrix} 3 & 2 \\ 1 & -4 \end{bmatrix}$, then the sum of the matrices A and B is $\begin{bmatrix} 5 & 0 \\ 1 & -1 \end{bmatrix}$ • *Recall* [1]

Reason (R) Let $A=[a_{ij}]$ and $B=[b_{ij}]$ be the two matrices of the same order say $m \times n$ their sum is defined as a matrix $C=[c_{ij}]_{m\times n}$, where $c_{ij}=a_{ij}+b_{ij}$ for all possible values of i and j. • *Analysis*

(a) Both A and R are true and R is the correct explanation of A.
(b) Both A and R are true and R is not the correct explanation of A.
(c) A is true but R is false.
(d) A is false but R is true.

(iii) **Statement I** If $P(A)=\frac{3}{10}$, $P(B)=\frac{2}{5}$ and $P(A\cup B)=\frac{3}{5}$, then $P(B/A)+P(A/B)$ is equal to $\frac{7}{12}$.

Statement II For any two events A and B, $P(A\cup B)=P(A)+P(B)-P(A\cap B)$.

Choose the correct option. • *Application* [1]

(a) Statement I is true.
(b) Statement II is true.
(c) Both Statements I and II are true.
(d) Both Statements I and II are false.

(iv) The graph of the function $f(x)$ is shown below. • *Application* [1]

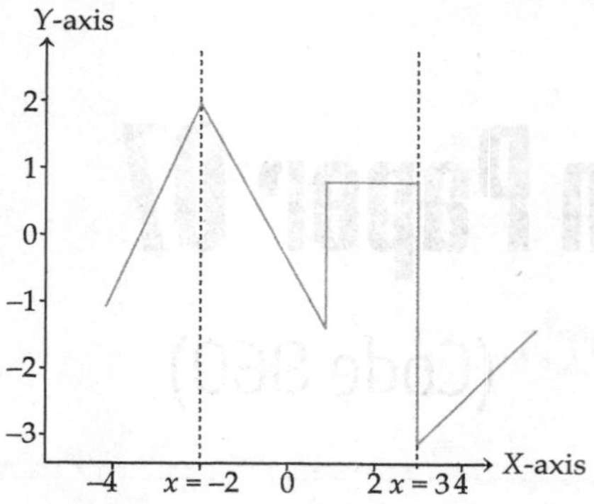

(a) $f(x)$ is continuous at $x=-2$ and discontinuous at $x=3$.
(b) $f(x)$ is continuous at $x=3$ and discontinuous at $x=-2$.
(c) $f(x)$ is differentiable at $x=-2$ and $x=3$.
(d) $f(x)$ is discontinuous at $x=-2$ and $x=3$.

(v) The function given by $f(x)=3-7x$ is strictly decreasing on R. • *Understanding* [1]

(a) True (b) False
(c) Cannot say (d) Partially true

(vi) Suppose 3×3 matrix $A=[a_{ij}]$, whose elements are given by $a_{ij}=i^2-j^2$, then a_{32} is equal to • *Understanding* [1]

(a) 5 (b) 1 (c) 2 (d) 3

(vii) The integrating factor of differential equation $(1-x^2)\dfrac{dy}{dx}-xy=1$ is • *Application* [1]

(a) $-x$ (b) $\dfrac{x}{1+x^2}$
(c) $\sqrt{1-x^2}$ (d) $\dfrac{1}{2}\log(1-x^2)$

(viii) If $y=\sqrt{\sin x+\sqrt{\sin x+\sqrt{\sin x+\ldots+\infty}}}$, then $\dfrac{dy}{dx}$ is equal to • *Application* [1]

(a) $\dfrac{\cos x}{2y+1}$ (b) $\dfrac{\cos x}{2y-1}$
(c) $\dfrac{\sin x}{2y-1}$ (d) None of these

(ix) **Statement I** The function $f(x)=\begin{cases}2x, & \text{if } x<0\\ 0, & \text{if } 0\le x\le 1\\ 4x, & \text{if } x>1\end{cases}$ is continuous everywhere except $x=1$.

Statement II A function $f(x)$ is said to be continuous in closed interval $[a, b]$. It is continuous for every value of x in the open interval (a, b) and $f(x)$ $f(x)$ is continuous at $x=a$ from right and continuous at $x=b$ from left.

Choose the correct option. • *Analysis* [1]

(a) Statement I is true; Statement II is true; Statement II is a correct explanation for Statement I.
(b) Statement I is true; Statement II is true; Statement II is not a correct explanation for Statement I.
(c) Statement I is true; Statement II is false.
(d) Statement I is false; Statement II is true.

(x) **Assertion** (A) The value of $\int_a^b f(t)\,dt$ and $\int_a^b f(u)\,du$ are equal.

Reason (R) The value of definite integral of a function over any particular interval depends on the function and the interval not on the variable of integration. • *Analysis* [1]

Choose the correct option.

(a) Both A and R are correct; R is the correct explanation of A
(b) Both A and R are correct; R is not the correct explanation of A
(c) A is correct; R is incorrect
(d) R is correct; A is incorrect

(xi) For the curve $\sqrt{x}+\sqrt{y}=1$, the value of $\dfrac{dy}{dx}$ at $\left(\dfrac{1}{4},\dfrac{1}{4}\right)$ is • *Evaluate* [1]

(a) 0 (b) $\dfrac{1}{2}$ (c) $-\dfrac{1}{2}$ (d) -1

(xii) Find the value of k for which the function $f(x)=\begin{cases}\dfrac{1-\cos 4x}{8x^2}, & \text{if } x\neq 0\\ k, & \text{if } x=0\end{cases}$ is continuous at $x=0$. • *Analysis* [1]

(xiii) State the reason for the relation R in the set $\{1, 2, 3\}$ given by $R=\{(1,2),(2,1)\}$ not to be transitive. • *Analysis* [1]

(xiv) Show that $(A-A')$ is skew-symmetric, if $A=\begin{bmatrix}2 & 4\\ 3 & 5\end{bmatrix}$. • *Application* [1]

(xv) Evaluate $\int \frac{\sin(x-\alpha)}{\sin(x+\alpha)} dx.$ • *Evaluate* [1]

2. (i) If $f(x)=\begin{cases} x^2 & , \text{if } x \ge 1 \\ x & , \text{if } x<1 \end{cases}$, then prove that f is not differentiable at $x=1$. • *Analysis* [2]

Or

(ii) If $e^y(x+1)=1$, then show that $\frac{dy}{dx}=-e^y$. • *Analysis* [2]

3. (i) Solve the differential equation $(x^2+3xy+y^2)dx-x^2dy=0$. • *Application* [2]

Or

(ii) Find the particular solution of the differential equation.
$\frac{dy}{dx}-2xy=3x^2e^{x^2}$; $y(0)=5$. • *Application* [2]

4. Find the points on the curve $x^2-y^2-2x-3=0$ at which tangent is parallel to X-axis. • *Application* [2]

5. Evaluate $\int \frac{dx}{(x+1)(2+2x+x^2)}$. • *Evaluate* [2]

6. (a) For what value of x, the matrix $\begin{bmatrix} 2x+4 & 4 \\ x+5 & 3 \end{bmatrix}$ is a singular matrix? • *Understanding*

(b) Evaluate $\begin{vmatrix} \cos 15^\circ & \sin 15^\circ \\ \sin 75^\circ & \cos 75^\circ \end{vmatrix}$. • *Evaluate* [2]

7. Using properties of determinants, prove that
$$\begin{vmatrix} 1+a & 1 & 1 \\ 1 & 1+b & 1 \\ 1 & 1 & 1+c \end{vmatrix} = abc+bc+ca+ab.$$
• *Application* [4]

8. Consider $f: R^+ \to [4, \infty)$ given by $f(x)=x^2+4$. Show that f is invertible with the inverse f^{-1} of f given by $f^{-1}(y)=\sqrt{y-4}$, where R^+ is the set of all non-negative real numbers. • *Analysis* [4]

9. (i) Probability of solving specific problem independently by A and B are 1/2 and 1/3, respectively. If both try to solve the problem independently, then find the probability that

(a) the problem is solved.

(b) exactly one of them solves the problem. • *Application* [4]

Or

(ii) 3 defective bulbs are mixed up with 7 good ones. 3 bulbs are drawn at random. Find the probability distribution of defective bulbs. • *Application*

10. (i) For inverse trigonometric functions, we have

I. $\sin^{-1}x+\cos^{-1}x=\frac{\pi}{2}$

II. $\tan^{-1}x+\cot^{-1}x=\frac{\pi}{2}$

III. $\text{cosec}^{-1}x+\sec^{-1}x=\frac{\pi}{2}$

On the basis of above information, answer the following questions. • *Recall* [4]

(a) If $\sin^{-1}x+\sin^{-1}y=\frac{\pi}{2}$, then find $\cos^{-1}x+\cos^{-1}y$.

(b) If $\tan^{-1}x+\tan^{-1}y=\frac{4\pi}{5}$, then find $\cot^{-1}x+\cot^{-1}y$.

(c) If $\tan^{-1}x-\cot^{-1}x=\tan^{-1}\frac{1}{\sqrt{3}}$, then find the value of x.

(d) If $\sin\left(\sin^{-1}\frac{1}{5}+\cos^{-1}x\right)=1$, then find the value of x.

Or

(ii) (a) If $\sin[\cot^{-1}(x+1)]=\cos(\tan^{-1}x)$, then find x.

(b) Find $\cos\left[\sin^{-1}\left(\frac{3}{4}\right)+\sec^{-1}\left(\frac{4}{3}\right)\right]$.

(c) Evaluate $\tan^{-1}\left(\frac{x}{y}\right)-\tan^{-1}\left(\frac{x-y}{x+y}\right)$.

• *Evaluate* [4]

11. Consider the function
$$y=\frac{4\sin\theta}{2+\cos\theta}-\theta,\ \theta\in\left(0,\frac{\pi}{2}\right).$$
Answer the following questions. • *Analysis* [6]

(i) Differentiate the function.

(ii) Find critical points.

(iii) Show that the given function is increasing in the given interval.

SP-07

12. (i) Evaluate $\int_0^{\pi} \frac{x}{a^2 \cos^2 x + b^2 \sin^2 x} dx.$ • *Evaluate* [6]

Or

(ii) Evaluate $\int \frac{1}{\cos^4 x + \sin^4 x} dx.$ • *Evaluate* [6]

13. (i) An insurance company insured 3000 scooters, 4000 cars and 5000 trucks. The probability of an accident involving a scooter, a car and a truck are 0.02, 0.03 and 0.04, respectively. One of the insured vehicles meets with an accident. Find the probability that it is a scooter, it is a car and it is a truck. • *Application* [6]

Or (ii) If A and B are two independent events such that $P(\overline{A} \cap B) = \frac{2}{15}$ and $P(A \cap \overline{B}) = \frac{1}{6}$, then find $P(A)$ and $P(B)$. • *Application* [6]

14. A building has a gate in the form of a rectangle is inscribed in a semi-circle of radius r with one of its sides on the diameter of the semi-circle. • *Application* [6]

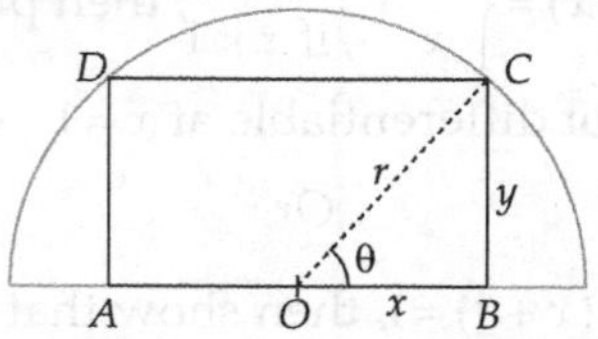

On the basis of above information, answer the following questions.

(i) Find the values of x and y in terms of θ and r.

(ii) If area of rectangle A is expressed in terms of θ and r, then find the value of A.

(iii) When A is maximum, then find the value of θ.

(iv) For maximum value of A, find the dimensions of rectangle.

Section B (15 Marks)

15. In subparts (i) to (iii) choose the correct options and in subparts (iv) and (v), answer the questions as instructed. [5]

(i) The unit vector normal to the plane $x + 2y + 3z - 6 = 0$ is • *Understanding*

(a) $\frac{1}{\sqrt{14}}(\hat{i} + 2\hat{j} - 3\hat{k})$ (b) $\frac{1}{\sqrt{14}}(\hat{i} + 2\hat{j} + 3\hat{k})$

(c) $\frac{1}{\sqrt{14}}(-\hat{i} + \hat{j} + \hat{k})$ (d) None of these

(ii) If the vector $\vec{b}$ is collinear with the vector $\vec{a} = (2\sqrt{2}, -1, 4)$ and $|\vec{b}| = 10$, then • *Understanding*

(a) $\vec{a} \pm \vec{b} = 0$ (b) $\vec{a} \pm 2\vec{b} = 0$

(c) $-\vec{b} \pm 2\vec{a} = 0$ (d) None of these

(iii) **Statement I** If $\vec{a}$ and $\vec{b}$ are two vectors, such that $|\vec{a} \cdot \vec{b}| = |\vec{a} \times \vec{b}|$, then the angle between $\vec{a}$ and $\vec{b}$ is $\frac{\pi}{4}$.

Statement II If $\vec{a}$ and $\vec{b}$ are two non-zero vectors, then $\vec{a} \cdot \vec{b} = |a||b| \cos \theta$ and $\vec{a} \times \vec{b} = |a||b| \sin \theta \, \hat{n}$.

Choose the correct option.

(a) Statement I is true.

(b) Statement II is true.

(c) Both Statements I and II are true.

(d) Both Statements I and II are false.

(iv) If A, B and C are the vertices of a ΔABC, as shown in the figure, then what is the value of $\overrightarrow{AB} + \overrightarrow{BC} + \overrightarrow{CA}$?

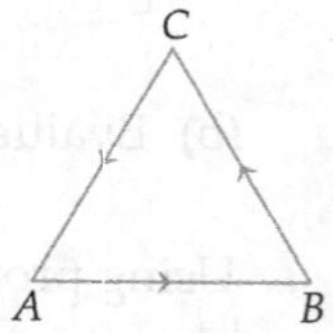

• *Application*

(v) Find the vector equation of the line passing through the point $A(1, 2, -1)$ and parallel to the line $5x - 25 = 14 - 7y = 35z$. • *Understanding*

16. (i) If $\vec{a} = 3\hat{i} + 5\hat{j} - 2\hat{k}$ and $\vec{b} = 2\hat{i} + \hat{j} + 3\hat{k}$, then find $|\vec{a} \times \vec{b}|$. • *Recall* [2]

Or

(ii) In any ΔABC, prove by vector method that $\cos A = \frac{b^2 + c^2 - a^2}{2bc}$. • *Recall* [2]

SP-07

17. (i) A variable plane which remains at a constant distance p from the origin cuts the coordinate axes at A, B and C. Show that the locus of the centroid of ΔABC is $\frac{1}{x^2}+\frac{1}{y^2}+\frac{1}{z^2}=\frac{9}{p^2}$ • *Analysis* [4]

Or

(ii) Find the points on the line $\frac{x+2}{3}=\frac{y+1}{2}=\frac{z-3}{2}$ at a distance of 5 units from the point $P(1,3,3)$. • *Understanding* [4]

18. Draw a rough sketch and find the area enclosed by the parabola $y^2=x$ and the line $y+x=6$. • *Application* [4]

Section C (15 Marks)

19. In subparts (i) and (ii) choose the correct options and in subparts (iii) to (v), answer the questions as instructed. [5]

(i) A profit making company wants to launch a new product. It observes that the fixed cost of the new product is ₹ 35000 and the variable cost per unit is ₹ 500. The revenue received on the sale of x units is given by $5000x-100x^2$, then the profit function is • *Application*

(a) $p(x)=4500x-100x^2-35000$
(b) $p(x)=45000x-100$
(c) $p(x)=4500x-3500x^2+100$
(d) $p(x)=4500x-100x^2$

(ii) If the lines of regression are parallel to coordinate axes, then the coefficient of correlation is • *Understanding*

(a) 1
(b) 0
(c) -1
(d) 1/2

(iii) If the regression coefficient of y on x is 1.8 and that of x on y is 0.8, then check this statement is true or false and also give the reason. • *Analysis*

(iv) A company produces a commodity with ₹ 22000 as fixed cost. The variable cost, estimated to be 20% of the total revenue received on selling the product, at the rate of ₹ 10 per unit. Find the break-even point. • *Application*

(v) For manufacturing a certain item, the fixed cost is ₹ 5000 and the cost of producing each unit is ₹ 30. What is the total cost and average cost of producing 10 units? • *Application*

20. (i) For the demand function $x=\frac{b-p}{a}$, where x denotes the number of units sold at the price p per unit. Find • *Understanding*

(a) slope of average revenue curve.
(b) slope of marginal revenue curve.

Or

(ii) The cost function of a firm is given by $C(x)=4x^3-2x+6$. Find • *Understanding*

(a) average cost function
(b) marginal cost function [2]

21. Find the equation of the regression line of y on x, if the observations (x_i, y_i) are the following (1, 4), (2, 8), (3, 2), (4, 12), (5, 10), (6, 14), (7, 16), (8, 6), (9, 18). Draw the regression line of y on x. • *Recall* [4]

22. (i) Solve minimum value of $Z=x+y$ graphically under the following constraints $3x+2y\ge 12$, $x+3y\ge 11$ and $x\ge 0, y\ge 0$ • *Analysis* [4]

Or

(ii) A manufacturer makes two products A and B. Product A sells at ₹ 200 each and takes 1/2 h to make. Product B sells at ₹ 300 each and takes 1 h to make. There is a permanent order for 14 units of product A and 16 units of product B. A working week consists of 40 h of production and the weekly turnover must not be less than ₹ 10000. If the profit on each of product A is ₹ 20 and on product B is ₹ 30, then how many of each should be produced so that the profit is maximum? Also, find the maximum profit. • *Application* [4]

Solutions in Topper's Style

My Commitment *I affirm that I am reviewing these solutions only after I have solved the Sample Question Paper 7 on my own. My purpose of looking the solutions is solely to verify whether my answers/solutions were correct or not and to identify my mistakes in case my solutions were wrong or I could not solve that.*

1. (i) (a) We have, $\begin{vmatrix} \sin\theta & \cos\theta \\ -\cos\theta & \sin\theta \end{vmatrix} = \sin^2\theta + \cos^2\theta$

$$\left[\because \begin{vmatrix} a_{11} & a_{12} \\ a_{21} & a_{22} \end{vmatrix} = a_{11}a_{22} - a_{21}a_{12}\right]$$

$= 1$ $\quad [\because \sin\theta^2 + \cos^2\theta = 1]$

(ii) (a) Given, matrices are $A = \begin{bmatrix} 2 & -2 \\ 0 & 3 \end{bmatrix}$ and $B = \begin{bmatrix} 3 & 2 \\ 1 & -4 \end{bmatrix}$

Here, we see that both matrices are of same order, therefore sum of A and B is defined.

$$\therefore A + B = \begin{bmatrix} 2 & -2 \\ 0 & 3 \end{bmatrix} + \begin{bmatrix} 3 & 2 \\ 1 & -4 \end{bmatrix} = \begin{bmatrix} 2+3 & -2+2 \\ 0+1 & 3-4 \end{bmatrix}$$

[add corresponding elements of A and B]

$$= \begin{bmatrix} 5 & 0 \\ 1 & -1 \end{bmatrix}$$

(iii) (c) We have,

$P(A) = \frac{3}{10}$, $P(B) = \frac{2}{5}$ and $P(A \cup B) = \frac{3}{5}$

$\Rightarrow P(A) + P(B) - P(A \cap B) = \frac{3}{5}$

$\Rightarrow \frac{3}{10} + \frac{2}{5} - P(A \cap B) = \frac{3}{5}$

$\Rightarrow P(A \cap B) = \frac{3}{10} + \frac{2}{5} - \frac{3}{5} = \frac{1}{10}$

Now, $P(B/A) + P(A/B)$

$= \frac{P(A \cap B)}{P(A)} + \frac{P(A \cap B)}{P(B)}$

$= \frac{\frac{1}{10}}{\frac{3}{10}} + \frac{\frac{1}{10}}{\frac{2}{5}} = \frac{1}{3} + \frac{1}{4} = \frac{7}{12}$

Hence, both Statements are true.

(iv) (d) From the given figure,

At $x = -2$, there is a removable discontinuity.

$\lim_{x \to -2} f(x)$ exists but $f(-2)$ is not defined.

So, At $x = -2$, $f(x)$ is not continuous

and $x = 3$, there is a jump discontinuity.

i.e. $\lim_{x \to 3^-} f(x) \neq \lim_{x \to 3^+} f(x)$

Hence, $f(x)$ is not continuous at $x = -2$ and $x = 3$.

(v) (a) Let x_1 and x_2 be any two numbers in R. Then,

$$x_1 < x_2 \Rightarrow -7x_1 > -7x_2 \Rightarrow 3 - 7x_1 > 3 - 7x_2$$

$\Rightarrow \quad f(x_1) > f(x_2), \forall x_1, x_2 \in R$

Hence, $f(x)$ is strictly decreasing on R.

(vi) (a) We have, $a_{ij} = i^2 - j^2$

$\therefore \ a_{32} = (3)^2 - (2)^2 = 9 - 4 = 5$

(vii) (c) Given differential equation is

$(1 - x^2)\frac{dy}{dx} - xy = 1$

$\Rightarrow \quad \frac{dy}{dx} - \frac{x}{1-x^2} y = \frac{1}{1-x^2}$

which is a linear differential equation of the form $\frac{dy}{dx} + Py = Q$.

Here, $P = \frac{-x}{1-x^2}$ and $Q = \frac{1}{1-x^2}$

$\therefore \quad \text{IF} = e^{-\int \frac{x}{1-x^2} dx}$

Let $1 - x^2 = t \Rightarrow -2x dx = dt \Rightarrow xdx = -\frac{dt}{2}$

Then, $\text{IF} = e^{\frac{1}{2}\int \frac{dt}{t}} = e^{\frac{1}{2}\log t} = e^{\frac{1}{2}\log(1-x^2)} = \sqrt{1-x^2}$

$\left[\because \frac{1}{a}\log m = \log m^{1/a} \text{ and } e^{\log_e m} = m\right]$

(viii) (b) We have,

$$y = \sqrt{\sin x + \sqrt{\sin x + \sqrt{\sin x + \ldots + \infty}}}$$

$\Rightarrow \quad y = \sqrt{\sin x + y}$

$\Rightarrow \quad y^2 = \sin x + y$ $\quad$ [square both sides]

On differentiating both sides w.r.t. x, we get

$2y\frac{dy}{dx} = \cos x + \frac{dy}{dx}$

$\Rightarrow \quad 2y\frac{dy}{dx} - \frac{dy}{dx} = \cos x$

$\Rightarrow \quad \frac{dy}{dx}(2y - 1) = \cos x$

$\Rightarrow \quad \frac{dy}{dx} = \frac{\cos x}{2y-1}$

(ix) (b) I. Here, $f(x) = \begin{cases} 2x, \text{if } & x < 0 \\ 0, \text{if } & 0 \le x \le 1 \\ 4x, \text{if } & x > 1 \end{cases}$

is polynomial and constant function, so it is continuous in the given intervals. So, we have to check the continuity only at $x = 0$ and 1.

At $x = 0$, LHL $= \lim_{x \to 0^-} f(x) = \lim_{x \to 0^-} (2x)$

On putting $x = 0 - h$ as $x \to 0^-$, $h \to 0$

$\therefore$ LHL $= \lim_{h \to 0} [2(0 - h)] = \lim_{h \to 0} (-2h) = -2 \times 0 = 0,$

and $\quad \text{RHL} = \lim_{x \to 0^+} f(x) = \lim_{x \to 0^+} (0) = 0$

Also, $f(0) = 0$

$\because$ At $x = 0$, LHL = RHL = $f(0)$

Thus, $f(x)$ is continuous at $x = 0$

At $x = 1$, $\text{LHL} = \lim_{x \to 1^-} f(x) = \lim_{x \to 1^-} (0) = 0,$

$\text{RHL} = \lim_{x \to 1^+} f(x) = \lim_{x \to 1^+} (4x)$

On putting $x = 1 + h$ as $x \to 1^+$ when $h \to 0$

$\text{RHL} = \lim_{h \to 0} [4(1+h)] = \lim_{h \to 0} (4 + 4h)$

$= 4 + 4 \times 0 = 4$

$\because$ *at* $x = 1$, LHL $\neq$ RHL

Thus, $f(x)$ is continuous everywhere except at $x = 1$.

(x) (a) The value of definite integral of a function over any particular interval depends on the function and the interval, but not on the variable of intergration that we choose to represent the independent variable. If the independent variable is denoted by t or u instead of x, we simply write the integral as $\int_a^b f(t)dt$ or $\int_a^b f(u)du$ instead of $\int_a^b f(x)dx$.

Hence, both A and R, true and R is the correct explanation of A.

(xi) (d) We have, $\sqrt{x} + \sqrt{y} = 1$

On differentiating both sides, w.r.t. x, we get

$$\frac{1}{2\sqrt{x}} + \frac{1}{2\sqrt{y}}\frac{dy}{dx} = 0 \Rightarrow \frac{dy}{dx} = -\frac{\sqrt{y}}{\sqrt{x}}$$

$$\therefore \text{ At } \left(\frac{1}{4}, \frac{1}{4}\right), \left(\frac{dy}{dx}\right)_{\left(\frac{1}{4}, \frac{1}{4}\right)} = \frac{-\frac{1}{2}}{\frac{1}{2}} = -1$$

(xii) Given, $f(x) = \begin{cases} \dfrac{1 - \cos 4x}{8x^2}, & \text{if } x \neq 0 \\ k, & \text{if } x = 0 \end{cases}$

The function $f(x)$ is continuous at $x = 0$

If $\lim_{x \to 0} f(x) = f(0)$ ...(i)

We have, $f(0) = k$ ...(ii)

$$\text{Now, } \lim_{x \to 0} f(x) = \lim_{x \to 0}\left(\frac{1 - \cos 4x}{8x^2}\right)$$

$$= \lim_{x \to 0}\left(\frac{2\sin^2 2x}{8x^2}\right) \quad [\because \cos 2\theta = 1 - 2\sin^2\theta]$$

$$= \lim_{x \to 0}\left(\frac{\sin^2 2x}{4x^2}\right)$$

$$= \lim_{x \to 0}\left(\frac{\sin 2x}{2x}\right)^2 = 1 \quad \text{...(iii)}$$

Hence, from Eqs. (i), (ii) and (iii), we get

$k = 1$

(xiii) We know that for a relation to be transitive, $(x, y) \in R$ and $(y, z) \in R \Rightarrow (x, z) \in R$.

Here, $(1, 2) \in R$ and $(2, 1) \in R$ but $(1, 1) \notin R$.

$\therefore$ R is not transitive.

(xiv) We have, $A = \begin{bmatrix} 2 & 4 \\ 3 & 5 \end{bmatrix}$, then $A' = \begin{bmatrix} 2 & 3 \\ 4 & 5 \end{bmatrix}$

$$\text{Now, } A - A' = \begin{bmatrix} 2 & 4 \\ 3 & 5 \end{bmatrix} - \begin{bmatrix} 2 & 3 \\ 4 & 5 \end{bmatrix} = \begin{bmatrix} 0 & 1 \\ -1 & 0 \end{bmatrix}$$

$$(A - A')' = \begin{bmatrix} 0 & 1 \\ -1 & 0 \end{bmatrix}' = \begin{bmatrix} 0 & -1 \\ 1 & 0 \end{bmatrix}$$

$$\Rightarrow (A - A')' = -\begin{bmatrix} 0 & 1 \\ -1 & 0 \end{bmatrix} = -(A - A')$$

Hence, $(A - A')$ is skew-symmetric matrix.

(xv) We have, $\int \frac{\sin(x - \alpha)}{\sin(x + \alpha)} dx = \int \frac{\sin(x + \alpha - 2\alpha)}{\sin(x + \alpha)} dx$

$$= \int \frac{\sin(x + \alpha)\cos 2\alpha - \cos(x + \alpha)\sin 2\alpha}{\sin(x + \alpha)} dx$$

$[\because \sin(A - B) = \sin A \cos B - \cos A \sin B]$

$= \int [\cos 2\alpha - \sin 2\alpha \cot(x + \alpha)] dx$

$= \cos 2\alpha \int 1 dx - \sin 2\alpha \int \cot(x + \alpha) dx$

$= x \cos 2\alpha - \sin 2\alpha \log|\sin(x + \alpha)| + C$

$[\because \int \cot\theta \, d\theta = \log \sin\theta]$

2. (i) Given, $f(x) = \begin{cases} x^2, & \text{if } x \geq 1 \\ x, & \text{if } x < 1 \end{cases}$

$$\text{Now, } Lf'(1) = \lim_{h \to 0} \frac{f(1-h) - f(1)}{-h}$$

$$= \lim_{h \to 0} \frac{(1-h) - (1)^2}{-h} = \lim_{h \to 0} \frac{1 - h - 1}{-h}$$

$$= \lim_{h \to 0}\left(\frac{-h}{-h}\right) = \lim_{h \to 0}(1) = 1$$

$$\text{and } Rf'(1) = \lim_{h \to 0} \frac{f(1+h) - f(1)}{h} = \lim_{h \to 0} \frac{(1+h)^2 - (1)^2}{h}$$

$$= \lim_{h \to 0} \frac{(1 + h^2 + 2h) - 1}{h}$$

$$= \lim_{h \to 0} \frac{h^2 + 2h}{h} = \lim_{h \to 0}(h + 2) = 0 + 2 = 2$$

Since, $Lf'(1) \neq Rf'(1)$

Hence, $f(x)$ is not differentiable at $x = 1$.

Hence proved.

Or

(ii) Given, $e^y(x + 1) = 1$ ...(i)

On differentiating both sides w.r.t. x, we get

$$e^y + (x + 1)e^y \frac{dy}{dx} = 0$$

$$\Rightarrow e^y + 1 \cdot \frac{dy}{dx} = 0 \quad \text{[using Eq. (i)]}$$

$$\Rightarrow e^y + \frac{dy}{dx} = 0$$

$$\Rightarrow \frac{dy}{dx} = -e^y$$

Hence proved.

3. (i) Given differential equation is

$(x^2+3xy+y^2)dx-x^2dy=0$

$\Rightarrow \quad \dfrac{dy}{dx}=\dfrac{x^2+3xy+y^2}{x^2}$ ...(i)

which is a homogeneous differential equation.

Put $y=vx \Rightarrow \dfrac{dy}{dx}=v+x\dfrac{dv}{dx}$

On substituting the values of y and $\dfrac{dy}{dx}$ in Eq. (i), we get

$$v+x\frac{dv}{dx}=1+3v+v^2$$

$$\Rightarrow x\frac{dv}{dx}=1+2v+v^2=(v+1)^2$$

$$\Rightarrow \frac{1}{(v+1)^2}dv=\frac{dx}{x}$$

On integrating both sides, we get

$$\int\frac{1}{(v+1)^2}dv=\int\frac{dx}{x}+C$$

$$\Rightarrow -\frac{1}{v+1}=\log|x|+C$$

$$\Rightarrow -\frac{1}{\frac{y}{x}+1}=\log|x|+C \quad \left[\because v=\frac{y}{x}\right]$$

$$\Rightarrow -\frac{x}{y+x}=\log|x|+C,$$

where C is an arbitrary constant.

(ii) Given differential equation is

$$\frac{dy}{dx}-2xy=3x^2e^{x^2}$$

which a linear differential equation of the form $\dfrac{dy}{dx}+Py=Q$

Here, $P=-2x$ and $Q=3x^2e^{x^2}$

$$\therefore \text{IF}=e^{\int Pdx}=e^{-2\int x\,dx}=e^{-2\left(\frac{x^2}{2}\right)}=e^{-x^2}$$

The solution of differential equation is given by

$$y\times\text{IF}=\int(Q\times\text{IF})\,dx+C$$

$$\Rightarrow y\times e^{-x^2}=\int(3x^2\cdot e^{x^2})\times e^{-x^2}dx+C$$

$$=\int 3x^2dx+C=3\left(\frac{x^3}{3}\right)+C$$

$$\Rightarrow y\times e^{-x^2}=x^3+C \quad \text{...(i)}$$

Now, given $y(0)-5$ i.e. when $x=0$, then $y=5$

From Eq. (i), we get $5e^0=0+C \Rightarrow C=5$

On putting the value of C in Eq. (i), we get

$ye^{-x^2}=x^3+5$

Which is the required solution.

4. Given, equation of curve is

$$x^2+y^2-2x-3=0 \quad \text{...(i)}$$

On differentiating both sides of Eq. (i) w.r.t. x, we get

$$2x+2y\frac{dy}{dx}-2=0$$

$$\Rightarrow 2y\frac{dy}{dx}=2-2x$$

$$\Rightarrow \frac{dy}{dx}=\frac{2-2x}{2y}$$

$$\Rightarrow \frac{dy}{dx}=\frac{1-x}{y}$$

We know that when a tangent to the curve is parallel to X-axis, then $\dfrac{dy}{dx}=0.$

On putting $\dfrac{dy}{dx}=0$, we get $1-x=0 \Rightarrow x=1$

Now, on putting $x=1$ in Eq. (i), we get

$$1+y^2-2-3=0 \Rightarrow y^2-4=0$$

$$\Rightarrow y^2=4 \Rightarrow y=\pm 2$$

Hence, the required points are (1, 2) and (1, –2).

5. Let $I=\displaystyle\int\frac{dx}{(x+1)(2+2x+x^2)}=\int\frac{dx}{(x+1)[(x+1)^2+1]}$

Put $x+1=t \Rightarrow dx=dt$

Then, we have $I=\displaystyle\int\frac{dt}{t(t^2+1)}=\int\frac{t\,dt}{t^2(t^2+1)}$

Again, on putting $t^2+1=z \Rightarrow 2t\,dt=dz$

$$\Rightarrow t\,dt=\frac{1}{2}dz$$

Then, $\quad I=\dfrac{1}{2}\displaystyle\int\frac{dz}{(z-1)z}=\frac{1}{2}\int\left(\frac{1}{z-1}-\frac{1}{z}\right)dz$

[using partial fractions]

$$=\frac{1}{2}[\log|z-1|-\log|z|]+C$$

$$=\frac{1}{2}\log\left|\frac{z-1}{z}\right|+C=\frac{1}{2}\log\left|\frac{t^2}{t^2+1}\right|+C$$

$$[\because z=t^2+1]$$

$$=\frac{1}{2}\log\left[\frac{(x+1)^2}{(x+1)^2+1}\right]+C\,[\because t=x+1]$$

6. (a) Let $A=\begin{bmatrix}2x+4 & 4\\ x+5 & 3\end{bmatrix}$

If matrix A is singular, then $|A|=0$

$$\Rightarrow \begin{vmatrix}2x+4 & 4\\ x+5 & 3\end{vmatrix}=0$$

$$\Rightarrow (2x+4)\times 3-(x+5)\times 4=0$$

$$\Rightarrow 6x+12-4x-20=0 \Rightarrow 2x=8$$

$$\therefore x=4$$

(b) Let $\Delta = \begin{vmatrix} \cos 15° & \sin 15° \\ \sin 75° & \cos 75° \end{vmatrix}$

On expanding, we get

$$\Delta = (\cos 15° \cos 75° - \sin 15° \sin 75°)$$
$$= \cos(15° + 75°) \quad [\because \cos x \cos y - \sin x \sin y = \cos(x+y)]$$
$$= \cos 90° = 0 \quad [\because \cos 90° = 0]$$

7. $\text{LHS} = \begin{vmatrix} 1+a & 1 & 1 \\ 1 & 1+b & 1 \\ 1 & 1 & 1+c \end{vmatrix}$

On applying $R_1 \to \frac{1}{a} R_1$, $R_2 \to \frac{1}{b} R_2$ and $R_3 \to \frac{1}{c} R_3$, we get

$$\text{LHS} = abc \begin{vmatrix} \frac{1}{a}+1 & \frac{1}{a} & \frac{1}{a} \\ \frac{1}{b} & \frac{1}{b}+1 & \frac{1}{b} \\ \frac{1}{c} & \frac{1}{c} & \frac{1}{c}+1 \end{vmatrix}$$

On applying $R_1 \to R_1 + R_2 + R_3$, we get

$$\text{LHS} = abc \begin{vmatrix} 1+\frac{1}{a}+\frac{1}{b}+\frac{1}{c} & \frac{1}{a}+\frac{1}{b}+\frac{1}{c}+1 & \frac{1}{a}+\frac{1}{b}+\frac{1}{c}+1 \\ \frac{1}{b} & \frac{1}{b}+1 & \frac{1}{b} \\ \frac{1}{c} & \frac{1}{c} & \frac{1}{c}+1 \end{vmatrix}$$

On taking $\left(1+\frac{1}{a}+\frac{1}{b}+\frac{1}{c}\right)$ common from R_1, we get

$$\text{LHS} = abc\left(1+\frac{1}{a}+\frac{1}{b}+\frac{1}{c}\right) \begin{vmatrix} 1 & 1 & 1 \\ \frac{1}{b} & \frac{1}{b}+1 & \frac{1}{b} \\ \frac{1}{c} & \frac{1}{c} & \frac{1}{c}+1 \end{vmatrix}$$

On applying $C_2 \to C_2 - C_1$, $C_3 \to C_3 - C_1$, we get

$$\text{LHS} = abc\left(1+\frac{1}{a}+\frac{1}{b}+\frac{1}{c}\right) \begin{vmatrix} 1 & 0 & 0 \\ \frac{1}{b} & 1 & 0 \\ \frac{1}{c} & 0 & 1 \end{vmatrix}$$

$$= abc\left(1+\frac{1}{a}+\frac{1}{b}+\frac{1}{c}\right)[1(1-0)]$$

[expanding along R_1]

$= abc + bc + ca + ab = \text{RHS}$ **Hence proved.**

8. Here, function $f: R^+ \to [4, \infty)$ is given by $f(x) = x^2 + 4$.

One-one function Let $x, y \in R^+$, such that $f(x) = f(y)$.

$$\Rightarrow \quad x^2 + 4 = y^2 + 4 \Rightarrow x^2 = y^2 \Rightarrow x = y$$

[we take only positive sign as $x, y \in R^+$]

Therefore, f is a one-one function.

Onto function For $y \in [4, \infty)$, let $y = x^2 + 4$

$$\Rightarrow \quad x^2 = y - 4 \geq 0 \quad [\because y \geq 4]$$
$$\Rightarrow \quad x = \sqrt{y-4} \geq 0$$

[we take only positive sign, as $x \in R^+$]

Therefore, for any $y \in R^+$, (codomain), there exists $x = \sqrt{y-4} \in R^+$ (domain) such that

$$f(x) = f(\sqrt{y-4}) = (\sqrt{y-4})^2 + 4$$
$$= y - 4 + 4 = y$$

Therefore, f is onto function.

Since, f is one-one and onto, therefore f^{-1} exists.

$\therefore \quad x = f^{-1}(y) = \sqrt{y-4}$ or $f^{-1}(x) = \sqrt{x-4}, x \in [4, \infty)$

9. (i) Let $= E_1 =$ problem solved by A and $E_2 =$ problem solved by B

Then, we have

$P(E_1) = \frac{1}{2}$ and $P(E_2) = \frac{1}{3}$

$\therefore P(\overline{E}_1) = 1 - P(E_1) = 1 - \frac{1}{2} = \frac{1}{2}$

and $P(\overline{E}_2) = 1 - P(E_2) = 1 - \frac{1}{3} = \frac{2}{3}$

(a) P (problem is solved)

= P (atleast one of them will solve the problem)

= $1 - P$ (none of them solve the problem)

$= 1 - P(\overline{E}_1) \cdot P(\overline{E}_2)$

[$\because$ E_1 and E_2 are independent events, then $\overline{E}_1$ and $\overline{E}_2$ are also independent events]

$$= 1 - \frac{1}{2} \times \frac{2}{3} = 1 - \frac{1}{3} = \frac{2}{3}$$

(b) P (exactly one of them solves the problem)

$= P(E_1 \cap \overline{E}_2) + P(\overline{E}_1 \cap E_2)$

$= P(E_1) \cdot P(\overline{E}_2) + P(\overline{E}_1) \cdot P(E_2)$

[$\because$ E_1 and E_2 are independent events, then $E_1, \overline{E}_2$ and $\overline{E}_1, E_2$ are also independent events]

$$= \frac{1}{2} \times \frac{2}{3} + \frac{1}{2} \times \frac{1}{3} = \frac{3}{6} = \frac{1}{2}$$

Or

(ii) Given, defective bulbs = 3 and good bulbs = 7

Here, total number of bulbs = 3 + 7 = 10

Let X denotes the number of defective bulbs drawn.

Then, X takes the values 0, 1, 2 and 3.

Now, $P(X = 0) = P$ (getting 0 defective bulb)

$$= \frac{({}^3C_0 \times {}^7C_3)}{{}^{10}C_3} = \frac{\left(1 \times \frac{7 \times 6 \times 5}{3 \times 2 \times 1}\right)}{\left(\frac{10 \times 9 \times 8}{3 \times 2 \times 1}\right)}$$

$$=\frac{7\times6\times5}{10\times9\times8}=\frac{7}{24}$$

$P(X=1)=P$ (getting 1 defective bulbs)

$$=\frac{({}^3C_1\times{}^7C_2)}{{}^{10}C_3}=\frac{\left(3\times\frac{7\times6}{2\times1}\right)}{\left(\frac{10\times9\times8}{3\times2\times1}\right)}$$

$$=\frac{3\times7\times6\times3}{10\times9\times8}=\frac{21}{40}$$

$P(X=2)=P$ (getting 2 defective bulbs)

$$=\frac{({}^3C_2\times{}^7C_1)}{{}^{10}C_3}=\frac{\left(\frac{3\times2}{2\times1}\times7\right)}{\left(\frac{10\times9\times8}{3\times2\times1}\right)}$$

$$=\frac{3\times2\times7\times3}{10\times9\times8}=\frac{7}{40}$$

$P(X=3)=P$ (getting 3 defective bulbs)

$$=\frac{({}^3C_3\times{}^7C_0)}{{}^{10}C_3}=\frac{1\times1}{\left(\frac{10\times9\times8}{3\times2\times1}\right)}$$

$$=\frac{3\times2\times1}{10\times9\times8}=\frac{1}{120}$$

Hence, required probability distribution is

X	0	1	2	3
P(X)	7/24	21/40	7/40	1/120

10. (i) (a) We have, $\sin^{-1}x+\sin^{-1}y=\frac{\pi}{2}$

$$\Rightarrow \frac{\pi}{2}-\cos^{-1}x+\frac{\pi}{2}-\cos^{-1}y=\frac{\pi}{2}$$

$$\left[\because \sin^{-1}x+\cos^{-1}x=\frac{\pi}{2}\right]$$

$$\cos^{-1}x+\cos^{-1}y=\frac{\pi}{2}$$

(b) We have, $\tan^{-1}x+\tan^{-1}y=\frac{4\pi}{5}$

$$\Rightarrow \frac{\pi}{2}-\cot^{-1}x+\frac{\pi}{2}-\cot^{-1}y=\frac{4\pi}{5}$$

$$\left[\because \tan^{-1}x+\cot^{-1}x=\frac{\pi}{2}\right]$$

$$\Rightarrow \cot^{-1}x+\cot^{-1}y=\pi-\frac{4\pi}{5}=\frac{\pi}{5}$$

(c) We have, $\tan^{-1}x-\cot^{-1}x=\tan^{-1}\frac{1}{\sqrt{3}}$

$$\Rightarrow \tan^{-1}x-\left(\frac{\pi}{2}-\tan^{-1}x\right)=\frac{\pi}{6}$$

$$\left[\because \tan^{-1}x+\cot^{-1}x=\frac{\pi}{2}\right]$$

$$\Rightarrow 2\tan^{-1}x=\frac{\pi}{6}+\frac{\pi}{2}$$

$$\Rightarrow \tan^{-1}x=\frac{\pi}{3}\Rightarrow x=\tan\frac{\pi}{3}=\sqrt{3}$$

(d) We have, $\sin\left(\sin^{-1}\frac{1}{5}+\cos^{-1}x\right)=1$

$$\Rightarrow \sin^{-1}\frac{1}{5}+\cos^{-1}x=\sin^{-1}1$$

$$\Rightarrow \sin^{-1}\frac{1}{5}+\cos^{-1}x=\frac{\pi}{2} \qquad \left[\because \sin\frac{\pi}{2}=1\right]$$

$$\Rightarrow \sin^{-1}\frac{1}{5}=\frac{\pi}{2}-\cos^{-1}x=\sin^{-1}\frac{1}{5}=\sin^{-1}x$$

$$\therefore \quad x=\frac{1}{5}$$

Or

(ii) (a) Given, $\sin[\cot^{-1}(x+1)]=\cos(\tan^{-1}x)$ ...(i)

Let $\theta_1=\cot^{-1}(x+1)$ and $\theta_2=\tan^{-1}x$

Then, $\cot\theta_1=x+1$ and $\tan\theta_2=x$.

Also, $\theta_1\in(0,\pi)$ and $\theta_2\in\left(\frac{-\pi}{2},\frac{\pi}{2}\right)$.

Now consider, $\text{cosec}^2\,\theta_1=1+\cot^2\theta_1$

$$=1+(x+1)^2$$

$$\Rightarrow \text{cosec}\,\theta_1=\sqrt{1+(x+1)^2}$$

[on taking positive square root only, as $\theta_1\in(0,\pi)$]

$$\Rightarrow \sin\theta_1=\frac{1}{\sqrt{1+(x+1)^2}}$$

$$\Rightarrow \theta_1=\sin^{-1}\left(\frac{1}{\sqrt{1+(x+1)^2}}\right)$$

and $\sec^2\theta_2=1+\tan^2\theta_2=1+x^2$

[take positive square root only, as $\theta_2\in\left(\frac{-\pi}{2},\frac{\pi}{2}\right)$]

$$\Rightarrow \sec\theta_2=\sqrt{1+x^2}$$

$$\Rightarrow \cos\theta_2=\frac{1}{\sqrt{1+x^2}}$$

$$\Rightarrow \theta_2=\cos^{-1}\left(\frac{1}{\sqrt{1+x^2}}\right)$$

From Eq. (i), we get $\sin\theta_1=\cos\theta_2$

$$\Rightarrow \sin\left[\sin^{-1}\left(\frac{1}{\sqrt{1+(x+1)^2}}\right)\right]=\cos\left[\cos^{-1}\left(\frac{1}{\sqrt{1+x^2}}\right)\right]$$

$$\Rightarrow \frac{1}{\sqrt{1+(x+1)^2}}=\frac{1}{\sqrt{1+x^2}}$$

On squaring both sides, we get

$$\frac{1}{1+(x+1)^2}=\frac{1}{1+x^2}$$

$$\Rightarrow \quad 1+x^2=1+x^2+1+2x$$

$$\Rightarrow \quad 1+2x=0 \Rightarrow x=-\frac{1}{2}$$

(b) We have, $\cos\left[\sin^{-1}\left(\frac{3}{4}\right)+\sec^{-1}\left(\frac{4}{3}\right)\right]$

$$=\cos\left[\sin^{-1}\left(\frac{3}{4}\right)+\cos^{-1}\left(\frac{3}{4}\right)\right]$$

$$\left[\because \cos^{-1}x=\sec^{-1}\left(\frac{1}{x}\right)\right]$$

$$=\cos\frac{\pi}{2} \quad \left[\because \sin^{-1}x+\cos^{-1}x=\frac{\pi}{2}\right]$$

$$=0 \quad \left[\because \cos\frac{\pi}{2}=0\right]$$

(c) We have, $\tan^{-1}\left(\frac{x}{y}\right)-\tan^{-1}\left(\frac{x-y}{x+y}\right)$

$$=\tan^{-1}\left(\frac{x}{y}\right)-\tan^{-1}\left[\frac{y\left(\frac{x}{y}-1\right)}{y\left(\frac{x}{y}+1\right)}\right]$$

$$=\tan^{-1}\left(\frac{x}{y}\right)-\tan^{-1}\left[\frac{\left(\frac{x}{y}\right)-1}{1+\left(\frac{x}{y}\right)\times 1}\right]$$

$$=\tan^{-1}\left(\frac{x}{y}\right)-\left\{\tan^{-1}\left(\frac{x}{y}\right)-\tan^{-1}(1)\right\}$$

$$\left[\because \tan^{-1}\theta_1-\tan^{-1}\theta_2=\tan^{-1}\left(\frac{\theta_1-\theta_2}{1+\theta_1\theta_2}\right)\right]$$

$$=\tan^{-1}\left(\frac{x}{y}\right)-\tan^{-1}\left(\frac{x}{y}\right)+\tan^{-1}(1)$$

$$=\tan^{-1}\left(\tan\frac{\pi}{4}\right) \quad \left[\because 1=\tan\frac{\pi}{4}\right]$$

$$=\frac{\pi}{4}$$

11. (i) Given function is $y=\frac{4\sin\theta}{2+\cos\theta}-\theta$ ...(i)

On differentiating both sides of Eq. (i) w.r.t. θ, we get

$$\frac{dy}{d\theta}=\frac{\left[(2+\cos\theta)\times\frac{d}{d\theta}(4\sin\theta)-4\sin\theta\times\frac{d}{d\theta}(2+\cos\theta)\right]}{(2+\cos\theta)^2}-1$$

[using quotient rule of derivative]

$$=\frac{(2+\cos\theta)(4\cos\theta)-4\sin\theta(0-\sin\theta)}{(2+\cos\theta)^2}-1$$

$$=\frac{[8\cos\theta+4\cos^2\theta+4\sin^2\theta-(2+\cos\theta)^2]}{(2+\cos\theta)^2}$$

$$=\frac{[8\cos\theta+4(\cos^2\theta+\sin^2\theta)-(4+\cos^2\theta+4\cos\theta)]}{(2+\cos\theta)^2}$$

$$=\frac{8\cos\theta+4-4-\cos^2\theta-4\cos\theta}{(2+\cos\theta)^2}$$

$$[\because \sin^2\theta+\cos^2\theta=1]$$

$$=\frac{4\cos\theta-\cos^2\theta}{(2+\cos\theta)^2}=\frac{\cos\theta(4-\cos\theta)}{(2+\cos\theta)^2}$$

(ii) Now, we have $\frac{dy}{d\theta}=\frac{\cos\theta(4-\cos\theta)}{(2+\cos\theta)^2}$

For critical points, putting $\frac{dy}{d\theta}=0$, we get

$$\frac{\cos\theta(4-\cos\theta)}{(2+\cos\theta)^2}=0 \Rightarrow \cos\theta(4-\cos\theta)=0$$

$$\Rightarrow \cos\theta=0=\cos\frac{\pi}{2}$$

$$\left[\because \cos\theta\neq 4 \text{ and } \cos\frac{\pi}{2}=0\right]$$

$$\Rightarrow \quad \theta=\frac{\pi}{2}$$

(iii) We know that a function $y=f(x)$ is said to be an increasing function, if $\frac{dy}{dx}>0$, for all values of x.

Here, $\cos\theta>0, \forall\, \theta\in\left(0,\frac{\pi}{2}\right)$

and $(2+\cos\theta)^2$ being a perfect square is always positive for all $\theta\in\left(0,\frac{\pi}{2}\right)$.

Also, for $\theta\in\left(0,\frac{\pi}{2}\right)$, we know that $0<\cos\theta<1$

$\therefore \quad 4-\cos\theta>0, \forall\, \theta\in\left(0,\frac{\pi}{2}\right)$

Thus, we conclude that

$$\frac{\cos\theta(4-\cos\theta)}{(2+\cos\theta)^2}>0, \forall\, \theta\in\left(0,\frac{\pi}{2}\right)$$

$$\Rightarrow \quad \frac{dy}{d\theta}>0, \forall\, \theta\in\left(0,\frac{\pi}{2}\right).$$

Hence, y is an increasing function in $\left(0,\frac{\pi}{2}\right)$.

12. (i) Let $I=\int_0^{\pi}\frac{x}{a^2\cos^2x+b^2\sin^2x}dx$ ...(i)

$$\Rightarrow \quad I=\int_0^{\pi}\frac{(\pi-x)}{a^2\cos^2(\pi-x)+b^2\sin^2(\pi-x)}dx$$

$$\left[\because \int_0^a f(x)\,dx=\int_0^a f(a-x)\,dx\right]$$

$$\Rightarrow \quad I=\int_0^{\pi}\frac{(\pi-x)}{a^2\cos^2x+b^2\sin^2x}dx \quad \text{...(ii)}$$

$[\because \cos(\pi-\theta) = -\cos\theta$ and $\sin(\pi-\theta) = \sin\theta]$

On adding Eqs. (i) and (ii), we get

$$2I = \int_0^{\pi} \frac{(x+\pi-x)}{a^2\cos^2 x + b^2\sin^2 x}dx$$

$$\Rightarrow 2I = \pi\int_0^{\pi} \frac{dx}{a^2\cos^2 x + b^2\sin^2 x}$$

Now, we know that

$$\int_0^{2a} f(x)\,dx = 2\int_0^a f(x)\,dx,$$

if $f(2a-x) = f(x)$.

Here, $a^2\cos^2(\pi-x) + b^2\sin^2(\pi-x)$

$$= a^2\cos^2 x + b^2\sin^2 x$$

$$\therefore \quad 2I = 2\pi\int_0^{\pi/2} \frac{dx}{a^2\cos^2 x + b^2\sin^2 x}$$

On dividing numerator and denominator by $\cos^2 x$, we get

$$2I = 2\pi\int_0^{\pi/2} \frac{\sec^2 x}{a^2 + b^2\tan^2 x}dx$$

Let $\tan x = t \Rightarrow \sec^2 x\,dx = dt$

Lower limit When $x = 0$, then $t = \tan 0 = 0$

Upper limit When $x = \frac{\pi}{2}$, then $t = \tan\frac{\pi}{2} = \infty$

$$\therefore \quad I = \pi\int_0^{\infty} \frac{dt}{a^2 + b^2t^2}$$

$$= \pi\int_0^{\infty} \frac{dt}{a^2 + (bt)^2} = \frac{\pi}{b^2}\int_0^{\infty} \frac{dt}{\left(\frac{a}{b}\right)^2 + t^2}$$

$$\Rightarrow \quad I = \frac{\pi}{ab}\left[\tan^{-1}\frac{bt}{a}\right]_0^{\infty} \quad \left[\because \int\frac{dx}{a^2+x^2} = \frac{1}{a}\tan^{-1}\frac{x}{a}\right]$$

$$\Rightarrow \quad I = \frac{\pi}{ab}[\tan^{-1}\infty - \tan^{-1}0]$$

$$\Rightarrow \quad I = \frac{\pi}{ab}\left[\frac{\pi}{2} - 0\right]$$

$$\left[\begin{array}{l}\because \tan^{-1}\infty = \tan^{-1}\left(\tan\frac{\pi}{2}\right) = \frac{\pi}{2} \\ \text{and } \tan^{-1}0 = \tan^{-1}(\tan 0) = 0\end{array}\right]$$

$$\therefore \quad I = \frac{\pi^2}{2ab}$$

Common Mistake

In solving the definite integral problem by substitution method, don't forget to change the limit.

Or

(ii) Let $I = \int \frac{1}{\cos^4 x + \sin^4 x}dx$

On dividing numerator and denominator by $\cos^4 x$ in RHS, we get

$$I = \int \frac{\sec^4 x}{1+\tan^4 x}dx \Rightarrow I = \int \frac{(\sec^2 x)(\sec^2 x)}{1+(\tan^2 x)^2}dx$$

$$\Rightarrow I = \int \frac{\sec^2 x(1+\tan^2 x)}{1+(\tan^2 x)^2}dx \quad [\because 1+\tan^2\theta = \sec^2\theta]$$

Let $\tan x = t \Rightarrow \sec^2 x\,dx = dt$

$$\therefore \quad I = \int \frac{1+t^2}{1+t^4}dt$$

Again, on dividing numerator and denominator by t^2 in RHS, we get

$$I = \int \frac{1+\frac{1}{t^2}}{t^2+\frac{1}{t^2}+2-2}dt = \int \frac{1+\frac{1}{t^2}}{\left(t-\frac{1}{t}\right)^2+2}dt$$

Again, let $t - \frac{1}{t} = u \Rightarrow \left(1+\frac{1}{t^2}\right)dt = du$

Then, $I = \int \frac{du}{u^2+(\sqrt{2})^2} \Rightarrow I = \frac{1}{\sqrt{2}}\tan^{-1}\left(\frac{u}{\sqrt{2}}\right) + C$

$$\left[\because \int\frac{dx}{x^2+a^2} = \frac{1}{a}\tan^{-1}\left(\frac{x}{a}\right) + C\right]$$

$$\Rightarrow \quad I = \frac{1}{\sqrt{2}}\tan^{-1}\left(\frac{t-\frac{1}{t}}{\sqrt{2}}\right) + C \quad \left[\text{putting } u = t - \frac{1}{t}\right]$$

$$\Rightarrow \quad I = \frac{1}{\sqrt{2}}\tan^{-1}\left(\frac{t^2-1}{\sqrt{2}t}\right) + C$$

$$\therefore \quad I = \frac{1}{\sqrt{2}}\tan^{-1}\left(\frac{\tan^2 x - 1}{\sqrt{2}\tan x}\right) + C$$

[putting $t = \tan x$]

13. (i) Let E_1, E_2 and E_3 be the events that the insured vehicle is a scooter, a car and a truck, respectively. Let A be the event that an insured vehicle meets an accident.

Then, $P(E_1) = \frac{3000}{3000+4000+5000} = \frac{3}{12}$,

$$P(E_2) = \frac{4000}{3000+4000+5000} = \frac{4}{12}$$

and $P(E_3) = \frac{5000}{3000+4000+5000} = \frac{5}{12}$

Also, given $P(A/E_1) = 0.02$, $P(A/E_2) = 0.03$, $P(A/E_3) = 0.04$

Probability that it is a scooter

$$= P(E_1/A) = \frac{P(E_1)\cdot P(A/E_1)}{\left[\begin{array}{l}P(E_1)\cdot P(A/E_1) + P(E_2)\cdot P(A/E_2) \\ \quad + P(E_3)\cdot P(A/E_3)\end{array}\right]}$$

$$= \frac{\frac{3}{12}\times 0.02}{\frac{3}{12}\times 0.02 + \frac{4}{12}\times 0.03 + \frac{5}{12}\times 0.04}$$

$$= \frac{0.06}{0.06 + 0.12 + 0.20} = \frac{0.06}{0.38} = \frac{3}{19}$$

Probability that it is a car

$$= P(E_2/A) = \frac{P(E_2) \cdot P(A/E_2)}{[P(E_1) \cdot P(A/E_1) + P(E_2) \cdot P(A/E_2) + P(E_3) \cdot P(A/E_3)]}$$

$$= \frac{\frac{4}{12} \times 0.03}{\frac{3}{12} \times 0.02 + \frac{4}{12} \times 0.03 + \frac{5}{12} \times 0.04}$$

$$= \frac{0.12}{0.06 + 0.12 + 0.20} = \frac{0.12}{0.38} = \frac{6}{19}$$

Probability that it is a truck

$$= P(E_3/A) = \frac{P(E_3) \cdot P(A/E_3)}{[P(E_1) \cdot P(A/E_1) + P(E_2) \cdot P(A/E_2) + P(E_3) \cdot P(A/E_3)]}$$

$$= \frac{\frac{5}{12} \times 0.04}{\frac{3}{12} \times 0.02 + \frac{4}{12} \times 0.03 + \frac{5}{12} \times 0.04}$$

$$= \frac{0.20}{0.06 + 0.12 + 0.20} = \frac{0.20}{0.38} = \frac{10}{19}$$

Or

(ii) Given, A and B are two independent events with

$$P(\overline{A} \cap B) = \frac{2}{15} \text{ and } P(A \cap \overline{B}) = \frac{1}{6}$$

We know that if A and B are independent events, then $\overline{A}$, B and A, $\overline{B}$ are independent events.

Now, $P(\overline{A} \cap B) = \frac{2}{15}$

$\Rightarrow P(B) \cdot P(\overline{A}) = \frac{2}{15}$

$\Rightarrow P(B) \cdot [1 - P(A)] = \frac{2}{15}$

$\Rightarrow P(B) - P(A) \cdot P(B) = \frac{2}{15}$ ...(i)

and $P(A \cap \overline{B}) = \frac{1}{6} \Rightarrow P(A) \cdot P(\overline{B}) = \frac{1}{6}$

$\Rightarrow P(A) \cdot [1 - P(B)] = \frac{1}{6}$

$\Rightarrow P(A) - P(A)P(B) = \frac{1}{6}$ ...(ii)

On subtracting Eq. (i) from Eq. (ii), w get

$$P(A) - P(B) = \frac{1}{6} - \frac{2}{15} = \frac{5-4}{30} = \frac{1}{30}$$

$\Rightarrow P(A) = \frac{1}{30} + P(B)$ ...(iii)

Now, substituting the value of $P(A)$ in Eq. (i), we get

$$P(B) - \left[\frac{1}{30} + P(B)\right] \cdot P(B) = \frac{2}{15}$$

Let $P(B) = x$, then

$$x - \left(\frac{1}{30} + x\right) x = \frac{2}{15}$$

$\Rightarrow 30x - (1 + 30x)x = 4$

$\Rightarrow 30x - x - 30x^2 = 4$

$\Rightarrow 30x^2 - 29x + 4 = 0$

$\Rightarrow (6x - 1)(5x - 4) = 0$

$\Rightarrow x = \frac{1}{6} \text{ or } \frac{4}{5}$ $[\because x = P(B)]$

Now, if $x = P(B) = \frac{1}{6}$, then from Eq. (iii), we get

$P(A) = \frac{1}{30} + \frac{1}{6}$

$\Rightarrow P(A) = \frac{1+5}{30} \Rightarrow P(A) = \frac{1}{5}$

and if $x = P(B) = \frac{4}{5}$, then from Eq. (iii), we get

$P(A) = \frac{1}{30} + \frac{4}{5} = \frac{1+24}{30}$

$\Rightarrow P(A) = \frac{5}{6}$

14. We have, radius, $OC = r$

$OB = x$, $BC = y$

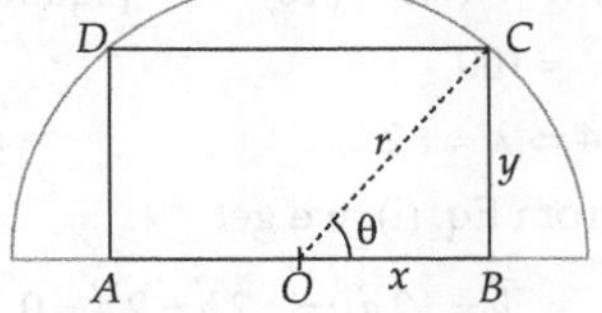

(i) In ΔOBC,

$\sin\theta = \frac{y}{r}$ and $\cos\theta = \frac{x}{r}$

$\Rightarrow y = r\sin\theta$ and $x = r\cos\theta$

$\therefore (x, y) = (r\cos\theta, r\sin\theta)$

(ii) Area of rectangle is given by

$A = l \times b$

$= 2x \times y = 2xy$

$= 2(r\cos\theta)(r\sin\theta)$

$= 2r^2 \sin\theta\cos\theta$

$= r^2 \sin 2\theta$

(iii) Now, we have $A = r^2 \sin 2\theta$

On differentiating w.r.t. θ two times, we get

$$\frac{dA}{d\theta} = r^2 (\cos 2\theta \cdot 2) = 2\cos 2\theta \cdot r^2$$

and $\frac{d^2A}{d\theta^2} = 2r^2(-\sin 2\theta)2 = -4r^2 \sin 2\theta$

For maxima, put $\frac{dA}{d\theta} = 0$

$\Rightarrow \quad 2\cos 2\theta \cdot r^2 = 0 \Rightarrow \cos 2\theta = 0$

$\Rightarrow \quad 2\theta = \frac{\pi}{2} \Rightarrow \theta = \frac{\pi}{4} \quad \left[\because \cos\frac{\pi}{2} = 0\right]$

For this value of θ, we have $\frac{d^2A}{d\theta^2} = -4r^2 < 0$

$\therefore$ A is maximum at $\theta = \frac{\pi}{4}$

(iv) We have, a A has maximum value at $\theta = \pi/4$

$\therefore$ Length $= 2x = 2r\cos\theta = 2r\cos\frac{\pi}{4} = \sqrt{2}\,r$

and breadth $= y = r\sin\theta = r\sin\frac{\pi}{4} = \frac{1}{\sqrt{2}}r$

15. (i) (b) We have, $\vec{n} = \hat{i} + 2\hat{j} + 3\hat{k}$

$\therefore$ Required unit vector, $\hat{n} = \frac{\hat{i} + 2\hat{j} + 3\hat{k}}{\sqrt{1^2 + 2^2 + 3^2}}$

$= \frac{\hat{i}}{\sqrt{14}} + \frac{2\hat{j}}{\sqrt{14}} + \frac{3\hat{k}}{\sqrt{14}} = \frac{1}{\sqrt{14}}(\hat{i} + 2\hat{j} + 3\hat{k})$

(ii) (c) Given that $\vec{b}$ is collinear with the vector $\vec{a}$ and $\vec{a} = (2\sqrt{2}, -1, 4)$ i.e. $\vec{a} = 2\sqrt{2}i - j + 4k$.

$\therefore \quad \vec{b} = \lambda\vec{a} = 2\sqrt{2}\,\lambda\hat{i} - \lambda\hat{j} + 4\lambda\hat{k} \quad \ldots(i)$

Also given, $|\vec{b}| = 10$

$\Rightarrow \sqrt{[(2)\sqrt{2}\lambda]^2 + (-\lambda)^2 + (4\lambda)^2} = 10$

$\Rightarrow 8\lambda^2 + \lambda^2 + 16\lambda^2 = (10)^2$ [square both sides]

$\Rightarrow 25\lambda^2 = 100$

$\Rightarrow \lambda^2 = 4 \Rightarrow \lambda = \pm 2$

Then, from Eq. (i), we get

$\vec{b} = \pm 2\vec{a} \Rightarrow 2\vec{b} \pm 2\vec{a} = 0$

(iii) (c) Given, $|\vec{a}\cdot\vec{b}| = |\vec{a}\times\vec{b}|$

$\Rightarrow \quad |\vec{a}||\vec{b}|\cos\theta = |\vec{a}||\vec{b}|\sin\theta \quad [\because |\hat{n}| = 1]$

$\Rightarrow \quad \cos\theta = \sin\theta \Rightarrow \tan\theta = 1$

$\Rightarrow \quad \tan\theta = \tan\frac{\pi}{4} \quad \left[\because 1 = \tan\frac{\pi}{4}\right]$

$\Rightarrow \quad \theta = \frac{\pi}{4}$

Hence, the angle between $\vec{a}$ and $\vec{b}$ is $\frac{\pi}{4}$.

(iv) By triangle law of vector addition, we get

$\overrightarrow{AB} + \overrightarrow{BC} = \overrightarrow{AC}$

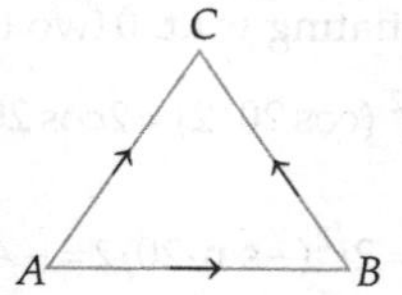

$\Rightarrow \quad \overrightarrow{AB} + \overrightarrow{BC} + \overrightarrow{CA} = \overrightarrow{CA} + \overrightarrow{AC}$

$\Rightarrow \quad \overrightarrow{AB} + \overrightarrow{BC} + \overrightarrow{CA} = \overrightarrow{CA} - \overrightarrow{CA} \quad [\because \overrightarrow{AC} = -\overrightarrow{CA}]$

$\Rightarrow \quad \overrightarrow{AB} + \overrightarrow{BC} + \overrightarrow{CA} = \vec{0}$

(v) Given equation of line is $5x - 25 = 14 - 7y = 35z$

$\Rightarrow \quad \frac{x-5}{1/5} = \frac{2-y}{1/7} = \frac{z}{1/35}$

$\Rightarrow \quad \frac{x-5}{1/5} = \frac{y-2}{-1/7} = \frac{z}{1/35}$

$\Rightarrow$ Now, direction ratios of the given line are $\frac{1}{5}, -\frac{1}{7}, \frac{1}{35}$.

Then, direction ratios of a line parallel to the given line are $\frac{1}{5}, -\frac{1}{7}, \frac{1}{35}$.

Hence, the required equation of a line passing through the point $A(1, 2, -1)$ and parallel to the given line is $\frac{x-1}{1/5} = \frac{y-2}{-1/7} = \frac{z+1}{1/35}$.

Common Mistake

In finding the direction ratio of a line in cartesian form don't forget to convert the cartesian form of equation of line into standard form.

16. (i) We have, $\vec{a} = 3\hat{i} + 5\hat{j} - 2\hat{k}$ and $\vec{b} = 2\hat{i} + \hat{j} + 3\hat{k}$

Now, $\vec{a}\times\vec{b} = \begin{vmatrix} \hat{i} & \hat{j} & \hat{k} \\ 3 & 5 & -2 \\ 2 & 1 & 3 \end{vmatrix}$

$= \hat{i}(15 + 2) - \hat{j}(9 + 4) + \hat{k}(3 - 10)$

$= 17\hat{i} - 13\hat{j} - 7\hat{k}$

$\therefore \quad |\vec{a}\times\vec{b}| = \sqrt{289 + 169 + 49} = \sqrt{507} = 13\sqrt{3}$

Or

(ii) Let ABC be a triangle, where $\overrightarrow{BC} = \vec{a}$, $\overrightarrow{CA} = \vec{b}$ and $\overrightarrow{AB} = \vec{c}$

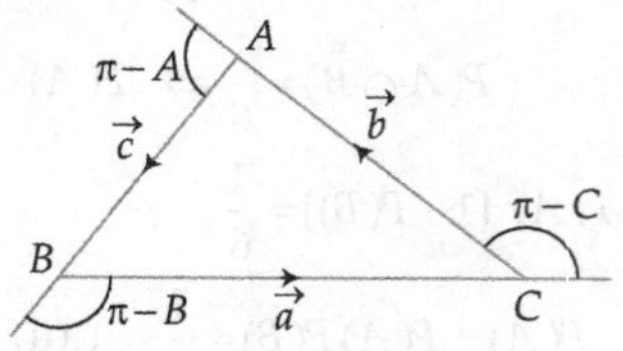

Then, $\quad \overrightarrow{BC} + \overrightarrow{CA} = \overrightarrow{BA}$ [triangle law of addition]

$\Rightarrow \quad \overrightarrow{BC} + \overrightarrow{CA} = -\overrightarrow{AB}$

$\Rightarrow \quad \overrightarrow{CA} + \overrightarrow{AB} = -\overrightarrow{BC} \Rightarrow \vec{b} + \vec{c} = -\vec{a}$

$\Rightarrow \quad (\vec{b} + \vec{c})^2 = (-\vec{a})$ [square both sides]

$\Rightarrow \quad |\vec{b}|^2 + |\vec{c}|^2 + 2\vec{b}\cdot\vec{c} = |\vec{a}|^2$

$[\because \vec{a}\cdot\vec{a} = |\vec{a}|^2 = a^2 \text{ and } \vec{a}\cdot\vec{b} = \vec{b}\cdot\vec{a}]$

$\Rightarrow \quad b^2 + c^2 + 2|\vec{b}|\,|\vec{c}|\cos(\pi - A) = a^2$

[by definition of scalar product of two vectors]

$\Rightarrow \quad b^2 + c^2 - 2bc\cos A = a^2$

$\Rightarrow \quad 2bc\cos A = b^2 + c^2 - a^2$

$\Rightarrow \quad \cos A = \dfrac{b^2 + c^2 - a^2}{2bc}$ **Hence proved.**

17. (i) Let the equation of variable plane is

$$\frac{x}{a} + \frac{y}{b} + \frac{z}{c} = 1 \quad \ldots(i)$$

Clearly, above plane (i) meets the X-axis, Y-axis and Z-axis at the points $A(a, 0, 0)$, $B(0, b, 0)$ and $C(0, 0, c)$, respectively.

Now, let (α, β, γ) be the coordinates of the centroid of ΔABC.

Then, $\alpha = \dfrac{a+0+0}{3}, \beta = \dfrac{0+b+0}{3}$ and $\gamma = \dfrac{0+0+c}{3}$

$\Rightarrow \quad \alpha = \dfrac{a}{3}, \beta = \dfrac{b}{3}$ and $\gamma = \dfrac{c}{3}$

$\Rightarrow \quad a = 3\alpha, b = 3\beta$ and $c = 3\gamma \quad \ldots(ii)$

$\because p =$ Length of the perpendicular from $(0, 0, 0)$ to the plane (i)

$$\therefore \quad p = \frac{\left|\frac{0}{a} + \frac{0}{b} + \frac{0}{c} - 1\right|}{\sqrt{\frac{1}{a^2} + \frac{1}{b^2} + \frac{1}{c^2}}}$$

$$\Rightarrow \quad p = \frac{1}{\sqrt{\frac{1}{a^2} + \frac{1}{b^2} + \frac{1}{c^2}}} \Rightarrow \frac{1}{p} = \sqrt{\frac{1}{a^2} + \frac{1}{b^2} + \frac{1}{c^2}}$$

$$\Rightarrow \quad \frac{1}{p^2} = \frac{1}{a^2} + \frac{1}{b^2} + \frac{1}{c^2}$$

$$\Rightarrow \quad \frac{1}{p^2} = \frac{1}{(3\alpha)^2} + \frac{1}{(3\beta)^2} + \frac{1}{(3\gamma)^2} \quad \text{[using Eq. (ii)]}$$

$$\Rightarrow \quad \frac{1}{p^2} = \frac{1}{9\alpha^2} + \frac{1}{9\beta^2} + \frac{1}{9\gamma^2}$$

$$\Rightarrow \quad \frac{9}{p^2} = \frac{1}{\alpha^2} + \frac{1}{\beta^2} + \frac{1}{\gamma^2}$$

Hence, the locus of centroid is

$$\frac{1}{x^2} + \frac{1}{y^2} + \frac{1}{z^2} = \frac{9}{p^2}$$

Or

(ii) Given equation of line is $\dfrac{x+2}{3} = \dfrac{y+1}{2} = \dfrac{z-3}{2}$

We find any random point on the line as follows

$$\frac{x+2}{3} = \frac{y+1}{2} = \frac{z-3}{2} = \lambda \text{ (say)}$$

$$\Rightarrow \quad \frac{x+2}{3} = \lambda, \frac{y+1}{2} = \lambda \text{ and } \frac{z-3}{2} = \lambda$$

$$\Rightarrow \quad x = 3\lambda - 2, y = 2\lambda - 1 \text{ and } z = 2\lambda + 3$$

So, the required point will be of the form,

$$Q(3\lambda - 2, 2\lambda - 1, 2\lambda + 3) \quad \ldots(i)$$

Now, given that distance between two points $P(1, 3, 3)$ and $Q(3\lambda - 2, 2\lambda - 1, 2\lambda + 3)$ is 5 units i.e. $PQ = 5$

$$\Rightarrow \sqrt{[(3\lambda - 2 - 1)^2 + (2\lambda - 1 - 3)^2 + (2\lambda + 3 - 3)^2]} = 5$$

$$[\because \text{Distance} = \sqrt{(x_2 - x_1)^2 + (y_2 - y_1)^2 + (z_2 - z_1)^2}]$$

$$\Rightarrow \quad \sqrt{(3\lambda - 3)^2 + (2\lambda - 4)^2 + (2\lambda)^2} = 5$$

On squaring both sides, we get

$$(3\lambda - 3)^2 + (2\lambda - 4)^2 + (2\lambda)^2 = 25$$

$$\Rightarrow 9\lambda^2 + 9 - 18\lambda + 4\lambda^2 + 16 - 16\lambda + 4\lambda^2 = 25$$

$$\Rightarrow \quad 17\lambda^2 - 34\lambda = 0$$

$$\Rightarrow \quad 17\lambda(\lambda - 2) = 0$$

$\Rightarrow$ Either $17\lambda = 0$ or $\lambda - 2 = 0 \Rightarrow \lambda = 0$ or 2

On putting $\lambda = 0$ and $\lambda = 2$ in Eq .(i), we get the required points as $Q(-2, -1, 3)$ or $Q(4, 3, 7)$.

18. Given, equation of the parabola is

$$y^2 = x \quad \ldots(i)$$

It represents a right hand parabola with vertex at (0, 0).

The given line is $y + x = 6$

i.e. $\quad x = 6 - y \quad \ldots(ii)$

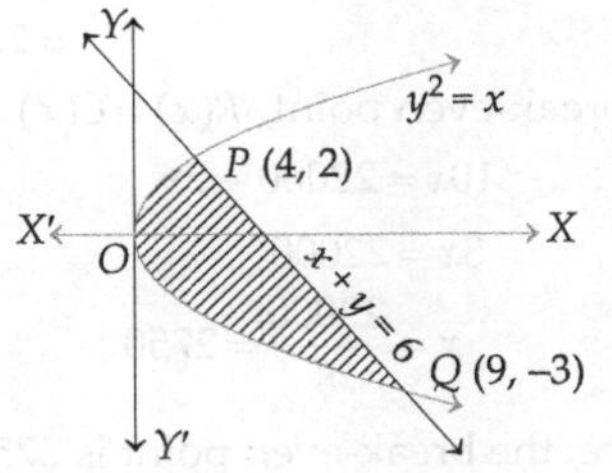

From Eqs. (i) and (ii), we get

$$y^2 = 6 - y$$

$$\Rightarrow \quad y^2 + y - 6 = 0$$

$$\Rightarrow \quad (y - 2)(y + 3) = 0 \Rightarrow y = 2 \text{ or } -3$$

When $y = 2$, then $x = 4$ and when $y = -3$, then $x = 9$ [using Eq. (i)]

Thus, the points of intersection of parabola and line are $P(4, 2)$ and $Q(9, -3)$.

$\therefore$ Required area = Area of the shaded region

$$= \int_{-3}^{2} (x_2 - x_1)\,dy$$

$$= \int_{-3}^{2} [(6 - y) - y^2]\,dy = \left[6y - \frac{y^2}{2} - \frac{y^3}{3}\right]_{-3}^{2}$$

$$= 12 - 2 - \frac{8}{3} + 18 + \frac{9}{2} - \frac{27}{3}$$

$$= 28 + \frac{9}{2} - \frac{35}{3} = \frac{125}{6} \text{ sq units}$$

19. (i) (a) Given that fixed cost is ₹ 35000 and variable cost is ₹ 500 per unit

$\therefore$ Total cost = Fixed cost + Variable cost per unit

$\Rightarrow \quad C(x) = 35000 + 500x$

Also, given $R(x) = 5000x - 100x^2$

$\therefore$ Profit function, $P(x) = R(x) - C(x)$

$= 5000x - 100x^2 - 35000 - 500x$

$= 4500x - 100x^2 - 35000$

(ii) (b) If the lines of regression are parallel to coordinate axes, then the coefficient of correlation is zero.

(iii) We have, $b_{yx} = 1.8$ and $b_{xy} = 0.8$

Now, $r^2 = b_{yx} \times b_{xy} = 1.8 \times 0.8 = 1.44 > 1$

Since, r^2 must be ≤ 1.

Therefore, the given statement is false.

(iv) Given, fixed cost of the commodity = ₹ 22000

Let the number of units produced by company be x and p be the price per unit.

The total revenue, $R = xp = 10x$

Since, the variable cost is 20% of the total revenue.

Therefore, variable cost = 20% of $10x = \frac{20}{100} \times 10x$

$= ₹\, 2x$

Total cost $C(x)$ = Fixed cost of the commodity + Variable cost of the commodity

$= 22000 + 2x$

For break-even point, $R(x) = C(x)$

$\Rightarrow \quad 10x = 22000 + 2x$

$\Rightarrow \quad 8x = 22000$

$\Rightarrow \quad x = \frac{22000}{8} = 2750$

Hence, the break-even point is 2750.

(v) Given, total fixed cost = ₹ 5000

Variable cost of producing one unit = ₹30

Let x be the number of units produced.

Then, total cost, TC = ₹ $(5000 + 30x)$

Total cost of producing 10 units $= 5000 + 30 \times 10$

$= ₹\, 5300$

$\therefore$ Average cost of producing 10 units $= ₹\frac{5300}{10}$

$= ₹\, 530$

20. (i) Given, $x = \frac{b-p}{a} \Rightarrow p = b - ax$

Then, total revenue (TR) = px

$= (b - ax)x = bx - ax^2$

(a) Average revenue (AR) $= \frac{TR}{x} = \frac{bx - ax^2}{x} = b - ax$

$\therefore$ Slope of AR curve $= \frac{d}{dx}(\text{AR})$

$= \frac{d}{dx}(b - ax) = -a \ldots$(i)

(b) Now, marginal revenue (MR) curve

$= \frac{d\,(\text{TR})}{dx}$

$= \frac{d}{dx}(bx - ax^2) = b - 2ax$

$\therefore$ Slope of MR curve $= \frac{d}{dx}(b - 2ax)$

$= -2a \quad \ldots$(ii)

Or

(ii) Given, $C(x) = 4x^3 - 2x + 6$

(a) Average Cost (AC) $= \frac{C(x)}{x} = \frac{4x^3 - 2x + 6}{x}$

$= 4x^2 - 2 + \frac{6}{x}$

(b) Marginal Cost (MC) $= \frac{d}{dx}[(Cx)]$

$= \frac{d}{dx}[4x^3 - 2x + 6]$

$= 12x^2 - 2$

21. Given observations in table form are

x	1	2	3	4	5	6	7	8	9	$\Sigma x = 45$
y	4	8	2	12	10	14	16	6	18	$\Sigma y = 90$
x^2	1	4	9	16	25	36	49	64	81	$\Sigma x^2 = 285$
xy	4	16	6	48	50	84	112	48	162	$\Sigma xy = 530$

Here, $n = 9$

$\therefore \bar{x} = \frac{\Sigma x}{n} = \frac{45}{9} = 5, \bar{y} = \frac{\Sigma y}{n} = \frac{90}{9} = 10$

$$b_{yx} = \frac{\Sigma xy - \frac{1}{n}\Sigma x \cdot \Sigma y}{\Sigma x^2 - \frac{1}{n}(\Sigma x)^2}$$

$$= \frac{530 - \frac{1}{9}(45)(90)}{285 - \frac{1}{9}(45)^2}$$

$$= \frac{530 - 450}{285 - 225} = \frac{80}{60} = \frac{4}{3}$$

$\therefore$ The equation of regression line of y on x is

$y - \bar{y} = b_{yx}(x - \bar{x})$

$\Rightarrow \quad y - 10 = \frac{4}{3}(x - 5)$

$\Rightarrow \quad 4x - 3y + 10 = 0,$

which is the required equation of regression line.

The table for line $4x - 3y + 10 = 0$ or $y = \frac{4x + 10}{3}$ is

x	0	2
y	10/3	6

Plot the points (0, 10/3) and (2, 6), and join them to get the line of regression as below

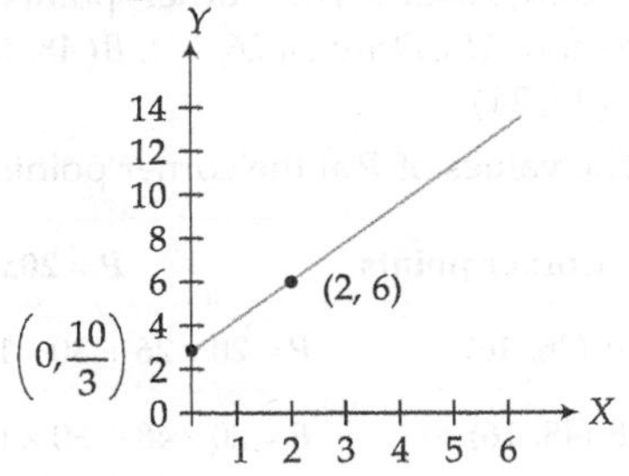

22. (i) Given, minimise $Z = x + y$

Subject to constraints

$$3x + 2y \geq 12 \quad \text{...(i)}$$

$$x + 3y \geq 11 \quad \text{...(ii)}$$

and $$x \geq 0, y \geq 0 \quad \text{...(iii)}$$

Table for line $3x + 2y = 12$ is

x	0	4
y	6	0

So, the line $3x + 2y = 12$ is passing through the points $(0, 6)$ and $(4, 0)$.

On putting $(0, 0)$ in the inequality $3x + 2y \geq 12$, we get $0 + 0 \geq 12$, which is not true.

So, the half plane is away from the origin.

Table for line $x + 3y = 11$ is

x	2	11
y	3	0

So, the line $x + 3y = 11$ is passing through the points $(2, 3)$ and $(11, 0)$.

On putting $(0, 0)$ in the inequality $x + 3y \geq 11$, we get $0 + 0 \geq 11$, which is not true.

So, the half plane is away from the origin.

Also, $x \geq 0$ and $y \geq 0$, so the region lies in I quadrant.

The intersection point of lines corresponding to Eqs. (i) and (ii) is $B(2, 3)$.

Now, plot all the inequalities on the graph paper as shown below. The shaded region represents the feasible region. The corner points of the boundary of the graph ABD are $A(0, 6)$, $B(2, 3)$ and $D(11, 0)$.

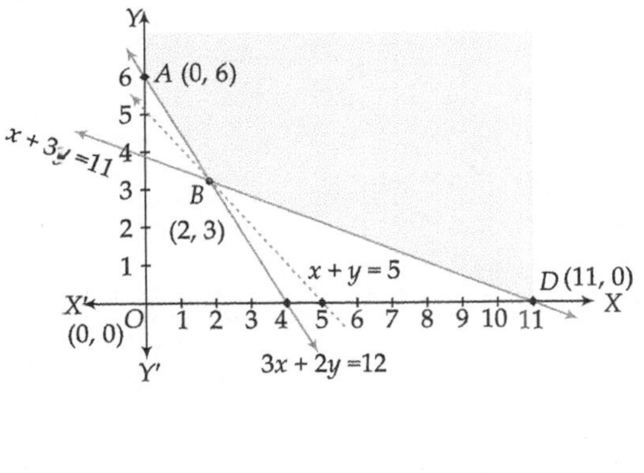

The values of Z at corner points are given below

Corner points	$Z = x + y$
$A(0, 6)$	$Z = 0 + 6 = 6$
$B(2, 3)$	$Z = 2 + 3 = 5$ (Minimum)
$D(11, 0)$	$Z = 11 + 0 = 11$

Thus, the minimum value of Z is 5 at the point $B(2, 3)$.

As the feasible region is unbounded, therefore 5 may or may not be the minimum value of Z. For this, we draw a dotted graph of the inequality $x + y < 5$ and check whether the resulting half plane has points in common with a feasible region or not. It can be seen that the feasible region has no common point with $x + y < 5$. Therefore, the minimum value of Z is 5 at $B(2, 3)$.

Or

(ii) Let x and y be the number of units manufactured of products A and B, respectively.
Then, total profit, $P = 20x + 30y$ (in ₹).

Now, the problem can be formulated as an LPP as follows

Maximise $P = 20x + 30y$

Subject to the constraints,

$200x + 300y \geq 10000$ i.e. $2x + 3y \geq 100$ [turnover constraint]

$\frac{1}{2}x + 1 \cdot y \leq 40$ [time constraint]

i.e. $x + 2y \leq 80$

$x \geq 14, y \geq 16$, product constraints $x \geq 0, y \geq 0$

Table for line $2x + 3y = 100$ or $y = \frac{100 - 2x}{3}$ is

x	0	50
y	100/3	0

So, the line passes through the points (0, 100/3) and (50, 0).

Put (0, 0) in the inequality $2x + 3y \geq 100$, we get

$0 + 0 \geq 100$ [false]

So, the half plane is away from the origin.

Table for line $x + 2y = 80$ or $y = \frac{80 - x}{2}$ is

x	0	80
y	40	0

So, the line passes through the points (0, 40) and (80, 0).

Put (0, 0) in the inequality $x + 2y \leq 80$, we get

$0 + 0 \leq 80$ [true]

So, the half plane is towards the origin.

Now, line $x = 14$ is perpendicular to the X-axis.

Put (0, 0) in the inequality $x \geq 14$, we get

$0 \geq 14$ [false]

So, the half plane is away from the origin.

Now, line $y = 16$ is perpendicular to the Y-axis.

Put (0, 0) in the inequality $y \geq 16$, we get

$0 \geq 16$ [false]

So, the half plane is away from the origin.

The points of intersection of given lines are $A(26, 16)$, $B(48, 16)$, $C(14, 33)$ and $D(14, 24)$.

Now, plot all the inequalities on a graph paper as shown below

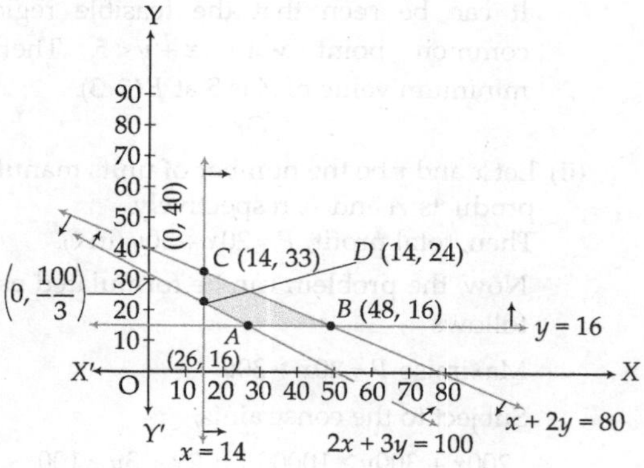

The shaded region shows the bounded feasible region $ABCD$. The corner points of the feasible region $ABCD$ are $A(26, 16)$, $B(48, 16)$, $C(14, 33)$ and $D(14, 24)$.

The values of P at the corner points are

Corner points	$P = 20x + 30y$
A (26, 16)	$P = 20 \times 26 + 30 \times 16 = 1000$
B (48, 16)	$P = 20 \times 48 + 30 \times 16 = 1440$ (maximum)
C (14, 33)	$P = 20 \times 14 + 30 \times 33 = 1270$
D (14, 24)	$P = 20 \times 14 + 30 \times 24 = 1000$

Thus, maximum value of P is 1440 at the point B (48, 16)

Hence, the manufacturer should produce 48 units of product A and 16 units of product B to get the maximum profit of ₹ 1440.

SQP Code : **PB-8/15** Series **i-Succeed 8-25/15** Roll No.

Sample Question Paper 08

Mathematics 12th (Code 860)

General Instructions

1. The Question Paper consists of three sections A, B and C.
2. Candidates are required to attempt all questions from Section A and all questions either from Section B Or Section C.
3. Section A Internal choice has been provided in two questions of two marks each, two questions of four marks each and two questions of six marks each.
4. Section B Internal choice has been provided in one questions of two marks and one question of four marks.
5. Section C Internal choice has been provided in one question of two marks and one question of four marks.
6. All working, including rough work, should be done on the same sheet as, and adjacent to the rest of the answer.
7. The intended marks for questions or parts of questions are given in brackets [].
8. Mathematical tables and graph papers are provided.

Time : 3 Hrs.

Max. Marks : 80

Section A (65 Marks)

1. In subparts (i) to (x) choose the correct options and in subparts (xi) to (xv), answer the questions as instructed.

(i) The function $f(x) = 4x^3 - 18x^2 + 27x - 7$ is always .... on R. • *Analysis* [1]

(a) increasing (b) decreasing

(c) strictly decreasing (d) None of these

(ii) If $P(A) = \frac{2}{5}$, $P(B) = \frac{3}{10}$ and $P(A \cap B) = \frac{1}{5}$, then $P(A'/B)$ is equal to • *Application* [1]

(a) $\frac{5}{6}$ (b) $\frac{5}{7}$

(c) $\frac{25}{42}$ (d) 1

(iii) **Assertion** (A) $\int_0^{\pi} \sin^{50} x \cos^{49} x\, dx$ is equal to 0.

Reason (R) By properties of definite integral, $\int_0^a f(x)dx = \int_0^a f(a-x)dx$. • *Analysis* [1]

(a) Both A and R are correct and R is the correct explanation of A.

(b) Both A and R are correct and R is not the correct explanation of A.

(c) A is correct but R is incorrect.

(d) A is incorrect but R is correct.

(iv) If $\tan^{-1}\left(\frac{3}{4}\right) = A$, then $\cos A$ is equal to • *Understanding* [1]

(a) $\frac{3}{5}$ (b) $\frac{4}{5}$ (c) $\frac{4}{3}$ (d) $\frac{5}{4}$

(v) **Statement I** The general solution of $e^x \cos y dx - e^x \sin y dy = 0$ is $e^x \cos y = K$.

Statement II The general solution of the differential equation is the relation between the variables x and y which is obtained after removing the derivatives when the relation constant arbitrary constant to denote the order of an equation. • *Analysis* [1]

(a) Both Statements I and II are true.

(b) Both Statements I and II are false.

(c) Statement I is true but II is false.

(d) Statement II is true but I is false.

(vi) Given below are the graphs of $f(x)$ along with the statements. Which one of the following statement is correct about the graphs? • *Application* [1]

(a)

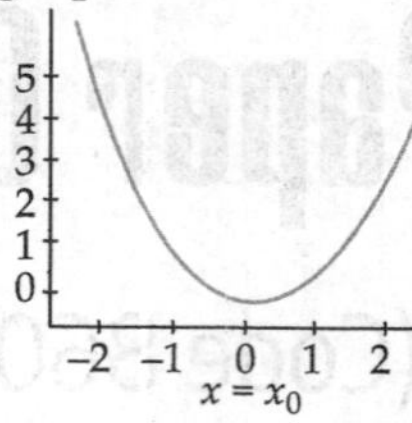

$\lim_{x \to x_0^-} f(x) \neq \lim_{x \to x_0^+} f(x)$

(b)

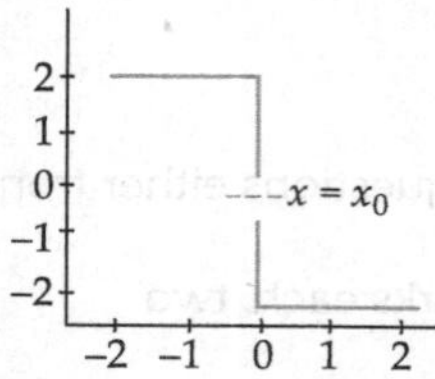

The function $f(x)$ is continuous at $x = x_0$.

(c)

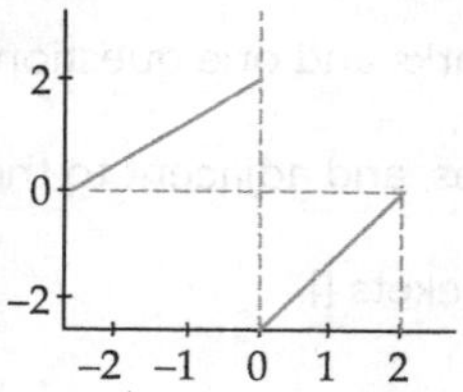

$\lim_{x \to x_0^+} f(x) \neq \lim_{x \to x_0^-} f(x)$

(d)

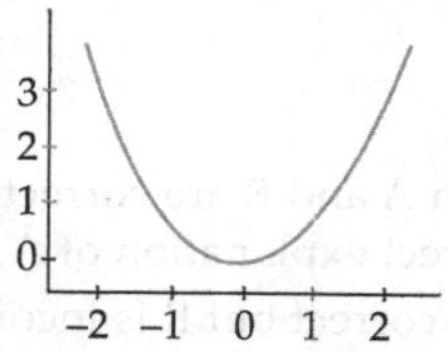

$f(x)$ is not continuous.

(vii) The graph of the function is given below. • *Application* [1]

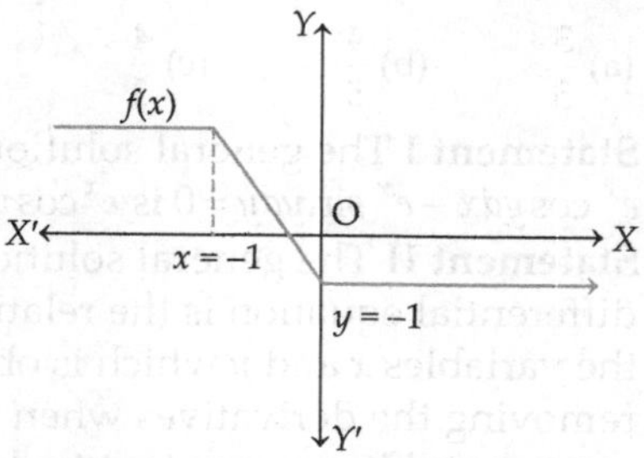

Choose the correct option.

(a) The function $f(x)$ is continuous for all values of x except $x = 0$.

(b) The function $f(x)$ is continuous for all values of x.

(c) The function is discontinuous for all values of x.

(d) The function is differentiable but not continuous.

(viii) If $x = at^2$ and $y = 2at$, then $\frac{dy}{dx}$ is equal to • *Understanding* [1]

(a) t (b) $1/t$

(c) $\frac{-1}{t^2}$ (d) None of these

(ix) **Statement I** Method of integration by parts does not work for $\int \sqrt{x} \sin x \, dx$.

Statement II It is not possible to find the derivative of $\sqrt{x}$.

Choose the correct option. • *Analysis* [1]

(a) Both the statements are correct; Statement II is the correct explanation of Statement I.

(b) Both the statements are correct; Statement II is not the correct explanation of Statement I.

(c) Statement I is correct; Statement II is incorrect

(d) Statement II is correct; Statement I is incorrect

(x) **Assertion** (A) If $f(x) = \frac{\sin(ax+b)}{\cos(cx+d)}$, then

$f'(x) = a\cos(ax+b)\sec(cx+d) + c\sin(ax+b)\tan(cx+d)\sec(cx+d)$.

Reason (R) If $f(x) = \frac{u}{v}$, then

$f'(x) = \frac{vu' - uv'}{v^2}$

Choose the correct option. • *Analysis* [1]

(a) Both A and R are correct; R is the correct explanation of A

(b) Both A and R are correct; R is not the correct explanation of A

(c) A is correct; R is incorrect

(d) R is correct; A is incorrect

(xi) Solve $\int a^{5\log_a x} dx$. • *Evaluate* [1]

(xii) Find the values of a and b, if $A = B$, where $A = \begin{bmatrix} a+4 & 3b \\ 8 & -6 \end{bmatrix}$ and $B = \begin{bmatrix} 2a+2 & b^2+2 \\ 8 & b^2-5b \end{bmatrix}$. • *Evaluate* [1]

(xiii) If $y = Ae^{5x} + Be^{-5x}$, then prove that $\frac{d^2y}{dx^2} - 25y = 0$. • *Analysis* [1]

(xiv) Find the value of $\tan^{-1}\left(\tan\frac{2\pi}{3}\right)$.
• *Recall* [1]

(xv) Find the order and degree of the differential equation $\frac{dy}{dx} + \tan x = 0$.
• *Recall* [1]

2. (i) The table below shows some of the values of differentiable functions f and g and their derivatives.

x	$f(x)$	$f'(x)$	$g(x)$	$g'(x)$
1	3	1	4	8
3	5	16	3	9
4	1	5	5	10
5	4	4	1	15

If $h(x) = f[g(x)]$, then find $h'(3)$.
• *Understanding*

Or

(ii) A company's profit $p(x)$, in thousands of dollars, as a function of the amount of money spent on advertising x, in thousands of dollars, is given by $p(x) = -2x^3 + 15x^2 + 36x - 100$. Find the interval where the profit is decreasing. • *Analysis* [2]

3. Solve the differential equation $(1-\cos 2x)dy + (1+\cos 2y)\,dx = 0$.
• *Application* [2]

4. Write the value of $\tan^{-1}\left(\tan\frac{3\pi}{4}\right)$. • *Recall* [2]

5. Find minors and cofactors of all the elements of the determinant $\begin{vmatrix} 3 & -2 \\ 1 & 4 \end{vmatrix}$.
• *Recall* [2]

6. (i) If $A = \begin{bmatrix} 3 & 1 \\ -1 & 2 \end{bmatrix}$ and $I = \begin{bmatrix} 1 & 0 \\ 0 & 1 \end{bmatrix}$, then find λ so that $A^2 = 5A + \lambda I$. [2]

Or

(ii) Find the values of a, b and c, if $\begin{bmatrix} a+b+c \\ a+c \\ b+c \end{bmatrix} = \begin{bmatrix} 6 \\ 5 \\ 3 \end{bmatrix}$. [2]

7. The table below shows the probability distribution of a random variable X which represents the number of defective items found in a sample of 4 items selected from a production line.

X (Number of defective items)	0	1	2	3	4
P(X)	0.41	0.37	K	0.05	0.01

Find the value of K, then find the probability that there are at most of 2 defective items in the sample. • *Evaluate* [4]

8. Using properties of determinants, prove that $\begin{vmatrix} 1 & a & a^3 \\ 1 & b & b^3 \\ 1 & c & c^3 \end{vmatrix} = (a-b)(b-c)(c-a)(a+b+c)$
• *Application* [4]

9. (i) Show that the relation S in set $A = \{x \in Z : 0 \le x \le 12\}$ given by $S = \{(a, b) : a, b \in A, |a-b| \text{ is divisible by } 4\}$ is an equivalence relation. Find the set of all elements related to 1. • *Analysis* [4]

Or

(ii) Show that $f : N \to N$, given by $f(x) = \begin{cases} x+1, & \text{if } x \text{ is odd} \\ x-1, & \text{if } x \text{ is even} \end{cases}$ is bijective (both one-one and onto). • *Analysis* [4]

10. (i) Consider the function $f(x) = [x(x-2)]^2$. Answer the following questions.

(a) Differentiate the given function with respect to x.
(b) Find the critical points.
(c) Find the interval at which the function is strictly increasing.
(d) Find the interval at which the function is strictly decreasing. • *Application* [4]

Or

(ii) Consider the function $f(x) = \sin x + \cos x$, $x \in \left(0, \frac{\pi}{2}\right)$

Answer the following questions.

(a) Find $f'(x)$.
(b) Find the critical points.
(c) Find interval(s) in which the function $f(x) = \sin x + \cos x$, $x \in \left(0, \frac{\pi}{2}\right)$ is strictly increasing or decreasing. • *Application* [4]

SP-08

11. Consider a scenario, a right angled triangle with constant area S and the length of hypotenuse is l as show in figure.

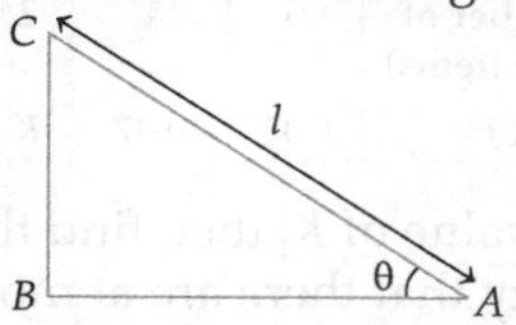

Based on the above information, answer the following questions. • *Application* [6]

(i) Establish a relation between l, S and θ.

(ii) Find the point at which hypotenuse is least.

(iii) Prove that the hypotenuse of the triangle is least when tiangle is isosceles.

12. (i) Find $\int \dfrac{\sin^{-1}\sqrt{x}-\cos^{-1}\sqrt{x}}{\sin^{-1}\sqrt{x}+\cos^{-1}\sqrt{x}}\,dx, x \in [0, 1]$. • *Evaluate* [6]

Or (ii) Evaluate $\int \dfrac{\tan x+\tan^3 x}{1+\tan^3 x}\,dx$. • *Evaluate* [6]

13. (i) Suppose a girl throws a die. If she gets 5 or 6, she tosses a coin 3 times and notes the number of heads. If she gets 1, 2, 3 or 4, she tosses a coin once and notes whether a head or tail is obtained. If she obtained exactly one head, then what is the probability that she threw 1, 2, 3 or 4 with the die? • *Application* [6]

Or

(ii) Two dice are thrown together and the total score is noted. The events A, B and C are 'a total of 4', 'a total of 9 or more' and 'a total divisible by 5', respectively. Calculate $P(A)$, $P(B)$ and $P(C)$ and decide which pairs of events, if any are independent? • *Application* [6]

14. Consider the following function.

$$f(x)=\begin{cases} x, & \text{if } x \le 1 \\ 5, & \text{if } x > 1 \end{cases}$$

Based on the above information, answer the following questions. • *Application* [6]

(i) Check whether the given function is continuous at $x=0$.

(ii) Prove that f is discontinuous at $x=1$.

(iii) Prove that f is continuous at $x=2$.

Section B (15 Marks)

15. In subparts (i) to (iii) choose the correct options and in subparts (iv) and (v), answer the questions as instructed. [5]

(i) The value of λ for which the vectors $3\hat{i}-6\hat{j}+\hat{k}$ and $2\hat{i}-4\hat{j}+\lambda\hat{k}$ are parallel, is • *Understanding*

(a) $\frac{2}{3}$ (b) $\frac{3}{2}$ (c) $\frac{5}{2}$ (d) $\frac{2}{5}$

(ii) The vector equation of a plane passing through a point having position vector $\hat{i}+\hat{j}-\hat{k}$ and perpendicular to the vector $\hat{i}-\hat{j}+\hat{k}$ is • *Understanding*

(a) $\vec{r}\cdot(\hat{i}+\hat{j}+\hat{k})=1$ (b) $\vec{r}\cdot(\hat{i}-\hat{j}+\hat{k})=-1$

(c) $\vec{r}\cdot(\hat{i}+\hat{j}+\hat{k})=-1$ (d) None of these

(iii) If $\vec{a}=2\hat{i}+3\hat{j}-4\hat{k}$ and $\vec{b}=5\hat{i}+2\hat{j}+3\hat{k}$, Then,

Statement I The value of $\vec{a}\cdot\vec{b}$ is 4.

Statement II The value of $\vec{a}\times\vec{b}$ is $17\hat{i}-6\hat{j}+11\hat{k}$. • *Understanding*

Choose the correct option.

(a) Only Statement I is true.

(b) Only Statement II is true.

(c) Both Statements I and II are true.

(d) Neither Statement I nor Statement II is true.

(iv) Find the angle between pair of lines $\vec{r}=3\hat{i}+2\hat{j}-4\hat{k}+\lambda(\hat{i}+2\hat{j}+2\hat{k})$ and $\vec{r}=5\hat{i}-2\hat{k}+\mu(3\hat{i}+2\hat{j}+6\hat{k})$. • *Recall*

(v) Find the area of triangle whose two adjacent sides are given by $\vec{a}=2\hat{i}+4\hat{j}-3\hat{k}$ and $\vec{b}=2\hat{i}+\hat{j}+4\hat{k}$. • *Application*

16. (i) The scalar product of the vector $\vec{a}=\hat{i}+\hat{j}+\hat{k}$ with a unit vector along the sum of vectors $\vec{b}=2\hat{i}+4\hat{j}-5\hat{k}$ and $\vec{c}=\lambda\hat{i}+2\hat{j}+3\hat{k}$ is equal to one. Find the value of λ and hence, find the unit vector along $\vec{b}+\vec{c}$. • *Understanding* [2]

Or

(ii) Find $\vec{a} \cdot \vec{b}$, if $|\vec{a}|=4$, $|\vec{b}|=3$ and $|\vec{a} \times \vec{b}|=6$.

• *Recall* [2]

17. (i) If the product of distances of the point (1, 1, 1) from origin and the plane $x-y+z+k=0$ be 5 units, then find the values of k. • *Understanding* [4]

Or

(ii) Find the coordinates of the point, where the line through the points (5, 1, 6) and (3, 4, 1) crosses the YZ-plane.

• *Understanding* [4]

18. Sketch the region lying in the first quadrant and bounded by $y=4x^2$, $x=0$, $y=2$ and $y=4$. Find the area of the region, using integration. • *Application* [4]

Section C (15 Marks)

19. In subparts (i) and (ii) choose the correct options and in subparts (iii) to (v), answer the questions as instructed. [5]

(i) The total cost function for x units of a commodity is $C(x)=\dfrac{x^3}{3}+3x^2-7x+16$, then the marginal cost (MC) function is

• *Understanding*

(a) x^2-6x+7 (b) x^2+6x-7

(c) x^2-8x+7 (d) None of these

(ii) If $\bar{x}=10$, $\bar{y}=9$ and $b_{yx}=3.1$, then the regression equation y on x is • *Recall*

(a) $y=3.1x+22$ (b) $y=3.1x-22$

(c) $y=x-22$ (d) None of these

(iii) For manufacturing a certain item, the fixed cost is ₹5000 and the cost of producing each unit is ₹15. • *Application*

(a) What is the cost function?

(b) What is the total cost and average cost of producing 20 units?

(iv) The total cost function for x units of a commodity is $C(x)=\dfrac{1}{5}x^3+6x^2-14x+6$.

Find (a) marginal cost function.

(b) average cost function.

• *Application*

(v) Calculate the coefficient of correlation and standard deviation of y (σ_y), where $x=0.85\,y$, $y=0.89\,x$ and $\sigma_x=3$. • *Recall*

20. (i) A product can be manufactured at a total cost $C(x)=\dfrac{x^2}{100}+100x+40$, where x is the number of units produced. The price at which each unit can be sold is given by $P=\left(200-\dfrac{x}{400}\right)$. Determine the production level x at which the profit is maximum. What is the price per unit and total profit at the level of production? • *Application* [2]

Or

(ii) The total cost and the total revenue of a company that produces and sells x units of particular product are respectively $C(x)=20x+350$ and $R(x)=65x-x^2$.

• *Application* [2]

Find

(a) the break-even values.

(b) the value of x that produce a profit.

21. The lines of regression of a set of data are: $8x-10y+66=0$, $40x-18y=214$

The variance of x is 9. Find [4]

(i) the mean value of x and y.

(ii) coefficient of correlation between x and y.

22. (i) Maximise and minimise $Z=x+2y$, subject to the constraints are $x+2y\geq 100$, $2x-y\leq 0$, $2x+y\leq 200$ and $x, y\geq 0$

Solve the above LPP graphically. [4]

Or

(ii) A manufacturer makes ₹ 600 profit on each 21″ TV set he produces and ₹ 400 profit on each 14″ TV set. A 21″ TV requires 1 h on machine X, 1 h on machine Y and 4 h on machine Z. The 14″ TV requires 2 h on X, 1 h on Y and 1 h on Z. In a given day, machines X, Y and Z can work a maximum of 16, 9 and 24 h, respectively. How many 21″ and 14″ TV sets should be produced per day to maximise the profit? [4]

Solutions *in Topper's Style*

My Commitment *I affirm that I am reviewing these solutions only after I have solved the Sample Question Paper 8 on my own. My purpose of looking the solutions is solely to verify whether my answers/solutions were correct or not and to identify my mistakes in case my solutions were wrong or I could not solve that.*

1. (i) (a) Given, $f(x) = 4x^3 - 18x^2 + 27x - 7$

On differentiating both sides w.r.t. x, we get

$$f'(x) = 12x^2 - 36x + 27$$

$$\Rightarrow \quad f'(x) = 12\left(x^2 - 3x + \frac{9}{4}\right) = 12\left[\left(x - \frac{3}{2}\right)^2\right]$$

$$= 12\left(x - \frac{3}{2}\right)^2 \geq 0, \forall x \in R$$

$\therefore$ $f(x)$ is always increasing on R.

Common Mistake

Be careful in observing the sign of $f'(x)$ in the interval before deciding the value of function.

(ii) (b) Given, $P(A) = \frac{2}{5}$, $P(B) = \frac{3}{10}$

and $P(A \cap B) = \frac{1}{5}$

$$\therefore \quad P(A'/B') = \frac{P(A' \cap B')}{P(B')} = \frac{1 - P(A \cup B)}{1 - P(B)}$$

$$= \frac{1 - [P(A) + P(B) - P(A \cap B)]}{1 - P(B)}$$

$$= \frac{1 - \left(\frac{2}{5} + \frac{3}{10} - \frac{1}{5}\right)}{1 - \frac{3}{10}}$$

$$= \frac{1 - \left(\frac{4+3-2}{10}\right)}{\frac{7}{10}} = \frac{1 - \frac{1}{2}}{\frac{7}{10}} = \frac{5}{7}$$

(iii) (a) Let $I = \int_0^{\pi} \sin^{50} x \cos^{49} x \, dx$ ...(i)

$$\Rightarrow \quad I = \int_0^{\pi} \sin^{50}(\pi - x) \cos^{49}(\pi - x) \, dx$$

$$\left[\because \int_0^a f(x)\,dx = \int_0^a f(a - x)\,dx\right]$$

$$\Rightarrow \quad I = -\int_0^{\pi} \sin^{50} x \cos^{49} x \, dx \quad \text{...(ii)}$$

On adding Eqs. (i) and (ii), we get

$$2I = \int_0^{\pi} 0 \, dx$$

$$\therefore \quad I = 0$$

Hence, A and R both are correct and R is correct explanation of A.

(iv) (b) Given, $\tan^{-1}\left(\frac{3}{4}\right) = A$

$$\Rightarrow \quad \frac{3}{4} = \tan A$$

$$\Rightarrow \quad \tan A = \frac{3}{4} = \frac{P}{B}$$

$$\therefore \quad \cos A = \frac{B}{H} = \frac{B}{\sqrt{B^2 + P^2}} = \frac{4}{\sqrt{4^2 + 3^2}} = \frac{4}{5}$$

(v) (a) Given, differential equation is

$$e^x \cos y dx - e^x \sin y dy = 0$$

$$\Rightarrow \quad e^x \cos y dx = e^x \sin y dy$$

$$\Rightarrow \quad \frac{dx}{dy} = \tan y$$

$$\Rightarrow \quad dx = \tan y dy$$

On integrating both sides, we get

$$\int 1 dx = \int \tan y dy$$

$$\Rightarrow \quad x = \log \sec y + C$$

$$\Rightarrow \quad x - C = \log \sec y$$

$$\Rightarrow \quad \sec y = e^{x - C}$$

$$\Rightarrow \quad \sec y = e^x e^{-C}$$

$$\Rightarrow \quad \frac{1}{\cos y} = \frac{e^x}{e^C}$$

$$\Rightarrow \quad e^x \cos y = e^C$$

$$\Rightarrow \quad e^x \cos y = K \quad [\text{where, } K = e^C]$$

Hence, both the statements are true.

(vi) (c) From option (a),

The graph is continuous, therefore

$$\lim_{x \to x_0^-} f(x) = \lim_{x \to x_0^+} f(x)$$

which is not a correct option.

From option (b),

The graph of function has a discontinuity at $x = x_0$.

Therefore, $f(x)$ is discontinuous.

From option (c)

The graph is not continuous at $x = x_0$.

Therefore, $\lim_{x \to x_0^+} f(x) \neq \lim_{x \to x_0^+} f(x)$

which is correct option.

From option (d),

The graph of the function is continuous.

(vii) (b) Clearly from the graph, $f(x)$ is continuous for all values of x.

(viii) (b) Given, $x = at^2$ and $y = 2at$

On differentiating w.r.t. t, we get

$$\frac{dx}{dt} = 2at \text{ and } \frac{dy}{dt} = 2a$$

Therefore, $\frac{dy}{dx}=\frac{\frac{dy}{dt}}{\frac{dx}{dt}}=\frac{2a}{2at}=\frac{1}{t}$

(ix) (c) It is worth mentioning that integration by parts is not applicable to product of function in all cases. For instance the method does not work for $\int\sqrt{x}\sin x\,dx$. The reason is that there does not exist any function whose differentiation is $\sqrt{x}\sin x$.

(x) (a) Let $y=\frac{\sin(ax+b)}{\cos(cx+d)}$

On differentiating both sides w.r.t. x, we get

$$\frac{dy}{dx}=\frac{d}{dx}\left(\frac{\sin(ax+b)}{\cos(cx+d)}\right)$$

$$=\frac{\cos(cx+d)\frac{d}{dx}\{\sin(ax+b)\}-\sin(ax+b)\frac{d}{dx}\cos(cx+d)}{[\cos(cx+d)]^2}$$

[by quotient rule]

$$=\frac{\cos(cx+d)\cos(ax+b).(a+0)+\sin(ax+b)\sin(cx+d)(c+0)}{\cos^2(cx+d)}$$

[by chain rule,
$\frac{d}{dx}\sin(ax+b)=\cos(ax+b)\frac{d}{dx}(ax+b)$
$=\cos(ax+b)\times(a\times1+0)$
$\frac{d}{dx}\cos(cx+d)=-\sin(cx+d)\frac{d}{dx}(cx+d)$
$=-\sin(cx+d)\times(c\times1+0)$]

$$=\frac{a\cos(cx+d)\cos(ax+b)+c\sin(ax+b)\sin(cx+d)}{\cos^2(cx+d)}$$

$$=\frac{a\cos(cx+d)\cos(ax+b)}{\cos^2(cx+d)}+\frac{c\sin(ax+b)\sin(cx+d)}{\cos^2(cx+d)}$$

$$=\frac{a\cos(ax+b)}{\cos(cx+d)}+\frac{c\sin(ax+b)\sin(cx+d)}{\cos(cx+d)\cos(cx+d)}$$

$$=a\cos(ax+b)\sec(cx+d)+c\sin(ax+b)\tan(cx+d)\sec(cx+d)$$

(xi) Let $I=\int a^{5\log_a x}\,dx$

$=\int a^{\log_a x^5}\,dx$ $\quad$ [$\because n\log m=\log m^n$]

$=\int x^5\,dx=\frac{x^6}{6}+C$ $\quad$ [$\because a^{\log_a m}=m$]

(xii) We have,

$$A=\begin{bmatrix}a+4 & 3b\\ 8 & -6\end{bmatrix}_{2\times2} \text{ and } B=\begin{bmatrix}2a+2 & b^2+2\\ 8 & b^2-5b\end{bmatrix}_{2\times2}$$

If $A=B$ then,

by equality of matrices, each element of A is equal to the corresponding element of B that is $a_{ij}=b_{ij},\ \forall\, i,j$.

$\therefore\quad a_{11}=b_{11}\Rightarrow a+4=2a+2\Rightarrow a=2$

$a_{12}=b_{12}\Rightarrow 3b=b^2+2\Rightarrow b^2=3b-2$

and $\quad a_{22}=b_{22}\Rightarrow -6=b^2-5b$

$\Rightarrow\quad -6=3b-2-5b$ $\quad$ [$\because b^2=3b-2$]

$\Rightarrow\quad 2b=4\Rightarrow b=2$

Hence, $\quad a=2$ and $b=2$

(xiii) We have, $y=Ae^{5x}+Be^{-5x}$ $\quad$ ...(i)

On differentiating w.r.t. to x, we get

$$\frac{dy}{dx}=5Ae^{5x}-5Be^{-5x}$$

Again, on differentiating w.r.t. x, we get

$$\frac{d^2y}{dx^2}=25Ae^{5x}+25Be^{-5x}$$

$\Rightarrow\quad \frac{d^2y}{dx^2}=25(Ae^{5x}+Be^{-5x})$

$\Rightarrow\quad \frac{d^2y}{dx^2}=25y$ $\quad$ [from Eq.(i)]

$\therefore\quad \frac{d^2y}{dx^2}-25y=0$ $\quad$ **Hence proved.**

(xiv) We have, $\tan^{-1}\left(\tan\frac{2\pi}{3}\right)=\tan^{-1}\tan\left(\pi-\frac{\pi}{3}\right)$

$=\tan^{-1}\left(-\tan\frac{\pi}{3}\right)$

$=-\tan^{-1}\tan\frac{\pi}{3}=-\frac{\pi}{3}$ $\quad$ [$\because \tan^{-1}(-x)=-\tan^{-1}x$]

[$\because \tan^{-1}(\tan x)=x, x\in\left(\frac{-\pi}{2},\frac{\pi}{2}\right)$]

Note Remember that $\tan^{-1}\left(\tan\frac{2\pi}{3}\right)\neq\frac{2\pi}{3}$

Since, $\tan^{-1}(\tan x)=x$, if $x\in\left(-\frac{\pi}{2},\frac{\pi}{2}\right)$ and $\frac{2\pi}{3}\notin\left(\frac{-\pi}{2},\frac{\pi}{2}\right)$.

(xv) Given differential equation is $\frac{dy}{dx}+\tan x=0$

The highest order derivative occurring in the differential equation is $\frac{dy}{dx}$ and highest power raised to $\frac{dy}{dx}$ is 1. So, its order is 1 and degree is 1.

2. (i) We have,

$$h(x)=f[g(x)]$$

On differentiating w.r.t. x, we get

$h'(x)=f'[g(x)]g'(x)$ $\quad$ [by chain rule]

On substituting $x=3$

$h'(3)=f'[g(3)].g'(3)$

$=f'(3).9$ $\quad$ [$\because g(3)=3, g'(3)=9$]

$=16\times9$ $\quad$ [$\because f'(3)=16$]

$=144$

Hence, $h'(3)=144$.

Or

(ii) We have,

$$p(x) = -2x^3 + 15x^2 + 36x - 100$$

On differentiating w.r.t. x, we get

$$p'(x) = -6x^2 + 30x + 36$$

For decreasing, put $p'(x) \le 0$.

$\Rightarrow \quad -6x^2 + 30x + 36 = 0 \Rightarrow x^2 - 5x - 6 = 0$

$\Rightarrow \quad (x-6)(x+1) = 0 \Rightarrow x = -1, 6$

Now, we check the sign of $p'(x)$.

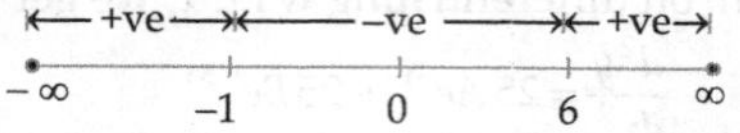

Thus, the profit is decreasing in the interval [–1, 6].

3. Given, differential equation is

$$(1 - \cos 2x)dy + (1 + \cos 2y)\, dx = 0$$

$\Rightarrow \quad 2\sin^2 x\, dy + 2\cos^2 y\, dx = 0$

$[\because \cos 2\theta = 1 - 2\sin^2\theta = 2\cos^2\theta - 1]$

On dividing both sides by $2\sin^2 x \cos^2 y$, we get

$$\sec^2 y\, dy + \text{cosec}^2 x\, dx = 0$$

On integrating both sides, we get

$$\int \sec^2 y\, dy + \int \text{cosec}^2 x\, dx = 0$$

$\Rightarrow \quad \tan y + (-\cot x) = C$

$\therefore \quad \tan y = \cot x + C$

Which is the required solution.

4. We know that principal value branch of $\tan^{-1} x$ is $\left(\frac{-\pi}{2}, \frac{\pi}{2}\right)$.

Since, $\frac{3\pi}{4} \notin \left(-\frac{\pi}{2}, \frac{\pi}{2}\right)$, so write $\frac{3\pi}{4} = \pi - \frac{\pi}{4}$

Now, $\tan^{-1}\left(\tan \frac{3\pi}{4}\right) = \tan^{-1}\left[\tan\left(\pi - \frac{\pi}{4}\right)\right]$

$= \tan^{-1}\left(-\tan \frac{\pi}{4}\right)$

$[\because \tan(\pi - \theta) = -\tan\theta]$

$= \tan^{-1}\left[\tan\left(-\frac{\pi}{4}\right)\right]$

$[\because -\tan\theta = \tan(-\theta)]$

$= -\frac{\pi}{4} \in \left(-\frac{\pi}{2}, \frac{\pi}{2}\right)$

$\left[\because \tan^{-1}(\tan\theta) = \theta, \forall\, \theta \in \left(-\frac{\pi}{2}, \frac{\pi}{2}\right)\right]$

$\therefore \quad \tan^{-1}\left(\tan \frac{3\pi}{4}\right) = -\frac{\pi}{4}$

5. Minors of elements of determinants $\begin{vmatrix} 3 & -2 \\ 1 & 4 \end{vmatrix}$ are

$M_{11} = 4$ [minor of an element a_{11} i.e. 3]

$M_{12} = 1$ [minor of an element a_{12} i.e. – 2]

$M_{21} = -2$ [minor of an element a_{21} i.e. 1]

and $M_{22} = 3$ [minor of an element a_{22} i.e. 4]

Cofactors of elements of determinant $\begin{vmatrix} 3 & -2 \\ 1 & 4 \end{vmatrix}$ are

$C_{11} = (-1)^{1+1} M_{11} = (-1)^2 \times 4 = 4$

[Cofactors of an element a_{11} i.e. 3]

$C_{12} = (-1)^{1+2} M_{12} = (-1)^3 \times 1 = -1$

[Cofactor of an element a_{12} i.e. – 2]

$C_{21} = (-1)^{2+1} M_{21} = (-1)^3 \times (-2) = 2$

[Cofactor of an element a_{21} i.e. 1]

and $C_{22} = (-1)^{2+2} M_{22} = (-1)^{2+2}(3) = 3$

[Cofactor of an element a_{22} i.e. 4]

6. (i) Given, $A = \begin{bmatrix} 3 & 1 \\ -1 & 2 \end{bmatrix}, I = \begin{bmatrix} 1 & 0 \\ 0 & 1 \end{bmatrix}$

and $\quad A^2 = 5A + \lambda I$

$\Rightarrow \begin{bmatrix} 3 & 1 \\ -1 & 2 \end{bmatrix}\begin{bmatrix} 3 & 1 \\ -1 & 2 \end{bmatrix} = 5\begin{bmatrix} 3 & 1 \\ -1 & 2 \end{bmatrix} + \lambda\begin{bmatrix} 1 & 0 \\ 0 & 1 \end{bmatrix}$

$\Rightarrow \begin{bmatrix} 9-1 & 3+2 \\ -3-2 & -1+4 \end{bmatrix} = \begin{bmatrix} 15 & 5 \\ -5 & 10 \end{bmatrix} + \begin{bmatrix} \lambda & 0 \\ 0 & \lambda \end{bmatrix}$

$\Rightarrow \begin{bmatrix} 8 & 5 \\ -5 & 3 \end{bmatrix} = \begin{bmatrix} 15+\lambda & 5 \\ -5 & 10+\lambda \end{bmatrix}$

On equating the corresponding elements from both sides, we get

$$15 + \lambda = 8 \Rightarrow \lambda = 8 - 15 \Rightarrow \lambda = -7$$

Hence $\quad \lambda = -7$

Or

(ii) Given, two matrices are equal. Therefore, equating the corresponding elements of two matrices, we get

$a + b + c = 6$ ...(i)

$a + c = 5$ ...(ii)

and $\quad b + c = 3$ ...(iii)

On subtracting Eq. (ii) from Eq. (i), we get

$b = 6 - 5 = 1$

On putting $b = 1$ in Eq. (iii), we get

$1 + c = 3 \Rightarrow c = 3 - 1 = 2$

On putting $c = 3$ in Eq. (ii), we get

$a + 2 = 5$

$\Rightarrow \quad a = 5 - 2 = 3$

Hence, $a = 3, b = 1$ and $c = 2$.

7. We know that the sum of all probabilities must equal to 1 for a valid distribution.

Therefore,

$P(X=0) + P(X=1) + P(X=2) + P(X=3) + P(X=4) = 1$

$\Rightarrow 0.41 + 0.37 + K + 0.05 + 0.01 = 1$

$\Rightarrow \quad K = 1 - 0.84 = 0.16$

Now, the probability that there are at most 2 defective items $= P(X \le 2)$

$= P(X=0) + P(X=1) + P(X=2)$

$= 0.41 + 0.37 + 0.16 = 0.94$

8. LHS $= \begin{vmatrix} 1 & a & a^3 \\ 1 & b & b^3 \\ 1 & c & c^3 \end{vmatrix}$

Expanding along first row, we get

$$\text{LHS} = 1(bc^3 - cb^3) - a(c^3 - b^3) + a^3(c-b)$$
$$= -bc(b^2 - c^2) - a(c-b)(b^2 + c^2 + bc) + a^3(c-b)$$
$$= (b-c)[-bc(b+c) + a(b^2 + c^2 + bc) - a^3]$$
$$= (b-c)[-b^2c - bc^2 + ab^2 + ac^2 + abc - a^3]$$
$$= (b-c)[(-b^2c + abc) + (-bc^2 + ac^2) - (a^3 - ab^2)]$$
$$= (b-c)[bc(a-b) + c^2(a-b) - a(a-b)(a+b)]$$
$$= (b-c)(a-b)[bc + c^2 - a^2 - ab]$$
$$= (a-b)(b-c)[(bc - ab) + (c^2 - a^2)]$$
$$= (a-b)(b-c)[b(c-a) + (c-a)(c+a)]$$
$$= (a-b)(b-c)(c-a)(a+b+c) = \text{RHS}$$

Hence proved.

9. (i) Given relation is $S = \{(a,b) : |a-b| \text{ is divisible by 4 and } a, b \in A\}$ and $A = \{x : x \in Z \text{ and } 0 \le x \le 12\}$

Now, A can be written as $A = \{0, 1, 2, 3, \ldots, 12\}$

Reflexive As for any $x \in A$, we get $|x - x| = 0$, which is divisible by 4.

$\Rightarrow \quad (x, x) \in S, \forall x \in A$

Therefore, S is reflexive.

Symmetric As for any $(x, y) \in S$, we get $|x - y|$ is divisible by 4. [by using definition of given relation]

$\Rightarrow \quad |x - y| = 4\lambda$, for some $\lambda \in Z$

$\Rightarrow \quad |y - x| = 4\lambda$, for some $\lambda \in Z \Rightarrow (y, x) \in S$

Thus, $(x, y) \in S \Rightarrow (y, x) \in S, \forall x, y \in A$

Therefore, S is symmetric.

Transitive For any $(x, y) \in S$ and $(y, z) \in S$, we get $|x - y|$ is divisible by 4 and $|y - z|$ is divisible by 4. [by using definition of given relation]

$\Rightarrow \quad |x - y| = 4\lambda$ and $|y - z| = 4\mu$, for some $\lambda, \mu \in Z$.

Now, $x - z = (x - y) + (y - z) = \pm 4\lambda \pm 4\mu$

$= \pm 4(\lambda + \mu)$

$\Rightarrow \quad |x - z|$ is divisible by 4.

$\Rightarrow \quad (x, z) \in S$

Thus, $(x, y) \in S$ and $(y, z) \in S$

$\Rightarrow \quad (x, z) \in S, \forall x, y, z \in A$

Therefore, S is transitive.

Since, S is reflexive, symmetric and transitive, so it is an equivalence relation. Now, set of all elements related to 1 is $\{1,5,9\}$.

Or

(ii) Given, $f : N \rightarrow N$, defined by

$$f(x) = \begin{cases} x + 1, & \text{if } x \text{ is odd} \\ x - 1, & \text{if } x \text{ is even} \end{cases}$$

For one-one Let $x_1, x_2 \in N$ (domain) such that

$$f(x_1) = f(x_2)$$

Now, following cases arise

***Case* I** When both x_1 and x_2 are odd

In this case, $f(x_1) = f(x_2) \Rightarrow x_1 + 1 = x_2 + 1 \Rightarrow x_1 = x_2$

***Case* II** When both x_1 and x_2 are even

In this case, $f(x_1) = f(x_2) \Rightarrow x_1 - 1 = x_2 - 1 \Rightarrow x_1 = x_2$

***Case* III** When one of them is odd and other is even

Let x_1 is odd and x_2 is even.

Then, $\quad f(x_1) = f(x_2) \Rightarrow x_1 + 1 = x_2 - 1$

$\Rightarrow$ even integer = odd integer, which is false.

So, $\quad f(x_1) \ne f(x_2)$

Thus, $x_1 \ne x_2 \Rightarrow f(x_1) \ne f(x_2)$.

From above three cases, it follows that f is one-one.

For onto Let $y \in N$ (codomain) be any arbitrary element.

Clearly, when y is odd then there exist $y + 1$, which is even and belongs to N (domain), such that

$$f\{(y+1)\} = (y+1) - 1 = y$$

and when y is even then there exist $y - 1$, which is odd and belongs to N (domain), such that

$$f\{(y-1)\} = (y-1) + 1 = y$$

Thus, from both cases we find that every element in the codomain of f has its pre-image in the domain of f, so f is onto.

Hence, the given function is bijective.

10. (i) (a) Given function is $f(x) = [x(x-2)]^2 = [x^2 - 2x]^2$.

On differentiating both sides w.r.t. x, we get

$$\frac{d}{dx}\{f(x)\} = 2(x^2 - 2x)\frac{d}{dx}(x^2 - 2x)$$

$$\Rightarrow \quad f'(x) = 2(x^2 - 2x)(2x - 2)$$
$$= 4x(x-2)(x-1)$$

(b) We have, $f'(x) = 4x(x-1)(x-2)$

On putting $f'(x) = 0$, we get

$$4x(x-2)(x-1) = 0$$

$\Rightarrow \quad x = 0, 1$ and 2

Which are the required critical points.

(c) Now, we find interval in which $f(x)$ is strictly increasing or strictly decreasing.

Interval	$f'(x) = 4x(x-2)(x-1)$	Sign of $f'(x)$
$(-\infty, 0)$	$(-)(-)(-)$	– ve
$(0, 1)$	$(+)(-)(-)$	+ ve
$(1, 2)$	$(+)(-)(+)$	– ve
$(2, \infty)$	$(+)(+)(+)$	+ ve

Hence, y is strictly increasing in $(0, 1)$ and $(2, \infty)$.

Hence, y is increasing in $(0, 1) \cup (2, \infty)$.

(d) From the above table, the given function is strictly decreasing in $(-\infty, 0)$ and $(1, 2)$.
Hence, y is decreasing in $(-\infty, 0) \cup (1, 2)$.

Common Mistake

Be careful in observing the sign of $f'(x)$ in the interval before deciding the value of function.

Or

(ii) (a) Given function is $f(x) = \sin x + \cos x$
On differentiating both sides w.r.t. x, we get
$$f'(x) = \cos x - \sin x$$
(b) We have, $f'(x) = \cos x - \sin x$
Put $f'(x) = 0 \Rightarrow \cos x - \sin x = 0$
$$\Rightarrow \quad \tan x = 1$$
$$\Rightarrow \quad x = \frac{\pi}{4} \in \left(0, \frac{\pi}{2}\right)$$
Which is the required critical points.
(c) Now, $\frac{\pi}{4}$ divides the interval $\left(0, \frac{\pi}{2}\right)$ into two sub intervals $\left(0, \frac{\pi}{4}\right)$ and $\left(\frac{\pi}{4}, \frac{\pi}{2}\right)$.

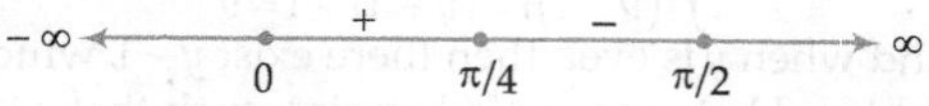

In interval $\left(0, \frac{\pi}{4}\right)$, $\cos x > \sin x$
$$\therefore \quad \cos x - \sin x > 0$$
$$\Rightarrow \quad f'(x) > 0$$
So, $f(x)$ is strictly increasing function in $\left(0, \frac{\pi}{4}\right)$.
In interval $\left(\frac{\pi}{4}, \frac{\pi}{2}\right)$, $\cos x < \sin x$
$$\therefore \quad \cos x - \sin x < 0$$
$$\Rightarrow \quad f'(x) < 0$$
So, $f(x)$ is strictly decreasing function in $\left(\frac{\pi}{4}, \frac{\pi}{2}\right)$.

11. (i) Given, l is the length of the hypotenuse of the given right angled ΔABC right angled at B and $\angle CAB = \theta$, where $0 < \theta < \frac{\pi}{2}$.

Then, $\cos\theta = \frac{AB}{l}$ and $\sin\theta = \frac{BC}{l} \Rightarrow AB = l\cos\theta$ and $BC = l\sin\theta$

$$\therefore \quad \text{Area of } \Delta ABC = \frac{1}{2} \times AB \times BC$$
$$= \frac{1}{2} \cdot l\cos\theta \cdot l\sin\theta = S \quad \text{[given]}$$
$$\Rightarrow \quad \frac{l^2}{2 \cdot 2} \cdot 2\cos\theta \cdot \sin\theta = S$$
$$\Rightarrow \quad \frac{l^2}{4}\sin 2\theta = S \Rightarrow l^2 = \frac{4s}{\sin 2\theta}$$
$$\Rightarrow \quad l^2 = 4S\operatorname{cosec} 2\theta$$

(ii) Now, l is least when l^2 is least. So, we need to find the value of θ for which l^2 is least.
Let us write l^2 as $f(\theta)$
Then, $\quad f(\theta) = 4S\operatorname{cosec} 2\theta \quad$ ...(i)
On differentiating both sides of Eq. (i) w.r.t. θ two times, we get
$$f'(\theta) = 4S(-\operatorname{cosec} 2\theta \cot 2\theta) \cdot 2$$
$$= -8S\operatorname{cosec} 2\theta \cot 2\theta$$
and $f''(\theta) = -8S[\operatorname{cosec} 2\theta(-\operatorname{cosec}^2 2\theta) \cdot 2$
$+ \cot 2\theta(-\operatorname{cosec} 2\theta \cot 2\theta) \cdot 2]$
[by using product rule of derivative]
$$= 16S\operatorname{cosec} 2\theta(\operatorname{cosec}^2 2\theta + \cot^2 2\theta)$$
Now, put $f'(\theta) = 0$
$$\Rightarrow \quad -8S\operatorname{cosec} 2\theta \cot 2\theta = 0$$
$$\Rightarrow \quad \operatorname{cosec} 2\theta \cot 2\theta = 0$$
$$\Rightarrow \quad \frac{1}{\sin 2\theta} \cdot \frac{\cos 2\theta}{\sin 2\theta} = 0$$
$$\Rightarrow \quad \cos 2\theta = 0 \Rightarrow 2\theta = \frac{\pi}{2} \Rightarrow \theta = \frac{\pi}{4}$$
Also, At $\theta = \frac{\pi}{4}, f''\left(\frac{\pi}{4}\right) = 16S\operatorname{cosec}\frac{\pi}{2}\left(\operatorname{cosec}^2\frac{\pi}{2} + \cot^2\frac{\pi}{2}\right)$
$$= 16S \cdot 1 \cdot (1 + 0)$$
$$= 16S > 0$$
So, $\quad f(\theta)$ is least, when $\theta = \frac{\pi}{4}$
$\Rightarrow \quad l$ is least, when $\theta = \frac{\pi}{4}$

(iii) When $\theta = \frac{\pi}{4}$, then
$$AB = l\cos\frac{\pi}{4} = \frac{l}{\sqrt{2}} \quad \text{and} \quad BC = l\sin\frac{\pi}{4} = \frac{l}{\sqrt{2}}$$
Hence, the hypotenuse is least when $AB = BC$ i.e. when the triangle is isosceles. **Hence proved.**

Value Point

If $f''\left(\frac{\pi}{4}\right) > 0$, then $f(\theta)$ is least when $\theta = \frac{\pi}{4}$.

12. (i) Let $I = \int \frac{\sin^{-1}\sqrt{x} - \cos^{-1}\sqrt{x}}{\sin^{-1}\sqrt{x} + \cos^{-1}\sqrt{x}} dx$

We know that $\sin^{-1}\theta + \cos^{-1}\theta = \frac{\pi}{2}$
$$\therefore \sin^{-1}\sqrt{x} + \cos^{-1}\sqrt{x} = \pi/2$$
$$\Rightarrow \quad \cos^{-1}\sqrt{x} = \frac{\pi}{2} - \sin^{-1}\sqrt{x}$$
Then, $I = \int \frac{\sin^{-1}\sqrt{x} - \left(\frac{\pi}{2} - \sin^{-1}\sqrt{x}\right)}{\pi/2} dx$
$$= \int \frac{2\sin^{-1}\sqrt{x} - \frac{\pi}{2}}{\frac{\pi}{2}} dx = \frac{2}{\pi}\int\left(2\sin^{-1}\sqrt{x} - \frac{\pi}{2}\right) dx$$

$$=\frac{4}{\pi}\int \sin^{-1}\sqrt{x}\,dx - \int 1dx$$

$$=\frac{4}{\pi}\int \sin^{-1}\sqrt{x}\,dx - x + C$$

$$\Rightarrow \quad I = \frac{4}{\pi}I_1 - x + C \quad \ldots(i)$$

where, $I_1 = \int \sin^{-1}\sqrt{x}\,dx$

On putting $\sqrt{x} = t \Rightarrow x = t^2$ and $dx = 2t\,dt$

$$\therefore\ I_1 = \int \sin^{-1}t\, 2t\,dt = 2\int \sin^{-1}t \cdot t\,dt$$

$$= 2\left[\sin^{-1}t \int t\,dt - \int\left\{\frac{d}{dt}(\sin^{-1}t)\int t\,dt\right\}dt\right]$$

[using integration by parts]

$$= 2\left[\sin^{-1}t \cdot \frac{t^2}{2} - \int \frac{1}{\sqrt{1-t^2}}\cdot\frac{t^2}{2}\,dt\right]$$

$$= t^2\sin^{-1}t + \int \frac{(1-t^2)-1}{\sqrt{1-t^2}}\,dt$$

$$= t^2\sin^{-1}t + \int \sqrt{1-t^2}\,dt - \int \frac{1}{\sqrt{1-t^2}}\,dt$$

$$= t^2\sin^{-1}t + \frac{t\sqrt{1-t^2}}{2} + \frac{1}{2}\sin^{-1}t - \sin^{-1}t$$

$$\left[\because \int \sqrt{a^2-y^2}\,dy = \frac{y}{2}\sqrt{a^2-y^2} + \frac{a^2}{2}\sin^{-1}\frac{y}{a} + C\right]$$

$$= \left(t^2 - \frac{1}{2}\right)\sin^{-1}t + \frac{1}{2}t\sqrt{1-t^2}$$

$$= \frac{1}{2}[(2x-1)\sin^{-1}\sqrt{x} + \sqrt{x}\sqrt{1-x}] \quad [\text{putting } t = \sqrt{x}]$$

$$= \frac{1}{2}[(2x-1)\sin^{-1}\sqrt{x} + \sqrt{x-x^2}]$$

On putting the value of I_1 in Eq. (i), we get

$$I = \frac{2}{\pi}[(2x-1)\sin^{-1}\sqrt{x} + \sqrt{x-x^2}] - x + C$$

Common Mistake

In solving the integral problem by substitution method don't forget to put the value of t in terms of x.

Or

(ii) Let $I = \int \frac{\tan x + \tan^3 x}{1+\tan^3 x}dx = \int \frac{\tan x(1+\tan^2 x)}{1+\tan^3 x}dx$

$$= \int \frac{\tan x \sec^2 x}{1+\tan^3 x}dx \quad [\because 1+\tan^2 x = \sec^2 x]$$

On putting $\tan x = t \Rightarrow \sec^2 x\,dx = dt$

$$\therefore \quad I = \int \frac{t\,dt}{1+t^3} = \int \frac{t\,dt}{(1+t)(1+t^2-t)}$$

$$[\because (a^3+b^3) = (a+b)(a^2-ab+b^2)]$$

Using partial fraction, let

$$\frac{t}{(1+t)(1+t^2-t)} = \frac{A}{1+t} + \frac{Bt+C}{t^2-t+1}$$

$$\Rightarrow \quad t = A(t^2-t+1) + (Bt+C)(1+t) \quad \ldots(i)$$

$$\Rightarrow \quad t = (A+B)t^2 + (-A+B+C)t + (A+C) \quad \ldots(ii)$$

On putting $t = -1$ in Eq. (i), we get

$$-1 = A(1+1+1) + 0 \Rightarrow A = \frac{-1}{3}$$

On equating the coefficients of t^2 and constant terms from both sides in Eq. (ii), we get

$$A + B = 0 \Rightarrow \frac{-1}{3} + B = 0 \Rightarrow B = \frac{1}{3}$$

and $\quad A + C = 0$

$$\Rightarrow \quad -\frac{1}{3} + C = 0 \Rightarrow C = \frac{1}{3}$$

Then, $$\frac{t}{(1+t)(1+t^2-t)} = \frac{\left(\frac{-1}{3}\right)}{1+t} + \frac{\left(\frac{1}{3}t + \frac{1}{3}\right)}{t^2-t+1}$$

$$\therefore \quad I = \int \frac{(-1/3)}{1+t}dt + \int \frac{\frac{1}{3}t + \frac{1}{3}}{t^2-t+1}dt$$

$$= -\frac{1}{3}\int \frac{dt}{1+t} + \frac{1}{3}\int \frac{t+1}{t^2-t+1}dt$$

$$= -\frac{1}{3}\int \frac{dt}{1+t} + \frac{1}{6}\int \frac{2t-1+3}{t^2-t+1}dt$$

$$= -\frac{1}{3}\int \frac{dt}{1+t} + \frac{1}{6}\int \frac{2t-1}{t^2-t+1}dt + \frac{3}{6}\int \frac{dt}{t^2-t+1+\frac{1}{4}-\frac{1}{4}}$$

On putting $z = t^2 - t + 1 \Rightarrow dz = (2t-1)dt$ in middle integral, we get

$$I = -\frac{1}{3}\int \frac{dt}{1+t} + \frac{1}{6}\int \frac{1}{z}dz + \frac{1}{2}\int \frac{dt}{\left(t-\frac{1}{2}\right)^2 + \frac{3}{4}}$$

$$\Rightarrow \quad I = -\frac{1}{3}\log|1+t| + \frac{1}{6}\log|z| + \frac{1}{2}\int \frac{dt}{\left(t-\frac{1}{2}\right)^2 + \left(\frac{\sqrt{3}}{2}\right)^2}$$

$$= -\frac{1}{3}\log|1+t| + \frac{1}{6}\log|t^2-t+1|$$

$$+ \frac{1}{2}\cdot\frac{1}{\frac{\sqrt{3}}{2}}\tan^{-1}\left(\frac{t-\frac{1}{2}}{\sqrt{3}/2}\right) + C$$

$$\left[\because \int \frac{dx}{x^2+a^2} = \frac{1}{a}\tan^{-1}\left(\frac{x}{a}\right) + C\right]$$

$$= -\frac{1}{3}\log|1+\tan x| + \frac{1}{6}\log|\tan^2 x - \tan x + 1|$$

$$+ \frac{1}{\sqrt{3}}\tan^{-1}\left(\frac{2\tan x - 1}{\sqrt{3}}\right) + C$$

[putting $t = \tan x$]

13. (i) Let E_1, E_2 and A be the events defined as follows

E_1 : Girl gets 5 or 6 on throw of a die

E_2 : Girl gets 1, 2, 3 or 4 on throw of a die

and A: The girl gets exactly one head

Then, $P(E_1)=\frac{2}{6}=\frac{1}{3}$ and $P(E_2)=\frac{4}{6}=\frac{2}{3}$

If E_1 has occurred, then the girl tosses a coin three times and the sample space for this experiment is {*HHH, HHT, HTH, THH, HTT, THT, TTH, TTT*}

Thus, sample space contains 8 equally likely outcomes, out of which exactly one head occurs 3 times.

$\therefore$ $P(A/E_1)$ = Probability of getting exactly one head when E_1 has already occurred $=\frac{3}{8}$

When E_2 has occurred, the girl tosses a coin once and the sample space for this experiment = {*H, T*}

$\therefore$ $P(A/E_2)$ = Probability of getting exactly one head when E_2 has already occurred $=\frac{1}{2}$

We want to find $P\left(\frac{E_2}{A}\right)$.

By Baye's theorem, we get

$$P\left(\frac{E_2}{A}\right)=\frac{P(E_2)P(A/E_2)}{P(E_1)\,P\left(\frac{A}{E_1}\right)+P(E_2)\,P\left(\frac{A}{E_2}\right)}$$

$$=\frac{\frac{2}{3}\times\frac{1}{2}}{\frac{1}{3}\times\frac{3}{8}+\frac{2}{3}\times\frac{1}{2}}=\frac{1}{3}\times\frac{24}{11}=\frac{8}{11}$$

Or

(ii) Two dice are thrown together, so number of outcomes in the sample space is 36.

$\Rightarrow$ $n(S)=36$

Event, $A=$ Total of $4=\{(2,2),(3,1),(1,3)\}$

$\Rightarrow$ $n(A)=3$

Event, $B=$ Total of 9 or more

$$=\begin{Bmatrix}(3,6),(6,3),(4,5),(5,4),(4,6),\\(6,4),(5,5),(5,6),(6,5),(6,6)\end{Bmatrix}$$

$\Rightarrow$ $n(B)=10$

and event $C=$ Total divisible by 5

$=\{(1,4),(4,1),(2,3),(3,2),(4,6),(6,4),(5,5)\}$

$\Rightarrow n(C)=7$

Here, $(A\cap B)=\phi$ and $(A\cap C)=\phi$

Also, $(B\cap C)=\{(4,6),(6,4),(5,5)\}$

$\Rightarrow$ $n(B\cap C)=3$ and $(A\cap B\cap C)=\phi$

$\therefore$ $P(A)=\frac{n(A)}{n(S)}=\frac{3}{36}=\frac{1}{12}$

$P(B)=\frac{n(B)}{n(S)}=\frac{10}{36}=\frac{5}{18}$ and $P(C)=\frac{n(C)}{n(S)}=\frac{7}{36}$

$P(B\cap C)=\frac{3}{36}=\frac{1}{12}$

and $P(B)\cdot P(C)=\frac{5}{18}\times\frac{7}{36}=\frac{35}{648}$

Here, we see that $P(B\cap C)\neq P(B)\cdot P(C)$

[$\because$ only B and C have common events, so only B and C are used here]

Hence, there is no pair which is independent.

14. (i) We have, $f(x)=\begin{cases}x, & \text{if } x\le 1\\ 5, & \text{if } x>1\end{cases}$

At $x=0$, $\lim_{x\to 0} f(x)=\lim_{x\to 0} x$

[$\because$ in the neighbourhood of 0, $f(x)=x$]

$=0$

and $f(0)=0$

$\because$ $f(0)=\lim_{x\to 0} f(x)$

$\therefore$ f is continuous at $x=0$. **Hence proved.**

(ii) At $x=1$,

LHL $=\lim_{x\to 1^-} f(x)=\lim_{h\to 0} f(1-h)=\lim_{h\to 0}(1-h)$

[$\because$ for $x<1$, $f(x)=x$]

[put $x=1-h$, hen$x\to 1^-$, then $h\to 0$]

$=1$

RHL $=\lim_{x\to 1^+} f(x)=\lim_{x\to 1^+} 5$ [$\because$ for $x>1$, $f(x)=5$]

$=5$

and $f(1)=1$

$\because$ LHL $\neq$ RHL

$\therefore$ f is not continuous at $x=1$. **Hence proved.**

(iii) At $x=2$, $\lim_{x\to 2} f(x)=\lim_{x\to 2} 5$

[$\because$ in the neighbourhood of 2, $f(x)=5$]

$=5$

and $f(2)=5$

$\because$ $f(2)=\lim_{x\to 2} f(x)$

$\therefore$ f is continuous at $x=2$. **Hence proved.**

15. (i) (a) The condition for two vectors to be parallel is

$$(3\hat{i}-6\hat{j}+\hat{k})\times(2\hat{i}-4\hat{j}+\lambda\hat{k})=\vec{0}$$

$$\Rightarrow \begin{vmatrix}\hat{i} & \hat{j} & \hat{k}\\ 3 & -6 & 1\\ 2 & -4 & \lambda\end{vmatrix}=\vec{0}$$

$\Rightarrow \hat{i}(-6\lambda+4)-\hat{j}(3\lambda-2)+\hat{k}(-12+12)=\vec{0}$

$\Rightarrow$ $(-6\lambda+4)\hat{i}-(3\lambda-2)\hat{j}=\vec{0}$

$\Rightarrow$ $-6\lambda+4=0$ and $3\lambda-2=0$

$\Rightarrow$ $\lambda=\frac{2}{3}$ and $\lambda=\frac{2}{3}$

(ii) (b) We have,

$$\vec{a}=\hat{i}+\hat{j}-\hat{k} \text{ and } \vec{n}=\hat{i}-\hat{j}+\hat{k}$$

$\therefore$ Required equation of plane is $\vec{r}\cdot\vec{n}=\vec{a}\cdot\vec{n}$

$\Rightarrow \quad \vec{r}\cdot(\hat{i}-\hat{j}+\hat{k})=(\hat{i}+\hat{j}-\hat{k})\cdot(\hat{i}-\hat{j}+\hat{k})$

$\Rightarrow \quad \vec{r}\cdot(\hat{i}-\hat{j}+\hat{k})=1-1-1$

$\Rightarrow \quad \vec{r}\cdot(\hat{i}-\hat{j}+\hat{k})=-1$

(iii) (a) Given, $\vec{a}=2\hat{i}+3\hat{j}-4\hat{k}$ and $\vec{b}=5\hat{i}+2\hat{j}+3\hat{k}$

$\therefore \quad \vec{a}\cdot\vec{b}=(2\hat{i}+3\hat{j}-4\hat{k})\cdot(5\hat{i}+2\hat{j}+3\hat{k})$

$=10+6-12=4$

Now, $\vec{a}\times\vec{b}=\begin{vmatrix}\hat{i} & \hat{j} & \hat{k}\\ 2 & 3 & -4\\ 5 & 2 & 3\end{vmatrix}$

$=\hat{i}(9+8)-\hat{j}(6+20)+\hat{k}(4-15)$

$=17\hat{i}-26\hat{j}-11\hat{k}$

Here, only Statement I is true.

(iv) Given pair of lines is

$\vec{r}=3\hat{i}+2\hat{j}-4\hat{k}+\lambda(\hat{i}+2\hat{j}+2\hat{k})$

and $\quad \vec{r}=5\hat{i}-2\hat{k}+\mu(3\hat{i}+2\hat{j}+6\hat{k})$

Given, first line is parallel to the vector $\vec{b_1}=\hat{i}+2\hat{j}+2\hat{k}$ and second line is parallel to the vector $\vec{b_2}=3\hat{i}+2\hat{j}+6\hat{k}$.

Let θ be the angle between the lines, then

$$\cos\theta=\frac{\vec{b_1}\cdot\vec{b_2}}{|\vec{b_1}|\,|\vec{b_2}|}$$

$$=\frac{1\times3+2\times2+2\times6}{\sqrt{1^2+2^2+2^2}\sqrt{3^2+2^2+6^2}}$$

$$=\frac{3+4+12}{\sqrt{1+4+4}\sqrt{9+4+36}}$$

$$=\frac{19}{\sqrt{9}\sqrt{49}}=\frac{19}{3\times7}=\frac{19}{21}$$

$$\Rightarrow \quad \theta=\cos^{-1}\left(\frac{19}{21}\right)$$

(v) We have adjacent sides of a triangle are

$\vec{a}=2\hat{i}+4\hat{j}-3\hat{k}$

and $\quad \vec{b}=2\hat{i}+\hat{j}+4\hat{k}$

$\therefore$ Area of triangle $=\frac{1}{2}|\vec{a}\times\vec{b}|=\frac{1}{2}\begin{Vmatrix}\hat{i} & \hat{j} & \hat{k}\\ 2 & 4 & -3\\ 2 & 1 & 4\end{Vmatrix}$

$=\frac{1}{2}|\hat{i}(16+3)-\hat{j}(8+6)+\hat{k}(2-8)|$

$=\frac{1}{2}|19\hat{i}-14\hat{j}-6\hat{k}|$

$=\frac{1}{2}\sqrt{(19)^2+(-14)^2+(-6)^2}$

$=\frac{1}{2}\sqrt{361+196+36}=\frac{1}{2}\sqrt{593}$ sq units

16. (i) Given, $\vec{a}=\hat{i}+\hat{j}+\hat{k}$, $\vec{b}=2\hat{i}+4\hat{j}-5\hat{k}$

and $\quad \vec{c}=\lambda\hat{i}+2\hat{j}+3\hat{k}$.

Now, $\vec{b}+\vec{c}=2\hat{i}+4\hat{j}-5\hat{k}+\lambda\hat{i}+2\hat{j}+3\hat{k}$

$=(2+\lambda)\hat{i}+6\hat{j}-2\hat{k}$

$\therefore \quad |\vec{b}+\vec{c}|=\sqrt{(2+\lambda)^2+(6)^2+(-2)^2}$

$=\sqrt{4+\lambda^2+4\lambda+36+4}$

$=\sqrt{\lambda^2+4\lambda+44}$

The unit vector along $\vec{b}+\vec{c}$

$$=\frac{\vec{b}+\vec{c}}{|\vec{b}+\vec{c}|}=\frac{(2+\lambda)\hat{i}+6\hat{j}-2\hat{k}}{\sqrt{\lambda^2+4\lambda+44}} \quad \text{...(i)}$$

Given, scalar product of $(\hat{i}+\hat{j}+\hat{k})$ with unit vector along $(\vec{b}+\vec{c})$ is 1.

$$\therefore \quad (\hat{i}+\hat{j}+\hat{k})\cdot\frac{\vec{b}+\vec{c}}{|\vec{b}+\vec{c}|}=1$$

$$\Rightarrow \quad (\hat{i}+\hat{j}+\hat{k})\cdot\frac{(2+\lambda)\hat{i}+6\hat{j}-2\hat{k}}{\sqrt{\lambda^2+4\lambda+44}}=1 \quad \text{[using Eq. (i)]}$$

$$\Rightarrow \quad \frac{1(2+\lambda)+1(6)+1(-2)}{\sqrt{\lambda^2+4\lambda+44}}=1$$

$$\Rightarrow \quad \frac{(2+\lambda)+6-2}{\sqrt{\lambda^2+4\lambda+44}}=1$$

$$\Rightarrow \quad \lambda+6=\sqrt{\lambda^2+4\lambda+44}$$

$$\Rightarrow \quad (\lambda+6)^2=\lambda^2+4\lambda+44 \quad \text{[square both sides]}$$

$$\Rightarrow \quad \lambda^2+36+12\lambda=\lambda^2+4\lambda+44$$

$$\Rightarrow \quad 8\lambda=8 \Rightarrow \lambda=1$$

Hence, the value of λ is 1.

Or

(ii) Given, $|\vec{a}\times\vec{b}|=6$, $|\vec{a}|=4$ and $|\vec{b}|=3$

We know that $\vec{a}\times\vec{b}=|\vec{a}||\vec{b}|\sin\theta\cdot\hat{n}$

$\Rightarrow \quad |\vec{a}\times\vec{b}|=|\vec{a}||\vec{b}|\sin\theta \quad [\because \hat{n}=1]$

$$\Rightarrow \quad \sin\theta=\frac{|\vec{a}\times\vec{b}|}{|\vec{a}||\vec{b}|}$$

$$\Rightarrow \quad \sin\theta=\frac{6}{4\times3}=\frac{1}{2}$$

$$\therefore \cos\theta=\sqrt{1-\sin^2\theta}=\sqrt{1-\left(\frac{1}{2}\right)^2}=\sqrt{\frac{3}{4}}=\frac{\sqrt{3}}{2}$$

Now, $\vec{a}\cdot\vec{b}=|\vec{a}||\vec{b}|\cos\theta=4\times3\times\frac{\sqrt{3}}{2}=6\sqrt{3}$

17. (i) Distance of the point (1, 1, 1) from origin

$$=\sqrt{(1-0)^2+(1-0)^2+(1-0)^2}=\sqrt{3} \text{ units}$$

Distance of the point (1, 1, 1) from the plane $x-y+z+k=0$ is

$$\frac{|1-1+1+k|}{\sqrt{(1)^2+(-1)^2+(1)^2}}=\frac{|1+k|}{\sqrt{3}} \text{ units}$$

According to the given condition,

$$\sqrt{3}\cdot\frac{|1+k|}{\sqrt{3}}=5$$

$\Rightarrow \quad |1+k|=5 \Rightarrow 1+k=\pm 5$

$\therefore \quad k=4,-6$

Or

(ii) Directions ratios of the line passing through the points (5, 1, 6) and (3, 4, 1) are

$$<3-5, 4-1, 1-6>$$

i.e. $\quad <-2, 3, -5>$

i.e. $\quad <2, -3, 5>$

$\therefore$ The equation of line passing through the given points is

$$\frac{x-5}{2}=\frac{y-1}{-3}=\frac{z-6}{5}=\lambda \text{ (say)} \quad \text{...(i)}$$

$\Rightarrow x=2\lambda+5, y=-3\lambda+1, z=5\lambda+6$

Any point on the line (i) is $(5+2\lambda, 1-3\lambda, 6+5\lambda)$.

If this point lies on YZ-plane, then its x-coordinate is zero.

$\Rightarrow \quad 5+2\lambda=0 \Rightarrow \lambda=\frac{-5}{2}$

Hence, the required point is

$$\left(0, 1+3\cdot\frac{5}{2}, 6-5\cdot\frac{5}{2}\right) \text{ i.e. } \left(0, \frac{17}{2}, \frac{-13}{2}\right).$$

18. Given curve $y=4x^2$ is symmetrical with regard to the Y-axis and open upwards.

$y=2$ and $y=4$ are lines parallel to X-axis.

Thus, the required bounded region is $ABCDA$.

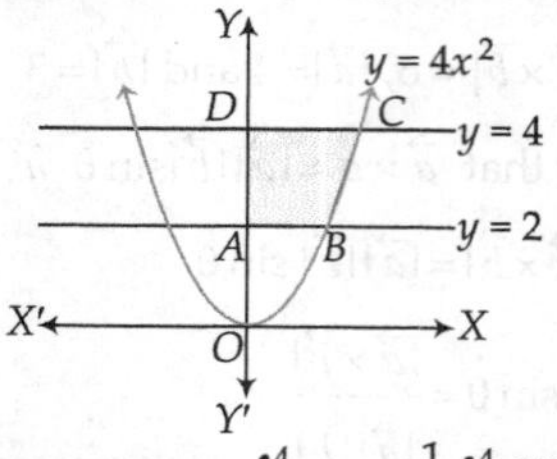

Hence, required area $=\int_2^4 x\,dy=\frac{1}{2}\int_2^4 y^{1/2}dy$

$$\left[\because y^2=4x^2 \Rightarrow x=\frac{1}{2}y^{\frac{1}{2}}\right]$$

$$=\frac{1}{2}\left[\frac{y^{3/2}}{3/2}\right]_2^4=\frac{1}{2}\times\frac{2}{3}(4^{3/2}-2^{3/2})$$

$$=\frac{1}{3}(8-2\sqrt{2}) \text{ sq units}$$

19. (i) (b) We have, $C(x)=\frac{x^3}{3}+3x^2-7x+16$

Marginal cost

$$(\text{MC})=\frac{dC}{dx}(x)=\frac{d}{dx}\left(\frac{x^3}{3}+3x^2-7x+16\right)$$

$$=\frac{3x^2}{3}+6x-7=x^2+6x-7$$

(ii) (b) We have, $\bar{x}=10, \bar{y}=9$ and $b_{yx}=3.1$

The regression equation y on x is

$$y-\bar{y}=b_{yx}(x-\bar{x})$$

$\Rightarrow \quad y-9=3.1(x-10)=3.1x-31 \Rightarrow y=3.1x-22$

(iii) (a) Given, total fixed cost = ₹ 5000

Variable cost of producing one unit = ₹ 15

$\therefore$ Total cost function, TC = ₹ $(5000+15x)$ where x is the number of units produced.

(b) Now, total cost of producing 20 units $=(\text{TC})_{x=20}$

$=5000+15\times 20=5000+300=$ ₹ 5300

and average cost of 20 units $=\frac{5300}{20}=$ ₹ 265

(iv) Given, cost function, $C(x)=\frac{1}{5}x^3+6x^2-14x+6$

(a) Now, marginal cost function,

$$\text{MC}=\frac{d}{dx}C(x)=\frac{1}{5}\times 3x^2+12x-14$$

$$=\frac{3}{5}x^2+12x-14$$

(b) Average cost function,

$$=\frac{C(x)}{x}=\frac{1}{5}x^2+6x-14+\frac{6}{x}.$$

(v) Given, $x=0.85y$ and $y=0.89x$ and $\sigma_x=3$

$\therefore \quad b_{xy}=0.85, b_{yx}=0.89$

Coefficient of correlation,

$$r=\sqrt{b_{xy}\times b_{yx}}=\sqrt{0.85\times 0.89}$$

$$=\sqrt{0.7565}=0.8698$$

Also, we know that $b_{xy}=r\times\frac{\sigma_x}{\sigma_y} \Rightarrow 0.85=0.8698\times\frac{3}{\sigma_y}$

$$\Rightarrow 0.85=\frac{2.6094}{\sigma_y} \Rightarrow \sigma_y=\frac{2.6094}{0.85}=3.0699$$

20. (i) Given, cost function $C(x)=\frac{x^2}{100}+100x+40$,

Selling function, $P=200-\frac{x}{400}$

We know that $R(x)=P\cdot x$

$$\therefore \quad R(x)=200x-\frac{x^2}{400}$$

Then, profit function, $P(x)=R(x)-C(x)$

$$=200x-\frac{x^2}{400}-\frac{x^2}{100}-100x-40$$

$$\Rightarrow \quad P(x)=100x-\frac{x^2}{80}-40$$

On differentiating w.r.t. x two times, we get

$$\frac{d}{dx}P(x) = 100 - \frac{2x}{80} = 100 - \frac{x}{40}$$

and $\frac{d^2}{dx^2}P(x) = \frac{-1}{40}$

for any value of x $\frac{d^2}{dx^2}P(x) < 0$, profit is maximum.

For maximum and minimum profit, put

$$\frac{d}{dx}P(x) = 0 \Rightarrow 100 - \frac{x}{40} = 0$$

$$\Rightarrow \quad 100 = \frac{x}{40}$$

$$\Rightarrow \quad x = 4000$$

Total profit at the level of production, when $x = 4000$

$$P(x) = 100 \times 4000 - \frac{(4000)^2}{80} - 40$$

$$= 400000 - \frac{4000 \times 4000}{80} - 40$$

$$= 400000 - 200000 - 40$$

$$\Rightarrow \quad P(x) = ₹\,199960$$

$\therefore$ Price per unit at $x = 4000$ is $P = 200 - \frac{4000}{400}$

$$= 200 - 10 = ₹190$$

Or

(ii) Given, total cost, $C(x) = 20x + 350$ and total revenue, $R(x) = 65x - x^2$

(a) At break-even values, $R(x) = C(x)$

$$\Rightarrow \quad 65x - x^2 = 20x + 350$$

$$\Rightarrow \quad x^2 - 45x + 350 = 0$$

$$\Rightarrow \quad x^2 - 35x - 10x + 350 = 0$$

$$\Rightarrow \quad x(x - 35) - 10(x - 35) = 0$$

$$\Rightarrow \quad (x - 35)(x - 10) = 0$$

$$\Rightarrow \quad x = 10 \text{ or } x = 35$$

Hence, the break-even values are

$$x = 10 \text{ and } x = 35.$$

(b) For profit, $R(x) > C(x)$

$\Rightarrow 65x - x^2 > 20x + 350$

$\Rightarrow \quad x^2 - 45x + 350 < 0$

$\Rightarrow \quad (x - 10)(x - 35) < 0 \Rightarrow 10 < x < 35$

21. (i) We know that two lines of regression intersect at point $(\bar{x}, \bar{y})$.

The given equations of lines of regressions are

$$8x - 10y = -66 \quad \ldots(\text{i})$$

and $$40x - 18y = 214 \quad \ldots(\text{ii})$$

On multiplying Eq. (i) by 5 and then subtracting from Eq (ii), we get

$$-18y + 50y = 214 + 330$$

$$32y = 344$$

$$\Rightarrow \quad y = \frac{544}{32} = 17$$

On putting the value of y in Eq. (i), we get

$$8x - 10(17) = -66$$

$$\Rightarrow \quad 8x = -66 + 170 = 104$$

$$\Rightarrow \quad x = \frac{104}{8} = 13$$

Hence, mean value of $x = 13$ and mean value of $y = 17$.

(ii) Eq. (i) can be rewritten as $y = \frac{8}{10}x + \frac{66}{10}$

$\therefore$ Regression coefficient of y on x is $b_{yx} = \frac{8}{10} = 0.8$

Eq. (ii) can be rewritten as, $x = \frac{18}{40}y + \frac{214}{40}$

$\therefore$ Regression coefficient of x on y is

$$b_{xy} = \frac{18}{40} = 0.45$$

We know that $r^2 = b_{xy} \cdot b_{yx} = 0.45 \times 0.8$

$$\Rightarrow \quad r^2 = 0.36$$

$$\Rightarrow \quad r = \pm\sqrt{0.36}$$

$$\therefore \quad r = 0.6$$

[as b_{xy} and b_{yx} are positive, so we take r positive]

22. (i) Given, problem is to minimise and maximise

$$Z = x + 2y \quad \ldots(\text{i})$$

Subject to constraints,

$$x + 2y \geq 100 \quad \ldots(\text{ii})$$

$$2x - y \leq 0 \quad \ldots(\text{iii})$$

$$2x + y \leq 200 \quad \ldots(\text{iv})$$

and $$x, y \geq 0 \quad \ldots(\text{v})$$

Table for line $x + 2y = 100$ is

x	0	100
y	50	0

So, the line $x + 2y = 100$ is passing through the points (0, 50) and (100, 0).

On putting (0, 0) in the inequality $x + 2y \geq 100$, we get

$$0 + 2 \times 0 \geq 100$$

$$\Rightarrow \quad 0 \geq 100 \quad \text{[false]}$$

So, the half plane is away from the origin.

Table for line $2x - y = 0$ is

x	0	10
y	0	20

So, the line $2x - y = 0$ is passing through the points (0, 0) and (10, 20).

On putting (5, 0) in the inequality $2x - y \leq 0$, we get

$$2 \times 5 - 0 \leq 0$$

$$\Rightarrow \quad 10 \leq 0 \quad \text{[false]}$$

So, the half plane is towards Y-axis.

Table for line $2x + y = 200$ is

x	0	100
y	200	0

So, the line $2x + y = 200$ is passing through the points (0, 200) and (100, 0).

On putting (0, 0) in the inequality $2x + y \le 200$, we get

$$2 \times 0 + 0 \le 200 \Rightarrow 0 \le 200 \quad \text{[true]}$$

So, the half plane is towards the origin.

Also, $x, y \ge 0$.

So, the region lies in the I quadrant.

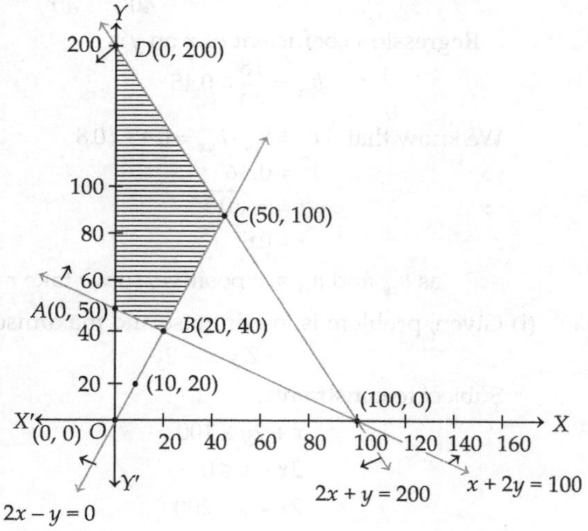

On solving equations $2x - y = 0$ and $x + 2y = 100$, we get the intersection point $B(20, 40)$.

Again, solving the equations $2x - y = 0$ and $2x + y = 200$, we get the intersection point $C(50, 100)$.

On plotting the above in equality on the graph paper, we get the bounded feasible region *ABCD*.

The corner points of the feasible region are $A(0, 50)$, $B(20, 40)$, $C(50, 100)$ and $D(0, 200)$.

The values of Z at corner points are given below

Corner points	Value of $Z = x + 2y$
$A(0, 50)$	$Z = 0 + 2 \times 50 = 100$
$B(20, 40)$	$Z = 20 + 2 \times 40 = 100$
$C(50, 100)$	$Z = 50 + 2 \times 100 = 250$
$D(0, 200)$	$Z = 0 + 2 \times 200 = 400$ (Maximum)

The maximum value of Z is 400, which occurs at $D(0, 200)$ and the minimum value of Z is 100, which occurs at all the points on the line segment joining $A(0, 50)$ and $B(20, 40)$.

Value Point

Always mention the point that if $x, y \ge 0$ then, the feasible region lies in the first quadrant only.

Or

(ii) Let x be the number of 21'' TV sets and y be the number of 14'' TV sets produced (and sold). Then, the problem can be formulated as

Maximise $Z = 600x + 400y$

Subject to the constraints

$x + 2y \le 16$ [machine X constraint]

$x + y \le 9$ [machine Y constraint]

$4x + y \le 24$ [machine Z constraint]

$x \ge 0, y \ge 0$

[number of TV sets cannot be negative]

The table for line $x + 2y = 16$ or $y = \dfrac{16 - x}{2}$ is

x	0	16
y	8	0

So, the line passes through the points (0, 8) and (16, 0).

Put (0, 0) in the inequality $x + 2y \le 16$, we get

$$0 + 0 \le 16 \quad \text{[true]}$$

So, the half plane is towards the origin.

The table for line $x + y = 9$ or $y = 9 - x$ is

x	0	9
y	9	0

So, the line passes through the points (0, 9) and (9, 0).

Put (0, 0) in the inequality $x + y \le 9$, we get

$$0 + 0 \le 9 \quad \text{(true)}$$

So, the half plane is towards the origin.

The table for line $4x + y = 24$ or $y = 24 - 4x$ is

x	0	6
y	24	0

So, the line passes through the points (0, 24) and (6, 0).

Put (0, 0) in the inequality $4x + y \le 24$, we get

$$0 + 0 \le 24 \quad \text{[true]}$$

Also, $x \ge 0$, $y \ge 0$, so feasible region lies in Ist quadrant.

On solving the equation, $4x + y = 24$ and $x + y = 9$, we get the intersection point $B(5, 4)$, and on solving the equation $x + 2y = 16$ and $x + y = 9$, we get the intersection point $C(2, 7)$.

On plotting the above inequality on the graph paper, we get the bounded feasible region *OABCDO*.

The corner points of the feasible region are $O(0, 0)$, $A(6, 0)$, $B(5, 4)$, $C(2, 7)$ and $D(0, 8)$.

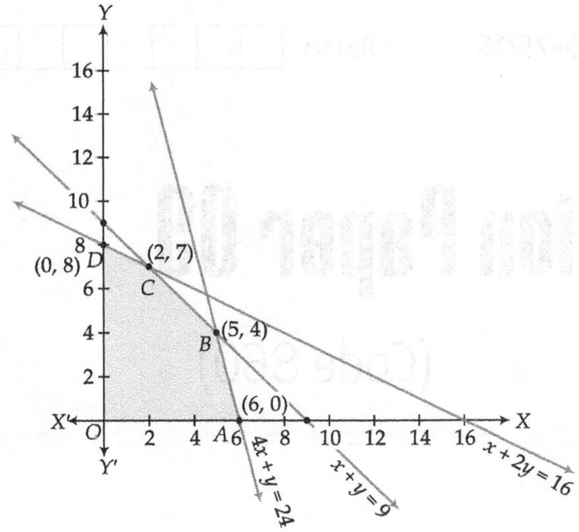

The value of Z at these corner points are as follows

Corner points	$Z = 600x + 400y$
O (0, 0)	$Z = 600 \times 0 + 400 \times 0 = 0$
A (6, 0)	$Z = 600 \times 6 + 400 \times 0 = 3600$
B (5, 4)	$Z = 600 \times 5 + 400 \times 4 = 4600$ (maximum)
C (2, 7)	$Z = 600 \times 2 + 400 \times 7 = 4000$
D (0, 8)	$Z = 600 \times 0 + 400 \times 8 = 3200$

Here, Z is maximum at (5, 4).

Hence, for maximum profit ₹ 4600 per day five 21″ TV sets and four 14″ TV sets should be produced.

SQP Code : **PB-9/15** | Series **i-Succeed 9-25/15** | Roll No.

Sample Question Paper 09

Mathematics 12th (Code 860)

General Instructions

1. The Question Paper consists of three sections A, B and C.
2. Candidates are required to attempt all questions from Section A and all questions either from Section B Or Section C.
3. Section A Internal choice has been provided in two questions of two marks each, two questions of four marks each and two questions of six marks each.
4. Section B Internal choice has been provided in one questions of two marks and one question of four marks.
5. Section C Internal choice has been provided in one question of two marks and one question of four marks.
6. All working, including rough work, should be done on the same sheet as, and adjacent to the rest of the answer.
7. The intended marks for questions or parts of questions are given in brackets [].
8. Mathematical tables and graph papers are provided.

Time : 3 Hrs.

Max. Marks : 80

Section A (65 Marks)

1. In subparts (i) to (xi) choose the correct options and in subparts (xii) to (xv), answer the questions as instructed.

(i) If a matrix has 18 elements, then the number of its possible order is • *Recall* [1]

(a) 2 (b) 4 (c) 6 (d) 8

(ii) The value of $\tan^{-1}\left[2\sin\left(2\cos^{-1}\frac{\sqrt{3}}{2}\right)\right]$ is • *Application* [1]

(a) $\frac{\pi}{3}$ (b) $\frac{2\pi}{3}$ (c) $\frac{-\pi}{3}$ (d) $\frac{\pi}{6}$

(iii) **Statement I** The relation R defined in the set

$$A = \{1, 2, 3, 4, 5, 6, 7\}$$

by $R = \{(a, b)$: both a and b are either odd or even$\}$. Then, R is an equivalence relation.

Statement II A relation R on a set A is said to be an equivalence relation if it is simultaneously reflexive, symmetric and transitive. • *Recall* [1]

(a) Statement I is true.

(b) Both Statements I and II are true.

(c) Statement II is true.

(d) Both Statements I and II are true.

(iv) The function $f(x) = \cot x$ is discontinuous on the set • *Recall* [1]

(a) $\{x = n\pi : n \in Z\}$ (b) $\{x = 2n\pi : n \in Z\}$

(c) $\left\{x = (2n+1)\frac{\pi}{2}; n \in Z\right\}$ (d) $\left\{x = \frac{n\pi}{2}; n \in Z\right\}$

(v) The order and degree of differential equation $\left[1 + \left(\frac{dy}{dx}\right)^2\right] = \frac{d^2y}{dx^2}$ are • *Analysis* [1]

(a) 2 and $\frac{3}{2}$ (b) 2 and 3

(c) 2 and 1 (d) 3 and 4

(vi) If $P(A)=\frac{7}{13}$, $P(B)=\frac{9}{13}$ and $P(A\cap B)=\frac{4}{13}$, then $P\left(\frac{A}{B}\right)$ is equal to • *Understanding* [1]

(a) $\frac{3}{2}$ (b) $\frac{9}{4}$ (c) $\frac{4}{9}$ (d) $\frac{2}{3}$

(vii) $\int \frac{x^3}{x+1}dx$ is equal to • *Analysis* [1]

(a) $x+\frac{x^2}{2}+\frac{x^3}{3}-\log|1-x|+C$

(b) $x+\frac{x^2}{2}-\frac{x^3}{3}-\log|1-x|+C$

(c) $x-\frac{x^2}{2}-\frac{x^3}{3}-\log|1+x|+C$

(d) $x-\frac{x^2}{2}+\frac{x^3}{3}-\log|1+x|+C$

(viii) If $y=\sqrt{3x+2}+\frac{1}{\sqrt{2x^2+4}}$, then $\frac{dy}{dx}$ is equal to • *Application* [1]

(a) $\frac{3}{2\sqrt{3x+2}}-\frac{2x}{(2x^2+4)^{3/2}}$

(b) $\frac{3}{2\sqrt{3x+2}}+\frac{2x}{(2x^2+4)^{3/2}}$

(c) $\frac{3}{2\sqrt{3x+2}}+\frac{2}{(2x^2+4)^{3/2}}$

(d) None of the above

(ix) Consider the following statements.

Statement I $\int_{-1}^{1} 5x^4\sqrt{x^5+1}\,dx=\frac{4\sqrt{2}}{3}$

Statement II $\int_0^1 \frac{\tan^{-1}x}{1+x^2}dx=\frac{\pi^2}{32}$

Choose the correct option • *Application* [1]

(a) Statement I is true.
(b) Statement II is true.
(c) Both statements are true.
(d) Both statements are false.

(x) **Assertion** (A) A square matrix A is invertible iff $\det(A)\neq 0$.

Reason (R) If a square matrix A is invertible, then its inverse A^{-1} is given by $\frac{1}{\det(A)}\cdot \text{adj}(A)$. • *Recall* [1]

(a) Both A and R are true and R is the correct explanation of A.
(b) Both A and R are true but R is not the correct explanation of A.
(c) A is true but R is false.
(d) A is false but R is true.

(xi) **Assertion** (A) The probability that Isha gets scholarship is 0.9 and Priti get is 0.8. Then, the probability that atleast one of them gets the scholarship is 0.98.

Reason (R) The probability of complementary event to A is $P(\bar{A})=(-P(A))$. • *Analysis* [1]

(a) Both A and R are true and R is the correct explanation of A.
(b) Both A and R are true and R is not the correct explanation of A.
(c) A is true but R is false.
(d) A is false but R is true.

(xii) Show that all the diagonal elements of a skew-symmetric matrix are zero. • *Understanding* [1]

(xiii) Show that $2\tan^{-1}(-3)=\frac{-\pi}{2}+\tan^{-1}\left(\frac{-4}{3}\right)$. • *Application [1]*

(xiv) Evaluate x, if $\begin{vmatrix}2 & 4\\5 & 1\end{vmatrix}=\begin{vmatrix}2x & 4\\6 & x\end{vmatrix}$. • *Evaluate* [1]

(xv) Let $f:R\to R$ be the function defined by $f(x)=2x-3$, $\forall\, x\in R$. Write f^{-1}. • *Understanding* [1]

2. (i) Solve the equation $\sin^{-1}(1-x)-2\sin^{-1}x=\frac{\pi}{2}$. • *Evaluate* [2]

Or

(ii) Prove that $\sin[\cot^{-1}\{\cos(\tan^{-1}x)\}]=\sqrt{\frac{x^2+1}{x^2+2}}$. • *Application* [2]

3. Solve the differential equation $(x+2y^3)\frac{dy}{dx}=y$. • *Application* [2]

4. The table below shows some of the values of differentiable functions p and q and their derivatives. • *Application* [2]

x	$p(x)$	$p'(x)$	$q(x)$	$q'(x)$
0	3.5	16	4	15
2	4	20	2	25
3.5	0	18	3.5	35
4	2	12	0	18.5

If $r(x)=p[q(x)]$, then find $r'(0)$.

SP-09

5. (i) If A and B are two events associated with the same random experiment such that $P(A \cup B) = \frac{3}{5}, P(A \cap B) = \frac{1}{5}$ and $P(\overline{A}) = \frac{3}{4}$, then find the value of $P(\overline{A} \cap B)$. • *Analysis* [2]

Or

(ii) Two integers are selected at random from integers 1 to 11. Then, find • *Analysis* [2]

(a) the probability that both numbers are odd.

(b) the probability that sum of numbers is even.

6. If $x \in R, 0 \le x \le \frac{\pi}{2}$ and $\begin{vmatrix} \sin\alpha & -1 \\ 1 & 2\sin\alpha \end{vmatrix} = \begin{vmatrix} \sin\alpha & 0 \\ -4 & 3 \end{vmatrix}$, then find the value of α. • *Evaluate* [2]

7. Let $A = \{1, 2, 3\}$. Then, show that the number of relations containing (1, 2) and (2, 3) which are reflexive and transitive but not symmetric is, three. • *Application* [4]

8. Solve the differential equation $e^x\sqrt{1-y^2}\,dx + \frac{y}{x}\,dy = 0$. • *Application* [4]

9. (i) Find the intervals in which the function $f(x) = \frac{x^4}{4} - x^3 - 5x^2 + 24x + 12$ is

(a) strictly increasing.

(b) strictly decreasing. • *Evaluate* [4]

Or

(ii) A ladder 5 m long is leaning against a wall. Bottom of ladder is pulled along the ground away from wall at the rate of 2 m/s. How fast is the height on the wall decreasing, when the foot of ladder is 4 m away from the wall? • *Evaluate* [4]

10. (i) Consider the function defined by

$$f(x) = \begin{cases} \lambda(x^2+2), & \text{if } x \le 0 \\ 4x+6, & \text{if } x > 0 \end{cases}$$

• *Application* [4]

(a) If the function f is continuous at $x = 0$, then find the value of λ.

(b) Using the value of λ (if any), check the differentiability of the function at $x = 0$.

(c) Using the value of λ, differentiate the function $f(x)$, when $x \le 0$.

Or

(ii) If $y = \sqrt{\frac{1-x}{1+x}}$, then answer the following questions. • *Application* [4]

(a) Find $\frac{dy}{dx}$.

(b) Prove that $(1-x^2)\frac{dy}{dx} + y = 0$.

(c) Find $\frac{dy}{dx}$, at (0, 2).

11. Two farmers Ramkishan and Gurucharan Singh cultivates only three varieties of rice namely Basmati, Permal and Naura. The sales (in ₹) of these varieties of rice by both the farmers in the months of September and October are given by in matrices form A and B. • *Understanding Analysis*

September sales (in ₹)

$$A = \begin{array}{c} \text{Basmati} \quad \text{Permal} \quad \text{Naura} \\ \begin{bmatrix} 10000 & 20000 & 30000 \\ 50000 & 30000 & 10000 \end{bmatrix} \end{array} \begin{array}{l} \text{Ramkishan} \\ \text{Gurucharan Singh} \end{array}$$

October sales (in ₹)

$$B = \begin{array}{c} \text{Basmati} \quad \text{Permal} \quad \text{Naura} \\ \begin{bmatrix} 5000 & 10000 & 6000 \\ 20000 & 10000 & 10000 \end{bmatrix} \end{array} \begin{array}{l} \text{Ramkishan} \\ \text{Gurucharan Singh} \end{array}$$

On the basis of above information, answer the following question

(i) Find the combined sales in September and October for each farmer in each variety.

(ii) Find the decrease in sales from September to October.

(iii) If both farmers receive 2% profit on gross sales, then find the profit for each farmer and for each variety sold in October. [6]

12. (i) A group of class XI students designed a game for class XII students to be played at the lab activity program. They kept two sets of cards on the stage. Each set contained four cards numbered 1, 2, 3 and 4. Each student of class XII had to arrow one card from each set simultaneously. • *Analysis*

The score a student received was defined as the sum of the number shown on the cards. The possible outcomes of the score are given in the table below.

Number on Cards	1	2	3	4
1	2	3	r	5
2	3	4	5	6
3	4	5	6	7
4	5	6	7	s

(a) Calculate the values of r and s in the above table.

(b) Anil plays the game once. Let the random variable S represents Anil's score. Construct the probability distribution of S.

S	2	3	4	5	6	7	8
$P(S=s)$							

(c) Find the probability that Anil's score is atleast 6. [6]

Or

(ii) If A and B are two independent events such that $P(\bar{A}\cap B)=\dfrac{2}{15}$ and $P(A\cap\bar{B})=\dfrac{1}{6}$, then find $P(A)$ and $P(B)$. • *Analysis* [6]

13. (i) Evaluate $\int \dfrac{x^2}{(x^2+4)(x^2+9)}dx$. • *Evaluate* [6]

Or

(ii) Prove that $\int_0^{\pi/4}(\sqrt{\tan x}+\sqrt{\cot x})dx=\sqrt{2}\cdot\dfrac{\pi}{2}$ • *Evaluate* [6]

14. Consider the scenario, let $ABCD$ be a trapezium. The length of three sides are 10 cm each as shown in figure. • *Evaluate* [6]

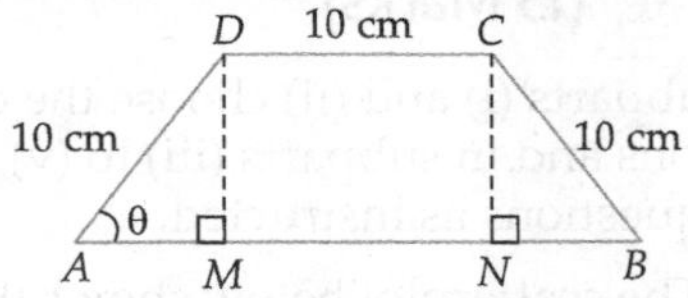

Based on the above information, answer the following questions.

(i) Find the area of trapezium in terms of θ.

(ii) From the obtained equation in terms of θ, find the critical points.

(iii) Find the point at which the area of trapezium is maximum.

(iv) Find the maximum area of trapezium.

Section B (15 Marks)

15. In subparts (i) to (iii) choose the correct options and in subparts (iv) and (v), answer the questions as instructed. [5]

(i) The cartesian equation of plane $\vec{r}\cdot(-\hat{i}+\hat{j}+2\hat{k})=5$ is • *Understanding*

(a) $-x+y+z=5$ (b) $-x+y+2z=5$

(c) $x+y-2z=5$ (d) None of these

(ii) The vector in the direction of vector $\hat{i}-2\hat{j}+2\hat{k}$ that has magnitude 12 is • *Application*

(a) $\hat{i}-2\hat{j}+2\hat{k}$ (b) $\dfrac{\hat{i}-2\hat{j}+2\hat{k}}{3}$

(c) $4(\hat{i}-2\hat{j}+2\hat{k})$ (d) $9(\hat{i}-2\hat{j}+2\hat{k})$

(iii) **Statement I** The length of perpendicular from origin to the plane $\vec{r}\cdot(3\hat{i}-4\hat{j}-12\hat{k})+52=0$ is 4. Also, the unit vector normal to this plane directed from origin to the plane is $\dfrac{-3\hat{i}+4\hat{j}+12\hat{k}}{13}$.

Statement II Let the equation plane be $\vec{r}\cdot\vec{n}=d$. The perpendicular distance from a point P whose position vector is $\vec{a}$, to the plane is $\dfrac{|\vec{a}\cdot\vec{n}-d|}{|\vec{n}|}$. • *Application*

(a) Statement I is true.

(b) Statement II is true.

(c) Both Statements I and II are true.

(d) Both Statements I and II are false.

(iv) Equation of line is $\dfrac{4-x}{2}=\dfrac{y+3}{2}=\dfrac{z+2}{1}$. Find the direction cosines of a line parallel to above line. • *Understanding*

(v) The two vectors $\hat{j}+\hat{k}$ and $3\hat{i}-\hat{j}+4\hat{k}$ represent the two sides AB and AC, respectively of ΔABC. Find the length of the median through A. • *Evaluate*

16. (i) If G is the centroid of ΔABC, using vectors, then prove that

Area of $\Delta AGB=$ Area of ΔBGC

$=$ Area of $\Delta CGA=\dfrac{1}{3}$ (Area of ΔABC). • *Analysis* [2]

Or (ii) Find a unit vector perpendicular to both the vectors $\vec{a}$ and $\vec{b}$, where $\vec{a} = \hat{i} - 7\hat{j} + 7\hat{k}$ and $\vec{b} = 3\hat{i} - 2\hat{j} + 2\hat{k}$. • *Analysis* [2]

17. (i) Find the vector equation of the plane containing the line $\frac{x+2}{2} = \frac{y+3}{3} = \frac{z-4}{-2}$ and the point $(0, 6, 0)$. • *Application* [4]

Section C (15 Marks)

19. In subparts (i) and (ii) choose the correct options and in subparts (iii) to (v), answer the questions as instructed. [5]

(i) The scatterplot below shows the relationship between games played and tickets won. Which of the graphs below represents the line of best fit? • *Recall*

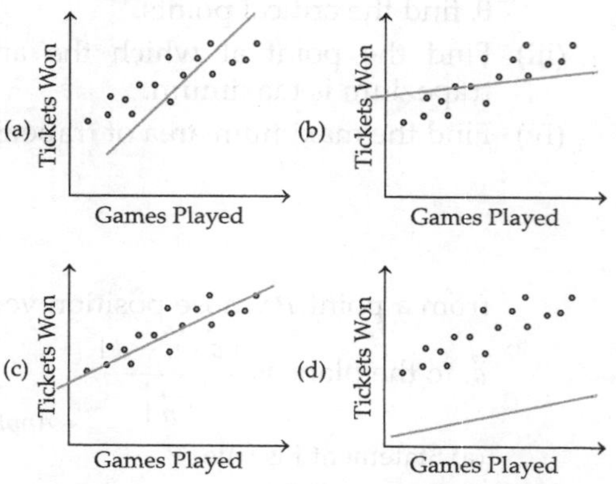

(ii) A monopolist demand function is $p = 500 - 7x$, then the marginal revenue function is • *Understanding*

(a) $500x - 7x^2$ (b) $500 - 14x$
(c) $500x - 14$ (d) None of these

(iii) The total cost function for a company is given by $C(x) = \frac{5}{4}x^2 - 7x + 5$. Find the level of output for which MC = AC. • *Understanding*

(iv) The average cost function of AC for a commodity is given by $AC = 2x + 3 + \frac{1}{x}$ in terms of output x, find the marginal cost as a function of x. • *Understanding*

(v) For 5 observations of pairs (x, y) of variables x and y, the following results are obtained $\Sigma x = 15$, $\Sigma y = 25$, $\Sigma x^2 = 55$, $\Sigma y^2 = 135$ and $\Sigma xy = 83$. Find the equation of the lines of regression and estimate the values of x and y, if $y = 12$. • *Application*

Or (ii) Prove that the lines $x = ay + b, z = cy + d$ and $x = a'y + b', z = c'y + d'$ are perpendicular, if $aa' + cc' + 1 = 0$. • *Application* [4]

18. Sketch the region lying in the first quadrant and bounded by $y = 9x^2$, $x = 0$, $y = 1$ and $y = 4$. Find the area of region using integration. • *Evaluate* [4]

20. (i) The average cost function AC for a commodity is given by $AC = x + 5 + \frac{36}{x}$ in terms of output x. Then, find the output for which AC increases. • *Application* [2]

Or

(ii) The cost of manufacturing x units of a commodity is $27 + 15x + 3x^2$. Find the output for which AC is

(a) decreasing

(b) increasing. • *Application* [2]

21. Fit a straight line to the following data, treating y as the dependent variable

x	14	12	13	14	12
y	22	23	22	24	24

Hence, predict the value of y, when $x = 16$. • *Application* [4]

22. (i) A company manufactures two types of sweaters type *A* and type *B*. It costs ₹ 360 to make a type *A* sweater and ₹ 120 to make a type *B* sweater. The company can make atmost 300 sweaters and spend atmost ₹ 72000 a day. The number of sweaters of type *B* cannot exceed the number of sweaters of type *A* by more than 100. The company makes a profit of ₹ 200 for each sweater of type *A* and ₹ 120 for every sweater of type *B*. Formulate this problem as a LPP and find the maximum. • *Analysis* [4]

SP-09

Or

(ii) A company makes two types of sets, FM set and AM/FM set. The company has enough number of equipments to make any number of FM sets upto and including 600 per month, or any number of AM/FM sets upto and including 525 per month. It takes 30 men hours of labour to produce one FM set and 40 men hours to produce an AM/FM set. The company has upto 24000 men hours available for radio production per month. If the profit on each FM set is ₹ 180 and on each AM/FM set is ₹ 240, then find

(a) maximum profit that could be made each month.

(b) Find the number of each kind of radio sets that the company should make to earn this profit. • *Analysis* [4]

Solutions *in Topper's Style*

My Commitment *I affirm that I am reviewing these solutions only after I have solved the Sample Question Paper 9 on my own. My purpose of looking the solutions is solely to verify whether my answers/solutions were correct or not and to identify my mistakes in case my solutions were wrong or I could not solve that.*

1. (i) (c) Given, the matrix has 18 elements.

Therefore, following are the possible orders

$1\times18,\ 18\times1,\ 2\times9,\ 9\times2,\ 3\times6$ and 6×3

Hence, the number of possible orders are 6.

(ii) (a) Given, $\tan^{-1}\left[2\sin\left(2\cos^{-1}\frac{\sqrt{3}}{2}\right)\right]$

$$=\tan^{-1}\left[2\sin\left(2\times\frac{\pi}{6}\right)\right]=\tan^{-1}\left(2\sin\frac{\pi}{3}\right)$$

$$=\tan^{-1}\left(2\times\frac{\sqrt{3}}{2}\right)=\tan^{-1}\sqrt{3}=\frac{\pi}{3}$$

(iii) (c) Given, $A=\{1, 2, 3, 4, 5, 6, 7\}$, $R=\{(a, b)$: both a and b are either odd or even$\}$ for any element a in A, both a and a must be either odd or even so that $(a, a)\in R$. So, R is reflexive.

Further, $(a, b)\in R\Rightarrow$ Both a and b must be either odd or even $\Rightarrow (b, a)\in R$.

So, R is symmetry.

Similarly, $(a, b)\in R$ and $(b, c)\in R$

$\Rightarrow$ All elements a, b and c must be either even or odd simultaneously $\Rightarrow (a, c)\in R$.

So, R is transitive.

Hence, R is an equivalence relation.

(iv) (a) We know that $f(x)=\cot x$ is continuous in $R-\{n\pi: n\in Z\}$.

$\because\ f(x)=\cot x=\dfrac{\cos x}{\sin x}$ $\quad[\because \sin x=0$ at $n\pi, n\in Z]$

Hence, $f(x)=\cot x$ is discontinuous on the set $\{x=n\pi: n\in Z\}$.

(v) (c) Given differential equation is $\left[1+\left(\dfrac{dy}{dx}\right)^2\right]=\dfrac{d^2y}{dx^2}$

$\therefore$ Order $=2$ and degree $=1$

(vi) (c) We know that

$$P\left(\frac{A}{B}\right)=\frac{P(A\cap B)}{P(B)}$$

$$\therefore\quad P\left(\frac{A}{B}\right)=\frac{\frac{4}{13}}{\frac{9}{13}}=\frac{4}{9}\left[\because P(A\cap B)=\frac{4}{13}, P(B)=\frac{9}{13}\right]$$

(vii) (d) Let $I=\int\dfrac{x^3}{x+1}dx=\int\left((x^2-x+1)-\dfrac{1}{(x+1)}\right)dx$

[dividing x^3 by $(x+1)$]

$$=\frac{x^3}{3}-\frac{x^2}{2}+x-\log|x+1|+C$$

(viii) (a) We have, $y=\sqrt{3x+2}+\dfrac{1}{\sqrt{2x^2+4}}$

$$=(3x+2)^{\frac{1}{2}}+(2x^2+4)^{-\frac{1}{2}}$$

On differentiating both sides w.r.t. x, we get

$$\frac{dy}{dx}=\frac{1}{2}(3x+2)^{\frac{1}{2}-1}\cdot\frac{d}{dx}(3x+2)+\left(-\frac{1}{2}\right)(2x^2+4)^{-\frac{1}{2}-1}\cdot\frac{d}{dx}(2x^2+4)$$

$$=\frac{1}{2}(3x+2)^{-\frac{1}{2}}\cdot(3)-\left(\frac{1}{2}\right)(2x^2+4)^{-\frac{3}{2}}\cdot 4x$$

$$=\frac{3}{2\sqrt{3x+2}}-\frac{2x}{(2x^2+4)^{3/2}}$$

(ix) (c) I. On putting $t = x^5 + 1 \Rightarrow dt = 5x^4 dx$.

Therefore, $\int 5x^4\sqrt{x^5+1}\,dx$

$$= \int \sqrt{t}\,dt = \frac{2}{3}t^{\frac{3}{2}} = \frac{2}{3}(x^5+1)^{\frac{3}{2}}$$

Hence, $\int_{-1}^{1} 5x^4\sqrt{x^5+1}\,dx = \left[\frac{2}{3}(x^5+1)^{\frac{3}{2}}\right]_{-1}^{1}$

$$= \frac{2}{3}\left[(1^5+1)^{\frac{3}{2}} - [(-1)^5+1]^{\frac{3}{2}}\right]$$

$$= \frac{2}{3}\left[2^{\frac{3}{2}} - 0^{\frac{3}{2}}\right] = \frac{2}{3}(2\sqrt{2}) = \frac{4\sqrt{2}}{3}$$

Alternate Method

Let $t = x^5 + 1$.

$\Rightarrow dt = 5x^4 dx$.

Also, when $x = -1, t = 0$ and when $x = 1, t = 2$

Hence, $\int_{-1}^{1} 5x^4\sqrt{x^5+1}\,dx = \int_0^2 \sqrt{t}\;dt$

$$= \frac{2}{3}\left[t^{\frac{3}{2}}\right]_0^2 = \frac{2}{3}\left[2^{\frac{3}{2}} - 0^{\frac{3}{2}}\right] = \frac{2}{3}(2\sqrt{2}) = \frac{4\sqrt{2}}{3}$$

II. Let $t = \tan^{-1}x, \Rightarrow dt = \frac{1}{1+x^2}dx$.

Also, when $x = 0, t = 0$ and when $x = 1, t = \frac{\pi}{4}$.

Hence, $\int_0^1 \frac{\tan^{-1}x}{1+x^2}dx = \int_0^{\frac{\pi}{4}} t\;dt = \left[\frac{t^2}{2}\right]_0^{\frac{\pi}{4}}$

$$= \frac{1}{2}\left[\frac{\pi^2}{16} - 0\right] = \frac{\pi^2}{32}$$

(x) (a) A is true because a square matrix A is invertible iff $|A| \neq 0$ i.e. if A is a non-singular matrix.

R is true and correctly explains the assertion.

$A^{-1} = \frac{1}{|A|}\text{adj}(A)$ shows that the existence of the inverse directly depends on the non-zero determinant of A.

(xi) (a) Let A be the event that Isha gets scholarship and B be the event that Priti gets scholarship.

Then, given $P(A) = 0.9$ and $P(B) = 0.8$.

The probability that none of them gets the scholarship $= \{1 - P(A)\}\{1 - P(B)\} = (1 - 0.9)(1 - 0.8)$
$= 0.1 \times 0.2 = 0.02$

Hence, Probability that atleast one of them gets the scholarship $= 1 - 0.02 = 0.98$

(xii) Let $A = [a_{ij}]$ be a skew-symmetric matrix.

Then, $\quad a_{ij} = -a_{ji}, \forall i, j$

$\Rightarrow \quad a_{ii} = -a_{ii}, \forall i \Rightarrow 2a_{ii} = 0$

$\Rightarrow \quad a_{ii} = 0, \forall i \quad$ [for diagonal elements, $i = j$]

$\Rightarrow \quad a_{11} = a_{22} = a_{33} = \ldots = a_{nn} = 0$

$\Rightarrow$ All the diagonal elements of a skew-symmetric matrix are zero.

(xiii) LHS $= 2\tan^{-1}(-3) = -2\tan^{-1}3$

[$\because \tan^{-1}(-x) = -\tan^{-1}x, x \in R$]

$$= -\left[\cos^{-1}\frac{1-3^2}{1+3^2}\right]$$

$\left[\because 2\tan^{-1}x = \cos^{-1}\frac{1-x^2}{1+x^2}, x \geq 0\right]$

$$= -\left[\cos^{-1}\left(\frac{-8}{10}\right)\right] = -\left[\cos^{-1}\left(\frac{-4}{5}\right)\right]$$

$$= -\left[\pi - \cos^{-1}\left(\frac{4}{5}\right)\right]$$

[$\because \cos^{-1}(-x) = \pi - \cos^{-1}x, x \in [-1, 1]$]

$$= -\pi + \cos^{-1}\left(\frac{4}{5}\right) = -\pi + \tan^{-1}\left(\frac{3}{4}\right)$$

$\left[\text{let } \cos^{-1}\left(\frac{4}{5}\right) = \theta \Rightarrow \cos\theta = \frac{4}{5} \Rightarrow \tan\theta = \frac{3}{4} \Rightarrow \theta = \tan^{-1}\frac{3}{4}\right]$

$$= \pi + \left[\frac{\pi}{2} - \cot^{-1}\left(\frac{3}{4}\right)\right]$$

$\left[\because \tan^{-1}x + \cot^{-1}x = \frac{\pi}{2}\right]$

$$= -\frac{\pi}{2} - \cot^{-1}\frac{3}{4} = -\frac{\pi}{2} - \tan^{-1}\frac{4}{3}$$

$\left[\because \tan^{-1}x = \cot^{-1}\frac{1}{x}\right]$

$$= -\frac{\pi}{2} + \tan^{-1}\left(\frac{-4}{3}\right) \quad [\because \tan^{-1}(-x) = -\tan^{-1}x]$$

$=$ RHS

(xiv) Given, $\begin{vmatrix} 2 & 4 \\ 5 & 1 \end{vmatrix} = \begin{vmatrix} 2x & 4 \\ 6 & x \end{vmatrix}$

$\Rightarrow \quad 2 \times 1 - 5 \times 4 = 2x \times x - 6 \times 4$

$\Rightarrow \quad 2 - 20 = 2x^2 - 24$

$\Rightarrow \quad 18 = 2x^2 - 24$

$\Rightarrow \quad 2x^2 = 6$

$\Rightarrow \quad x^2 = 3$

$\therefore \quad x = \pm\sqrt{3} \quad$ [take square root]

(xv) Given that $f(x) = 2x - 3, \forall x \in R$

Now, let $\quad y = 2x - 3$

$\Rightarrow \quad 2x = y + 3 \Rightarrow x = \frac{y+3}{2}$

$\therefore \quad f^{-1}(x) = \frac{x+3}{2}$

2. (i) We have, $\sin^{-1}(1-x) - 2\sin^{-1}x = \frac{\pi}{2}$

$\Rightarrow \quad \sin^{-1}(1-x) = \frac{\pi}{2} + 2\sin^{-1}x$

$\Rightarrow \quad 1 - x = \sin\left(\frac{\pi}{2} + 2\sin^{-1}x\right)$

$\Rightarrow \quad 1 - x = \cos(2\sin^{-1}x)$

$\left[\because \sin\left(\frac{\pi}{2} + \theta\right) = \cos\theta\right]$

$\Rightarrow \quad 1-x=\cos\{\cos^{-1}(1-2x^2)\}$
$[\because 2\sin^{-1}x=\cos^{-1}(1-2x^2)]$

$\Rightarrow \quad 1-x=(1-2x^2)$

$\Rightarrow \quad x=2x^2$

$\Rightarrow \quad x(2x-1)=0$

$\Rightarrow \quad x=0 \text{ or } x=\frac{1}{2}$

For $x=\frac{1}{2}$, LHS $=\sin^{-1}(1-x)-2\sin^{-1}x$

$=\sin^{-1}\frac{1}{2}-2\sin^{-1}\frac{1}{2}$

$=-\sin^{-1}\frac{1}{2}=\frac{-\pi}{6}\neq$ RHS

So, $x=\frac{1}{2}$ is not a root of the given equation.

For $x=0$, LHS $=\sin^{-1}(1-0)-2\sin^{-1}0$

$=\sin^{-1}1-0$

$=\frac{\pi}{2}=$ RHS

Hence, $x=0$ is a root of the given equation.

Common Mistake

Check whether the obtained solution satisfies the given equation or not.

Or

(ii) Consider $\cos(\tan^{-1}x)=\cos\left\{\cos^{-1}\frac{1}{\sqrt{1+x^2}}\right\}$

$\left[\because \tan^{-1}x=\cos^{-1}\frac{1}{\sqrt{1+x^2}}\right]$

$=\frac{1}{\sqrt{1+x^2}}$ ...(i)

LHS $=\sin[\cot^{-1}\{\cos(\tan^{-1}x)\}]$

$=\sin\left\{\cot^{-1}\frac{1}{\sqrt{1+x^2}}\right\}$ [from Eq. (i)]

$=\sin\left\{\sin^{-1}\frac{1}{\sqrt{1+\left(\frac{1}{\sqrt{1+x^2}}\right)^2}}\right\}$

$\left[\because \cot^{-1}x=\sin^{-1}\frac{1}{\sqrt{1+x^2}}\right]$

$=\sin\left\{\sin^{-1}\frac{\sqrt{1+x^2}}{\sqrt{2+x^2}}\right\}$

$=\frac{\sqrt{1+x^2}}{\sqrt{2+x^2}}=\sqrt{\frac{x^2+1}{x^2+2}}$

$=$ RHS

3. Given differential equation is $(x+2y^3)\frac{dy}{dx}=y$ can be rewritten as

$$x+2y^3=y\frac{dx}{dy}\Rightarrow \frac{x}{y}+2y^2=\frac{dx}{dy}$$

$$\Rightarrow \frac{dx}{dy}-\frac{x}{y}=2y^2$$

$$\Rightarrow \frac{dx}{dy}-\frac{1}{y}\cdot x=2y^2 \quad ...(i)$$

which is a linear differential equation of the form $\frac{dx}{dy}+Px=Q$, where P and Q are the functions of y or constants.

Here, $P=-\frac{1}{y}$ and $Q=2y^2$

$\therefore \quad \text{IF}=e^{\int P\,dy}=e^{\int\frac{-1}{y}dy}$

$=e^{-\log y}=e^{\log y^{-1}}=y^{-1}=\frac{1}{y}$

The solution is given by

$x\cdot\text{IF}=\int Q\cdot\text{IF}.\,dy+C$

$\Rightarrow x\cdot\frac{1}{y}=\int\frac{1}{y}\cdot 2y^2dy+C$

$\Rightarrow \frac{x}{y}=2\int y\,dy+C$

$\Rightarrow \frac{x}{y}=2\cdot\frac{y^2}{2}+C$

$\Rightarrow x=y(y^2+C)$, which is the required solution.

4. We have, $r(x)=p[q(x)]$

On differentiating w.r.t. x, we get

$r'(x)=p'[q(x)]\cdot q'(x)$

On substituting $x=0$, we get

$r'(0)=p'[q(0)]\cdot q'(0)$

$=p'(4)\cdot 15$ $[\because q(0)=4, q'(0)=15]$

$=12\times 15$ $[\because p'(4)=12]$

$=180$

Hence, $r'(0)=180$

5. (i) Given, $P(A\cup B)=\frac{3}{5}$, $P(A\cap B)=\frac{1}{5}$ and $P(\overline{A})=\frac{3}{4}$

Now, $P(A\cup B)=P(A)+P(B)-P(A\cap B)$

$\Rightarrow \frac{3}{5}=\left(1-\frac{3}{4}\right)+P(B)-\frac{1}{5}$ $[\because P(\overline{A})=1-P(A)]$

$\Rightarrow \frac{3}{5}+\frac{1}{5}=\frac{1}{4}+P(B)$

$\Rightarrow \frac{4}{5}=\frac{1}{4}+P(B)$

$\Rightarrow P(B)=\frac{4}{5}-\frac{1}{4}=\frac{11}{20}$

Hence, $P(\overline{A}\cap B)=P(B)-P(A\cap B)=\frac{11}{20}-\frac{1}{5}=\frac{7}{20}$

Or

(ii) The integers from 1 to 11 are 1, 2, 3, 4, 5, 6, 7, 8, 9, 10, 11.
Out of these, there are 5 even and 6 odd integers.
Let A be the event that both numbers chosen are odd and B be the event that the sum of the numbers chosen is even.

(a) Then, $P(A)=\dfrac{^6C_2}{^{11}C_2}=\dfrac{\frac{6\times5}{2}}{\frac{11\times10}{2}}=\dfrac{3}{11}$

(b) We know that the sum of two integers will be even, if either both the chosen integers are even or both are odd.

Therefore, $P(B)=\dfrac{^6C_2+{^5C_2}}{^{11}C_2}$

$$=\frac{\frac{6\times5}{2}+\frac{5\times4}{2}}{\frac{11\times10}{2}}$$

$$=\frac{30+20}{110}=\frac{50}{110}=\frac{5}{11}$$

6. Given, $\begin{vmatrix}\sin\alpha & -1\\ 1 & 2\sin\alpha\end{vmatrix}=\begin{vmatrix}\sin\alpha & 0\\ -4 & 3\end{vmatrix}$

$\Rightarrow \quad 2\sin^2\alpha+1=3\sin\alpha-0$

$\Rightarrow \quad 2\sin^2\alpha-3\sin\alpha+1=0$

$\Rightarrow \quad 2\sin^2\alpha-2\sin\alpha-\sin\alpha+1=0$

$\Rightarrow \quad 2\sin\alpha(\sin\alpha-1)-1(\sin\alpha-1)=0$

$\Rightarrow \quad (2\sin\alpha-1)(\sin\alpha-1)=0$

$\Rightarrow \quad \sin\alpha=\dfrac{1}{2}$ or $\sin\alpha=1$

$\Rightarrow \quad \sin\alpha=\sin30^\circ$ or $\sin\alpha=\sin90^\circ$

$\Rightarrow \quad \alpha=30^\circ$ or $\alpha=90^\circ$

7. The smallest relation R containing (1, 2) and (2, 3), which is reflexive and transitive but not symmetric is $R=\{(1,1),(2,2),(3,3),(1,2),(2,3),(1,3)\}$.

Now, we are left with three pairs, (2, 1), (3, 1) and (3, 2). If we add the ordered pair (2, 1) to R, then we get the relation say R_1.

It can be observed that, the relation R_1 will be reflexive, transitive but not symmetric.

Similarly, if we add the ordered pair (3, 2) to R, then we get the relation say R_2, which will be reflexive, transitive but not symmetric.

But if we add two ordered pairs (2, 1), (3, 2) or (2, 1), (3, 1) or (3, 1), (3, 2) or single ordered pair (3, 1) to R at a time, then we have to add some other ordered pair to maintain the condition of transitivity, but in this process the relation become symmetric also which is not required.

Hence, the total number of desired relations is three.

8. Given differential equation is

$$e^x\sqrt{1-y^2}\,dx+\frac{y}{x}\,dy=0$$

$\Rightarrow \quad e^x\sqrt{1-y^2}\,dx=\dfrac{-y}{x}\,dy$

$\Rightarrow \quad xe^x\,dx=\dfrac{-y}{\sqrt{1-y^2}}\,dy$

On integrating both sides, we get

$$\int xe^x\,dx=-\int\frac{y}{\sqrt{1-y^2}}\,dy \quad \ldots\text{(i)}$$

Now, $\int \underset{\text{I}}{x}\,\underset{\text{II}}{e^x}\,dx=x\int e^x dx-\int\left[\dfrac{d}{dx}x\int e^x\,dx\right]dx$

[use integration by parts]

$\Rightarrow \quad \int xe^x dx=xe^x-\int e^x\,dx=xe^x-e^x+C_1$

and for $\int\dfrac{y}{\sqrt{1-y^2}}\,dy$

On putting $1-y^2=t^2 \Rightarrow -2y\,dy=2t \Rightarrow y\,dy=t\,dt$

$\therefore \int\dfrac{y}{\sqrt{1-y^2}}\,dy=-\int t\dfrac{dt}{t}=-\int dt=-t+C_2$ then

$\Rightarrow \int\dfrac{y}{\sqrt{1-y^2}}\,dy=-\sqrt{1-y^2}+C_2$

On putting these values in Eq. (i), we get

$$xe^x-e^x+C_1=\sqrt{1-y^2}-C_2$$

$\Rightarrow \quad xe^x-e^x=\sqrt{1-y^2}+C$, where $C=-C_1-C_2$

which is the required solution.

9. (i) We have,

$$f(x)=\frac{x^4}{4}-x^3-5x^2+24x+12$$

On differentiating both sides w.r.t. x, we get

$$f'(x)=x^3-3x^2-10x+24=(x-2)(x^2-x-12)$$
$$=(x-2)(x^2-4x+3x-12)$$
$$=(x-2)\{x(x-4)+3(x-4)\}$$
$$=(x-2)(x-4)(x+3) \quad [1]$$

Now, put $f'(x)=0$, which gives $x=2$, 4 and -3.

The points $x=-3$, $x=2$ and $x=4$ divide the whole real line into four disjoint intervals namely,

$$(-\infty,-3),(-3,2),(2,4),(4,\infty)$$

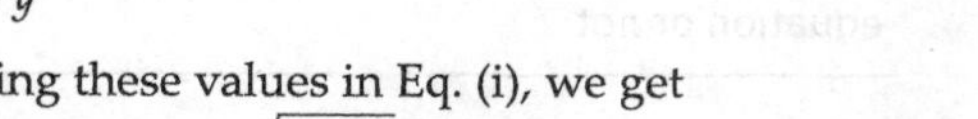

[1]

for $x\in(-\infty,-3)$, $f'(x)<0$

for $x\in(-3,2)$, $f'(x)>0$

for $x\in(2,4)$, $f'(x)<0$

and for $x\in(4,\infty)$, $f'(x)>0$ [1]

Hence, $f(x)$ is strictly increasing in the intervals $(-3,2)$ and $(4,\infty)$ and strictly decreasing in the intervals $(-\infty,-3)$ and $(2,4)$.

Or

(ii) Let AC be the ladder, $BC = x$ and height of the wall, $AB = y$.

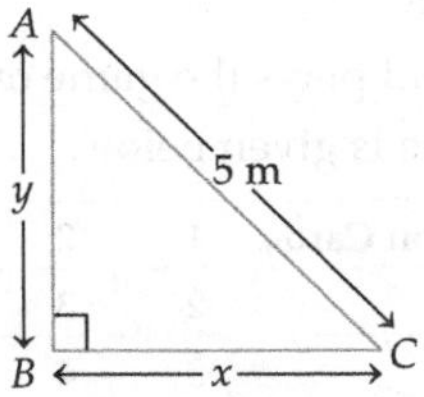

As the ladder is pulled along the ground away from the wall at the rate of 2 m /s.

So, $\frac{dx}{dt} = 2\text{ m /s}$

To find $\frac{dy}{dt}$, when $x = 4$. [1]

In right angled ΔABC, by Pythagoras theorem, we get

$(AB)^2 + (BC)^2 = (AC)^2 \Rightarrow x^2 + y^2 = 25$ ...(i)

When $x = 4$, then $(4)^2 + y^2 = 25 \Rightarrow 16 + y^2 = 25$

$\Rightarrow y^2 = 9 \Rightarrow y = \sqrt{9}$

[take positive square root]

$\therefore y = 3$ [1]

On differentiating both sides of Eq. (i) w.r.t. t, we get

$$2x\frac{dx}{dt} + 2y\frac{dy}{dt} = 0$$

$$\Rightarrow x\frac{dx}{dt} + y\frac{dy}{dt} = 0 \quad ...(ii)$$

[divide both sides by 2]

On substituting the values of x, y and $\frac{dx}{dt}$ in Eq. (ii), we get

$$(4 \times 2) + 3 \times \frac{dy}{dt} = 0 \Rightarrow 8 + 3 \times \frac{dy}{dt} = 0$$ [1]

$$\Rightarrow \frac{dy}{dt} = \frac{-8}{3}\text{ m /s}$$

Hence, the height of the wall is decreasing at the rate of $\frac{8}{3}$ m /s. [1]

Note In a rate of change of a quantity, +ve sign shows that it is increasing and – ve sign shows that it is decreasing.

10. (i) Given function is

$$f(x) = \begin{cases} \lambda(x^2 + 2), & \text{if } x \le 0 \\ 4x + 6, & \text{if } x > 0 \end{cases}.$$

(a) Since, $f(x)$ is continuous at $x = 0$.

$\therefore$ LHL = RHL = $f(0)$ ...(i)

Here, RHL = $\lim_{x \to 0^+} f(x) = \lim_{x \to 0^+} (4x + 6)$

$= \lim_{h \to 0} [4(0 + h) + 6]$

[put $x = 0 + h$; when $x \to 0^+$, then $h \to 0$]

$= \lim_{h \to 0} (4h + 6) = 4 \times 0 + 6 = 6$

and $f(0) = \lambda(0^2 + 2) = 2\lambda$

From Eq. (i), We have RHL = $f(0)$

$\Rightarrow 2\lambda = 6$

$\Rightarrow \lambda = 3$

(b) On putting the value of $\lambda = 3$, given function becomes

$$f(x) = \begin{cases} 3(x^2 + 2), & \text{if } x \le 0 \\ 4x + 6, & \text{if } x > 0 \end{cases}$$

Now, let us check the differentiability at $x = 0$.

$$\text{LHD} = \lim_{h \to 0} \frac{f(0 - h) - f(0)}{-h}$$

$$= \lim_{h \to 0} \frac{3[(0 - h)^2 + 2] - 3(0 + 2)}{-h}$$

$$= \lim_{h \to 0} \frac{3[h^2 + 2] - 6}{-h} = \lim_{h \to 0} (-3h) = 0$$

and $$\text{RHD} = \lim_{h \to 0} \frac{f(0 + h) - f(0)}{h}$$

$$= \lim_{h \to 0} \frac{[4(0 + h) + 6] - 3(0 + 2)}{h}$$

$$= \lim_{h \to 0} \frac{4h}{h} = 4$$

$\because$ LHD $\ne$ RHD

$\therefore f(x)$ is not differentiable at $x = 0$.

(c) When $x \le 0$ we have, the function,

$$f(x) = 3(x^2 + 2)$$

On differentiating w.r.t. x, we get

$$f'(x) = 3\frac{d}{dx}(x^2 + 2)$$

$$= 3\left[\frac{d}{dx}(x^2) + \frac{d}{dx}(2)\right]$$

$$= 3[2x + 0] = 6x$$

Or

(ii) (a) We have, $y = \sqrt{\frac{1 - x}{1 + x}}$

On differentiating both sides w.r.t. x, we get

$$\frac{dy}{dx} = \frac{1}{2}\left(\frac{1 - x}{1 + x}\right)^{-\frac{1}{2}} \frac{d}{dx}\left(\frac{1 - x}{1 + x}\right)$$

$$= \frac{1}{2} \times \sqrt{\frac{1 + x}{1 - x}} \times \frac{(1 + x)(-1) - (1 - x) \cdot 1}{(1 + x)^2}$$

$$\Rightarrow \frac{dy}{dx} = \frac{1}{2}\sqrt{\frac{1 + x}{1 - x}} \times \frac{-1 - x - 1 + x}{(1 + x)^2}$$

$$= \frac{-1}{2}\sqrt{\frac{1 + x}{1 - x}} \times \frac{2}{(1 + x)^2} = \frac{-1}{\sqrt{1 - x}\,(1 + x)\sqrt{1 + x}}$$

$$= \frac{-1}{(1 + x)\sqrt{1 - x^2}}$$

(b) We have, $\frac{dy}{dx}=-\frac{1}{2}\sqrt{\frac{1+x}{1-x}}\times\frac{2}{(1+x)^2}$

$\Rightarrow (1-x^2)\frac{dy}{dx}=-\sqrt{\frac{1+x}{1-x}}\times\frac{1}{(1+x)^2}(1-x^2)$

[multiplying both sides by $(1-x^2)$]

$\Rightarrow (1-x^2)\frac{dy}{dx}=-\sqrt{\frac{1+x}{1-x}}\times\frac{1}{(1+x)^2}\times(1-x)(1+x)$

$\Rightarrow (1-x^2)\frac{dy}{dx}=-\sqrt{\frac{1+x}{1-x}}\times\frac{(1-x)}{(1+x)}$

$\Rightarrow (1-x^2)\frac{dy}{dx}=-\sqrt{\frac{1-x}{1+x}}$

$\Rightarrow (1-x^2)\frac{dy}{dx}+y=0 \quad \left[\because y=\sqrt{\frac{1-x}{1+x}}\right]$

Hence proved.

(c) We have, $\frac{dy}{dx}=\frac{-1}{(1+x)\sqrt{1-x^2}}$ [from part (a)]

On putting $x=0$ and $y=2$, we get

$$\left[\frac{dy}{dx}\right]_{(0,2)}=\frac{-1}{(1+0)\sqrt{1-0}}=-1$$

11. (i) Combined sales in September and October for each farmer in each variety is given by

$$A+B=\begin{bmatrix}10000 & 20000 & 30000\\ 50000 & 30000 & 10000\end{bmatrix}+\begin{bmatrix}5000 & 10000 & 6000\\ 20000 & 10000 & 10000\end{bmatrix}$$

	Basmati	Permal	Naura
Ramkishan	15000	30000	36000
Gurucharan Singh	70000	40000	20000

$$=\begin{bmatrix}15000 & 30000 & 36000\\ 70000 & 40000 & 20000\end{bmatrix}$$

(ii) Changes in sales from September to October is given by

$$A-B=\begin{bmatrix}10000 & 20000 & 30000\\ 50000 & 30000 & 10000\end{bmatrix}-\begin{bmatrix}5000 & 10000 & 6000\\ 20000 & 10000 & 10000\end{bmatrix}$$

	Basmati	Permal	Naura
Ramkishan	5000	10000	24000
Gurucharan Singh	30000	20000	0

(iii) Profit for each farmer and for each variety = 2% of October sale = 2% of $B=\frac{2}{100}\times B=0.02\times B$

	Basmati	Permal	Naura
Ramkishan	5000	10000	6000
Gurucharan Singh	20000	10000	10000

(the above matrix multiplied by 0.02)

	Basmati	Permal	Naura
Ramkishan	100	200	120
Gurucharan Singh	400	200	200

12. (i) (a) According to the question, the score is the sum of the numbers shown on the cards.

Therefore from the table, $r=3+1=4$ and $s=4+4=8$

(b) Given, Anil plays the game once.

Now, table is given below.

Number on Cards	1	2	3	4
1	2	3	$r=4$	5
2	3	4	5	6
3	4	5	6	7
4	5	6	7	$s=8$

Here, total outcomes = 16

S = Anil's score

So, probability distribution of S is

S	2	3	4	5	6	7	8
$P(S=s)$	$\frac{1}{16}$	$\frac{2}{16}=\frac{1}{8}$	$\frac{3}{16}$	$\frac{4}{16}=\frac{1}{4}$	$\frac{3}{16}$	$\frac{2}{16}=\frac{1}{8}$	$\frac{1}{16}$

(c) Probability that Anil's score is atleast 6

i.e. $P(S\geq 6)=P(S=6)+P(S=7)+P(S=8)$

$=\frac{3}{16}+\frac{2}{16}+\frac{1}{16}=\frac{6}{16}=\frac{3}{8}$

Or

(ii) Given, A and B are two independent events with $P(\overline{A}\cap B)=\frac{2}{15}$ and $P(A\cap\overline{B})=\frac{1}{6}$.

We know that if A and B are independent events, then $\overline{A}, B$ and $A, \overline{B}$ are independent events.

So, $P(\overline{A}\cap B)=\frac{2}{15}\Rightarrow P(B)\cdot P(\overline{A})=\frac{2}{15}$

$\Rightarrow \quad P(B)\cdot[1-P(A)]=\frac{2}{15}$

$[\because P(A)+P(\overline{A})=1]$

$\Rightarrow \quad P(B)-P(A)\cdot P(B)=\frac{2}{15}$ ...(i)

and $P(A\cap\overline{B})=\frac{1}{6}\Rightarrow P(A)\cdot P(\overline{B})=\frac{1}{6}$

$\Rightarrow \quad P(A)\cdot[1-P(B)]=\frac{1}{6}$

$[\because P(B)+P(\overline{B})=1]$

$\Rightarrow \quad P(A)-P(A)P(B)=\frac{1}{6}$ ...(ii)

On subtracting Eq. (i) from Eq. (ii), we get

$$P(A)-P(B)=\frac{1}{6}-\frac{2}{15}=\frac{5-4}{30}=\frac{1}{30}$$

$\Rightarrow \quad P(A)=\frac{1}{30}+P(B)$ ...(iii)

Now, substituting the value of $P(A)$ in Eq. (i), we get

$$P(B)-\left[\frac{1}{30}+P(B)\right]\cdot P(B)=\frac{2}{15}$$

Let $P(B)=x$, then equation becomes

$$x-\left(\frac{1}{30}+x\right)x=\frac{2}{15}$$

$\Rightarrow$ $30x-(1+30x)x=4$

$\Rightarrow$ $30x-x-30x^2=4$

$\Rightarrow$ $30x^2-29x+4=0$

$\Rightarrow$ $(6x-1)(5x-4)=0$

$\Rightarrow$ $x=\frac{1}{6}$ or $\frac{4}{5}$

$\Rightarrow$ $P(B)=\frac{1}{6}$ or $\frac{4}{5}$ $[\because x=P(B)]$

Now, if $P(B)=\frac{1}{6}$, then

$$P(A)=\frac{1}{30}+\frac{1}{6}=\frac{1+5}{30}=\frac{6}{30}=\frac{1}{5} \quad \text{[from Eq. (iii)]}$$

and if $P(B)=\frac{4}{5}$, then

$$P(A)=\frac{1}{30}+\frac{4}{5}=\frac{1+24}{30}=\frac{25}{30}=\frac{5}{6} \quad \text{[from Eq. (iii)]}$$

13. (i) Let $I=\int\frac{x^2}{(x^2+4)(x^2+9)}dx$

Consider $\frac{x^2}{(x^2+4)(x^2+9)}$ and put $x^2=t$,

Then, $\frac{x^2}{(x^2+4)(x^2+9)}=\frac{t}{(t+4)(t+9)}$

Now, let $\frac{t}{(t+4)(t+9)}=\frac{A}{(t+4)}+\frac{B}{(t+9)}$

$\Rightarrow$ $t=A(t+9)+B(t+4)$

On putting $t=-9$, we get

$$-9=-5B\Rightarrow B=\frac{9}{5}$$

On putting $t=-4$, we get

$$-4=5A\Rightarrow A=\frac{-4}{5}$$

Thus, $\frac{t}{(t+4)(t+9)}=\frac{-4}{5(t+4)}+\frac{9}{5(t+9)}$

Then, $\frac{x^2}{(x^2+4)(x^2+9)}=\frac{-4}{5(x^2+4)}+\frac{9}{5(x^2+9)}$

$\therefore$ $I=\int\frac{x^2}{(x^2+4)(x^2+9)}dx$

$$=\int\frac{-4}{5(x^2+4)}dx+\int\frac{9}{5(x^2+9)}dx$$

$$=\frac{-4}{5}\int\frac{dx}{x^2+(2)^2}+\frac{9}{5}\int\frac{dx}{x^2+(3)^2}$$

$$=\frac{-4}{5}\cdot\frac{1}{2}\tan^{-1}\left(\frac{x}{2}\right)+\frac{9}{5}\cdot\frac{1}{3}\cdot\tan^{-1}\left(\frac{x}{3}\right)+C$$

$$\left[\because\int\frac{1}{x^2+a^2}dx=\frac{1}{a}\tan^{-1}\frac{x}{a}+C\right]$$

$$=\frac{3}{5}\tan^{-1}\left(\frac{x}{3}\right)-\frac{2}{5}\tan^{-1}\left(\frac{x}{2}\right)+C$$

Or

(ii) Let $I=\int_0^{\pi/4}(\sqrt{\tan x}+\sqrt{\cot x})dx$

$$=\int_0^{\pi/4}\left(\frac{\sqrt{\sin x}}{\sqrt{\cos x}}+\frac{\sqrt{\cos x}}{\sqrt{\sin x}}\right)dx$$

$$=\int_0^{\pi/4}\frac{(\sin x+\cos x)}{\sqrt{\sin x\cos x}}dx$$

$$=\sqrt{2}\int_0^{\pi/4}\frac{(\sin x+\cos x)}{\sqrt{2\sin x\cos x}}dx$$

[multiply and divide by $\sqrt{2}$]

$$=\sqrt{2}\int_0^{\pi/4}\frac{(\sin x+\cos x)}{\sqrt{1+2\sin x\cos x-1}}dx$$

[add and subtract 1 in denominator]

$$=\sqrt{2}\int_0^{\pi/4}\frac{(\sin x+\cos x)}{\sqrt{1-(1-2\sin x\cos x)}}dx$$

$$=\sqrt{2}\int_0^{\pi/4}\frac{(\sin x+\cos x)}{\sqrt{1-(\sin x-\cos x)^2}}dx$$

$[\because(\sin x-\cos x)^2=\sin^2x+\cos^2x-2\sin x\cos x$
$=1-2\sin x\cos x]$

Now, on putting $\sin x-\cos x=t$

$\Rightarrow$ $(\cos x+\sin x)dx=dt$

Also, when $x=0$, then $t=-1$

and when $x=\frac{\pi}{4}$, then $t=0$

$\therefore$ $I=\sqrt{2}\int_{-1}^{0}\frac{dt}{\sqrt{1-t^2}}=\sqrt{2}[\sin^{-1}t]_{-1}^{0}$

$$=\sqrt{2}[\sin^{-1}(0)-\sin^{-1}(-1)]$$

$$=\sqrt{2}[\sin^{-1}(0)+\sin^{-1}(1)]$$

$[\because\sin^{-1}(-\theta)=-\sin^{-1}\theta]$

$=\sqrt{2}\cdot\frac{\pi}{2}$ **Hence proved.**

14. (i) Given $ABCD$ be a trapezium. The length of whose three sides are 10 cm each as shown in figure.

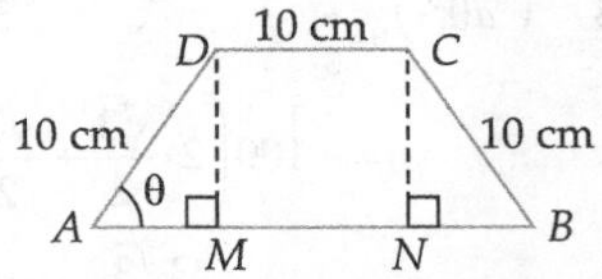

$\because$ DM and CN are perpendicular on AB.

So, $\Delta AMD\cong\Delta BNC$ [RHS axiom of congruency]

$\therefore$ $AM=BN$

Let $\angle DAM=\theta$ [in radian measure]

When $0<\theta<\frac{\pi}{2}$, then $AM=BN=10\cos\theta$

In ΔAMD,

$\cos\theta=\frac{AM}{AD}\Rightarrow AM=10\cos\theta$, $\sin\theta=\frac{MD}{AD}$

$\Rightarrow MD=10\sin\theta$ and $MD=10\sin\theta$

Let A be the area of the trapezium, then

$$A=\frac{1}{2}\text{(Sum of parallel sides)}\times\text{Height}$$

$$=\frac{1}{2}(AB+DC)\times MD$$

$$= \frac{1}{2}(AM + MN + NB + DC) \times MD$$

$$= \frac{1}{2}(10\cos\theta + 10 + 10\cos\theta + 10) \times 10\sin\theta$$

$$\Rightarrow A = 50(2\cos\theta + 2)\sin\theta = 50(\sin 2\theta + 2\sin\theta)$$

$[\because 2\sin\theta\cos\theta = \sin 2\theta]$

(ii) We have, The equation in terms of θ is

$A = 50(\sin 2\theta + 2\sin\theta)$. ...(i)

On differentiating both sides of Eq. (i) w.r.t. θ, we get

$$\frac{dA}{d\theta} = 50(2\cos 2\theta + 2\cos\theta) = 100(\cos 2\theta + \cos\theta) \quad ...(ii)$$

For critical points, put $\frac{dA}{d\theta} = 0$

$$\Rightarrow 100(\cos\theta + \cos 2\theta) = 0 \Rightarrow \cos\theta + \cos 2\theta = 0$$

$$\Rightarrow 2\cos\frac{3\theta}{2}\cos\frac{\theta}{2} = 0$$

$$\left[\because \cos C + \cos D = 2\cos\left(\frac{C+D}{2}\right)\cdot\cos\left(\frac{C-D}{2}\right)\right]$$

$$\Rightarrow \cos\frac{3\theta}{2} = 0 \text{ or } \cos\frac{\theta}{2} = 0$$

$$\Rightarrow \frac{3\theta}{2} = \frac{\pi}{2} \text{ or } \frac{\theta}{2} = \frac{\pi}{2} \Rightarrow \theta = \frac{\pi}{3} \text{ or } \pi$$

but $0 < \theta < \frac{\pi}{2}$ So, $\theta = \frac{\pi}{3}$

Thus, the critical point is $\frac{\pi}{3}$.

(iii) On differentiating Eq. (ii), w.r.t θ, we get

$$\frac{d^2A}{d\theta^2} = 100(-2\sin 2\theta - \sin\theta)$$

$$= -100(2\sin 2\theta + \sin\theta)$$

At $\theta = \frac{\pi}{3}$, $\left(\frac{d^2A}{d\theta^2}\right)_{\theta=\frac{\pi}{3}} = -100\left(2\sin\frac{2\pi}{3} + \sin\frac{\pi}{3}\right)$

$$= -100\left(2\cdot\frac{\sqrt{3}}{2} + \frac{\sqrt{3}}{2}\right)$$

$$= -100 \times \frac{3\sqrt{3}}{2} = -150\sqrt{3} < 0$$

So, A is maximum, when $\theta = \frac{\pi}{3}$.

(iv) We have, $A = 50(\sin 2\theta + 2\sin\theta)$

At $\theta = \frac{\pi}{3}$,

$$A = 50\left(\sin 2\times\frac{\pi}{3} + 2\sin\frac{\pi}{3}\right) = 50\left(\frac{\sqrt{3}}{2} + 2\times\frac{\sqrt{3}}{2}\right)$$

$$= 75\sqrt{3}$$

Hence, the maximum area of the trapezium is $75\sqrt{3}$ cm².

15. (i) (b) We have, $\vec{r}\cdot(-\hat{i} + \hat{j} + 2\hat{k}) = 5$

$$\Rightarrow (x\hat{i} + y\hat{j} + z\hat{k}).(-\hat{i} + \hat{j} + 2\hat{k}) = 5$$

$$\Rightarrow -x + y + 2z = 5$$

(ii) (c) Let $\vec{a} = \hat{i} - 2\hat{j} + 2\hat{k}$

Unit vector in the direction of vector $\vec{a}$ is given by $\frac{\vec{a}}{|\vec{a}|}$

$$= \frac{\hat{i} - 2\hat{j} + 2\hat{k}}{\sqrt{1^2 + (-2)^2 + 2^2}} = \frac{\hat{i} - 2\hat{j} + 2\hat{k}}{3}$$

∴ Vector in the direction of $\vec{a}$ with magnitude 12

$$= 12\cdot\frac{\hat{i} - 2\hat{j} + 2\hat{k}}{3} = 4(\hat{i} - 2\hat{j} + 2\hat{k})$$

(iii) (c) Given, equation of plane is

$$\vec{r}\cdot(3\hat{i} - 4\hat{j} - 12\hat{k}) = -52$$

$$\Rightarrow \vec{r}.(-3\hat{i} + 4\hat{j} + 12\hat{k}) = 52 \Rightarrow \vec{r}\cdot\vec{n} = 52,$$

where $\vec{n} = -3\hat{i} + 4\hat{j} + 12\hat{k}$

$$\Rightarrow \vec{r}\cdot\frac{\vec{n}}{|\vec{n}|} = \frac{52}{|\vec{n}|} \Rightarrow \vec{r}\cdot\hat{n} = p,$$

where $p = \frac{52}{|\vec{n}|} = \frac{52}{\sqrt{(-3)^2 + (4)^2 + (12)^2}}$

$$= \frac{52}{\sqrt{9 + 16 + 144}}$$

$$= \frac{52}{\sqrt{169}} = \frac{52}{13} = 4$$

Hence, the length of perpendicular from origin to the plane is 4 units and the unit vector normal to the given plane is $\frac{\vec{n}}{|\vec{n}|}$ i.e. $\left(\frac{-3\hat{i} + 4\hat{j} + 12\hat{k}}{13}\right)$.

Hence, both Statements are true.

(iv) Given equation of line can be written as

$$\frac{x-4}{-2} = \frac{y+3}{2} = \frac{z+2}{1}$$

Here, direction ratios of this line are (−2,2,1).

∴ Direction cosine of line parallel to above line are given by

$$\left(\frac{-2}{\sqrt{(-2)^2 + (2)^2 + (1)^2}}, \frac{2}{\sqrt{(-2)^2 + (2)^2 + (1)^2}}, \frac{1}{\sqrt{(-2)^2 + (2)^2 + (1)^2}}\right)$$

$$= \left(\frac{-2}{\sqrt{4+4+1}}, \frac{2}{\sqrt{4+4+1}}, \frac{1}{\sqrt{4+4+1}}\right)$$

$$= \left(\frac{-2}{\sqrt{9}}, \frac{2}{\sqrt{9}}, \frac{1}{\sqrt{9}}\right) = \left(-\frac{2}{3}, \frac{2}{3}, \frac{1}{3}\right)$$

Hence, the required direction cosines of a line parallel to the given line are $\left(-\frac{2}{3}, \frac{2}{3}, \frac{1}{3}\right)$.

Common Mistake

Make sure that equation of line should be in proper symmetrical form.

(v) Given, $\overrightarrow{AB} = \hat{j} + \hat{k}$ and $\overrightarrow{AC} = 3\hat{i} - \hat{j} + 4\hat{k}$.

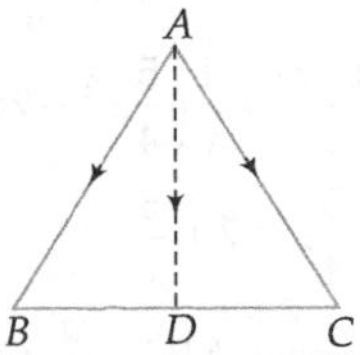

We know that median vector,

$$\overrightarrow{AD} = \frac{\overrightarrow{AB} + \overrightarrow{AC}}{2} \Rightarrow \overrightarrow{AD} = \frac{(\hat{j} + \hat{k}) + (3\hat{i} - \hat{j} + 4\hat{k})}{2}$$

$$= \frac{3\hat{i} - 5\hat{k}}{2}$$

Now, length of median $= |\overrightarrow{AD}| = \sqrt{\left(\frac{3}{2}\right)^2 + \left(\frac{5}{2}\right)^2}$

$$= \frac{1}{2}\sqrt{9 + 25} = \frac{\sqrt{34}}{2}$$

$$= \frac{\sqrt{17} \times \sqrt{2}}{2} = \sqrt{\frac{17}{2}} \text{ units}$$

16. (i) Taking A as origin, let $\vec{b}$ and $\vec{c}$ be the position vectors of B and C, respectively.

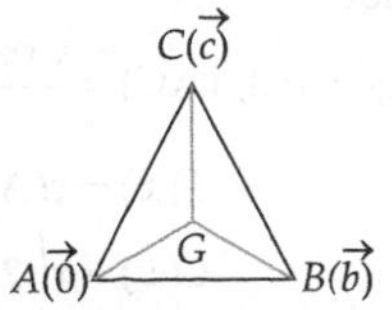

Then, position vector of centroid

$$G = \frac{\vec{0} + \vec{b} + \vec{c}}{3} = \frac{\vec{b} + \vec{c}}{3}$$

$\therefore$ Area of $\Delta ABC = \frac{1}{2} |\vec{b} \times \vec{c}|$

and area of $\Delta AGB = \frac{1}{2} |\overrightarrow{AB} \times \overrightarrow{AG}| = \frac{1}{2}\left|\vec{b} \times \left(\frac{\vec{b} + \vec{c}}{3}\right)\right|$

$$= \frac{1}{6}|(\vec{b} \times \vec{b} + \vec{b} \times \vec{c})|$$

$$= \frac{1}{6}|\vec{b} \times \vec{c}| = \frac{1}{3} \times \frac{1}{2}|\vec{b} \times \vec{c}| \quad [\because \vec{b} \times \vec{b} = \vec{0}]$$

$$= \frac{1}{3}(\text{Area of } \Delta ABC) \quad \ldots\text{(i)}$$

Similarly, area of $\Delta CGA = \frac{1}{3}(\text{Area of } \Delta ABC)$ ...(ii)

Now, ar (ΔAGB) + ar (ΔCGA) + ar (ΔGBC) = ar (ΔABC)

$\Rightarrow$ ar (ΔBGC) = ar $(\Delta ABC) - \frac{1}{3}$ ar $(\Delta ABC) - \frac{1}{3}$ ar (ΔABC)

[using Eqs. (i) and (ii)]

$\Rightarrow$ ar (ΔBGC) = ar $(\Delta ABC)\left(1 - \frac{2}{3}\right)$

$$= \frac{1}{3} \text{ ar } (\Delta ABC) \quad \ldots\text{(iii)}$$

Hence, from Eqs. (i), (ii) and (iii), we get

ar (ΔAGB) = ar (ΔBGC) = ar (ΔCGA)

$= \frac{1}{3}$ ar (ΔABC) **Hence proved.**

Or

(ii) Given, $\vec{a} = \hat{i} - 7\hat{j} + 7\hat{k}$ and $\vec{b} = 3\hat{i} - 2\hat{j} + 2\hat{k}$.

Then, $\vec{a} \times \vec{b} = \begin{vmatrix} \hat{i} & \hat{j} & \hat{k} \\ 1 & -7 & 7 \\ 3 & -2 & 2 \end{vmatrix}$

$$= \hat{i}(-14 + 14) - \hat{j}(2 - 21) + \hat{k}(-2 + 21)$$

$$= 0\hat{i} + 19\hat{j} + 19\hat{k}$$

$\therefore \quad |\vec{a} \times \vec{b}| = \sqrt{0^2 + 19^2 + 19^2}$

$$= \sqrt{361 + 361} = 19\sqrt{2}$$

Hence, a unit vector perpendicular to $\vec{a}$ and $\vec{b}$ is

$$\hat{n} = \frac{\vec{a} \times \vec{b}}{|\vec{a} \times \vec{b}|}$$

$$= \frac{19\hat{j} + 19\hat{k}}{19\sqrt{2}}$$

$\Rightarrow \quad \hat{n} = \frac{1}{\sqrt{2}}\hat{j} + \frac{1}{\sqrt{2}}\hat{k}$

17. (i) Equation of any plane through the point $(0, 6, 0)$ is

$a(x - 0) + b(y - 6) + c(z - 0) = 0$

$\Rightarrow \quad ax + b(y - 6) + cz = 0$ ...(i)

The plane (i) will contain the given line

$$\frac{x + 2}{2} = \frac{y + 3}{3} = \frac{z - 4}{-2} \quad \ldots\text{(ii)}$$

It means plane passing through $(-2, -3, 4)$ and normal to the plane is perpendicular to the line (ii)

i.e. $\quad a(-2) + b(-9) + c \cdot 4 = 0$

$\Rightarrow \quad -2a - 9b + 4c = 0$ ...(iii)

and $\quad 2a + 3b - 2c = 0$ ...(iv)

[$\because$ two lines with direction ratios a_1, b_1, c_1 and a_2, b_2, c_2 are perpendicular, iff $a_1a_2 + b_1b_2 + c_1c_2 = 0$]

On solving Eqs. (iii) and (iv), we get

$$\frac{a}{18 - 12} = \frac{b}{8 - 4} = \frac{c}{-6 + 18}$$

$\Rightarrow \quad \frac{a}{6} = \frac{b}{4} = \frac{c}{12}$

$\Rightarrow \quad \frac{a}{3} = \frac{b}{2} = \frac{c}{6} = k$ (constant)

$\Rightarrow \quad a = 3k, b = 2k$ and $c = 6k$

On substituting these values in Eq. (i), we get

$3kx + 2k(y - 6) + 6kz = 0$

$\Rightarrow \quad 3x + 2y + 6z - 12 = 0$

In vector form, this equation can be written as

$$\vec{r} \cdot (3\hat{i} + 2\hat{j} + 6\hat{k}) = 12$$

which is the required equation of plane, where $\vec{r} = x\hat{i} + y\hat{j} + z\hat{k}$.

Or

(ii) We first express the given equations in symmetrical form.

$$x = ay + b \Rightarrow \frac{x-b}{a} = y$$

and $$z = cy + d \Rightarrow \frac{z-d}{c} = y$$

Now, the equation of line $x = ay + b$ and $z = cy + d$ can be expressed in the symmetrical form as

$$\frac{x-b}{a} = \frac{y-0}{1} = \frac{z-d}{c}$$

Similarly, the equations $x = a'y + b'$ and $z = c'y + d'$ can be expressed in the symmetrical form as

$$\frac{x-b'}{a'} = \frac{y-0}{1} = \frac{z-d'}{c'}$$

Since, the direction ratios of these lines are a, 1, c and a', 1, c', respectively. Therefore, they will be perpendicular to each other, if $a \cdot a' + 1 \cdot 1 + c \cdot c' = 0$ i.e. $aa' + cc' + 1 = 0$. **Hence proved.**

18. Given curve is $y = 9x^2 \Rightarrow x^2 = \frac{1}{9}y \Rightarrow x = \frac{1}{3}\sqrt{y}$ ...(i)

It is a parabolic curve, which open upwards, symmetrical about Y-axis and passes through the origin.

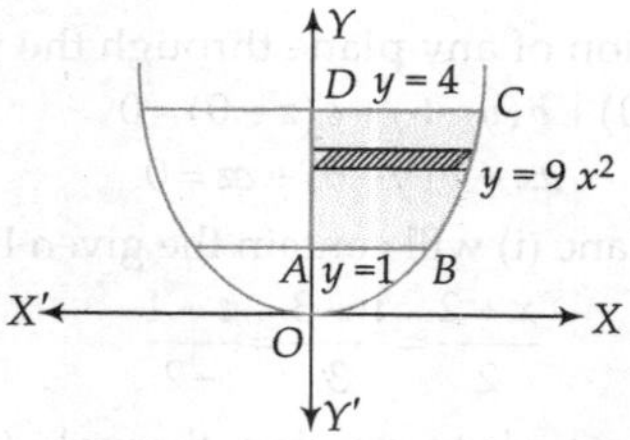

$\therefore$ Required area = Area of bounded region $ABCDA$

$$= \int_1^4 x\,dy = \frac{1}{3}\int_1^4 \sqrt{y}\,dy \quad \text{[from Eq. (i)]}$$

$$= \frac{1}{3}\left[\frac{y^{3/2}}{3/2}\right]_1^4 = \frac{1}{3} \times \frac{2}{3}[(4)^{3/2} - (1)^{3/2}] \quad [1]$$

$$= \frac{2}{9}[(2)^3 - 1]$$

$$= \frac{14}{9} \text{ sq units}$$

Hence, the required area is $\frac{14}{9}$ sq units.

19. (i) (c) A line of best fit is a straight line that minimises the distance between it and some data.

From the given plots it can be observed that only option (c) could be a line of best fit.

(ii) (b) Given demand function, $p = 500 - 7x$

We know that revenue function, $R = px$

$$= (500 - 7x)x$$
$$= 500x - 7x^2$$

Now, marginal revenue function.

$$MR = \frac{dR}{dx} = \frac{d}{dx}(500x - 7x^2) = 500 - 14x$$

(iii) Given, cost function $C(x) = \frac{5}{4}x^2 - 7x + 5$

Then, $AC = \frac{C(x)}{x} = \frac{1}{x}\left(\frac{5}{4}x^2 - 7x + 5\right)$

$\Rightarrow \quad AC = \frac{5}{4}x - 7 + \frac{5}{x}$

and marginal cost, $MC = \frac{d}{dx}C(x)$

$$= \frac{d}{dx}\left[\frac{5}{4}x^2 - 7x + 5\right] = \frac{5}{2}x - 7$$

Now, consider AC = MC

$\Rightarrow \quad \frac{5}{4}x - 7 + \frac{5}{x} = \frac{5}{2}x - 7$

$\Rightarrow \quad \frac{5}{x} = \frac{5}{2}x - \frac{5}{4}x \Rightarrow \frac{5}{x} = \frac{5}{4}x$

$\Rightarrow \quad x^2 = 4$

$\Rightarrow \quad x = 2$

Hence, at $x = 2$, MC = AC

(iv) Given, average cost function of the commodity is

$$AC = 2x + 3 + \frac{1}{x}$$

We know that

$$\text{Average Cost, (AC)} = \frac{\text{Cost function } C(x)}{x}$$

$\Rightarrow \quad C(x) = x(AC)$

$\Rightarrow \quad C(x) = x\left(2x + 3 + \frac{1}{x}\right)$

$\Rightarrow \quad C(x) = 2x^2 + 3x + 1$

Now, marginal cost function is given by,

$$MC = \frac{dC}{dx} = \frac{d}{dx}(2x^2 + 3x + 1)$$

$\Rightarrow \quad MC = 4x + 3$

(v) We have, $\Sigma x = 15, \Sigma y = 25, \Sigma x^2 = 55, \Sigma y^2 = 135$ and $\Sigma xy = 83$

Here, $n = 5$

then, $\bar{x} = \frac{\Sigma x}{n} = \frac{15}{5} = 3, \bar{y} = \frac{\Sigma y}{n} = \frac{25}{5} = 5$

$$\therefore \quad b_{xy} = \frac{\Sigma xy - \frac{\Sigma x \, \Sigma y}{n}}{\Sigma y^2 - \frac{1}{n}(\Sigma y)^2}$$

$$= \frac{83 - \frac{1}{5}(15)(25)}{135 - \frac{1}{5}(25)^2}$$

$$= \frac{83 - 75}{135 - 125} = \frac{8}{10} = 0.8$$

Hence, the regression line of x on y is $x - \bar{x} = b_{xy}(y - \bar{y})$

$\Rightarrow \quad x - 3 = 0.8(y - 5)$

$\Rightarrow \quad x = 0.8y - 1$ ...(i)

The predicted value of x when $y = 12$ is

$x = 0.8 \times 12 - 1 = 9.6 - 1 = 8.6$ [using Eq. (i)]

20. (i) Given, $AC = x + 5 + \dfrac{36}{x}$

Now, $\dfrac{d}{dx}(AC) = \dfrac{d}{dx}\left(x + 5 + \dfrac{36}{x}\right) = 1 - \dfrac{36}{x^2}$

For AC to be increasing,

$$\frac{d}{dx}(AC) > 0$$

$\Rightarrow \quad 1 - \dfrac{36}{x^2} > 0$

$\Rightarrow \quad x^2 - 36 > 0$

$\Rightarrow \quad (x-6)(x+6) > 0$

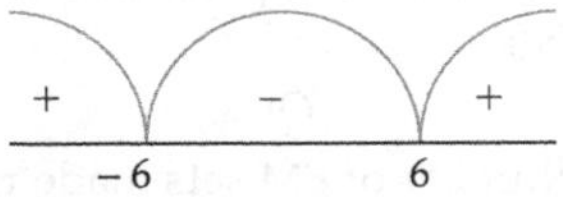

$\Rightarrow \quad x < -6$ or $x > 6$

$\Rightarrow \quad x > 6 \quad [\because x > 0]$

Hence, the average cost increases if the output $x > 6$.

Or

(ii) Given, $C(x) = 27 + 15x + 3x^2$

Now, $AC = \dfrac{C}{x} = \dfrac{27 + 15x + 3x^2}{x}$

$= \dfrac{27}{x} + 15 + 3x$

$\therefore \quad \dfrac{d}{dx}(AC) = -\dfrac{27}{x^2} + 3$

(a) AC decreases, when $\dfrac{d}{dx}(AC) < 0$

$\Rightarrow \quad 3 - \dfrac{27}{x^2} < 0$

$\Rightarrow \quad 3 < \dfrac{27}{x^2}$

$\Rightarrow \quad 1 < \dfrac{9}{x^2}$

$\Rightarrow \quad x^2 < 9$

[multiply both sides of inequality by x^2]

$\Rightarrow \quad x^2 - 9 < 0 \Rightarrow (x+3)(x-3) < 0$

$\Rightarrow \quad -3 < x < 3$

As x is positive, AC decreases in the range from $0 < x < 3$.

(b) AC increases, when $\dfrac{d}{dx}(AC) > 0$

$\Rightarrow \quad 3 - \dfrac{27}{x^2} > 0 \Rightarrow 1 > \dfrac{9}{x^2} \Rightarrow x^2 > 9$

$\Rightarrow \quad x^2 - 9 > 0 \Rightarrow (x+3)(x-3) > 0$

$\Rightarrow \quad x < -3$ or $x > 3$

As x is positive, AC increases, when $x > 3$.

21. To convert x and y into small numbers, let $X = x - 10$ and $Y = y - 20$.

Let the regression line of Y on X be $Y = a + bX$.

The normal equations are

$$\Sigma Y = na + b\Sigma X \quad \ldots(i)$$

and

$$\Sigma XY = a\Sigma X + b\Sigma X^2 \quad \ldots(ii)$$

x	$X = x - 10$	y	$Y = y - 20$	XY	X^2
14	4	22	2	8	16
12	2	23	3	6	4
13	3	22	2	6	9
14	4	24	4	16	16
12	2	24	4	8	4
	$\Sigma X = 15$		$\Sigma Y = 15$	$\Sigma XY = 44$	$\Sigma X^2 = 49$

On putting the values from table in Eqs. (i) and (ii), we get

$15 = 5a + 15b \Rightarrow a + 3b = 3 \quad \ldots(iii)$

and $\quad 44 = 15a + 49b \Rightarrow 15a + 49b = 44 \quad \ldots(iv)$

On multiplying Eq. (iii) by 15 and then subtracting from Eq. (iv), we get

$$4b = -1$$

$\Rightarrow \quad b = -\dfrac{1}{4}$

From Eq. (iii), $a = 3 - 3b = 3 - 3\left(-\dfrac{1}{4}\right) = 3 + \dfrac{3}{4} = \dfrac{15}{4}$

Hence, the regression line of Y on X is

$$Y = \frac{15}{4} - \frac{1}{4}X \Rightarrow y - 20 = \frac{15}{4} - \frac{1}{4}(x - 10)$$

$[\because X = x - 10 \text{ and } Y = y - 20]$

$\Rightarrow \quad y = -\dfrac{1}{4}x + \dfrac{15}{4} + \dfrac{10}{4} + 20 \Rightarrow y = -\dfrac{1}{4}x + \dfrac{105}{4}$

When $x = 16$, then $y = -\dfrac{1}{4}(16) + \dfrac{105}{4} = \dfrac{105}{4} - 4 = \dfrac{89}{4}$

22. (i) Let the company manufactures x number of type A sweaters and y number of type B sweaters.

From the given information we see that cost to make a type A sweater is ₹360 and cost to make a type B sweater is ₹ 120.

Also, the company spend atmost ₹ 72000 a day.

$\therefore \quad 360x + 120y \le 72000$

$\Rightarrow \quad 3x + y \le 600 \quad \ldots(i)$

Company can make atmost 300 sweaters.

$\therefore \quad x + y \le 300 \quad \ldots(ii)$

Further, the number of sweaters of type B cannot exceed the number of sweaters of type A by more than 100

i.e. $\quad x + 100 \ge y$

$\Rightarrow \quad x - y \ge -100 \quad \ldots(iii)$

Also, we have non-negative constraints for x and y

i.e. $\quad x, y \ge 0 \quad \ldots(iv)$

Hence, the company makes a profit of ₹200 for each sweater of type A and ₹120 for each sweater of type B

i.e. profit, $Z = 200x + 120y$

Thus, the required LPP to maximise the profit is

Maximise $Z = 200x + 120y$

and subject to constraints,

$3x + y \le 600$, $x + y \le 300$, $x - y \ge -100$ and $x, y \ge 0$

Table for line $3x+y=600$ or $y=600-3x$ is

x	0	200
y	600	0

So, it passes through the points (0, 600) and (200, 0).
On putting (0, 0) in the inequality $3x+y \le 600$, we get

$0 \le 600$ (true)

So, the half plane is towards the origin.
Table for line $x+y \le 300$ is

x	0	300
y	300	0

So, it passes through the points (0, 300) and (300, 0)
On putting (0, 0) in the inequality $x+y \le 300$, we get

$0 \le 300$ (true)

So, the half plane is towards the origin.
Table for line $x-y=-100$ or $y=x+100$ is

x	0	-100
y	100	0

So, it passes through the points (0, 100) and (−100, 0).
On putting (0, 0) in the inequality $x-y \ge -100$, we get

$0 \ge -100$ (true)

So, the half plane is towards the origin.
On solving equation $3x+y=600$ and $x+y=300$
We get the intersection point (150, 150).
On solving $3x+y=600$ and $x-y=-100$, we get the intersection point (125, 225). On solving $x+y=300$ and $x-y=-100$, we get the intersection point (100, 200).

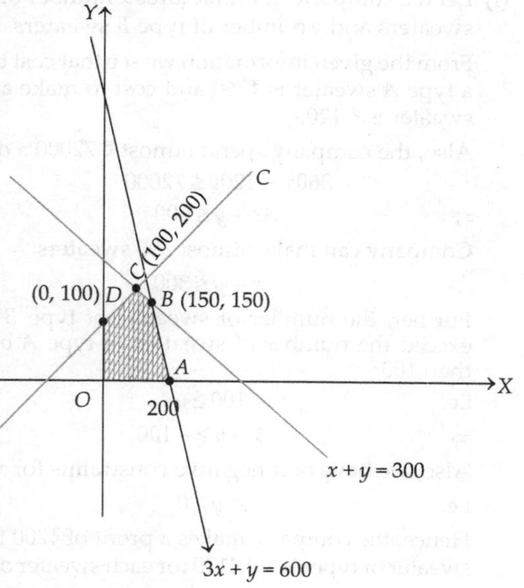

Also, $x \ge 0$, $y \ge 0$, so the feasible region lies in 1st quadrant. On plotting the graph of these constraints we get the feasible region $OABCD$.

The corner points of the feasible region are $O(0,0)$, $A(200,0)$, $B(150,150)$, $C(100,200)$ and $D(0,100)$.
The values of Z at corner points are

Corner Points	$Z=200x+120y$
$O(0,0)$	$Z=200\times0+120\times0=0$
$A(200,0)$	$Z=200\times200+120\times0=40{,}000$
$B(150,150)$	$Z=200\times150+120\times150$ $=48{,}000$ (Max).
$C(100,200)$	$Z=200\times100+200\times110$ $=44{,}000$
$D(0,100)$	$Z=200\times0+120\times100=12{,}000$

Hence the maximum profit is ₹ 48,000 at $B(150,150)$.

Or

(ii) Let x = Number of FM sets made per month and y = Number of AM/FM sets made per month.
So, profit per month, $P=₹(180x+240y)$
Now, the value of x and y should satisfy the following linear constraints
$x \le 600$ (number per month constraint)
$y \le 525$ (number per month constraint)
$30x+40y \le 24000$ (men house constraint)
$\Rightarrow 3x+4y \le 2400$
$x \ge 0$, $y \ge 0$, (non-negative constraint)
The table for line $3x+4y=2400$ or $y=\dfrac{2400-3x}{4}$ is

x	0	800
y	600	0

So, it passes through the points (0, 600) and (800, 0).
On Putting (0, 0) in the inequality $3x+4y \le 2400$, we get

$0+0 \le 24000$ [true]

So, the half plane is towards the origin.
Line $x=600$ is perpendicular to the X-axis.
Put (0, 0) in the inequality $x \le 600$, we get

$0 \le 600$ [true]

So, the half plane is towards the origin.
Also, line $y=525$ is perpendicular to the Y-axis.
On putting (0, 0) in the inequality $y \le 525$, we get

$0 \le 525$ [true]

So, the half plane is towards the origin.
Also, $x \ge 0$ and $y \ge 0$, so the feasible region lies in Ist quadrant.
On solving equation $3x+4y=2400$ and $x=600$
We get the intersection point $B(600,150)$ and on solving equation $3x+4y=2400$ and $y=525$ we get the intersection point $C(100,525)$.
On plotting the graph of these constraints, we get the feasible region $OABCD$.

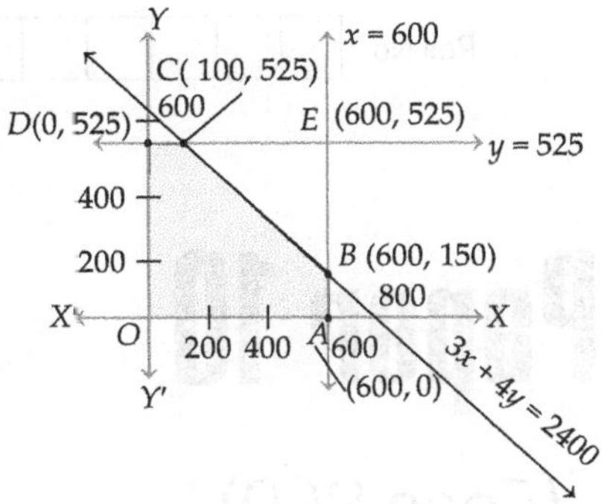

The corner points of the feasible region are $O(0, 0)$, $A(600, 0)$, $B(600, 150)$, $C(100, 525)$ and $D(0, 525)$. Hence, 10 corn maximum profit company can make XM 600 to 100 FM per month and 150 to 525 AM/FM per month.

Now, the value of $P = 180x + 240y$ at each of the corner points are as follows

Corner points	$P = ₹ (180x + 240y)$
$O(0, 0)$	$P = (180 \times 0 + 240 \times 0) = ₹\,0$
$A(600, 0)$	$P = (180 \times 600 + 240 \times 0) = ₹\,108000$
$B(600, 150)$	$P = (180 \times 600 + 240 \times 150) = ₹\,144000$
$C(100, 525)$	$P = (180 \times 100 + 240 \times 525) = ₹\,144000$
$D(0, 525)$	$P = (180 \times 0 + 240 \times 525) = ₹\,126000$

(a) Clearly, the maximum profit is ₹ 144000 per month.

(b) The maximum profit will be obtained at line joining the point $B(600, 150)$ and $C(100, 525)$.

Hence, the number of FM sets and the number of AM/FM sets are 600 and 150 or 100 and 525, respectively.

SQP Code : **PB-10/15** Series **i-Succeed 10-25/15** Roll No.

Sample Question Paper 10

Mathematics 12th (Code 860)

General Instructions

1. The Question Paper consists of three sections A, B and C.
2. Candidates are required to attempt all questions from Section A and all questions either from Section B Or Section C.
3. Section A Internal choice has been provided in two questions of two marks each, two questions of four marks each and two questions of six marks each.
4. Section B Internal choice has been provided in one questions of two marks and one question of four marks.
5. Section C Internal choice has been provided in one question of two marks and one question of four marks.
6. All working, including rough work, should be done on the same sheet as, and adjacent to the rest of the answer.
7. The intended marks for questions or parts of questions are given in brackets [].
8. Mathematical tables and graph papers are provided.

Time : 3 Hrs.

Max. Marks : 80

Section A (65 Marks)

1. In subparts (i) to (xi) choose the correct options and in subparts (xii) to (xv), answer the questions as instructed.

(i) The differentiation of 10^x w.r.t. x is [1]

(a) $\log x$ (b) $10^x \log x$

(c) $10^x \log 10$ (d) $x^{10} \log 10$

• *Recall*

(ii) $\sin\left[\frac{\pi}{3} - \sin^{-1}\left(\frac{-1}{2}\right)\right]$ is equal to [1]

(a) $\frac{1}{2}$ (b) $\frac{1}{3}$

(c) $\frac{1}{4}$ (d) 1

• *Understanding*

(iii) If $P(A) = \frac{3}{13}$, $P(B) = \frac{8}{13}$ and $P(A \cap B) = \frac{4}{13}$, then $P(A' / B)$ is equal to [1]

(a) $\frac{6}{13}$ (b) $\frac{4}{13}$

(c) $\frac{1}{2}$ (d) $\frac{8}{13}$

• *Application*

(iv) Shown below is the graph of a function $h(x)$.

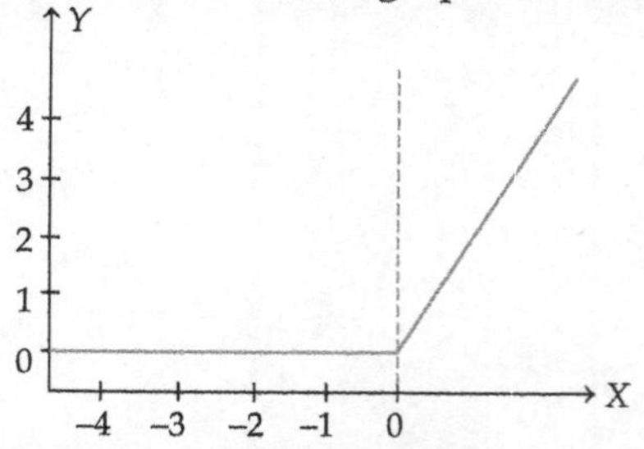

(a) $h(x)$ is differentiable at $x = 0$.

(b) $h(x)$ is not continuous at $x = 0$.

(c) $h(x)$ is continuous at $x = 0$.

(d) $h(x)$ is continuous but not differentiable at $x = 0$.

• *Understanding*

(v) Let $R = \{(3,1),(1,3),(3,3)\}$ be a relation defined on the set $A = \{1,2,3\}$. Then, R is symmetric, transitive but not reflexive. [1]

(a) True (b) False

(c) Cannot say (d) Partially true/false

• *Analysis*

(vi) $y = x(x-3)^2$ decreases for the values of x given by [1]

(a) $1 < x < 3$ (b) $x < 0$
(c) $x > 0$ (d) $0 < x < \frac{3}{2}$

• *Evaluate*

(vii) **Statement I** The area of the triangle, whose vertices are (3, 8), (–4, 2) and (5, 1) is 61 sq. units.

Statement II The area of triangle whose vertices are $(x_1, y_1), (x_2, y_2)$ and (x_3, y_3) is given by, $\Delta = \begin{vmatrix} x_1 & y_1 & 1 \\ x_2 & y_2 & 1 \\ x_3 & y_3 & 1 \end{vmatrix}$ • *Application*

(a) Only Statement I is true.
(b) Only Statement II is true.
(c) Both Statements I and II are true.
(d) Neither Statement I nor II is true.

(viii) $\int_{-100}^{100} (x^3 + x^5) dx$ is equal to [1]

(a) 1 (b) 0 (c) 100 (d) 200

• *Evaluate*

(ix) Consider the following statements

Statement I The order of the differential equation $\frac{dy}{dx} = e^x$ is 1.

Statement II The order of the differential equation $\left(\frac{d^3y}{dx^3}\right) + x^2\left(\frac{d^2y}{dx^2}\right)^3 = 0$ is 3.

• *Recall*

Choose correct option. [1]

(a) Only I is true
(b) Only II is true
(c) I and II both are true
(d) I and II both are false

(x) **Assertion** (A) If $A = \begin{bmatrix} 2 & 3 & -1 \\ 1 & 4 & 2 \end{bmatrix}$ and $B = \begin{bmatrix} 2 & 3 \\ 4 & 5 \\ 2 & 1 \end{bmatrix}$, then AB and BA both are defined.

Reason (R) For the two matrices A and B, the product AB is defined, if number of columns in A is equal to the number of rows in B. • *Recall*

Choose the correct option.

(a) Both A and R are correct; R is the correct explanation of A
(b) Both A and R are correct; R is not the correct explanation of A
(c) A is correct ; R is incorrect
(d) A is incorrect ; R is correct

(xi) **Assertion** (A) $\int \frac{1}{9x^2 + 6x + 5} dx = \frac{1}{6} \tan^{-1}\left(\frac{3x+1}{2}\right) + c$

Reason (R) $\int \frac{dx}{a^2 + x^2} = \frac{1}{a} \tan^{-1}\left(\frac{x}{a}\right)$

• *Application*

(a) Both A and R are correct and R is correct explanation of A.
(b) Both A and R are correct but R is not correct explanation of A.
(c) A is correct but R is incorrect
(d) A is incorrect but R is correct [1]

(xii) Evaluate $\int e^x (\tan x + \sec^2 x)\, dx$ [1]

• *Evaluate*

(xiii) Prove that $\sin^{-1}\frac{3}{5} - \sin^{-1}\frac{8}{17} = \cos^{-1}\frac{84}{85}$.

• *Analysis* [1]

(xiv) A bag X contains 3 white balls and 2 black balls and another bag Y contains 2 white balls and 4 black balls. A bag and a ball out of it are picked at random, what is the probability that the ball is white? • *Analysis* [1]

(xv) Let R be a relation on Z (set of integers) defined by $R = \{(a, b) : a, b \in Z, |a - b| \le 4\}$. Check whether R is reflexive and symmetric. • *Understanding* [1]

SP-10

2. (i) A stone is dropped into a quiet lake and waves move in circles at a speed of 3.5 cm/s. At the instant when the radius of the circular wave is 9 cm, how fast is the enclosed area increasing? • *Application* [2]

Or

(ii) Let I be an interval disjoint from $(-1, 1)$. Prove that function $f(x) = \left(x + \frac{1}{x}\right)$ is strictly increasing on I. • *Application* [2]

3. Find value of k, if

$\sin^{-1}\left[k \tan\left(2 \cos^{-1}\frac{\sqrt{3}}{2}\right)\right] = \frac{\pi}{3}$ • *Evaluate* [2]

4. If $y = \tan x + \sec x$, then prove that $\dfrac{d^2y}{dx^2} = \dfrac{\cos x}{(1-\sin x)^2}$. • *Analysis* [2]

5. (i) Solve the given differential equation

$$\frac{dy}{dx} + \frac{y}{x\log x} = \frac{1}{x}.$$ • *Application* [2]

Or

(ii) Solve the differential equation

$$3e^x \tan y\, dx + (1-e^x)\sec^2 y\, dy = 0$$ [2] • *Application*

6. Without expanding, prove that

$$\begin{vmatrix} (2^x+2^{-x})^2 & (2^x-2^{-x})^2 & 1 \\ (3^x+3^{-x})^2 & (3^x-3^{-x})^2 & 1 \\ (4^x+4^{-x})^2 & (4^x-4^{-x})^2 & 1 \end{vmatrix} = 0, \text{ where}$$

$x \in R$. • *Analysis* [2]

7. If $P(B) = \dfrac{3}{5}$, $P(A/B) = \dfrac{1}{2}$ and $P(A \cup B) = \dfrac{4}{5}$, then find $P(A \cup B)' + P(A' \cup B)$. • *Analysis* [4]

8. Evaluate

$$\int \frac{1}{\sin^4 x + \sin^2 x \cos^2 x + \cos^4 x}\, dx.$$ [4] • *Evaluate*

9. (i) Solve the differential equation

$$(1+x^2)\frac{dy}{dx} + 2xy - 4x^2 = 0,$$

subject to the initial condition $y(0) = 0$. • *Application* [4]

Or

(ii) Evaluate $\displaystyle\int \frac{\sin x - \cos x}{\sqrt{\sin 2x}}\, dx.$ • *Evaluate* [4]

10. (i) The given integral $\int f(x)dx$ can be transformed into another form by changing the independent variable x to t by substituting $x = g(t)$. • *Application*

Consider $I = \int f(x)dx$

Put $x = g(t)$ so that $\dfrac{dx}{dt} = g'(t)$

We write $dx = g'(t)dt$

Thus, $I = \int f(x)dx = \int f[g(t)]g'(t)dt$

This change of variable formula is one of the important tools available to us in the name of integration by substitution.

On the basis of above information, answer the following questions.

(a) Evaluate $\displaystyle\int \frac{x}{\sqrt{32-x^2}}\, dx.$

(b) Evaluate $\displaystyle\int \frac{\sin(2\tan^{-1} x)}{1+x^2}\, dx.$

(c) Solve $\displaystyle\int \frac{\sqrt{1+x^2}}{x^4}\, dx.$

(d) Evaluate $\displaystyle\int \frac{\cos^{-1} x}{\sqrt{1-x^2}}\, dx.$ [4]

Or

(ii) Let f be a continuous function defined on the closed interval $[a, b]$ and F be an antiderivative of f, then

$$\int_a^b f(x)\, dx = [F(x)]_a^b = F(b) - F(a)$$

Based on the above information, answer the following questions. • *Application*

(a) Find $\displaystyle\int_2^3 x^2\, dx.$

(b) Find $\displaystyle\int_1^{\sqrt{3}} \frac{dx}{1+x^2}.$

(c) Evaluate $\displaystyle\int_{-1}^{1} (x+1)\, dx.$

(d) $\displaystyle\int_0^{\pi/2} \sin x\, dx$ [4]

11. Find the value of a for which the function f is defined as

$$f(x) = \begin{cases} a\sin\dfrac{\pi}{2}(x+1), & x \le 0 \\ \dfrac{\tan x - \sin x}{x^3}, & x > 0 \end{cases}$$

is continuous at $x = 0$. • *Evaluate* [6]

12. (i) Prove that the height of the cylinder of maximum volume that can be inscribed in a sphere of radius R is $\dfrac{2R}{\sqrt{3}}$. Also, find the maximum volume. • *Application* [6]

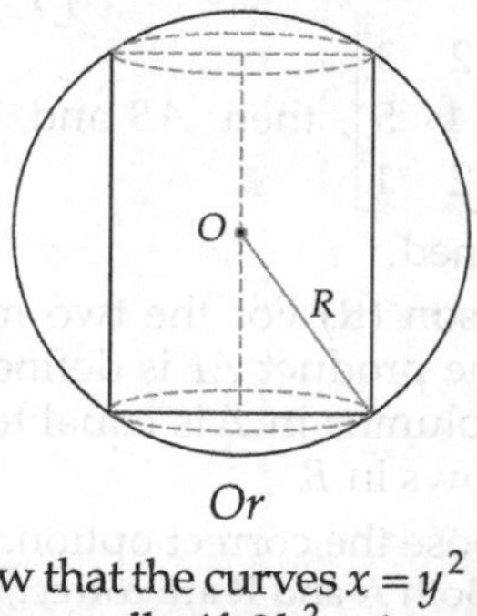

Or

(ii) Show that the curves $x = y^2$ and $xy = k$ cut orthogonally, if $8k^2 = 1$. • *Application* [6]

13. (i) In a test, an examinee either guess or copies or knows the answer to a multiple choice question with four choices and only one correct option. The probability that he makes a guess is $\frac{1}{3}$. The probability that he copies the answer is $\frac{1}{6}$. The probability that the answer is correct given that he copied it is $\frac{1}{8}$. Find the probability that he knows the answer to the question, given that he correctly answered it. • *Analysis* [6]

Or

(ii) A problem in Mathematics is given to three students A, B and C. Their chances of solving the problem are $\frac{1}{2}, \frac{2}{3}, \frac{3}{4}$ and $\frac{1}{4}$ respectively. Find the probability that

(a) exactly two students will solve the problem.

(b) atleast two of them will solve the problem. • *Analysis* [6]

14. If $A=\begin{pmatrix} \cos\alpha & -\sin\alpha & 0 \\ \sin\alpha & \cos\alpha & 0 \\ 0 & 0 & 1 \end{pmatrix}$, then answer the following questions. • *Application*

(i) Find adj A. (ii) Find det A.

(iii) Verify that $A[\text{adj } A]=[\text{adj } A]\,A$.

(iv) Also verify that $A(\text{adj } A)=(\text{adj } A)\,A=|A|\,I_3$. [6]

Section B (15 Marks)

15. In subparts (i) to (iii) choose the correct options and in subparts (iv) and (v), answer the questions as instructed. [5]

(i) If the plane $2x+\lambda y+3z=5$ is perpendicular to the plane $x+y+3z=9$, then the value of λ is • *Understanding*

(a) 11 (b) – 11

(c) 12 (d) 0

(ii) If $|\vec{a}|=3|\vec{b}|$ and $(\vec{a}+\vec{b})\cdot(\vec{a}-\vec{b})=32$, then value of $|\vec{b}|$ is • *Evaluate*

(a) 2 (b) 3

(c) 4 (d) 12

(iii) **Statement I** The angle between the planes $2x-y+z=6$ and $x+y+2z=7$ is $\frac{\pi}{3}$.

Statement II The angle between the planes $\vec{r}\cdot\vec{n}_1=d_1$ and $\vec{r}\cdot\vec{n}_2=d_2$ is $\cos\theta=\left|\frac{\vec{n}_1\cdot\vec{n}_2}{|\vec{n}_1|\cdot|\vec{n}_2|}\right|$ • *Application*

(a) Only Statement I is true.

(b) Only Statement II is true.

(c) Both Statements I and II are true.

(d) Neither I nor II is true.

(iv) Show that the points whose position vectors are $(-2\hat{i}+3\hat{j}+5\hat{k}), (\hat{i}+2\hat{j}+3\hat{k})$ and $(7\hat{i}-\hat{k})$ are collinear. • *Understanding*

(v) Vectors $\vec{a}, \vec{b}, \vec{c}$ and $\vec{d}$ are given by $\vec{a}=\hat{i}+\hat{j}+\hat{k}, \vec{b}=2\hat{i}+3\hat{j}, \vec{c}=3\hat{i}+5\hat{j}-2\hat{k}$ and $\vec{d}=\hat{k}-\hat{j}$. Prove that the vectors $\vec{b}-\vec{a}$ and $\vec{d}-\vec{c}$ are parallel and find the ratio of their lengths. • *Application*

16. (i) If $\vec{a}, \vec{b}$ and $\vec{c}$ are three vectors such that $\vec{a}\times\vec{b}=\vec{c}, \vec{b}\times\vec{c}=\vec{a}$, then prove that $\vec{a}, \vec{b}$ and $\vec{c}$ are mutually at right angles and $|\vec{b}|=1$, $|\vec{c}|=|\vec{a}|$. • *Application* [2]

Or

(ii) Find the angle θ between the vectors $\vec{a}=\hat{i}+\hat{j}-\hat{k}$ and $\vec{b}=\hat{i}-\hat{j}+\hat{k}$. • *Evaluate* [2]

17. (i) Show that the lines $\frac{x-1}{3}=\frac{y+1}{2}=\frac{z-1}{5}$ and $\frac{x-2}{4}=\frac{y-1}{3}=\frac{z+1}{-2}$ do not intersect each other. • *Application* [4]

Or

(ii) Find the equation of plane passing through the point $(-1,-1,2)$ and perpendicular to the planes $3x+2y-3z=1$ and $5x-4y+z=5$. [4] • *Application*

18. Find the area of the region bounded by the curves $y=x^2+2$, $y=x$, $x=0$ and $x=3$. [4] • *Analysis & Evaluate*

SP-10

Section C (15 Marks)

19. In subparts (i) and (ii) choose the correct options and in subparts (iii) to (v), answer the questions as instructed. [5]

(i) By using the data $\overline{x}=5, \overline{y}=13$ and $b_{yx}=2.5$, the regression equation y on x is • *Recall*

(a) $y=2.5x-0.5$

(b) $y=0.5x+2.5$

(c) $y=0.5x-2.5$

(d) $y=2.5x+0.5$

(ii) If $p=50-3x$ when p is monopolist demand function, then marginal revenue at $x=0$ is • *Understanding*

(a) 200 (b) 500 (c) 50 (d) 100

(iii) In a factory, it is found that the number of units (x) produced in a day depends upon the number of workers (n) is obtained by the relation $x=\frac{5n}{\sqrt{n+5}}$. The demand function of product is $p=\frac{2}{x}+x$. Determine the marginal revenue, when $n=44$. • *Understanding*

(iv) Given the cost function and revenue function, respectively as $C(x)=2x+40$ and $R(x)=11x-0.2x^2$, then find the break-even point. • *Evaluate*

(v) For the given lines of regression, $2x-3y=6$ and $5x-4y=20$, find regression coefficients b_{yx} and b_{xy}. • *Understanding*

20. (i) Given the total cost function for x units of a commodity as $C(x)=\frac{x^3}{3}+3x^2-7x+16$.

Find (a) the marginal cost.

(b) the average cost. • *Application* [2]

Or

(ii) Given, the total cost function for x units of commodity, $C(x)=ax^3+bx^2-cx+d$, where $a>0, b<0, c>0$, show that average variable cost and marginal cost curves intersect at minimum average variable cost. • *Application* [2]

21. Given the observations

$$(10,-5),(10,-3),(11,-2),(11,0),$$
$$(12,1),(15,6),(16,4),(11,-2).$$

Find

(i) b_{yx} and b_{xy}

(ii) predict the value of y corresponding to the value 14 of x.

(iii) predict the value of x, when the value of y is 3. • *Application* [4]

22. (i) A dietician has to develop a special diet using two foods P and Q. Each packet (containing 30 g) of food P contains 12 units of calcium, 4 units of iron, 6 units of cholestrol and 6 units of vitamin A. Each packet of the same quantity of food Q contains 3 units of calcium, 20 units of iron, 4 units of cholestrol and 3 units of vitamin A. The diet requires atleast 240 units of calcium, atleast 460 units of iron and atmost 300 units of cholestrol.

How many packets of each food should be used to minimise the amount of vitamin A in the diet and what is the minimum amount of vitamin A? • *Analysis* [4]

Or

(ii) Solve the following linear programming problem graphically.

Maximise $Z=x+y$

subject to constraints

$$x-y\le -1, -x+y\le 0 \text{ and } x,y\ge 0$$

• *Analysis* [4]

Solutions *in Topper's Style*

My Commitment *I affirm that I am reviewing these solutions only after I have solved the Sample Question Paper 10 on my own. My purpose of looking the solutions is solely to verify whether my answers/solutions were correct or not and to identify my mistakes in case my solutions were wrong or I could not solve that.*

1. (i) (c) Let $y = 10^x$

On taking log both sides, we get

$$\log y = \log 10^x$$

$$\Rightarrow \quad \log y = x \log 10$$

On differentiating both sides w.r.t. x, we get

$$\frac{1}{y}\frac{dy}{dx} = 1 \log 10$$

$$\therefore \quad \frac{dy}{dx} = 10^x \log 10$$

(ii) (d) $\sin\left[\frac{\pi}{3} - \sin^{-1}\left(\frac{-1}{2}\right)\right]$

$$= \sin\left[\frac{\pi}{3} + \frac{\pi}{6}\right] \quad \left[\because \sin^{-1}\left(\frac{-1}{2}\right) = \frac{-\pi}{6}\right]$$

$$= \sin\frac{\pi}{2} = 1$$

(iii) (c) Given, $P(A) = \frac{3}{13}$, $P(B) = \frac{8}{13}$ and $P(A \cap B) = \frac{4}{13}$

$$\therefore \quad P(A'/B) = \frac{P(A' \cap B)}{P(B)} = \frac{P(B) - P(A \cap B)}{P(B)}$$

$$= \frac{\frac{8}{13} - \frac{4}{13}}{\frac{8}{13}} = \frac{\frac{4}{13}}{\frac{8}{13}} = \frac{4}{8} = \frac{1}{2}$$

(iv) (b) By observing the graph of function $h(x)$, we consider

$$h(x) = \begin{cases} 0, & x < 0 \\ x, & x \geq 0 \end{cases}$$

The function $h(x)$ is not continuous at $x = 0$ because at $x = 0$, the function changes its behaviour suddenly.

(v) (b) Given that, $R = \{(3,1), (1,3), (3,3)\}$ be defined on the set $A = \{1, 2, 3\}$

Here, $(1,1) \notin R$

So, R is not reflexive.

Here, $(3,1) \in R \Rightarrow (1,3) \in R$

So, R is symmetric.

Here, $(1,3) \in R$, $(3,1) \in R$

But $(1,1) \notin R$

So, R is not transitive.

(vi) (a) We have, $y = x(x-3)^2$

$$\therefore \quad \frac{dy}{dx} = x \cdot 2(x-3) \cdot 1 + (x-3)^2 \cdot 1$$

$$= 2x^2 - 6x + x^2 + 9 - 6x = 3x^2 - 12x + 9$$

$$= 3(x^2 - 3x - x + 3) = 3(x-3)(x-1)$$

So, $y = x(x-3)^2$ decreases for $x \in (1, 3)$.

$[\because y' < 0$ for all $x \in (1, 3)$,
$\therefore y$ is decreasing on $(1, 3)]$

(vii) (d) Given vertices of a triangle are $(x_1, y_1) = (3, 8)$, $(x_2, y_2) = (-4, 2)$ and $(x_3, y_3) = (5, 1)$

Then, the area of triangle

$$= \frac{1}{2}\begin{vmatrix} x_1 & y_1 & 1 \\ x_2 & y_2 & 1 \\ x_3 & y_3 & 1 \end{vmatrix} = \frac{1}{2}\begin{vmatrix} 3 & 8 & 1 \\ -4 & 2 & 1 \\ 5 & 1 & 1 \end{vmatrix}$$

$$= \frac{1}{2}[3(2-1) - 8(-4-5) + (-4-10)]$$

$$= \frac{1}{2}[3 + 72 - 14] = \frac{61}{2} \text{ sq. units}$$

Hence, both Statements are incorrect.

(viii) (b) Let $I = \int_{-100}^{100} (x^3 + x^5)\, dx$

Let $f(x) = x^3 + x^5$

$$\therefore \quad f(-x) = (-x)^3 + (-x)^5$$

$$= -x^3 - x^5 = -(x^3 + x^5) = -f(x)$$

$\Rightarrow f(x)$ is an odd function.

$$\therefore \quad I = \int_{-100}^{100} (x^3 + x^5)\, dx = 0$$

(ix) (c) I. The differential equation $\frac{dy}{dx} = e^x$ involves the highest derivative of first order.

$\therefore$ Its order is 1.

II. The differential equation $\left(\frac{d^3y}{dx^3}\right) + x^2\left(\frac{d^2y}{dx^2}\right)^3 = 0$ involves highest derivative of third order.

$\therefore$ Its order is 3.

(x) (a) The given matrices are

$$A = \begin{bmatrix} 2 & 3 & -1 \\ 1 & 4 & 2 \end{bmatrix} \text{ and } B = \begin{bmatrix} 2 & 3 \\ 4 & 5 \\ 2 & 1 \end{bmatrix}$$

Here, order of $A = 2 \times 3$

and order of $B = 3 \times 2$

Since, number of columns in A is equal to the number of rows in B.

So, AB is defined.

Also, number of columns in B is equal to the number of rows in A.

$\therefore$ The product BA is also defined.

Hence, A and R both are correct and R is the correct explanation of A.

(xi) (a) Let $I=\int\frac{1}{9x^2+6x+5}dx$

$=\frac{1}{9}\int\frac{1}{x^2+\frac{2}{3}x+\frac{5}{9}}dx$

[take 9 common from denominator]

$=\frac{1}{9}\int\frac{1}{x^2+2\cdot\frac{1}{3}x+\left(\frac{1}{3}\right)^2+\frac{5}{9}-\left(\frac{1}{3}\right)^2}dx$

[add and subtract $\left(\frac{1}{3}\right)^2$ from denominator]

$=\frac{1}{9}\int\frac{1}{x^2+\frac{2}{3}x+\left(\frac{1}{3}\right)^2+\frac{5}{9}-\frac{1}{9}}dx$

$=\frac{1}{9}\int\frac{1}{\left(x+\frac{1}{3}\right)^2+\left(\frac{2}{3}\right)^2}dx$

$=\frac{1}{9}\left(\frac{1}{2/3}\right)\tan^{-1}\left(\frac{x+\frac{1}{3}}{\frac{2}{3}}\right)+c$

$\left[\because\int\frac{dx}{a^2+x^2}=\frac{1}{a}\tan^{-1}\left(\frac{x}{a}\right)\right]$

$=\frac{1}{6}\tan^{-1}\left(\frac{3x+1}{2}\right)+c$

Hence, both A and R are correct and R is correct explanation of A.

(xii) Let $I=\int e^x(\tan x+\sec^2 x)\,dx$

$=e^x\tan x+C$

$[\because\int e^x\{f(x)+f'(x)\}dx=e^x f(x)+C]$

(xiii) LHS $=\sin^{-1}\frac{3}{5}-\sin^{-1}\frac{8}{17}$

$=\sin^{-1}\left[\frac{3}{5}\sqrt{1-\frac{64}{289}}-\frac{8}{17}\sqrt{1-\frac{9}{25}}\right]$

$[\because\sin^{-1}x-\sin^{-1}y=\sin^{-1}(x\sqrt{1-y^2}-y\sqrt{1-x^2})]$

$=\sin^{-1}\left[\frac{3}{5}\cdot\frac{15}{17}-\frac{8}{17}\cdot\frac{4}{5}\right]$

$=\sin^{-1}\left[\frac{45-32}{85}\right]=\sin^{-1}\left[\frac{13}{85}\right]$

$=\cos^{-1}\sqrt{1-\left(\frac{13}{85}\right)^2}$ $\quad[\because\sin^{-1}x=\cos^{-1}\sqrt{1-x^2}]$

$=\cos^{-1}\sqrt{\frac{7225-169}{(85)^2}}=\cos^{-1}\sqrt{\frac{7056}{(85)^2}}$

$=\cos^{-1}\left[\frac{84}{85}\right]$

= RHS **Hence proved.**

(xiv) Either of the bags is picked up, then the ball is drawn.

***Case* I** Bag X is picked up, then

P(white ball) $=\frac{1}{2}\times\frac{3}{5}=\frac{3}{10}$

***Case* II** Bag Y is picked up, then

P(white ball) $=\frac{1}{2}\times\frac{2}{6}=\frac{2}{12}$

Hence, required probability, P(white ball)

$=\frac{3}{10}+\frac{2}{12}=\frac{18+10}{60}=\frac{28}{60}=\frac{7}{15}$

(xv) Given relation is $R=\{(a,b):a,b\in Z,|a-b|\le 4\}$

Let $a\in Z$, then $|a-a|=0\le 4\Rightarrow(a,a)\in R$

Hence R is reflexive.

Let $(a,b)\in R$, then $|a-b|\le 4\Rightarrow|b-a|\le 4$

$\Rightarrow(b,a)\in R$

Hence, R is symmetric.

2. (i) Let r be the radius of the circular wave and A be the area enclosed by it at any time t, then

$A=\pi r^2$ ...(i)

Given, $\frac{dr}{dt}=3.5$ cm/s $=\frac{7}{2}$ cm/s ...(ii)

On differentiating Eq. (i) w.r.t. t, we get

$\frac{dA}{dt}=\pi\cdot 2r\frac{dr}{dt}$

$\Rightarrow\frac{dA}{dt}=2\pi r\cdot\frac{7}{2}=7\pi r$ [using Eq. (ii)]

When $r=9$ cm, then $\frac{dA}{dt}=7\pi\times 9=63\pi$ cm^2/s

Hence, the enclosed area is increasing at the rate of 63π cm^2/s when the radius of the wave is 9 cm.

Or

(ii) We have, $f(x)=x+\frac{1}{x}$ ...(i)

and $I=R-(-1,1)$

$=(-\infty,-1]\cup[1,\infty)$.

On differentiating Eq. (i) w.r.t. x, we get

$f'(x)=1-\frac{1}{x^2}=\frac{x^2-1}{x^2}>0,\forall x\in I$

$[\because x^2>1,\forall x\in I$ and $x^2-1>0,\forall x\in I]$

Hence, $f(x)$ is strictly increasing on I.

Hence Proved.

3. We have,

$\sin^{-1}\left[k\tan\left(2\cos^{-1}\frac{\sqrt{3}}{2}\right)\right]=\frac{\pi}{3}$

$\Rightarrow\sin^{-1}\left[k\tan\left(2\times\frac{\pi}{6}\right)\right]=\frac{\pi}{3}$ $\quad\left[\because\cos^{-1}\frac{\sqrt{3}}{2}=\frac{\pi}{6}\right]$

$\Rightarrow\sin^{-1}\left[k\tan\left(\frac{\pi}{3}\right)\right]=\frac{\pi}{3}$

$\Rightarrow\sin^{-1}(k\sqrt{3})=\frac{\pi}{3}$ $\quad\left[\because\tan\frac{\pi}{3}=\sqrt{3}\right]$

$\Rightarrow k\sqrt{3}=\sin\frac{\pi}{3}$

$\Rightarrow k\sqrt{3}=\frac{\sqrt{3}}{2}$

$\Rightarrow k=\frac{1}{2}$

4. Given, $y=\tan x+\sec x$

$$\Rightarrow \quad y=\frac{\sin x}{\cos x}+\frac{1}{\cos x}=\frac{\sin x+1}{\cos x}$$

On differentiating both sides w.r.t. x, we get

$$\frac{dy}{dx}=\frac{\cos x\frac{d}{dx}(\sin x+1)-(\sin x+1)\frac{d}{dx}(\cos x)}{(\cos x)^2}$$

$$=\frac{\cos x(\cos x)-(\sin x+1)(-\sin x)}{\cos^2 x}$$

$$=\frac{\cos^2 x+\sin^2 x+\sin x}{\cos^2 x}=\frac{1+\sin x}{\cos^2 x}$$

$[\because \cos^2\theta+\sin^2\theta=1]$

$$\Rightarrow \frac{dy}{dx}=\frac{1+\sin x}{1-\sin^2 x}=\frac{1}{1-\sin x} \quad [\because a^2-b^2=(a-b)(a+b)]$$

[2]

Again, on differentiating w.r.t. x, we get

$$\frac{d^2y}{dx^2}=\frac{(1-\sin x)(0)-1(0-\cos x)}{(1-\sin x)^2}$$

$$=\frac{\cos x}{(1-\sin x)^2}$$

Hence proved. [1]

5. (i) Given differential equation is

$$\frac{dy}{dx}+\frac{y}{x\log x}=\frac{1}{x} \quad \ldots(i)$$

On comparing Eq. (i) with $\frac{dy}{dx}+Py=Q$, we get

$$P=\frac{1}{x\log x} \text{ and } Q=\frac{1}{x}$$

$$\therefore \text{ IF}=e^{\int P\,dx}=e^{\int \frac{1}{x\log x}dx}=e^{\log(\log x)}=\log x$$

Now, solution is $y\times \text{IF}=\int \text{IF}\times Q+C$

$$\Rightarrow \quad y\log x=\int \frac{\log x}{x}dx=\int t\,dt$$

$[\because$ putting in RHS $\log x=t \Rightarrow \frac{1}{x}dx=dt]$

$$\Rightarrow y\log x=\frac{t^2}{2}+C=\frac{(\log x)^2}{2}+C \text{ [put } t=\log x]$$

$$\Rightarrow \quad y=\frac{1}{2}(\log x)+\frac{C}{\log x}$$

which is the required solution.

Value Point

Precisely describe the form of differential equation present.

Or

(ii) Given differential equation is

$$3e^x\cdot\tan y\,dx+(1-e^x)\sec^2 y\,dy=0$$

$$\Rightarrow \quad (1-e^x)\cdot\sec^2 y\,dy=-3e^x\cdot\tan y\,dx$$

$$\Rightarrow \quad \frac{\sec^2 y}{\tan y}dy=-3\frac{e^x}{1-e^x}dx$$

On integrating both sides, we get

$$\int\frac{\sec^2 y}{\tan y}dy=-3\int\frac{e^x}{1-e^x}dx$$

Put $\tan y=u \Rightarrow \sec^2 y\,dy=du$

and $1-e^x=v \Rightarrow -e^x dx=dv$

Then, we get $\int\frac{du}{u}=-3\int\frac{-dv}{v}$

$$\Rightarrow \quad \log u=3\log v+\log C$$

$$\Rightarrow \log|\tan y|=3\log|1-e^x|+\log C \quad \left[\begin{array}{l}\text{put } u=\tan y\\ \text{and } v=1-e^x\end{array}\right]$$

$$\Rightarrow \log|\tan y|=\log[|1-e^x|^3 C]$$

$[\because m\log n=\log n^m$ and $\log m+\log n=\log mn]$

$$\Rightarrow \quad \tan y=C\cdot(1-e^x)^3$$

which is the required solution.

6. Let $\Delta=\begin{vmatrix}(2^x+2^{-x})^2 & (2^x-2^{-x})^2 & 1\\ (3^x+3^{-x})^2 & (3^x-3^{-x})^2 & 1\\ (4^x+4^{-x})^2 & (4^x-4^{-x})^2 & 1\end{vmatrix}$

On applying $C_1\to C_1-C_2$, we get

$$\Delta=\begin{vmatrix}(2^x+2^{-x})^2-(2^x-2^{-x})^2 & (2^x-2^{-x})^2 & 1\\ (3^x+3^{-x})^2-(3^x-3^{-x})^2 & (3^x-3^{-x})^2 & 1\\ (4^x+4^{-x})^2-(4^x-4^{-x})^2 & (4^x-4^{-x})^2 & 1\end{vmatrix}$$

$$=\begin{vmatrix}4(2^x2^{-x}) & (2^x-2^{-x})^2 & 1\\ 4(3^x3^{-x}) & (3^x-3^{-x})^2 & 1\\ 4(4^x4^{-x}) & (4^x-4^{-x})^2 & 1\end{vmatrix}$$

$[\because (a+b)^2-(a-b)^2=4ab]$

$$=\begin{vmatrix}4 & (2^x-2^{-x})^2 & 1\\ 4 & (3^x-3^{-x})^2 & 1\\ 4 & (4^x-4^{-x})^2 & 1\end{vmatrix} \quad [\because a^x\cdot a^{-x}=a^0=1]$$

On taking 4 common from C_1, we get

$$\Delta=4\begin{vmatrix}1 & (2^x-2^{-x})^2 & 1\\ 1 & (3^x-3^{-x})^2 & 1\\ 1 & (4^x-4^{-x})^2 & 1\end{vmatrix}=0$$

$[\because$ column C_1 and C_3 are identical]

Hence proved.

7. Given, $P(B)=\frac{3}{5}$, $P(A/B)=\frac{1}{2}$ and $P(A\cup B)=\frac{4}{5}$

We know that $P(A/B)=\frac{P(A\cap B)}{P(B)}$

$$\Rightarrow \quad P(A\cap B)=P(A/B)\cdot P(B)=\frac{1}{2}\times\frac{3}{5}=\frac{3}{10}$$

Also, $P(A\cup B)=P(A)+P(B)-P(A\cap B)$

$$\Rightarrow \quad \frac{4}{5}=P(A)+\frac{3}{5}-\frac{3}{10}$$

$$\Rightarrow \quad P(A)=\frac{4}{5}-\frac{3}{5}+\frac{3}{10}=\frac{1}{2}$$

$$\therefore \quad P(A\cup B)'=1-P(A\cup B)=1-\frac{4}{5}=\frac{1}{5}$$

and $P(A'\cup B)=1-P(A\cap B')$

$$=1-P(A)\cdot P(B')$$

$$=1-\frac{1}{2}\cdot\frac{2}{5}=\frac{4}{5} \quad \left[\begin{array}{l}\because P(B')=1-P(B)\\ \qquad =1-\frac{3}{5}=\frac{2}{5}\end{array}\right]$$

Hence, $P(A\cup B)'+P(A'\cup B)=\frac{1}{5}+\frac{4}{5}=\frac{5}{5}=1$

8. Let $I=\int \frac{1}{\sin^4 x+\sin^2 x\cos^2 x+\cos^4 x}dx$

On dividing numerator and denominator by $\cos^4 x$ in RHS, we get

$$I=\int \frac{\sec^4 x}{\tan^4 x+\tan^2 x+1}dx$$

$$\Rightarrow \quad I=\int \frac{(\sec^2 x)(\sec^2 x)}{\tan^4 x+\tan^2 x+1}dx$$

Put $\tan x = t \Rightarrow \sec^2 x\,dx = dt$

and $\sec^2 x = 1+\tan^2 x = 1+t^2$

$$\therefore \quad I=\int \frac{1+t^2}{t^4+t^2+1}dt=\int \frac{1+\frac{1}{t^2}}{t^2+\frac{1}{t^2}+1}dt$$

[dividing numerator and denominator by t^2]

$$=\int \frac{1+\frac{1}{t^2}}{t^2+\frac{1}{t^2}-2+2+1}dt=\int \frac{\left(1+\frac{1}{t^2}\right)}{\left(t-\frac{1}{t}\right)^2+3}dt$$

Again, put $u=t-\frac{1}{t} \Rightarrow \left(1+\frac{1}{t^2}\right)dt=du$

$$\therefore \quad I=\int \frac{du}{u^2+(\sqrt{3})^2} \Rightarrow I=\frac{1}{\sqrt{3}}\tan^{-1}\left(\frac{u}{\sqrt{3}}\right)+C$$

$$\left[\because \int \frac{dx}{x^2+a^2}=\frac{1}{a}\tan^{-1}\left(\frac{x}{a}\right)+C\right]$$

$$=\frac{1}{\sqrt{3}}\tan^{-1}\left(\frac{t-\frac{1}{t}}{\sqrt{3}}\right)+C \quad \left[\because u=t-\frac{1}{t}\right]$$

$$=\frac{1}{\sqrt{3}}\tan^{-1}\left(\frac{t^2-1}{\sqrt{3}t}\right)+C$$

$$\therefore \quad I=\frac{1}{\sqrt{3}}\tan^{-1}\left(\frac{\tan^2 x-1}{\sqrt{3}\tan x}\right)+C \quad [\because t=\tan x]$$

9. (i) Given differential equation is

$$(1+x^2)\frac{dy}{dx}+2xy-4x^2=0$$

$$\Rightarrow \quad \frac{dy}{dx}+\frac{2x}{1+x^2}y=\frac{4x^2}{1+x^2}$$

which is the equation of the form

$$\frac{dy}{dx}+Py=Q,$$

where $P=\frac{2x}{1+x^2}$ and $Q=\frac{4x^2}{1+x^2}$

$$\therefore \text{IF}=e^{\int P\,dx}=e^{\int \frac{2x}{1+x^2}dx}=e^{\log(1+x^2)}=1+x^2$$

The general solution is

$$y\cdot \text{IF}=\int Q\cdot \text{IF}\,dx+C$$

$$\Rightarrow \quad y\cdot(1+x^2)=\int (1+x^2)\frac{4x^2}{(1+x^2)}dx+C$$

$$\Rightarrow \quad (1+x^2)y=\int 4x^2\,dx+C$$

$$\Rightarrow \quad (1+x^2)y=\frac{4x^3}{3}+C$$

$$\Rightarrow \quad y=\frac{4x^3}{3(1+x^2)}+C(1+x^2)^{-1} \quad \text{...(i)}$$

Now, given $y(0)=0$, so put $x=0$, $y=0$ in Eq. (i), we get

$$0=\frac{4\cdot 0^3}{3(1+0^2)}+C(1+0^2)^{-1} \Rightarrow C=0$$

On putting the value of C in Eq. (i), we get

$$y=\frac{4x^3}{3(1+x^2)},$$

which is the required solution.

Or

(ii) Let $I=\int \frac{\sin x-\cos x}{\sqrt{\sin 2x}}dx=\int \frac{\sin x-\cos x}{\sqrt{1+\sin 2x-1}}dx$

$$=\int \frac{\sin x-\cos x}{\sqrt{\sin^2 x+\cos^2 x+2\sin x\cos x-1}}dx$$

$$\left[\begin{array}{l}\because \sin^2\theta+\cos^2\theta=1\\ \text{and } \sin 2\theta=2\sin\theta\cos\theta\end{array}\right]$$

$$=\int \frac{\sin x-\cos x}{\sqrt{(\sin x+\cos x)^2-1}}dx$$

Put $\sin x+\cos x=t \Rightarrow (\cos x-\sin x)\,dx=dt$

$$\therefore \quad I=\int \frac{-dt}{\sqrt{t^2-1}}=-\log\left|t+\sqrt{t^2-1}\right|+C$$

$$\left[\because \int \frac{dx}{\sqrt{x^2-a^2}}=\log\left|x+\sqrt{x^2-a^2}\right|+C\right]$$

$$\Rightarrow \quad I=-\log|(\sin x+\cos x)+\sqrt{(\sin x+\cos x)^2-1}|+C$$

$$[\because t=\sin x+\cos x]$$

$$=-\log|(\sin x+\cos x)+\sqrt{\sin^2 x+\cos^2 x+2\sin x\cos x-1}|+C$$

$$=-\log|(\sin x+\cos x)+\sqrt{\sin 2x}|+C$$

10. (i) (a) Let $I=\int \frac{x}{\sqrt{32-x^2}}dx$

Put $32-x^2=t \Rightarrow -2x\,dx=dt$

$$\Rightarrow \quad x\,dx=\frac{-1}{2}dt$$

$$\therefore \quad I=-\frac{1}{2}\int \frac{dt}{\sqrt{t}}=\frac{-1}{2}\cdot 2\sqrt{t}+C$$

$$=-\sqrt{t}+C=-\sqrt{32-x^2}+C$$

(b) Let $I=\int \frac{\sin(2\tan^{-1}x)}{1+x^2}dx$

Put $\tan^{-1}x=t \Rightarrow \frac{1}{1+x^2}dx=dt$

$$\therefore \quad I=\int \sin 2t\,dt=-\frac{\cos 2t}{2}+C$$

$$=\frac{-[\cos 2(\tan^{-1}x)]}{2}+C$$

(c) Let $I=\int \frac{\sqrt{1+x^2}}{x^4}dx=\int \frac{\sqrt{1+x^2}}{x}\cdot\frac{1}{x^3}dx$

$=\int\sqrt{\frac{1+x^2}{x^2}}\cdot\frac{1}{x^3}dx=\int\sqrt{\frac{1}{x^2}+1}\cdot\frac{1}{x^3}dx$

Now, put $1+\frac{1}{x^2}=t^2$

$\Rightarrow \frac{-2}{x^3}dx=2t\,dt \Rightarrow -\frac{1}{x^3}dx=t\,dt$

$\therefore \quad I=\int -t^2dt=-\frac{t^3}{3}+C$

$=-\frac{1}{3}\left(1+\frac{1}{x^2}\right)^{3/2}+C$

(d) Let $I=\int\frac{\cos^{-1}x}{\sqrt{1-x^2}}dx$

Put $\cos^{-1}x=t \Rightarrow \frac{-1}{\sqrt{1-x^2}}dx=dt$

$\Rightarrow \frac{1}{\sqrt{1-x^2}}dx=-dt$

$\therefore \quad I=\int t(-dt)=-\int t\,dt$

$=\frac{-t^2}{2}+C=\frac{-(\cos^{-1}x)^2}{2}+C$

Or

(ii) (a) We have, $\int_2^3 x^2\,dx=\left[\frac{x^3}{3}\right]_2^3=\left(\frac{3^3}{3}-\frac{2^3}{3}\right)$

$=\left(9-\frac{8}{3}\right)=\frac{19}{3}$

(b) We have, $\int_1^{\sqrt{3}}\frac{dx}{1+x^2}=[\tan^{-1}x]_1^{\sqrt{3}}$

$=[\tan^{-1}(\sqrt{3})-\tan^{-1}(1)]$

$=\frac{\pi}{3}-\frac{\pi}{4}=\frac{\pi}{12}$

(c) We have, $\int_{-1}^{1}(x+1)\,dx=\int_{-1}^{1}x\,dx+\int_{-1}^{1}1(dx)$

$=\left[\frac{x^2}{2}\right]_{-1}^{1}+[x]_{-1}^{1}$

$=\left(\frac{1}{2}-\frac{1}{2}\right)+(1+1)=2$

(d) We have, $\int_0^{\pi/2}\sin x\,dx=[-\cos x]_0^{\pi/2}$

$=\left[-\cos\frac{\pi}{2}+\cos 0\right]$

$=-0+1=1$

11. Given $f(x)=\begin{cases} a\sin\frac{\pi}{2}(x+1), & x\le 0\\ \frac{\tan x-\sin x}{x^3}, & x>0\end{cases}$ is continuous at $x=0$.

$\therefore$ LHL = RHL = $f(0)$ ...(i)

Here, LHL = $\lim_{x\to 0^-} f(x)$

$\Rightarrow$ LHL = $\lim_{h\to 0} a\sin\frac{\pi}{2}(-h+1)$

[put $x=0-h$; when $x\to 0^-$, then $h\to 0$]

$=a\sin\frac{\pi}{2}=a$ $\left[\because \sin\frac{\pi}{2}=1\right]$

and $f(0)=a\sin\frac{\pi}{2}=a$

Now, RHL = $\lim_{x\to 0^+} f(x)$

$\Rightarrow$ RHL = $\lim_{h\to 0}\frac{\tan h-\sin h}{h^3}$

[put $x=0+h=h$; when $x\to 0^+$, then $h\to 0$]

$=\lim_{h\to 0}\frac{\frac{\sin h}{\cos h}-\sin h}{h^3}=\lim_{h\to 0}\frac{\sin h-\sin h\cos h}{h^3\cos h}$

$=\lim_{h\to 0}\frac{\sin h(1-\cos h)}{h^3\cos h}$

$=\lim_{h\to 0}\frac{\sin h}{h}\cdot\lim_{h\to 0}\frac{1-\cos h}{h^2}\cdot\lim_{h\to 0}\frac{1}{\cos h}$

$=1\times\lim_{h\to 0}\frac{1-\cos h}{h^2}\times 1$

$\left[\because \lim_{\theta\to 0}\frac{\sin\theta}{\theta}=1 \text{ and } \lim_{\theta\to 0}\frac{1}{\cos\theta}=\frac{1}{\cos 0}=\frac{1}{1}=1\right]$

$=\lim_{h\to 0}\frac{1-\cos h}{h^2}=\lim_{h\to 0}\frac{2\sin^2\frac{h}{2}}{h^2}$

$\left[\because 1-\cos\theta=2\sin^2\frac{\theta}{2}\right]$

$=\lim_{h\to 0}\frac{2\times\sin^2\frac{h}{2}}{\left(\frac{h^2}{4}\times 4\right)}=\lim_{h\to 0}\frac{2}{4}\times\lim_{h\to 0}\frac{\sin^2\frac{h}{2}}{\frac{h^2}{4}}$

$=\frac{1}{2}\times\lim_{h\to 0}\left(\frac{\sin\frac{h}{2}}{\frac{h}{2}}\right)^2=\frac{1}{2}\times 1\left[\because \lim_{x\to 0}\frac{\sin x}{x}=1\right]$

$\Rightarrow$ RHL $=\frac{1}{2}$

From Eq. (i), we get LHL = RHL $\Rightarrow a=\frac{1}{2}$

12. (i) Let h be the height and a be the radius of base of cylinder inscribed in the given sphere of radius (R).

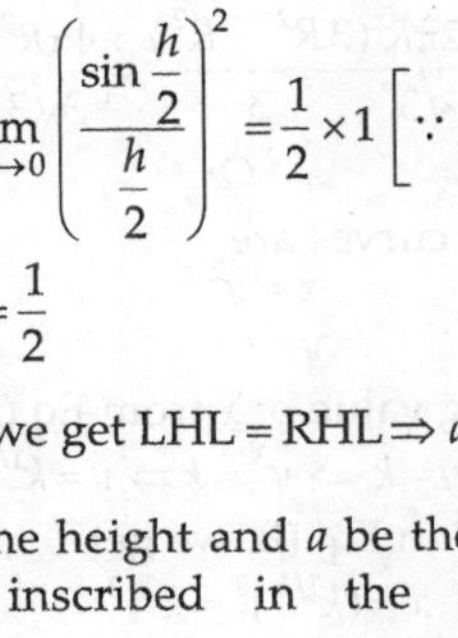

In ΔBAC, $AB^2+AC^2=BC^2$

[by Pythagoras theorem]

$\Rightarrow \quad a^2+\left(\frac{h}{2}\right)^2=R^2 \Rightarrow a^2=R^2-\frac{h^2}{4}$

Volume of cylinder,

$$V=\pi a^2h=\pi h\left(R^2-\frac{h^2}{4}\right)=\frac{\pi}{4}(4R^2h-h^3)$$

On differentiating both sides two times w.r.t. h, we get

$$\frac{dV}{dh}=\frac{\pi}{4}(4R^2-3h^2)$$

and $$\frac{d^2V}{dh^2}=\frac{\pi}{4}(-6h)=-\frac{3\pi h}{2} \quad \ldots(i)$$

For maxima or minima, put $\frac{dV}{dh}=0$.

$$\Rightarrow \quad \frac{\pi}{4}(4R^2-3h^2)=0$$

$$\Rightarrow \quad h^2=\frac{4}{3}R^2$$

$$\Rightarrow \quad h=\frac{2}{\sqrt{3}}R$$

[height is always positive, so we do not take '–' sign]

On substituting the value of h in Eq. (i), we get

$$\frac{d^2V}{dh^2}=\frac{-3\pi}{2}\cdot\frac{2}{\sqrt{3}}R=-\sqrt{3}\pi R<0$$

$\Rightarrow V$ is maximum.

Hence, the required height of cylinder is $\frac{2R}{\sqrt{3}}$.

Hence proved.

Now, maximum volume of cylinder,

$$V=\pi h\left(R^2-\frac{h^2}{4}\right)=\pi\frac{2R}{\sqrt{3}}\left(R^2-\frac{1}{4}\cdot\frac{4}{3}R^2\right) \quad \left[\text{put } h=\frac{2}{\sqrt{3}}R\right]$$

$$=\frac{2\pi R\,(3R^2-R^2)}{\sqrt{3}\cdot 3}=\frac{4\pi R^3}{3\sqrt{3}} \text{ cu units}$$

Or

(ii) The given curves are

$$x=y^2 \quad \ldots(i)$$

and $$xy=k \quad \ldots(ii)$$

On putting value of x from Eq (i) in Eq (ii), we get

$$y^2\cdot y=k\Rightarrow y^3=k\Rightarrow y=k^{1/3}$$

Put $y=k^{1/3}$ in Eq. (i), we get

$$x=(k^{1/3})^2=k^{2/3}$$

Thus, the given curves intersect at the point $P(k^{2/3},k^{1/3})$.

On differentiating Eqs. (i) and (ii) w.r.t. x respectively, we get

$$1=2y\frac{dy}{dx}$$

$$\Rightarrow \quad \frac{dy}{dx}=\frac{1}{2y} \quad \ldots(iii)$$

and $$x\cdot\frac{dy}{dx}+y=0$$

$$\Rightarrow \quad \frac{dy}{dx}=-\frac{y}{x} \quad \ldots(iv)$$

The slope of the tangent to curve (i) at P is $m_1=\frac{1}{2k^{1/3}}$ and the slope of the tangent to curve (ii) at P is $m_2=-\frac{k^{1/3}}{k^{2/3}}=-\frac{1}{k^{1/3}}$.

Now, the given curves (i) and (ii) will cut orthogonally at P, if

$$m_1m_2=-1$$

$$\Rightarrow \quad \frac{1}{2k^{1/3}}\cdot\left(-\frac{1}{k^{1/3}}\right)=-1$$

$$\Rightarrow \quad 2k^{2/3}=1$$

$$\Rightarrow \quad (2k^{2/3})^3=1^3$$

$$\Rightarrow \quad 8k^2=1$$

Hence proved.

13. (i) Let E_1, E_2, E_3 and A be the events defined as follows

E_1: The examinee guesses the answer,

E_2: The examinee copies the answer,

E_3: The examinee knows the answer and

A: The examinee has answered the question correctly

Then, $P(E_1)=\frac{1}{3}, P(E_2)=\frac{1}{6}$ [given]

As E_1, E_2 and E_3 are mutually exclusive and exhaustive events, therefore

$$P(E_1)+P(E_2)+P(E_3)=1$$

$$\Rightarrow \quad P(E_3)=1-P(E_1)-P(E_2)$$

$$=1-\frac{1}{3}-\frac{1}{6}=\frac{3}{6}=\frac{1}{2}$$

Since, there are four choices and only one is correct, so the probability that he answers correctly given that he has made a guess is $\frac{1}{4}$.

i.e. $$P(A/E_1)=\frac{1}{4}$$

$P(A/E_2)=$ Probability that he answers correctly given that he has copied $=\frac{1}{8}$ [given]

When E_3 has occurred i.e. the examinee knows the answer, then the probability that he answers correctly given that he knows the answer is 1 (sure event) i.e. $P(A/E_3)=1$

We want to find $P(E_3/A)$.

By Baye's theorem, we get

$$P(E_3/A)=\frac{P(E_3)\,P(A/E_3)}{P(E_1)\,P(A/E_1)+P(E_2)\,P(A/E_2)+P(E_3)\,P(A/E_3)}$$

$$=\frac{\frac{1}{2}\cdot 1}{\frac{1}{3}\cdot\frac{1}{4}+\frac{1}{6}\cdot\frac{1}{8}+\frac{1}{2}\cdot 1}=\frac{\frac{1}{2}}{\frac{1}{12}+\frac{1}{48}+\frac{1}{2}}$$

$$=\frac{1}{2}\times\frac{48}{4+1+24}=\frac{24}{29}$$

Or

(ii) Let E_1 = problem solved by A,

E_2 = problem solved by B

and E_3 = problem solved by C.

Given, $P(E_1)=\frac{1}{2}$ $P(E_2)=\frac{2}{3}$ and $P(E_3)=\frac{3}{4}$

(a) P(exactly two students will solve the problem)

$$= P(E_1E_2\overline{E_3}) + P(E_1\overline{E_2}E_3) + P(\overline{E_1}E_2E_3)$$
$$= P(E_1)P(E_2)P(\overline{E_3}) + P(E_1)P(\overline{E_2})P(E_3) + P(\overline{E_1})P(E_2)P(E_3)$$
$$= P(E_1)P(E_2)\{1-P(E_3)\} + P(E_1)\{1-P(E_2)\}P(E_3) + \{1-P(E_1)\}P(E_2)P(E_3)$$
$$= \frac{1}{2}\times\frac{2}{3}\times\left(1-\frac{3}{4}\right)+\frac{1}{2}\times\left(1-\frac{2}{3}\right)\times\frac{3}{4}+\left(1-\frac{1}{2}\right)\times\frac{2}{3}\times\frac{3}{4}$$
$$= \frac{2}{6}\times\frac{1}{4}+\frac{3}{8}\times\frac{1}{3}+\frac{1}{2}\times\frac{6}{12}$$
$$= \frac{2+3+6}{24}=\frac{11}{24}$$

(b) P(atleast two of them will solve the problem)

$$= P(E_1E_2\overline{E_3}) + P(E_1\overline{E_2}E_3) + P(\overline{E_1}E_2E_3) + P(E_1E_2E_3)$$
$$= P(E_1)P(E_2)\{1-P(E_3)\} + P(E_1)\{1-P(E_2)\}P(E_3) + \{1-P(E_1)\}P(E_2)P(E_3) + P(E_1)P(E_2)P(E_3)$$
$$= \frac{1}{2}\times\frac{2}{3}\times\left(1-\frac{3}{4}\right)+\frac{1}{2}\times\left(1-\frac{2}{3}\right)\times\frac{3}{4}+\left(1-\frac{1}{2}\right)\times\frac{2}{3}\times\frac{3}{4}+\frac{1}{2}\times\frac{2}{3}\times\frac{3}{4}$$
$$= \frac{2}{6}\times\frac{1}{4}+\frac{3}{8}\times\frac{1}{3}+\frac{6}{12}\times\frac{1}{2}+\frac{6}{24}$$
$$= \frac{2}{24}+\frac{3}{24}+\frac{6}{24}+\frac{6}{24}$$
$$= \frac{2+3+6+6}{24}=\frac{17}{24}$$

14. (i) We have, $A=\begin{bmatrix}\cos\alpha & -\sin\alpha & 0\\ \sin\alpha & \cos\alpha & 0\\ 0 & 0 & 1\end{bmatrix}$

Clearly, the cofactors of elements of matrix A are given by

$A_{11}=\cos\alpha$; $A_{12}=-\sin\alpha$; $A_{13}=0$;

$A_{21}=\sin\alpha$; $A_{22}=\cos\alpha$; $A_{23}=0$

$A_{31}=0$; $A_{32}=0$ and $A_{33}=\cos^2\alpha+\sin^2\alpha=1$

$$\therefore \text{adj } A=\begin{bmatrix}A_{11} & A_{12} & A_{13}\\ A_{21} & A_{22} & A_{23}\\ A_{31} & A_{32} & A_{33}\end{bmatrix}^T$$
$$=\begin{bmatrix}\cos\alpha & -\sin\alpha & 0\\ \sin\alpha & \cos\alpha & 0\\ 0 & 0 & 1\end{bmatrix}^T=\begin{bmatrix}\cos\alpha & \sin\alpha & 0\\ -\sin\alpha & \cos\alpha & 0\\ 0 & 0 & 1\end{bmatrix}$$

(ii) Now,

$$|A|=\begin{vmatrix}\cos\alpha & -\sin\alpha & 0\\ \sin\alpha & \cos\alpha & 0\\ 0 & 0 & 1\end{vmatrix}=1\cdot(\cos^2\alpha+\sin^2\alpha)=1$$

[expanding along R_3]

(iii) Now, $A(\text{adj } A)$

$$=\begin{bmatrix}\cos\alpha & -\sin\alpha & 0\\ \sin\alpha & \cos\alpha & 0\\ 0 & 0 & 1\end{bmatrix}\begin{bmatrix}\cos\alpha & \sin\alpha & 0\\ -\sin\alpha & \cos\alpha & 0\\ 0 & 0 & 1\end{bmatrix}$$
$$=\begin{bmatrix}\cos^2\alpha+\sin^2\alpha & 0 & 0\\ 0 & \sin^2\alpha+\cos^2\alpha & 0\\ 0 & 0 & 1\end{bmatrix}$$
$$=\begin{bmatrix}1 & 0 & 0\\ 0 & 1 & 0\\ 0 & 0 & 1\end{bmatrix} \quad [\because \cos^2\theta+\sin^2\theta=1]$$
$$(\text{adj } A)\cdot(A)=\begin{bmatrix}\cos\alpha & \sin\alpha & 0\\ -\sin\alpha & \cos\alpha & 0\\ 0 & 0 & 1\end{bmatrix}\begin{bmatrix}\cos\alpha & -\sin\alpha & 0\\ \sin\alpha & \cos\alpha & 0\\ 0 & 0 & 1\end{bmatrix}$$
$$=\begin{bmatrix}\cos^2\alpha+\sin^2\alpha & 0 & 0\\ 0 & \sin^2\alpha+\cos^2\alpha & 0\\ 0 & 0 & 1\end{bmatrix}$$
$$=\begin{bmatrix}1 & 0 & 0\\ 0 & 1 & 0\\ 0 & 0 & 1\end{bmatrix}$$

Hence, $A[\text{adj } A]=[\text{adj } A]\,A$

(iv) From parts (i), (ii) and (iii), we get

$A(\text{adj } A)=(\text{adj } A)\cdot A=|A|\,I_3$

Common Mistake Remember that adjoint of a matrix is the transpose of a matrix formed by its cofactors.

15. (i) (b) Given planes are

$$2x+\lambda y+3z=5 \quad \text{...(i)}$$
and $$x+y+3z=9 \quad \text{...(ii)}$$

Here, $a_1=2$, $b_1=\lambda$, $c_1=3$

and $a_2=1$, $b_2=1$, $c_2=3$

$\because$ Condition of perpendicular is

$$a_1a_2+b_1b_2+c_1c_2=0$$
$$\Rightarrow 2(1)+\lambda(1)+3(3)=0$$
$$\Rightarrow 2+\lambda+9=0 \Rightarrow \lambda=-11$$

(ii) (a) Given, $|\vec{a}|=3|\vec{b}|$ and $(\vec{a}+\vec{b})\cdot(\vec{a}-\vec{b})=32$

$$\Rightarrow |\vec{a}|^2-|\vec{b}|^2=32$$
$$\Rightarrow (3|\vec{b}|)^2-|\vec{b}|^2=32$$

[given, $|\vec{a}|=3|\vec{b}|$]

$$\Rightarrow 9|\vec{b}|^2-|\vec{b}|^2=32 \Rightarrow 8|\vec{b}|^2=32$$
$$\Rightarrow |\vec{b}|^2=4 \Rightarrow |\vec{b}|=2$$

(iii) (c) Given equations of planes are

$$2x-y+z=6 \text{ and } x+y+2z=7$$

The direction ratios of normals to the given planes are

$$\langle a_1,b_1,c_1\rangle=\langle 2,-1,1\rangle$$
and $$\langle a_2,b_2,c_2\rangle=\langle 1,1,2\rangle$$

Let θ be the angle between them, then

$$\cos\theta = \frac{a_1 \cdot a_2 + b_1 \cdot b_2 + c_1 \cdot c_2}{\sqrt{a_1^2 + b_1^2 + c_1^2}\sqrt{a_2^2 + b_2^2 + c_2^2}}$$

$$= \frac{2 \times 1 + (-1) \times 1 + 1 \times 2}{\sqrt{2^2 + (-1)^2 + (1)^2}\sqrt{(1)^2 + (1)^2 + (2)^2}}$$

$$= \frac{2 - 1 + 2}{\sqrt{4 + 1 + 1}\sqrt{1 + 1 + 4}} = \frac{3}{\sqrt{6}\sqrt{6}}$$

$$\Rightarrow \cos\theta = \frac{3}{6} = \frac{1}{2} \Rightarrow \theta = \frac{\pi}{3}$$

(iv) Given points are A, B and C whose position vectors are $\overrightarrow{OA} = (-2\hat{i} + 3\hat{j} + 5\hat{k})$, $\overrightarrow{OB} = (\hat{i} + 2\hat{j} + 3\hat{k})$ and $\overrightarrow{OC} = (7, \hat{i}, \hat{k})$.

Now, $\overrightarrow{AB} = \overrightarrow{OE} - \overrightarrow{OA} = (\hat{i} + 2\hat{j} + 3\hat{k}) - (-2\hat{i} + 3\hat{j} + 5\hat{k})$

$= 3\hat{i} - \hat{j} - 2\hat{k}$

$\therefore (\overrightarrow{AB}) = \sqrt{(3)^2 + (-1)^2 + (-2)^2} = \sqrt{9 + 1 + 4} = \sqrt{14}$

$\overrightarrow{BC} = \overrightarrow{OC} - \overrightarrow{OE} = (7\hat{i} - \hat{k}) - (\hat{i} + 2\hat{j} + 3\hat{k})$

$= 6\hat{i} - 2\hat{j} - 4\hat{k}$

$\therefore \quad |\overrightarrow{BC}| = \sqrt{(6)^2 + (-2)^2 + (-4)^2} = \sqrt{36 + 4 + 16}$

$= \sqrt{56} = 2\sqrt{14}$

and $\overrightarrow{AC} = \overrightarrow{OC} - \overrightarrow{OA} = (7\hat{i} - \hat{k}) - (-2\hat{i} + 3\hat{j} + 5\hat{k})$

$= 9\hat{i} - 3\hat{j} - 6\hat{k}$

$\therefore \quad |\overrightarrow{AC}| = \sqrt{(9)^2 + (-3)^2 + (-6)^2}$

$= \sqrt{81 + 9 + 36} = \sqrt{126} = 3\sqrt{14}$

Now, $|\overrightarrow{AB}| + |\overrightarrow{BC}| = \sqrt{14} + 2\sqrt{14} = 3\sqrt{14} = |\overrightarrow{AC}|$

$\Rightarrow |\overrightarrow{AB}| + |\overrightarrow{BC}| = |\overrightarrow{AC}|$

Hence, the points A, B and C are collinear.

(v) Given vectors are

$$\vec{a} = \hat{i} + \hat{j} + \hat{k}, \vec{b} = 2\hat{i} + 3\hat{j}, \vec{c} = 3\hat{i} + 5\hat{j} - 2\hat{k}$$

and $\vec{d} = \hat{k} - \hat{j}$

Now, $\vec{b} - \vec{a} = 2\hat{i} + 3\hat{j} - (\hat{i} + \hat{j} + \hat{k}) = \hat{i} + 2\hat{j} - \hat{k}$ ...(i)

$\therefore \quad |\vec{b} - \vec{a}| = \sqrt{(1)^2 + (2)^2 + (-1)^2}$

$\Rightarrow \quad |\vec{b} - \vec{a}| = \sqrt{1 + 4 + 1} = \sqrt{6}$

and $\quad \vec{d} - \vec{c} = \hat{k} - \hat{j} - (3\hat{i} + 5\hat{j} - 2\hat{k})$

$= -3\hat{i} - 6\hat{j} + 3\hat{k}$ ...(ii)

$\therefore \quad |\vec{d} - \vec{c}| = \sqrt{(-3)^2 + (-6)^2 + (3)^2}$

$= \sqrt{9 + 36 + 9} = \sqrt{54}$

$\Rightarrow \quad |\vec{d} - \vec{c}| = 3\sqrt{6}$

From Eqs. (i) and (ii), we get

$$\vec{d} - \vec{c} = -3(\hat{i} + 2\hat{j} - \hat{k}) = -3(\vec{b} - \vec{a})$$

Hence, $\vec{d} - \vec{c}$ is parallel to $\vec{b} - \vec{a}$.

Now, $\dfrac{\text{Length of } (\vec{b} - \vec{a})}{\text{Length of } (\vec{d} - \vec{c})} = \dfrac{|\vec{b} - \vec{a}|}{|\vec{d} - \vec{c}|} = \dfrac{\sqrt{6}}{3\sqrt{6}} = \dfrac{1}{3}$

16. (i) Given, $\vec{a} \times \vec{b} = \vec{c} \Rightarrow \vec{c}$ is perpendicular to both $\vec{a}$ and $\vec{b}$.

Also, $\vec{b} \times \vec{c} = \vec{a} \Rightarrow \vec{a}$ is perpendicular to both $\vec{b}$ and $\vec{c}$.

From above conclusions, it follows that $\vec{a}, \vec{b}$ and $\vec{c}$ are mutually perpendicular vectors. Further,

$$\vec{a} \times \vec{b} = \vec{c} \Rightarrow |\vec{a} \times \vec{b}| = |\vec{c}|$$

$\Rightarrow \quad |\vec{a}|\,|\vec{b}| \sin\frac{\pi}{2} = |\vec{c}| \quad [\because \vec{a} \perp \vec{b}]$

$\Rightarrow \quad |\vec{a}|\,|\vec{b}| = |\vec{c}| \quad [\because \sin\frac{\pi}{2} = 1]$ ...(i)

Also, $\vec{b} \times \vec{c} = \vec{a} \Rightarrow |\vec{b} \times \vec{c}| = |\vec{a}|$

$\Rightarrow \quad |\vec{b}|\,|\vec{c}| \sin\frac{\pi}{2} = |\vec{a}| \quad [\because \vec{b} \perp \vec{c}]$

$\Rightarrow \quad |\vec{b}|\,|\vec{c}| = |\vec{a}|$

$\Rightarrow \quad |\vec{b}|(|\vec{a}|\,|\vec{b}|) = |\vec{a}|$ [using Eq. (i)]

$\Rightarrow \quad |\vec{b}|^2\,|\vec{a}| = |\vec{a}|$

$\Rightarrow \quad |\vec{b}|^2 = 1 \quad [\because |\vec{a}| \neq 0]$

$\therefore \quad |\vec{b}| = 1$

On substituting this value of $|\vec{b}|$ in Eq. (i), we get $|\vec{a}| \cdot 1 = |\vec{c}|$ i.e. $|\vec{c}| = |\vec{a}|$. **Hence proved.**

Or

(ii) Given, $\vec{a} = \hat{i} + \hat{j} - \hat{k}$ and $\vec{b} = \hat{i} - \hat{j} + \hat{k}$

Then, $|\vec{a}| = |\hat{i} + \hat{j} - \hat{k}|$

$= \sqrt{1^2 + 1^2 + (-1)^2} = \sqrt{1 + 1 + 1} = \sqrt{3}$

and $\quad |\vec{b}| = |\hat{i} - \hat{j} + \hat{k}|$

$= \sqrt{(1)^2 + (-1)^2 + (1)^2} = \sqrt{1 + 1 + 1} = \sqrt{3}$

Also, $\vec{a} \cdot \vec{b} = (\hat{i} + \hat{j} - \hat{k}) \cdot (\hat{i} - \hat{j} + \hat{k})$

$= (1)(1) + (1)(-1) + (-1)(1)$

$= 1 - 1 - 1 = -1$

Now, let the angle between two vectors $\vec{a}$ and $\vec{b}$ be θ.

Then, $\cos\theta = \dfrac{\vec{a} \cdot \vec{b}}{|\vec{a}|\,|\vec{b}|} = \dfrac{-1}{\sqrt{3}\sqrt{3}}$

$\Rightarrow \quad \cos\theta = -\dfrac{1}{3} \Rightarrow \theta = \cos^{-1}\left(\dfrac{-1}{3}\right)$

17. (i) Given lines are,

$$\frac{x - 1}{3} = \frac{y + 1}{2} = \frac{z - 1}{5} = r \quad \text{[say]...(i)}$$

and $\quad \dfrac{x - 2}{4} = \dfrac{y - 1}{3} = \dfrac{z + 1}{-2} = r_1 \quad$ [say] ...(ii)

Direction ratios of these lines are (3, 2, 5) and (4, 3, − 2). Since, $3 : 2 : 5 \neq 4 : 3 : -2$, therefore the lines are not parallel. They may intersect or may not.

Any point on line (i) is

$P(3r+1, 2r-1, 5r+1)$

Any point on line (ii) is

$Q(4r_1+2, 3r_1+1, -2r_1-1)$

The lines given by Eqs. (i) and (ii) intersect, if the points P and Q coincide for some values of r and r_1

i.e.

$$\left.\begin{array}{l}3r+1=4r_1+2\\2r-1=3r_1+1\\5r+1=-2r_1-1\end{array}\right\} \Rightarrow \left.\begin{array}{l}3r-4r_1=1\\2r-3r_1=2\\5r+2r_1=-2\end{array}\right\}$$

On solving first two equations, we get

$$r=-5 \text{ and } r_1=-4$$

But the values $r=-5$ and $r_1=-4$ do not satisfy the 3rd equation $5r+2r_1=-2$.

Hence, the given lines do not intersect each other.

Hence proved.

Or

(ii) Given, plane passes through the point $(-1,-1,2)$.

Therefore, equation of plane is

$$a(x+1)+b(y+1)+c(z-2)=0 \quad \ldots\text{(i)}$$

As, the plane is perpendicular to the planes

$$3x+2y-3z=1 \text{ and } 5x-4y+z=5 \quad \text{[given]}$$

$$\therefore \quad 3a+2b-3c=0 \quad \ldots\text{(ii)}$$

[$\because$ condition of perpendicular is $a_1a_2+b_1b_2+c_1c_2=0$]

and $$5a-4b+c=0 \quad \ldots\text{(iii)}$$

[$\because$ condition of perpendicular $a_1a_2+b_1b_2+c_1c_2=0$]

On solving Eqs. (iii) and (ii), we get

$$\frac{a}{2-12}=\frac{b}{-15-3}=\frac{c}{-12-10}$$

$$\Rightarrow \quad \frac{a}{-10}=\frac{b}{-18}=\frac{c}{-22} \Rightarrow \frac{a}{5}=\frac{b}{9}=\frac{c}{11}$$

$$\Rightarrow \quad a=\frac{5c}{11} \text{ and } b=\frac{9c}{11}$$

On putting the values of a and b in Eq. (i), we get

$$\frac{5c}{11}(x+1)+\frac{9c}{11}(y+1)+c(z-2)=0$$

$$\Rightarrow \quad \frac{c}{11}(5x+5+9y+9+11z-22)=0$$

$$\Rightarrow \quad 5x+9y+11z-8=0$$

which is the required equation of plane.

18. Given equations of curves are

$$y=x^2+2 \text{ or } x^2=y-2 \quad \ldots\text{(i)}$$

$$y=x \quad \ldots\text{(ii)}$$

$$x=0 \quad \ldots\text{(iii)}$$

and $$x=3 \quad \ldots\text{(iv)}$$

Eq. (i) represents a parabola of the form $X^2=4aY$ with vertex at (0, 2) and axis along positive direction of Y-axis.

Eq. (ii) represents a line which intersects the coordinate axes at (0, 0).

Eqs. (iii) and (iv) represent the lines perpendicular to the X-axis

The line $x=3$ intersects $y=x$ at $(3,3)$ and $y=x^2+2$ at (3, 11).

The graph of given curves is shown below.

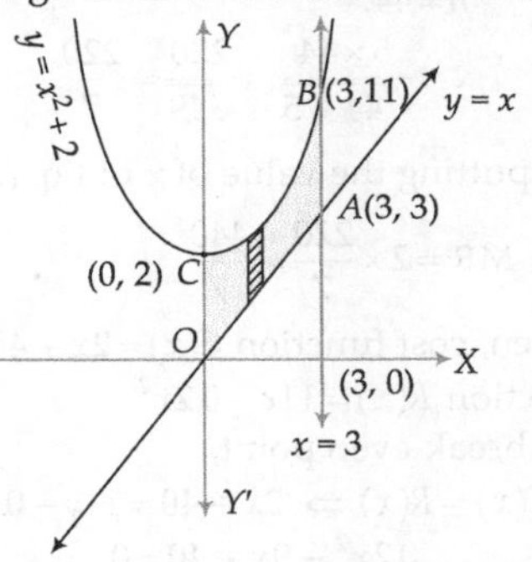

It is clear from the figure that the required region is *OABCO*.

$\therefore$ Required area = Area of shaded portion *OABCO*

$$=\int_0^3 [y_2 \text{ (parabola)} - y_1 \text{ (line)}]\,dx$$

$$=\int_0^3 (x^2+2-x)\,dx=\left[\frac{x^3}{3}-\frac{x^2}{2}+2x\right]_0^3$$

$$=\frac{27}{3}-\frac{9}{2}+6=9+6-\frac{9}{2}=15-\frac{9}{2}$$

$$=\frac{30-9}{2}=\frac{21}{2} \text{ sq. units}$$

Hence, the required area is $\frac{21}{2}$ sq. units.

Value Point

Precisely draw and mark the graph and point of intersection respectively.

19. (i) (d) We have, $\bar{x}=5, \bar{y}=13$ and $b_{yx}=2.5$

The regression equation y on x is

$$y-\bar{y}=b_{yx}(x-\bar{x})$$

$$\Rightarrow \quad y-13=2.5(x-5)=2.5x-12.5$$

$$\Rightarrow \quad y=2.5x+0.5$$

(ii) (c) Given, $p=50-3x$

We know that revenue function $(R)=px$

$$\Rightarrow \quad R=50x-3x^2$$

Now, marginal revenue, $\text{MR}=\frac{dR}{dx}=\frac{d}{dx}(50x-3x^2)$

$$=50-6x$$

$$\Rightarrow \quad \text{MR}=50-6x$$

At $x=0$, $[\text{MR}]_{x=0}=50$

(iii) We have, $x=\frac{5n}{\sqrt{n+5}}$ and $p=\frac{2}{x}+x$

Now, total revenue,

$$R=px=\left(\frac{2}{x}+x\right)x=2+x^2$$

$\therefore$ Marginal Revenue,

$$(\text{MR})=\frac{dR}{dx}=\frac{d}{dx}(2+x^2)=2x \quad \ldots\text{(i)}$$

$$\because \quad x=\frac{5n}{\sqrt{n+5}} \quad \text{[given]}$$

At $n = 44$,

$$x = \frac{5 \times 44}{\sqrt{44+5}} = \frac{220}{\sqrt{49}} = \frac{220}{7}$$

On putting the value of x in Eq. (i), we get

$$MR = 2 \times \frac{220}{7} = \frac{440}{7}$$

(iv) Given, cost function $C(x) = 2x + 40$ and revenue function $R(x) = 11x - 0.2x^2$

For break-even point,

$C(x) = R(x) \Rightarrow 2x + 40 = 11x - 0.2x^2$

$\Rightarrow 0.2x^2 - 9x + 40 = 0$

$\Rightarrow x^2 - 45x + 200 = 0$ [multiply by 5]

$\Rightarrow x^2 - 40x - 5x + 200 = 0$

$\Rightarrow x(x-40) - 5(x-40) = 0$

$\Rightarrow (x-5)(x-40) = 0$

$\Rightarrow x = 40, 5$

Hence, break-even points are 40 and 5.

(v) Given, regression lines are $2x - 3y = 6$

and $5x - 4y = 20$

Let the line of regression y on x is

$$3y = 2x - 6 \text{ or } y = \frac{2}{3}x - 2$$

$\therefore$ Regression coefficient of y on x is

$$b_{yx} = \frac{2}{3}$$

and the line of regression x on y is

$$5x = 4y + 20 \text{ or } x = \frac{4}{5}y + 4$$

$\therefore$ Regression coefficient of x on y is

$$b_{xy} = \frac{4}{5}$$

20. (i) Given, $C(x) = \frac{1}{3}x^3 + 3x^2 - 7x + 16$

(*a*) Marginal Cost (MC)

$$= \frac{dC(x)}{dx} = \frac{d}{dx}\left(\frac{1}{3}x^3 + 3x^2 - 7x + 16\right)$$

$$= x^2 + 6x - 7$$

(*b*) Average Cost (AC)

$$= \frac{C(x)}{x} = \frac{1}{x}\left(\frac{1}{3}x^3 + 3x^2 - 7x + 16\right)$$

$$= \frac{1}{3}x^2 + 3x - 7 + \frac{16}{x}$$

Or

(ii) Given, $C(x) = ax^3 + bx^2 - cx + d$,

then variable cost (VC) $= ax^3 + bx^2 - cx$

$\therefore$ Average variable cost

$$(AVC) = \frac{VC}{x} = \frac{ax^3 + bx^2 - cx}{x}$$

$$= ax^2 + bx - c$$

On differentiating w.r.t. x two times, we get

$$\frac{d}{dx}(AVC) = 2ax + b$$

and $\frac{d^2}{dx^2}(AVC) = 2a$

For maxima or minima, put $\frac{d}{dx}(AVC) = 0$,

$\Rightarrow 2ax + b = 0 \Rightarrow x = -\frac{b}{2a}$

At $x = -\frac{b}{2a}$, $\frac{d^2}{dx^2}(AVC) = 2a > 0$, for all x.

[$\because a > 0$, given]

Hence, AVC is minimum, when $x = -\frac{b}{2a}$.

To show that average variable cost (AVC) and marginal cost (MC) curves intersect at minimum average variable cost, we have to show that

$$AVC = MC \text{ at } x = -\frac{b}{2a}.$$

Now, $MC = \frac{dC}{dx} = \frac{d}{dx}(ax^3 + bx^2 - cx + d)$

$= 3ax^2 + 2bx - c$

$AVC - MC = (ax^2 + bx - c) - (3ax^2 + 2bx - c)$

$= -2ax^2 - bx$

If AVC = MC, then AVC − MC = 0

$\Rightarrow -2ax^2 - bx = 0$

$\Rightarrow x(2ax + b) = 0$

$\Rightarrow x = 0 \text{ or } x = -\frac{b}{2a}$.

Hence, AVC = MC at $x = -\frac{b}{2a}$.

21. Here, we make the following table :

x	x^2	y	y^2	xy
10	100	−5	25	−50
10	100	−3	9	−30
11	121	−2	4	−22
11	121	0	0	0
12	144	1	1	12
15	225	6	36	90
16	256	4	16	64
11	121	−2	4	−22
$\Sigma x = 96$	$\Sigma x^2 = 1188$	$\Sigma y = -1$	$\Sigma y^2 = 95$	$\Sigma xy = 42$

$$\therefore \bar{x} = \frac{\Sigma x}{n} = \frac{96}{8} = 12,\ \bar{y} = \frac{\Sigma y}{n} = \frac{-1}{8} = -0.125$$

(i) $$b_{yx} = \frac{\Sigma xy - \frac{1}{n}\Sigma x \Sigma y}{\Sigma x^2 - \frac{1}{n}(\Sigma x)^2} = \frac{42 - \frac{1}{8}(96)(-1)}{1188 - \frac{1}{8}(96)^2}$$

$$= \frac{42 + 12}{1188 - 1152} = \frac{54}{36} = \frac{3}{2} = 1.5$$

and $b_{xy} = \dfrac{\Sigma xy - \frac{1}{n}\Sigma x \Sigma y}{\Sigma y^2 - \frac{1}{n}(\Sigma y)^2} = \dfrac{42 - \frac{1}{8}\times 96 \times (-1)}{95 - \frac{1}{8}(-1)^2}$

$= \dfrac{42+12}{95-0.125} = \dfrac{54}{94.88} = 0.569$

(ii) The regression line of y on x is

$$y - \bar{y} = b_{yx}(x - \bar{x})$$

$\Rightarrow \quad y + 0.125 = 1.5(x - 12)$

On substituting $x = 14$, we get

$$y = 1.5(14-12) - 0.125 = 3 - 0.125 = 2.875$$

(iii) The regression line of x on y is

$$x - \bar{x} = b_{xy}(y - \bar{y})$$

$\Rightarrow \quad x = 0.569(y + 0.125) + 12$

On substituting $y = 3$, we get

$$x = 0.569(3 + 0.125) + 12 = 13.778$$

Common Mistake

For regression line of y on x use b_{yx} and for regression line of x on y use b_{xy}.

22. (i) Let x packets of food P and y packets of food Q be mixed, then this problem can be formulated as an LPP as follows

Optimal function (units of vitamin A).

$$Z = 6x + 3y$$

Subject to the constraints

$12x + 3y \geq 240$ [units of calcium constraint]

$\Rightarrow \quad 4x + y \geq 80,$

$4x + 20y \geq 460$ [units of iron constraint]

$\Rightarrow \quad x + 5y \geq 115,$

$6x + 4y \leq 300$ [units of cholestrol constraint]

$\Rightarrow \quad 3x + 2y \leq 150,$

$x \geq 0, y \geq 0$ [non-negativity constraints]

The table for line $4x + y = 80$ or $y = 80 - 4x$ is

x	0	20
y	80	0

So, the line passes through the points (0, 80) and (20, 0).

Put (0, 0) in the inequality $4x + y \geq 80$, we get

$0 + 0 \geq 80$ [false]

So, the half plane is away from the origin.

The table for line $x + 5y = 115$ or $y = \dfrac{115 - x}{5}$ is

x	0	115
y	23	0

So, the line passes through the points (0, 23) and (115, 0).

Put (0, 0) in the inequality $x + 5y \geq 115$, we get

$0 + 0 \geq 115$ [false]

So, the half plane is away from the origin.

The table for line $3x + 2y = 150$ or $y = \dfrac{150 - 3x}{2}$ is

x	0	50
y	75	0

So, the line passes through the points (0, 75) and (50, 0).

Put (0, 0) in the inequality $3x + 2y \leq 150$, we get

$0 + 0 \leq 150$ [true]

So, the half plane is towards the origin.

Also, $x \geq 0$, $y \geq 0$, so the region lies in the first quadrant.

The point of intersection of given inequalities are $A(15, 20)$, $B(40, 15)$ and $C(2, 72)$.

Now, we plots the inequalities on the graph paper which is shown below.

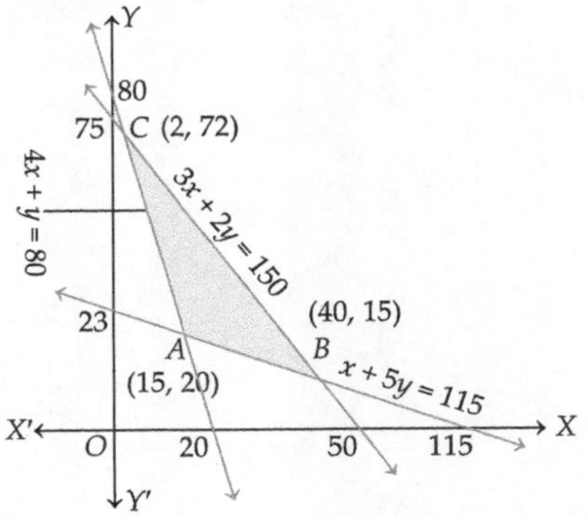

The feasible region is ABC, which is bounded. The corner points are $A(15, 20)$, $B(40, 15)$ and $C(2, 72)$.

The values of Z at these corner points are given below.

Corner points	$Z = 6x + 3y$
$A(15, 20)$	$Z = 6 \times 15 + 3 \times 20 = 150$ (Minimum)
$B(40, 15)$	$Z = 6 \times 40 + 3 \times 15 = 285$
$C(2, 72)$	$Z = 6 \times 2 + 3 \times 72 = 228$

Minimum units of vitamin $A = 150$, when 15 packets of food P and 20 packets of food Q are mixed.

Or

(ii) Given problem is to maximise

$$Z = x + y \quad \text{...(i)}$$

subject to constraints,

$$x - y \leq -1 \quad \text{...(ii)}$$

$$-x + y \leq 0 \quad \text{...(iii)}$$

and $\quad x \geq 0, y \geq 0 \quad$ ...(iv)

Table for line $x - y = -1$ or $y = x + 1$ is

x	0	−1
y	1	0

So, the line $x - y = -1$ is passing through the points (0, 1) and (– 1, 0).

On putting (0, 0) in the inequality $x - y \le -1$, we get

$$0 - 0 \le -1$$

$\Rightarrow$ $0 \le -1$, which is not true.

So, the half plane is away from the origin.

Table for line $-x + y = 0$ or $y = x$ is

x	0	1
y	0	1

So, the line $-x + y = 0$ is passing through (0, 0) and (1, 1).

On putting (2, 0) in the inequality $-x + y \le 0$, we get

$$-2 + 0 \le 0$$

$\Rightarrow$ $-2 \le 0$, which is true.

So, the half plane is towards the X-axis.

Also, $x, y \ge 0$.

So, the region lies in the I quadrant. Now, plot all the inequalities on the graph paper as shown.

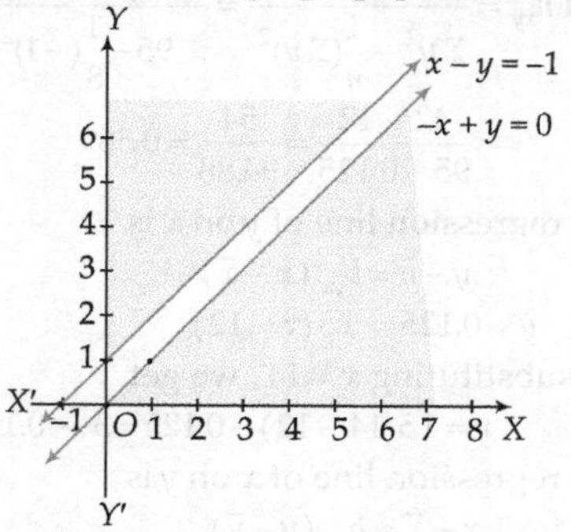

From the above graph, it is clear that there is no common region.

Hence, there is no feasible region and thus Z has no maximum value.

SQP Code : **PB-11/15** Series **i-Succeed 11-25/15** Roll No. | | | | | | | |

Sample Question Paper 11

Mathematics 12th (Code 860)

General Instructions

1. The Question Paper consists of three sections A, B and C.
2. Candidates are required to attempt all questions from Section A and all questions either from Section B Or Section C.
3. Section A Internal choice has been provided in two questions of two marks each, two questions of four marks each and two questions of six marks each.
4. Section B Internal choice has been provided in one questions of two marks and one question of four marks.
5. Section C Internal choice has been provided in one question of two marks and one question of four marks.
6. All working, including rough work, should be done on the same sheet as, and adjacent to the rest of the answer.
7. The intended marks for questions or parts of questions are given in brackets [].
8. Mathematical tables and graph papers are provided.

Time : 3 Hrs.

Max. Marks : 80

Section A (65 Marks)

1. In subparts (i) to (xi) choose the correct options and in subparts (xii) to (xv), answer the questions as instructed.

(i) The relation R in the set of natural numbers N defined as $R=\{(x,y): x>y\}$ is • *Recall* [1]

(a) an equivalence relation
(b) reflexive, symmetric but not transitive
(c) reflexive, transitive but not symmetric
(d) transitive but neither reflexive nor symmetric

(ii) **Assertion** (A) The value of

$\cos^{-1}\left(\frac{1}{2}\right)+2\sin^{-1}\left(\frac{1}{2}\right)$ is $\frac{2\pi}{3}$

Reason (R) Principal values branch of $\cos^{-1}$ is $[0, \pi]$ and $\sin^{-1}$ is $\left[-\frac{\pi}{2},\frac{\pi}{2}\right]$. • *Understanding* [1]

(a) Both A and R are correct and R is the correct explanation of A.
(b) Both A and R are correct but R is not the correct explanation of A.
(c) A is correct but R is incorrect.
(d) A is incorrect but R is correct.

(iii) If $A=[a_{ij}]_{3\times 4}$ is matrix given by

$$A=\begin{bmatrix}4 & -2 & 1 & 3\\ 5 & 7 & 9 & 6\\ 21 & 15 & 18 & -25\end{bmatrix}$$

Then, $a_{23}+a_{24}$ will be equal to the element • *Analysis* [1]

(a) a_{14}
(b) a_{44}
(c) a_{13}
(d) a_{32}

(iv) If $f(x)=2x$ and $g(x)=\frac{x^2}{2}+1$, then which of the following can be a discontinuous function? • *Recall* [1]

(a) $f(x)+g(x)$
(b) $f(x)-g(x)$
(c) $f(x)\cdot g(x)$
(d) $\frac{g(x)}{f(x)}$

(v) The values of x for which $y=[x(x-2)]^2$ is an increasing function, are • *Application* [1]

(a) $0<x<1$ and $x>2$

(b) $0<x<2$ and $x>3$

(c) $0<x<\frac{1}{2}$ and $x>\frac{3}{2}$

(d) $0<x<\frac{3}{2}$ and $x>4$

(vi) **Statement I** $\int \frac{2dx}{1+\cos 2x}$ is equal to $\tan x + C$ [1]

Statement II $\int \sqrt{ax+b}\,dx$ is equal to $\frac{2}{a}(ax+b)^{3/2}+C$

Choose the correct option. • *Evaluate*

(a) Only Statement I is true.

(b) Only Statement II is true.

(c) Both Statements I and II are true.

(d) Neither I nor II is true.

(vii) $\int \frac{dx}{x(x^7+1)}$ is equal to • *Application* [1]

(a) $\log\left(\frac{x^7}{x^7+1}\right)+C$ (b) $\frac{1}{7}\log\left(\frac{x^7}{x^7+1}\right)+C$

(c) $\log\left(\frac{x^7+1}{x^7}\right)+C$ (d) $\frac{1}{7}\log\left(\frac{x^7+1}{x^7}\right)+C$

(viii) The value of $\int_0^1 \frac{dx}{e^x+e}$ is • *Evaluate* [1]

(a) $\frac{1}{e}\log\left(\frac{1+e}{2}\right)$ (b) $\log\left(\frac{1+e}{2}\right)$

(c) $\frac{1}{e}\log(1+e)$ (d) $\log\left(\frac{2}{1+e}\right)$

(ix) **Assertion** (A) The general solution of the differential equation $\frac{dy}{dx}+y=e^x$ is $y=Ce^{-x}+e^x$. where C is an arbitrary constant.

Reason (R) The method of integrating factors can be used to solve first order linear differential equation of the form $\frac{dy}{dx}+P(x)y=Q(x)$. • *Recall*

(a) Both A and R are correct and R is the correct explanation of A.

(b) Both A and R are correct but R is not the correct explanation of A.

(c) A is correct but R is false.

(d) A is false but R is correct.

(x) Consider the following statements.

Statement I The mean of a random variable X is also called the expectation of X, denoted by $E(X)$.

Statement II The mean or expectation of a random variable X is not equal to the products of all possible values of X by their respective probabilities.

Choose the correct option. • *Recall* [1]

(a) Statement I is true; Statement II is true; Statement II is a correct explanation for Statement I

(b) Statement I is true; Statement II is true; Statement II is not a correct explanation for Statement I

(c) Statement I is true; Statement II is false.

(d) Statement I is false; Statement II is true.

(xi) If $P=\begin{bmatrix}\sin x & \cos x\\ -\cos x & \sin x\end{bmatrix}$ and $P(\text{adj } P)=k\begin{bmatrix}1 & 0\\ 0 & 1\end{bmatrix}$, then the value of k is • *Evaluate* [1]

(a) 0 (b) 1

(c) -1 (d) 2

(xii) Is $g=\{(1,1),(2,3),(3,5),(4,7)\}$ a function? If g is described by $g(x)=\alpha x+\beta$, then what value should be assigned to α and β? • *Understanding* [1]

(xiii) Differentiate $\sin x^2$ w.r.t. x^2. [1] • *Application*

(xiv) Evaluate $\int_{-2}^{1}\frac{|x|}{x}\,dx$. • *Evaluate* [1]

(xv) One card is drawn at random from a pack of well-shuffled deck of cards.

Let E: The card drawn is a spade.

F: The card drawn is an ace.

Are the events E and F independent? • *Analysis* [1]

2. (i) Find the point on the curve $y^2=8x$ for which the abscissa and ordinate change at the same rate. • *Analysis* [2]

Or

(ii) Prove that the function f is given by $f(x)=\log\cos x$ is strictly decreasing. • *Analysis* [2]

3. Prove that

$$\cot^{-1}\left[\frac{\sqrt{1+\sin x}+\sqrt{1-\sin x}}{\sqrt{1+\sin x}-\sqrt{1-\sin x}}\right]=\frac{x}{2},\ x\in\left(0,\frac{\pi}{4}\right).$$

• *Application* [2]

4. If $A=\begin{bmatrix} 2 & 3 \\ -1 & 2 \end{bmatrix}$, then find $A^2 - 4A + I$. • *Evaluate* [2]

5. (i) Prove that
$$\int_0^1 \sin^{-1}\left(\frac{2x}{1+x^2}\right) dx = \frac{\pi}{2} - \log 2.$$
• *Application* [2]

Or

(ii) Evaluate $\int_0^1 \log\left|\frac{1}{x} - 1\right| dx$. • *Evaluate* [2]

6. If $x = a(\cos t + t \sin t)$ and $y = a(\sin t - t \cos t)$, then find $\frac{dy}{dx}$. • *Understanding* [2]

7. Let $f : N \to N$ be a function defined as $f(x) = 9x^2 + 6x - 5$. Show that $f : N \to S$, where S is the range of f, is invertible. Find the inverse of f and hence find $f^{-1}(43)$ and $f^{-1}(163)$. • *Evaluate* [4]

8. Solve the differential equation $(x-y)(dx+dy) = dx - dy, y(0) = -1$. • *Application* [4]

9. (i) Show that the function $f(x) = |x-3|, x \in R$, is continuous but not differentiable at $x = 3$. • *Application* [4]

Or

(ii) Find $\frac{dy}{dx}$, when $y = x^{\cot x} + \frac{2x^2 - 3}{x^2 + x + 2}$. • *Application* [4]

10. (i) A and B are two candidates seeking admission in a college. The probability that A is selected, is 0.7 and the probability that exactly one of them is selected, is 0.6.
Based on the above information, answer the following questions. • *Analysis* [4]
(a) Find the probability that A is not selected.
(b) Find the probability that B is selected.
(c) Find the probability that both are selected.
(d) Find the probability that none of them selected.

Or

(ii) The odds against a husband who is 45 yr old, living till he is 70 are 7 : 5 and the against his wife who is now 36, living till she is 61 are 5 : 3. Find the probability that • *Analysis* [4]
(a) the husband will not be alive 25 yr.
(b) the couple will be alive 25 yr.
(c) atleast one of them will be alive 25 yr hence.

11. If $A=\begin{bmatrix} 1 & 1 & 1 \\ 1 & 0 & 2 \\ 3 & 1 & 1 \end{bmatrix}$ then,
(a) Check the matrix A is invertible or not
(b) Find A^{-1}.
(c) Solve the system of equations $x + y + z = 6$, $x + 2z = 7$ and $x + y + z = 12$. • *Application* [6]

12. (i) If the sum of the lengths of the hypotenuse and a side of a right angled triangle is given, then show that the area of the triangle is maximum when the angle between them is $(\pi/3)$. • *Application* [6]

Or

(ii) A metal box with a square base and vertical sides is to contain 1024 cm^3. If the material for the top and bottom costs ₹ 5 per cm^2 and the material for the sides costs ₹ 2.50 per cm^2. Then, find the least cost of the box. • *Application* [6]

13. (i) Find $\int \frac{\sin x}{\sin^3 x + \cos^3 x} dx$. • *Application* [6]

Or

(ii) Find the particular solution of the differential equation $\frac{dy}{dx} = \frac{xy}{x^2 + y^2}$ given that $y = 1$, when $x = 0$. • *Application* [6]

14. A factory produces electronic components and a quality control process is in place to ensure the components meet certain standards. The factory uses two machines to test the components. Each machine provides a score based on the quality of the component.
The score a component receives is defined as the product of the numbers shown on the machines.
The scores from the machines are recorded in the table below. Each number on machine

SP-11

1 and machine 2 represents a possible outcome for a component being tested.

• *Analysis* [6]

Number on machine 2 \ Number on machine 1	1	2	3	4
1	1	2	3	4
2	2	4	p	r
3	3	p	9	12
4	4	r	12	q

(i) Calculate the values of p, q and r in the above table.

(ii) If a component is tested once, let the random variable S represent the component's score. Construct the probability distribution for S.

S	
$P(S=s)$	

(iii) Find the probability that the component's score is at most 8.

Section B (15 Marks)

15. In subparts (i) to (iii) choose the correct options and in subparts (iv) and (v), answer the questions as instructed. [5]

(i) If $|\vec{a}|=4$ and $-3 \le \lambda \le 2$, then the range of $|\lambda \vec{a}|$ is • *Understanding*

(a) [0, 8] (b) [−12, 8]
(c) [0, 12] (d) [8, 12]

(ii) The vector equation of the plane passing through the point (a, b, c) and parallel to the plane $\vec{r}\cdot(\hat{i}+\hat{j}+\hat{k})=2$ is • *Recall*

(a) $\vec{r}\cdot(\hat{i}+\hat{j}+\hat{k})=a+b+c$
(b) $\vec{r}\cdot(\hat{i}-\hat{j}+\hat{k})=a+b+c$
(c) $\vec{r}\cdot(\hat{i}-\hat{j}-\hat{k})=a+b+c$
(d) None of the above

(iii) The equations of two lines are $\dfrac{x+1}{5}=\dfrac{y-2}{-2}=\dfrac{z-1}{2}$ and $\dfrac{x+3}{-2}=\dfrac{z-4}{3}, y=-5$. • *Analysis*

Statement I The angle between the above lines is $\dfrac{\pi}{2}$.

Statement II The given two lines are parallel.

Choose the correct statement.

(a) Only Statement I is true.
(b) Only Statement II is true.
(c) Both Statements I and II are true.
(d) Neither I nor II is true.

(iv) Find the distance of a point (3, −4, 8) from the plane $\vec{r}\cdot(6\hat{i}+3\hat{j}-2\hat{k})=4$.

• *Evaluate*

(v) Let $\vec{a}$, $\vec{b}$ and $\vec{c}$ be three vectors such that $|\vec{a}|=1, |\vec{b}|=2$ and $|\vec{c}|=3$. If the projection of $\vec{b}$ along $\vec{a}$ is equal to the projection of $\vec{c}$ along $\vec{a}$; and $\vec{b}$, $\vec{c}$ are perpendicular to each other, then find $|3\vec{a}-2\vec{b}+2\vec{c}|$.

• *Application*

16. (i) If $\vec{a}=\hat{i}+\hat{j}+\hat{k}$ and $\vec{b}=\hat{j}-\hat{k}$, then find a vector $\vec{c}$ such that $\vec{a}\times\vec{c}=\vec{b}$ and $\vec{a}\cdot\vec{c}=3$. • *Evaluate* [2]

Or

(ii) Find a vector of magnitude 9, which is perpendicular to both the vectors $4\hat{i}-\hat{j}+3\hat{k}$ and $-2\hat{i}+\hat{j}-2\hat{k}$. • *Evaluate* [2]

17. (i) Find the equation of the plane passing through the point (1, 1, −1) and perpendicular to the planes $x+2y+3z-7=0$ and $2x-3y+4z=0$. • *Application* [4]

Or

(ii) A line passes through (2, −1, 3) and is perpendicular to the line $\vec{r}=(\hat{i}+\hat{j}-\hat{k})+\lambda(2\hat{i}-2\hat{j}+\hat{k})$ and $\vec{r}=(2\hat{i}-\hat{j}-3\hat{k})+\mu(\hat{i}+2\hat{j}+2\hat{k})$. Obtain its equation is cartesian and vector form. • *Application* [4]

18. Find the area bounded by $y=x^2$, the X-axis and the lines $x=-1$ and $x=1$. • *Evaluate* [4]

Section C (15 Marks)

19. In subparts (i) to (ii) choose the correct options and in subparts (iii) to (v), answer the questions as instructed. [5]

(i) If $\bar{x}=10$, $\bar{y}=20$ and $b_{xy}=\frac{9}{20}$, then the equation of regression line of x on y is • *Recall*

(a) $x=\frac{9y}{20}+1$

(b) $x=\frac{y}{20}+1$

(c) $y=\frac{x}{50}+5$

(d) None of the above

(ii) A firm has cost function, $C=\frac{x^2}{2}-7x+111$ and demand function, $x=70-p$, then the total revenue in terms of x is • *Understanding*

(a) x^2-70x

(b) $70x-x^2$

(c) x^2+70x

(d) None of the above

(iii) The demand function is $x=\frac{17-2p}{4}$, where x is the number of units demanded and p is the price per unit. Find the revenue function R in term of p. • *Understanding*

(iv) If the cost function $C(x)$ of producing x quantities of a product is given by $C(x)=500x^2+2500x+5000$ and if each unit of the product is sold at ₹6000, then what are the break-even points? • *Evaluate*

(v) Given two regression lines $4x+3y+7=0$ and $3x+4y+8=0$. Determine • *Analysis*

(a) the regression line of y on x.

(b) the regression line of x on y.

20. (i) A cable TV operator has 5000 subscribers, each of them pays ₹100 per month. The operator proposes to increase the subscription and he found that for every increase of ₹ 0.50, 10 subscribers will discontinue the service. Find what increase in the subscription rate will increase maximum revenue and what will be maximum revenue? • *Application* [2]

Or

(ii) The demand function for a manufacture's product is $x=70-5p$, where x is the number of units and p is the price per unit. At what value of x will there be maximum revenue? What is the maximum revenue? • *Application* [2]

21. Find the regression coefficient of line x on y and y on x for the data

x	1	2	3	4	5
y	7	6	5	4	3

and hence find an estimate of variate y for $x=3.5$. • *Application* [4]

22. (i) If a young man rides his motorcycle at 30 km/h, then he had to spend ₹ 4 per km on petrol. If he rides at a faster speed of 45 km/h, then the petrol cost increases at ₹ 6 per km. He has ₹ 120 to spend on petrol and wishes to find what is the maximum distance, he can travel within 1 h. Express this as a linear programming problem and solve it graphically. • *Analysis* [4]

Or

(ii) Solve minimise $Z=5x+7y$, subject to constraints are $2x+y\geq 8$, $x+2y\geq 10$ and $x, y\geq 0$. • *Analysis* [4]

Solutions in Topper's Style

My Commitment *I affirm that I am reviewing these solutions only after I have solved the Sample Question Paper 11 on my own. My purpose of looking the solutions is solely to verify whether my answers/solutions were correct or not and to identify my mistakes in case my solutions were wrong or I could not solve that.*

1. (i) (d) Given, $R=\{(x,y): x>y\}$

Let $(x,x)\in R$.

For $x\,R\,x$, $x>x$ is not true for any $x\in N$.

Therefore, R is not reflexive.

Let $(x,y)\in R$

$\Rightarrow \quad xRy$

$\therefore \quad x>y$

But $y>x$ is not true for any $x, y\in N$.

Thus, R is not symmetric.

Let xRy and yRz

$\therefore \quad x>y$ and $y>z$

$\Rightarrow \quad x>z$

$\Rightarrow \quad xRz$

So, R is transitive.

(ii) (a) Let $\cos^{-1}\left(\frac{1}{2}\right)=x$

$\Rightarrow \quad \cos x=\frac{1}{2}=\cos\frac{\pi}{3}$

$\Rightarrow \quad x=\frac{\pi}{3}\in[0,\pi]$

$[\because$ principal value branch of $\cos^{-1}$ is $[0,\pi]]$

Again, let $\sin^{-1}\left(\frac{1}{2}\right)=y$

$\Rightarrow \quad \sin y=\frac{1}{2}=\sin\frac{\pi}{6}$

$\Rightarrow \quad y=\frac{\pi}{6}\in\left[-\frac{\pi}{2},\frac{\pi}{2}\right]$

$\left[\because \text{principal value branch of } \sin^{-1} \text{ is } \left[-\frac{\pi}{2},\frac{\pi}{2}\right]\right]$

Now, $\cos^{-1}\left(\frac{1}{2}\right)+2\sin^{-1}\left(\frac{1}{2}\right)=\frac{\pi}{3}+2\cdot\frac{\pi}{6}$

$=\frac{\pi}{3}+\frac{\pi}{3}=\frac{2\pi}{3}$

Hence, both A and R are correct and R is the correct explanation of A.

(iii) (d) The given matrix is $A=\begin{bmatrix}4 & -2 & 1 & 3\\ 5 & 7 & 9 & 6\\ 21 & 15 & 18 & -25\end{bmatrix}$.

Here, $a_{23}=9$ and $a_{24}=6$

$\therefore \; a_{23}+a_{24}=9+6=15$

Also, 15 lies in 3rd row and 2nd column.

$\therefore \quad a_{23}+a_{24}=15=a_{32}$

(iv) (d) We know that if f and g are continuous functions, then

(a) $f+g$ is continuous

(b) $f-g$ is continuous.

(c) fg is continuous

(d) $\frac{f}{g}$ is continuous at those points, where $g(x)\neq 0$.

Here, $\frac{g(x)}{f(x)}=\frac{\frac{x^2}{2}+1}{2x}=\frac{x^2+2}{4x}$

which is discontinuous at $x=0$.

(v) (a) Given function is

$y=[x(x-2)]^2=[x^2-2x]^2$

On differentiating w.r.t. x, we get

$\frac{dy}{dx}=2(x^2-2x)\frac{d}{dx}(x^2-2x)$

$=2(x^2-2x)(2x-2)=4x(x-2)(x-1)$

On putting $\frac{dy}{dx}=0$, we get

$4x(x-2)(x-1)=0$

$\Rightarrow \quad x=0, 1$ and 2

which divides real line in disjoint intervals $(-\infty,0)$, $(0,1)$, $(1,2)$ and $(2,\infty)$.

$-\infty \leftarrow$ –ve | 0 | +ve | 1 | –ve | 2 | +ve $\rightarrow \infty$

Intervals	Sign of $f'(x)$	Nature of $f(x)$
$(-\infty,0)$	(–) (–) (–) = – ve	Strictly decreasing
$(0,1)$	(+) (–) (–) = + ve	Strictly increasing
$(1,2)$	(+) (–) (+) = – ve	Strictly decreasing
$(2,\infty)$	(+) (+) (+) = + ve	Strictly increasing

Therefore, y is increasing in $(0,1)$ and $(2,\infty)$.

Hence, $0<x<1$ and $x>2$.

(vi) (a) **I.** Let $I=\int\frac{2}{1+\cos 2x}dx=\int\frac{2}{2\cos^2 x}dx$

$[\because \cos 2\theta=2\cos^2\theta-1]$

$=\int\sec^2 x\,dx=\tan x+C$

II. Let $I=\int\sqrt{ax+b}\,dx=\int(ax+b)^{1/2}dx$

$=\frac{(ax+b)^{(1/2)+1}}{\left(\frac{1}{2}+1\right)\cdot a}+C$

$$= \frac{2}{3} \cdot \frac{(ax+b)^{3/2}}{a} + C$$

$$= \frac{2}{3a}(ax+b)^{3/2} + C$$

Hence, only Statement I is true.

(vii) (b) Let $I = \int \frac{dx}{x(x^7+1)} = \int \frac{x^6 dx}{x^7(x^7+1)}$

[multiply and divide by x^6]

On putting $x^7 = t \Rightarrow 7x^6 dx = dt \Rightarrow x^6 dx = \frac{dt}{7}$

$\therefore \quad I = \frac{1}{7}\int \frac{dt}{t(t+1)} = \frac{1}{7}\int \left(\frac{1}{t} - \frac{1}{t+1}\right) dt$

[using partial fraction]

$$= \frac{1}{7}[\log t - \log(t+1)] + C$$

$$= \frac{1}{7}\log\left(\frac{t}{t+1}\right) + C = \frac{1}{7}\log\left(\frac{x^7}{x^7+1}\right) + C \; [\because t = x^7]$$

(viii) (a) Let $I = \int_0^1 \frac{dx}{e^x + e} = \int_0^1 \frac{dx}{e^x\left(1 + \frac{e}{e^x}\right)}$

Put $1 + \frac{e}{e^x} = t \Rightarrow 0 - \frac{e}{e^x}dx = dt$

$\Rightarrow \quad \frac{1}{e^x}dx = -\frac{1}{e}dt$

Also, when $x = 0$, then $t = 1 + e$

When $x = 1$, then $t = 2$

$\therefore \quad I = -\frac{1}{e}\int_{1+e}^{2} \frac{1}{t}dt = \frac{-1}{e}[\log t]_{1+e}^{2}$

$$= \frac{-1}{e}[\log 2 - \log(1+e)]$$

$$= \frac{-1}{e}\log\left(\frac{2}{1+e}\right) = \frac{1}{e}\log\left(\frac{1+e}{2}\right)$$

(ix) (d) The given differential equation is

$$\frac{dy}{dx} + y = e^x$$

which is in the form of $\frac{dy}{dx} + Py = Q$,

where $P(x) = 1$ and $Q(x) = e^x$

The integrating factor (IF) is

$$\text{IF} = e^{\int P dx} = e^{\int 1 dx} = e^x$$

Thus, the general solution is $y \cdot \text{IF} = \int Q \cdot \text{IF} dx + c$

$\Rightarrow \quad y \times e^x = \int e^x \cdot e^x \, dx + C$

$\Rightarrow \quad ye^x = \frac{e^{2x}}{2} + C \Rightarrow y = \frac{1}{2}e^x + Ce^{-x}$

So, Assertion is false, while Reason is true.

(x) (c) Let X be a random variable whose possible values $x_1, x_2, x_3, \ldots, x_n$ occur with probabilities $p_1, p_2, p_3, \ldots, p_n$, respectively. The mean of X, denoted by μ, is the number $\sum_{i=1}^{n} x_i p_i$ i.e. the mean of X is the weighted average of the possible values of X, each value being weighted by its probability with which it occurs.

$\therefore$ The mean of a random variable X is also called the expectation of X, denoted by $E(X)$.

Thus, $E(X) = \mu = \sum_{i=1}^{n} x_i p_i = x_1 p_1 + x_2 p_2 + \ldots + x_n p_n$

In other words, the mean or expectation of a random variable X is the sum of the products of all possible values of X by their respective probabilities.

Hence, Statement I is true; Statement II is false.

(xi) (b) We know that for a square matrix

$$P(\text{adj}P) = |P| I_2 \quad \ldots\text{(i)}$$

Now, $|P| = \begin{vmatrix} \sin x & \cos x \\ -\cos x & \sin x \end{vmatrix}$

$$= \sin^2 x + \cos^2 x = 1$$

But it is given $P(\text{adj } P) = k\begin{bmatrix} 1 & 0 \\ 0 & 1 \end{bmatrix} \quad \ldots\text{(ii)}$

$\therefore$ From Eqs. (i) and (ii), we get

$$|P| I_2 = k\begin{bmatrix} 1 & 0 \\ 0 & 1 \end{bmatrix}$$

$\Rightarrow \quad 1\begin{bmatrix} 1 & 0 \\ 0 & 1 \end{bmatrix} = k\begin{bmatrix} 1 & 0 \\ 0 & 1 \end{bmatrix}$

$\Rightarrow \quad k = 1$

(xii) Given that $g = \{(1, 1), (2, 3), (3, 5), (4, 7)\}$.

Here, each element of domain has unique image.

So, g is a function.

Now, given that $g(x) = \alpha x + \beta$

$\therefore \quad g(1) = \alpha + \beta$

$\Rightarrow \quad \alpha + \beta = 1 \quad \ldots\text{(i)}$

and $\quad g(2) = 2\alpha + \beta$

$\Rightarrow \quad 2\alpha + \beta = 3 \quad \ldots\text{(ii)}$

On putting the value of α from Eq. (i) in Eq (ii), we get

$$2(1-\beta) + \beta = 3$$

$\Rightarrow \quad 2 - 2\beta + \beta = 3$

$\Rightarrow \quad 2 - \beta = 3$

$\Rightarrow \quad \beta = -1$

If $\beta = -1$, then $\alpha = 2$ [from Eq. (i)]

Hence, $\alpha = 2$ and $\beta = -1$

(xiii) Let $u = \sin x^2$

On differentiating both sides w.r.t x, we get

$$\frac{du}{dx} = \frac{d}{dx}(\sin x^2) = \cos(x^2) \cdot \frac{d}{dx}(x^2) = 2x\cos x^2 \quad \ldots\text{(i)}$$

also let, $v = x^2$

On differentiating both sides w.r.t x, we get

$$\frac{dv}{dx}=2x \quad \ldots\text{(ii)}$$

Now, $\frac{du}{dv}=\frac{du}{dx}\times\frac{dx}{dv}=\frac{2x\cos x^2}{2x}=\cos x^2$

(xiv) Let $I=\int_{-2}^{1}\frac{|x|}{x}\,dx=\int_{-2}^{0}\frac{|x|}{x}\,dx+\int_{0}^{1}\frac{|x|}{x}\,dx$

$$=\int_{-2}^{0}\frac{(-x)}{x}\,dx+\int_{0}^{1}\frac{x}{x}\,dx \quad \left[\because |x|=\begin{cases}-x, & x<0\\ x, & x\geq 0\end{cases}\right]$$

$$=\int_{-2}^{0}(-1)\,dx+\int_{0}^{1}1\,dx=[-x]_{-2}^{0}+[x]_{0}^{1}$$

$$=[0-(2)]+[1-0]=-2+1=-1$$

(xv) Let S be the sample space.

Given, $E=$ The event that the card drawn is a spade

and $F=$ The event that the card drawn is an ace

Then, $E\cap F=$ The event that the card drawn is an ace and spade

Here, $n(S)={}^{52}C_1=52$,

$n(E)={}^{13}C_1=13, n(F)={}^{4}C_1=4$ and $n(E\cap F)=1$

Now, $P(E\cap F)=\frac{n(E\cap F)}{n(S)}=\frac{1}{52}$

$P(E)=\frac{n(E)}{n(S)}=\frac{13}{52}=\frac{1}{4}$ and $P(F)=\frac{n(F)}{n(S)}=\frac{4}{52}=\frac{1}{13}$

Here, we see that $P(E\cap F)=\frac{1}{52}=\frac{1}{4}\cdot\frac{1}{13}=P(E)\cdot P(F)$

Hence, the events E and F are independent.

2. (i) Let the required point be (x, y).

Given, $\frac{dy}{dt}=\frac{dx}{dt}$ ...(i)

and $y^2=8x$ ...(ii)

On differentiating both sides of Eq. (ii) w.r.t. t, we get

$$2y\frac{dy}{dt}=8\cdot\frac{dx}{dt}$$

$\Rightarrow$ $2y=8$ [from Eq. (i)]

$\Rightarrow$ $y=4$

On putting $y=4$ in Eq. (ii), we get

$8x=16\Rightarrow x=2$

Hence, the required point is $(2, 4)$.

Or

(ii) Given, $f(x)=\log\cos x$

On differentiating both sides w.r.t. x, we get

$$f'(x)=\frac{1}{\cos x}\cdot\frac{d}{dx}(\cos x)$$

$$=\frac{1}{\cos x}\cdot(-\sin x)$$

$$=-\tan x$$

We know that for $x\in\left(0,\frac{\pi}{2}\right)$, $\tan x>0$

$\therefore$ $f'(x)=-\tan x<0$

Hence, $f(x)$ is strictly decreasing. **Hence proved.**

3. LHS $=\cot^{-1}\left[\frac{\sqrt{1+\sin x}+\sqrt{1-\sin x}}{\sqrt{1+\sin x}-\sqrt{1-\sin x}}\right]$

$$=\cot^{-1}\left[\frac{\sqrt{\sin^2\frac{x}{2}+\cos^2\frac{x}{2}+2\sin\frac{x}{2}\cos\frac{x}{2}}+\sqrt{\sin^2\frac{x}{2}+\cos^2\frac{x}{2}-2\sin\frac{x}{2}\cos\frac{x}{2}}}{\sqrt{\sin^2\frac{x}{2}+\cos^2\frac{x}{2}+2\sin\frac{x}{2}\cos\frac{x}{2}}-\sqrt{\sin^2\frac{x}{2}+\cos^2\frac{x}{2}-2\sin\frac{x}{2}\cos\frac{x}{2}}}\right]$$

$$\left[\because 1=\sin^2\theta+\cos^2\theta \text{ and } \sin\theta=2\sin\frac{\theta}{2}\cos\frac{\theta}{2}\right]$$

$$=\cot^{-1}\left[\frac{\sqrt{\left(\cos\frac{x}{2}+\sin\frac{x}{2}\right)^2}+\sqrt{\left(\cos\frac{x}{2}-\sin\frac{x}{2}\right)^2}}{\sqrt{\left(\cos\frac{x}{2}+\sin\frac{x}{2}\right)^2}-\sqrt{\left(\cos\frac{x}{2}-\sin\frac{x}{2}\right)^2}}\right]$$

$$[\because a^2+b^2\pm 2ab=(a\pm b)^2]$$

$$=\cot^{-1}\left[\frac{\cos\frac{x}{2}+\sin\frac{x}{2}+\cos\frac{x}{2}-\sin\frac{x}{2}}{\cos\frac{x}{2}+\sin\frac{x}{2}-\cos\frac{x}{2}+\sin\frac{x}{2}}\right]$$

$$=\cot^{-1}\left[\frac{2\cos\frac{x}{2}}{2\sin\frac{x}{2}}\right]=\cot^{-1}\left(\cot\frac{x}{2}\right)$$

$=\frac{x}{2}=$ RHS $\left[\because 0<\frac{x}{2}<\frac{\pi}{8}\right]$ **Hence proved.**

4. Given, $A=\begin{bmatrix}2 & 3\\ -1 & 2\end{bmatrix}$

$\therefore$ $A^2=\begin{bmatrix}2 & 3\\ -1 & 2\end{bmatrix}\begin{bmatrix}2 & 3\\ -1 & 2\end{bmatrix}$

$$=\begin{bmatrix}4-3 & 6+6\\ -2-2 & -3+4\end{bmatrix}=\begin{bmatrix}1 & 12\\ -4 & 1\end{bmatrix}$$

Now, $A^2-4A+I=\begin{bmatrix}1 & 12\\ -4 & 1\end{bmatrix}-4\begin{bmatrix}2 & 3\\ -1 & 2\end{bmatrix}+\begin{bmatrix}1 & 0\\ 0 & 1\end{bmatrix}$

$$=\begin{bmatrix}1 & 12\\ -4 & 1\end{bmatrix}-\begin{bmatrix}8 & 12\\ -4 & 8\end{bmatrix}+\begin{bmatrix}1 & 0\\ 0 & 1\end{bmatrix}$$

$$=\begin{bmatrix}1-8+1 & 12-12+0\\ -4+4+0 & 1-8+1\end{bmatrix}$$

$$=\begin{bmatrix}-6 & 0\\ 0 & -6\end{bmatrix}=-6I$$

5. (i) Let $I=\int_0^1\sin^{-1}\left(\frac{2x}{1+x^2}\right)dx$

Put $x=\tan\theta\Rightarrow dx=\sec^2\theta\,d\theta$

Also, when $x=0$, then $0=\tan\theta\Rightarrow\theta=0$

and when $x=1$, then $1=\tan\theta\Rightarrow\theta=\pi/4$

$\therefore$ $I=\int_0^{\pi/4}\sin^{-1}\left(\frac{2\tan\theta}{1+\tan^2\theta}\right)\cdot\sec^2\theta\,d\theta$

$\Rightarrow \quad I = \int_0^{\pi/4} \sin^{-1}(\sin 2\theta)\cdot \sec^2\theta\, d\theta$

$\left[\because \sin 2A = \dfrac{2\tan A}{1+\tan^2 A}\right]$

$= \int_0^{\pi/4} \underset{\text{I}}{2\theta}\cdot \underset{\text{II}}{\sec^2\theta}\, d\theta$

On applying the rule of integration by parts, we get

$$I = \left[2\theta \int \sec^2\theta\, d\theta - \int\left\{\frac{d}{d\theta}(2\theta)\int \sec^2\theta\, d\theta\right\}d\theta\right]_0^{\pi/4}$$

$= [2\theta \tan\theta]_0^{\pi/4} - \int_0^{\pi/4} 2\tan\theta\, d\theta$

$= \left[2\times\dfrac{\pi}{4}\tan\dfrac{\pi}{4} - 0\right] - 2[\log\sec\theta]_0^{\pi/4}$

$= \dfrac{\pi}{2} - 2\left[\log\sec\dfrac{\pi}{4} - \log\sec 0\right] \quad \left[\because \tan\dfrac{\pi}{4} = 1\right]$

$= \dfrac{\pi}{2} - 2[\log\sqrt{2} - \log 1] \quad \left[\because \sec\dfrac{\pi}{4} = \sqrt{2}, \sec 0 = 1\right]$

$= \dfrac{\pi}{2} - 2\cdot\dfrac{1}{2}\log 2 = \dfrac{\pi}{2} - \log 2$

$[\because \log m^n = n\log m \text{ and } \log 1 = 0]$

Hence proved.

Or

(ii) Let $I = \int_0^1 \log\left|\dfrac{1}{x} - 1\right| dx$

$\Rightarrow \quad I = \int_0^1 \log\left|\dfrac{1-x}{x}\right| dx \quad \ldots(i)$

$\Rightarrow \quad I = \int_0^1 \log\left|\dfrac{1-(1-x)}{1-x}\right| dx$

$\left[\because \int_0^a f(x)\,dx = \int_0^a f(a-x)\,dx\right]$

$\Rightarrow \quad I = \int_0^1 \log\left|\dfrac{x}{1-x}\right| dx \quad \ldots(ii)$

On adding Eqs. (i) and (ii), we get

$2I = \int_0^1 \log\left|\dfrac{1-x}{x}\right| dx + \int_0^1 \log\left|\dfrac{x}{1-x}\right| dx$

$\Rightarrow \quad 2I = \int_0^1 \left[\log\left|\dfrac{1-x}{x}\right| + \log\left|\dfrac{x}{1-x}\right|\right] dx$

$\Rightarrow \quad 2I = \int_0^1 \log\left|\left(\dfrac{1-x}{x}\times\dfrac{x}{1-x}\right)\right| dx$

$[\because \log m + \log n = \log(m\times n)]$

$\Rightarrow \quad 2I = \int_0^1 \log 1\, dx \Rightarrow 2I = \int_0^1 0\, dx = 0 \; [\because \log 1 = 0]$

$\therefore \quad I = 0$

6. Given, $x = a(\cos t + t\sin t)$

On differentiating both sides w.r.t. t, we get

$\dfrac{dx}{dt} = a\left[-\sin t + \dfrac{d}{dt}(t)\cdot\sin t + t\dfrac{d}{dt}(\sin t)\right]$

[using product rule of derivative]

$\Rightarrow \quad \dfrac{dx}{dt} = a(-\sin t + 1\cdot\sin t + t\cos t) = at\cos t$

Also, given $y = a(\sin t - t\cos t)$

On differentiating both sides w.r.t. t, we get

$\dfrac{dy}{dt} = a\left[\cos t - \dfrac{d}{dt}(t)\cos t - t\dfrac{d}{dt}(\cos t)\right]$

[by using product rule of derivative]

$\Rightarrow \quad \dfrac{dy}{dt} = a(\cos t - \cos t\cdot 1 + t\sin t) = at\sin t \quad \ldots(i)$

Now, $\quad \dfrac{dy}{dx} = \dfrac{\dfrac{dy}{dt}}{\dfrac{dx}{dt}} = \dfrac{at\sin t}{at\cos t} = \tan t$

7. We have a mapping $f: N \to N$ given by

$f(x) = 9x^2 + 6x - 5$

One-one function Let $x_1, x_2 \in N$, such that $f(x_1) = f(x_2)$

Then, $\quad 9x_1^2 + 6x_1 - 5 = 9x_2^2 + 6x_2 - 5$

$\Rightarrow \quad 9x_1^2 + 6x_1 = 9x_2^2 + 6x_2$

$\Rightarrow \quad 9(x_1^2 - x_2^2) + 6(x_1 - x_2) = 0$

$\Rightarrow \quad 3(x_1 - x_2)(x_1 + x_2) + 2(x_1 - x_2) = 0 \quad$ [divide by 3]

$\Rightarrow \quad (x_1 - x_2)(3x_1 + 3x_2 + 2) = 0$

$\Rightarrow \quad x_1 - x_2 = 0$ or $3x_1 + 3x_2 + 2 = 0$

But $3x_1 + 3x_2 + 2 \neq 0 \quad [\because x_1, x_2 \in N]$

$\therefore \quad x_1 - x_2 = 0 \Rightarrow x_1 = x_2$

So, f is one-one function.

Onto function Obviously, $f: N \to S$ is an onto function because S is the range of f.

Thus, $f: N \to S$ is one-one and onto function.

Hence, f is invertible function, so its inverse exists.

Let $f(x) = y$, then $\quad y = 9x^2 + 6x - 5$

$\Rightarrow \quad y = (3x)^2 + 2\cdot 3x\cdot 1 + 1 - 6 \Rightarrow y = (3x+1)^2 - 6$

$\Rightarrow \quad (3x+1)^2 = y + 6 \Rightarrow 3x + 1 = \sqrt{y+6}$

[taking positive square root as $x \in N$]

$\Rightarrow \quad x = \dfrac{\sqrt{y+6} - 1}{3}$

$\therefore \quad f^{-1}(y) = \dfrac{\sqrt{y+6} - 1}{3}$

or $\quad f^{-1}(x) = \dfrac{\sqrt{x+6} - 1}{3}$, where $x \in S$

Now, $f^{-1}(43) = \dfrac{\sqrt{43+6} - 1}{3} = \dfrac{\sqrt{49} - 1}{3} = \dfrac{7-1}{3} = 2$

and $f^{-1}(163) = \dfrac{\sqrt{163+6} - 1}{3} = \dfrac{\sqrt{169} - 1}{3} = \dfrac{13-1}{3} = \dfrac{12}{3} = 4$

8. The given differential equation is

$(x - y)(dx + dy) = dx - dy$

$\Rightarrow \quad (x - y - 1)\,dx = -(x - y + 1)\,dy$

$\Rightarrow \quad \dfrac{dy}{dx} = -\dfrac{x - y - 1}{x - y + 1} \quad \ldots(i)$

Let $x-y=v$. Then,
$$1-\frac{dy}{dx}=\frac{dv}{dx}\Rightarrow\frac{dy}{dx}=1-\frac{dv}{dx}$$

On putting $x-y=v$ and $\frac{dy}{dx}=1-\frac{dv}{dx}$ in Eq. (i), we get
$$1-\frac{dv}{dx}=-\frac{v-1}{v+1}\Rightarrow\frac{dv}{dx}=\frac{v-1}{v+1}+1$$
$$\Rightarrow\quad \frac{dv}{dx}=\frac{2v}{v+1}\Rightarrow\frac{v+1}{v}dv=2\,dx$$
$$\Rightarrow\quad \left(1+\frac{1}{v}\right)dv=2\,dx$$

On integrating both sides, we get
$$\int\left(1+\frac{1}{v}\right)dv=2\int 1\,dx$$
$$\Rightarrow\quad v+\log|v|=2x+C$$
$$\Rightarrow\quad x-y+\log|x-y|=2x+C \quad [\text{put } v=x-y]$$
$$\Rightarrow\quad \log|x-y|=x+y+C \quad \ldots\text{(ii)}$$

It is given that $y(0)=-1$, i.e. when $x=0, y=-1$.

On putting $x=0$ and $y=-1$ in Eq. (ii), we get
$$\log 1=-1+C\Rightarrow C=1 \quad [\because \log 1=0]$$

On putting $C=1$ in Eq. (ii), we get
$$\log|x-y|=x+y+1\Rightarrow|x-y|=e^{x+y+1}$$
$$\Rightarrow\quad x-y=\pm e^{x+y+1}$$

which is the required solution.

9. (i) Given, $f(x)=|x-3|$

First, we check the continuity of $f(x)$ at $x=3$.

Here, $\text{LHL}=\lim_{x\to 3^-}|x-3|=\lim_{h\to 0}|3-h-3|$

[put $x=3-h$, when $x\to 3^-$, then $h\to 0$]

$$=\lim_{h\to 0}|-h|=0$$

$$\text{RHL}=\lim_{x\to 3^+}|x-3|=\lim_{h\to 0}|3+h-3|=\lim_{h\to 0}|h|=0$$

[put $x=3+h$, when $x\to 3^+$, then $h\to 0$]

and $f(3)=|3-3|=0$

Thus, LHL = RHL = $f(3)$

Hence, f is continuous at $x=3$.

Now, let us check the differentiability of $f(x)$ at $x=3$.
$$\text{LHD}=f'(3^-)=\lim_{h\to 0}\frac{f(3-h)-f(3)}{-h}$$
$$\left[\because Lf'(a)=\lim_{h\to 0}\frac{f(a-h)-f(a)}{-h}\right]$$
$$=\lim_{h\to 0}\frac{|3-h-3|-|3-3|}{-h}=\lim_{h\to 0}\frac{|-h|}{-h}=\lim_{h\to 0}\frac{h}{-h}=-1$$
$[\because |-x|=x, \text{ if } x>0]$
$$\text{RHD}=f'(3^+)=\lim_{h\to 0}\frac{f(3+h)-f(3)}{h}$$
$$\left[\because Rf'(a)=\lim_{h\to 0}\frac{f(a+h)-f(a)}{h}\right]$$
$$=\lim_{h\to 0}\frac{|3+h-3|-|3-3|}{h}$$
$$=\lim_{h\to 0}\frac{|h|}{h}=\lim_{h\to 0}\frac{h}{h}=1 \quad [\because |x|=x, \text{ if } x>0]$$

Here, LHD $\neq$ RHD at $x=3$.

Hence, f is not differentiable at $x=3$. **Hence proved.**

(ii) Given, $y=x^{\cot x}+\frac{2x^2-3}{x^2+x+2}$

Let $u=x^{\cot x}$ and $v=\frac{2x^2-3}{x^2+x+2}$

Then, given equation becomes
$$y=u+v$$
$$\Rightarrow\quad \frac{dy}{dx}=\frac{du}{dx}+\frac{dv}{dx} \quad \ldots\text{(i) [differentiating w.r.t. } x]$$

Consider $u=x^{\cot x}$

On taking log both sides, we get
$$\log u=\cot x\log x$$

On differentiating both sides w.r.t. x, we get
$$\frac{1}{u}\frac{du}{dx}=\cot x\cdot\frac{1}{x}-\operatorname{cosec}^2 x\cdot\log x$$
$$\Rightarrow\quad \frac{du}{dx}=u\left(\frac{\cot x}{x}-\operatorname{cosec}^2 x\cdot\log x\right)$$
$$=x^{\cot x}\left(\frac{\cot x}{x}-\operatorname{cosec}^2 x\cdot\log x\right) \quad \ldots\text{(ii)}$$

Now, consider $v=\frac{2x^2-3}{x^2+x+2}$

On differentiating both sides w.r.t. x, we get
$$\frac{dv}{dx}=\frac{(x^2+x+2)(4x)-(2x^2-3)(2x+1)}{(x^2+x+2)^2}$$
[using quotient rule of derivative]
$$=\frac{4x^3+4x^2+8x-4x^3-2x^2+6x+3}{(x^2+x+2)^2}$$
$$=\frac{2x^2+14x+3}{(x^2+x+2)^2} \quad \ldots\text{(iii)}$$

On substituting the values from Eqs. (ii) and (iii) into Eq. (i), we get
$$\frac{dy}{dx}=x^{\cot x}\left(\frac{\cot x}{x}-\operatorname{cosec}^2 x\cdot\log x\right)+\frac{2x^2+14x+3}{(x^2+x+2)^2}$$

10. (i) (a) Let E_1 be the event that A is selected.

The probability that A is selected = 0.7

i.e. $P(E_1)=0.7$

We know that
$$P(E_1)+P(\bar{E}_1)=1$$
$$\Rightarrow\quad 0.7+P(\bar{E}_1)=1$$
$$\Rightarrow\quad P(\bar{E}_1)=1-0.7=0.3$$

Hence, the probability that A is not selected is 0.3.

(b) Let E_2 : The event that candidate B is selected.

Then, we have

$$P(E_1)=0.7$$

and P(exactly one of A, B is selected) = 0.6

$$\Rightarrow \quad P((E_1\cap\bar{E}_2)\cup(\bar{E}_1\cap E_2))=0.6$$

$$\Rightarrow \quad P(E_1\cap\bar{E}_2)+P(\bar{E}_1\cap E_2)=0.6$$

[$\because$ events $E_1\cap\bar{E}_2$ and $\bar{E}_1\cap E_2$ are mutually exclusive]

$$\Rightarrow \quad P(E_1)\cdot P(\bar{E}_2)+P(\bar{E}_1)\cdot P(E_2)=0.6$$

[$\because$ E_1 and E_2 are independent events]

$$\Rightarrow \quad (0.7)P(\bar{E}_2)+(0.3)P(E_2)=0.6$$

[$\because P(\bar{E}_1)=0.3$]

$$\Rightarrow \quad 0.7(1-P(E_2))+0.3P(E_2)=0.6$$

[$\because P(E_2)+P(\bar{E}_2)=1$]

$$\Rightarrow \quad 0.7-0.7P(E_2)+0.3P(E_2)=0.6$$

$$\Rightarrow \quad 0.4P(E_2)=0.1$$

$$\Rightarrow \quad P(E_2)=\frac{1}{4} \text{ or } 0.25$$

(c) The probability that both A and B are selected

$= P(E_1)\times P(E_2)$ [from parts (a) and (b)]

$=0.7\times 0.25$

$=0.175$

(d) The probability that none of them selected

$=1-$ probability that both A and R are selected

$=1-0.175$ [from part (c)]

$=0.825$

Or

(ii) Let E: The event that the husband will be alive 25 yr hence.

F: The event that the wife will be alive 25 yr hence.

Then, $P(E)=\frac{5}{7+5}=\frac{5}{12}$ and $P(F)=\frac{3}{5+3}=\frac{3}{8}$.

Also, $P(\bar{E})=1-P(E)=1-\frac{5}{12}=\frac{7}{12}$

and $P(\bar{F})=1-P(F)=1-\frac{3}{8}=\frac{5}{8}$

(a) P(the husband will not be alive 25 yr) $= P(\bar{E})$

$=\frac{7}{12}$

Hence, required probability is $\frac{7}{12}$.

(b) P(couple will be alive 25 yr hence)

$=P(E \text{ and } F)=P(E\cap F)=P(E)\cdot P(F)$

$=\frac{5}{12}\times\frac{3}{8}=\frac{5}{32}$

(c) P(atleast one of them will be alive 25 yr hence)

$=1-P$(none will be alive 25 yr hence)

$=1-P[(\text{not } E) \text{ and } (\text{not } F)]$

$=1-P(\bar{E}\cap\bar{F})=1-P(\bar{E})\cdot P(\bar{F})$

[$\because$ events E and F are independent, $\therefore \bar{E}$ and $\bar{F}$ are also independent events]

$$=1-\left(\frac{7}{12}\times\frac{5}{8}\right)=1-\frac{35}{96}=\frac{61}{96}$$

11. (a) We have, $A=\begin{bmatrix}1&1&1\\1&0&2\\3&1&1\end{bmatrix}$

$$\therefore |A|=\begin{vmatrix}1&1&1\\1&0&2\\3&1&1\end{vmatrix}=1(0-2)-1(1-6)+1(1-0)$$

$$=-2+5+1$$

$$=4\neq 0$$

So, A is invertible.

(b) Cofactors of elements of $|A|$ are

$$A_{11}=(-1)^{1+1}\begin{vmatrix}0&2\\1&1\end{vmatrix}=0-2=-2$$

$$A_{12}=(-1)^{1+2}\begin{vmatrix}1&2\\3&1\end{vmatrix}=-(1-6)=5$$

$$A_{13}=(-1)^{1+3}\begin{vmatrix}1&0\\3&1\end{vmatrix}=1-0=1$$

$$A_{21}=(-1)^{2+1}\begin{vmatrix}1&1\\1&1\end{vmatrix}=1-1=0$$

$$A_{22}=(-1)^{2+2}\begin{vmatrix}1&1\\3&1\end{vmatrix}=1-3=-2$$

$$A_{23}=(-1)^{2+3}\begin{vmatrix}1&1\\3&1\end{vmatrix}=-(1-3)=2$$

$$A_{31}=(-1)^{3+1}\begin{vmatrix}1&1\\0&2\end{vmatrix}=2-0=2$$

$$A_{32}=(-1)^{3+2}\begin{vmatrix}1&1\\1&2\end{vmatrix}=(2-1)=1$$

$$A_{33}=(-1)^{3+3}\begin{vmatrix}1&1\\1&0\end{vmatrix}=0-1=-1$$

$$\text{adj}(A)=\begin{bmatrix}-2&5&1\\0&-2&2\\2&-1&-1\end{bmatrix}^T=\begin{bmatrix}-2&0&2\\5&-2&-1\\1&2&-1\end{bmatrix}$$

Hence, $A^{-1}=\frac{1}{|A|}\cdot\text{adj}\,A=\frac{1}{4}\begin{bmatrix}-2&0&2\\5&-2&-1\\1&2&-1\end{bmatrix}$

(c) Given, system of the equations is

$x+y+z=6$, $x+2z=7$, $3x+y+z=12$,

which can be written in matrix form as $AX=B$, where

$$A=\begin{bmatrix}1&1&1\\1&0&2\\3&1&1\end{bmatrix}, X=\begin{bmatrix}x\\y\\z\end{bmatrix} \text{ and } B=\begin{bmatrix}6\\7\\12\end{bmatrix}$$

Now, $AX=B$

$$\Rightarrow \quad X = A^{-1}B$$

$$\Rightarrow \quad X = \frac{1}{4}\begin{bmatrix} -2 & 0 & 2 \\ 5 & -2 & -1 \\ 1 & 2 & -1 \end{bmatrix}\begin{bmatrix} 6 \\ 7 \\ 12 \end{bmatrix} \quad \text{[from part (b)]}$$

$$\Rightarrow \quad X = \frac{1}{4}\begin{bmatrix} -12+0+24 \\ 30-14-12 \\ 6+14-12 \end{bmatrix} = \frac{1}{4}\begin{bmatrix} 12 \\ 4 \\ 8 \end{bmatrix} \Rightarrow \begin{bmatrix} x \\ y \\ z \end{bmatrix} = \begin{bmatrix} 3 \\ 1 \\ 2 \end{bmatrix}$$

Hence, $x = 3, y = 1$ and $z = 2$

12. (i) Let us consider a right angled triangle ACB with base $BC = x$ and hypotenuse $AB = y$ then $x + y = k$, where k is a constant. Again, let θ be the angle between the base and the hypotenuse and A be the area of the triangle.

Then, $\quad A = \frac{1}{2} \times BC \times AC = \frac{1}{2} x\sqrt{y^2 - x^2}.$

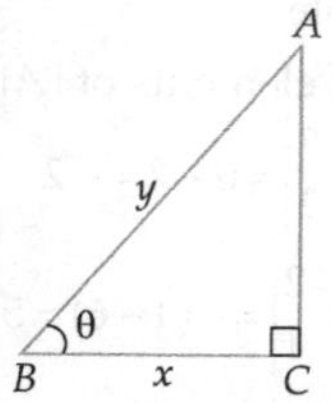

$$\Rightarrow \quad A^2 = \frac{x^2(y^2 - x^2)}{4} = \frac{x^2[(k-x)^2 - x^2]}{4}$$

[$\because$ put $y = (k - x)$]

$$\Rightarrow \quad A^2 = \frac{x^2(k^2 + x^2 - 2kx - x^2)}{4}$$

$$\Rightarrow \quad A^2 = \frac{k^2x^2 - 2kx^3}{4} \quad \text{...(i)}$$

On differentiating Eq. (i) w.r.t. x, we get

$$2A \cdot \frac{dA}{dx} = \frac{2k^2x - 6kx^2}{4} \quad \text{...(ii)}$$

$$\Rightarrow \quad \frac{dA}{dx} = \frac{k^2x - 3kx^2}{4A}$$

Now, put $\frac{dA}{dx} = 0$

$$\Rightarrow \quad (k^2x - 3kx^2) = 0 \Rightarrow kx(k - 3x) = 0$$

$$\Rightarrow \quad x = \frac{k}{3} \quad \text{[neglect } x = 0\text{]}$$

Now, on differentiating Eq. (ii) w.r.t. x, we get

$$2\left(\frac{dA}{dx}\right)^2 + 2A \cdot \frac{d^2A}{dx^2} = \frac{2k^2 - 12kx}{4} \quad \text{...(iii)}$$

On putting $\frac{dA}{dx} = 0$ and $x = \frac{k}{3}$ in Eq. (iii), we get

$$\frac{d^2A}{dx^2} = \frac{-k^2}{4A} < 0.$$

Thus, A is maximum when $x = \left(\frac{k}{3}\right)$.

Now, at $x = \frac{k}{3}$

$$y = \left(k - \frac{k}{3}\right) = \frac{2k}{3}.$$

$\therefore$ In ΔACB, $\cos\theta = \frac{x}{y}$

$$\Rightarrow \quad \cos\theta = \frac{(k/3)}{(2k/3)} = \frac{1}{2} \Rightarrow \theta = \frac{\pi}{3}$$

Hence, the area is maximum when $\theta = \frac{\pi}{3}$.

Hence proved.

Or

(ii) Given, volume of the box = 1024 cm^3

Let length of the side of square base be x cm and height of the box be y cm.

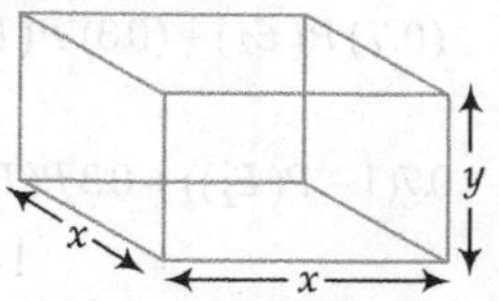

$\therefore$ Volume of the box $(V) = x^2 \cdot y = 1024$ [given]

$$\Rightarrow \quad y = \frac{1024}{x^2} \quad \text{...(i)}$$

Let C denotes the cost of the box.

Then, $\quad C = 2x^2 \times 5 + 4xy \times 2.50$

[$\because$ total area of top and bottom $= 2x^2$ and area of one side $= xy$]

$$= 10x^2 + 10xy$$

$$= 10x^2 + 10x\left(\frac{1024}{x^2}\right) \quad \text{[from Eq. (i)]}$$

$$\Rightarrow \quad C = 10x^2 + \frac{10240}{x} \quad \text{...(ii)}$$

On differentiating both sides w.r.t. x, we get

$$\frac{dC}{dx} = 20x - 10240(x)^{-2}$$

$$\Rightarrow \frac{dC}{dx} = 20x - \frac{10240}{x^2} \quad \text{...(iii)}$$

Now, for maxima or minima, put $\frac{dC}{dx} = 0$

$$\Rightarrow \quad 20x = \frac{10240}{x^2}$$

$$\Rightarrow \quad 20x^3 = 10240$$

$$\Rightarrow \quad x^3 = 512 = 8^3$$

$$\Rightarrow \quad x = 8$$

Again, on differentiating Eq. (iii) w.r.t. x, we get

$$\frac{d^2C}{dx^2} = 20 - 10240(-2) \cdot \frac{1}{x^3} = 20 + \frac{20480}{x^3}$$

Now, at $x = 8$, $\left(\frac{d^2C}{dx^2}\right)_{x=8} = 20 + \frac{20480}{512} = 60 > 0$

Thus, at $x = 8$, cost is minimum and the corresponding least cost of the box is

$$C(8) = 10 \cdot (8)^2 + \frac{10240}{8} \quad \text{[from Eq. (ii)]}$$

$$= 640 + 1280 = ₹\,1920$$

13. (i) Let $I=\int \frac{\sin x}{\sin^3 x+\cos^3 x}dx=\int \frac{\sin x/\cos^3 x}{\frac{\sin^3 x}{\cos^3 x}+\frac{\cos^3 x}{\cos^3 x}}dx$

[∵ divide numerator and denominator by $\cos^3 x$]

$$=\int \frac{\tan x \sec^2 x}{\tan^3 x+1}dx$$

On substituting $\tan x = t \Rightarrow \sec^2 x\, dx = dt$, we get

$$I=\int \frac{t}{t^3+1}dt=\int \frac{t}{(t+1)(t^2-t+1)}dt$$

Again, let $\frac{t}{(t+1)(t^2-t+1)}=\frac{A}{t+1}+\frac{Bt+C}{t^2-t+1}$

$\Rightarrow t = A(t^2-t+1)+(Bt+C)(t+1)$

$\Rightarrow t=(A+B)t^2+(-A+B+C)t+(A+C)$

On comparing the coefficient of t^2, t and constant term from both sides, we get

$A+B=0, -A+B+C=1$ and $A+C=0$

On solving these equations, we get

$A=-\frac{1}{3}, B=\frac{1}{3}$ and $C=\frac{1}{3}$

Then, $\frac{t}{(t+1)(t^2-t+1)}=\frac{-1/3}{t+1}+\frac{\frac{1}{3}t+\frac{1}{3}}{t^2-t+1}$

$$\therefore I=-\frac{1}{3}\int \frac{1}{t+1}dt+\frac{1}{3}\int \frac{t+1}{t^2-t+1}dt$$

$$=-\frac{1}{3}\log|t+1|+\frac{1}{6}\int \frac{(2t-1)+3}{t^2-t+1}dt \quad (1)$$

$$=-\frac{1}{3}\log|t+1|+\frac{1}{6}\int \frac{2t-1}{t^2-t+1}dt+\frac{1}{2}\int \frac{1}{t^2-t+1}dt$$

$$=-\frac{1}{3}\log|t+1|+\frac{1}{6}\log|t^2-t+1|$$

$$+\frac{1}{2}\int \frac{1}{\left(t-\frac{1}{2}\right)^2+\left(\frac{\sqrt{3}}{2}\right)^2}dt \quad (1)$$

$$\left[\because t^2-t+1=z \Rightarrow (2t-1)\,dt=dz \quad \therefore \int \frac{2t-1}{t^2-t+1}dt=\int \frac{dz}{z}=\log|z|=\log|t^2-t+1|\right]$$

$$=-\frac{1}{3}\log|t+1|+\frac{1}{6}\log|t^2-t+1|$$

$$+\frac{1}{\sqrt{3}}\tan^{-1}\left(\frac{2t-1}{\sqrt{3}}\right)$$

$$\left[\because \int \frac{dx}{x^2+a^2}=\frac{1}{a}\tan^{-1}\frac{x}{a}+C\right]$$

$$=-\frac{1}{3}\log|\tan x+1|+\frac{1}{6}\log|\tan^2 x-\tan x+1|$$

$$+\frac{1}{\sqrt{3}}\tan^{-1}\left(\frac{2\tan x-1}{\sqrt{3}}\right)+C \quad [\because t=\tan x]$$

(ii) Given, differential equation is

$$\frac{dy}{dx}=\frac{xy}{x^2+y^2}=\frac{\frac{y}{x}}{1+\frac{y^2}{x^2}} \quad \text{...(i)}$$

which is a homogeneous differential equation as $\frac{dy}{dx}=F\left(\frac{y}{x}\right)$.

Now, put $y=vx \Rightarrow \frac{dy}{dx}=v+x\frac{dv}{dx}$ in Eq. (i),

we get

$$v+x\frac{dv}{dx}=\frac{v}{1+v^2} \Rightarrow x\frac{dv}{dx}=\frac{v}{1+v^2}-v$$

$$\Rightarrow \quad x\frac{dv}{dx}=\frac{v-v-v^3}{1+v^2}$$

$$\Rightarrow \quad x\frac{dv}{dx}=-\frac{v^3}{1+v^2}$$

$$\Rightarrow \quad \frac{1+v^2}{v^3}dv=-\frac{dx}{x}$$

On integrating both sides, we get

$$\int\left(\frac{1}{v^3}+\frac{1}{v}\right)dv=-\int \frac{dx}{x}$$

$$\Rightarrow \quad -\frac{1}{2v^2}+\log|v|=-\log|x|+C$$

$$\Rightarrow \quad -\frac{x^2}{2y^2}+\log\left|\frac{y}{x}\right|=-\log|x|+C \quad \left[\text{put } v=\frac{y}{x}\right]$$

$$\Rightarrow -\frac{x^2}{2y^2}+\log|y|-\log|x|=-\log|x|+C$$

$$\left[\because \log\frac{m}{n}=\log m-\log n\right]$$

$$\Rightarrow \quad -\frac{x^2}{2y^2}+\log|y|=C \quad \text{...(ii)}$$

Also, it is given that $y=1$, when $x=0$.

Then, from Eq. (ii), we get

$$0+\log|1|=C \Rightarrow C=0 \quad [\because \log 1=0]$$

On putting $C=0$ in Eq. (ii), we get

$$-\frac{x^2}{2y^2}+\log|y|=0$$

$$\Rightarrow \quad \log|y|=\frac{x^2}{2y^2} \Rightarrow y=e^{\frac{x^2}{2y^2}}$$

which is the required solution.

14. (i) Given that the score is the product of the number shown on the machines.

For the entry at (2, 3),

$$p=2\times 3=6$$

For the entry at (2, 4),

$$r=2\times 4=8$$

For the entry at (4, 4),

$$q=4\times 4=16$$

Hence, $p=6, q=16$ and $r=8$.

(ii) Total possible outcomes = 16

Here, 1 appears 1 time.

$\Rightarrow \quad P(S=1)=\frac{1}{16}$

$\because \quad$ 2 appears 2 times $\Rightarrow P(S=2)=\frac{2}{16}$,

3 appears 2 times $\Rightarrow P(S=3)=\frac{2}{16}$,

4 appears 3 times. $\Rightarrow P(S=4)=\frac{3}{16}$,

6 appears 2 times $\Rightarrow P(S=6)=\frac{2}{16}$,

8 appears 2 times $\Rightarrow P(S=8)=\frac{2}{16}$,

9 appears 1 time $\Rightarrow P(S=9)=\frac{1}{16}$,

12 appears 2 times $\Rightarrow P(S=12)=\frac{2}{16}$,

and 16 appears 1 time

$\Rightarrow \quad P(S=16)=\frac{1}{16}$

Thus, probability distribution table is

S	1	2	3	4	6	8	9	12	16
$P(S=s)$	$\frac{1}{16}$	$\frac{2}{16}$	$\frac{2}{16}$	$\frac{3}{16}$	$\frac{2}{16}$	$\frac{2}{16}$	$\frac{1}{16}$	$\frac{2}{16}$	$\frac{1}{16}$

(iii) If the component scored at most 8. Then,

$$P(S\le 8)=P(S=1)+P(S=2)+P(S=3)+P(S=4)+P(S=6)+P(S=8)$$

$$=\frac{1}{16}+\frac{2}{16}+\frac{2}{16}+\frac{3}{16}+\frac{2}{16}+\frac{2}{16}=\frac{12}{16}=\frac{3}{4}$$

15. (i) (a) We have, $|\vec{a}|=4$

and $\quad -3\le\lambda\le 2$

$\therefore \quad |\lambda\vec{a}|=|\lambda||\vec{a}|=|\lambda|4$

$\Rightarrow \quad |\lambda\vec{a}|=|-3|4=12$, at $\lambda=-3$

$|\lambda\vec{a}|=|0|4=0$, at $\lambda=0$

$|\lambda\vec{a}|=|2|4=8$, at $\lambda=2$

So, the range of $|\lambda\vec{a}|$ is [0, 8].

(ii) (a) The required plane is passing through the point (a, b, c) whose position vector is $\vec{p}=a\hat{i}+b\hat{j}+c\hat{k}$ and is parallel to the plane $\vec{r}\cdot(\hat{i}+\hat{j}+\hat{k})=2$.

So, it is normal to the vector

$$\vec{n}=\hat{i}+\hat{j}+\hat{k}$$

Hence, the required equation of plane is

$$(\vec{r}-\vec{p})\cdot\vec{n}=0 \Rightarrow \vec{r}\cdot\vec{n}=\vec{p}\cdot\vec{n}$$

$\Rightarrow \quad \vec{r}\cdot(\hat{i}+\hat{j}+\hat{k})=(a\hat{i}+b\hat{j}+c\hat{k})\cdot(\hat{i}+\hat{j}+\hat{k})$

$\Rightarrow \quad \vec{r}\cdot(\hat{i}+\hat{j}+\hat{k})=a+b+c$

(iii) (d) Given, equations of lines are

$$\frac{x+1}{5}=\frac{y-2}{-2}=\frac{z-1}{2} \text{ and } \frac{x+3}{-2}=\frac{y+5}{0}=\frac{z-4}{3}$$

$\therefore$ The direction ratios of above lines are $<5,-2,2>$ and $<-2,0,3>$, respectively.

Let θ be the angle between the above lines, then

$$\cos\theta=\frac{|a_1a_2+b_1b_2+c_1c_2|}{\sqrt{a_1^2+b_1^2+c_1^2}\sqrt{a_2^2+b_2^2+c_2^2}}$$

$$=\frac{|5\times(-2)+(-2)\times 0+2\times 3|}{\sqrt{(5)^2+(-2)^2+(2)^2}\sqrt{(-2)^2+(0)^2+(3)^2}}$$

$$=\frac{|-10+0+6|}{\sqrt{25+4+4}\sqrt{4+9}}$$

$$=\frac{4}{\sqrt{33}\sqrt{13}}=\frac{4}{\sqrt{429}}$$

$\therefore \quad \theta=\cos^{-1}\left(\frac{4}{\sqrt{429}}\right)$

Also, $\frac{a_1}{a_2}=\frac{5}{-2}, \frac{b_1}{b_2}=\frac{-2}{0}$ and $\frac{c_1}{c_2}=\frac{2}{3}$

Since, $\frac{a_1}{a_2}\ne\frac{b_1}{b_2}\ne\frac{c_1}{c_2}$ so given lines are not parallel.

Hence, neither Statement I nor II is true.

(iv) Given, vector equation of the plane is

$$\vec{r}\cdot(6\hat{i}+3\hat{j}-2\hat{k})=4$$

Therefore, its cartesian equation is

$$(x\hat{i}+y\hat{j}+z\hat{k})\cdot(6\hat{i}+3\hat{j}-2\hat{k})=4$$

$\Rightarrow \quad 6x+3y-2z=4 \quad$ ...(i)

Now, the perpendicular distance from point $(3,-4,8)$ to the plane (i) is

$$\frac{|6\times 3+3(-4)-2(8)-4|}{\sqrt{(6)^2+(3)^2+(-2)^2}}=\frac{|18-12-16-4|}{\sqrt{36+9+4}}$$

$$=\frac{|-14|}{\sqrt{49}}=\frac{14}{7}=2 \text{ units}$$

(v) We have, $|\vec{a}|=1$, $|\vec{b}|=2$ and $|\vec{c}|=3$ ...(i)

It is given that

Projection of $\vec{b}$ along $\vec{a}$ = Projection of $\vec{c}$ along $\vec{a}$

$\Rightarrow \quad \frac{\vec{b}\cdot\vec{a}}{|\vec{a}|}=\frac{\vec{c}\cdot\vec{a}}{|\vec{a}|}$

$\Rightarrow \quad \vec{b}\cdot\vec{a}=\vec{c}\cdot\vec{a}$

$\Rightarrow \quad \vec{a}\cdot\vec{b}=\vec{a}\cdot\vec{c} \quad$ ...(ii)

Also, $\vec{b}$ and $\vec{c}$ are perpendicular to each other.

$\therefore \quad \vec{b}\cdot\vec{c}=0 \quad$ ...(iii)

Now, $|3\vec{a}-2\vec{b}+2\vec{c}|^2 = (3\vec{a}-2\vec{b}+2\vec{c})\cdot(3\vec{a}-2\vec{b}+2\vec{c})$

$= 9(\vec{a}\cdot\vec{a}) - 6(\vec{a}\cdot\vec{b}) + 6(\vec{a}\cdot\vec{c}) - 6(\vec{b}\cdot\vec{a}) + 4(\vec{b}\cdot\vec{b})$

$-4\vec{b}\cdot\vec{c} + 6\vec{c}\cdot\vec{a} - 4\vec{c}\cdot\vec{b} + 4(\vec{c}\cdot\vec{c})$

$= 9|\vec{a}|^2 + 4|\vec{b}|^2 + 4|\vec{c}|^2 + 2\{-6(\vec{a}\cdot\vec{b}) - 4(\vec{b}\cdot\vec{c}) + 6(\vec{a}\cdot\vec{c})\}$

$= 9\times 1^2 + 4\times 2^2 + 4\times 3^2 + 2\{-6(\vec{a}\cdot\vec{b}) - 4\times 0 + 6(\vec{a}\cdot\vec{b})\}$

[using Eqs. (i), (ii) and (iii)]

$= 9 + 16 + 36 + 2\times 0 = 61$

Hence, $|3\vec{a}-2\vec{b}+2\vec{c}| = \sqrt{61}$

16. (i) Given, $\vec{a} = \hat{i}+\hat{j}+\hat{k}$ and $\vec{b} = \hat{j}-\hat{k}$

Let $\vec{c} = x\hat{i} + y\hat{j} + z\hat{k}$

Then, $\vec{a}\times\vec{c} = \vec{b} \Rightarrow \begin{vmatrix} \hat{i} & \hat{j} & \hat{k} \\ 1 & 1 & 1 \\ x & y & z \end{vmatrix} = \hat{j}-\hat{k}$

$\Rightarrow \hat{i}(z-y) - \hat{j}(z-x) + \hat{k}(y-x) = \hat{j} - \hat{k}$

On comparing the coefficients of $\hat{i}$, $\hat{j}$ and $\hat{k}$ from both sides, we get

$z - y = 0$ ...(i)

$x - z = 1$ ...(ii)

and $x - y = 1$ ...(iii)

Also, $\vec{a}\cdot\vec{c} = 3 \Rightarrow (\hat{i}+\hat{j}+\hat{k})\cdot(x\hat{i}+y\hat{j}+z\hat{k}) = 3$

$\Rightarrow x + y + z = 3$ ...(iv)

On adding Eqs. (ii) and (iii), we get

$2x - y - z = 2$ ...(v)

On adding Eqs. (iv) and (v), we get

$3x = 5 \Rightarrow x = \frac{5}{3}$

Then, from Eq. (iii), we get

$y = \frac{5}{3} - 1 = \frac{2}{3}$ and from Eq. (i), we get $z = \frac{2}{3}$

Hence, $\vec{c} = \frac{5}{3}\hat{i} + \frac{2}{3}\hat{j} + \frac{2}{3}\hat{k} = \frac{1}{3}(5\hat{i} + 2\hat{j} + 2\hat{k})$

Or

(ii) Let $\vec{a} = 4\hat{i} - \hat{j} + 3\hat{k}$ and $\vec{b} = -2\hat{i} + \hat{j} - 2\hat{k}$.

Then, $\vec{a}\times\vec{b} = \begin{vmatrix} \hat{i} & \hat{j} & \hat{k} \\ 4 & -1 & 3 \\ -2 & 1 & -2 \end{vmatrix}$

$= (2-3)\hat{i} - (-8+6)\hat{j} + (4-2)\hat{k}$

$= -\hat{i} + 2\hat{j} + 2\hat{k}$

and $|\vec{a}\times\vec{b}| = \sqrt{(-1)^2 + 2^2 + 2^2} = \sqrt{1+4+4} = \sqrt{9} = 3$

$\therefore$ Required vector $= 9\left\{\frac{\vec{a}\times\vec{b}}{|\vec{a}\times\vec{b}|}\right\}$

$= \frac{9}{3}(-\hat{i} + 2\hat{j} + 2\hat{k})$

$= -3\hat{i} + 6\hat{j} + 6\hat{k}$

17. (i) Let the direction ratio of the normal to the required plane be a, b and c.

Since, the required plane passes through the point $(1, 1, -1)$. Then, its equation is

$a(x-1) + b(y-1) + c(z+1) = 0$ ...(i)

Also, plane (i) is perpendicular to each of the given planes $x + 2y + 3z - 7 = 0$

and $2x - 3y + 4z = 0$

$\therefore$ $a + 2b + 3c = 0$ ...(ii)

and $2a - 3b + 4c = 0$ ...(iii)

[$\because$ if two planes are perpendicular, then $a_1a_2 + b_1b_2 + c_1c_2 = 0$ where, a_1, b_1, c_1 and a_2, b_2, c_2 are the DR's of the normal to the planes]

On solving Eqs. (ii) and (iii) by cross-multiplication method, we get

$\frac{a}{8+9} = \frac{b}{6-4} = \frac{c}{-3-4}$

$\Rightarrow \frac{a}{17} = \frac{b}{2} = \frac{c}{-7} = \lambda$ (say)

$\Rightarrow a = 17\lambda,\ b = 2\lambda$ and $c = -7\lambda$

On putting the values of a, b and c in Eq. (i), we get

$17\lambda(x-1) + 2\lambda(y-1) + (-7\lambda)(z+1) = 0$

$\Rightarrow \lambda[17x - 17 + 2y - 2 - 7z - 7] = 0$

$\Rightarrow \lambda[17x + 2y - 7z - 26] = 0$

$\therefore 17x + 2y - 7z = 26$ [$\because \lambda \neq 0$]

which is the required equation of plane.

Or

(ii) Given lines are

$\vec{r} = (\hat{i}+\hat{j}-\hat{k}) + \lambda(2\hat{i} - 2\hat{j} + \hat{k})$

or $\frac{x-1}{2} = \frac{y-1}{-2} = \frac{z+1}{1} = \lambda$ ...(i)

and $\vec{r} = (2i - j - 3k) + \mu(i + 2j + 2k)$

or $\frac{x-2}{1} = \frac{y+1}{2} = \frac{z+3}{2} = \mu$ ...(ii)

Let the line passes through the point $(2, -1, 3)$ is

$\frac{x-2}{a} = \frac{y+1}{b} = \frac{z-3}{c}$ ...(iii)

If Eq. (iii) is perpendicular to Eqs. (i) and (ii), then

$2a - 2b + c = 0$

and $a + 2b + 2c = 0$

On solving these equations by cross-multiplication, we get

$\frac{a}{-4-2} = \frac{b}{1-4} = \frac{c}{4+2}$

$\Rightarrow \frac{a}{-6} = \frac{b}{-3} = \frac{c}{6} \Rightarrow \frac{a}{2} = \frac{b}{1} = \frac{c}{-2} = t$ (say)

$\Rightarrow a = 2t,\ b = t,\ c = -2t$

On putting these values in Eq. (iii), we get

$$\frac{x-2}{2t}=\frac{y+1}{t}=\frac{z-3}{-2t} \text{ or } \frac{x-2}{2}=\frac{y+1}{2}=\frac{z-3}{-2}$$

which is required equation of line in cartesian form.

and its vector form is, $\vec{r}=(2i-j-3k)+t(2i+j-2k)$

18. Given, curve is $y=x^2$ which is a parabola with centre at (0, 0) and upward.

The lines $x=-1$ and $x=1$ are perpendicular to X-axis. The graph of given curves is show below. It is clear from the figure that the required region is *OABO* and *OCDO*. It is symmetrical about Y-axis.

$\therefore$ Required area = 2 area of $OABO=2\int_0^1 y\,dx=2\int_0^1 x^2 dx$

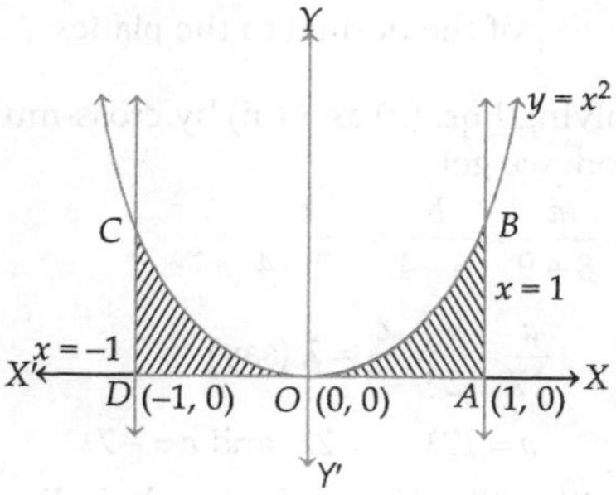

$$=2\left[\frac{x^3}{3}\right]_0^1=\frac{2}{3}[1-0]=\frac{2}{3} \text{ sq unit}$$

19. (i) (a) Given $\bar{x}=10, \bar{y}=20$ and $b_{xy}=\frac{9}{20}$

The equation of regression line of x on y is

$$x-\bar{x}=b_{xy}(y-\bar{y})$$

$\Rightarrow \quad x-10=\frac{9}{20}(y-20)$

$\Rightarrow \quad 20x-200=9y-180$

$\Rightarrow \quad 20x-9y=20$

$\Rightarrow \quad x=\frac{9y}{20}+1$

(ii) (b) Given cost function, $C=\frac{x^2}{2}-7x+111$

and demand function, $x=70-p \Rightarrow p=70-x$

We know that

Revenue function, $R=xp$

$\Rightarrow \quad R=x(70-x)=70x-x^2$

(iii) Given, demand function,

$$x=\frac{17-2p}{4}$$

$\therefore$ Revenue function,

$R(p)=$ Demand function $\times$ per unit price

$$=\left(\frac{17-2p}{4}\right)\times p$$

$$=\frac{17p-2p^2}{4}$$

(iv) Given cost function,

$$C(x)=500x^2+2500x+5000$$

Let production function be x. Then,

Revenue function, $R(x)=6000x$

$\therefore$ For break-even points, $R(x)=C(x)$

$\Rightarrow \quad 6000x=500x^2+2500x+5000$

$\Rightarrow \quad 500x^2-3500x+5000=0$

$\Rightarrow \quad x^2-7x+10=0$ [dividing by 500]

$\Rightarrow \quad x^2-5x-2x+10=0$

$\Rightarrow \quad x(x-5)-2(x-5)=0$

$\Rightarrow \quad (x-5)(x-2)=0$

$\Rightarrow \quad x=5, 2$

Hence, the break-even points are $x=5$ and $x=2$

(v) Given, lines are $4x+3y+7=0$ ...(i)

and $3x+4y+8=0$ ...(ii)

Let us consider Eq. (i) be regression line of x on y and Eq. (ii) be considered as regression line of y on x.

$\therefore$ From Eq. (i), we get

$$4x=-3y-7$$

$\Rightarrow \quad x=\frac{-3}{4}y-\frac{7}{4}$

$\therefore \quad b_{xy}=\frac{-3}{4}$

From Eq. (ii), we get $4y=-3x-8$

$\Rightarrow \quad y=\frac{-3}{4}x-\frac{8}{4}$

$\therefore \quad b_{yx}=\frac{-3}{4}$

Now, $\quad b_{yx}\times b_{xy}=\left(\frac{-3}{4}\right)\times\left(-\frac{3}{4}\right)=\frac{9}{16}<1$

Thus, our consideration is correct.

(*a*) The regression line of y on x is $3x+4y+8=0$

(*b*) The regression line of x on y is $4x+3y+7=0$

20. (i) Let the operator increase ₹x in monthly subscription. Then, the rate per subscriber $P=100+x$

Since, for each increase of ₹0.50, 10 subscribers will discontinue the service, therefore, for increase for ₹ x in monthly subscription the number of subscribers who will discontinue the service is

$$\frac{10x}{0.50}=20x$$

Therefore, total number of subscribers $=5000-20x$

Now, the total revenue R of the operator is given by

$R=$ Rate $\times$ Number of subscribers

$$=(100+x)(5000-20x)$$

$$=500000+3000x-20x^2 \quad \text{...(i)}$$

On differentiating w.r.t. x, two times, we get

$$\frac{dR}{dx} = 3000 - 40x \text{ and } \frac{d^2R}{dx^2} = -40$$

For R to be maximum, put $\frac{dR}{dx} = 0$

$\Rightarrow$ $3000 - 40x = 0$

$\Rightarrow$ $x = 75$

Also, At $x = 75$,

$$\left(\frac{d^2R}{dx^2}\right)_{x=75} = -40 < 0.$$

Therefore, R is maximum when $x = 75$.

On substituting $x = 75$ in Eq. (i), we get

the maximum revenue $= ₹\ 500000 + 3000 \times 75 - 20(75)^2$
$= ₹\ 612500.$

Or

(ii) Given, demand function is $x = 70 - 5p$, which can be rewritten as $p = \frac{70 - x}{5}$

Now, revenue function $R(x) = p \cdot x = \frac{70x - x^2}{5}$

On differentiating w.r.t. x, two times, we get

$$\frac{d[R(x)]}{dx} = \frac{1}{5}[70 - 2x] \text{ and } \frac{d^2R(x)}{dt^2} = \frac{-2}{5}$$

On putting $\frac{d}{dx}[R(x)] = 0, \Rightarrow \frac{70 - 2x}{5} = 0 \Rightarrow x = 35$

At $x = 35$, $\frac{d^2}{dx^2}[R(x)] = \frac{1}{5}(-2) < 0, \forall\, x$

$\therefore$ For maximum revenue, $x = 35$

and maximum revenue is given by

$$R(35) = ₹\ \frac{70(35) - (35)^2}{5} = ₹\ 245$$

21. The table for regression coefficient is shown below

x	y	xy	x^2	y^2
1	7	7	1	49
2	6	12	4	36
3	5	15	9	25
4	4	16	16	16
5	3	15	25	9
$\Sigma x = 15$	$\Sigma y = 25$	$\Sigma xy = 65$	$\Sigma x^2 = 55$	$\Sigma y^2 = 135$

Here, $n = 5$

Then, mean $\bar{x} = \frac{\Sigma x}{n} = \frac{15}{5} = 3$ and $\bar{y} = \frac{\Sigma y}{n} = \frac{25}{5} = 5$

Now, regression coefficient of y on x is

$$b_{yx} = \frac{n\Sigma xy - \Sigma x \cdot \Sigma y}{n\Sigma x^2 - (\Sigma x)^2}$$

$$= \frac{5 \times 65 - 15 \times 25}{5 \times 55 - 15^2}$$

$$= \frac{13 - 15}{11 - 9} = -1$$

and regression coefficient of x on y is

$$b_{xy} = \frac{n\Sigma xy - \Sigma x \cdot \Sigma y}{n\Sigma y^2 - (\Sigma y)^2}$$

$$= \frac{5 \times 65 - 15 \times 25}{5 \times 135 - 25^2}$$

$$= \frac{13 - 15}{27 - 25} = -1$$

$\therefore$ The regression line of y on x is

$y - \bar{y} = b_{yx}(x - \bar{x})$

$\Rightarrow$ $y - 5 = -1(x - 3)$

$\Rightarrow$ $x + y = 8$

when $x = 3.5$, then $y = 8 - 3.5 = 4.5$

22. (i) Let the distance covered at the speed of 30 km/h $= x$ km

and the distance covered at the speed of 45 km/h $= y$ km

Maximum distance $Z = x + y$

Subject to the constraints,

$4x + 6y \le 120$

$\Rightarrow$ $2x + 3y \le 60$ ...(i) [money constraint]

$\frac{x}{30} + \frac{y}{45} \le 1$ [time constraint]

$\Rightarrow$ $3x + 2y \le 90$ ...(ii)

and $x, y \ge 0$ ...(iii)

[non-negative constraint]

Table for the line $2x + 3y = 60$ or $y = \frac{60 - 2x}{3}$ is

x	0	30
y	20	0

So, the line $2x + 3y = 60$ passes through the points (0, 20) and (30, 0).

On putting (0, 0) in the inequality $2x + 3y \le 60$, we get $0 + 0 \le 60$ (true)

So, the region is towards the origin.

Table for line $3x + 2y = 90$ or $y = \frac{90 - 3x}{2}$ is

x	0	30
y	45	0

So, the line $3x + 2y = 90$ passes through the points (0, 45) and (30, 0).

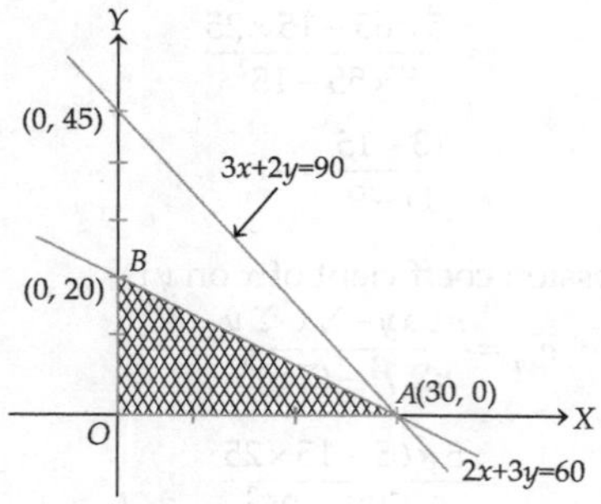

On putting (0, 0) in the inequality $3x + 2y \le 90$, we get $0 + 0 \le 90$ (true)

So, the region is towards the origin.

Also, $x \ge 0, y \ge 0$ so the region less in Ist quadrant.

On solving $2x + 3y = 60$ and $3x + 2y = 90$, we get the intersection point (30, 0).

On plotting the graph of above inequality we get the feasible region OAB. The corner points of feasible region are $O(0, 0)$, $A(30, 0)$ and $B(0, 20)$.

The value of z at corner points are given below.

Corner points	$Z = x + y$
$O(0, 0)$	$0 + 0 = 0$
$A(30, 0)$	$30 + 0 = 30$ (Maximum)
$B(0, 20)$	$0 + 20 = 20$

The maximum value of z is 30 at point $A(30, 0)$.

Hence, he can travel maximum distance of 30 km in 1 hour.

Or

(ii) Given LPP is

Minimise $Z = 5x + 7y$

Subject to constraints,

$2x + y \ge 8$ ...(i)

$x + 2y \ge 10$ ...(ii)

and $x, y \ge 0$ ...(iii)

Table for line $2x + y = 8$ or $y = 8 - 2x$ is

x	0	4
y	8	0

So, the line passes through the points (0, 8) and (4, 0).

On putting (0, 0) in the inequality $2x + y \ge 3$, we get $0 + 0 \ge 8$ (not true)

So, the region is away from the origin.

Table for line $x + 2y = 10$ or $y = \dfrac{10 - x}{2}$ is

x	0	10
y	5	0

So, the line passes through the points (0, 5) and (10, 0).

On putting (0, 0) in inequality $x + 2y \ge 10$, we get $0 + 0 \ge 10$ (not true).

So, the region is away, from the origin.

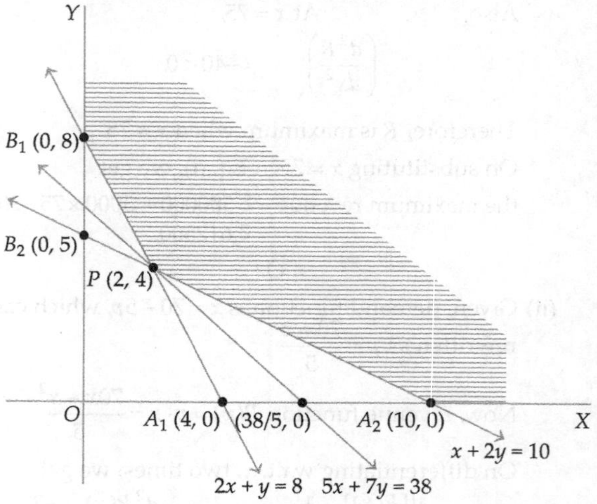

On solving the equations $2x + y = 8$ and $x + 2y = 10$, we get the intersection point $P(2, 4)$. Also, $x \ge 0, y \ge 0$ shows these feasible region lies in Ist quadrant.

On plotting the graph of above inequalities, we get the feasible region $A_2 B_1$.

As the feasible region is unbounded therefore 38 may or may not be the minimum value of Z. For this drive a dotted graph of the inequality $5x + 7y < 38$ and check whether the resulting half plane has points in common with a feasible region or not. It can be sun that the feasible region has no common point with $5x + 7y < 38$. Therefore, the minimum value of z is 38 at $P(2, 4)$.

The coordinates of the corner points of this region are $A_2(10, 0)$, $P(2, 4)$ and $B_1(0, 8)$.

The values of the objective function $Z = 5x + 7y$ at the corner points of the feasible region are given in the following table

Point (x, y)	Value of $Z = 5x + 7y$
$A_2(10, 0)$	$5 \times 10 + 7 \times 0 = 50$
$P(2, 4)$	$5 \times 2 + 7 \times 4 = 38$ (Minimum)
$B_1(0, 8)$	$5 \times 0 + 7 \times 8 = 56$

Clearly, Z is minimum at $x = 2$ and $y = 4$.

SQP Code : **PB-12/15** Series **i-Succeed 12-25/15** Roll No. | | | | | | | |

Sample Question Paper 12

Mathematics 12th (Code 860)

General Instructions

1. The Question Paper consists of three sections A, B and C.
2. Candidates are required to attempt all questions from Section A and all questions either from Section B Or Section C.
3. Section A Internal choice has been provided in two questions of two marks each, two questions of four marks each and two questions of six marks each.
4. Section B Internal choice has been provided in one questions of two marks and one question of four marks.
5. Section C Internal choice has been provided in one question of two marks and one question of four marks.
6. All working, including rough work, should be done on the same sheet as, and adjacent to the rest of the answer.
7. The intended marks for questions or parts of questions are given in brackets [].
8. Mathematical tables and graph papers are provided.

Time : 3 Hrs.

Max. Marks : 80

Section A Multiple Choice Questions *(Each Que. carries 1 M)*

1. In subparts (i) to (xi) choose the correct option and in subparts (xii) to (xv), answer the questions as instructed.

(i) Let $R = \{(1,3),(4,2),(2,4),(2,3),(3,1)\}$ be a relation on the set $A = \{1,2,3,4\}$. The relation R is • *Understanding* [1]

(a) a function
(b) transitive
(c) not symmetric
(d) reflexive

(ii) The value of $\tan^{-1}\left[2\sin\left(2\cos^{-1}\frac{\sqrt{3}}{2}\right)\right]$ is • *Application* [1]

(a) $\frac{\pi}{3}$ (b) $\frac{2\pi}{3}$ (c) $\frac{-\pi}{3}$ (d) $\frac{\pi}{6}$

(iii) Total number of possible matrices of order 3×3 with each entry 2 or 0 is • *Recall* [1]

(a) 9 (b) 27
(c) 81 (d) 512

(iv) **Assertion** (A) The function defined by $g(x) = x - [x]$ is discontinuous at all integer points.
Reason (R) Greatest integer function $\int(x) - [x]$, where $[x]$ upwards the greatest integer less than or equal be x.
In general, is $n < x < n+1$ for any integer n then $[x] = n$. • *Recall* [1]

(a) Both A and R are true and R is the correct explanation of A.
(b) Both A and R are true but R is not the correct explanation of A.
(c) A is true but R is false.
(d) A is false but R is true.

(v) In which interval, the function $f(x)$ is the always increasing, where $f(x) = 5 + 36x + 3x^2 - 2x^3$. • *Understanding* [1]

(a) $(-2, 3)$ (b) $[3, \infty)$
(c) $(-\infty, -2)\cup(3,\infty)$ (d) None of these

(vi) The value of $\int 2^{3\log_2 x} dx$ is • *Application* [1]

(a) $\frac{\log x}{x^4} + C$ (b) $\frac{x^4}{4} + C$

(c) $x^{-4} + C$ (d) $2^x \log x + C$

(vii) The value of $\int e^x(\cos x - \sin x)dx$ is • *Application* [1]

(a) $-e^x \sin x + C$ (b) $e^x \sin x + C$

(c) $-e^x \cos x + C$ (d) $e^x \cos x + C$

(viii) The graph of function $f(x) = x^{\frac{1}{3}}$ is shown below. • *Understanding* [1]

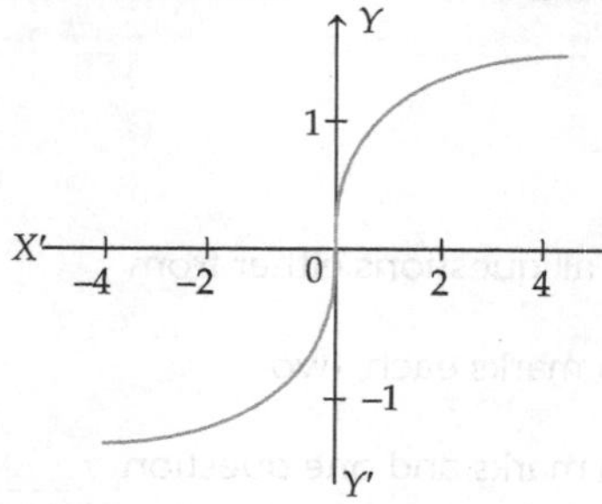

(a) $f(x)$ is continuous at $x = 0$.

(b) $f(x)$ is differentiable at $x = 0$.

(c) $f(x)$ is not differentiable at $x = 0$.

(d) $f(x)$ is not continuous but differentiable $x = 0$.

(ix) **Assertion** (A) The solution of the differential equation $\frac{d^2y}{dx^2} + y = 0$ is $y = \phi(x) = a \sin(x + b)$.

The function $y = \phi(x)$ is called general solution.

Reason (R) The solution which contains arbitrary constants, is called general solution.

Choose the correct option. • *Recall* [1]

(a) Both A and R are correct and R is the correct explanation of A.

(b) Both A and R are correct but R is not the correct explanation of A.

(c) A is correct but R is incorrect.

(d) R is correct but A is incorrect.

(x) Consider the function $f(x)$ is defined as follows. $\begin{cases} x^2 + 3x + 2, & \text{if } x < 1 \\ 2x + 1, & \text{if } x \geq 1 \end{cases}$.

Evaluate the following statements.

Statement I The function $f(x)$ is continuous at $x = 1$.

Statement II The function $f(x)$ is differentiable at $x = 1$.

Which of the following option is correct? • *Analysis* [1]

(a) Both the Statements are true.

(b) Statement I is true and Statement II is false.

(c) Statement I is false and Statement II is true.

(d) Both Statements are false.

(xi) **Statement I** If $y = \cot^{-1}(\sqrt{\cos x}) - \tan^{-1}(\sqrt{\cos x})$, then $\sin y = \tan^2 \frac{x}{2}$.

Statement II We have, $2\tan^{-1}\theta = \cos^{-1}\left(\frac{1-\theta^2}{1+\theta^2}\right)$, if $0 \leq \theta < \infty$ and $\tan^{-1}\theta + \cot^{-1}\theta = \frac{\pi}{2}, \theta \in R$ • *Application* [1]

(a) Only Statement I is true.

(b) Only Statement II is true.

(c) Both Statements I and II are true.

(d) Neither I nor II is true.

(xii) Let $A = \{0, 1, 2, 3\}$ and define a relation R on A as follows.

$R = \{(0,0)(0,1)(0,3)(1,0)(1,1)(2,2)(3,0)(3,3)\}$.

Is R reflexive, symmetric and transitive? • *Analysis* [1]

(xiii) If A is a skew-symmetric matrix of odd order n, then show that $|A| = 0$. • *Understanding* [1]

(xiv) Find $\int \frac{2^{x+1} - 5^{x-1}}{10^x} dx$. • *Evaluate* [1]

(xv) The random variable X can take only the values 0, 1, 2. Given that $P(X = 0) = P(X = 1) = p$ and that $E(X^2) = E(X)$, find the value of p. • *Evaluate* [1]

2. (i) Find the minimum value of $(\sec^{-1} x)^2 + (\operatorname{cosec}^{-1} x)^2$. • *Evaluate* [2]

Or (ii) Prove that $\tan^{-1}\left[\frac{\sqrt{1+x} - \sqrt{1-x}}{\sqrt{1+x} + \sqrt{1-x}}\right] = \frac{\pi}{4} - \frac{1}{2}\cos^{-1} x, -\frac{1}{\sqrt{2}} \leq x \leq 1$. • *Application* [2]

3. Find the value of k for which $f(x) = \begin{cases} kx + 5, & \text{when } x \leq 2 \\ x - 1, & \text{when } x > 2 \end{cases}$ is continuous at $x = 2$. • *Application* [2]

4. Simplify $4\begin{bmatrix} 1 & 3 \\ 1 & -4 \end{bmatrix} - \frac{1}{2}\begin{bmatrix} 8 & 4 \\ 4 & 8 \end{bmatrix}$. • *Analysis* [2]

5. (i) Find the intervals in which the function $f(x)=2x^3-15x^2+36x+17$ is increasing or decreasing. • *Application* [2]

Or

(ii) Find the point on the curve $y^2=8x$ for which the abscissa and ordinate change at the same line. • *Analysis*

6. Evaluate $\int_1^2 \log_e [x]\,dx$, where $[\cdot]$ denotes the greatest integer function. • *Evaluate* [2]

7. Let T be the set of all triangles in a plane. Let us define a relation $R=\{(T_1,T_2):T_1$ is similar to $T_2; T_1, T_2 \in T\}$. Show that R is an equivalence relation. • *Understanding* [4]

8. Find $\int \frac{(3\sin\theta-2)\cos\theta}{5-\cos^2\theta-4\sin\theta}\,d\theta$. • *Evaluate*

9. (i) Find the particular solution of the differential equation $(1+e^{2x})\,dy+(1+y^2)\,e^x\,dx=0$, given that $y=1$, when $x=0$. • *Application* [4]

Or

(ii) If $x=\tan\left(\frac{1}{a}\log y\right)$, then show that

$$(1+x^2)\frac{d^2y}{dx^2}+(2x-a)\frac{dy}{dx}=0.$$ • *Application* [4]

10. (i) If $f(x)$ is the continuous function, integral of $f(x)$ over the interval $[a, b]$ is denoted by $\int_a^b f(x)dx$.

$$\int_a^b f(x)dx=[F(x)]_a^b=[F(b)-F(a)]$$

On the basis of above information, answer the following questions. • *Evaluate* [4]

(a) Evaluate $\int_4^7 x^2 dx$.

(b) Evaluate $\int_1^{\sqrt{3}} \frac{1}{1+x^2}dx$.

(c) Evaluate $\int_{-1}^1 (x+3)dx$.

(d) Evaluate $\int_4^6 e^x dx$.

Or

(ii) Consider the function

$$f(x)=\frac{x^2+1}{(x-1)^2(x+3)}.$$

Answer the following questions.

(a) Decompose the function using partial fraction.

(b) Differentiate the decomposed function with respect to x.

(c) Evaluate $\int f(x)dx$. • *Evaluate* [4]

11. A company produces two types of products, product *A* and product *B*. To produce these products, the company, uses two resources: Resource 1 and Resource 2. The amount of each resource required for each product is given in the table below.

	Product *A*	Product *B*
Resource 1	3 units	2 units
Resource 2	5 units	4 units

The company has 18 units of Resources 1 and 28 units of Resource 2 available. • *Application* [6]

(i) Set up the system of equation using the given information.

(ii) Find the inverse of the coefficient matrix.

(iii) How many units of product *A* and product *B* the company should produce to utilise all resources completely?

12. (i) Find the mean of number of tails, when a coin is tossed thrice. • *Analysis* [6]

Or

(ii) Three bags contain a number of red and white balls as follows.
Bag I: 3 red balls, Bag II: 2 red balls and 1 white ball and Bag III: 3 white balls. The probability that bag will be chosen and a ball is selected from it is $\frac{i}{6}$, where $i=1,2,3$. • Analysis

(a) What is the probability that a red ball is selected?

(b) If a white ball is selected, then what is the probability that it came from bag III? [6]

13. (i) Show that the altitude of the right circular cone of maximum volume that can be inscribed in a sphere of radius r is $\frac{4r}{3}$. Also, show that the maximum volume of the cone is $\frac{8}{27}$ of the volume of the sphere. • *Application* [6]

SP-12

Or (ii) A window is in the form of a rectangle surmounted by a semicircular opening. The total perimeter of the window is 10 m. Find the dimensions of the window to admit maximum light through the whole opening.
• *Application* [6]

14. A medical test is used to diagnose a rare disease that affects 1 in 1000 people. The test is not perfect. It has a sensitivity (true positive rate) of 99% and a specifically (true negative rate) of 98%.
A patient tests positive and we want to analyse the implications.

(i) What is the probability that a randomly selected person has the prior disease?
(ii) What is the probability of a false positive result (i.e., the test indicating the disease when the person does not have it?)
(iii) Given that the patient tested positive, what is the probability that the patient actually has the disease?
(iv) If a patient tests negative, what is the probability that they do not have the disease? • *Analysis* [6]

Section B Very Short Answer Type Questions *(Each Que. carries 2 M)*

15. In subparts (i) to (iii) choose the correct options and in subparts (iv) and (v), answer the questions as instructed. [5]

(i) If $\vec{a}$ and $\vec{b}$ are any two vectors and k and m are any scalars, then which of the following is correct? • *Recall*

(a) $k\vec{a}+m\vec{a}=(k+m)\vec{a}$ (b) $k(m\vec{a})=(km)\vec{a}$
(c) $k(\vec{a}+\vec{b})=k\vec{a}+k\vec{b}$ (d) All of these

(ii) The intercept cut-off by plane $2x+y-z=5$ on X-axis is • *Recall*

(a) $\frac{5}{3}$ units (b) $\frac{5}{2}$ units
(c) 5 units (d) None of these

(iii) **Statement I** The vector and the cartesian equations of the plane passing through the point $(5,2,-4)$ and perpendicular to the line with direction ratios $<2,3,-1>$ are $\vec{r}\cdot(2i+3j-k)=20$ and $2x+3y-z=20$, respectively.
Statement II The vector equation of a plane passing through a given point A with position vector $\vec{a}$ and perpendicular to a given vector $\vec{n}$ is $(\vec{r}-\vec{a})\cdot\vec{n}=0$
Where, $\vec{r}$ is the position vector of any point $P(x,y,z)$ on the plane.
• *Understanding*

(a) Only Statement I is true.
(b) Only Statement II is true.
(c) Both Statements are true.
(d) Neither I nor II is true.

(iv) Show that the points $A(2,3,-4)$, $B(1,-2,3)$ and $C(3,8,-11)$ are collinear. • *Understanding*

(v) Find a vector in the direction of a vector $\vec{a}=\hat{i}-\hat{j}+\hat{k}$, which has magnitude 8 units. • *Understanding*

16. (i) If $|\vec{a}|=2, |\vec{b}|=7$ and $\vec{a}\times\vec{b}=3\hat{i}+2\hat{j}+6\hat{k}$, find the angle between $\vec{a}$ and $\vec{b}$.
• *Evaluate* [2]

Or

(ii) If $\vec{a}$, $\vec{b}$ and $\vec{c}$ are three mutually perpendicular vectors of the same magnitude, then prove that $\vec{a}+\vec{b}+\vec{c}$ is equally inclined with the vectors $\vec{a}$, $\vec{b}$ and $\vec{c}$. • *Analysis* [2]

17. (i) Find the coordinates of the point, where the line $\frac{x-2}{3}=\frac{y+1}{4}=\frac{z-2}{2}$ intersects the plane $x-y+z-5=0$. Also, find the angle between the line and the plane.
• *Application* [4]

Or (ii) Find the coordinates of the point where the line through the points $(3,-4,-5)$ and $(2,-3,1)$ crosses the plane $2x+y+z=7$. • *Application* [4]

18. Using integration, find the area of the triangular region whose sides have the equations $y=2x+1$, $y=3x+1$ and $x=4$.
• *Evaluate* [4]

SP-12

Section C Short Answer Type Questions *(Each Que. carries 3 M)*

19. In subparts (i) and (ii) choose the correct option and in subparts (iii) to (v), answer the questions as instructed. [5]

(i) Feasible region (shaded) for a LPP is shown in following figure, then the maximum value of $Z = x + y$ is

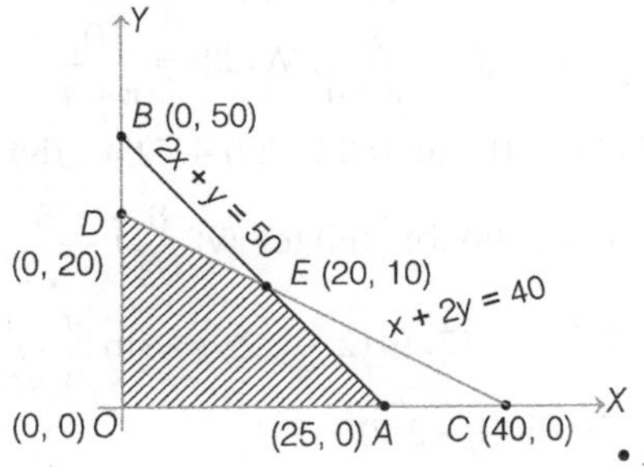

• *Analysis*

(a) 20 (b) 30
(c) 50 (d) 100

(ii) The total revenue (in ₹) received from the sale of x units of a product is given by $R(x) = 4x^3 + 6x^2 + 8x$, then the marginal revenue, when $x = 6$ is • *Understanding*

(a) 512 (b) 510
(c) 558 (d) 258

(iii) The total revenue (in ₹) received from the sale of x units of a product is given by $R(x) = 3x^3 + 7x^2 + 8x$. Find the marginal revenue, when $x = 8$. • *Understanding*

(iv) Find the total revenue from the sale of 12 units of output x from the marginal revenue given by $\text{MR} = 15 - x^2 + 7x$. • *Understanding*

(v) For lines of regression $4x - 2y = 3$ and $2x - 3y = 5$, find $r(x, y)$. • *Application*

20. (i) For the demand function $p = \dfrac{a}{x+b} - c$, where $ab > 0$, show that the marginal revenue decreases with the increase of x. • *Analysis* [2]

Or (ii) The relation between profit P of a firm and the selling price x of its goods is $P(x) = 2000x - 50x^2, 0 \le x \le 40$. For what range of selling price is profit increasing? For what selling price is profit maximised? • *Analysis* [2]

21. Given that the observations are $(9, -4)$, $(10, -3)$, $(11, -1)$, $(12, 0)$, $(13, 1)$, $(14, 3)$, $(15, 5)$, $(16, 8)$. Find the two lines of regression and estimate the value of y when $x = 13.5$. • *Application* [4]

22. (i) In order to supplement daily diet, a person wishes to take X and Y tablets. The contents (in milligrams per tablet) of iron, calcium and vitamins in X and Y are given as below.

Tablets	Iron	Calcium	Vitamin
X	6	3	2
Y	2	3	4

The person needs to supplement atleast 18 mg of iron, 21 mg of calcium and 16 mg of vitamins. The price of each tablet of X and Y is ₹ 2 and ₹ 1, respectively. How many tablets of each type should the person take in order to satisfy the above requirement at the minimum cost? Make an LPP and solve graphically. • *Analysis* [4]

Or

(ii) An aeroplane can carry a maximum of 200 passengers. A profit of ₹ m is made on each executive class ticket and a profit of ₹ n is made on each economy class ticket, where m and n are obtained on multiplying first term and common ratio by 100 of the geometric series 10, 60, 360, ………… times. The airline reserves atleast 20 seats for executive class. However atleast 4 times as many passengers prefer to travel by economy class than by the executive class. Determine how many tickets of each type must be sold in order to maximise the profit for the airline? What is the maximum profit? • *Analysis* [4]

Answer Key

1. (i) (c) (ii) (a) (iii) (d) (iv) (a)
(v) (a) (vi) (b) (vii) (d) (viii) (c)
(ix) (a) (x) (d) (xi) (c)
(xii) Reflexive and symmetric but not transitive
(xiv) $\frac{1}{5}\log 2(2^{-x}) - 2\log 5(5^{-x}) + C$ (xv) $\frac{1}{2}$

2. (i) $\frac{\pi^2}{8}$ **3.** -2

4. $\begin{bmatrix} 0 & 10 \\ 2 & -20 \end{bmatrix}$

5. (i) Increasing $(-\infty, 2]$ and $[3, \infty)$, Decreasing $[2, 3]$
Or (ii) $(2, 4)$

6. 0

8. $3\log|\sin\theta - 2| - \frac{4}{(\sin\theta - 2)} + C$

9. (i) $y = \frac{1}{e^x}$

10. (i) (a) 93 (b) $\frac{\pi}{12}$ (c) 6 (d) $e^6 - e^4$

Or (ii) (a) $\frac{3}{8}\cdot\frac{1}{(x-1)} + \frac{1}{2}\cdot\frac{1}{(x-1)^2} + \frac{5}{8}\cdot\frac{1}{(x+3)}$

(b) $-\frac{3}{8}\cdot\frac{1}{(x-1)^2} - \frac{1}{(x-1)^3} - \frac{5}{8}\cdot\frac{1}{(x+3)^2}$

(c) $\frac{3}{8}\log|x-1| - \frac{1}{2(x-1)} + \frac{5}{8}\log|x+3| + C$

11. (i) $3x + 2y = 18$ and $5x + 4y = 28$
(ii) $\frac{1}{2}\begin{bmatrix} 4 & -2 \\ -5 & 3 \end{bmatrix}$
(iii) Product $A = 8$ units, Product $B = -3$ unit.

12. (i) $\frac{3}{2}$ *Or* (ii) (a) $\frac{7}{18}$ (b) $\frac{9}{11}$

13. *Or* Length $= \frac{20}{\pi + 4}$, Width $= \frac{10}{\pi + 4}$

14. (i) 0.001 (ii) 0.02 (iii) 4.72% (iv) 99.9%

15. (i) (d) (ii) (b) (iii) (c) (v) $\frac{8}{\sqrt{3}}\hat{i} - \frac{8}{\sqrt{3}}\hat{j} + \frac{8}{\sqrt{3}}\hat{k}$

16. (i) $\frac{\pi}{6}$ **17.** (i) $(2, -1, 2)$, $\phi = \sin^{-1}\left(\frac{1}{\sqrt{87}}\right)$
Or (ii) $(1, -2, 7)$

18. 8 sq units **19.** (i) (b) (ii) (a) (iii) ₹ 696
(iv) ₹ 108 (v) $\sqrt{\frac{1}{3}}$

20. *Or* (ii) $[0, 20]$; ₹ 20

21. $919x - 548y = 10871, 137x - 84y = 1618$
and $y = 2.76$

22. (i) 1 tablet of type X and 6 tablets of type Y.
Or
(ii) Max. Profit = ₹ 136000

Scan this QR code from your mobile phone to get the explanations of this paper.

SQP Code : **PB-13/15** Series **i-Succeed 13-25/15** Roll No.

Sample Question Paper 13

Mathematics 12th (Code 860)

General Instructions

1. The Question Paper consists of three sections A, B and C.
2. Candidates are required to attempt all questions from Section A and all questions either from Section B Or Section C.
3. Section A Internal choice has been provided in two questions of two marks each, two questions of four marks each and two questions of six marks each.
4. Section B Internal choice has been provided in one questions of two marks and one question of four marks.
5. Section C Internal choice has been provided in one question of two marks and one question of four marks.
6. All working, including rough work, should be done on the same sheet as, and adjacent to the rest of the answer.
7. The intended marks for questions or parts of questions are given in brackets [].
8. Mathematical tables and graph papers are provided.

Time : 3 Hrs.
Max. Marks : 80

Section A (65 Marks)

1. In subparts (i) to (xi) choose the correct options and in subparts (xii) to (xv), answer the questions as instructed.

(i) Let R be the equivalence relation in the set $A = \{0, 1, 2, 3, 4, 5\}$ given by $R = \{(a, b) : 2$ divides $(a - b)\}$. Then, the equivalence class of [0] is • *Understanding* [1]

(a) {2, 4} (b) {0, 4}
(c) {0, 2, 4} (d) None of these

(ii) If $\sin\left(\sin^{-1}\frac{1}{5} + \cos^{-1}x\right) = 1$, then the value of x is • *Application* [1]

(a) $\frac{1}{2}$ (b) $\frac{1}{3}$ (c) $\frac{1}{5}$ (d) $\frac{1}{6}$

(iii) If $\begin{bmatrix} 1+x & 2 \\ y-1 & 3 \end{bmatrix} = \begin{bmatrix} 2 & 2 \\ 3 & 3 \end{bmatrix}$, then $x = -1$ and $y = 2$. • *Understanding* [1]

(a) True (b) False
(c) Cannot say (d) Partially True/False

(iv) **Assertion** (A) $y = \sin^{-1}x + \cos^{-1}x + \tan^{-1}x + \cot^{-1}x$, then $\frac{dy}{dx}$ is equal to 0.

Reason (R) $\tan^{-1}\theta + \cot^{-1}\theta = \frac{\pi}{2}$ and $\cos^{-1}\theta - \sin^{-1}\theta = \frac{\pi}{2}$ • *Analysis* [1]

(a) Both A and R are true and R is the correct explanation of A.
(b) Both A and R are true but R is not the correct explanation of A.
(c) A is true but R is false.
(d) A is false but R is true.

(v) If $f(x) = \begin{cases} mx + 1, & \text{if } x \le \frac{\pi}{2} \\ \sin x + n, & \text{if } x > \frac{\pi}{2} \end{cases}$ is continuous at $x = \frac{\pi}{2}$, then • *Application* [1]

(a) $m=1, n=0$ (b) $m=\frac{n\pi}{2}+1$

(c) $n=\frac{m\pi}{2}$ (d) $m=n=\frac{\pi}{2}$

(vi) **Statement I** $\int \frac{2x+3}{x^2+3x}dx$ is equal to $\log|(x^2+3x)|+C$

Statement II $\int \frac{(1+x)^2}{\sqrt{x}}dx$ is equal to $2\sqrt{x}+\frac{2}{5}x^{5/2}+\frac{4}{3}x^{3/2}+C.$ • *Evaluate* [1]

(a) Only Statement I is correct.
(b) Only Statement II is correct.
(c) Both Statements I and II are correct.
(d) Neither I nor II is correct.

(vii) If $x+4y=14$ is a normal to the curve $y^2=\alpha x^3-\beta$ at (2, 3), then the value of $\alpha+\beta$ is • *Evaluate* [1]

(a) 9 (b) 5
(c) 7 (d) –7

(viii) The graph of the function $f(x)$ is given below. • *Analysis* [1]

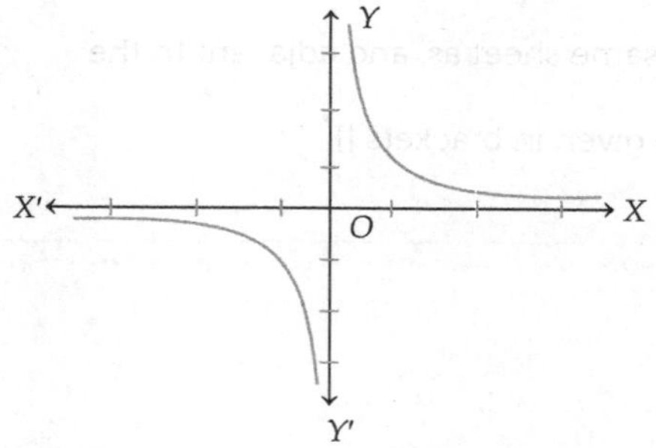

(a) $f(x)$ is continuous at $x=0$.
(b) $f(x)$ is differentiable at $x=0$.
(c) $f(x)$ is discontinuous but differentiable.
(d) $f(x)$ is not differentiable at $x=0$.

(ix) For the differential equation $\frac{d^2y}{dx^2}+y=0$, let its solution be $y=\phi_1(x)=2\sin\left(x+\frac{\pi}{4}\right)$

Assertion (A) The function $y=\phi_1(x)$ is called the particular solution.

Reason (R) The solution which is free from arbitrary constant, is called a particular solution.

Choose the correct option. • *Recall* [1]

(a) Both A and R are correct and R is the correct explanation of A.
(b) Both A and R are correct but R is not the correct explanation of A.
(c) A is correct but R is incorrect.
(d) R is correct but A is incorrect.

(x) A discrete random variable X has the probability distribution given as below.

X	0.5	1	1.5	2
P(X)	k	k^2	$2k^2$	k

Consider the following statements.

Statement I The value of k is $\frac{1}{3}$.

Statement II The mean of distribution is $\frac{23}{18}$.

Choose the correct option. • *Evaluate* [1]

(a) Statement I is true.
(b) Statement II is true.
(c) Both Statements are true.
(d) Both Statements are false.

(xi) If A and B are events such that $P(A)=\frac{1}{2}$, $P(B)=\frac{1}{3}$ and $P(A\cap B)=\frac{1}{4}$, $P\left(\frac{A'}{B'}\right)$ is equal to • *Application* [1]

(a) $\frac{2}{3}$ (b) $\frac{5}{12}$ (c) $\frac{5}{8}$ (d) $\frac{3}{4}$

(xii) Find the domain and the range of the function $f(x)=\sqrt{3-2x}$. • *Evaluate* [1]

(xiii) If $A'=\begin{bmatrix}-2 & 3\\ 1 & 2\end{bmatrix}$ and $B=\begin{bmatrix}-1 & 0\\ 1 & 2\end{bmatrix}$, then find $[A+2B]'$. • *Understanding* [1]

(xiv) Evaluate $\sin^{-1}(\sin 10)$. • *Evaluate* [1]

(xv) Evaluate $\int_{-\pi/6}^{\pi/6} x^3\cos^2 x\,dx$. • *Evaluate* [1]

2. (i) Prove that $\tan^{-1}\left(\frac{\cos x}{1-\sin x}\right)=\left(\frac{\pi}{4}+\frac{x}{2}\right), x\in\left(\frac{-\pi}{2},\frac{\pi}{2}\right)$ • *Application* [2]

Or

(ii) Find the value of $\tan^{-1}\left(-\frac{1}{\sqrt{3}}\right)+\cot^{-1}\left(\frac{1}{\sqrt{3}}\right)+\tan^{-1}\left[\sin\left(\frac{-\pi}{2}\right)\right]$. • *Application* [2]

3. Show that $f(x)=|x-2|+|x-3|$ is not differentiable at $x=2$. • *Analysis* [2]

4. Differentiate $\tan^{-1}\left(\frac{1+2x}{1-2x}\right)$ w.r.t. $\sqrt{1+4x^2}$.
• *Understanding* [2]

5. (i) The probabilities of two students A and B coming to the school in time are $\frac{3}{7}$ and $\frac{5}{7}$, respectively. Assuming that the events, 'A coming in time' and 'B coming in time' are independent, find the probability of only one of them coming to the school in time. • *Analysis* [2]

Or

(ii) In a college, 70% students pass in Physics, 75% pass in Mathematics and 10% students fail in both. One student is chosen at random. What is the probability that he passes in Physics and Mathematics? • *Analysis* [2]

6. If area of a triangle with vertices $(k, 0), (1, 1)$ and $(0, 3)$ is 5 sq units, then find the value(s) of k. • *Understanding* [2]

7. Find the intervals in which the function given by $f(x) = \sin x + \cos x, 0 \le x \le 2\pi$ is
(i) increasing. (ii) decreasing.
• *Application* [4]

8. If $x = a\cos\theta + b\sin\theta$, $y = a\sin\theta - b\cos\theta$, then show that $y^2\frac{d^2y}{dx^2} - x\frac{dy}{dx} + y = 0$. • *Analysis* [4]

9. (i) Find $\int \frac{\cos\theta}{(4+\sin^2\theta)(5-4\cos^2\theta)}d\theta$
• *Evaluate* [4]

Or (ii) Find $\int \frac{(x^2+1)(x^2+4)}{(x^2+3)(x^2-5)}dx$
• *Evaluate* [4]

10. (i) If $f(x)$ is a continuous function defined on $[0, a]$, then $\int_0^a f(x)\,dx = \int_0^a f(a-x)\,dx$.

Using the above information, answer the following questions.
• *Understanding & Evaluate* [4]

(a) Evaluate $\int_0^a \frac{f(x)\,dx}{f(x)+f(a-x)}$.

(b) If $f(x) = \frac{\sin x - \cos x}{1 + \sin x\cos x}$, then find $f\left(\frac{\pi}{2} - x\right)$.

(c) Evaluate $\int_0^{\pi/2} f(x)\,dx$.

(d) If $g(x) = \log(1 + \tan x)$, then find $g\left(\frac{\pi}{4} - x\right)$.

Or

(ii) The given integral $\int f(x)\,dx$ can be transformed into another form by changing the independent variable x to t by substituting $x = g(t)$.
Consider $I = \int f(x)\,dx$
Put $x = g(t) \Rightarrow dx = g'(t)\,dt$
Thus, $I = \int f[g(t)]\,g'(t)\,dt$
This process known as integration by substitution method.
Based on the above information, answer the following questions.
• *Understanding & Evaluate* [4]

(a) Evaluate $\int \frac{\cos(\tan^{-1}x)}{1+x^2}dx$.

(b) Evaluate $\int \sin(ax+b)\cos x\,(ax+b)dx$.

(c) Evaluate $\int \frac{1}{x + x\log x}dx$.

11. A factory produces three types of gadgets: Gadget X, Gadget Y and Gadget Z. Each gadget requires different amounts of three raw materials: Material A, Material B and Material C. The requirements for each gadget are given in the table below.

	Gadget X	Gadget Y	Gadget Z
Material A	2 units	1 unit	3 units
Material B	4 units	2 units	5 units
Material C	3 units	3 units	2 units

The factory has 20 units of Material A, 30 units of Material B and 25 units of Material C available. • *Application* [6]

On the basis of above information, answer the following questions.

(i) Set up the system of equations using the above information.

(ii) Find the inverse of the coefficient matrix.

(iii) Determine how many units of Gadget X, Gadget Y and Gadget Z the factory should produce to utilize all materials completely.

12. (i) Find the equation of tangents to the curve $y = \cos(x+y), -2\pi \le x \le 2\pi$, that are parallel to the line $x + 2y = 0$. • *Application* [6]

Or

(ii) Find the point P on the curve $y^2 = 4ax$, which is nearest to the point $(11a, 0)$. • *Application* [6]

13. (i) An insurance company insured 2000 scooter drivers, 4000 car drivers and 6000 truck drivers. The probabilities of an accident involving a scooter, a car and a truck are 0.01, 0.03 and 0.15, respectively. One of the insured persons meets with an accident. What is the probability that he is a scooter driver? • *Analysis* [6]

Or

(ii) There are 5 cards numbered 1 to 5, one number on one card. Two cards are drawn at random without replacement. Let X denotes the sum of the numbers on two cards drawn. Find the mean of X. • *Analysis* [6]

14. Polio drops are delivered to 50K children in a district. The rate at which polio drops are given is directly proportional to the number of children who have not been administered the drops. By the end of 2nd week half the children have been given the polio drops. How many will have been given the drops by the end of 3rd week can be estimated using the solution to the differential equation $\frac{dy}{dx} = k(50 - y)$ where x denotes the number of weeks and y the number of children who have been given the drops. • *Application* [6]

Answer the following questions, using the above information.

(i) State the order of the above given differential equation.

(ii) Find the solution of the differential equation $\frac{dy}{dx} = k(50 - y)$.

(iii) Find the value of C in the particular solution given that $y(0) = 0$ and $k = 0.049$.

(iv) Find the particular solution.

Section B (15 Marks)

15. In subparts (i) to (iii) choose the correct options and in subparts (iv) and (v), answer the questions as instructed. [5]

(i) In the given figure, which vectors are coinitial vectors • *Recall*

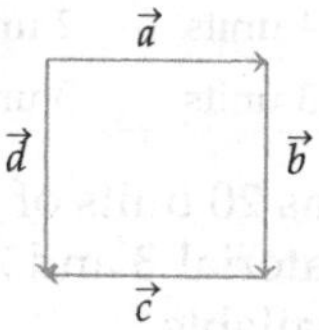

(a) $\vec{a}$ and $\vec{d}$
(b) $\vec{d}$ and $\vec{b}$
(c) $\vec{a}$ and $\vec{c}$
(d) $\vec{a}$ and $\vec{b}$

(ii) The equation of plane through the origin containing the line $\frac{x-1}{5} = \frac{y-2}{4} = \frac{z-3}{5}$ is • *Understanding*

(a) $2x + 5y - 6z = 0$
(b) $x + 5y - 5z = 0$
(c) $x - 5y + 3z = 0$
(d) $x + y + z = 0$

(iii) **Statement I** The position vector of the point while divide the line joining the two points $3\vec{a} - 2\vec{b}$ and $2\vec{a} - 5\vec{b}$ internally in the ratio, 3 : 2 is $\frac{12}{5}\vec{a} - \frac{19}{5}\vec{b}$.

Statement II Let a point C divides the line joining A, B internally in the ratio $m : n$. Then, position vector of point C is given by $\overrightarrow{OC} = \frac{m\overrightarrow{OB} + n\overrightarrow{OA}}{m+n}$, where m and n are position scalars.

(a) Only Statement I is correct.
(b) Only Statement II is correct.
(c) Both Statements are correct.
(d) Neither I nor II is correct.

(iv) The planes $\vec{r}\cdot(2\hat{i} - \lambda\hat{j} + \hat{k}) = 3$ and $\vec{r}\cdot(4\hat{i} + \hat{j} - \mu\hat{k}) = 5$ are parallel. Find λ and μ. • *Understanding*

SP-13

(v) If $\vec{a}$ and $\vec{b}$ are perpendicular vectors, $|\vec{a}+\vec{b}|=13$ and $|\vec{a}|=5$, then find the value of $|\vec{b}|$. • *Evaluate*

16. (i) Write the direction ratios of the vector $\vec{a}=\hat{i}+\hat{j}-2\hat{k}$ and hence calculate its direction cosines. • *Understanding* [2]

Or

(ii) If $\vec{a}=3\hat{i}-\hat{j}$ and $\vec{b}=2\hat{i}+\hat{j}-3\hat{k}$, then express $\vec{b}$ in the form of $\vec{b}=\vec{b_1}+\vec{b_2}$, where $\vec{b_1} \parallel \vec{a}$ and $\vec{b_2} \perp \vec{a}$. • *Understanding* [2]

17. (i) Find the angle between the lines whose direction cosines are given by the equations $3l+m+5n=0$ and $6mn-2nl+5lm=0$. • *Application* [4]

Or

(ii) Find the equation of the lines passing through the point (2, 1, 3) and perpendicular to the lines $\frac{x-1}{1}=\frac{y-2}{2}=\frac{z-3}{3}$ and $\frac{x}{-3}=\frac{y}{2}=\frac{z}{5}$. [4]

18. Find the area of the circle $x^2+y^2=16$, which is exterior to the parabola $y^2=6x$, by using integration. • *Analysis* [4]

Section C (15 Marks)

19. In subparts (i) and (ii) choose the correct options and in subparts (iii) to (v), answer the questions as instructed. [5]

(i) In a bivariate distribution, it was found $\sigma_x=3$, the regression line of y on x is $8x-10y+66=0$ while regression line of x on y is $40x-18y-214=0$, then b_{yx} equals to • *Understanding*

(a) 0.7 (b) 0.8
(c) 0.6 (d) None of these

(ii) The total revenue (in ₹) received from the sale of x units of a product is given by $R(x)=x^2+26x+10$, then the marginal revenue when $x=5$ is • *Understanding*

(a) 30 (b) 32
(c) 36 (d) 38

(iii) The total revenue (in ₹) received from the sale of x units of a product is given by $R(x)=13x^2+26x+15$. Find the marginal revenue when $x=7$. • *Understanding*

(iv) Find the slope of the average cost of function $C(x)=5e^{-x/5}$.

(v) Using the data $\bar{x}=24, \bar{y}=28, b_{yx}=-2.3$ and $b_{xy}=-0.25$, then find the regression equation y on x. Also, find the most likely value of y when $x=30$. • *Analysis*

20. (i) Profit function of a company is given as $P(x)=\frac{24x}{5}-\frac{x^2}{100}-500$, where x is the number of units produced. What is the maximum profit of the company? Company feels its social responsibility and decided to contribute 10% of its profit for a orphanage. Find the amount contributed to the orphanage. • *Application* [2]

Or

(ii) The marginal revenue function for a commodity is given by $MR=\frac{ab}{(x-b)^2}-c$.

Find the total revenue function and the demand function and prove that the average revenue function is given by $AR=\frac{a}{b-x}-c$. • *Application* [2]

21. In a partially destroyed laboratory record of an analysis of a correlation data the following results are only available.

Variance of $x=9$, regression equations are $8x-10y+66=0$ and $40x-18y=214$.

What were (*a*) the mean values of x and y and find b_{yx} and b_{xy} (*b*) the standard deviation of y. • *Application* [4]

22. (i) David wants to invest atmost ₹ 12000 in bonds *A* and *B*. According to the rule, he has to invest atleast ₹ 2000 in bond *A* and atleast ₹ 4000 in bond *B*. If the rates of interest on bonds *A* and *B*, respectively are 8% and 10% per annum.

Formulate the problem as linear programming problem and solve it graphically for maximum interest. Also, determine the maximum interest received in a year. • *Analysis* [4]

Or

(ii) A firm has to transport 1200 packages using large vans which can carry 200 packages each and small vans which can take 80 packages each. The cost for engaging each large van is ₹ 400 and each small van is ₹ 200. Not more than ₹ 3000 is to be spent on the job and the number of large vans cannot exceed the number of small vans. Formulate this problem as a LPP given that the objective is to minimise cost. What will be the minimum cost? • *Analysis* [4]

Answer Key

1. (i) (c) (ii) (c) (iii) (b) (iv) (c)
(v) (c) (vi) (c) (vii) (a) (viii) (d)
(ix) (a) (x) (c) (xi) (c)
(xii) Domain $= \left(-\infty, \frac{3}{2}\right]$ and Range $= [0, \infty)$
(xiii) $\begin{bmatrix} -4 & 5 \\ 1 & 6 \end{bmatrix}$ (xiv) $3\pi - 10$ (xv) 0

2. *Or* (ii) $\frac{\pi}{12}$ **4.** $\frac{1}{2x\sqrt{1+4x^2}}$

5. (i) $\frac{26}{49}$ *Or* (ii) $\frac{11}{20}$ **6.** $-\frac{7}{2}$ and $\frac{13}{2}$

7. (i) Increasing in $\left[0, \frac{\pi}{4}\right]$ and $\left[\frac{5\pi}{4}, 2\pi\right]$
(ii) Decreasing in $\left[\frac{\pi}{4}, \frac{5\pi}{4}\right]$

9. (i) $\frac{-1}{30}\tan^{-1}\left(\frac{\sin\theta}{2}\right) + \frac{2}{15}\tan^{-1}(2\sin\theta) + C$
(ii) $x + \frac{1}{4\sqrt{3}}\tan^{-1}\left(\frac{x}{\sqrt{3}}\right) + \frac{27}{8\sqrt{5}}\log\left|\frac{x-\sqrt{5}}{x+\sqrt{5}}\right| + C$

10. (i) (a) $\frac{a}{2}$ (b) $-f(x)$ (c) 0 (d) $\log 2 - g(x)$ *Or*
(ii) (a) $\sin(\tan^{-1} x) + C$
(b) $\frac{1}{2a}\sin^2(ax + b) + C$ (c) $\log[(1 + \log x)] + C$

11. (i) $2x + y + 3z = 20$
$4x + 2y + 5z = 30$
$3x + 3y + 2z = 25$
(ii) $A^{-1} = \frac{1}{3}\begin{bmatrix} -11 & 7 & -1 \\ 7 & -5 & 2 \\ 6 & -3 & 0 \end{bmatrix}$
(iii) $x = -12, y = 13, z = 10$

12. (i) $2x + 4y + 3\pi = 0$ and $2x + 4y - \pi = 0$ *Or* (ii) $(9a, 6a)$ and $(9a, -6a)$.

13. (i) $\frac{1}{52}$ *Or* (ii) 6

14. (i) 1 (ii) $-\log|50 - y| = kx + C$ (iii) $\log\frac{1}{50}$
(iv) $50\,(1 - e^{-kx})$

15. (i) (a) (ii) (c) (iii) (c) (iv) $\lambda = -\frac{1}{2}$ and $\mu = -2$ (v) 12

16. (i) 1, 1 and −2; $\left(\frac{1}{\sqrt{6}}, \frac{1}{\sqrt{6}}, \frac{-2}{\sqrt{6}}\right)$ *Or* (ii) $2\hat{i} + \hat{j} - 3\hat{k}$
$= \left(\frac{3}{2}\hat{i} - \frac{1}{2}\hat{j}\right) + \left(\frac{1}{2}\hat{i} + \frac{3}{2}\hat{j} - 3\hat{k}\right)$

17. (i) $\cos^{-1}\left(\frac{1}{6}\right)$ *Or* (ii) $\frac{x-2}{2} = \frac{y-1}{-7} = \frac{z-3}{4}$

18. $\left(\frac{32\pi}{3} - \frac{4}{3}\sqrt{3}\right)$ sq units

19. (i) (b) (ii) (c) (iii) ₹208 (iv) $\frac{-e^{-x/5}(x+5)}{x^2}$
(v) $y + 2.3x = 83.2$, $y = 14.2$

20. (i) ₹ 76 ₹ 7.6 *Or* (ii) $R = \frac{-ab}{(x-b)} - cx - a$
and $p = \frac{a}{b-x} - c$

21. (a) $\bar{x} = 13, \bar{y} = 17, b_{yx} = \frac{4}{5}, b_{xy} = \frac{9}{20}$ (b) 4

22. (i) ₹ 1160 *Or* (ii) ₹ 2571.43

Scan this QR code from your mobile phone to get the explanations of this paper.

SQP Code : **PB-14/15** Series **i-Succeed 14-25/15** Roll No. | | | | | | | | |

Sample Question Paper 14

Mathematics 12th (Code 860)

General Instructions

1. The Question Paper consists of three sections A, B and C.
2. Candidates are required to attempt all questions from Section A and all questions either from Section B Or Section C.
3. Section A Internal choice has been provided in two questions of two marks each, two questions of four marks each and two questions of six marks each.
4. Section B Internal choice has been provided in one questions of two marks and one question of four marks.
5. Section C Internal choice has been provided in one question of two marks and one question of four marks.
6. All working, including rough work, should be done on the same sheet as, and adjacent to the rest of the answer.
7. The intended marks for questions or parts of questions are given in brackets [].
8. Mathematical tables and graph papers are provided.

Time : 3 Hrs.

Max. Marks : 80

Section A (65 Marks)

1. In subparts (i) to (xi) choose the correct options and in subparts (xii) to (xv), answer the questions as instructed.

(i) If $R = \{(a, a^3) : a$ is a prime number less than $5\}$ be a relation. Then, the range of R is

(a) {8, 27} (b) {8, 9, 10}

(c) {4, 8, 27} (d) None of these

• *Understanding* [1]

(ii) Write the principal value of $\tan^{-1}\left[\sin\left(\frac{-\pi}{2}\right)\right]$.

(a) $\frac{\pi}{4}$ (b) $\frac{-\pi}{4}$

(c) $\frac{\pi}{6}$ (d) $\frac{\pi}{2}$

• *Recall* [1]

(iii) If $x\begin{bmatrix}2\\3\end{bmatrix} - y\begin{bmatrix}-1\\1\end{bmatrix} = \begin{bmatrix}10\\5\end{bmatrix}$, then the values of x and y are

(a) −4 and 3 (b) 3 and −4

(c) 3 and −3 (d) 4 and −4

• *Recall* [1]

(iv) For the curve $\sqrt{x} + \sqrt{y} = 1$, $\frac{dy}{dx}$ at $\left(\frac{1}{4}, \frac{1}{4}\right)$ is

• *Understanding* [1]

(a) −2 (b) 0

(c) −1 (d) 2

(v) The value of k for which

$$f(x) = \begin{cases} \frac{3x + 4\tan x}{x}, & \text{when } x \neq 0 \\ k, & \text{when } x = 0 \end{cases}$$ is continuous

at $x = 0$, is

• *Application* [1]

(a) 3 (b) 4

(c) 7 (d) None of these

(vi) If $\int e^x\left(\frac{x-1}{x^2}\right)dx = e^x f(x) + C$. Then, $f(x)$ satisfying the equation is

• *Analysis* [1]

(a) x (b) x^2

(c) $\frac{1}{x}$ (d) None of these

(vii) **Statement I** The slope of the normal to the curve $x=t^2+3t-8$ and $y=2t^2-2t-5$ at $t=2$ is $\frac{7}{8}$ • *Application* [1]

Statement II Slope of the normal at point $P=\frac{1}{\text{Slope of the tangent at point } P}$

(a) Only Statement I is correct.
(b) Only Statement II is correct.
(c) Both Statements I and II are correct.
(d) Neither Statement I nor II is correct.

(viii) **Assertion** (A) If a function $f(x)$ is continuous at $x=a$, then $f(x)$ is also differentiable at $x=a$.

Reason (R) For a function $f(x)$ to be differentiable at $x=a$, it must be continuous at $x=a$. • *Recall* [1]

(a) Both A and R are correct and R is the correct explanation of A.
(b) Both A and R are correct but R is not the correct explanation of A.
(c) A is false but R is true.
(d) A is true but R is false.

(ix) The graph of the function is shown below:

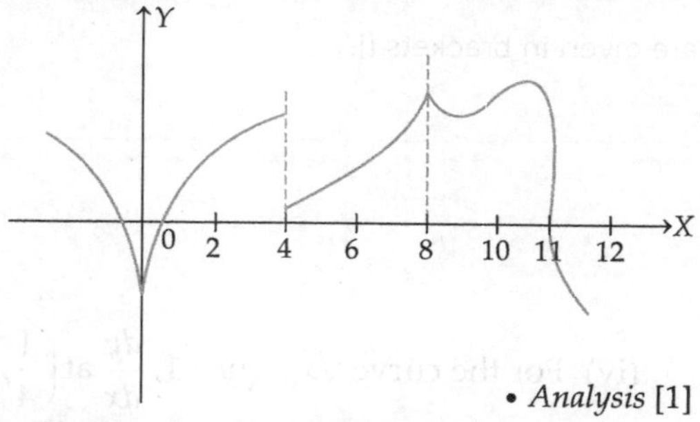

• *Analysis* [1]

Choose the correct option.

(a) $f(x)$ is continuous at $x=4$.
(b) $f(x)$ is not continuous at $x=4$ and not differentiable at $x=8$.
(c) $f(x)$ is differentiable at $x=8$.
(d) $f(x)$ is differentiable at $x=11$.

(x) Consider the probability distribution of a random variable X.

X	0	1	2	3	4
P(X)	0.1	0.25	0.3	0.2	0.15

Statement I The value of $V\left(\frac{X}{2}\right)$ is 0.3618.

Statement II The variance of X is 1.4475.

Choose the correct option. • *Understanding* [1]

(a) Statement I is true; Statement II is true; Statement II is the correct explanation for Statement I
(b) Statement I is true; Statement II is true; Statement II is not the correct explanation for Statement I
(c) Statement I is true but Statement II is false
(d) Statement I is false but Statement II is true

(xi) **Assertion** (A) The value of determinant $\Delta=\begin{vmatrix} \log_3 512 & \log_4 3 \\ \log_3 8 & \log_4 9 \end{vmatrix}$ is $\frac{15}{2}$. • *Application* [1]

Reason (R) We know that $\log_{a^p} m^n = \frac{n}{p}\log_a m$ and $\log_a b \times \log_b a = 1$.

(a) Both A and R are correct and R is the correct explanation of A.
(b) Both A and R are correct but R is not the correct explanation of A.
(c) A is correct but R is incorrect.
(d) A is incorrect but R is correct.

(xii) The radius of a circle is increasing at the rate of 0.7 cm/s. What is the rate of increase of its circumference? • *Application* [1]

(xiii) Show that the function $f(x)=\begin{cases} 1+x, & \text{if } x\le 2 \\ 5-x, & \text{if } x>2 \end{cases}$ is not differentiable at $x=2$. • *Application* [1]

(xiv) If $y=\sqrt{\log x+\sqrt{\log x+\sqrt{\log x+\ldots\infty}}}$, then find $\frac{dy}{dx}$. • *Application* [1]

(xv) The odds against A solving a certain problem are 4 to 3 and the odds in favour of B solving the same problem are 7 to 5. Find the probability that the problem will be solved. • *Analysis* [1]

2. Evaluate the following.

(i) $\sin^{-1}\left(\sin\frac{5\pi}{6}\right)$ • *Evaluate* [2]

Or

(ii) $\tan^{-1}\left(\tan\frac{3\pi}{4}\right)$ • *Evaluate* [2]

3. If $A=\begin{bmatrix} 3 & -2 \\ 4 & 5 \end{bmatrix}$ and $B=\begin{bmatrix} -2 & 4 \\ 3 & 1 \end{bmatrix}$, then verify $(AB)'=B'A'$. • *Application* [2]

4. If $y=\frac{\sin^{-1}x}{\sqrt{1-x^2}}$, then show that

$$(1-x^2)\frac{d^2y}{dx^2}-3x\frac{dy}{dx}-y=0.$$ • *Analysis* [2]

5. (i) Evaluate $\int \frac{dx}{\sin(x-a)\cdot\cos(x-b)}$. [2]

Or

(ii) Evaluate $\int \frac{xe^{2x}}{(1+2x)^2}dx$. • *Evaluate* [2]

6. Let X denotes the number of hours, you study during a randomly selected school day. The probability that X can take the values x has the following form, where k is any unknown constant. • *Analysis* [2]

$$P(x)=\begin{cases}0.1, & \text{if } x=0\\ kx, & \text{if } x=1 \text{ or } 2\\ k(5-x), & \text{if } x=3 \text{ or } 4\\ 0, & \text{otherwise}\end{cases}$$

(i) Find the value of k.

(ii) What is the probability that you study atleast 2 h?

7. (i) Solve the following differential equation $(1+x^2)\frac{dy}{dx}-2xy=(x^2+2)(x^2+1)\forall$, when $x=1$ and $y=2$. • *Application* [4]

(ii) Consider the given equation $\frac{dy}{dx}+Py=Q$.

The above equation is known as linear differential equation. Here, $\quad = e^{\int Pdx}$ and solution is given by $y\cdot \quad = \int Q\cdot \quad dx + C$

Now, consider the given equation $(1+\sin x)\frac{dy}{dx}+y\cos x+x=0$.

On the basis of above information, answer the following questions.

(a) Find the integrating factor of given differential equation.

(b) What is the solution of the given equation?

(c) If $y(0)=1$, then what is the value of $y\left(\frac{\pi}{2}\right)$? • *Application* [4]

8. Show that $f(x)=\log\sin x$ is increasing on $\left(0,\frac{\pi}{2}\right)$ and decreasing on $\left(\frac{\pi}{2},\pi\right)$. • *Analysis* [4]

9. (i) The table below shows some of the values of differentiable functions p and q and their derivatives at certain points.

x	$p(x)$	$p'(x)$	$q(x)$	$q'(x)$
0	2	1	3	−2
1	4	3	1	0
2	1	−1	2	1
3	3	2	4	−4

Given, $r(x)=p[q(x)]$

Based on the above information, answer the following questions.

(a) Find $r'(0)$

(b) Determinate the values of $r(x)$ at $x=1$ and $x=2$. • *Understanding* [4]

Or

(ii) Imagine a company manufactures and sells handmade candles. The company's profit depends on the number of candles produced and sold. Let's say the profit p (in ₹) for producing and selling x candles is given by

$$p(x)=-2x^2+120x-200$$

Find the maximum profit of the company • *Application* [4]

10. $P(x)=-6x^2+120x+25000$ (in ₹) is the total profit function of a company where x denotes the production of the company.

Based on the above information, answer the following questions.

(a) Find the profit of the company, when the production is 3 units.

(b) Find $P'(5)$.

(c) Find the interval in which the profit is strictly increasing.

(d) Find the production, when the profit is maximum. • *Application* [4]

SP-14

11. A small bakery makes three types of pastries. Pastry A, Pastry B and Pastry C. To make these pastries, the bakery uses three key ingredients: Flour, Sugar, and Butter. The amount of each ingredient required for each pastry is given in the table below.

	Pastry A	Pastry B	Pastry C
Flour	2 units	1 unit	3 units
Sugar	1 unit	3 units	2 units
Butter	4 units	2 units	1 unit

The bakery has 25 units of flour, 18 units of sugar and 20 units of butter available.

Based on the above information, answer the following questions.

(i) Set up the system of equation using the given information.

(ii) Find the inverse of the coefficient matrix.

(iii) Determine how many units of Pastry A, Pastry B and Pastry C the bakery should produce to utilise all ingredients completely. • *Application* [6]

12. (i) Find $\int \frac{\log|x|}{(x+1)^2}dx$. • *Evaluate* [6]

Or

(ii) Evaluate $\int_0^{\pi/2} \frac{x \sin x \cos x}{\sin^4 x + \cos^4 x}dx$. • *Evaluate* [6]

13. (i) A letter is known to have come from either 'TATANAGAR' or 'CALCUTTA'. On the envelope just two letters 'TA' are visible. What is the probability that the letter has come from

(a) TATANAGAR?

(b) CALCUTTA? • *Analysis* [6]

Or

(ii) Given three identical boxes *A*, *B* and *C*, box *A* contains 2 gold and 1 silver coin, box *B* contains 1 gold and 2 silver coins and box C contains 3 silver coins. A person chooses a box at random and takes out a coin. If the coin drawn is of silver, find the probability that it has been drawn from the box which also has the remaining two coins of silver. • *Analysis* [6]

14. Consider the scenario, let *H* be the height and *R* be the radius of cylinder inscribed in the cone of height *h* and radius *r* as shown in figure.

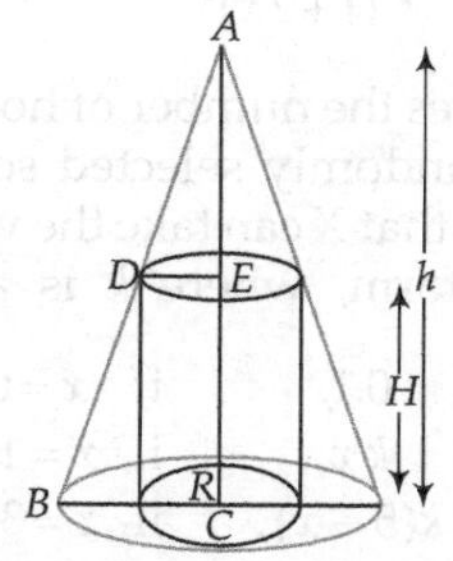

Based on the above information, answer the following questions.

(i) Write the curved surface area of cylinder in terms of *h*, *R* and *r*.

(ii) Prove that the radius of the right circular cylinder of greatest curved surface area which can be inscribed in a given cone is half of that of the cone.

(iii) Find the maximum curved surface area of cylinder.

(iv) If $r = 7$ m and $h = 14$ m, then find the curved surface area of cylinder. • *Application* [6]

Section B (15 Marks)

15. In subparts (i) to (iii) choose the correct options and in subparts (iv) and (v), answer the questions as instructed. [5]

(i) In the given parallelogram *ABCD*, identify the vectors $\vec{a}$ and $\vec{c}$ are

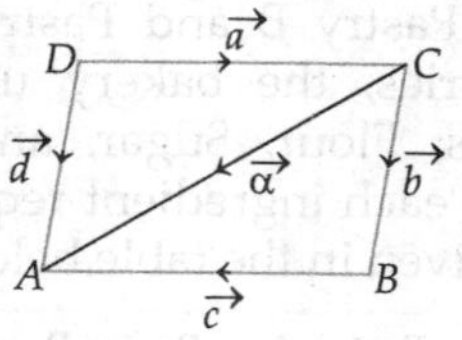

• *Recall*

(a) equal vectors.

(b) collinear but not equal.

(c) coinitial vector.

(d) None of the above

(ii) The equation of plane passing through a point $A(2, -1, 3)$ and parallel to the vectors $\vec{a} = (3, 0, -1)$ and $\vec{b} = (-3, 2, 2)$ is • *Understanding*

(a) $2x - 3y + 6z - 25 = 0$

(b) $2x - 3y + 6z + 25 = 0$

(c) $3x - 2y + 6z - 25 = 0$

(d) $3x - 2y + 6z + 25 = 0$

(iii) **Statement I** The angle between the line $\vec{r} = (-\hat{i} + 3\hat{k}) + \lambda(2\hat{i} + 3\hat{j} + 6\hat{k})$ and plane $\vec{r} \cdot (10\hat{i} + 2\hat{j} - 11\hat{k}) = 3$ is $\sin^{-1}\left(\frac{8}{21}\right)$

Statement II If the equation of a line is $\vec{r} = \vec{a} + \lambda\vec{b}$ and plane is $\vec{r} \cdot \vec{n} = \lambda$, then the angle between the line and normal is $\cos\theta = \frac{|\vec{n} \cdot \vec{b}|}{|\vec{n}| \cdot |\vec{b}|}$.

(a) Only Statement I is correct.

(b) Only Statement II is correct.

(c) Both Statements I and II are correct.

(d) Neither I nor II is correct.

(iv) Show that the three points $A(1,-2,-8)$, $B(5,0,-2)$ and $C(11,3,7)$ are collinear and also find the ratio in which B divides AC. • *Understanding*

(v) The x-coordinate of a point on the line joining the points $P(2,2,1)$ $Q(5,1,-2)$ is 4.
Find its z-coordinate. • *Application*

16. (i) Show that the points $A(6,-7,0)$, $B(16,-19,-4)$, $C(0,3,-6)$ and $D(2,-5,10)$ are such that $\overrightarrow{AB}$ and $\overrightarrow{CD}$ intersect at the point $P(1,-1,2)$. • *Analysis* [2]

Or

(ii) Find the values of a for which the vectors $\vec{r}=(a^2-4)\hat{i}+2\hat{j}-(a^2-9)\hat{k}$ makes an acute angles with the coordinate axes. • *Evaluate* [2]

17. (i) Find the equation of the plane passing through the intersection of the planes $2x+2y-3z-7=0$ and $2x+5y+3z-9=0$ such that the intercepts made by the resulting plane on the X-axis and Z-axis are equal. • *Application* [4]

Or

(ii) Find the image of the point having position vector $\hat{i}+3\hat{j}+4\hat{k}$ in the plane $\vec{r}\cdot(2\hat{i}-\hat{j}+\hat{k})+3=0$ • *Application* [4]

18. Find the area of the region enclosed by the parabola $y^2=x$ and the line $x+y=2$. • *Analysis* [4]

Section C (15 Marks)

19. In subparts (i) and (ii) choose the correct options and in subparts (iii) to (v), answer the questions as instructed. [5]

(i) You are given the following data

	x	y
Arithmetic mean	36	85
Standard deviation	11	8

Correlation coefficient between x and y is 0.66, then regression coefficient b_{xy} is • *Understanding*

(a) 0.9075 (b) 0.8075
(c) 0.7095 (d) 0.4875

(ii) The total revenue received from the sale of x units of a product is given by $R(x)=10x+x^2+1$, then the marginal revenue at $x=20$ is • *Understanding*

(a) 50 (b) 30 (c) 40 (d) 20

(iii) The cost function of a firm is given by $C(x)=3x^2+x+5$, find the average cost when $x=4$? • *Understanding*

(iv) The total variable cost of manufacturing x units in a firm is ₹ $\left(3x+\frac{x^5}{25}\right)$. Show that average variable cost increases with output x. • *Analysis*

(v) Out of the two regression lines $x+2y-5=0$, $2x+3y=8$, find the line of regression of y on x. • *Analysis*

20. (i) The cost of manufacturing a particular type of a cricket ball is given by $C(x)=x^2-1200x+360040$, where x denotes the number of balls produced. How many balls should the company manufacture at which cost is minimum and what would be cost per ball at this level of production? • *Application* [2]

Or

(ii) If the cost function of a product is given by $C(x)=x^3-45x^2-90x$, where x is the numbers of units produced, then how many units of the product must be produced to minimize the marginal cost? • *Application* [2]

21. For observation of pairs (x, y) of the variables X and Y, the following results are obtained: $\Sigma x=125$, $\Sigma y=100$, $\Sigma x^2=1650$, $\Sigma y^2=1500$, $\Sigma xy=50$ and $n=25$.
Find the equation of the line of regression of x on y. Estimate the value of x, if $y=5$. • *Application* [4]

22. (i) A factory manufactures two types of screws A and B, each type requiring the use of two machines, an automatic and a hand-operated. It takes 4 min on the automatic and 6 min on the hand-operated machines to manufacture a packet of screw 'A' while it takes 6 min on the automatic and 3 min on the hand-operated machine to manufacture a

SP-14

packet of screw *B*. Each machine is available for at most 4 h on any day. The manufacturer can sell a packet of screw *A* at a profit of 70 paise and screw *B* at a profit of ₹1.
Assuming that he can sell all the screws he manufactures, how many packets of each type should the factory owner produce in a day in order to maximise his profit? Formulate the above LPP and solve it graphically and find the maximum profit. • *Analysis*

Or

(ii) A company manufactures two types of screws *A* and *B*. All the screws have to pass through a threading machine and a slotting machine. A box of type *A* screws requires 2 min on the threading machine and 3 min on the slotting machine. A box of type *B* screws requires 8 min on the threading machine and 2 min on the slotting machine. In a week, each machine is available for 60 h. On selling these screws, the company gets a profit of ₹ 100 per box on type *A* screws and ₹ 170 per box on type *B* screws.
Formulate this problem as a LPP given that the objective is to maximise profit and solve it graphically. • *Analysis* [4]

Answer Key

1. (i) (a) (ii) (b) (iii) (b) (iv) (c)
(v) (c) (vi) (c) (vii) (d) (viii) (c)
(ix) (b) (x) (b) (xi) (a) (xii) 1.4π cm/s
(xiv) $\frac{1}{x(2y-1)}$ (xv) $\frac{16}{21}$

2. (i) $\frac{\pi}{6}$ *Or* (ii) $-\frac{\pi}{4}$

5. (i) $\frac{1}{\cos(b-a)}\log\left|\frac{\sin(x-a)}{\cos(x-b)}\right|+C$ *Or*
(ii) $\frac{e^{2x}}{4(1+2x)}+C$

6. (i) $\frac{3}{20}$ *Or* (ii) $\frac{3}{4}$

7. (i) $y=x(1+x^2)+(1+x^2)\tan^{-1}x-\frac{\pi}{4}(1+x^2)$
(ii) (a) $1+\sin x$ (b) $y(1+\sin x)=-\frac{x^2}{2}+C$ (c) $\frac{8-\pi^2}{16}$

9. (i) (a) –4 (b) 1 (ii) ₹1600

10. (i) (a) ₹ 25306 (b) 60 (c) (0, 10) (d) 10

11. (i) $2x+y+3z=25$
$x+3y+2z=18$
$4x+2y+z=20$
(ii) $A^{-1}=\frac{1}{25}\begin{bmatrix}1 & -5 & 7\\ -7 & 10 & 1\\ 10 & 0 & -5\end{bmatrix}$
(iii) $x=3, y=1$ and $z=5$.

12. (i) $-\frac{1}{x+1}\log|x|+\log\left|\frac{x}{x+1}\right|+C$ *Or* (ii) $\frac{\pi^2}{16}$

13. (i) (a) $\frac{7}{11}$ (b) $\frac{4}{11}$ *Or* (ii) $\frac{1}{2}$

14. (i) $2\pi h\left(R-\frac{R^2}{r}\right)$ (iii) $\frac{1}{2}\pi rh$ (iv) $154\ \text{m}^2$

15. (i) (b) (ii) (a) (iii) (c) (iv) 2 : 3 (v) –1

16. *Or* (ii) $a\in(-3,-2)\cup(2,3)$

17. (i) $12x+27y+12z=52$ *Or* (ii) $(-3,5,2)$

18. $\frac{9}{2}$ sq units

19. (i) (a) (ii) (a) (iii) ₹14.25 (v) $x+2y-5=0$

20. (i) 600, ₹40 per ball *Or* (ii) 15

21. $22x+9y=146, 4.591$

22. (i) 30 packets of screw *A* and 20 packets to screw *B*; Maximum profit = ₹ 41
Or
(ii) Maximum value 138600
1080 boxes of type A
180 boxes of type B.

Scan this QR code from your mobile phone to get the explanations of this paper.

SQP Code : **PB-15/15** Series **i-Succeed 15-25/15** Roll No.

Sample Question Paper 15

Mathematics 12th (Code 860)

Time : 3 Hrs.

Max. Marks : 80

General Instructions

1. The Question Paper consists of three sections A, B and C.
2. Candidates are required to attempt all questions from Section A and all questions either from Section B Or Section C.
3. Section A Internal choice has been provided in two questions of two marks each, two questions of four marks each and two questions of six marks each.
4. Section B Internal choice has been provided in one questions of two marks and one question of four marks.
5. Section C Internal choice has been provided in one question of two marks and one question of four marks.
6. All working, including rough work, should be done on the same sheet as, and adjacent to the rest of the answer.
7. The intended marks for questions or parts of questions are given in brackets [].
8. Mathematical tables and graph papers are provided.

Section A (65 Marks)

1. In subparts (i) to (xi) choose the correct options and in subparts (xii) to (xv), answer the questions as instructed.

(i) If $R=\{(x,y): x+2y=8\}$ is a relation on N, then the range of R is • *Understanding* [1]

(a) {4, 5} (b) {3, 2, 1}
(c) {1, 2} (d) None of these

(ii) If $\tan^{-1} x+\tan^{-1} y=\frac{\pi}{4}; xy<1$, then the value of $x+y+xy$ is • *Understanding* [1]

(a) 3 (b) 1
(c) 3 (d) None of these

(iii) If $f(x)=\begin{cases} \frac{\sin 5x}{x^2+2x}, & x\neq 0 \\ k+\frac{1}{2}, & x=0 \end{cases}$ is continuous at $x=0$, then the value of k is • *Application* [1]

(a) 1 (b) −2 (c) 2 (d) 1/2

(iv) A box contains 3 orange balls, 3 green balls and 2 blue balls. Three balls are drawn at random from the box without replacement. The probability of drawing 2 green balls and one blue ball is • *Analysis* [1]

(a) $\frac{3}{28}$ (b) $\frac{2}{21}$ (c) $\frac{1}{28}$ (d) $\frac{167}{168}$

(v) **Statement I** If

$$f(x)=\begin{cases} \frac{\sqrt{1+kx}-\sqrt{1-kx}}{x}, & \text{for } -1\leq x<0 \\ 2x^2+3x-2, & \text{for } 0\leq x\leq 1 \end{cases}$$ is

continuous at $x=0$, then k is equal to −2.

Statement II A function $f(x)$ is said to be continuous at $x=C$ if, $\lim_{x\to c} f(x)=\lim_{x\to c^+} f(x)=f(0)$ • *Recall* [1]

(a) Only Statement I is correct.
(b) Only Statement II is correct.
(c) Both Statements are correct.
(d) Neither I nor II is correct.

(vi) If $\int_0^a \frac{1}{4+x^2}dx = \frac{\pi}{8}$, then the value of a is • *Evaluate* [1]

(a) 1 (b) 0 (c) 2 (d) 3

(vii) Two matrices $A=[a_{ij}]$ and $B=[b_{ij}]$ are said to be equal, if they are of same order and for all i and j, their elements are • *Recall* [1]

(a) $a_{ij}=b_{ji}$ (b) $a_{ij}=b_{ij}$
(c) $a_{ij}=-b_{ij}$ (d) $a_{ij}+b_{ij}=0$

(viii) The solution of the differential equation $\frac{dy}{dx}=x^3e^{-2y}$ is • *Application* [1]

(a) $e^{2y}+x^4=C$
(b) $e^{2y}=x^4+C$
(c) $2e^{2y}=x^4+C$
(d) None of the above

(ix) **Assertion** (A) The differential equations $\frac{dx}{dy}+x=\cos y$ and $\frac{dx}{dy}+\frac{-2x}{y}=y^2e^{-y}$ are first order linear differential equations.
Reason (R) The differential equation of the form $\frac{dx}{dy}+P_1x=Q_1$, where P_1 and Q_1 are constants or functions of y only, is called first order linear differential equation.
Choose the correct option. • *Understanding* [1]

(a) Both A and R are correct and R is the correct explanation of A.
(b) Both A and R are correct but R is not the correct explanation of A.
(c) A is correct but R is incorrect.
(d) R is correct but A is incorrect.

(x) Symbolically, we write $\int f(x)dx = F(x)+C$
Statement I Symbol $\int f(x)\,dx$ represents the entire class of anti-derivatives.
Statement II If $\frac{dy}{dx}=f(x)$, then $dy=\int f(x)\,dx$.
Choose the correct option. • *Recall* [1]

(a) Statement I is true but Statement II is false.
(b) Statement I is false but Statement II is true.
(c) Both the statement are true.
(d) Both the statement are false.

(xi) **Assertion** (A) The volume of a sphere is increasing at the rate of 3 cm^3/s, the rate of increase of its surface area, when the radius is 2 cm is 3 cm^2/s.
Reason (R) Suppose quantity y varies with another quantity x, then, of change of y with respect to x at point $x=x_0$ is given by $\left(\frac{dy}{dx}\right)_{x=x_0}$ or $f(x_0)$. • *Application* [1]

(a) Both A and R are correct and R is the correct explanation of A.
(b) Both A and R are correct but R is not the correct explanation of A.
(c) A is correct but R is incorrect.
(d) A is incorrect but R is correct.

(xii) Write the value of $\int \frac{1-\sin x}{\cos^2 x}dx$.

(xiii) For what value of x, the matrix $A=\begin{bmatrix}0 & 3 & 4\\ -3 & 0 & 5\\ x & -5 & 0\end{bmatrix}$ is skew-symmetric matrix? • *Understanding* [1]

(xiv) Evaluate $\int \frac{1}{\sqrt{1+\sin 2x}}dx$. • *Evaluate* [1]

(xv) A die is thrown 6 times. If getting an odd number is a success, then what is the probability of 5 success? • *Analysis* [1]

2. (i) Using the properties of determinants, show that
$$\begin{vmatrix}y+z & x & y\\ z+x & z & x\\ x+y & y & z\end{vmatrix}=(x+y+z)(z-x)^2.$$
• *Application* [2]

Or

(ii) Find the value of θ satisfying
$$\begin{vmatrix}1 & 1 & \sin 3\theta\\ -4 & 3 & \cos 2\theta\\ 7 & -7 & -2\end{vmatrix}=0.$$
• *Application* [2]

3. Nidhi has a cup of hot coffee initially at a temperature of 90°C and leave it in a room where the ambient temperature is 25°C. Over time, the coffee will cool down to the room temperature.
The rate at which the coffee cools is proportional to the difference between its own temperature and ambient temperature.
(a) Set up the differential equation.
(b) Solve the differential equation. • *Analysis* [2]

SP-15

4. Find the intervals in which the function $f(x) = \frac{x^4}{4} - x^3 - 5x^2 + 24x + 12$ is
(i) strictly increasing.
(ii) strictly decreasing. • *Evaluate* [2]

5. (i) Examine the continuity of the function
$$f(x) = \begin{cases} \frac{|\sin x|}{x}, & x \neq 0 \\ 1, & \text{at } x = 0 \end{cases}$$
• *Application* [2]

Or

(ii) Find $\frac{dy}{dx}$, if $y = \sin^{-1}\left(\frac{1-x^2}{1+x^2}\right), 0 < x < 1$.
• *Application* [2]

6. Show that the function $f: R \to R$ defined by $f(x) = \frac{3x-1}{2}, x \in R$ is one-one and onto function. Also, find the inverse of the function f. • *Analysis* [2]

7. Find $\int \frac{x^2 + x + 1}{(x+2)(x^2+1)} dx$.
• *Evaluate*

8. If $y = e^{\sin^{-1} x}$ and $z = e^{-\cos^{-1} x}$, then prove that $\frac{dy}{dz} = e^{\pi/2}$.
• *Application* [4]

9. (i) Solve for x,
$$\tan^{-1}\left(\frac{x-1}{x-2}\right) + \tan^{-1}\left(\frac{x+1}{x+2}\right) = \frac{\pi}{4}.$$
• *Evaluate* [4]

Or

(ii) If $\sec^{-1} x = \text{cosec}^{-1} y$, then show that $\frac{1}{x^2} + \frac{1}{y^2} = 1$.
• *Analysis* [4]

10. (i) The given integral $\int f(x)\, dx$ can be transformed into another form by changing the independent variable 'x' to 't' by substitution $x = g(t)$.
Consider $I = \int f(x)\, dx$
Put $x = g(t)$
$\Rightarrow \quad \frac{dx}{dt} = g'(t)$
$\Rightarrow \quad dx = g'(t)\, dt$
Thus, $I = \int f[g(t)]\, g'(t)\, dt$

Based on the above information, answer the following questions.
(a) Evaluate $\int 2x \sin(x^2 + 1)\, dx$.
(b) Evaluate $\int \frac{\sin(\tan^{-1} x)}{1+x^2} dx$.
(c) Evaluate $\int \sin(ax+b)\cos(ax+b)\, dx$
(d) Evaluate $\int \frac{1}{m^2} \cos^2\left(\frac{1}{m} - 1\right) dm$
• *Evaluate* [4]

Or

(ii) Integrate $\frac{2e^x}{(e^x - 1)(2e^x + 3)}$. Show your work. • *Evaluate* [4]

11. A factory produces three types of widgets : widget *A*, widget *B* and widget *C*. To produce these widgets, the factory uses three essential materials : material *X*, material *Y* and material *Z*. The amount of each material required for each widget is given in the table below.

	Widget *A*	Widget *B*	Widget *C*
Material *X*	1 unit	2 units	3 units
Material *Y*	3 units	2 units	1 unit
Material *Z*	2 units	1 unit	2 units

The factory has 44 units of material *X*, 36 units of material *Y* and 34 units of material *Z* available.
Based on the above information, answer the following questions.
(i) Set up the system of equations using the given information.
(ii) Find the inverse of the coefficients matrix.
(iii) Determine how many units of widget *A*, widget *B* and widget *C*, the factory should produce to utilise all materials completely? • *Application* [6]

SP-15

12. (i) A 13 m long ladder is leaning against a wall, touching the wall at a certain height from the ground level. The bottom of the ladder is pulled away from the wall, along the ground, at the rate of 2 m/s. How fast is the height on the wall decreasing when the foot of the ladder is 5 m away from the wall?
• *Application* [6]

Or

(ii) A window has the shape of a rectangle surmounted by an equilateral triangle. If the perimeter of the window is 12 m, then find the dimensions of the rectangle that will produce the largest area of the window. • *Application* [6]

13. (i) In a factory producing light bulbs, 2% of the produced bulbs are defective. A quality control test is conducted, where

- If a bulb is defective, the test correctly identifies it as defective 98% of the time (true positive rate).
- If a bulb is not defective, the test incorrectly identifies it as defective 3% of the time (false positive rate).

What is the probability that a bulb is actually defective given that it is tested as defective? • *Analysis* [6]

Or

(ii) A weather forecasting model predicts that it will rain tomorrow. Historical data shows.

- It rains 30% of the days.
- When it rains, the model correctly predicts rain 90% of the time (true positive rate).
- When it does not rain, the model incorrectly predicts rain 20% of the time (false positive rate).

What is the probability that it will actually rain tomorrow given that the model predicts rain? • *Analysis* [6]

14. A function $F(x, y)$ is said to be homogenous function of degree n, if $F(x, y) = x^n g\left(\frac{y}{x}\right)$ or $y^n h\left(\frac{x}{y}\right)$ i.e. $F(x, y) = \frac{x+2y}{x-y}$ is a homogenous function of degree 0. As

$$F(x, y) = x^0 \left[\frac{1+2\left(\frac{y}{x}\right)}{1-\frac{y}{x}}\right]$$

Also, a differential equation of the form $\frac{dy}{dx} + Py = Q$, where P and Q are function of x only, where IF is given by $e^{\int P dx}$.

Consider the differential equation

$$(xy - x^2)dy = y^2 dx$$

Based on the above information, answer the following questions.

(i) Show that the given differential equation is homogenous.

(ii) Find the general solution of the given differential equation.

(iii) Find the particular solution for $y(1) = 1$.

(iv) If $\frac{dx}{dv} = \left(\frac{v-1}{v}\right)x$, then find integrating factor. • *Analysis* [6]

Section B (15 Marks)

15. In subparts (i) to (iii) choose the correct options and in subparts (iv) and (v), answer the questions as instructed. [5]

(i) The length of the perpendicular drawn from origin to the plane $3x - 2y + 5z + 10 = 0$ is • *Understanding*

(a) $\frac{1}{\sqrt{38}}$ unit (b) $\frac{10}{\sqrt{37}}$ units

(c) $\frac{5}{\sqrt{38}}$ unit (d) $\frac{10}{\sqrt{38}}$ units

(ii) The value of $\hat{i} \cdot (\hat{j} \times \hat{k}) + \hat{j} \cdot (\hat{k} \times \hat{i}) + \hat{k} \cdot (\hat{i} \times \hat{j})$ is • *Recall*

(a) 0 (b) -1

(c) 1 (d) 3

(iii) Find λ, if the scalar projection of $\vec{a} = \lambda\hat{i} + \hat{j} + 4\hat{k}$ on $\vec{b} = 2\hat{i} + 6\hat{j} + 3\hat{k}$ is 4 units. • *Understanding*

(iv) **Statement I** The vector equation of the line passing through the point (1, 2, 3) and perpendicular to the plane $\vec{r} \cdot (\hat{i} + 2\hat{j} - 5\hat{k}) + 9 = 0$ is $\vec{r} = (\hat{i} + 2\hat{j} + 3\hat{k}) + \lambda(\hat{i} + 2\hat{j} - 5\hat{k})$

Statement II If a line $\vec{r} = \vec{a} + \lambda\vec{b}$ lies in the plane $\vec{r} \cdot \vec{n} = d$, then $\vec{b} \cdot \vec{n} = 0$ • *Understanding*

(a) Only Statement I is correct.

(b) Only Statement II is correct.

(c) Both Statements I and II are correct.

(d) Neither I nor II is correct.

(v) Find the vector and the cartesian equations of the line passing through the point $(5, 2, -4)$, which is parallel to the vector $5\hat{i} + \hat{j} - 7\hat{k}$. • *Application*

16. (i) Let $\vec{a} = 2\hat{i} + \hat{k}$, $\vec{b} = \hat{i} + \hat{j} + \hat{k}$ and $\vec{c} = 4\hat{i} - 3\hat{j} + 7\hat{k}$ be three vectors. Find a vector $\vec{r}$ which satisfies $\vec{r} \times \vec{b} = \vec{c} \times \vec{b}$ and $\vec{r} \cdot \vec{a} = 0$. • *Application* [2]

Or

(ii) Let $\vec{a} = 4\hat{i} + 5\hat{j} - \hat{k}$, $\vec{b} = \hat{i} - 4\hat{j} + 5\hat{k}$ and $\vec{c} = 3\hat{i} + \hat{j} - \hat{k}$. Find a vector $\vec{d}$ which is perpendicular to both $\vec{b}$ and $\vec{c}$ and $\vec{d} \cdot \vec{a} = 21$. • *Application* [2]

Section C (15 Marks)

19. In subparts (i) and (ii) choose the correct options and in subparts (iii) to (v), answer the questions as instructed. [5]

(i) If the total revenue received from the sale of x units of a product is given by $R(x) = 4x^3 + 3x^2 + 7$, then the marginal revenue is • *Understanding*

(a) $12x^2 + 6x$ (b) $24x + 6$
(c) $12x^3 + 3x^2$ (d) $6x^2 + 12x + 5$

(ii) By using the data $\bar{x} = 15$, $\bar{y} = 10$ and $b_{yx} = 2.7$, the regression equation y on x is • *Recall*

(a) $3.7x + 30.5$ (b) $2.7x + 30.5$
(c) $2.7x - 30.5$ (d) $1.7x + 30.5$

(iii) The total cost $C(x)$ associated with the production of x units of an item is given by $C(x) = 0.005x^3 - 0.02x^2 + 30x + 5000$. Find the marginal cost when 3 units are produced. • *Understanding*

(iv) Calculate the value of b_{yx} for the following data.
$\{(x, y): (5, 2), (7, 4), (8, 3), (4, 2), (6, 4)\}$ • *Evaluate*

(v) Determine the cost of producing 300 cars, if the marginal cost (in ₹ per unit) is given by $MC(x) = 3x^2 + 10$ • *Understanding*

20. (i) The relation between total cost y and the output x is given by $y = 3x\left(\frac{x+7}{x+5}\right) + 5$. Prove that the marginal cost falls continuously as the output increases. • *Analysis* [2]

Or

(ii) The relationship between sales, TR(x) and advertising cost, ₹x is given by $TR(x) = \frac{32000x}{500 + x}$. It is known that gross profit is 25% of the sales. Determine

(a) the corresponding net profit as a function of x, $P(x)$.
(b) the value of x which maximises $P(x)$ and
(c) maximised $P(x)$. • *Analysis* [2]

17. (i) From the point $P(1, 2, 4)$, a perpendicular is drawn on the plane $2x + y - 2z + 3 = 0$. Find the length and the coordinates of the foot of the perpendicular. • *Evaluate* [4]

Or

(ii) Find the image of a point having position vector $3\hat{i} - 2\hat{j} + \hat{k}$ in the plane $\vec{r} \cdot (3\hat{i} - \hat{j} + 4\hat{k}) = 2$. • *Evaluate* [4]

18. Draw a rough sketch of $y^2 = x + 1$ and $y^2 = -x + 1$ and determine the area enclosed by the two curves. • *Analysis* [6]

21. The data for marks in Physics and History obtained by ten students are given below.

Marks in Physics	15	12	8	8	7	7	7	6	5	3
Marks in History	10	25	17	11	13	17	20	13	9	15

Using this data

(i) Find the line of regression in which Physics is taken as the independent variable.

(ii) A candidate had scored 10 marks in Physics but was absent from the History test. Estimate his probable score for the latter test. • *Application* [4]

22. (i) Solve the following linear programming problem graphically.
Maximise $Z = 34x + 45y$
Subject to constraints are
$x + y \leq 300, 2x + 3y \leq 70$ and $x, y \geq 0$ • *Analysis* [4]

Or

(ii) Determine graphically the minimum value of the objective function $Z = -50x + 20y$, subject to constraints are $2x - y \geq -5, 3x + y \geq 3, 2x - 3y \leq 12$ and $x \geq 0, y \geq 0$. • *Analysis* [4]

Answer Key

1. (i) (b) (ii) (b) (iii) (c) (iv) (a)
(v) (a) (vi) (c) (vii) (b) (viii) (c)
(ix) (a) (x) (a) (xi) (a) (xii) $\tan x - \sec x + C$
(xiii) -4 (xiv) $\frac{1}{\sqrt{2}}\log\left|\tan\left(\frac{\pi}{8}+\frac{x}{2}\right)\right|+C$ (xv) $\frac{1}{60}$

2. *Or* (ii) $n\pi+(-1)^n\frac{\pi}{6}, n\pi$ **3.** (a) $\frac{dT}{dt}=k(T-25), T(0)=90°C$ (b) $T(t)=25+65e^{kt}$

4. (i) $(-3, 2)$ and $(4, \infty)$ (ii) $(-\infty, -3)$ and $(2, 4)$

5. (i) Discontinuous at $x=0$ *Or* (ii) $\frac{-2}{1+x^2}$ **6.** $f^{-1}(x)=\frac{2x+1}{3}$

7. $\frac{3}{5}\log|x+2|+\frac{1}{5}\log|x^2+1|+\frac{1}{5}\tan^{-1}x+C$

9. (i) $\pm\frac{1}{\sqrt{2}}$ **10.** (i) (a) $-\cos^2(x+1)+C$ (b) $-\cos(\tan^{-1}x)+C$ (c) $\frac{1}{4a}\cos(2ax+2b)+C$

(d) $-\frac{1}{4}\sin\left[\sin 2\left(\frac{1}{m}-1\right)\right]\frac{1}{2}\left(\frac{1}{m}-1\right)+C$ *Or* (ii) $\frac{2}{5}\log(e^x-1)-\frac{2}{5}\log\left(e^x+\frac{3}{2}\right)+C$

11. (i) $x+2y+3z=44, 3x+2y+z=36, 2x+y+2z=34$

(ii) $A^{-1}=-\frac{1}{8}\begin{bmatrix}3 & -1 & -4\\ -4 & -4 & 8\\ -1 & 3 & -4\end{bmatrix}$ (iii) $x=5, y=6, z=9$

12. (i) $\frac{5}{6}$ m/s *Or* (ii) $\frac{18-6\sqrt{3}}{6-\sqrt{3}}$ and $\frac{12}{6-\sqrt{3}}$.

13. (i) 40% *Or* (ii) 65.85% **14.** (ii) $\frac{y}{x}-\log|y|=C$ (iii) $\frac{y}{x}-\log|y|=1$ (iv) $v e^{-v}$

15. (i) (d) (ii) (d) (iii) 5 (iv) (c)

(v) $\vec{r}=5\hat{i}+2\hat{j}-4\hat{k}+\lambda(5\hat{i}+\hat{j}-7\hat{k})$ and $\frac{x-5}{5}=\frac{y-2}{1}=\frac{z+4}{-7}$

16. (i) $-\hat{i}-8\hat{j}+2\hat{k}$ *Or* (ii) $-\frac{1}{3}(\hat{i}-16\hat{j}-13\hat{k})$ **17.** (i) $\frac{1}{3}$ unit and $\left(\frac{11}{9},\frac{19}{9},\frac{34}{9}\right)$ *Or* (ii) $(0, -1, -3)$

18. $\frac{8}{3}$ sq units **19.** (i) (a) (ii) (c) (iii) ₹ 30.015 (iv) 0.4 (v) ₹ 27003000

20. *Or* (ii) (a) $\frac{8000x}{500+x}-x$ (b) ₹ 1500 (c) ₹ 4500

21. (i) $24y=5x+321$ (ii) 15.5 (approx.)

22. (i) Maximum value $=1190$ which occurs at (35, 0) *Or* (ii) No minimum value exists.

Scan this QR code from your mobile phone to get the explanations of this paper.

Knowledge Booster Zone

Welcome to the Knowledge Booster Zone !

This section is dedicated to enhancing your understanding of key concepts. Here, you will find chapter-wise revision notes designed to solidify your **foundational knowledge**. Use these notes to review and reinforce what you've learned, ensuring you're well-prepared for each topic.

Progress Tracker **Tick the papers as you complete them.**

- ☐ Relations and Functions
- ☐ Inverse Trigonometric Functions
- ☐ Matrices
- ☐ Determinants
- ☐ Continuity and Differentiability
- ☐ Differentiation
- ☐ Application of Derivatives
- ☐ Indefinite Integrals
- ☐ Definite Integrals
- ☐ Differential Equations
- ☐ Probability
- ☐ Vector Algebra
- ☐ Three-Dimensional Geometry
- ☐ Applications of Integrals
- ☐ Application of Calculus in Commerce and Economics
- ☐ Linear Regression
- ☐ Linear Programming

Chapter 1 : **Relations and Functions**

1. Relation on a Set

Let A be a non-empty set, then a relation R from A to itself, i.e. a subset of $A \times A$, is called a relation on set A (or a relation in set A).

e.g. Let $A = \{1, 2, 3, 4\}$, then

$$R = \{(a, b) \in A \times A : a - b = 3\} = \{(4\ 1)\}$$

is a relation on set A.

Suppose a relation R is defined on two non-empty sets from A to B such that it is a subset of $A \times B$. Then, set A is called **domain** and set B is called **codomain**.

2. Empty or Void Relation

Relation R on a set A is called an empty relation, if no element of A is related to any element of A.

i.e. $R = \phi \subset A \times A$.

Note Empty relation is always a smallest relation on set A.

3. Universal Relation

Relation R on a set A is called a universal relation, if each element of A is related to every element of A

i.e. $R = A \times A$.

Note (i) A universal relation is always a largest relation on set A.
(ii) Both the relations empty and universal are sometimes known as **trivial relations.**

4. Identity Relation

Relation R on a set A is called an identity relation, if each element of A is related to itself only and it is denoted by I_A.

i.e. $I_A = R = \{(a, a) : a \in A\}$.

5. Reflexive Relation

Relation R on a set A is called reflexive relation, f $(a, a) \in R$, for every $a \in A$, i.e. $aRa, \forall a \in A$.

6. Symmetric Relation

Relation R on a set A is called symmetric relation, if $(a, b) \in R$ $\Rightarrow (b, a) \in R$, for every $a, b \in A$.

i.e. $aRb \Rightarrow bRa,\ \forall a, b \in A$.

7. Transitive Relation

Relation R on a set A is called transitive relation, if $(a, b) \in R$ and $(b, c) \in R \Rightarrow (a, c) \in R, \forall a, b, c \in A$,

i.e. aRb and $bRc \Rightarrow aRc, \forall a, b, c \in A$.

Note Identity relation is always reflexive, symmetric and transitive.

8. Equivalence Relation

A relation R on a set A is said to be an equivalence relation iff it is

(i) **reflexive** i.e. aRa or $(a, a) \in R, \forall a \in A$.

(ii) **symmetric** i.e. $aRb \Rightarrow bRa$ or $(a, b) \in R \Rightarrow (b, a) \in R$, where $a, b \in A$.

(iii) **transitive** i.e. if aRb and bRc, then aRc or $(a, b) \in R$ and $(b, c) \in R \Rightarrow (a, c) \in R$, where $a, b, c \in A$.

Note Identity relation on a non-empty set is always an equivalence relation.

10. Function as a Special Relation

Let A and B be two non-empty sets. A function from set A to set B is a relation from A to B (denoted by f) satisfying the following conditions

(i) for each $a \in A$, there exists $b \in B$ such that $(a, b) \in f$.

(ii) no two distinct ordered pairs in f have the same first element.

e.g. If $A = \{1, 2, 3\}$ and $B = \{4, 5\}$, then $f = \{(1, 4), (2, 5), (3, 4)\}$ is a function but $f = \{(1, 4), (1, 5), (2, 4), (3, 5)\}$ is not a function, because the ordered pairs (1, 4) and (1, 5) have the same first element.

If f is a function from A to B and $(a, b) \in f$, then we can write $f(a) = b$, where b is called the **image** of a under f and a is called the **pre-image** of b under f.

Note Every function is a relation but converse is not always true. e.g. If $A = \{1, 2, 3\}$ and $B = \{1, 4\}$, then $R = \{(1, 1), (1, 4), (2, 4)\}$ is a relation but not a function.

11. Function as a Rule

For any two non-empty sets A and B, a function f from A to B is a rule which associates each element of set A to a unique element of set B. It is represented by

$$f : A \to B \text{ or } A \xrightarrow{f} B.$$

Note If $n(A) = p$ and $n(B) = q$, then the **number of functions** defined from A to B is q^p.

12. The Notation $y = f(x)$

Let $x \in A$ is associated to $y \in B$ under the function $f : A \to B$, then the value of y depends upon the choice of x. So, we can say that y is a function of x and write it as $y = f(x)$.

13. Domain, Codomain and Range of a Function

Consider a function $f : A \to B$, then elements of set A are called **domain** of f and elements of set B are called **codomain** of f, and the set of all f-images obtained in set B corresponding to each element belongs to set A is called **range** of f.

14. Real Valued Function

A function, whose codomain is a set (or a subset) of real numbers, is known as real valued function and a function whose domain and codomain both are the sets (or subsets) of real numbers, is known as **real function**.

Note that every real function is a real valued function, but converse may not be true.

15. Some Special Real Functions

Function	Graph
Identity function $f(x) = x, \forall x \in R$ Domain $\to R$ Range $\to R$	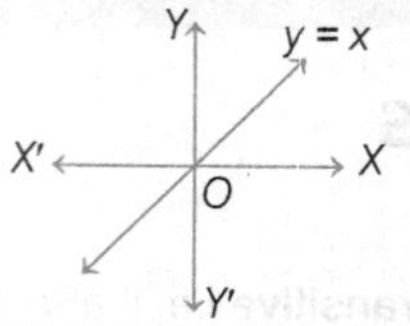
Constant function $f(x) = c, \forall x \in R$ Domain $\to R$ Range $\to \{c\}$	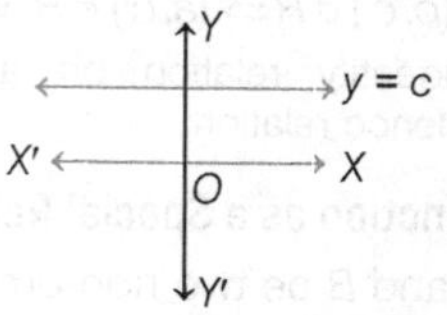
Reciprocal function $f(x) = \frac{1}{x}, \forall x \in R - \{0\}$ Domain $\to R - \{0\}$ Range $\to R - \{0\}$	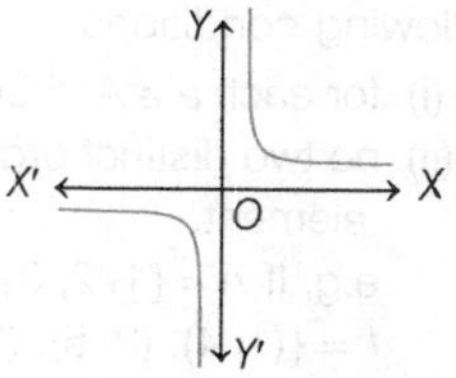
Greatest integer function $f(x) = [x], \forall x \in R$ Domain $\to R$ Range $\to I$	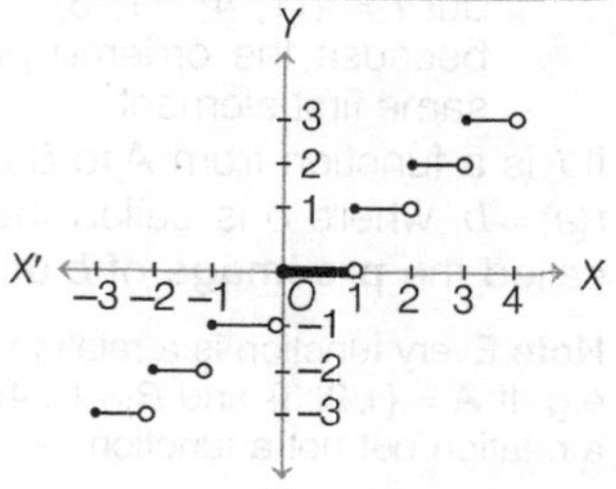

Properties of greatest integer function

If $n < x < n + 1$, where n is a greatest integer less than x and x is a real number, then

- $[x] = n$
- $[-x] = -[x] - 1$
- $[x + m] = [x] + m$, for any integer m.

Function	Graph
Modulus function $f(x) = \lvert x \rvert, \forall x \in R = \begin{cases} x, & \text{if } x \ge 0 \\ -x, & \text{if } x < 0 \end{cases}$ Domain $\to R$ Range $\to [0, \infty)$	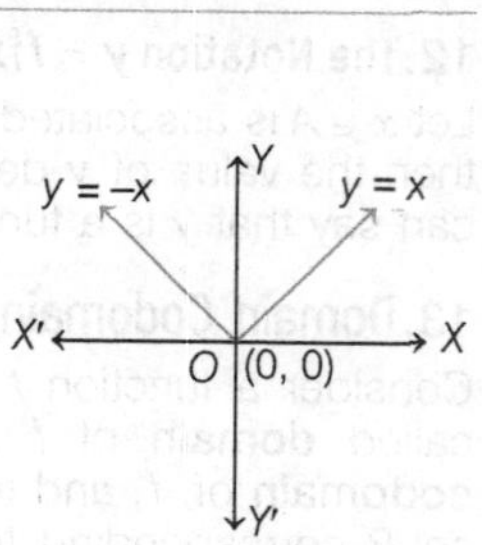

Properties of modulus function

Let $x, y \in R$ (set of real numbers).

Then,

- $\sqrt{x^2} = |x|$
- $x^2 \le a^2 \Leftrightarrow |x| \le a \Leftrightarrow -a \le x \le a$
- $x^2 \ge a^2 \Leftrightarrow |x| \ge a \Leftrightarrow x \le -a$ or $x \ge a$
- $|x \pm y| \le |x| + |y|$
- $|x - y| \ge ||x| - |y||$

Function	Graph
Signum function $f(x) = \text{sgn}(x) = \frac{\lvert x \rvert}{x}$ or $f(x) = \begin{cases} -1, & \text{for } x < 0 \\ 0, & \text{for } x = 0 \\ 1, & \text{for } x > 0 \end{cases}$ Domain $\to R$ Range $\to \{-1, 0, 1\}$	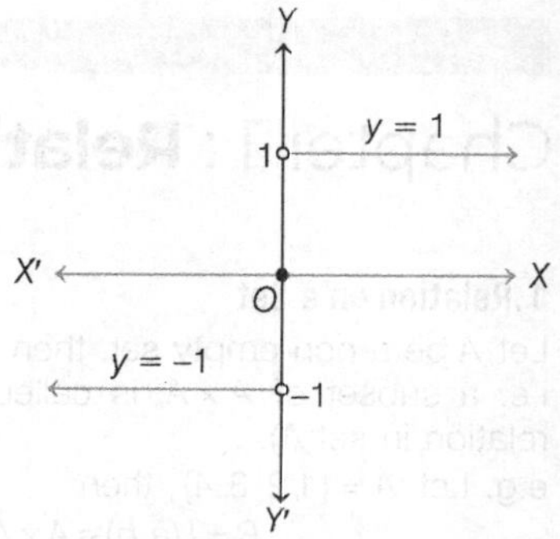
Exponential function $f(x) = a^x$, where $a > 0$ and $a \ne 1 \forall x \in R$ *Case* I When $a > 1$, $f(x) = a^x \to \begin{cases} < 1, & \text{for } x < 0 \\ = 1, & \text{for } x = 0 \\ > 1, & \text{for } x > 0 \end{cases}$	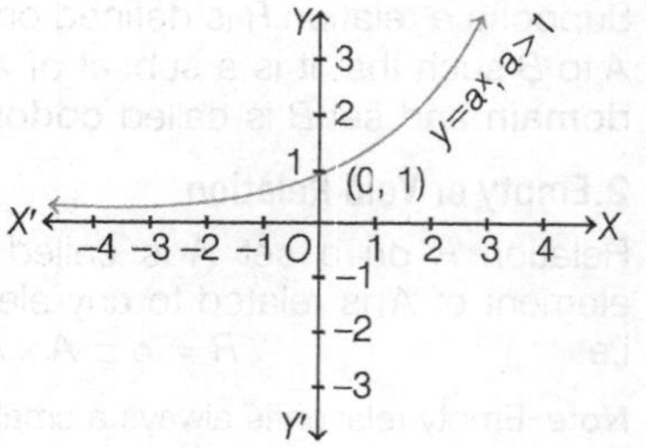
Case II When $0 < a < 1$, $f(x) = a^x \to \begin{cases} > 1, & \text{for } x < 0 \\ = 1, & \text{for } x = 0 \\ < 1, & \text{for } x > 0 \end{cases}$ Domain $\to R$ Range $\to (0, \infty)$	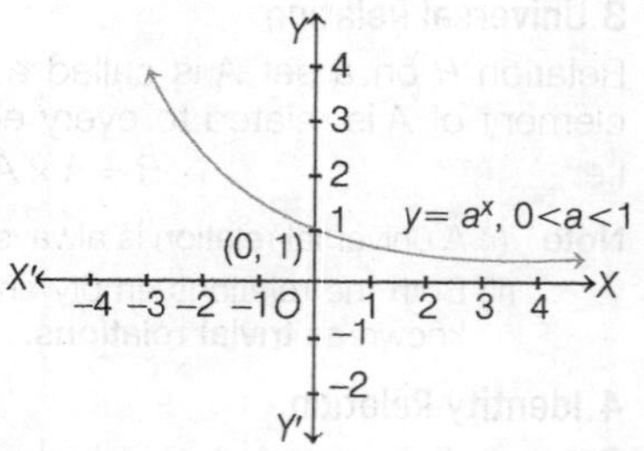
Logarithmic function $f(x) = \log_a x, \forall x > 0$, where $a > 0$ and $a \ne 1$ *Case* I When $a > 1$, $f(x) = \log_a x = \begin{cases} < 0, & \text{for } 0 < x < 1 \\ = 0, & \text{for } x = 1 \\ > 0, & \text{for } x > 1 \end{cases}$	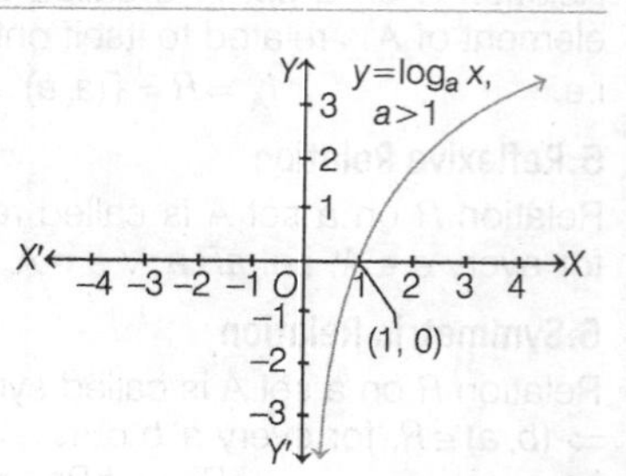
Case II When $0 < a < 1$, $f(x) = \log_a x = \begin{cases} > 0, & \text{for } 0 < x < 1 \\ = 0, & \text{for } x = 1 \\ < 0, & \text{for } x > 1 \end{cases}$ Domain $\to R^+$ Range $\to R$	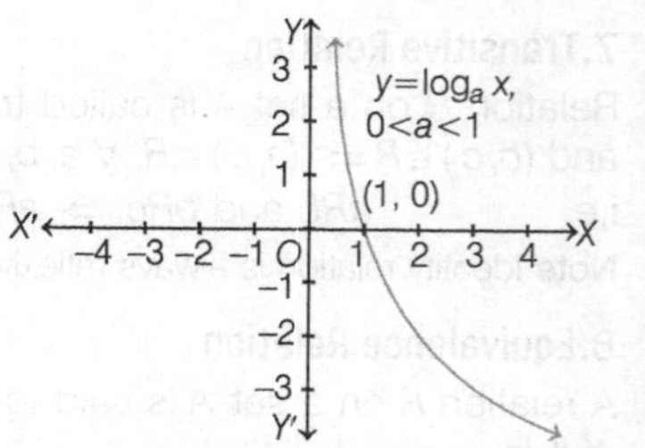

16. Types of Functions

One-One (Injective) Function

A function $f: A \rightarrow B$ is called a one-one or injective function, if distinct elements of A have distinct images in E, i.e. for every $a_1, a_2 \in A$, if $a_1 \neq a_2$, then $f(a_1) \neq f(a_2)$ and if $f(a_1) = f(a_2)$, then $a_1 = a_2$.

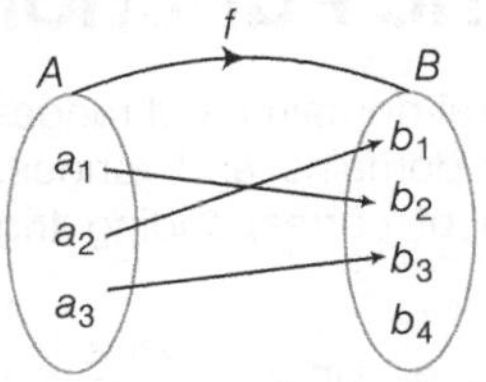

Many-One Function

A function $f: A \rightarrow B$ is called a many-one function, if there exist atleast two distinct elements in A, whose images are same in B, i.e. if there exist $a_1, a_2 \in A$, such that $a_1 \neq a_2$ and $f(a_1) = f(a_2)$, then f is many-one. In other words, a function $f: A \rightarrow B$ is called a many-one function, if it is not one-one.

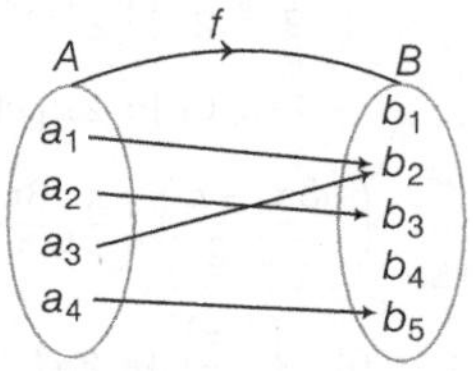

17. Methods to Check Whether a Function is One-One or Many-One

Method I In this we use the following steps

I. First, consider any two arbitrary elements, say $a_1, a_2 \in$ (domain of function).

II. Put $f(a_1) = f(a_2)$ and simplify the equation.

III. If we get $a_1 = a_2$, then f is one-one, otherwise f is many-one.

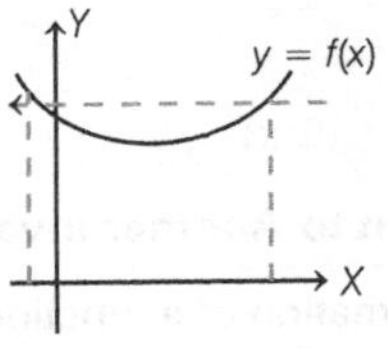

Method II (Horizontal line test) If a horizontal line intersects the graph of function more than once, then f is not one-one.

18. Onto (Surjective) and Into Function

A function $f: A \rightarrow B$ is said to be onto (or surjective), if every element of B is the image of at least one element of A under f, i.e. for every $b \in B$, there exists an element a in A such that $f(a) = b$.

In other words, $f: A \rightarrow B$ is onto iff Range of $f = B$

i.e. Range = Codomain

A function $g: X \rightarrow Y$ is an into function, if there exists one element in Y, which have no pre-image in X. In other words, if a function is not onto then it is an into function.

Let $f: A \rightarrow B$ and $g: X \rightarrow Y$ be two functions represented by the following diagrams.

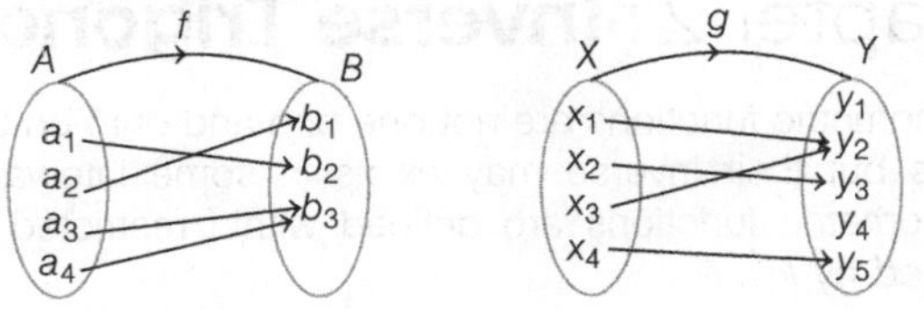

Here, f is an onto function and g is an into function because y_1 and y_4 are elements of Y, which do not have pre-image in X.

19. Bijective (One-to-One Correspondence)

A function $f: A \rightarrow B$ is said to be bijective, if f is both one-one and onto, i.e. all elements of A have distinct images in B and every element of B is the image of some elements of A.

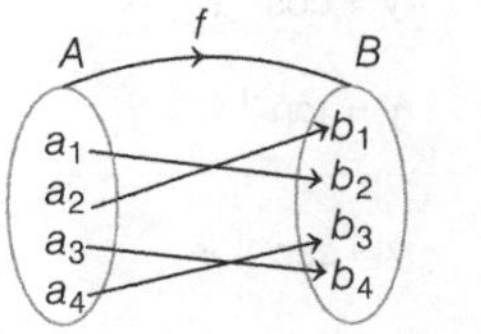

Note If A and B are finite sets having the same number of elements n. Then, number of bijections from A to B is $n!$.

20. Invertible Functions

A function $f: A \rightarrow B$ is defined to be invertible, if there exists a function $g: B \rightarrow A$, such that $gof = I_A$ and $fog = I_B$. Here, the function g is called the **inverse of f** and denoted by f^{-1}.

A function whose inverse exists, is called an invertible function or **invertible**.

(i) Domain (f^{-1}) = Range (f)

(ii) Range (f^{-1}) = Domain (f)

(iii) If $f(x) = y$, then $f^{-1}(y) = x$ and *vice-versa*.

21. Conditions of Invertibility

A function f is invertible, if and only if f is one-one and onto.

Properties of Inverse Functions

(i) The inverse of a invertible function is unique.

(ii) The inverse of a bijective function is also a bijective function.

(iii) If f is an invertible function, then $(f^{-1})^{-1} = f$.

(iv) If $f: A \rightarrow B$ is bijective, then $f^{-1} of = I_A$ and $fof^{-1} = I_B$.

Chapter 2 : **Inverse Trigonometric Functions**

Trigonometric functions are not one-one and onto on their natural domains and ranges, so their inverse does not exist in all values but their inverse may exists in some interval of their domains and ranges. Thus, we can say that, inverse of trigonometric functions are defined within restricted domains of corresponding trigonometric functions. Inverse of f is denoted by f^{-1}.

Let $y = f(x) = \sin x$ be a function. Then, its inverse is $x = \sin^{-1} y$, or $\sin x \xrightarrow{\text{inverse}} \sin^{-1} x$.

Domain, Range and Principal Values of Inverse Trigonometric Functions

S.No.	Function	Domain	Principal value branch (Range)	Other possible ranges
1.	$y = \sin^{-1} x$	$[-1, 1]$	$\left[-\frac{\pi}{2}, \frac{\pi}{2}\right]$	$\left[\frac{-3\pi}{2}, \frac{-\pi}{2}\right], \left[\frac{\pi}{2}, \frac{3\pi}{2}\right]$ etc.
2.	$y = \cos^{-1} x$	$[-1, 1]$	$[0, \pi]$	$[-\pi, 0]$, $[\pi, 2\pi]$ etc.
3.	$y = \tan^{-1} x$	R	$\left(-\frac{\pi}{2}, \frac{\pi}{2}\right)$	$\left(\frac{-3\pi}{2}, \frac{-\pi}{2}\right), \left(\frac{\pi}{2}, \frac{3\pi}{2}\right)$ etc.
4.	$y = \sec^{-1} x$	$R - (-1, 1)$	$[0, \pi] - \left\{\frac{\pi}{2}\right\}$	$[-\pi, 0] - \left\{-\frac{\pi}{2}\right\}$, $[\pi, 2\pi] - \left\{\frac{3\pi}{2}\right\}$ etc.
5.	$y = \operatorname{cosec}^{-1} x$	$R - (-1, 1)$	$\left[\frac{-\pi}{2}, \frac{\pi}{2}\right] - \{0\}$	$\left[\frac{-3\pi}{2}, \frac{-\pi}{2}\right] - \{-\pi\}$, $\left[\frac{\pi}{2}, \frac{3\pi}{2}\right] - \{\pi\}$, etc.
6.	$y = \cot^{-1} x$	R	$(0, \pi)$	$(-\pi, 0)$, $(\pi, 2\pi)$, etc.

Transformation of Inverse Trigonometric Function to Another Inverse Trigonometric Functions

Function	Transformation of a function				
(i) $\sin^{-1} x$	$\cos^{-1}(\sqrt{1-x^2})$	$\tan^{-1}\left(\frac{x}{\sqrt{1-x^2}}\right)$	$\cot^{-1}\left(\frac{\sqrt{1-x^2}}{x}\right)$	$\sec^{-1}\left(\frac{1}{\sqrt{1-x^2}}\right)$	$\operatorname{cosec}^{-1}\left(\frac{1}{x}\right)$
(ii) $\cos^{-1} x$	$\sin^{-1}(\sqrt{1-x^2})$	$\tan^{-1}\left(\frac{\sqrt{1-x^2}}{x}\right)$	$\cot^{-1}\left(\frac{x}{\sqrt{1-x^2}}\right)$	$\sec^{-1}\left(\frac{1}{x}\right)$	$\operatorname{cosec}^{-1}\left(\frac{1}{\sqrt{1-x^2}}\right)$
(iii) $\tan^{-1} x$	$\sin^{-1}\left(\frac{x}{\sqrt{1+x^2}}\right)$	$\cos^{-1}\left(\frac{1}{\sqrt{1+x^2}}\right)$	$\cot^{-1}\left(\frac{1}{x}\right)$	$\sec^{-1}\sqrt{1+x^2}$	$\operatorname{cosec}^{-1}\left(\frac{\sqrt{1+x^2}}{x}\right)$

Elementary Properties of Inverse Trigonometric Functions

Property I

(i) $\sin^{-1}(\sin\theta) = \theta$, $\theta \in \left[-\frac{\pi}{2}, \frac{\pi}{2}\right]$

(ii) $\cos^{-1}(\cos\theta) = \theta$, $\theta \in [0, \pi]$

(iii) $\tan^{-1}(\tan\theta) = \theta$, $\theta \in \left(-\frac{\pi}{2}, \frac{\pi}{2}\right)$

(iv) $\cot^{-1}(\cot\theta) = \theta$, $\theta \in (0, \pi)$

(v) $\operatorname{cosec}^{-1}(\operatorname{cosec}\theta) = \theta$, $\theta \in \left[-\frac{\pi}{2}, \frac{\pi}{2}\right] - \{0\}$

(vi) $\sec^{-1}(\sec\theta) = \theta$, $\theta \in [0, \pi] - \left\{\frac{\pi}{2}\right\}$

(vii) $\sin(\sin^{-1} x) = x$, $x \in [-1, 1]$

(viii) $\cos(\cos^{-1} x) = x$, $x \in [-1, 1]$

(ix) $\tan(\tan^{-1} x) = x$, $x \in R$

(x) $\cot(\cot^{-1} x) = x$, $x \in R$

(xi) $\operatorname{cosec}(\operatorname{cosec}^{-1} x) = x$, $x \in (-\infty, -1] \cup [1, \infty)$ or $|x| \geq 1$

(xii) $\sec(\sec^{-1} x) = x$, $x \in (-\infty, -1] \cup [1, \infty)$ or $|x| \geq 1$

Property II

(i) $\sin^{-1}(-x) = -\sin^{-1} x$, $x \in [-1, 1]$

(ii) $\cos^{-1}(-x) = \pi - \cos^{-1} x$, $x \in [-1, 1]$

(iii) $\tan^{-1}(-x) = -\tan^{-1} x$, $x \in R$

(iv) $\cot^{-1}(-x) = \pi - \cot^{-1} x, x \in R$

(v) $\operatorname{cosec}^{-1}(-x) = -\operatorname{cosec}^{-1} x, |x| \geq 1$ or $x \in (-\infty, -1] \cup [1, \infty)$

(vi) $\sec^{-1}(-x) = \pi - \sec^{-1} x, |x| \geq 1$ or $x \in (-\infty, -1] \cup [1, \infty)$

Property III

(i) $\sin^{-1}(1/x) = \operatorname{cosec}^{-1} x, x \geq 1$ or $x \leq -1$

(ii) $\cos^{-1}(1/x) = \sec^{-1} x, x \geq 1$ or $x \leq -1$

(iii) $\tan^{-1} \frac{1}{x} = \begin{cases} \cot^{-1} x, & x > 0 \\ -\pi + \cot^{-1} x, & x < 0 \end{cases}$

Property IV

(i) $\sin^{-1} x + \cos^{-1} x = \frac{\pi}{2}, x \in [-1, 1]$

(ii) $\tan^{-1} x + \cot^{-1} x = \frac{\pi}{2}, x \in R$

(iii) $\operatorname{cosec}^{-1} x + \sec^{-1} x = \frac{\pi}{2}, x \in (-\infty, -1] \cup [1, \infty)$

Property V

(i) $\sin^{-1} x + \sin^{-1} y = \sin^{-1}[x\sqrt{1-y^2} + y\sqrt{1-x^2}]$, [if $-1 \leq x, y \leq 1$ and $x^2 + y^2 \leq 1$ or if $xy < 0$ and $x^2 + y^2 > 1$]

(ii) $\sin^{-1} x - \sin^{-1} y = \sin^{-1}[x\sqrt{1-y^2} - y\sqrt{1-x^2}]$, [if $-1 \leq x, y \leq 1$ and $x^2 + y^2 \leq 1$ or if $xy > 0$ and $x^2 + y^2 > 1$]

(iii) $\cos^{-1} x + \cos^{-1} y = \cos^{-1}[xy - \sqrt{1-x^2}\sqrt{1-y^2}]$, [if $-1 \leq x, y \leq 1$ and $x + y \geq 0$]

(iv) $\cos^{-1} x - \cos^{-1} y = \cos^{-1}[xy + \sqrt{1-x^2}\sqrt{1-y^2}]$, [if $-1 \leq x, y \leq 1$ and $x \leq y$]

(v) $\tan^{-1} x + \tan^{-1} y = \tan^{-1}\left(\frac{x+y}{1-xy}\right), xy < 1$

(vi) $\tan^{-1} x - \tan^{-1} y = \tan^{-1}\left(\frac{x-y}{1+xy}\right), xy > -1$

Property VI

(i) $2\sin^{-1} x = \sin^{-1}(2x\sqrt{1-x^2}), -\frac{1}{\sqrt{2}} \leq x \leq \frac{1}{\sqrt{2}}$

(ii) $2\cos^{-1} x = \cos^{-1}(2x^2 - 1), 0 \leq x \leq 1$

(iii) $2\tan^{-1} x = \sin^{-1}\left(\frac{2x}{1+x^2}\right), |x| \leq 1$ or $-1 \leq x \leq 1$

(iv) $2\tan^{-1} x = \cos^{-1}\left(\frac{1-x^2}{1+x^2}\right), 0 \leq x$

(v) $2\tan^{-1} x = \tan^{-1}\left(\frac{2x}{1-x^2}\right), -1 < x < 1$

Property VII

(i) $3\sin^{-1} x = \sin^{-1}(3x - 4x^3)$, if $-\frac{1}{2} \leq x \leq \frac{1}{2}$

(ii) $3\cos^{-1} x = \cos^{-1}(4x^3 - 3x)$, if $\frac{1}{2} \leq x \leq 1$

(iii) $3\tan^{-1} x = \tan^{-1}\left(\frac{3x - x^3}{1 - 3x^2}\right)$, if $-\frac{1}{\sqrt{3}} < x < \frac{1}{\sqrt{3}}$

Chapter 3 : Matrices

1. Matrix

A matrix is an ordered rectangular array of numbers or functions arranged in rows and columns and enclosed by [ ] or ( ). Matrix is represented by single capital letter like A, B, X, Y etc. The number or functions are called the elements or the entries of the matrix.

2. Order of Matrix

A matrix of order $m \times n$ is of the form

$$A = \begin{bmatrix} a_{11} & a_{12} & a_{13} & \cdots & a_{1n} \\ a_{21} & a_{22} & a_{23} & \cdots & a_{2n} \\ \vdots & \vdots & \vdots & \cdots & \vdots \\ a_{m1} & a_{m2} & a_{m3} & \cdots & a_{mn} \end{bmatrix}_{m \times n}$$

In notation form It can be rewritten as $A = [a_{ij}]_{m \times n}$, where $1 \leq i \leq m, 1 \leq j \leq n$ and $i, j \in N$.

Its element laying in the ith row and jth column is a_{ij}.

3. Types of Matrices

(i) **Row matrix** A matrix having only one row and many columns, is called a row matrix.

(ii) **Column matrix** A matrix having only one column and many rows, is called a column matrix.

(iii) **Zero matrix or null matrix** If all the elements of a matrix are zero, then it is called a zero or null matrix. It is denoted by symbol O.

(iv) **Square matrix** A matrix in which number of rows and number of columns are equal, is called a square matrix.

(v) **Diagonal matrix** A square matrix having all the elements lying outside the diagonal elements as zero and atleast one diagonal element is non-zero, is called a diagonal matrix. The diagonal elements of a diagonal matrix are also called principal diagonal elements.

(vi) **Scalar matrix** A diagonal matrix in which all principal diagonal elements are equal, is called a scalar matrix.

(vii) **Unit matrix or identity matrix** A square matrix having 1 (one) on its principal diagonal and 0 (zero) elsewhere, is called an identity matrix. It is denoted by symbol I.

(viii) **Compatibility of matrices** Two matrices are said to be compatible, if both matrices have same order.

(ix) **Equality of matrix** Two matrices are said to be equal, if their order is same and their corresponding elements are equal.

4. Addition of Matrices

Let A and B be two matrices each of order $m \times n$. Then, the sum of matrices $A+B$ is defined, (if matrices A and B are of same order).

If $A=[a_{ij}]_{m\times n}$ and $B=[b_{ij}]_{m\times n}$, then $A+B=[a_{ij}+b_{ij}]_{m\times n}$

5. Negative of a Matrix

If $A=[a_{ij}]_{m\times n}$ is a matrix, then $-A=[-a_{ij}]_{m\times n}$ is called the negative of matrix A. In negative of A, each element is multiplied by (–1).

6. Difference of Matrices

If $A=[a_{ij}]$ and $B=[b_{ij}]$ are two matrices of the same order $m\times n$, then difference, $A-B$ is defined as a matrix $D=[d_{ij}]$, where $d_{ij}=a_{ij}-b_{ij}, \forall\, i, j$.

7. Properties of Addition of Matrices

If A, B and C are three matrices of same order $m\times n$, then

(i) **Commutative law** $A+B=B+A$

(ii) **Associative law** $(A+B)+C=A+(B+C)$

(iii) **Existence of additive identity** A zero matrix (O) of order $m\times n$ (same as of A), is additive identity, if $A+O=A=O+A$.

(iv) **Existence of additive inverse** If A is a square matrix, then the matrix $(-A)$ is additive inverse, if $A+(-A)=O=(-A)+A$, where $-A$ is negative of matrix A.

Note If A and B are not of same order, then $A+B$ is not defined.

8. Multiplication of a Matrix by a Scalar

Let $A=[a_{ij}]_{m\times n}$ be a matrix and k be any scalar. Then, the matrix obtained by multiplying each element of A by k is called the scalar multiplication of A by k, i.e. $kA=[ka_{ij}]_{m\times n}$.

9. Properties of Scalar Multiplication

If A and B are the two matrices of same order. Then,

(i) $k(A+B)=kA+kB$ (ii) $(k+l)A=kA+lA$

(iii) $(kl)A=k(lA)=l(kA)$, where k and l are scalars.

(iv) $(-1)A=-A$

10. Multiplication of Matrices

Let $A=[a_{ij}]$ be the $m\times n$ matrix and $B=[b_{jk}]$ be the $n\times p$ matrix such that, the **number of columns of A is equal to the number of rows of B**. Then, the product AB of the matrices A and B is matrix C of order $m\times p$.

Thus, $C=[c_{ik}]_{m\times p}=AB=[a_{ij}]m\times n \quad [b_{jk}]n\times p$

Same number

Order of resulting matrix

To get the (i, k)th element c_{ik} of the matrix C, we take the ith row of A and kth column of B, multiply them elementwise and take the sum of all these products.

Generally, it is not commutative, i.e. $AB \neq BA$.

11. Properties of Multiplication of Matrices

Let A, B and C be matrices of suitable order.

(i) **Associative law** $(AB)C=A(BC)$

(ii) **Existence of multiplicative identity**

$A\cdot I=A=I\cdot A$, I is called multiplicative identity.

(iii) **Distributive law** $A(B+C)=AB+AC$

or $(A+B)C=AC+BC$

12. Existence of Two Non-zero Matrices whose Product is a Zero Matrix

We know that, for real numbers a, b, if $ab=0$, then either $a=0$ or $b=0$. This need not be true for product of matrices.

e.g. If $A=\begin{bmatrix}0 & -1\\ 0 & 2\end{bmatrix}$ and $B=\begin{bmatrix}3 & 5\\ 0 & 0\end{bmatrix}$, then $AB=\begin{bmatrix}0 & 0\\ 0 & 0\end{bmatrix}$

13. Matrix Polynomial

Let $f(x)=a_0x^n+a_1x^{n-1}+a_2x^{n-2}+\ldots+a_{n-1}x+a_n$ be a polynomial in x and A be a square matrix. Then, $f(A)=a_0A^n+a_1A^{n-1}+a_2A^{n-2}+\ldots+a_{n-1}A+a_nI$ is called a matrix polynomial, where I is the identity matrix of order of A.

14. Transpose of a Matrix

The matrix obtained by interchanging the rows and columns of a given matrix A, is called transpose of a matrix. It is denoted by A' or A^T. i.e. if $A=[a_{ij}]$ is $m\times n$ matrix then $A^T=[a_{ji}]_{n\times m}$.

15. Properties of Transpose of Matrices

For any matrices A and B of suitable orders, we have

(i) $(A\pm B)'=A'\pm B'$ (ii) $(kA)'=kA'$, where k is a scalar.

(iii) $(AB)'=B'A'$ (iv) $(-A)'=-A'$

(v) $(A')'=A$

Note $(A^n)^T=(A^T)^n$, where n is a positive integer.

16. Symmetric and Skew-symmetric Matrix

A square matrix A is called symmetric, iff $A'=A$.

A square matrix A is called skew-symmetric, iff $A'=-A$.

17. Properties of Symmetric and Skew-symmetric Matrix

(i) For any square matrix A with real number entries, $A+A'$ is a symmetric matrix and $A-A'$ is a skew-symmetric matrix.

(ii) Any square matrix can be expressed as the sum of symmetric and skew-symmetric matrix.

i.e. $A = \frac{1}{2}(A + A') + \frac{1}{2}(A - A')$,

where $\frac{1}{2}(A + A')$ is symmetric and $\frac{1}{2}(A - A')$ is skew-symmetric.

(iii) The principal diagonal elements of a skew-symmetric matrix are always zero.

18. Equivalent Matrices

Two matrices A and B are called equivalent, if one can be obtained from the other by applying a finite number of elementary operations and it is denoted by $A \sim B$.

19. Invertible Matrices

If A is a square matrix of order m and there exists another square matrix B of the same order m, such that $AB = BA = I$, where I is a unit matrix of same order m, then B is called the inverse matrix of A and it is denoted by A^{-1}.

Note ▪ A rectangular matrix does not posses inverse matrix.
▪ If B is an inverse of A, then A is also the inverse of B.

20. Some Important Theorems

Theorem 1. (*Uniqueness of Inverse*) Inverse of a square matrix, if it exists, is unique.

Theorem 2. If A and B are invertible matrices of the same order, then $(AB)^{-1} = B^{-1}A^{-1}$.

Chapter 4 : **Determinants**

1. Determinant

Every square matrix A is associated with a number or expression, called its determinant and it is denoted by det(A) or $|A|$.

2. Order of a Determinant

The number of rows and columns in a determinant is called the order of a determinant.

3. Expansion of Determinant of Order (2×2)

$$\det(A) = \begin{vmatrix} a_{11} & a_{12} \\ a_{21} & a_{22} \end{vmatrix} = a_{11}a_{22} - a_{12}a_{21}$$

4. Expansion of Determinant of Order (3×3)

$$\det(A) = \begin{vmatrix} a_{11} & a_{12} & a_{13} \\ a_{21} & a_{22} & a_{23} \\ a_{31} & a_{32} & a_{33} \end{vmatrix} = a_{11}(a_{22}a_{33} - a_{32}a_{23}) - a_{12}(a_{21}a_{33} - a_{31}a_{23}) + a_{13}(a_{21}a_{32} - a_{31}a_{22})$$

We use the following sign (+, −), while expanding the determinant. $\begin{vmatrix} + & - & + \\ - & + & - \\ + & - & + \end{vmatrix}$

Note Similarly, we can expand the above determinant corresponding to any row or column.

5. Properties of Determinant

(i) If all the elements of any row or column of a determinant are zero, then the value of such determinant becomes zero.

(ii) If the rows and columns of a determinant are interchanged, the value of the determinant does not change.

(iii) If any two rows (columns) of a determinant are interchanged, the sign of determinant changes.

(iv) If any two rows (columns) of a determinant are identical (or same), the value of the determinant is zero.

(v) If each element of a row (column) of a determinant is multiplied by a non-zero number k, the value of the new determinant becomes k times the original determinant.
By this property, we can take out any common factor from any one row (column) of a given determinant.

Note If A is an $n \times n$ matrix, then $|kA| = k^n \cdot |A|$, where $n = 1, 2, 3, \ldots$.

(vi) If all the elements of any two rows or columns of a determinant are proportional, then the value of such determinant becomes zero.

(vii) If each element of any row (column) of a determinant is added to k times the corresponding elements of another row (column), then the value of the determinant remains unchanged.

(viii) If some or all elements of a row (column) of a determinant are expressed as sum of two (more) terms, the determinant can be expressed as sum of two (or more) determinants of the same order.

6. Minors

Minor of an element a_{ij} of a determinant is the determinant obtained by deleting ith row and jth column. It is denoted by M_{ij}.

If $A = \begin{vmatrix} a_{11} & a_{12} & a_{13} \\ a_{21} & a_{22} & a_{23} \\ a_{31} & a_{32} & a_{33} \end{vmatrix}$, then minors of A are

$$M_{11} = \begin{vmatrix} a_{22} & a_{23} \\ a_{32} & a_{33} \end{vmatrix}, M_{12} = \begin{vmatrix} a_{21} & a_{23} \\ a_{31} & a_{33} \end{vmatrix}, M_{13} = \begin{vmatrix} a_{21} & a_{22} \\ a_{31} & a_{32} \end{vmatrix}, \text{etc.}$$

Note The minor of an element of a determinant of order n ($n \geq 2$) is a determinant of order ($n - 1$).

7.Cofactor

If M_{ij} is the minor of an element a_{ij}, then the cofactor of a_{ij} is denoted by C_{ij} or A_{ij} and defined as follows

$$A_{ij} = C_{ij} = (-1)^{i+j} M_{ij}$$

where, $i = 1, 2, 3, \ldots, n$ and $j = 1, 2, 3, \ldots, n$

Note
- If elements of a row (column) are multiplied with cofactors of same row (column), then their sum is equal to the value of that determinant, i.e. $\Delta = a_{11}C_{11} + a_{12}C_{12} + a_{13}C_{13}$.
- If elements of a row (column) are multiplied with cofactors of any other row (column), then their sum is zero.
i.e. $a_{11}C_{21} + a_{12}C_{22} + a_{13}C_{23} = 0$

8.Singular and Non-Singular Matrices

A square matrix A is said to be a singular matrix, if $|A| = 0$ and if $|A| \neq 0$, then matrix A is said to be non-singular matrix.

e.g. Let $A = \begin{bmatrix} 2 & 1 \\ 6 & 3 \end{bmatrix}$.

Then, $|A| = 6 - 6 = 0$

So, the matrix A is a singular matrix.

9.Adjoint of a Matrix

The adjoint of a square matrix $A = [a_{ij}]_{n \times n}$ is defined as the transpose of the matrix formed by cofactors of the elements a_{ij} and it is denoted by adj (A).

e.g. If $A = \begin{bmatrix} a_{11} & a_{12} & a_{13} \\ a_{21} & a_{22} & a_{23} \\ a_{31} & a_{32} & a_{33} \end{bmatrix}$.

Then, adj (A) = Transpose of $\begin{bmatrix} C_{11} & C_{12} & C_{13} \\ C_{21} & C_{22} & C_{23} \\ C_{31} & C_{32} & C_{33} \end{bmatrix}$

or adj $(A) = \begin{bmatrix} C_{11} & C_{21} & C_{31} \\ C_{12} & C_{22} & C_{32} \\ C_{13} & C_{23} & C_{33} \end{bmatrix}$

where, C_{ij} is the cofactor of element a_{ij}.

Note For a square matrix of order 2 given by $A = \begin{bmatrix} a_{11} & a_{12} \\ a_{21} & a_{22} \end{bmatrix}$, adj (A) can also be obtained by interchanging a_{11} and a_{22} and by changing signs of a_{12} and a_{21}, i.e. adj $(A) = \begin{bmatrix} a_{22} & -a_{12} \\ -a_{21} & a_{11} \end{bmatrix}$.

10.Some Important Theorems

Theorem 1. If A is any given square matrix of order n, then $A(\text{adj } A) = (\text{adj } A)A = |A| I_n$, where I is the identity matrix of order n. Thus, for a square matrix A of order 2 and 3, we can write respectively,

$$A(\text{adj } A) = (\text{adj } A)\, A = |A|\, I_2$$

and $$A(\text{adj } A) = (\text{adj } A)\, A = |A|\, I_3$$

Theorem 2. If A and B are non-singular matrices of the same order, then AB and BA are also non-singular matrices of the same order.

Theorem 3. The determinant of the product of matrices is equal to the product of their respective determinants, i.e. $|AB| = |A||B|$

where, A and B are square matrices of the same order.

11.Properties of Adjoint of a Matrix

Suppose A and B are two non-singular matrices of same order n. Then,

(i) adj $(A^T) = [\text{adj } (A)]^T$

(ii) adj $(kA) = k^{n-1}$ (adj A), $k \in R$

(iii) adj $(AB) = [\text{adj } (B)]\, [\text{adj } (A)]$

(iv) $|\text{adj } A| = |A|^n$

(v) $|\text{adj } [\text{adj } (A)]| = |A|^{(n-1)^2}$

(vi) adj (adj A) $= |A|^{n-2} \cdot A$

Theorem 3. A square matrix A is invertible if and only if A is non-singular matrix.

Note If A is a square matrix of order n and there exists a square matrix B of order n such that $AB = BA = I_n \Rightarrow B = A^{-1}$ and $A = B^{-1}$.

Theorem 4. If A, B and C are all square matrices of order n and A is non-singular, then

(i) $AB = AC \Rightarrow B = C$ [left cancellation law]

(ii) $BA = CA \Rightarrow B = C$ [right cancellation law]

12.Properties of Inverse of a Matrix

Let A and B be two square invertible matrices of same order. Then,

(i) $(A^{-1})^{-1} = A$

(ii) $(AB)^{-1} = B^{-1}A^{-1}$ [reversal law]

(iii) $(A^T)^{-1} = (A^{-1})^T$

(iv) $|A^{-1}| = |A|^{-1}$

(v) $AA^{-1} = A^{-1}A = I$

(vi) $(kA)^{-1} = \frac{1}{k} A^{-1}, k \neq 0$

Note (i) Only square matrices have adjoint or inverse.

(ii) $(AA)^{-1} = A^{-1}A^{-1} \Rightarrow (A^2)^{-1} = (A^{-1})^2$

(iii) If A, B and C are invertible matrices of the same order, then $(ABC)^{-1} = C^{-1}B^{-1}A^{-1}$.

13. The area of triangle whose vertices are (x_1, y_1), (x_2, y_2) and (x_3, y_3) is given by

$$\Delta = \frac{1}{2}\begin{vmatrix} x_1 & y_1 & 1 \\ x_2 & y_2 & 1 \\ x_3 & y_3 & 1 \end{vmatrix}$$

Chapter 5 : Continuity and Differentiability

If we can draw the graph of a function around the given fixed point without lifting the pen from the plane of paper, then the function is said to be **continuous** at that point.

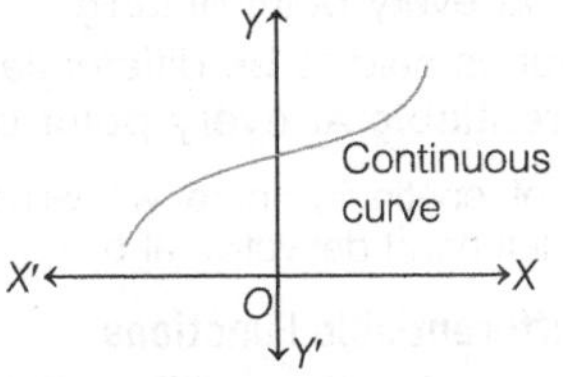

1. Continuity of a Real Function at a Point

A function $f(x)$ is said to be continuous at $x = c$, if

$$\lim_{x \to c^-} f(x) = \lim_{x \to c^+} f(x) = f(c).$$

Note (i) A function $f(x)$ is said to be left continuous or continuous at $x = c$ from left, if $\lim_{x \to c^-} f(x) = f(c)$.

(ii) A function $f(x)$ is said to be right continuous or continuous at $x = c$ from right, if $\lim_{x \to c^+} f(x) = f(c)$.

2. Working Rule to Check Continuity of a Function at Given Point

I. Write the given function say $f(x)$ and given point say $x = c$, at which we have to check continuity.

II. Find the value of $f(x)$ at $x = c$.

III. Find LHL (Left Hand Limit) of $f(x)$ at $x = c$.

IV. Find RHL (Right Hand Limit) of $f(x)$ at $x = c$.

V. Now, if LHL = RHL = $f(c)$. Then, f is continuous at $x = c$, otherwise not continuous.

Note (i) If a function is not continuous at $x = c$, then it is said to be discontinuous at c and c is called the point of discontinuity of the function.

(ii) $f(x)$ is discontinuous at $x = c$, if any one of the following cases arise.

(a) $f(c)$ is not defined.

(b) $\lim_{x \to c} f(x)$ does not exist.

(c) $\lim_{x \to c} f(x) \neq f(c)$.

Some Standard Results Based on Limits

(i) $\lim_{x \to a} \frac{x^n - a^n}{x - a} = na^{n-1}$

(ii) $\lim_{x \to 0} \frac{\sin x}{x} = 1$

(iii) $\lim_{x \to 0} \frac{\tan x}{x} = 1$

(iv) $\lim_{x \to 0} \frac{\sin^{-1} x}{x} = 1$

(v) $\lim_{x \to 0} \frac{\tan^{-1} x}{x} = 1$

(vi) $\lim_{x \to 0} \frac{e^x - 1}{x} = 1$

(vii) $\lim_{x \to 0} \frac{a^x - 1}{x} = \log_e a$

(viii) $\lim_{x \to 0} \frac{\log (1 + x)}{x} = 1$

(ix) $\lim_{x \to 0} (1 + x)^{1/x} = e$

(x) $\lim_{x \to \infty} \left(1 + \frac{1}{x}\right)^x = e$

(xi) $\lim_{x \to \infty} \frac{\sin x}{x} = \lim_{x \to \infty} \frac{\cos x}{x} = 0$

3. Removable Discontinuity

When $\lim_{x \to a} f(x)$ exists but either $f(a)$ does not exist or $\lim_{x \to a} f(x) \neq f(a)$, then f has a removable discontinuity at $x = a$, otherwise f has non-removable discontinuity at $x = a$.

4. Continuous Function

A function f is said to be continuous, if it is continuous at every point of its domain.

Note (i) The domain of continuous function may be a proper subset of domain of the function.

(ii) The set of all points where the function is continuous is called its **domain of continuity**.

5. Continuity of a Function in an Interval

(i) A function $f(x)$ is said to be **continuous in open interval (a, b)**, if it is continuous for every value of x in the interval (a, b).

(ii) A function $f(x)$ is said to be **continuous in closed interval $[a, b]$**, if

(a) it is continuous for every value of x in the open interval (a, b).

(b) $f(x)$ is continuous at $x = a$ from right, i.e. $\lim_{x \to a^+} f(x) = f(a)$.

(c) $f(x)$ is continuous at $x = b$ from left, i.e. $\lim_{x \to b^-} f(x) = f(b)$.

Note (i) If the domain of function f is a singleton set, i.e. it is defined only at one point, then it is a continuous function.

(ii) A continuous function in a closed interval has a least and greatest value.

6. Properties of Continuous Functions

(i) Constant function is continuous everywhere.

(ii) Identity function is continuous everywhere.

(iii) Polynomial function is continuous everywhere.

(iv) Rational function is continuous at every point of its domain.

(v) Modulus (or absolute) function $f(x) = |x|$ is continuous everywhere.

(vi) All trigonometric functions are continuous at every point of their respective domain of definition.

(vii) The greatest integer function is continuous everywhere except at integers.

(viii) The basic inverse trigonometric functions are continuous at every point of their respective domain of definition.

7. Algebra of Continuous Functions

Theorem 1. Let f and g be two real functions continuous at a real number c, then

(i) $(f + g)$ is continuous at $x = c$.

(ii) $(f - g)$ is continuous at $x = c$.

(iii) fg is continuous at $x = c$.

(iv) f/g is continuous at $x = c$, provided that $g(c) \neq 0$.

(v) αf is continuous at $x = c$, for all $\alpha \in R$.

Theorem 2. Let D_1 and D_2 be the domains of continuity of the functions f and g, respectively, then

(i) αf is continuous on D_1 for all $\alpha \in R$.

(ii) $(f+g)$, $(f-g)$ and fg are continuous on $D_1 \cap D_2$.

(iii) f/g is also continuous on $D_1 \cap D_2$ except those points, where $g(x) = 0$.

(iv) f^n is continuous on D_1 for all $n \in N$.

(v) $\frac{1}{f}$ is continuous on D_1 except at those points where $f(x) = 0$.

Theorem 3. The composition of two continuous function is continuous. Suppose f and g are real valued functions such that (fog) is defined at c. If g is continuous at c and if f is continuous at $g(c)$, then (fog) is continuous at c.

Note If f and g are two real valued functions, then $(fog)(x) = f(g(x))$ is defined, whenever the range of g is a subset of domain of f.

8. Differentiability or Derivability

A real function f is said to be derivable or differentiable at a point c in its domain, if $\lim_{x \to c} \frac{f(x)-f(c)}{x-c}$ exist or $\lim_{h \to 0} \frac{f(c+h)-f(c)}{h}$ exist or its **left hand** and **right hand derivatives** at c exist (i.e. finite and unique) and are equal, i.e. $Lf'(c) = Rf'(c)$.

Here, at $x = c$ left hand derivative,

$$\text{LHD} = \lim_{x \to c^-} \frac{f(x)-f(c)}{x-c} = \lim_{h \to 0} \frac{f(c-h)-f(c)}{-h} = Lf'(c)$$

and right hand derivative,

$$\text{RHD} = \lim_{x \to c^+} \frac{f(x)-f(c)}{x-c} = \lim_{h \to 0} \frac{f(c+h)-f(c)}{h} = Rf'(c).$$

9. Differentiable Function

A function f is said to be a differentiable function iff it is differentiable at every point of its domain.

A function is said to be **differentiable in an interval (a, b)**, if it is differentiable at every point of (a, b).

Similarly, a function is said to be differentiable in an interval $[a, b]$, if it is **differentiable at every point of $[a, b]$**.

Note As in case of continuity, here we will take right hand derivative at a and left hand derivative at b.

10. Some Basic Differentiable Functions

(i) Every polynomial function is differentiable at each $x \in R$.

(ii) The exponential function $a^x, a > 0$ is differentiable at each $x \in R$.

(iii) Every constant function is differentiable at each $x \in R$.

(iv) The logarithmic function is differentiable at each point in its domain.

(v) The trigonometric and inverse trigonometric functions are differentiable in their respective domains.

(vi) The sum, difference, product and quotient of two differentiable functions is differentiable.

(vii) The composition of differentiable functions is a differentiable function.

Note The function $f(x) = |x-a_1| + |x-a_2| + |x-a_3| + \ldots + |x-a_n|$ is not differentiable at $x = a_1, a_2, a_3, \ldots, a_n$.

11. Relation between Differentiability and Continuity

Theorem If a function is differentiable at any point, it is necessarily continuous at that point.

Note The converse of the above theorem may not be true, i.e. a function is continuous at a point but may not be derivable at that point, e.g. $f(x) = |x|$.

Chapter 6 : **Differentiation**

1. Differentiation

The process of finding derivative of a function is called differentiation.

2. Derivatives of Algebraic Functions

(i) $\frac{d}{dx}(\text{constant}) = 0$ (ii) $\frac{d}{dx}(x^n) = nx^{n-1}$

(iii) $\frac{d}{dx}(cx^n) = cnx^{n-1}$, where c is a constant.

3. Derivative of Trigonometric Functions

(i) $\frac{d}{dx}(\sin x) = \cos x$

(ii) $\frac{d}{dx}(\cos x) = -\sin x$

(iii) $\frac{d}{dx}(\tan x) = \sec^2 x$

(iv) $\frac{d}{dx}(\text{cosec } x) = -\text{cosec } x \cot x$

(v) $\frac{d}{dx}(\sec x) = \sec x \tan x$

(vi) $\frac{d}{dx}(\cot x) = -\text{cosec}^2 x$

4. Derivatives of Two or More Functions

(i) $\frac{d}{dx}(u \pm v) = \frac{du}{dx} \pm \frac{dv}{dx}$

(ii) $\frac{d}{dx}(u \pm v \pm w \pm \ldots) = \frac{du}{dx} \pm \frac{dv}{dx} \pm \frac{dw}{dx} \pm \ldots$

(iii) $\frac{d}{dx}(u \cdot v) = u\frac{d}{dx}(v) + v\frac{d}{dx}(u)$

[product rule of derivative]

(iv) $\frac{d}{dx}\left(\frac{u}{v}\right) = \frac{v\frac{d}{dx}(u) - u\frac{d}{dx}(v)}{v^2}$

[quotient rule of derivative]

5. Differentiation by Substitution

Substitution is useful to reduce the function into simple form. For problems involving inverse trigonometric functions, first try for a suitable substitution to simplify it and then differentiate it. If no substitution is found, then differentiate directly.

Some standard substitutions are given below

Expressions	Substitutions
$\sqrt{a^2 - x^2}$	$x = a \tan \theta$ or $x = a \cot \theta$
$\sqrt{a^2 - x^2}$	$x = a \sin \theta$ or $x = a \cos \theta$
$\sqrt{x^2 - a^2}$	$x = a \sec \theta$ or $x = a \operatorname{cosec} \theta$
$\frac{a+x}{a-x}$ or $\frac{a-x}{a+x}$	$x = a \tan \theta$ or $x = a \cot \theta$
$\sqrt{\frac{a+x}{a-x}}$ or $\sqrt{\frac{a-x}{a+x}}$	$x = a \cos \theta$ or $x = a \cos 2\theta$
$\frac{2x}{1+x^2}$ or $\frac{2x}{1-x^2}$	$x = \tan \theta$
$a \sin x + b \cos x$	$a = r \cos \alpha$, $b = r \sin \alpha$
$\sqrt{x-\alpha}$ and $\sqrt{\beta - x}$	$x = \alpha \sin^2 \theta + \beta \cos^2 \theta$
$\sqrt{2ax - x^2}$	$x = a(1 - \cos \theta)$

9. Derivatives of Absolute Value Function

If $y = |x| = \sqrt{x^2}$, then on differentiating y w.r.t. x, we get

$$\frac{dy}{dx} = \frac{1}{2}(x^2)^{-1/2}\frac{d}{dx}(x^2) = \frac{1}{2} \times \frac{1}{\sqrt{x^2}} \times 2x = \frac{x}{|x|}, \; x \neq 0$$

$[\because |x| = \sqrt{x^2}]$

10. Differentiation of a Function with Respect to Another Function

If $y = f(x)$ and $z = g(x)$ are two functions of x. Then, to find the derivative of $f(x)$ w.r.t. $g(x)$ i.e. $\frac{dy}{dz}$ use the following formula, $\frac{dy}{dz} = \frac{dy/dx}{dz/dx} = \frac{f'(x)}{g'(x)}$

11. Differentiation of Parametric Functions

Sometimes x and y are separately given as functions of a single variable t (called a parameter), i.e. $y = f(t)$ and $x = g(t)$. In this case,

derivative, $\frac{dy}{dx} = \frac{dy/dt}{dx/dt} = \frac{f'(t)}{g'(t)}$

12. Derivative of Exponential Functions

(i) $\frac{d}{dx}(e^x) = e^x$ (ii) $\frac{d}{dx}(a^x) = a^x \log_e a, \; a > 0$

13. Derivative of Logarithmic Functions

(i) $\frac{d}{dx}(\log_e x) = \frac{1}{x}, \; x > 0$

(ii) $\frac{d}{dx}(\log_a x) = \frac{1}{x \log_e a}, \; x > 0, a > 0$ and $a \neq 1$

14. Derivative of Inverse Trigonometric Functions

(i) $\frac{d}{dx}(\sin^{-1} x) = \frac{1}{\sqrt{1-x^2}}, \; -1 < x < 1$

(ii) $\frac{d}{dx}(\cos^{-1} x) = \frac{-1}{\sqrt{1-x^2}}, \; -1 < x < 1$

(iii) $\frac{d}{dx}(\tan^{-1} x) = \frac{1}{1+x^2}, \; x \in R$

(iv) $\frac{d}{dx}(\cot^{-1} x) = \frac{-1}{1+x^2}, \; x \in R$

(v) $\frac{d}{dx}(\sec^{-1} x) = \frac{1}{|x|\sqrt{x^2-1}}, \; |x| > 1$

(vi) $\frac{d}{dx}(\operatorname{cosec}^{-1} x) = \frac{-1}{|x|\sqrt{x^2-1}}, \; |x| > 1$

15. Useful Logarithmic Formulae

(i) $\log_a mn = \log_a m + \log_a n$

(ii) $\log_a \frac{m}{n} = \log_a m - \log_a n$

(iii) $\log_a m^n = n \log_a m$

} $m > 0, n > 0, a > 0, a \neq 1$

(iv) $\log_a a = 1, \; a > 0$ and $a \neq 1$

(v) $\log_a m = \log_a b \cdot \log_b m, \; a > 0, b > 0, a \neq 1, b \neq 1$ and $m > 0$

(vi) $\log_a m \times \log_m a = 1, \; a > 0, m > 0, a \neq 1$ and $m \neq 1$

(vii) $\log_{b^m} a = \frac{1}{m}\log_b a, \; a > 0, b > 0, m \neq 0$ and $b \neq 1$

(viii) $\log_b a = \frac{\log_m a}{\log_m b}, \; a > 0, b > 0, b \neq 1, m > 0$ and $m \neq 1$

(ix) $a^{\log_a m} = m, \; a > 0, m > 0$ and $a \neq 1$

16. Logarithmic Differentiation

The functions, which can be evaluated by using logarithmic differentiation, are of type

$$y = [f(x)]^{g(x)} \text{ or } y = f_1(x) f_2(x) f_3(x) \cdots$$

or $$y = \frac{f_1(x) f_2(x) f_3(x) \cdots}{g_1(x) g_2(x) g_3(x) \cdots}$$

For this type of function, firstly we take the logarithm in the following way given below and then differentiate both sides.

(i) If the function is given as the product of a number of functions like $y = u(x) v(x) w(x)$, then taking log on both sides, we get

$$\log y = \log u(x) + \log v(x) + \log w(x)$$

(ii) If the function is given as the division of two functions like $y = \frac{u(x)}{v(x)}$, then taking log on both sides, we get

$$\log y = \log u(x) - \log v(x).$$

(iii) If the function is given as one function with a power of other function like $y = [f(x)]^{g(x)}$, then taking log on both sides, we get $\log y = g(x) \log [f(x)]$.

Thus, the derivative of such functions can be easily obtained by taking the logarithm of the function. This process is called logarithmic differentiation.

Here, $\frac{d}{dx}(\log y) = \frac{1}{y} \cdot \frac{dy}{dx}$

Note If $y = [f(x)]^{g(x)}$ then

$$\frac{dy}{dx} = [f(x)]^{g(x)}\left[\frac{g(x)}{f(x)} f'(x) + \log f(x) \cdot g'(x)\right]$$

17. Derivative of Implicit Function

If the relation between the variables x and y is given by an equation containing of the form $\phi(x, y) = 0$ and this equation is not immediately solvable for y, i.e. it is not possible to express y as a function of x in the form $y = \phi(x)$, then y is called an implicit function of x. In such a case to find dy/dx, differentiate both sides of the given relation w.r.t. x keeping in mind that the derivative of $f(y)$ w.r.t. x is $\frac{df}{dy} \cdot \frac{dy}{dx}$.

18. Successive Differentiation

If the function f is defined by $y = f(x)$, then its first and second derivatives are denoted by

$$f'(x), f''(x) \text{ or } \frac{dy}{dx}, \frac{d^2y}{dx^2} \text{ or } y_1, y_2 \text{ or } y', y'', \text{ respectively.}$$

The process of finding the derivatives of higher order (> 1) is called successive differentiation.

Note $\frac{dy}{dx} = \frac{dy/d\theta}{dx/d\theta}$

but $\frac{d^2y}{dx^2} \neq \frac{d^2y/d\theta^2}{d^2x/d\theta^2}$

Chapter 7 : **Application of Derivatives**

1. Tangents and Normals

A tangent is a straight line, which touches the curve $y = f(x)$ at a point.

A normal is a straight line perpendicular to a tangent to the curve $y = f(x)$ intersecting at the point of contact.

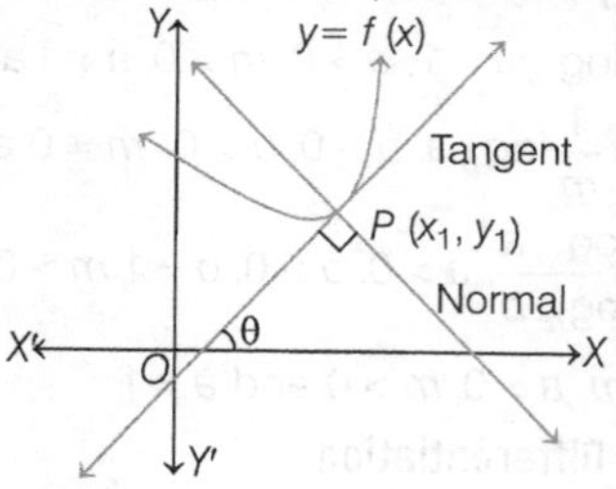

2. Slope of Tangent and Normal

Suppose the given curve is $y = f(x)$. Then, the slope (or gradient) of tangent to this curve at point (x_1, y_1) is given by $\left(\frac{dy}{dx}\right)_{(x_1, y_1)}$ or $f'(x_1)$.

Also, slope of the normal to the curve $y = f(x)$ at point (x_1, y_1) $= \frac{-1}{\text{slope of tangent}}$, i.e. $\frac{-1}{\left(\frac{dy}{dx}\right)_{(x_1, y_1)}}$.

Particular Cases

Case I If slope of the tangent line is zero, i.e. $dy/dx = 0$ $\Rightarrow \tan\theta = 0 \Rightarrow \theta = 0$, then it means the **tangent line** is **parallel to *X*-axis**.

Case II If $\theta \to \frac{\pi}{2}$, then $\frac{dy}{dx} = \tan\theta \to \infty$, which means the **tangent line is perpendicular to *X*-axis**, i.e. **parallel to *Y*-axis**.

3. Equations of Tangents and Normals

Let $y = f(x)$ be a curve and $P(x_1, y_1)$ be a point on curve. Then, the equations of tangent and normal at P according to slope are given below

(i) **When slope is *m***

If the slope of tangent is $m = dy/dx$ at point (x_1, y_1), then
(a) the equation of tangent is $(y - y_1) = m(x - x_1)$.
(b) the equation of normal is $y - y_1 = m_1(x - x_1)$ where, $m_1 = -1/m$.

(ii) **When slope is zero**

If the slope of tangent is $dy/dx = 0$, i.e. $\theta = 0$, then
(a) the equation of tangent is $y = y_1$.
(b) the equation of normal is $x = x_1$.

(iii) **When slope is tends to infinity.**

If the slope of tangent is $dy/dx \to \infty$, i.e. $\theta \to \pi/2$, then
(a) the equation of tangent is $x = x_1$.
(b) the equation of normal is $y = y_1$.

4. Angle between Intersection of Two Curves

Angle between the intersection of two curves is equal to an angle between their tangents at the point of intersection.

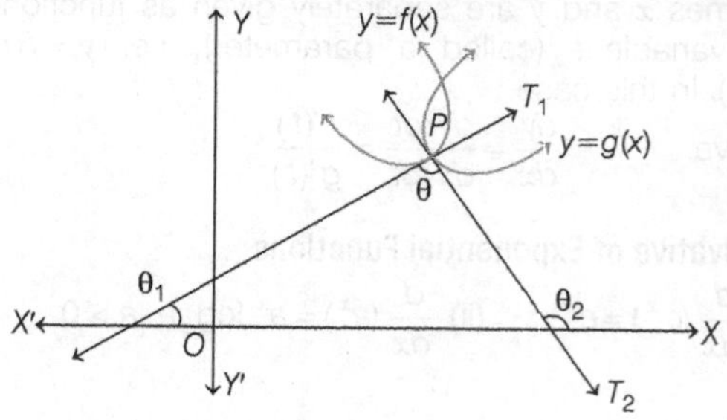

Let $y = f(x)$ and $y = g(x)$ be two curves and let PT_1 and PT_2 be two tangents at their point of intersection (P).
Let slope of tangents of two curves at any point P are m_1, m_2 and θ be the angle between the two curves at any point P. Then, the angle between two curves is given by

$$\tan\theta = \left|\frac{m_1 - m_2}{1 + m_1 m_2}\right|$$

(i) Tangents are parallel, if $m_1 = m_2$.
(ii) Tangents are perpendicular (orthogonally), if $m_1 m_2 = -1$.

Note Angle between intersection of the curves is defined as acute angle between their tangents.

5. Rate of Change of Quantities (Rate Measure)

Suppose one quantity y (dependent quantity) varies with another quantity, say x (independent) satisfying some rule $y = f(x)$, then $\frac{dy}{dx}$ **or** $f'(x)$ **represents the rate of change of** y **with respect to** x.

6. Rate of Change of a Quantity at a Point

Suppose quantity y varies with another quantity x, then rate of change of y with respect to x at point $x = x_0$ is given by $\left(\frac{dy}{dx}\right)_{x = x_0}$ or $f'(x_0)$, i.e. firstly, find the derivative of y with respect to x and then put x_0 in place of x in $\frac{dy}{dx}$.

7. Rate of Change of Two Variables

Suppose two variables are varying with respect to another variable t, i.e. $y = f(t)$ and $x = g(t)$. Then, rate of change of y with respect to x is given by

$$\frac{dy}{dx} = \frac{dy/dt}{dx/dt}, \text{ provided that } \frac{dx}{dt} \neq 0$$

or

$$\frac{dy}{dx} = \frac{dy}{dt} \cdot \frac{dt}{dx}. \text{ [by chain rule of derivative]}$$

Thus, the rate of change of y with respect to x can be calculated using the rate of change of y and x both with respect to t.

Another method by chain rule, $\frac{dy}{dx} = \frac{dy/dt}{dx/dt} \Rightarrow \frac{dy}{dt} = \frac{dy}{dx} \cdot \frac{dx}{dt}$

$\Rightarrow$ Rate of change of $y = \frac{dy}{dx} \times$ Rate of change of x.

Note (i) The term 'rate of change' means the instantaneous rate of change.
(ii) $\frac{dy}{dx}$ is positive, if y increases as x increases and is negative, if y decreases as x increases.
(iii) For rate of change of shadow, use the concept of similar triangles to establish the relationship between the variables.

8. Increasing Function

A function f is called a increasing function in I, if $x_1 < x_2 \Rightarrow f(x_1) \leq f(x_2)$ for all $x_1, x_2 \in I$. The graphical representation of such function is given below

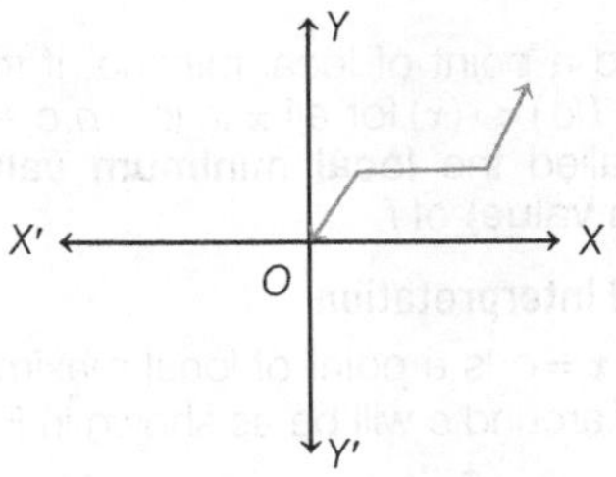

9. Strictly Increasing Function

A function f is called a strictly increasing function in I, if $x_1 < x_2 \Rightarrow f(x_1) < f(x_2)$ for all $x_1, x_2 \in I$. The graphical representation of such function is given below

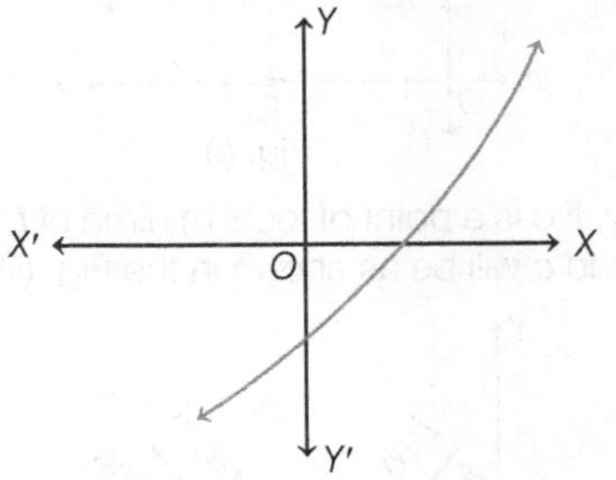

10. Decreasing Function

A function f is called a decreasing function in I, if $x_1 < x_2 \Rightarrow f(x_1) \geq f(x_2)$ for all $x_1, x_2 \in I$.
The graphical representation of such function is given below

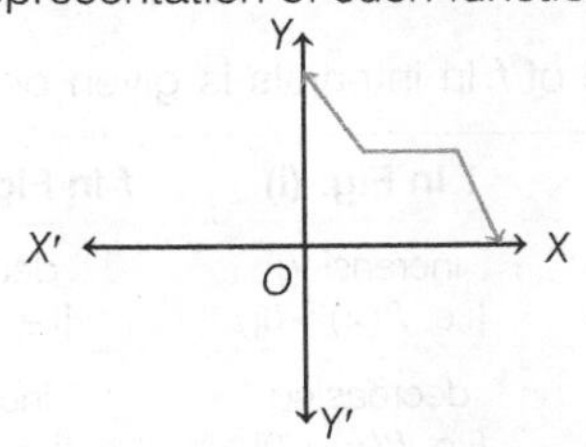

11. Strictly Decreasing Function

A function f is called a strictly decreasing function in I, if $x_1 < x_2 \Rightarrow f(x_1) > f(x_2)$ for all $x_1, x_2 \in I$. The graphical representation of such function is given below

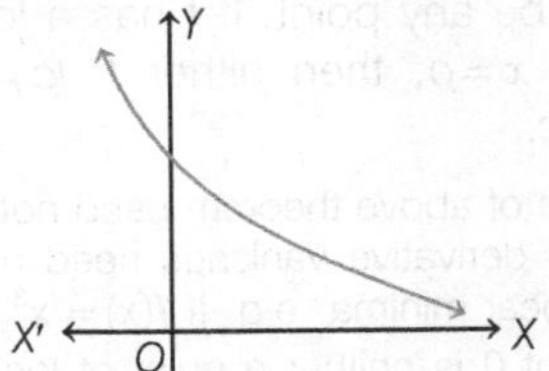

12. Local Maxima and Local Minima

Definition Let f be a real valued function and c be an interior point in the domain of f, then

(i) c is called a point of local maxima, if there is an $h > 0$ such that $f(c) > f(x)$ for all x in $(c - h, c + h)$. Here, value $f(c)$ is called the **local maximum value (or relative maximum value)** of f.

(ii) c is called a point of local minima, if there is an $h > 0$ such that $f(c) < f(x)$ for all x in $(c-h, c+h)$. Here, value $f(c)$ is called the **local minimum value (or relative minimum value)** of f.

13. Geometrical Interpretation

(i) Suppose $x = c$ is a point of local maxima of f, then the graph of f around c will be as shown in Fig. (i).

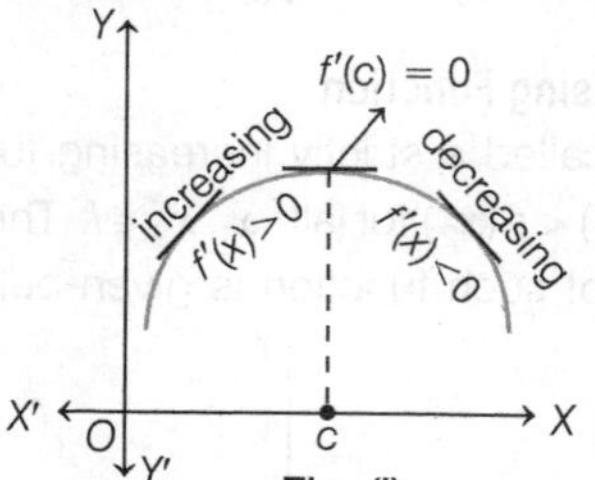

Fig. (i)

(ii) Similarly, if c is a point of local minima of f, then the graph of f around c will be as shown in the Fig. (ii).

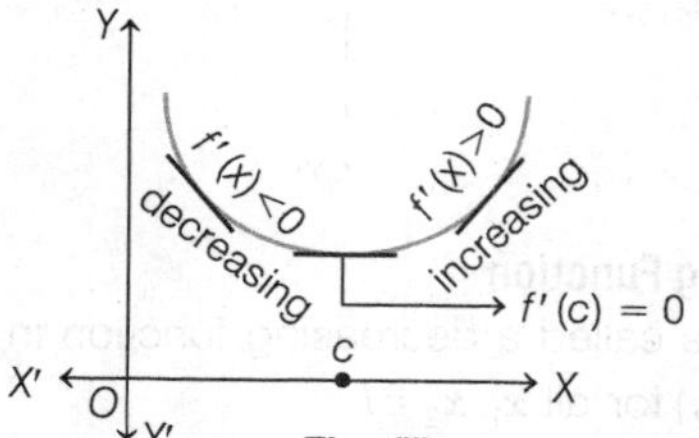

Fig. (ii)

Thus, the nature of f in intervals is given below

Interval	f in Fig. (i)	f in Fig. (ii)
$(c-h, c)$	increasing [i.e. $f'(x) > 0$]	decreasing [i.e. $f(x) < 0$]
$(c, c+h)$	decreasing [i.e. $f'(x) < 0$]	increasing [i.e. $f(x) > 0$]

Thus, this suggest that $f'(c)$ must be zero.

14. Some Important Theorems

Theorem 1. Let f be a function defined on an open interval I. Suppose $c \in I$ be any point. If f has a local maxima or a local minima at $x = c$, then either $f'(c) = 0$ or f is not differentiable at c.

Note The converse of above theorem need not be true that is a point at which the derivative vanishes need not be a point of local maxima or local minima. e.g. If $f(x) = x^3$, then $f'(x) = 3x^2$ and so $f'(0) = 0$. But 0 is neither a point of local maxima nor a point of local minima.

Critical Point A point c in the domain of a function f at which either $f'(c) = 0$ or f is not differentiable, is called a critical point of f. If f is continuous at point c and $f'(c) = 0$, then there exists a $h > 0$ such that f is differentiable in the interval $(c-h, c+h)$.

Theorem 2. (First Derivative Test) Let f be a function defined on an open interval I and f be continuous at a critical point c in I.

(i) If $f'(x)$ changes sign from positive to negative as x increases through point c, i.e. if $f'(x) > 0$ at every point sufficiently close to and to the left of c and $f'(x) < 0$ at every point sufficiently close to and to the right of c, then c is a point of local maxima.

(ii) If $f'(x)$ changes sign from negative to positive as x increases through point c, i.e. if $f'(x) < 0$ at every point sufficiently close to and to the left of c and $f'(x) > 0$ at every point sufficiently close to and to the right of c, then c is a point of local minima.

Theorem 3 (Second Derivative Test) Let f be a function defined on an interval I and $c \in I$ and f be twice differentiable at c. Then,

(i) $x = c$ is a point of local maxima, if

$$f'(c) = 0 \text{ and } f''(c) < 0$$

The value $f(c)$ is local maximum value of f.

(ii) $x = c$ is a point of local minima, if $f'(c) = 0$ and $f''(c) > 0$.

The value $f(c)$ is local minimum value of f.

(iii) The test fails, if $f'(c) = 0$ and $f''(c) = 0$.

In this case, we go back to the first derivative test and find whether c is a point of local maxima, local minima or a point of inflexion.

15. Maximum and Minimum Values of a Function in Closed Interval

If a function $f(x)$ is continuous on a closed interval, say $[a, b]$, then it attains the **absolute** maximum value or **global** maximum (absolute minimum value or global minimum) at critical points or at the end points of the interval $[a, b]$.

Thus, to find the absolute maximum (absolute minimum) value of the function, we choose the largest and smallest amongst the numbers $f(a), f(c_1), f(c_2), f(b)$, where c_1 and c_2 are the critical points.

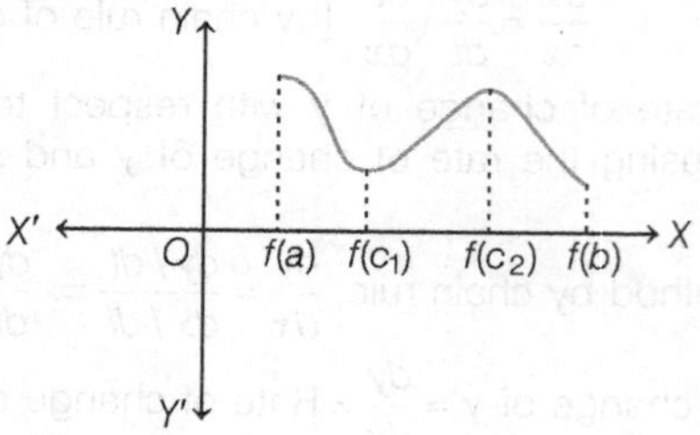

21. Important Theorems

Theorem 1. Let f be a continuous function on an interval $I = [a, b]$. Then, f has the absolute maximum value and f attains it atleast once in I.

Also, f has the absolute minimum value and attains it atleast once in I.

Theorem 2. Let f be a differentiable function on a closed interval I and c be any interior point of I. Then,

(i) $f'(c) = 0$, if f attains its absolute maximum value at c.

(ii) $f'(c) = 0$, if f attains its absolute minimum value at c.

22. Method to Find Absolute Maximum /Minimum Values in an Interval [a, b]

Let $f(x)$ be the given function. Then,

I. Find all critical points of f in the interval, i.e. find points at which either $f'(x) = 0$ or f is not differentiable.

II. Take the end points of the interval.

III. At all these points listed in steps I and II, calculate the values of f.

IV. Identify the maximum and minimum values of f out of the values calculated in step III. This maximum value will be the absolute maximum (greatest) value of f and the minimum value will be the absolute minimum (least) value of f.

Chapter 8 : **Indefinite Integrals**

1. Indefinite Integral

Let $F(x)$ and $f(x)$ be two functions connected together, such that $\frac{d}{dx}[F(x)] = f(x)$, then $F(x)$ is called **integral** of $f(x)$ or indefinite integral or **anti-derivative**.

Thus, $\int f(x)dx = F(x) + C$

where, C is an arbitrary constant (also called constant of integration) and symbol '$\int$' stands for the sign of integration.

2. Important Results

(i) $\int x^n\,dx = \frac{x^{n+1}}{n+1} + C,\ n \neq -1$

(ii) $\int \frac{1}{x}dx = \log|x| + C,\ x \neq 0$

(iii) $\int e^x\,dx = e^x + C$

(iv) $\int a^x\,dx = \frac{a^x}{\log a} + C$

(v) $\int \sin x\,dx = -\cos x + C$

(vi) $\int \cos x\,dx = \sin x + C$

(vii) $\int \tan x\,dx = \log|\sec x| + C$

(viii) $\int \cot x\,dx = \log|\sin x| + C$

(ix) $\int \sec x\,dx = \log|\sec x + \tan x| + C$

$= \log|\tan(\pi/4 + x/2)| + C$

(x) $\int \text{cosec}\,x\,dx = \log|\text{cosec}\,x - \cot x| + C$

$= \log|\tan(x/2)| + C$

(xi) $\int \sec^2 x\,dx = \tan x + C$

(xii) $\int \text{cosec}^2\,x\,dx = -\cot x + C$

(xiii) $\int \sec x \tan x\,dx = \sec x + C$

(xiv) $\int \text{cosec}\,x \cot x\,dx = -\text{cosec}\,x + C$

(xv) $\int \frac{1}{\sqrt{1-x^2}}dx = \sin^{-1} x + C$

(xvi) $\int \frac{-1}{\sqrt{1-x^2}}dx = \cos^{-1} x + C$

(xvii) $\int \frac{dx}{1+x^2} = \tan^{-1} x + C$

(xviii) $\int \frac{-1}{1+x^2}dx = \cot^{-1} x + C$

(xix) $\int \frac{dx}{x\sqrt{x^2-1}} = \sec^{-1} x + C$

(xx) $\int \frac{-1}{x\sqrt{x^2-1}}dx = \text{cosec}^{-1} x + C$

3. Properties of Indefinite Integral

(i) The process of differentiation and integration are inverse of each other.

i.e. $\frac{d}{dx}\int f(x)dx = f(x)$ and $\int f'(x)dx = f(x) + C$

where, C is an arbitrary constant.

(ii) $\int \{f(x) \pm g(x)\}\,dx = \int f(x)dx \pm \int g(x)dx$

(iii) $\int k\,f(x)dx = k\int f(x)dx$, where k is any non-zero real number.

(iv) In general, if $f_1, f_2, \ldots, f_n$ are functions and $k_1, k_2, \ldots, k_n$ are numbers, then

$\int [k_1 f_1(x) + k_2 f_2(x) + \cdots + k_n f_n(x)]dx$

$= k_1\int f_1(x)dx + k_2\int f_2(x)dx + \cdots + k_n\int f_n(x)dx + C$

where, C is the constant of integration.

Note If more than one constant of integration is used while solving the integral, then at the end of the solution write only one constant of integration.

4. Integration by Substitution

The method of reducing a given integral into one of the other standard integral by proper substitution is called method of substitution.

Thus, $\int f(x)dx = \int f\{g(t)\} \cdot g'(t)dt$, if we substitute $x = g(t)$, such that $dx = g'(t)\,dt$.

In particular,

(i) $\int f'(x)[f(x)]^n dx = \frac{[f(x)]^{n+1}}{n+1} + C,\ n \neq -1$

(ii) $\int \frac{f'(x)}{f(x)}dx = \log|f(x)| + C$

5. Integration Using Partial Fractions

	Form of the rational functions	Form of the partial fractions
(i)	$\frac{px \pm q}{(x \pm a)(x \pm b)}, a \neq b$	$\frac{A}{x \pm a} + \frac{B}{x \pm b}$
(ii)	$\frac{px \pm q}{(x \pm a)^2}$	$\frac{A}{(x \pm a)} + \frac{B}{(x \pm a)^2}$
(iii)	$\frac{px^2 \pm qx \pm r}{(x \pm a)(x \pm b)^2}$	$\frac{A}{(x \pm a)} + \frac{B}{(x \pm b)} + \frac{C}{(x \pm b)^2}$
(iv)	$\frac{px^2 \pm qx \pm r}{(x \pm a)(x^2 \pm bx \pm c)}$	$\frac{A}{(x \pm a)} + \frac{Bx + C}{(x^2 \pm bx \pm c)}$, where $x^2 \pm bx \pm c$ cannot be factorised further.

Note To integrate $\int \frac{x^2}{(x^2+a^2)(x^2+b^2)} dx$, firstly consider $x^2 = y$ and proceed for partial fraction of $\frac{y}{(y+a^2)(y+b^2)}$.

6. Integration by Parts

Let u and v be two differentiable functions of a single variable x, then the integral of the product of two functions is

$$\int \underset{\text{I}}{u} \underset{\text{II}}{v}\, dx = u \int v\, dx - \int \left(\frac{d}{dx} u \int v\, dx \right) dx$$

If two functions are of different types, then consider the 1st function (i.e. u) which comes first in word ILATE, where

I : Inverse trigonometric function e.g. $\sin^{-1} x, \cos^{-1} x$
L : Logarithmic function. e.g. $\log x, \log_a x$
A : Algebraic function. e.g. $1, x, x^2$
T : Trigonometric function. e.g. $\sin x, \cos x$
E : Exponential function. e.g. e^x, a^x

7. Some Important Integrals

(i) $\int \frac{dx}{x^2 + a^2} = \frac{1}{a} \tan^{-1} \frac{x}{a} + C$

(ii) $\int \frac{dx}{x^2 - a^2} = \frac{1}{2a} \log \left| \frac{x-a}{x+a} \right| + C$

(iii) $\int \frac{dx}{a^2 - x^2} = \frac{1}{2a} \log \left| \frac{a+x}{a-x} \right| + C$

(iv) $\int \frac{dx}{\sqrt{x^2 - a^2}} = \log |x + \sqrt{x^2 - a^2}| + C$

(v) $\int \frac{dx}{\sqrt{a^2 - x^2}} = \sin^{-1} \left(\frac{x}{a} \right) + C$

(vi) $\int \frac{dx}{\sqrt{x^2 + a^2}} = \log \left| x + \sqrt{x^2 + a^2} \right| + C$

(vii) $\int \sqrt{a^2 - x^2}\, dx = \frac{x}{2} \sqrt{a^2 - x^2} + \frac{a^2}{2} \sin^{-1} \frac{x}{a} + C$

(viii) $\int \sqrt{x^2 - a^2}\, dx = \frac{x}{2} \sqrt{x^2 - a^2} - \frac{a^2}{2} \log \left| x + \sqrt{x^2 - a^2} \right| + C$

(ix) $\int \sqrt{x^2 + a^2}\, dx = \frac{x}{2} \sqrt{x^2 + a^2} + \frac{a^2}{2} \log \left| x + \sqrt{x^2 + a^2} \right| + C$

Some Standard Substitutions

	Expression	Substitution
(i)	$a^2 - x^2$	$x = a\sin\theta$ or $a\cos\theta$
(ii)	$a^2 + x^2$	$x = a\tan\theta$ or $a\cot\theta$
(iii)	$x^2 - a^2$	$x = a\sec\theta$ or $a\operatorname{cosec}\theta$
(iv)	$\sqrt{\frac{a+x}{a-x}}$ or $\sqrt{\frac{a-x}{a+x}}$	$x = a\cos\theta$ or $x = a\cos 2\theta$
(v)	$\sqrt{\frac{x-\alpha}{\beta-x}}$ or $\sqrt{(x-\alpha)(\beta-x)}$	$x = \alpha\cos^2\theta + \beta\sin^2\theta$

8. Integral of the Type $\int [e^x [f(x) + f'(x)]] dx$

To evaluate such integral, we directly use the result

$$\int e^x [f(x) + f'(x)]\, dx = e^x f(x) + c$$

9. Integrals of the types $\int \frac{dx}{ax^2 + bx + c}$ or $\int \frac{dx}{\sqrt{ax^2 + bx + c}}$

It can be transformed into standard form by expressing

$$ax^2 + bx + c = a\left[x^2 + \frac{b}{a}x + \frac{c}{a} \right] = a\left[\left(x + \frac{b}{2a} \right)^2 + \left(\frac{c}{a} - \frac{b^2}{4a^2} \right) \right]$$

10. Integrals of the types $\int (px + q)\sqrt{ax^2 + bx + c}\, dx$ or $\int \frac{px + q}{ax^2 + bx + c} dx$ or $\int \frac{px + q}{\sqrt{ax^2 + bx + c}} dx$

It can be transformed into standard form by expressing

$$px + q = A\frac{d}{dx}(ax^2 + bx + c) + B = A(2ax + b) + B,$$

where A and B are determined by comparing coefficients and constants of both sides.

11. Integration of Irrational and Trigonometric Functions

	Integral	Substitution
(i)	$\int \frac{dx}{a \pm b\cos x}$	Put $\cos x = \frac{1 - \tan^2 \frac{x}{2}}{1 + \tan^2 \frac{x}{2}}$, then put $\tan \frac{x}{2} = t$
(ii)	$\int \frac{dx}{a \pm b\sin x}$	Put $\sin x = \frac{2\tan \frac{x}{2}}{1 + \tan^2 \frac{x}{2}}$, then put $\tan \frac{x}{2} = t$
(iii)	$\int \frac{dx}{a\sin x + b\cos x}$	Put $a = r\cos\theta$ and $b = r\sin\theta$, where $r = \sqrt{a^2 + b^2}$ and $\theta = \tan^{-1}\left(\frac{b}{a} \right)$
(iv)	$\int \frac{a\sin x + b\cos x + c}{p\sin x + q\cos x} dx$	Put $a\sin x + b\cos x + c = A\frac{d}{dx}(p\sin x + q\cos x) + B(p\sin x + q\cos x)$

	Integral	Substitution
(v)	$\int \dfrac{a\sin x + b\cos x}{p\sin x + q\cos x + r}dx$	Put $a\sin x + b\cos x$ $= A\dfrac{d}{dx}(p\sin x + q\cos x + r)$ $+ B(p\sin x + q\cos x + r)$
(vi)	$\int \dfrac{dx}{(ax+b)\sqrt{px+q}}$	Put $\sqrt{px+q} = t$
(vii)	$\int \dfrac{dx}{(ax^2+bx+c)\sqrt{px+q}}$	Put $\sqrt{px+q} = t$
(viii)	$\int \dfrac{dx}{(px+q)(\sqrt{ax^2+bx+c})}$	Put $px+q = \dfrac{1}{t}$
(ix)	$\int \dfrac{dx}{(px^2+q)\sqrt{ax^2+b}}$	Put $x = \dfrac{1}{t}$ and then put $\sqrt{a+bt^2} = U$

12. Integrals of the type

$$\int \frac{dx}{a\sin^2 x + b\cos^2 x}, \int \frac{dx}{a + b\sin^2 x}, \int \frac{dx}{a + b\cos^2 x},$$
$$\int \frac{dx}{(a\sin x + b\cos x)^2}, \int \frac{dx}{a\cos^2 x + b\sin^2 x + c}$$

To evaluate these type of integrals divide numerator and denominator both by $\cos^2 x$, replace $\sec^2 x$, if any, in denominator by $(1+\tan^2 x)$ and put $\tan x = t$, so that $\sec^2 x\,dx = dt$.

13. Integral of the type $\int \dfrac{1 \pm x^2}{1+x^4}dx$

To evaluate this type of integral, we proceed as follows

(i) Divide numerator and denominator by x^2.

(ii) Express the denominator of integrand in the form of $\left(x + \dfrac{1}{x}\right)^2 \pm k^2$.

(iii) Introduce $d\left(x+\dfrac{1}{x}\right)$ or $d\left(x - \dfrac{1}{x}\right)$ in numerator.

(iv) Put $x + \dfrac{1}{x} = t$ or $x - \dfrac{1}{x} = t$, as the case may be.

(v) Integral reduced to the form of $\int \dfrac{dx}{x^2+a^2}$ or $\int \dfrac{dx}{x^2-a^2}$.

14. Integral of the type $\int \dfrac{dx}{1+x^4}$

To evaluate this type of integral, we proceed as follows

(i) Multiply and divide by 2 in integrand.

(ii) Write 2 as $(1+x^2)+(1-x^2)$, the integral reduced to the form of $\dfrac{1}{2}\int \dfrac{1+x^2}{1+x^4} + \dfrac{1}{2}\int \dfrac{1-x^2}{1+x^4}$ say $I_1 + I_2$.

(iii) Evaluate I_1 and I_2 by the method discussed above.

15. Integral of the type $\int \sqrt{\tan x}\,dx$ **and** $\int \sqrt{\cot x}\,dx$

To evaluate this type of integral, put $\tan x = t^2$, that reduces the integral into the form of

$$\int \frac{2t^2}{t^4+1}dt = \int \frac{t^2+1}{t^4+1}dt + \int \frac{t^2-1}{t^4+1}dt$$

which can be done by the method discussed above.

Chapter 9 : **Definite Integrals**

1. Definite Integral

An integral of the form of $\int_a^b f(x)dx$ is known as definite integral and is given by $\int_a^b f(x)dx = [g(x)]_a^b = g(b) - g(a)$

where, a and b are lower and upper limits of the definite integral, respectively and $g'(x) = f(x)$.

2. (i) First Fundamental Theorem of Integral Calculus

Let f be a continuous function defined on the closed interval $[a, b]$ and $A(x)$ be the area of function, i.e. $A(x) = \int_a^x f(x)dx$. Then, $A'(x) = f(x)$, for all $x \in [a, b]$.

(ii) Second Fundamental Theorem of Integral Calculus

Let f be a continuous function defined on the closed interval $[a, b]$ and F be an anti-derivative of f.

Then, $\int_a^b f(x)dx = [F(x)]_a^b = F(b) - F(a)$

3. Properties of Definite Integral

(i) $\int_a^b f(x)dx = \int_a^b f(t)dt$ (ii) $\int_a^b f(x)dx = -\int_b^a f(x)dx$

(iii) $\int_a^b f(x)dx = \int_a^c f(x)dx + \int_c^b f(x)dx$, where $a < c < b$.

(iv) $\int_a^b f(x)dx = \int_a^b f(a+b-x)dx$

(v) $\int_0^a f(x)dx = \int_0^a f(a-x)dx$

(vi) $\int_0^{2a} f(x)dx = \begin{cases} 2\int_0^a f(x)dx, & \text{if } f(2a-x) = f(x) \\ 0, & \text{if } f(2a-x) = -f(x) \end{cases}$

(vii) $\int_{-a}^a f(x)dx = \begin{cases} 2\int_0^a f(x)dx, & \text{if } f(-x) = f(x) \\ 0, & \text{if } f(-x) = -f(x) \end{cases}$

Note Some special cases are as follows

(i) $\int_a^a f(x)dx = 0$ (ii) $\int_0^{2a} f(x)dx = \int_0^a f(x)dx + \int_0^a f(2a-x)dx$

Chapter 10 : Differential Equations

1. Differential Equation

An equation containing an independent variable, dependent variable and derivative of dependent variable with respect to independent variable, is called a differential equation. The derivatives are denoted by the symbols

$$\frac{dy}{dx}, \frac{d^2y}{dx^2}, \dots, \frac{d^ny}{dx^n} \text{ or } y', y'', \dots, y'''^{\dots n} \text{ or } y_1, y_2, \dots, y_n.$$

2. Order of a Differential Equation

The order of the differential equation is the highest order of the derivative occuring in it.

3. Degree of a Differential Equation

The greatest exponent of the highest order derivative in the differential equation, is called degree.

4. Solution of a Differential Equation

A relation between the dependent and independent variables which, when substituted in the differential equation reduces it to an identity, is called a solution.

5. General Solution of a Differential Equation

A solution of a differential equation which contains as many arbitrary constants as the order of the differential equation, is called the general solution or primitive solution of the differential equation.

6. Particular Solution of a Differential Equation

The solution obtained from the general solution giving particular values to the arbitrary constants, is called a particular solution of the differential equation.

7. Equation in Variable Separable Form

If the equation can be reduced into the form

$$f(x)\,dx + g(y)\,dy = 0,$$

we say that the variables have been separated.

Then, $\int f(x)\,dx + \int g(y)\,dy = C$

8. Equation Reducible to Variables Separable

If the given differential equation is of the form $\frac{dy}{dx} = f(ax + by + c)$, put $v = ax + by + c$ and it will be reduced to variables separable.

9. Homogeneous Differential Equation

A differential equation of the form $\frac{dy}{dx} = \frac{f(x, y)}{g(x, y)}$, where $f(x, y)$ and $g(x, y)$ are homogeneous functions of x and y are of the same order.

To solve such differential equation we make substitution $y = vx$ and proceed further to find the general solution.

Note If the homogeneous differential equation is in the form $\frac{dx}{dy} = \frac{f(x, y)}{g(x, y)}$, where $f(x, y)$ and $g(x, y)$ are homogeneous functions of same order, then we make substitution $\frac{x}{y} = v$, i.e. $x = vy$ and proceed further to find the general solution.

10. Equation Reducible to Homogeneous Form

The differential equations of the form

$$\frac{dy}{dx} = \frac{a_1x + b_1y + c_1}{a_2x + b_2y + c_2} \quad \dots(i)$$

Put, $x = X + h$ and $y = Y + k$

$$\therefore \quad \frac{dY}{dX} = \frac{a_1X + b_1Y + (a_1h + b_1k + c_1)}{a_2X + b_2Y + (a_2h + b_2k + c_2)} \quad \dots(ii)$$

We choose h and k, such that it satisfies

$$a_1h + b_1k + c_1 = 0 \text{ and } a_2h + b_2k + c_2 = 0.$$

On solving, we get

$$\frac{h}{b_1c_2 - b_2c_1} = \frac{k}{c_1a_2 - c_2a_1} = \frac{1}{a_1b_2 - a_2b_1}$$

$$\therefore \quad h = \frac{b_1c_2 - b_2c_1}{a_1b_2 - a_2b_1}$$

and $$k = \frac{c_1a_2 - c_2a_1}{a_1b_2 - a_2b_1}$$

Provided $a_1b_2 - a_2b_1 \neq 0$ or $\frac{a_1}{a_2} \neq \frac{b_1}{b_2}$.

Then, Eq. (ii) reduces to $\frac{dy}{dx} = \frac{a_1X + b_1Y}{a_2X + b_2Y}$, which is a homogeneous form and will be solved easily.

11. Linear Differential Equation

A first order and first degree differential equation in which the degree of dependent variable and its derivative is one and they do not get multiplied together, is called a linear differential equation.

There are two types of linear differential equations.

***Type* I** Form $\frac{dy}{dx} + Py = Q$, where P and Q are constants or functions of x only. We find integrating factor (IF) $= e^{\int P\,dx}$. Now, solution is given by $y \times (\text{IF}) = \int [Q \times (\text{IF})]\,dx + C$.

***Type* II** Form $\frac{dx}{dy} + Px = Q$, where P and Q are constants or functions of y only, then IF $= e^{\int P\,dy}$

Its solution is given by $x \times (\text{IF}) = \int [Q \times (\text{IF})]\,dy + C$.

Chapter 11 : **Probability**

1. Some Basic Definitions

There are some basic definitions given below

(i) **Experiment** An operation in which results are some well-defined outcomes, is called an experiment.

(ii) **Random experiment** An experiment in which total outcomes are known in advance but occurrence of specific outcome can be told only after completion of the experiment, is known as a random experiment.

(iii) **Trial** When a random experiment is repeated under identical conditions and it does not give the same result each time but may result in any one of the several possible outcomes, then such experiment is called a trial.

(iv) **Sample space** The set of all possible outcomes of a random experiment is called its sample space. It is usually denoted by S.

(v) **Discrete sample space** A sample space is called a discrete sample space, if S is a finite set.

2. Event

A subset of the sample space associated with a random experiment is called an event (or **case**).

3. Types of Events

There are following types of events

(i) **Sure event** Sure event is the sample space S itself.

(ii) **Impossible event** Impossible event corresponds to null set ϕ.

(iii) **Equally likely events** The given events are said to be equally likely, if none of them is expected to occur in preference to the other.

(iv) **Mutually exclusive events** A set of events is said to be mutually exclusive, if the happening of one excludes the happening of the other, i.e. if A and B are mutually exclusive, then $(A \cap B) = \phi$.

(v) **Exhaustive events** A set of events is said to be exhaustive, if the performance of the experiment always results in the occurrence of atleast one of the events. If $E_1, E_2, \dots, E_n$ are exhaustive events, then $E_1 \cup E_2 \cup \dots \cup E_n = S$.

(vi) **Complement of an event** Let A be an event in a sample space S, then complement of A is the set of all sample points of the space other than the sample point in A and it is denoted by A' or $\overline{A}$.

i.e. $A' = \{n : n \in S, n \notin A\}$.

4. Probability of an Event

If there are n elementary equally likely events associated with a random experiment and m of them are favourable to an event A, then the **probability of happening or occurrence of A** is denoted by $P(A)$ and defined as

$$P(A) = \frac{m}{n} = \frac{\left[\text{Number of elementary events favourable to event } A\right]}{\left[\text{Total number of elementary events to the experiment}\right]}$$

Note (i) $0 \le P(A) \le 1$ (ii) $P(A \cup A') = 1$

(iii) $P(A \cap A') = 0$ (iv) $P((A')') = P(A)$

(v) Probability of impossible event is zero.

(vi) Probability of sure event is 1.

(vii) Sometimes, we have to select r objects from n distinct objects, then we use the formula,

$$^nC_r = \frac{n!}{r!(n-r)!}, \quad 0 \le r \le n.$$

5. Laws on Probability

A. Addition Theorem of Probability

(i) For two events A and B,

$$P(A \cup B) = P(A) + P(B) - P(A \cap B)$$
$$= P(A-B) + P(B-A) + P(A \cap B)$$
$$= P(A) + P(B-A)$$
$$= P(B) + P(A-B)$$

If A and B are mutually exclusive events, then

$$P(A \cup B) = P(A) + P(B)$$

[for mutually exclusive events, $P(A \cap B) = 0$]

(ii) For three events A, B and C,

$$P(A \cup B \cup C) = P(A) + P(B) + P(C) - P(A \cap B) - P(B \cap C) - P(A \cap C) + P(A \cap B \cap C)$$

If A, B and C are mutually exclusive events, then

$$P(A \cup B \cup C) = P(A) + P(B) + P(C)$$

[$\because$ for mutually exclusive events, $P(A \cap B) = P(B \cap C) = P(C \cap A) = P(A \cap B \cap C) = 0$]

Note If $A_1, A_2, A_3, \dots, A_n$ are mutually exclusive events associated with a random experiment, then

$$P(A_1 \cup A_2 \cup A_3 \cup \dots \cup A_n) = P(A_1) + P(A_2) + P(A_3) + \dots + P(A_n).$$

B. If A and B are two events associated with a random experiment, then

(i) $P(\overline{A} \cap B) = P(B) - P(A \cap B)$

(ii) $P(A \cap \overline{B}) = P(A) - P(A \cap B)$

(iii) $P[(A \cap \overline{B}) \cup (\overline{A} \cap B)] = P(A) + P(B) - 2P(A \cap B)$

(iv) $P(\overline{A} \cap \overline{B}) = 1 - P(A \cup B)$

(v) $P(\overline{A} \cup \overline{B}) = 1 - P(A \cap B)$

(vi) $P(A) = P(A \cap B) + P(A \cap \overline{B}) = P(A-B) + P(A \cap B)$

(vii) $P(B)=P(A\cap B)+P(B\cap \bar{A})=P(B-A)+P(A\cap B)$

(viii) P(exactly one of A, B occurs)

$$= P(A)+P(B)-2P(A\cap B)$$
$$= P(A\cup B)-P(A\cap B)$$

C. If A, B and C are three events, then

P(exactly one of A, B, C occurs)

$$= P(A)+P(B)+P(C)-2P(A\cap B)-2P(B\cap C) -2P(A\cap C)+3P(A\cap B\cap C)$$

D. $P(\bar{A})=1-P(A)$

Note If $A\subseteq B$, then

(i) $P(A)\le P(B)$ (ii) $P(B-A)=P(B)-P(A)$

6. Conditional Probability

Let E and F be two events associated with a random experiment. Then, probability of occurrence of event E, when the event F has already occurred, is called conditional probability of event E over F and is denoted by $P(E/F)$.

$$P(E/F)=\frac{P(E\cap F)}{P(F)}, \text{ where } P(F)\neq 0.$$

7. Properties of Conditional Probability

Let A, B and C be the events of a sample space S. Then,

(i) $P(S/A)=P(A/A)=1$

(ii) $P\{(A\cup B)/C\}=P(A/C)+P(B/C)-P\{(A\cap B)/C\}$, $P(C)\neq 0$

(iii) $P(A'/B)=1-P(A/B)$, where A' is complement of A.

8. Multiplication Theorem on Probability

Let A and B be two events associated with a random experiment, then

$$P(A\cap B)=\begin{cases} P(A)\cdot P(B/A), \text{ where } P(A)\neq 0 \\ P(B)\cdot P(A/B), \text{ where } P(B)\neq 0 \end{cases}$$

The above result is known as the multiplication rule of probability.

Multiplication probability for more than two events

Let E, F and G are three events of sample space S, then

$$P(E\cap F\cap G)=P(E)\cdot P\left(\frac{F}{E}\right)\cdot P(G/(E\cap F))$$

9. Independent Events

Two events A and B are said to be independent, if the occurrence or non-occurrence of one event does not affect the occurrence or non-occurrence of another event.

Then, $P(A\cap B)=P(A)\cdot P(B)$, $P(A/B)=P(A)$

and $P(B/A)=P(B)$

10. Dependent Events

Two events are said to be dependent, if the occurrence or non-occurrence of the one event in any trial affects the probability of the other subsequent trials.

11. Some Important Results

1. Two events E and F are said to be dependent, if they are not independent, i.e. $P(E\cap F)\neq P(E)\cdot P(F)$
2. Two experiments are said to be independent, if for every pair of events E and F, where E is associated with the first experiment and F with the second experiment, the probability of the simultaneous occurrence of the events E and F is the product of $P(E)$ and $P(F)$ calculated separately on the basis of two experiments,

   i.e. $P(E\cap F)=P(E)\cdot P(F)$
3. Three events A, B and C are said to be mutually independent, if

$$P(A\cap B)=P(A)\cdot P(B)$$
$$P(A\cap C)=P(A)\cdot P(C)$$
$$P(B\cap C)=P(B)\cdot P(C)$$
and $$P(A\cap B\cap C)=P(A)\cdot P(B)\cdot P(C)$$

If atleast one of the above is not true for three given events, then events are not independent. i.e. dependent.

12. Properties of Independent Events

If A and B are independent events, then

(i) A and B' are also independent events.

(ii) A' and B are also independent events.

(iii) A' and B' are also independent events.

13. Partition of Sample Space

A set of events $E_1, E_2, \ldots, E_n$ is said to represent a partition of the sample space S, if it satisfies the following conditions

(i) $E_i\cap E_j=\phi, i\neq j,\ i, j=1,2,\ldots,n$

(ii) $E_1\cup E_2\cup\ldots\cup E_n=S$

(iii) $P(E_i)>0$, for all $i=1,2,\ldots,n$

14. Theorem of Total Probability

Let S be the sample space and $E_1, E_2, E_3, \ldots, E_n$ be n mutually exclusive and exhaustive events associated with a random experiment.

If E is any event which occurs with $E_1, E_2, E_3, \ldots, E_n$.

Then, $$P(E)=P(E_1)\cdot P(E/E_1)+P(E_2)\cdot P(E/E_2) + P(E_3)\cdot P(E/E_3)+\cdots+P(E_n)\cdot P(E/E_n)$$

or $$P(E)=\sum_{i=1}^{n} P(E_i)\cdot P\left(\frac{E}{E_i}\right)$$

15. Baye's Theorem

Let S be the sample space and $E_1, E_2, \ldots, E_n$ be n mutually exclusive and exhaustive events associated with a random experiment. If A is any event which occurs with $E_1, E_2, \ldots, E_n$, then probability of occurrence of E_i when A has occurred, is

$$P(E_i/A)=\frac{P(E_i)P(A/E_i)}{\sum_{i=1}^{n} P(E_i)P(A/E_i)},\ i=1,2,\ldots,n$$

If $P(E_1)=P(E_2)=P(E_3)=\ldots=P(E_n)$,

then $$P(E_i/E)=\frac{P(E/E_i)}{\sum_{i=1}^{n} P(E/E_i)}$$

16. Random Variable

A random variable is a real valued function, whose domain is the sample space of a random experiment. Generally, it is denoted by capital letter X. Also, more than one random variables can be defined on the same sample space.

17. Probability Distribution of a Random Variable

The system in which the value of a random variable are given along with their corresponding probability is called probability distribution. If X is a random variable and takes the values $x_1, x_2, x_3, \ldots, x_n$ with respective probabilities $p_1, p_2, p_3, \ldots, p_n$. Then, the probability distribution of X is represented by

X	x_1	x_2	x_3	...	x_n
$P(X)$	p_1	p_2	p_3	...	p_n

such that $\Sigma\, p_i = 1$

Note If x_i is one of the possible values of a random variable X, then statement $X = x_i$ is true only at some point(s) of the sample space. Hence, the probability that X takes value x_i is always non-zero, i.e. $P(X = x_i) \neq 0$.

18. Mean of a Random Variable

Mean of a random variable is $\sum_{i=1}^{n} x_i\, p_i$. It is also called expectation of X, i.e. $E(X) = \sum_{i=1}^{n} x_i\, p_i$.

Chapter 12 : Vector Algebra

1. Vector and Scalar

A quantity that has magnitude as well as direction, is called a vector. Since, the length is never negative, so the notation $|\vec{a}| < 0$ has no meaning.

A quantity that has magnitude only, is called scalar.

Types of Vectors

There are various types of vectors as given below

(i) **Like Vectors** Two vectors $\vec{a}$ and $\vec{b}$ are said to be like vectors, if they have the same directions and are said **unlike vectors**, if they have opposite directions.

(ii) **Zero or Null Vector** A vector whose magnitude is zero, i.e whose initial and terminal points coincide, is called a null vector or zero vector.

(iii) **Unit Vector** A vector whose magnitude is one unit (i.e. unity) is called a unit vector.

(iv) **Proper Vector** A vector, which is not a zero vector, is called proper vector. i.e. If $|\vec{a}| \neq 0$.

(v) **Coinitial Vectors** Two or more vectors having the same initial point are called coinitial vectors.

Note Two equal coinitial vectors must coincide.

(vi) **Collinear or Parallel Vectors** Two or more vectors are said to be collinear, if they are parallel to same line, irrespective of their magnitudes and directions.

(vii) **Non-collinear Vectors** Those vectors whose directions are neither parallel nor coincident, are called non-collinear vectors.

(viii) **Equal Vectors** Two vectors are said to be equal, if they have same magnitude and direction regardless of the positions of their initial points. Symbolically if $\vec{a}$ and $\vec{b}$ are equal, then it is written as $\vec{a} = \vec{b}$.

(ix) **Negative of a Vector** A vector whose magnitude is same as that of a given vector but the direction is opposite to that of it, is called negative of the given vector.

(x) **Localised Vectors** Those vectors which are restricted to pass through a given point (origin) are called localised vectors.

(xi) **Reciprocal Vectors** Two vectors are said to be reciprocal vectors, if they have the same direction but whose magnitude (or modulus or length) are reciprocal of each other. Thus, if $\hat{a}$ denotes the unit vector in the direction of a vector $\vec{a}$, then $\vec{a} = |\vec{a}|\,\hat{a}$ and $\dfrac{1}{\vec{a}} = \dfrac{\hat{a}}{|\vec{a}|}$.

Note If the value of a vector depends only on its magnitude and direction and is independent of its position in the space, it is called free or non-localised vector. Throughout this chapter, we will be dealing with free vectors only.

Position Vector of a Point

Let $O\ (0, 0, 0)$ be the origin and P be a point in space having coordinates (x, y, z) with respect to the origin O. Then, the vector $\overrightarrow{OP}$ or $\vec{r}$ is called the position vector of the point P with respect to O.

2. Triangle Law of Vectors Addition

If two vectors are represented along two sides of a triangle taken in order, then their resultant is represented by the third side taken in opposite direction, i.e. in ΔABC, by using triangle law of vector addition, we have

$$\overrightarrow{BC} + \overrightarrow{CA} = \overrightarrow{BA}$$

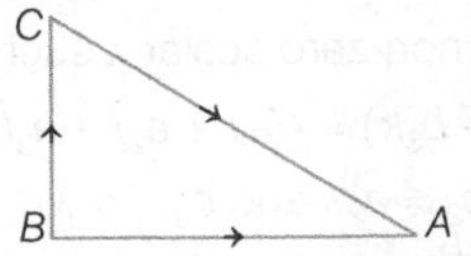

3. Parallelogram Law of Vectors Addition

If two vectors are represented along the two adjacent sides of a parallelogram, then their resultant is represented by the diagonal of these sides.

If the sides OA and OC of parallelogram $OABC$ represents $\overrightarrow{OA}$ and $\overrightarrow{OC}$, respectively, then we get

$$\overrightarrow{OA}+\overrightarrow{OC}=\overrightarrow{OB} \text{ or } \overrightarrow{OA}+\overrightarrow{AB}=\overrightarrow{OB} \quad [\because \overrightarrow{AB}=\overrightarrow{OC}]$$

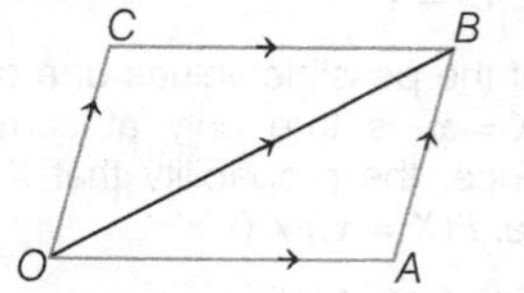

Thus, we may say that the two laws of vectors addition are equivalent to each other.

Properties of Vector Addition

Suppose $\vec{a}$, $\vec{b}$ and $\vec{c}$ are any three vectors, then

(i) Vector addition is **commutative,**

i.e. $\vec{a}+\vec{b}=\vec{b}+\vec{a}$

(ii) Vector addition is **associative**,

i.e. $(\vec{a}+\vec{b})+\vec{c}=\vec{a}+(\vec{b}+\vec{c})$

(iii) **Existence of additive identity**

$\vec{a}+\vec{0}=\vec{a}=\vec{0}+\vec{a}$,

where $\vec{0}$ is called additive identity.

(iv) **Existence of additive inverse**

$(\vec{a})+(-\vec{a})=\vec{0}=(-\vec{a})+(\vec{a})$

where, vector $-\vec{a}$ is called the negative (or additive inverse) of $\vec{a}$.

Note The associative property of vector addition enables us to write the sum of three vectors $\vec{a}$, $\vec{b}$ and $\vec{c}$ as $\vec{a}+\vec{b}+\vec{c}$ without using brackets.

Important Results in Component Form

If $\vec{a}$ and $\vec{b}$ are any two vectors given in the component form such that $\vec{a}=a_1\hat{i}+a_2\hat{j}+a_3\hat{k}$ and $\vec{b}=b_1\hat{i}+b_2\hat{j}+b_3\hat{k}$.

Then,

(i) the sum (or resultant) of the vectors $\vec{a}$ and $\vec{b}$ is given by $\vec{a}+\vec{b}=(a_1+b_1)\hat{i}+(a_2+b_2)\hat{j}+(a_3+b_3)\hat{k}$.

(ii) the difference of the vectors $\vec{a}$ and $\vec{b}$ is given by $\vec{a}-\vec{b}=(a_1-b_1)\hat{i}+(a_2-b_2)\hat{j}+(a_3-b_3)\hat{k}$.

(iii) the vectors $\vec{a}$ and $\vec{b}$ are equal, if and only if $a_1=b_1$, $a_2=b_2$ and $a_3=b_3$.

(iv) the multiplication of vector $\vec{a}$ by any scalar λ is given by $\lambda\vec{a}=(\lambda a_1)\hat{i}+(\lambda a_2)\hat{j}+(\lambda a_3)\hat{k}$.

(v) The vectors $\vec{a}$ and $\vec{b}$ are collinear (or parallel) if and only if there exists a non-zero scalar λ such that $\vec{b}=\lambda\vec{a}$.

$\Rightarrow (b_1\hat{i}+b_2\hat{j}+b_3\hat{k})=\lambda(a_1\hat{i}+a_2\hat{j}+a_3\hat{k})$

$\Rightarrow b_1=a_1\lambda,\ b_2=a_2\lambda$ and $b_3=a_3\lambda$

$\Rightarrow \dfrac{b_1}{a_1}=\dfrac{b_2}{a_2}=\dfrac{b_3}{a_3}=\lambda$

Thus, the vectors $\vec{a}$ and $\vec{b}$ are collinear (or parallel) iff

$$\frac{b_1}{a_1}=\frac{b_2}{a_2}=\frac{b_3}{a_3}=\lambda \quad \text{[non-zero constant]}$$

4. Direction Cosines and Direction Ratios of a Vector

Suppose $\overrightarrow{OP}$ (or $\vec{r}$) is the position vector of a point $P(x, y, z)$ shown in the figure.

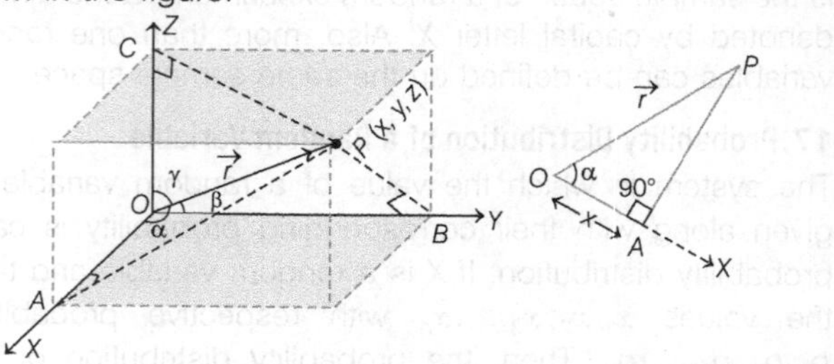

Here, the angles α, β and γ made by the vector $\overrightarrow{OP}$ with positive directions of coordinates axes OX, OY and OZ, respectively, are called **direction angles**.

Generally, they are denoted by l, m and n, respectively, i.e. $l=\cos\alpha$, $m=\cos\beta$ and $n=\cos\gamma$.

In point $P(lr, mr, nr)$, the numbers lr, mr and nr are proportional to the direction cosines, so these numbers are called the direction ratios of vector $\vec{r}$ and denoted as x, y and z, respectively.

Suppose a position vector is $\vec{a}=a_1\hat{i}+a_2\hat{j}+a_3\hat{k}$, then a_1, a_2 and a_3 are called the direction ratios of $\vec{a}$.

Note (i) In general, it may be noted that $l^2+m^2+n^2=1$ but $x^2+y^2+z^2\neq 1$.

(ii) If it is given that l, m and n are direction cosines of a vector, then $l\hat{i}+m\hat{j}+n\hat{k}=(\cos\alpha)\hat{i}+(\cos\beta)\hat{j}+(\cos\gamma)\hat{k}$ is the unit vector in the direction of that vector, where α, β and γ are the angles which the vector makes with X, Y and Z-axes, respectively.

5. Section Formulae

(i) Internal Division

Let a point C divide the line joining A, B internally in the ratio of $m:n$. Then, the position vector of point C is given by

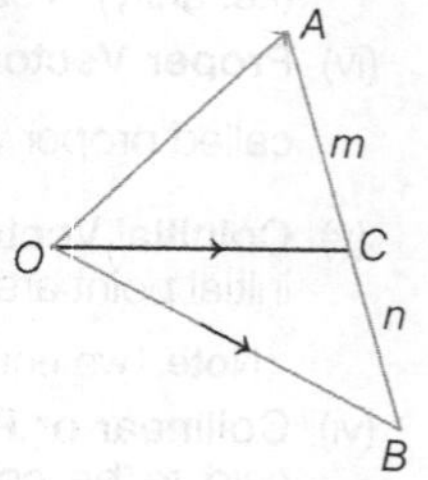

$$\overrightarrow{OC}=\frac{m\overrightarrow{OB}+n\overrightarrow{OA}}{m+n}$$

where, m and n are positive scalars.

(ii) External Division

Let a point C divide the line joining AB externally in the ratio of $m:n$. Then, the position vector of point C is given by

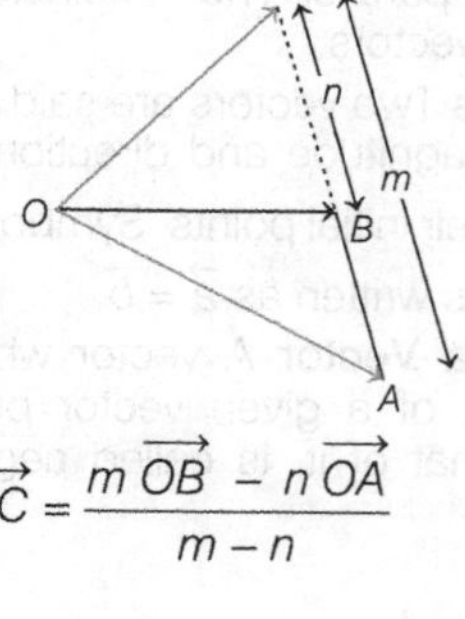

$$\overrightarrow{OC}=\frac{m\overrightarrow{OB}-n\overrightarrow{OA}}{m-n}$$

where, m and n are positive scalars.

Note If C is a mid-point, then the position vector of point C is given by $\overrightarrow{OC} = \dfrac{\overrightarrow{OB} + \overrightarrow{OA}}{2}$.

6. Scalar (or Dot) Product of Two Vectors

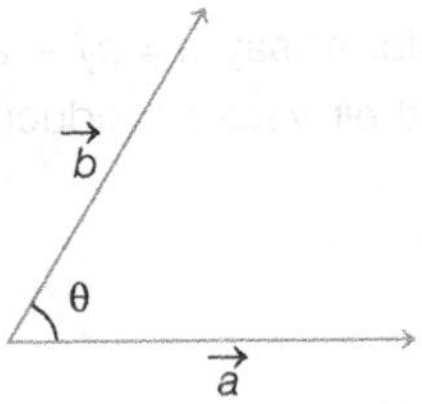

Let $\vec{a}$ and $\vec{b}$ be two non-zero vectors inclined at an angle θ. Then, the scalar product or dot product of $\vec{a}$ and $\vec{b}$ is denoted by $\vec{a} \cdot \vec{b}$ and defined as

$$\vec{a} \cdot \vec{b} = |\vec{a}||\vec{b}| \cos \theta,\ 0 \le \theta \le \pi$$

Note If either $\vec{a} = 0$ or $\vec{b} = 0$, then θ is not defined and in this case we define, $\vec{a} \cdot \vec{b} = 0$.

7. Important Results on Scalar Product of Two Vectors

(i) The scalar product of two vectors (i.e. $\vec{a} \cdot \vec{b}$) is a real number.

(ii) Let $\vec{a}$ and $\vec{b}$ be two non-zero vectors, then $\vec{a} \cdot \vec{b} = 0$ if and only if $\vec{a}$ and $\vec{b}$ are perpendicular to each other, i.e. $\vec{a} \cdot \vec{b} = 0 \Leftrightarrow \vec{a} \perp \vec{b}$ i.e. $a_1b_1 + a_2b_2 + a_3b_3 = 0$.

(iii) Two vectors $\vec{a}$ and $\vec{b}$ are parallel, if there exists a scalar λ such that $\vec{a} = \lambda \vec{b}$,

i.e. $\dfrac{a_1}{b_1} = \dfrac{a_2}{b_2} = \dfrac{a_3}{b_3} = \lambda$.

In other words, two vectors are parallel, if their corresponding components are proportional.

(iv) If $\theta = 0$, then $\vec{a} \cdot \vec{b} = |\vec{a}||\vec{b}|$. Also, $\vec{a} \cdot \vec{a} = |\vec{a}|^2$.

(v) If $\theta = \pi$, then $\vec{a} \cdot \vec{b} = -|\vec{a}||\vec{b}|$.

Also, $\vec{a} \cdot (-\vec{a}) = -|\vec{a}|^2$.

(vi) For mutually perpendicular unit vectors $\hat{i}, \hat{j}$ and $\hat{k}$, $\hat{i} \cdot \hat{i} = \hat{j} \cdot \hat{j} = \hat{k} \cdot \hat{k} = 1$ and $\hat{i} \cdot \hat{j} = \hat{j} \cdot \hat{k} = \hat{k} \cdot \hat{i} = 0$.

(vii) The angle between two non-zero vectors $\vec{a}$ and $\vec{b}$ is given by $\cos \theta = \dfrac{\vec{a} \cdot \vec{b}}{|\vec{a}||\vec{b}|}$

or $\qquad \theta = \cos^{-1}\left(\dfrac{\vec{a} \cdot \vec{b}}{|\vec{a}||\vec{b}|}\right)$.

8. Some Results Related to Projection of a Vector

(i) **Projection of vector $\vec{a}$ on $\vec{b}$** is given by $\vec{a} \cdot \hat{b}$ or $\dfrac{\vec{a} \cdot \vec{b}}{\vec{b}}$ and **projection of vector $\vec{b}$ on $\vec{a}$** is given by $\vec{b} \cdot \hat{a}$ or $\dfrac{\vec{a} \cdot \vec{b}}{\vec{a}}$

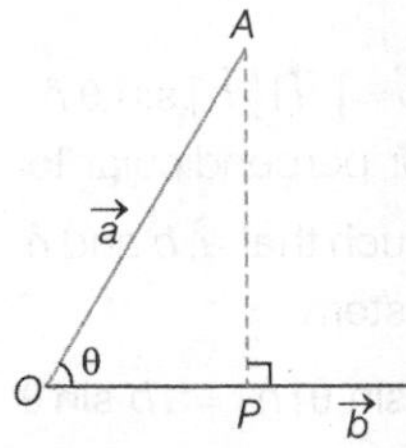

(ii) If $\theta = 0$, then the projection vector of $\overrightarrow{AO}$ will be $\overrightarrow{AO}$ itself and if $\theta = \pi$, then the projection vector of $\overrightarrow{AO}$ will be $\overrightarrow{AO}$.

(iii) If $\theta = \dfrac{\pi}{2}$ or $\theta = \dfrac{3\pi}{2}$, then the projection vector of $\overrightarrow{AO}$ will be zero vector.

(iv) Let α, β and γ be the direction angles of vector $\vec{a} = a_1\hat{i} + a_2\hat{j} + a_3\hat{k}$, then its direction cosines may be given as

$$\cos \alpha = \frac{\vec{a} \cdot \hat{i}}{|\vec{a}||\hat{i}|} = \frac{a_1}{|\vec{a}|}, \cos \beta = \frac{\vec{a} \cdot \hat{j}}{|\vec{a}||\hat{j}|} = \frac{a_2}{|\vec{a}|}$$

and $\cos \gamma = \dfrac{\vec{a} \cdot \hat{k}}{|\vec{a}||\hat{k}|} = \dfrac{a_3}{|\vec{a}|}$.

Note (i) If $\hat{a}$ is a unit vector, then it may be expressed as

$$\hat{a} = \cos \alpha \hat{i} + \cos \beta \hat{j} + \cos \gamma \hat{k}.$$

(ii) Square of a vector is always equal to square of its modulus.

9. Properties of Scalar Product of Two Vectors

(i) Scalar product of two vectors is **commutative**, i.e. for vectors $\vec{a}$ and $\vec{b}$, we have $\vec{a} \cdot \vec{b} = \vec{b} \cdot \vec{a}$.

(ii) Scalar product of vectors is **distributive over addition**, i.e. for vectors $\vec{a}$, $\vec{b}$ and $\vec{c}$, we have

$$\vec{a} \cdot (\vec{b} + \vec{c}) = \vec{a} \cdot \vec{b} + \vec{a} \cdot \vec{c}.$$

(iii) If m is any scalar and $\vec{a}$ and $\vec{b}$ be two non-zero vectors. Then, $(m\vec{a}) \cdot (\vec{b}) = m(\vec{a} \cdot \vec{b}) = (\vec{a}) \cdot (m\vec{b})$

Note For any two vectors $\vec{a}$ and $\vec{b}$,

(i) $\vec{a} \cdot (-\vec{b}) = -(\vec{a} \cdot \vec{b}) = (-\vec{a}) \cdot (\vec{b})$

(ii) $(-\vec{a}) \cdot (-\vec{b}) = \vec{a} \cdot \vec{b}$

(iv) **Scalar product of two vectors in component form**

Suppose two vectors $\vec{a}$ and $\vec{b}$ are given in component form, say $\vec{a} = a_1\hat{i} + a_2\hat{j} + a_3\hat{k}$ and $\vec{b} = b_1\hat{i} + b_2\hat{j} + b_3\hat{k}$.

Then, their scalar product is given by

$$\vec{a} \cdot \vec{b} = (a_1\hat{i} + a_2\hat{j} + a_3\hat{k}) \cdot (b_1\hat{i} + b_2\hat{j} + b_3\hat{k})$$
$$= a_1b_1 + a_2b_2 + a_3b_3$$

10. Vector (or Cross) Product of Two Vectors

Let $\vec{a}$ and $\vec{b}$ be two non-zero vectors inclined at an angle θ. Then, the vector (or cross) product of $\vec{a}$ and $\vec{b}$ is denoted by $\vec{a} \times \vec{b}$, read as $\vec{a}$ cross $\vec{b}$ and defined as

$$\vec{a} \times \vec{b} = |\vec{a}||\vec{b}| \sin \theta \, \hat{n}$$

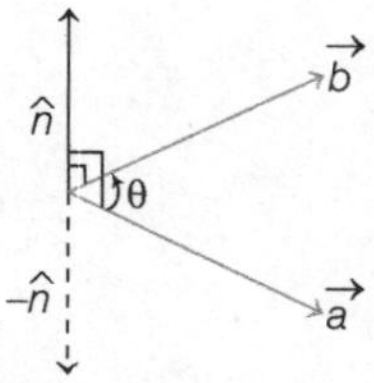

where, $\hat{n}$ is a unit vector perpendicular to both vectors $\vec{a}$ and $\vec{b}$, such that $\vec{a}, \vec{b}$ and $\hat{n}$ form a right handed system.

Also, $|\vec{a} \times \vec{b}| = |\vec{a}||\vec{b}| \sin \theta |\hat{n}| = ab \sin \theta$

$[\because |\vec{a}| = a, |\vec{b}| = b \text{ and } |\hat{n}| = 1]$

Note (i) Either $\vec{a} = \vec{0}$ or $\vec{b} = \vec{0}$, then θ is not defined as $\vec{0}$ has no direction and in this case $\vec{a} \times \vec{b} = \vec{0}$.

(ii) Unit vector perpendicular of two vectors $\vec{a}$ and $\vec{b}$ is given by $\hat{n} = \dfrac{\vec{a} \times \vec{b}}{|\vec{a} \times \vec{b}|}$

(iii) **Lagrange's Identity** If $\vec{a}$ and $\vec{b}$ are two vectors, then $(\vec{a} \times \vec{b})^2 = |\vec{a}|^2 |\vec{b}|^2 - (\vec{a} \cdot \vec{b})^2$ which are known as relation between dot and cross product.

11. Important Results on Vector Product of Two Vectors

(i) The vector product of two vectors $(\vec{a} \times \vec{b})$ is a vector.

(ii) Let $\vec{a}$ and $\vec{b}$ be two non-zero vectors. Then, $\vec{a} \times \vec{b} = \vec{0}$ if and only if $\vec{a}$ and $\vec{b}$ are parallel (or **collinear**) to each other,

i.e. $\vec{a} \times \vec{b} = \vec{0} \Leftrightarrow \vec{a} \parallel \vec{b}$.

(iii) $\vec{a} \times \vec{a} = \vec{0}$, as $\theta = 0°$ and $\vec{a} \times (-\vec{a}) = \vec{0}$, as $\theta = \pi$.

(iv) If $\theta = \dfrac{\pi}{2}$, then $|\vec{a} \times \vec{b}| = |\vec{a}||\vec{b}|$.

(v) For mutually perpendicular unit vectors $\hat{i}, \hat{j}$ and $\hat{k}$,

$$\hat{i} \times \hat{i} = \hat{j} \times \hat{j} = \hat{k} \times \hat{k} = \vec{0}$$

and $\hat{i} \times \hat{j} = \hat{k}, \hat{j} \times \hat{k} = \hat{i}, \hat{k} \times \hat{i} = \hat{j}$,

$\hat{j} \times \hat{i} = -\hat{k}, \hat{k} \times \hat{j} = -\hat{i}$

and $\hat{i} \times \hat{k} = -\hat{j}$.

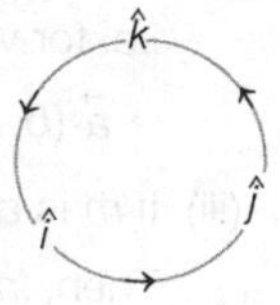

(vi) The angle between two non-zero vectors $\vec{a}$ and $\vec{b}$ in terms of vector product is given by $\sin \theta = \dfrac{|\vec{a} \times \vec{b}|}{|\vec{a}||\vec{b}|}$.

(vii) Vectors of magnitude λ normal to the plane of $\vec{a}$ and $\vec{b}$ are given as $\dfrac{\pm \lambda (\vec{a} \times \vec{b})}{|\vec{a} \times \vec{b}|}$.

12. Properties of Vector Product of Two Vectors

(i) The vector product is not **commutative**, for vectors $\vec{a}$ and $\vec{b}$, we have $(\vec{a} \times \vec{b}) = -(\vec{b} \times \vec{a})$

(ii) The vector product is distributive over addition, i.e. for vectors $\vec{a}, \vec{b}$ and $\vec{c}$, we have

$$\vec{a} \times (\vec{b} + \vec{c}) = \vec{a} \times \vec{b} + \vec{a} \times \vec{c}$$

(iii) If m is any scalar and $\vec{a}$ and $\vec{b}$ be the two non-zero vectors, then $(m\vec{a}) \times \vec{b} = m(\vec{a} \times \vec{b}) = \vec{a} \times (m\vec{b})$

13. Vector Product of Two Vectors in Component Form

Suppose two vectors $\vec{a}$ and $\vec{b}$ are given in component form, say $\vec{a} = a_1\hat{i} + a_2\hat{j} + a_3\hat{k}$ and $\vec{b} = b_1\hat{i} + b_2\hat{j} + b_3\hat{k}$, then their vector product is given by

$$\vec{a} \times \vec{b} = \begin{vmatrix} \hat{i} & \hat{j} & \hat{k} \\ a_1 & a_2 & a_3 \\ b_1 & b_2 & b_3 \end{vmatrix}$$

14. Applications of Vector Product of Two Vectors

Vector product of two vectors can be used to find the area of some geometrical figures which are given below

(i) **Area of a triangle** The area of triangle having adjacent sides $\vec{a}$ and $\vec{b}$ is given by

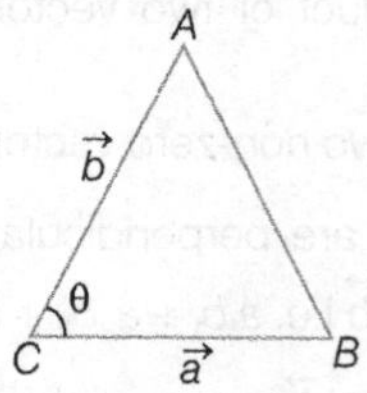

$$\text{Area} = \frac{1}{2}|\vec{a} \times \vec{b}|$$

(ii) **Area of a triangle** The area of ΔABC is

$\dfrac{1}{2}|\overrightarrow{AB} \times \overrightarrow{AC}|$ or $\dfrac{1}{2}|\overrightarrow{BC} \times \overrightarrow{BA}|$ or $\dfrac{1}{2}|\overrightarrow{CB} \times \overrightarrow{CA}|$.

(iii) **Area of a parallelogram** The area of a parallelogram having adjacent sides $\vec{a}$ and $\vec{b}$ is given by

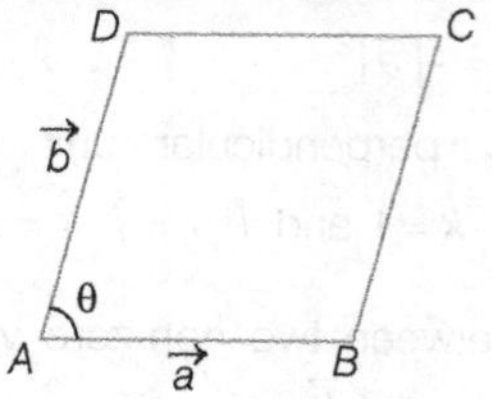

$$\text{Area} = |\vec{a} \times \vec{b}|$$

(iv) **Area of a parallelogram** The area of a parallelogram having diagonals $\vec{d_1}$ and $\vec{d_2}$ is given by

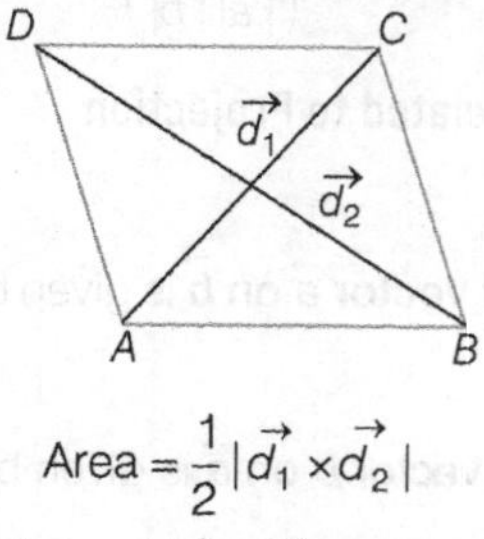

$$\text{Area} = \frac{1}{2}|\vec{d_1} \times \vec{d_2}|$$

where, $\overrightarrow{AC} = \vec{d_1}$ and $\overrightarrow{BD} = \vec{d_2}$ are diagonals.

Chapter 13 : **Three-Dimensional Geometry**

1. Direction Cosines and Direction Ratios

If a line make angles α, β and γ with X-axis, Y-axis and Z-axis, respectively, then $l = \cos\alpha$, $m = \cos\beta$ and $n = \cos\gamma$ are called the direction cosines of the line.

(i) We always have, $l^2 + m^2 + n^2 = 1$.

(ii) **Angle between two lines** If θ is the angle between two lines with direction cosines l_1, m_1, n_1 and l_2, m_2, n_2, then $\cos\theta = l_1 l_2 + m_1 m_2 + n_1 n_2$.

Numbers proportional to the direction cosines of a line are called the direction ratios of the line.

(a) If a, b and c are the direction ratios of a line, then

$$l = \frac{a}{\sqrt{a^2 + b^2 + c^2}},\quad m = \frac{b}{\sqrt{a^2 + b^2 + c^2}}$$

and $$n = \frac{c}{\sqrt{a^2 + b^2 + c^2}}$$

(b) In any line, direction cosines are unique but direction ratios are not unique.

2. Direction Cosines and Direction Ratios of a Line

The direction cosines and direction ratios of the line segment joining $P(x_1, y_1, z_1)$ and $Q(x_2, y_2, z_2)$ are respectively given by

$$\frac{x_2 - x_1}{PQ}, \frac{y_2 - y_1}{PQ}, \frac{z_2 - z_1}{PQ} \text{ and } (x_2 - x_1, y_2 - y_1, z_2 - z_1)$$

where, $PQ = \sqrt{(x_2 - x_1)^2 + (y_2 - y_1)^2 + (z_2 - z_1)^2}$

3. Direction Ratios and Direction Cosines of a Vector

Let $\vec{r} = a\hat{i} + b\hat{j} + c\hat{k}$ be a vector, then coefficients of $\hat{i}, \hat{j}, \hat{k}$ i.e. a, b, c are called direction ratios of $\vec{r}$ and the direction cosines of $\vec{r}$ are given by

$$\frac{a}{\sqrt{a^2 + b^2 + c^2}}, \frac{b}{\sqrt{a^2 + b^2 + c^2}}, \frac{c}{\sqrt{a^2 + b^2 + c^2}}$$

4. Line

A straight line is the locus of the intersection of two planes. A line is uniquely determined, if

(i) it passes through a given point and has given direction.

(ii) it passes through two given points.

5. Equation of Line in Vector Form

(i) Equation of a line through a given point A with position vector $\vec{a}$ and parallel to a given vector $\vec{b}$ is given by $\vec{r} = \vec{a} + t\vec{b}$, where t is a scalar. If $\vec{b} = a\hat{i} + b\hat{j} + c\hat{k}$, then a, b and c are direction ratios of the line and conversely, if a, b and c are direction ratios of a line, then $\vec{b} = a\hat{i} + b\hat{j} + c\hat{k}$ will be parallel to the line.

(ii) The vector equation of a line passing through two points with position vectors $\vec{a}$ and $\vec{b}$ is given by $\vec{r} = \vec{a} + t(\vec{b} - \vec{a})$, where t is a scalar.

(iii) **Angle between two lines** If θ is the angle between two lines $\vec{r} = \vec{a} + t\vec{b}$ and $\vec{r} = \vec{c} + s\vec{d}$,

then $$\cos\theta = \frac{\vec{b}\cdot\vec{d}}{|\vec{b}||\vec{d}|},$$

where t and s are parameters.

If two lines are perpendicular, then $\vec{b_1}\cdot\vec{b_2} = 0$.

And if two lines are parallel, then $\vec{b_1} = \lambda\vec{b_2}$

6. Equation of Line in Cartesian Form

(i) The equation of a line passing through a point $A(x_1, y_1, z_1)$ and having direction ratios a, b and c is

$$\frac{x - x_1}{a} = \frac{y - y_1}{b} = \frac{z - z_1}{c}.$$

These types of equations are called the symmetrical form of a line.

(ii) The equation of a line passing through a point $A(x_1, y_1, z_1)$ and having l, m and n as the direction cosines, is

$$\frac{x - x_1}{l} = \frac{y - y_1}{m} = \frac{z - z_1}{n}$$

(iii) The equation of a line passing through two points $A(x_1, y_1, z_1)$ and $B(x_2, y_2, z_2)$ is

$$\frac{x - x_1}{x_2 - x_1} = \frac{y - y_1}{y_2 - y_1} = \frac{z - z_1}{z_2 - z_1}$$

(iv) If a_1, b_1, c_1 and a_2, b_2, c_2 are direction ratios of two lines respectively, then the angle θ between the lines is given by

$$\cos\theta = \left|\frac{a_1a_2 + b_1b_2 + c_1c_2}{\sqrt{a_1^2 + b_1^2 + c_1^2}\cdot\sqrt{a_2^2 + b_2^2 + c_2^2}}\right|$$

or $$\sin\theta = \frac{\sqrt{(a_1b_2 - a_2b_1)^2 + (b_1c_2 - b_2c_1)^2 + (c_1a_2 - c_2a_1)^2}}{\sqrt{a_1^2 + b_1^2 + c_1^2}\sqrt{a_2^2 + b_2^2 + c_2^2}}$$

(v) Two lines with direction ratios a_1, b_1, c_1 and a_2, b_2, c_2 are

(a) perpendicular, if $a_1a_2 + b_1b_2 + c_1c_2 = 0$.

(b) parallel, if $\dfrac{a_1}{a_2} = \dfrac{b_1}{b_2} = \dfrac{c_1}{c_2}$.

7. Conditions for Two Given Lines to be Intersect

(i) **Equation of lines in vector form** Let the two given lines L_1 and L_2 be $\vec{r} = \vec{a_1} + \lambda\vec{b_1}$ and $\vec{r} = \vec{a_2} + \mu\vec{b_2}$, where λ and μ are parameters of real numbers. Now, the given lines will intersect, iff vectors $\vec{b_1}$ and $\vec{b_2}$ are non-parallel and $(\vec{a_2} - \vec{a_1})\cdot(\vec{b_1}\times\vec{b_2}) = 0$.

(ii) **Equation of lines in cartesian form** Let the two given lines L_1 and L_2 be $\frac{x-x_1}{a_1}=\frac{y-y_1}{b_1}=\frac{z-z_1}{c_1}$ and $\frac{x-x_2}{a_2}=\frac{y-y_2}{b_2}=\frac{z-z_2}{c_2}$, respectively.

Now, the lines L_1 and L_2 will intersect, iff

$a_1:b_1:c_1 \neq a_2:b_2:c_2$ and $\begin{vmatrix} x_2-x_1 & y_2-y_1 & z_2-z_1 \\ a_1 & b_1 & c_1 \\ a_2 & b_2 & c_2 \end{vmatrix}=0.$

8. Plane

A plane is a surface such that a line segment joining any two points on it lies wholly on it. A plane is determined uniquely, if any one of the following is known.

(i) The normal to the plane and its distance from the origin is given, i.e. equation of a plane in normal form.

(ii) It passes through a point and is perpendicular to a given direction.

(iii) It passes through three given non-collinear points.

9. Equation of Plane in Cartesian Form

(i) **General form** The general equation of a plane is

$$ax+by+cz+d=0.$$

The direction ratios of the normal to this plane are a, b and c.

(ii) **Intercept form** If a plane cuts (intercepts) a, b and c with the coordinate axes, then the equation of the plane is $\frac{x}{a}+\frac{y}{b}+\frac{z}{c}=1.$

(iii) **Equation of a plane passing through a point and perpendicular to a given vector** The equation of a plane passing through a point (x_1, y_1, z_1) is

$$a(x-x_1)+b(y-y_1)+c(z-z_1)=0,$$

where a, b and c are direction ratios of perpendicular vector.

(iv) **Equation of a plane passing through three non-collinear points** The equation of a plane passing through three non-collinear points $A(x_1, y_1, z_1)$, $B(x_2, y_2, z_2)$ and $C(x_3, y_3, z_3)$ is given by

$$\begin{vmatrix} x-x_1 & y-y_1 & z-z_1 \\ x_2-x_1 & y_2-y_1 & z_2-z_1 \\ x_3-x_1 & y_3-y_1 & z_3-z_1 \end{vmatrix}=0.$$

10. Equation of Plane in Vector Form

(i) Let O be the origin and $\hat{n}$ be a unit vector in the direction of the normal ON to the plane and let $ON=p$. Then, the equation of the plane is $\vec{r}\cdot\hat{n}=p$.

Note If $\vec{r}\cdot(a\hat{i}+b\hat{j}+c\hat{k})=d$ is the vector equation of a plane, then $ax+by+cz=d$ is the cartesian equation of the plane, where a, b and c are the direction ratios of the normal to the plane.

(ii) **Equation of a plane perpendicular to a given vector and passing through a given point** The equation of a plane passing through the point $\vec{a}$ and perpendicular to the given vector $\vec{n}$ is

$$(\vec{r}-\vec{a})\cdot\vec{n}=0.$$

(iii) **Equation of plane passing through three non-collinear points** The equation of plane passing through three non-collinear points $\vec{a}, \vec{b}$ and $\vec{c}$ is

$$(\vec{r}-\vec{a})\cdot[(\vec{b}-\vec{a})\times(\vec{c}-\vec{a})]=0.$$

11. Coplanarity of Two Lines

(i) **Equation of lines in vector form**

Two lines $\vec{r}=\vec{a_1}+\lambda\vec{b_1}$ and $\vec{r}=\vec{a_2}+\mu\vec{b_2}$ are coplanar, iff $(\vec{a_2}-\vec{a_1})\cdot(\vec{b_1}\times\vec{b_2})=0$

Note The equation of plane containing above lines is

$$(\vec{r}-\vec{a_1})\cdot(\vec{b_1}\times\vec{b_2})=0 \text{ or } (\vec{r}-\vec{a_2})\cdot(\vec{b_1}\times\vec{b_2})=0$$

(ii) Equation of lines in cartesian form

Two lines $\frac{x-x_1}{a_1}=\frac{y-y_1}{b_1}=\frac{z-z_1}{c_1}$

and $\frac{x-x_2}{a_2}=\frac{y-y_2}{b_2}=\frac{z-z_2}{c_2}$

are coplanar, if and only if

$$\begin{vmatrix} x_2-x_1 & y_2-y_1 & z_2-z_1 \\ a_1 & b_1 & c_1 \\ a_2 & b_2 & c_2 \end{vmatrix}=0$$

Note The equation of plane containing the above lines is

$$\begin{vmatrix} x-x_1 & y-y_1 & z-z_1 \\ a_1 & b_1 & c_1 \\ a_2 & b_2 & c_2 \end{vmatrix}=0. \text{ or } \begin{vmatrix} x-x_2 & y-y_2 & z-z_2 \\ a_1 & b_1 & c_1 \\ a_2 & b_2 & c_2 \end{vmatrix}=0$$

12. Angle between two Planes

(i) **Cartesian form** The angle between two planes is the angle between their normals.

If θ is the angle between the normals of the planes $a_1x+b_1y+c_1z+d_1=0$ and $a_2x+b_2y+c_2z+d_2=0$, then

$$\cos\theta=\frac{a_1a_2+b_1b_2+c_1c_2}{\sqrt{a_1^2+b_1^2+c_1^2}\sqrt{a_2^2+b_2^2+c_2^2}}$$

If two planes are perpendicular, then $a_1a_2+b_1b_2+c_1c_2=0$ and if they are parallel, then $\frac{a_1}{a_2}=\frac{b_1}{b_2}=\frac{c_1}{c_2}$.

(ii) **Vector form** Angle between the planes $\vec{r}\cdot\vec{n}_1=p_1$ and $\vec{r}\cdot\vec{n}_2=p_2$ is given by $\cos\theta=\frac{\vec{n}_1\cdot\vec{n}_2}{|\vec{n}_1||\vec{n}_2|}$, where θ is the angle between their normals.

Note Two planes are perpendicular to each other, if $\vec{n_1}\cdot\vec{n_2}=\vec{0}$ and parallel, if $\vec{n_1}\times\vec{n_2}=\vec{0}$.

13. Distance of a Point from a Plane

(i) **Cartesian form**

(a) Distance of a point $P(x_1, y_1, z_1)$ from a plane $ax + by + cz + d = 0$ is given by

$$p = \frac{|ax_1 + by_1 + cz_1 + d|}{\sqrt{a^2 + b^2 + c^2}}.$$

(b) The length of perpendicular from origin O to the plane $ax + by + cz + d = 0$ is $\dfrac{|d|}{\sqrt{a^2 + b^2 + c^2}}$.

(ii) **Vector form**

(a) The perpendicular distance of a point $\vec{a}$ from the plane $\vec{r} \cdot \vec{n} = d$, where $\vec{n}$ is normal to the plane, is $\dfrac{|\vec{a} \cdot \vec{n} - d|}{|\vec{n}|}$.

(b) The length of the perpendicular from origin O to the plane $\vec{r} \cdot \vec{n} = d$ is $\dfrac{|d|}{|\vec{n}|}$.

14. Angle between a Line and a Plane

The angle between a line and a plane is the complement of the angle between the line and normal to the plane.

(i) **Cartesian form**

Let the equation of a line is $\dfrac{x - x_1}{a_1} = \dfrac{y - y_1}{b_1} = \dfrac{z - z_1}{c_1}$ and equation of a plane is $a_2x + b_2y + c_2z = d_2$.

Then, the angle 'θ' between the line and normal to the plane is

$$\cos\theta = \frac{a_1a_2 + b_1b_2 + c_1c_2}{\sqrt{a_1^2 + b_1^2 + c_1^2}\sqrt{a_2^2 + b_2^2 + c_2^2}}$$

And the angle 'ϕ' between the line and plane is $\sin\phi = \sin(90 - \theta)$

$$= \cos\theta = \frac{a_1a_2 + b_1b_2 + c_1c_2}{\sqrt{a_1^2 + b_1^2 + c_1^2}\sqrt{a_2^2 + b_2^2 + c_2^2}}.$$

Deduction

(i) If line is perpendicular to plane, then $\dfrac{a_1}{a_2} = \dfrac{b_1}{b_2} = \dfrac{c_1}{c_2}$.

(V) If the line is parallel to the plane, the $a_1a_2 + b_1b_2 + c_1c_2 = 0$.

(ii) **Vector form** Let the equation of line $\vec{r} = \vec{a} + \lambda\vec{b}$ and plane is $\vec{r} \cdot \vec{n} = d$. Then, the angle 'θ' between the line and normal to the plane is

$$\cos\theta = \left|\frac{\vec{b} \cdot \vec{n}}{|\vec{b}||\vec{n}|}\right|$$

And the angle 'ϕ' between the line and plane is

$$\sin\phi = \sin(90 - \theta) = \cos\theta = \left|\frac{\vec{b} \cdot \vec{n}}{|\vec{b}| \cdot |\vec{n}|}\right|$$

Here, $\phi = 90° - \theta$,

where ϕ is the angle between the line and plane.

15. Foot of Perpendicular

Foot of the perpendicular from a point (x_1, y_1, z_1) on the plane $ax + by + cz + d = 0$ is (x, y, z), where

$$\frac{x - x_1}{a} = \frac{y - y_1}{b} = \frac{z - z_1}{c} = \frac{(ax_1 + by_1 + cz_1 + d)}{a^2 + b^2 + c^2}.$$

Cartesian Form

Let $P(x_1, y_1, z_1)$ be the given point and $ax + by + cz = d$ be the cartesian equation of the given plane, then perpendicular distance $= \dfrac{|ax_1 + by_1 + cz_1 - d|}{\sqrt{a^2 + b^2 + c^2}}$

16. Distance between Parallel Planes

Let $a_1x + b_1y + c_1z + d_1 = 0$ and $a_1x + b_1y + c_1z + d_2 = 0$ be two parallel planes. Then the distance between the two parallel planes is $\dfrac{|d_2 - d_1|}{\sqrt{a_1^2 + b_1^2 + c_1^2}}$

17. Condition for a Line to Lie in a Plane (Vector Form)

If the line $\vec{r} = \vec{a} + \lambda\vec{b}$ lies in the plane $\vec{r} \cdot \vec{n} = d$, then

(i) $\vec{b} \cdot \vec{n} = 0$ (ii) $\vec{a} \cdot \vec{n} = d$

Cartesian Form

If the line $\dfrac{x - x_1}{l} = \dfrac{y - y_1}{m} = \dfrac{z - z_1}{n}$ lies in the plane $ax + by + cz + d = 0$, then

(i) $ax_1 + by_1 + cz_1 + d = 0$

(ii) $al + bm + cn = 0$

Chapter 14 : **Applications of Integrals**

Curve Sketching

For curve sketching of the function $y = f(x)$, we follow the following steps

1. Symmetry

(i) **Symmetry about the Y-axis** If the given equation remains same when x is replaced by $(-x)$ or equation of the curve contains only even power of x, then the given curve is symmetrical about Y-axis.

(ii) **Symmetry about the X-axis** If the given equation remains same when y is replaced by $(-y)$ or equation of the curve contains only even power of y, then the given curve is symmetrical about X-axis.

(iii) **Symmetry about the origin** If the given equation remains same when both x and y are replaced by $-x$ and $-y$, respectively, then the given curve is symmetrical about origin.

(iv) **Symmetry about the line $y = x$** If the given equation remains same when x and y are interchanged with each other, then the given curve is symmetrical about the line $y = x$.

(v) **Symmetry about the line $y = -x$** If the given equation remains same, when x and y are replaced with $-y$ and $-x$, then the given curve is symmetrical about the line $y = -x$.

2. Points of Intersection with the Axes

For finding the intersecting points with X-axis and Y-axis, put $y = 0$ and $x = 0$, respectively.

3. Origin

If the curve satisfies $(0, 0)$, then it will pass through origin.

4. Turning Points

Put $f'(x) = 0$ for obtaining the turning points. Turning points gives the position of maxima or minima point and nature of curve.

Applications of Integrals

(i) The area enclosed by the curve $y = f(x)$, the X-axis and the ordinates at $x = a$ and $x = b$, is given by $\int_a^b y\,dx$.

(ii) The area enclosed by the curve $x = f(y)$, the Y-axis and the abscissae at $y = c$ and $y = d$, is given by $\int_c^d x\,dy$.

(iii) If the curve $y = f(x)$ lies below the X-axis, then area bounded by the curve $y = f(x)$, X-axis and the ordinates at $x = a$ and $x = b$, is given by $\left|\int_a^b y\,dx\right|$.

(iv) Generally, it may happen that some position of the curve is above X-axis and some is below the X-axis which is shown in the figure. The area A bounded by the curve $y = f(x)$, X-axis and the ordinates at $x = a$ and $x = b$, is given by $A = |A_2| + A_1$.

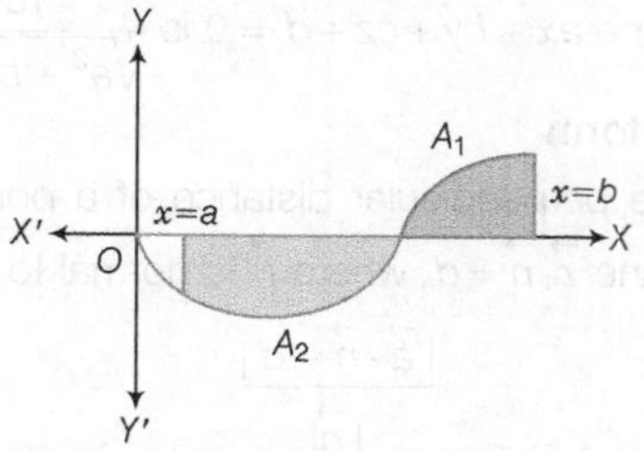

(v) The area enclosed between two curves, $y_1 = f(x)$ and $y_2 = g(x)$ and the ordinates at $x = a$ and $x = b$, is given by $\int_a^b (y_2 - y_1)\,dx$.

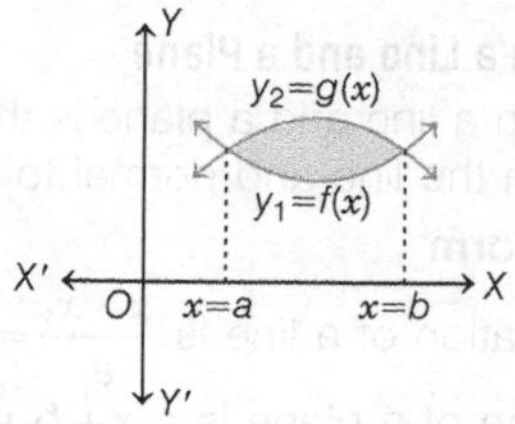

(vi) The area enclosed between two curves, $x_1 = f(y)$ and $x_2 = g(y)$ and the abscissae at $y = c$ and $y = d$, is given by $\int_c^d (x_2 - x_1)\,dy$.

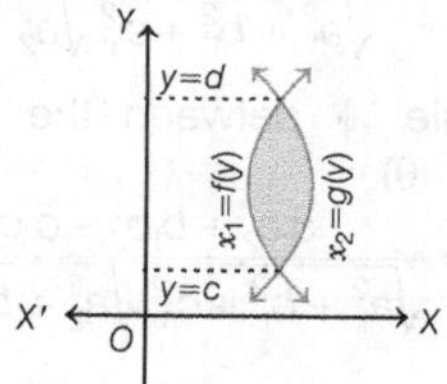

(vii) Area bounded by the two curves, $y = f(x)$ and $y = g(x)$ between the abscissae at $x = a$ and $x = b$, is given by $\int_a^c f(x)dx + \int_c^b g(x)dx$.

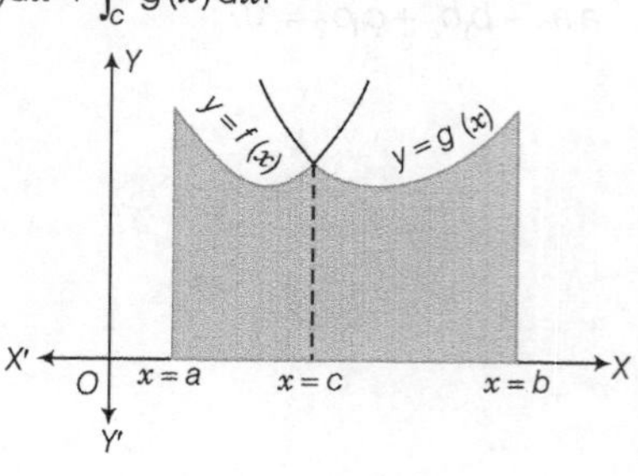

Chapter 15 : **Application of Calculus in Commerce and Economics**

1. Cost Function (CF)

If x denotes the quantity produced of a certain commodity at total cost C, then the total cost function (C) is expressed as $C = C(x)$ explicitly and $f(C, x) = 0$ is the implicit form. The total cost (TC) is broken into two parts, the fixed cost and the variable cost.

(i) **Fixed Cost** Fixed costs are those which are incurred regardless of the level of production like interest, rent, wages of permanent staff etc. These costs are not zero at zero level of output.

Thus, total fixed cost (TFC) = TC, when output is zero.

Fixed cost does not change whether there is any increase or decrease in the level of production.

(ii) **Variable Cost** Variable costs are those which vary with output. e.g. Raw materials and wages of casual labour etc. Thus,

Total Cost = Total Fixed Cost + Total Variable Cost

or TC = TFC + TVC

2. Demand Function

The demand function represents the functional relationship between demand and price of a commodity. If P denotes the price per unit and x is the number of units demanded by a consumer at that price, the demand function in explicit form will be written as $x = f(P)$ and in implicit form as $f(x, P) = 0$.

Note (i) If the demand of the item depends upon the price of the item, the demand function is $x = f(P)$.

(ii) If the price of the item depends upon the demand of the item, the demand is $P = f(x)$.

3. Revenue Function

Revenue means the amount received by a company on selling a certain number of units of a commodity. Let P be the price per unit and x be the number of units sold. Then, total revenue (TR) $= R(x) = P \cdot x$

4. Profit Function

Profit function is the difference of revenue function and cost function, i.e. $P(x) = R(x) - C(x)$.

5. Break-even Point

The break-even point is that point where total revenue equals to total cost incurred, i.e. $R(x) = C(x)$. Beyond the level of break-even point, a company begins to earn a profit.

6. Average Cost (AC)

The average cost (AC) represents the cost per unit, i.e. $AC = \frac{C}{x}$, where C = total cost, x = number of units.

7. Marginal Cost (MC)

The marginal cost is the rate of change of the total cost with respect to x (output), It can be computed by differentiating total cost (C),

i.e. $$MC = \frac{d}{dx}(C) = \frac{dC}{dx}$$

8. Marginal Average Cost (MAC)

It is the rate of change in average cost when one additional unit is produced, i.e. $MAC = \frac{d}{dx}\left(\frac{C}{x}\right)$

9. Relation between Average Cost (AC) and Marginal Cost (MC)

The following relation is observed between AC and MC

(i) When MC>AC $\Rightarrow$ AC increases with increase in output.

(ii) When MC=AC $\Rightarrow$ AC is constant at all levels of output.

(iii) When MC< AC $\Rightarrow$ AC decreases with increase in output.

If C is the total cost of producing x units of commodity, then the following equation always holds true.

$$\frac{d}{dx}(AC) = \frac{1}{x}(MC - AC)$$

10. Average Revenue (AR)

It is the revenue generated per unit of output sold and is computed as

$$AR = \frac{\text{Total revenue}}{\text{Number of units sold}}$$

Note Average revenue is same as the price of the commodity.

11. Marginal Revenue (MR)

It is the rate of change of total revenue with respect to quantity sold,

i.e. $$MR = \frac{d}{dx}(TR).$$

12. Relation between AR and MR

(i) In perfect competition market, AR and MR are equal and constant at all level of sales.

(ii) In monopolistic market, $MR < AR$

13. For Minimization of AC

Step I First, find $\frac{d}{dx}(AC)$.

Step II Put $\frac{d}{dx}(AC) = 0$ and solve for x.

Step III Now, find $\frac{d^2}{dx^2}(AC)$.

***Step* IV** The value of x for which $\frac{d^2}{dx^2}$ (AC) > 0, is the required value.

Similar, steps can be defined for minimization of MC.

14. For Maximization of $R(x)$ (Revenue Function)

In this method, we use the following steps

***Step* I** First, find $\frac{d}{dx}(R(x))$.

***Step* II** Put $\frac{d}{dx}(R(x)) = 0$ and solve for x.

***Step* III** Now, find $\frac{d^2}{dx^2}(R(x))$.

***Step* IV** The value of x for which $\frac{d^2}{dx^2}(R(x)) < 0$, is the required value.

Similar steps can be defined for maximization of profit function, $P(x)$.

Chapter 16 : **Linear Regression**

1. Linear Regression

It helps to estimate or predict the unknown value of one variable from the known value of the other value of the related variables called regression.

Line of Regression

A line of regression is the straight line which gives the best fit in the least square sense to the given sets of data.

2. Scatter Diagram

It is a technique for visually examining the form of relationship, without calculating any numerical value. To construct a scatter diagram, x variable is taken on X-axis and y variable is taken on Y-axis. The cluster of points, plotted is referred to as a scatter diagram.

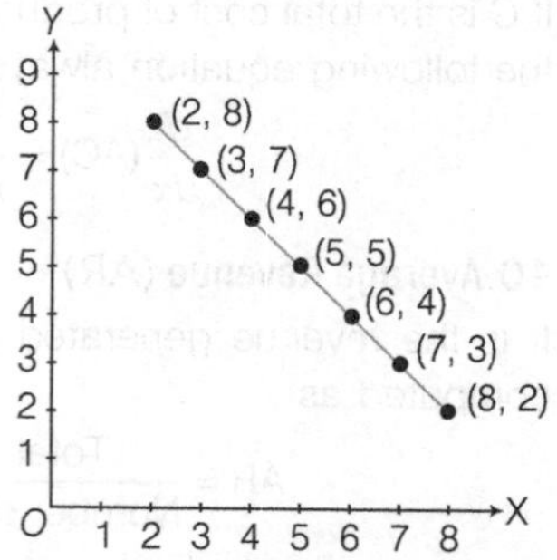

e.g. Let us draw a scatter diagram for observations, (2, 8), (3, 7), (4, 6), (5, 5), (6, 4), (7, 3), (8, 2)

Note Data connecting two variables are known as bivariate data.

3. Curve Fitting

If data $(x_1, y_1), (x_2, y_2), \ldots, (x_n, y_n)$ is plotted on a scatter diagram and then visualise a smooth curve which is approximating the data is called curve fitting.

The main purpose of curve fitting **is to estimate one of the variable from the other.** It is shown in the following diagram.

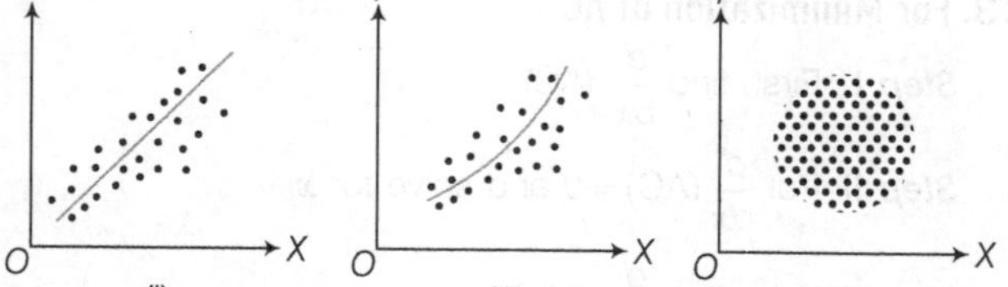

(i) (ii) (iii)

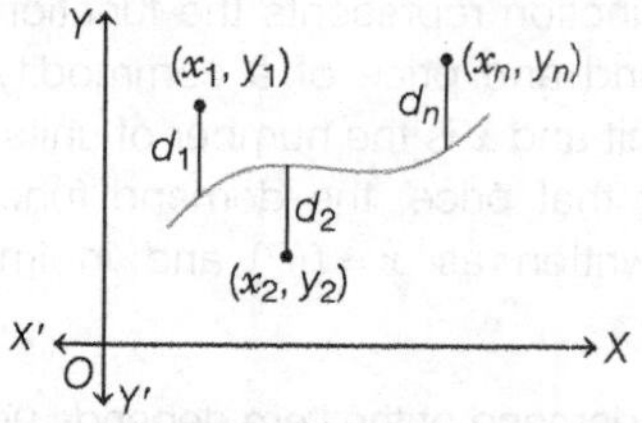

In above diagram the function $y = f(x)$ is called regression function. Also, the best fitting line is called **regression line** of y on x.

4. Least Squares Method

Under this method a regression line is fitted through different points in such a way that the sum of squares of the deviations of the observed value from the fitted line shall be least.

The line drawn by this method is called **line of best fit.**

In the above diagram, clearly all the curves approximately a given set of data point, where $d_1^2 + d_2^2 + \ldots + d_n^2$ is minimum and it is best fitting curve. It is estimating correctly (very least error) on average.

5. Regression Coefficient For Two Variables x and y

There are two regression coefficients.

(i) **Regression Coefficient of y on x** It is a unit change in the value of x variable and the average change in the value of y variable. Thus, it is represented by b_{yx}:

$$\therefore \quad b_{yx} = r \cdot \frac{\sigma_y}{\sigma_x} = \frac{\Sigma xy - \frac{\Sigma x \cdot \Sigma y}{n}}{\Sigma x^2 - \frac{(\Sigma x)^2}{n}}$$

The value of b_{yx} can also be found out by other formulae.

(ii) **Regression Coefficient of x on y** It is a unit change in the value of y variable, and the average change in the value of x variable. It is represented by b_{xy}.

$$\therefore \quad b_{xy} = r \cdot \frac{\sigma_x}{\sigma_y} = \frac{\Sigma xy - \frac{\Sigma x \cdot \Sigma y}{n}}{\Sigma y^2 - \frac{(\Sigma y)^2}{n}}$$

The value of b_{xy} can also be found out by other formulae.

6. Relation between Regression Coefficients of y on x and x on y

$b_{xy} \times b_{yx} = r^2,\ 0 \le b_{xy} \times b_{yx} \le 1$

and r is known as correlation coefficient.

Note Correlation studies and measures the direction and intensities of relationship between two variables in which change in the value of one variable, are associated with changes in the value of the other variable.

7. Types of Correlation

(i) **Positive correlation** When two related variables move together in the same direction, it is said to be positive correlation.

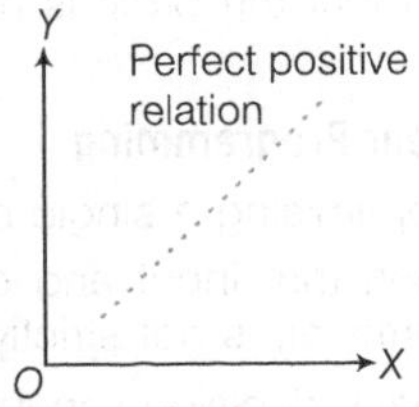

(ii) **Negative correlation** When two variables move in the opposite direction, it is said to be negative correlation.

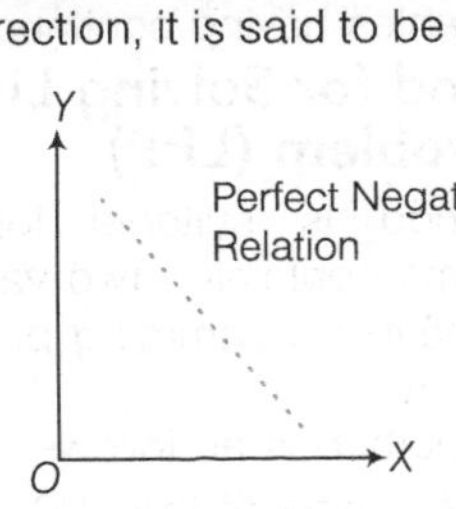

8. Regression Equation (Equation of line of Regression)

Regression equations are the algebraic formulation of regression lines. Regression equations represent regression lines.

Lines of regression can be fixed in following ways

(i) **Lines of regression equation of y on x** This equation is used to estimate the probable values of y on the basis of the given values of x.

i.e. $y = a + bx$

where, a and b are constants.

Line of regression of y on x can also be written as or

$$y - \bar{y} = b_{yx}(x - \bar{x}) \left[\text{where, } \bar{x} = \frac{\Sigma x}{n}, \bar{y} = \frac{\Sigma y}{n} \right]$$

where, b_{yx} = Regression coefficient of y on x.

(ii) **Lines of regression equation of x on y** This equation is used to estimate the probable values of x on the basis of the given values of y.

i.e. $x = a_0 + b_0 y$

where, a_0 and b_0 are constants.

Line of regression of x on y can also be written as

or $x - \bar{x} = b_{xy}(y - \bar{y}) \left[\text{where, } \bar{x} = \frac{\Sigma x}{n}, \bar{y} = \frac{\Sigma y}{n} \right]$

where, b_{xy} = Regression coefficient of x on y.

9. Identification of Regression Equations

Suppose two equations $a_1 x + b_1 y + c_1 = 0$ and $a_2 x + b_2 y + c_2 = 0$ are given and we have to identify the regression line of y on x or x on y, *we use the following steps*

***Step* I** First, we consider any one of the equations say first, i.e. $a_1 x + b_1 y + c_1 = 0$ as y on x and other equation say second, i.e. $a_2 x + b_2 y + c_2 = 0$ as x on y.

***Step* II** Adjust the first equation y on x such that y should be on left side with coefficient 1 and rest of the terms be on right side (i.e. $y = -\frac{a_1}{b_1}x - \frac{c_1}{b_1}$). The coefficient of x will considered as regression coefficient y on x, i.e. $b_{yx} = \frac{-a_1}{b_1}$. Similarly, for another equation x on y, adjust equation like as $x = -\frac{b_2}{a_2}y - \frac{c_2}{a_2}$. The coefficient of y will give regression coefficient of x on y i.e. $b_{xy} = \frac{-b_2}{a_2}$.

***Step* III** If b_{xy} and b_{yx} are not of same sign, then we do not determine the regression line. If they have the same sign, then determine coefficient by using the formula, $r = \sqrt{b_{yx} \times b_{xy}},\ 0 \le b_{yx} \times b_{xy} \le$

***Step* IV** If $r^2 \in [0, 1]$, then our consideration is true, otherwise we have to change the considering equations.

10. Properties of Regression Coefficient and Lines of Regression

(i) **Coefficient of correlation** is the geometric mean of the regression coefficients,

i.e. $r = \sqrt{b_{xy} \times b_{yx}}$

(ii) Both the regression coefficients must have the same algebraic signs.

(iii) The **coefficient of correlation** will have the same sign as that of regression coefficients.

(iv) Both the regression coefficients cannot be greater than unity.

(v) Arithmetic mean of two regression coefficients is either equal to or greater than the **correlation coefficient.**

i.e. $\frac{b_{yx} + b_{xy}}{2} \ge r$

(vi) The two regression lines coincide if and only if there is perfect linear relation between x and y.

i.e. $\rho(x, y) = r = \pm 1$

(vii) The intersection points of two regression lines is at means, i.e. $(\bar{x}, \bar{y})$.

Chapter 17 : **Linear Programming**

1. Linear Programming Problem

A linear programming problem is one that is concerned with finding the optimal value (maximum or minimum value) of a linear function (called **objective function**) of several variables (say x and y called **decision variables**), subject to the conditions that the variables are non-negative and satisfy a set of linear inequalities (called **linear constraints**).

2. Some Terms Related to LPP

There are some terms related to LPP given below

(i) **Constraints** The linear inequations or inequalities or restrictions on the variables of a linear programming problem are called constraints. The conditions $x \geq 0$, $y \geq 0$ are called non-negative restrictions.

(ii) **Optimisation problem** A problem which seeks to maximise (or minimise) a linear function subject to certain constraints, determined by a set of linear inequalities, is called an optimisation problem. Linear programming problems are special type of optimisation problems.

(iii) **Objective function** A linear function of two or more variables which has to be maximised or minimised under the given restrictions in the form of linear inequations (or **linear constraints**) is called the objective function. The variables used in the objective function are called **decision variables.**

(iv) **Optimal values** The maximum or minimum value of an objective function is known as its optimal value.

(v) **Solution** A set of values of the variables which satisfy the constraints of given linear function (objective function) of several variables, subject to the conditions that the variables are **non-negative**, is called a solution of the linear programming problem.

(vi) **Feasible solution** Any solution to the given linear programming problem which also satisfies the non-negative restrictions of the problem, is called a feasible solution. Any solution outside the feasible solution is called an **infeasible solution.**

(vii) **Feasible region** The set of all feasible solutions constitutes a region which is called the feasible region. Each point in this region represents a feasible choice. The region other than feasible region is called an **infeasible region**.

(viii) **Bounded region** A feasible region of a system of linear inequalities is said to be bounded, if it can be enclosed within a circle. Otherwise, it is said to be **unbounded region**.

(ix) **Optimal solution** A feasible solution at which the objective function has optimal value, is called the optimal solution of the linear programming problem.

(x) **Optimisation technique** The process of obtaining the optimal solution is called optimisation technique.

3. Advantages of Linear Programming

The linear programming helps in the following points

(i) Linear programming is used in solving different problems like diet problems, manufacturing problems, investment problems, transportation problems, blending problems and advertising media selection problems.

(ii) It is used in determining shortest routes for **travelling salesmen**.

(iii) It helps a farmer to produce the best crop by minimising risk and maximising profit.

(iv) It helps to choose the best alternative amongst a set of alternatives, so that the profit is maximised or cost is minimised.

4. Limitations of Linear Programming

(i) It deals with optimising a single objective only.

(ii) The assumption that input and output variables are directly proportional, is not strictly true.

(iii) In practice, many decision variables assume integral values. e.g. Number of workers. Linear programming deals with variables having continuous values.

Graphical Method for Solving Linear Programming Problem (LPP)

The graphical method is suitable for solving linear programming problems containing two variables only. This method of solving linear programming problem is referred as corner point method.

The process of this method is as follows

1. Find the feasible region of the LPP and determine its corner points (vertices) either by inspection or by solving the two equations of the lines intersecting at that point.
2. Find the value of objective function $Z = ax + by$ at each corner point. Let M and m respectively, denote the largest and the smallest values at these points.
   (i) When the feasible region is **bounded**, then M and m are the maximum and minimum values of Z.
   (ii) When the feasible region is **unbounded**, then
      (a) M is the maximum value of Z, if the open half plane determined by $ax + by > M$ has no point in common with the feasible region. Otherwise, Z has no maximum value.
      (b) m is the minimum value of Z, if the open half plane determined by $ax + by < m$ has no point in common with the feasible region. Otherwise, Z has no minimum value.

Note (i) A half plane (if a line divides XY-plane into two parts, then each part is known as half plane) in XY-plane is called an open half plane, if the line separating the plane is not included in the half plane.

(ii) If two corner points of the feasible region are both optimal solution of the same type, i.e. both produce the same maximum or minimum, then any point on the line segment joining these two points is also an optimal solution of the same type.